PRINCIPLES
OF WEED CONTROL
IN CALIFORNIA

Second Edition

Sponsored By
CALIFORNIA WEED CONFERENCE
P.O. Box 609
Fremont, CA 94537-0609

Thomson Publications
P.O. Box 9335
Fresno, CA 93791

Copies are available from:
Thomson Publications
P.O. Box 9335
Fresno, CA 93791
(209) 435-2163

The California Weed Conference proudly dedicates this book to those who preceded us in establishing this discipline. May the knowledge and skills they provided be passed on in turn to our successors with the hope that this vital transfer of information will be perpetuated.

TABLE OF CONTENTS

PREFACE

In 1988, it was decided to revise The Principles of Weed Control in California published by the California Weed Conference. This decision was made partly as a result of the demand from a number of educational institutions in California that use this volume as a textbook, and partly because of the needs of those who use it as a working guide in weed science both here and abroad. Additionally, it was felt that there had been a number of substantial changes in technology since the first edition, and that it would be in the best interests of those who wish to remain up-to-date on this valuable science to provide them with the latest developments in weed control.

The second edition contains one new chapter, Chapter 6—Biochemical Control Methods, and three chapters with major revisions, Chapter 1—Plants, Chapter 8—Herbicides, and the Regulation and Registration section of Chapter 9—Safety and Regulation. Other chapters have been revised by including current information, moving individual sections to more appropriate chapters, and attempting to provide references only to currently registered herbicides. The latter problem is one which commanded considerable attention, and the final decision was to delete references to those herbicides (other than those retained for historical purposes) that were known to have had their registration withdrawn or canceled in California at the time the chapters were revised. The authors recognize that the registration of herbicides in California is an ever-changing process, and advise the reader that what is presented was current when the chapter was revised. A list of herbicides that were deleted from the first edition is provided in Chapter 8—Herbicides.

References to common names for weeds are taken from the Weed Science Society of America's *Composite List of Weeds* (Volume 32, Supplement 2, 1984). Chemical and common names for the herbicides mentioned are taken from the Weed Science Society of America's *Weed Science* (Volume 36, Number 3, May 1988).

A number of authors who contributed to the first edition have passed away, while others are no longer in weed control or have moved from California since the first edition was published. The California Weed Conference takes this opportunity to recognize these individuals for their valuable contributions. The editors elected to retain all references to the original authors, regardless of their participation in preparing the second edition.

The editors wish to thank all of those who contributed to the publication of this volume and hereby acknowledge their contributions. As with the first edition, we solicit any opinions or criticisms the reader may have that would add emphasis to or clarify the discussions that follow.

Edward A. Kurtz
Chairman, Textbook Committee, Second Edition

Members of the textbook committee for the second edition:

Floyd O. Colbert
David Lester
Joanna Lynch
Linda L. Romander
Andi Stein
W.T. Thomson

PREFACE TO FIRST EDITION

Early in 1982, a conclave of unsuspecting souls decided that the sum total of knowledge available within the membership of the California Weed Conference could form the basis for the publication of a textbook dealing primarily with the applied aspects of weed control in California. They speculated that the end result would benefit anyone interested in pursuing or continuing a career in weed science and, further, that such an undertaking could be accomplished in a relatively short period (i.e., less than two years). Although the goal never changed, a number of editorial and publication schedules did, and the following comments are deemed appropriate to indicate to the reader the basic thinking that accompanied the many months of dedicated effort represented by this book.

The purpose of this textbook is to provide access to the fundamental principles and concepts of weed control in California as understood by individual experts and based on their research, experimentation, observations, and practical experience. Some 70 authors contributed to the success of this book. Their individual areas of expertise and writing styles are reflected within their respective chapters and sections.

The literature of plant and weed science is rich in journal articles, bulletins, manuals, and books dealing with both specific and general aspects of weed control. We hope that this book, concentrating as it does on weed control in California, will contribute significantly to the knowledge in this field.

Numerous weeds affect crop production and noncrop areas in California under a multitude of environmental conditions. To define all of the interrelationships that exist under such various conditions is beyond the scope of this book. What is provided, however, is information relating to weed control practices currently existing in selected crops and noncrop areas, with emphasis on the use of weed-control systems that allow for optimum crop production and/or management of noncrop areas.

Although the book deals only with weed control in California, the diverse conditions that exist within the state and the importance of weed control in the production of food, feed, fiber, and fuel, and in noncrop and recreational areas should make its contents of worldwide interest.

As a text, the book is designed for use at the freshman college level by students who have an interest in pursuing a plant science or associated background of course work. It is also designed to aid those involved in the process of controlling weeds on a day-to-day basis. It is not intended as a manual or a set of recommendations for controlling weeds in California, but it can be used by growers, pest control advisers, and others as a guide to existing weed-control practices. Further, it is hoped that what is presented will stimulate the reader to explore all of the various available alternatives prior to making decisions regarding the use of weed-control methods or techniques.

A glossary, provided in part by the Weed Science Society of America from its *Herbicide Handbook* for 1983, is included to assist the reader in the comprehension of selected terms used throughout the book. Naturally, opinions and local variations as to the precise definition of a term may differ, and the editors acknowledge this. Where any confusion may result, we ask the reader's indulgence.

Likewise, discrepancies between common names of weeds and "local" names is also an area of concern. Scientific names are also subject to periodic changes. In the interest of clarity, we have elected to use the common names listed in the Weed Science Society of America's *Composite List of Weeds* (Volume 19, Issue 4, 1971). Those interested in the corresponding scientific names can also refer to that document.

Because many of the weed-control systems described in the text are subject to change, as is the case with any highly technical endeavor, it is the intent of the California Weed Conference to publish updated editions of this book as the need arises. In this regard, the editors solicit any opinions and criticisms the reader may have that would add emphasis or clarification to the discussions herein presented.

Edward A. Kurtz
Chairman, Editorial Review Committee

Floyd O. Colbert
Co-chairman, Textbook Committee

ACKNOWLEDGEMENTS

Many individuals and committees participated in the publication of this book. The California Weed Conference is indebted to all these individuals and wishes to acknowledge with gratitude the able assistance provided by the following persons:

California Weed Conference Executive Committee
1982–1983, 1983–1984, and 1984–1985

Textbook Committee—Co-chairmen Floyd O. Colbert and Edward M. Rose

Chapter Coordinators—Chairman Floyd O. Colbert

Harry S. Agamalian	Harold M. Kempen	Howard Rhoads
Robert W. Brazelton	Edward A. Kurtz	Sara S. Rosenthal
Clyde L. Elmore	John E. Marcroft	John T. Schlesselman
Bill B. Fischer	W.B. McHenry	Edwin E. Sieckert
William A. Harvey	Jack P. Orr	Dennis J. Stroud
F.A. Holmes	Steven R. Radosevich	

Technical Review Committee—Chairman Howard Rhoads

Harry S. Agamalian	George Gowgani	Larry W. Mitich
David E. Bayer	Thomas Heffernan	Jack P. Orr
Ken W. Dunster	James E. Hill	Vincent H. Schweers
Bill B. Fischer	F.A. Holmes	Leslie W. Sonder
Donald H. Ford	Wesley A. Humphrey	L.K. Stromberg
James Greil	Lester B. Kreps	

Publications Committee—Chairman W.B. McHenry
Linda L. Romander
W.T. Thomson
Stanley V. Walton

Photos and Figures Committee—Chairman Clyde L. Elmore
Jack K. Clark
John T. Schlesselman

Editorial Review Committee—Chairman Edward A. Kurtz

Bill Berkson	Harold M. Kempen	Linda L. Romander
Floyd O. Colbert	David Lester	Edward M. Rose
Clyde L. Elmore	Karen Miner	W.T. Thomson
George Gowgani	Michael H. Pickett	

Special acknowledgement is extended to Floyd O. Colbert for his patience, perseverance, and tireless efforts throughout the course of preparing this book for publication, and to Linda L. Romander for her editorial guidance.

In addition to the aforementioned committees and individuals, a special thanks is extended to Bill Berkson for editing all the various drafts that went toward the making of this book.

INTRODUCTION

by William A. Harvey[1]

This book exemplifies the present stage in the evolution of what we now call weed science. It represents the efforts of a great many people, not only the listed authors, who are to be commended, but also those forerunners whose work provided a foundation for this science.

Weeds are a category of plant that has been with us since humans first began selecting their food from among the many wild plants in their environment. A simple and common definition of a weed is a plant out of place. Serious efforts to minimize the growth and numbers of unwanted plants and to maximize the production of useful plants began slowly in early historical times.

As human populations increased and cultivation of food crops became essential for survival, the recognition of losses due to weeds resulted in weed control being tolerated as a laborious but natural part of good crop husbandry. This tolerance contributed to the slow development of weed control as a science.

A detailed history of the worldwide development of weed control is not the aim of this publication. Excellent general histories are available elsewhere. There are, however, milestones in the development of weed science, particularly in California, which should be mentioned.

Although for many people weed control began with the development of 2,4-D in 1945, there were important beginnings long before. Hand pulling was probably the earliest method of removing undesirable plants, followed by the development of crude cultivation implements. The latter have evolved into more sophisticated equipment, and this evolution continues today.

1. University of California Cooperative Extension, Davis, CA.

The recognition by botanists of weeds as a category of the plant world began at least a century ago. Publications on identification of weeds began to appear in the United States before 1900. Some included limited discussions of control methods. These bulletins were often published to meet farmers' needs, and the control information was based on field experiments rather than research programs. Two of the earliest publications on weed control in the state were *The California Agricultural Experiment Station Report for 1890,* which included a 15-page section on "The Weeds of California," by E.W. Hilgard, and, in 1911, Frederic T. Bioletti's California Agricultural Experiment Station Circular 69 titled *The Extermination of Morningglory.*

By the 1920s most states had weed manuals of some sort. In 1922, the California Department of Agriculture published *Weeds of California and Methods of Control* by F.J. Smiley, with contributions by members of the department. This was succeeded by the 1941 publication of *Weeds of California* by W.W. Robbins, Margaret K. Bellue, and Walter S. Ball. In the foreword to that publication, W.C. Jacobsen stated, "The year 1922 marked the beginning of a real and active interest in weeds and weed control on the part of official agencies in California."

It was in 1922 that W.W. "Doc" Robbins came from Colorado to teach botany at the University of California at Davis. His background had included work on weed control, and in 1929 he persuaded the California Department of Agriculture to bring Walter S. Ball from Colorado to act as the department's specialist in that subject. This early core group was further strengthened in 1931 when Alden S. Crafts was hired in the botany department as a full-time research botanist to work on weed control. Thus, by 1931 California had a nucleus of trained people to develop a weed-control program that included teaching, research, and regulation.

Let us see where weed control stood in the early 1930s—some 55 years ago. The conversion of agricultural systems to tractor power was proceeding rapidly, making possible new improvements in cultivation equipment, much of which was developed by the farmers themselves to meet their needs. Different kinds of blades and the rod weeder developed earlier could now be used for numerous weeding chores on a large scale. The potential for using tractor-mounted sprayers to treat large areas now existed.

Herbicides were just then beginning to become part of farming practice. Selective weed control in crops with herbicides was not yet an accepted practice, although copper sulfate, iron sulfate, and sulfuric acid had been tested. Limited use was made of sulfuric acid on cereals and onions, but the problems associated with handling a strong acid prevented a wide-scale use.

Nonselective herbicides, such as arsenic, orchard heating oil, salt (sodium chloride), sodium chlorate, and carbon bisulfide as a fumigant, were the available remedies, primarily for perennial weeds. The application rates of these compounds seem tremendous as compared to today's herbicide use rates. Salt was used at 20 tons/A or more; sodium chlorate at 600–1000 lb/A; carbon bisulfide at 320 gal (3200 lb)/A; heating oil at 100–300 gal/A; and arsenic in various forms—from several pounds as sodium arsenite to hundreds of pounds as dry white arsenic.

Biological control was under investigation, but no release of insects had been made in the United States. However, success in the control of prickly pear cactus with an introduced insect in Australia gave hope of future successes.

Seed and weed laws were enacted in many states by the early 1930s, but those pertaining to weeds were not always enforced, due in part to lack of suitable herbicides and of adequate funding. However, weed supervisors became important officials in a number of states, particularly in the Midwest, with the authority to enforce control of certain weeds. Specific weeds were often targeted for eradication, and sodium chlorate and carbon bisulfide were used in large quantities in the Midwest and the West for field bindweed control. The government programs were often used to provide work for the unemployed, but they had the side effect of stimulating research into both weeds and herbicides.

Farmer meetings on the subject of weeds led by experiment-station and extension-service personnel were common in almost every state as farmers became more conscious of losses caused by weeds. Basic farm practices, such as sowing clean seeds, preventing seed formation of existing weeds, cultivation, mowing, and hand hoeing of individual weeds, were emphasized in these meetings. W.W. Robbins became famous throughout California for his rallying cry of "Eternal Vigilance" uttered while brandishing a hoe.

Several state weed conferences were organized in the 1930s, including the Western Weed Control Conference in 1938, which was a spin-off from the Western Plant Quarantine Board, and a recognition by representatives of the 11 western states of the importance of weeds and the value of exchanging information among weed workers. Most state experiment stations had at least part-time weed-research workers in their botany or agronomy departments. In 1935, in response to congressional pressure and funding, the United States Department of Agriculture (USDA) set up a regional weed-research project with field research stations in five states.

Thus, by the start of the 1940s, there had begun a steady development of weed science in all of its aspects. This advance was slowed with the advent of World War II. The war years, nevertheless, brought the beginning of a revolution in weed science that stemmed from plant hormone research begun in the 1930s. The potential of vegetation control with chemicals was recognized and investigated under wartime secrecy. In late 1944, the secret was out: (2,4-dichlorophenoxy) acetic acid (now known as 2,4-D) had been found capable of destroying annual weeds at rates of a few ounces per acre, and certain perennial weeds at slightly higher rates. Moreover, it could be used selectively to control broadleaved weeds in corn, small grains, grass pastures, and lawns. The phenoxy compounds were translocated in the plant and could cause destruction of deep roots of perennial weeds; they could be applied at low volume by ground or air. Indeed, they appeared as miracles to those weed workers who had labored with pounds and tons per acre of non-selective, soil-acting herbicides. Weed science was never to be the same again. All that had gone before became ancient history.

Although the development of synthetic organic herbicides had begun in the late 1930s and early 1940s with dinitrophenol salts used as selective herbicides, such chemicals had the disadvantages of relatively high human toxicity, staining of skin and clothing, and the requirement of high volumes of solution per acre to give adequate wetting of the foliage. Nevertheless, prior to the introduction of 2,4-D, they were used extensively in California in small grains, often with spray rigs carrying 1000 gallons of solution and applying 70–100 gal/A. Despite the availability of 2,4-D, their use on onions continued, since their selectivity was based on plant wetting.

The selectivity of the phenoxy compounds was based on physiological factors within the plant, a phenomenon that excited plant physiologists throughout the world and generated large quantities of research. This was a breakthrough for the acceptance of weed research as a valid field of scientific enquiry. There were important facts to be learned from studying the action of herbicides on plants. Much of the work was aimed not necessarily at control of weeds but at understanding the physiology of plants, including both crops and weeds. Thus, weed control became weed science with the infusion of scientific studies of the physiology, biochemistry, and anatomy of weedy plants.

The increased interest in weed control that accompanied the wide acceptance of 2,4-D was not lost on chemical companies looking for postwar products. Screening programs were developed by major chemical and drug companies that previously had never thought to look for herbicidal activity in the multitude of organic compounds they produced or were capable of producing. Early screening and product development of herbicides became the province of the chemical industry, while the academic community moved toward field screening and adaptation to local crop and weed problems and into basic research studies (e.g., mode-of-action research).

New herbicides came on the market in ever-increasing numbers. Use recommendations became a major task for extension services, experiment stations, and the USDA. As farmers were eager to use the new herbicides and industry was interested in getting new products on the market and into use, a major issue regarding herbicide recommendation arose: how much local testing was adequate for such factors as soil type, organic matter, rainfall, irrigation practice, soil and air temperature, crop variety, etc.? Specialists were brought in to help provide such information, with the serendipitous result of broadening the scientific base of weed science. The need for pooling information led to the formation of many state and regional weed-control conferences.

The North Central Weed Control Conference was organized in 1944, the Northeastern in 1947, and the Southern in 1948. These regional conferences came together in 1949 as the Association of Regional Weed Control Conferences and in 1951 initiated the publication *Weeds*. A joint meeting was held in 1953, and the Weed Science Society of America organized in 1954, with the first meeting held in 1956.

The California Weed Conference was organized in 1949, largely through the efforts of W.W. Robbins and Walter Ball of the California Department of Agriculture. Participation by all interest groups and agencies was encouraged. The meeting was an instant success.

As the number of herbicides increased and field use expanded, the issue of weed science began to change. Early interest centered on finding herbicides that were effective in controlling weeds, and rates into the tons-per-acre range were accepted to accomplish this purpose. As herbicides that were selective on certain crops were discovered, concerns about crop injury spread. As a result, application rates were refined to provide weed control with crop safety. Wide-scale use of 2,4-D produced concerns about drift to nearby sensitive crops. It should be understood that there had never before been a herbicide whose chemical drift could damage such crops as grapes, cotton, melons, tomatoes, etc., miles away from the original application point. This hazard resulted in new government regulations and research into application techniques and air-mass movement. Crop-damage evaluations and estimates of crop losses resulting from non-target chemical applications produced a new breed of consultants skilled in legal testimony.

Pesticide drift, plus the commercial use of pesticides on many food crops, aroused public concern about food-supply contamination. This led to extensive efforts in residue analyses by both manufacturers and recommending agencies prior to registration approval. Analytic methods became highly sophisticated, with measurements of chemical residues possible in terms of parts per million, parts per billion, and in some instances, parts per trillion. Attempts to relate these values to human toxicity have required expanded toxicological studies and have aroused much controversy. Studies include research into exposure of field workers, wildlife, water supplies, and other, more general ecological effects. Weed science has integrated these new disciplines as needed to meet the questions posed by the public. Litigation has become commonplace, and laws and regulations have proliferated. More time and money are now invested in studies of potential peripheral effects than in studies of effectiveness and economic value. Conferences address technological problems but are also faced with political and social questions which are more difficult to resolve and which require skills not commonly part of the weed scientist's training.

Thus, weed science has come of age, a discipline in its own right. Much of its strength comes from its foundations in basic sciences. Its vitality comes from the cooperation of the many sectors involved—university, regulatory, and industry.

A study of the information in this book should prepare the reader to better understand weed science and to continue as an informed participant in the future of this rapidly expanding discipline.

1

PLANTS

By Jodie S. Holt[1] and Steven R. Radosevich[2]

Botany is the study of the many organisms in the plant kingdom. Botanists study numerous aspects of plants, including their classification, structure, function, inheritance, propagation, and interactions of plants with each other, with animals, and with their environment. Applied botanists, such as weed scientists, use basic information about plants to solve vegetation-management problems. This introductory chapter presents a brief overview of plant characteristics, which must be understood in order to develop effective weed control methods.

PLANT STRUCTURE

The plant kingdom is generally divided into several major groups that are interrelated. The simplest organisms in this kingdom are bacteria, fungi, and algae, which are sometimes aquatic weeds (see Chapter 16). Embryophytes, or higher plants, form embryos, and most have vascular or conducting tissues. Most weeds are in the category known as higher vascular plants, or seed plants, which includes both gymnosperms and angiosperms. These plants are highly complex and composed of different kinds of cells, tissues, tissue systems, and organs.

Plant Cells

The fundamental structural unit of a plant is the cell (fig. 1). Cells of higher plants are compartmentalized into discrete, membrane-bound

1. University of California, Riverside, CA. 2. Oregon State University, Corvallis, OR.

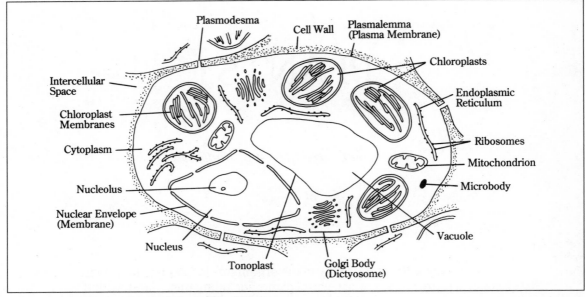

Figure 1. A typical plant cell and its parts.

particles called organelles, each of which has a unique structure and function. The organelles of a typical cell are the nucleus, containing the genetic material (DNA) of the plant and acting as the "control center" of the cell; mitochondria, the site of respiration; chloroplasts, the site of photosynthesis; vacuoles, fluid-filled organelles that regulate and store waste materials; and endoplasmic reticulum, which functions in cell wall synthesis. A nonliving, cellulose wall surrounds plant cells and provides structure, while a plasma membrane (plasmalemma) occurs inside the wall and completely surrounds the cell contents, or cytoplasm. The plasma membrane is semipermeable and is the major barrier to penetration of solutes into the cell. Other parts of a typical cell are plasmodesmata, ribosomes, Golgi bodies, microbodies, and other types of plastids (fig. 1).

There are many different types of plant cells that perform a variety of different functions. At maturity, some cells are still living (they contain cytoplasm), while others are dead. Collectively, all nonliving parts of plants, including cell walls, intercellular spaces, and nonliving cells, are called the apoplast, while all living portions of the plant, including the cytoplasm of living cells, are called the symplast. In general, water and solutes can flow freely through apoplastic regions of a plant, while flow into symplastic regions is regulated by the plasma membrane. Ultimately, in order to injure a plant, some aspect of proper functioning of the symplast must be disrupted. Herbicides exert their effect on plants by disrupting specific cellular and molecular sites and processes.

Plant Tissues

Groups of cells with a common origin that perform a particular collective function are called tissues. The major plant tissues are meristematic tissues, the sites of growth and differentiation; epidermis, which covers the entire plant body and protects it from drying out; vascular tissues (xylem, phloem), which transport water, minerals, and food materials throughout the plant; and ground tissues, which form the bulk of a plant and serve a variety of functions. Many herbicides act on a specific tissue; for example, the auxin-type growth regulators are especially toxic to meristematic tissues. Herbicides contact plants at the epidermis; for a herbicide to injure a plant, it must either act on the epidermis or be transported through the vascular tissue to another site of action. Thus, basic information about plant structure and function is necessary in order to select appropriate chemicals for weed control.

Plant Organs

Organs are the largest structural units of a plant and are composed of groups of tissues that perform a specific function. The aboveground plant organs (stems, leaves, buds, and flowers) are referred to as the shoot, while the root is the primary underground plant organ. Angiosperms, the group containing most terrestrial weeds and crops, are separated into two types based on the number of cotyledons in the seed. Dicotyledons (dicots), such as wild mustard and bean, contain two cotyledons, while monocotyledons (monocots), such as johnsongrass and corn, contain one. These two large groups of plants typically have different types, arrangements, and locations of organs. Dicots have broad leaves with veins radiating from a midvein, a taproot and/or fibrous root system, and flower parts in multiples of four or five. In contrast, monocots generally have long, narrow leaves with parallel veins, a fibrous root system, and flower parts in multiples of three. The structure of typical dicot and monocot plants is shown in figure 2. Because of pronounced structural differences between dicots and monocots, weed control methods can often be targeted specifically at one of these groups.

Roots

The roots of plants provide anchorage to the soil, absorb water and solutes, and conduct this material upward to the shoot via the xylem. Older roots may also act as storage organs for starch and sugars that are synthesized in the shoot and transported via the phloem to the root. Roots possess meristematic tissue, the apical meristem, near the root tip, from which primary root growth continues to occur during the life of the plant. In addition, lateral roots and sometimes underground shoots originate

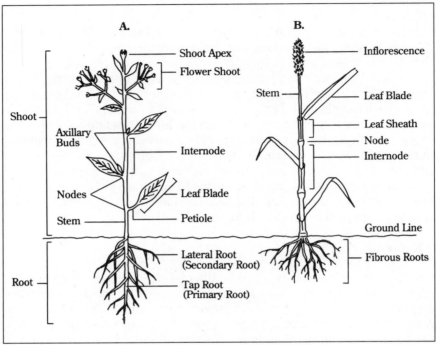

Figure 2. Structure of (a) a mature dicot and (b) a mature monocot plant.

from a specialized meristematic cell layer called the pericycle (fig. 3).

Epidermal tissue comprises the outer cell layer of all roots. Epidermal cells of the root near the tip produce root hairs, which are cellular extensions that increase the surface area, and thus, the absorbing capacity of the root. The vascular tissue in the root, as in all plant organs, is composed of xylem and phloem. Cells of the xylem, tracheids, and vessel elements, are elongated cells that form thick secondary walls (fig. 3). These cells die after the walls are formed, producing the xylem tissue in which water and nutrients are transported throughout the plant. The phloem tissue, generally located to the outside of the xylem, is composed of sieve-tube elements and companion cells (fig. 3). This tissue functions in the long-range transport of food materials, mostly sugars, which are produced in the upper portions of the plant. A major distinction between these two plant tissues is that at maturity, phloem cells are alive (symplastic) while xylem cells are dead (apoplastic); together they form the vascular cylinder of the plant.

Outside the vascular cylinder is a single cell layer, the endodermis, where plants regulate the flow of materials from the soil solution into the vascular tissue. This regulation is critically important to plant survival and occurs by means of specially modified walls of the endoder-

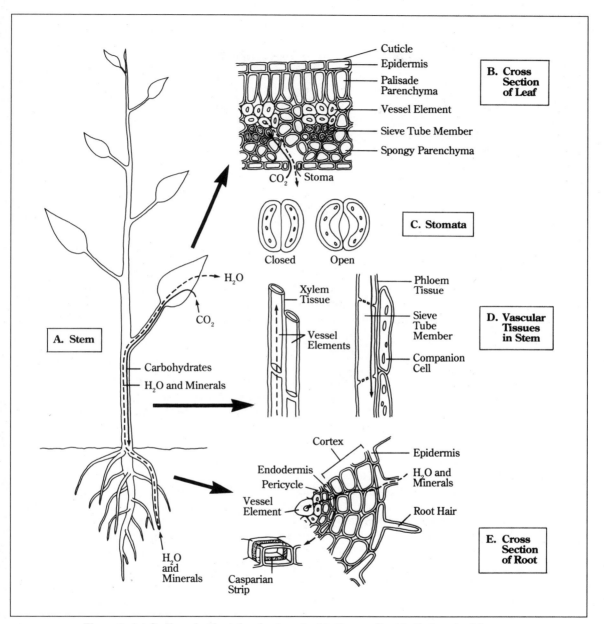

Figure 3. (a) Section of a plant showing transport pathways. Symplastic transport from leaves to roots is shown by solid line, apoplastic transport from roots to leaves is shown by broken line. (b) Leaf cross-section showing tissues and cell layers. (c) Stomata, closed and open, showing configuration of guard cells. (d) Vascular tissues in the stem, showing xylem (left) and phloem (right). (e) Root cross-section showing Casparian strip of the endodermis and other tissues and cell layers.

mal cells. These cell walls contain a continuous, impermeable, waxy band, called the Casparian strip (fig. 3), which forces absorbed material through the living portion, or symplast, of the endodermal cells via the plasma membrane. The cortex, a type of ground tissue, comprises the remainder of the root and functions in food storage.

The two types of root systems in plants are the taproot system, which are typical of dicots, and the fibrous root system, which are typical of monocots (fig. 2). Taproots develop from the seedling primary root and have lateral roots extending from them. Fibrous roots develop as adventitious roots from underground parts of stems after the seedling primary root dies. Many plants with taproots also form fibrous roots that are close to the soil surface. Roots can penetrate deep into the soil; the extent of the root system of a plant usually exceeds that of its shoot. However, fibrous root systems are generally more shallowly rooted than are taproot systems.

Stems

The main axis of the plant shoot is the stem (fig. 2). Stems function to support the aboveground plant parts, store and conduct water and solutes from the roots to the shoot, and store and conduct products of photosynthesis from the leaves to other aboveground plant parts and to the roots. In addition, green stems have the capacity to perform photosynthesis. Just as in roots, stems possess apical meristems, or buds, at the shoot tip, from which primary growth continues to occur. Axillary buds located in the axils of leaves grow into lateral branches on the plant (fig. 2). Buds on the plant shoot may grow into vegetative parts (stems and/or leaves) or may undergo transition to the floral state and produce flowers. Buds characteristically possess seasonal periods of inactivity, or dormancy, which are regulated by environmental conditions and internal hormones of the plant.

The anatomy of the plant stem is similar to that of the root but is more complex due to the presence of leaves and buds. Plant shoots are covered on their outer surfaces by a waxy cuticle that is secreted by the epidermal tissue. The cuticle is the primary barrier to gas and water movement into and out of the plant, and also represents the major barrier to entry of foliar-applied herbicides into plants. Inside the epidermis is a cortex similar to that of the root, except that these cells may engage in photosynthesis. The vascular bundles of the stem are dispersed throughout the cortex. As the cells of the stem and leaves develop, some differentiate to form sieve-tube elements for phloem and others to form xylem elements. This creates an interconnecting and continuous system for transport between roots and shoots (fig. 3). Stems do not have an endodermis, such as is found in roots. The innermost part of dicot stems is the ground tissue known as pith.

Stems are divided into nodes, where leaves are attached, and internodes, the areas between nodes. Many plants also possess stems that are modified for specialized functions. For example, horizontal stems, such as the underground rhizomes of quackgrass and the aboveground stolons of strawberry, can reproduce vegetatively, while enlarged underground stems, such as the tubers of yellow nutsedge and the bulbs of onion, can store food materials. Other types of modified stems include thorns and vines.

Leaves

The leaves of a plant are attached to the stems at the nodes and consist of a flattened blade and a petiole that supports the blade (fig. 2). In grass plants (monocots), the petiole forms a sheath around the stem for a short distance above the node, while in some dicots, the petiole is lacking entirely and the blade is sessile (attached directly at the node). Leaf blades may be simple, all in one unit, or compound, composed of a number of separate parts called leaflets. There are many types of compound leaves. Although leaf size and to some extent shape may vary considerably with environment, the type of leaf on a plant is often a good diagnostic clue to use in plant identification.

The primary function of leaves is photosynthesis, in which light, carbon dioxide (CO_2), and water (H_2O) are utilized to produce energy-rich food materials for the plant. Sandwiched between the upper and lower epidermis of the leaf are two types of ground tissue, both of which function in photosynthesis. The palisade parenchyma, near the upper surface, consists of elongated cells, while the spongy parenchyma, near the lower surface, is made up of irregularly shaped cells surrounded by air spaces (fig. 3). Cells of both tissues contain an abundance of chloroplasts. Both outer surfaces of the leaf are covered by the cuticle and epidermis. Movement of gases into and out of the leaf occurs through microscopic pores that are usually most abundant on the lower leaf surface. Two crescent-shaped guard cells surround each pore. This structure, or stoma, regulates the flow of CO_2 into the leaf, and oxygen (O_2) and H_2O out of the leaf. Thus, CO_2 for photosynthesis can enter the leaf directly, without having to pass through the epidermal cells and the cuticle. Vascular tissue is present in leaves as shown in figure 3.

PLANT FUNCTION

The many biochemical reactions occurring in an organism are known as metabolism. These processes occur within organelles in plant cells. Metabolic reactions are divided into anabolic, or synthesis, reactions that require energy, and catabolic, or degradation, reactions that release energy. The major anabolic reactions in plants include photosynthesis and synthesis of nitrogen-containing compounds, such as proteins and nucleotides. Catabolic reactions include respiration and breakdown of other energetic compounds accompanied by the release of available energy. Herbicides generally have a phytotoxic effect on plants by blocking or disrupting one or more metabolic reactions.

Photosynthesis—Food Production in Plants

Through photosynthesis, green plants convert the light energy of the sun to biochemical energy in the form of carbohydrates. The presence of CO_2 in the plant cell, as well as light, H_2O, and chlorophyll, are required for photosynthesis to occur. The general equation for photosynthesis is:

$$6\,CO_2 + 6\,H_2O \xrightarrow{\text{light}} C_6H_{12}O_6 + 6\,O_2$$

Photosynthesis in most higher plants occurs in chloroplasts as a twofold process involving light-dependent reactions, the light reactions, and light-independent reactions, the dark reactions. In the light reactions, energy-rich compounds are produced that are subsequently used in the dark reactions to produce sugars from CO_2. These six-carbon sugars can then be resynthesized into a variety of carbohydrates such as starch, sucrose, or cellulose. The food substances that plants produce become directly or indirectly the food supply of all animals on earth.

Respiration

In order to grow, plants also must derive energy from the carbohydrates they produce. The process of converting a carbohydrate to its simpler components of CO_2, H_2O, and energy is known as respiration and occurs in the mitochondria of the cell. The general equation for respiration is:

$$C_6H_{12}O_6 + 6\,O_2 \longrightarrow 6\,CO_2 + 6\,H_2O + \text{energy}$$

Respiration is a complex series of chemical reactions involving many different enzymes. All living cells depend on this process to provide energy for their life processes. Respiration in most plants is aerobic, utilizing free oxygen from the air to completely oxidize food substances. Aerobic respiration is essentially the chemical reverse of photosynthesis.

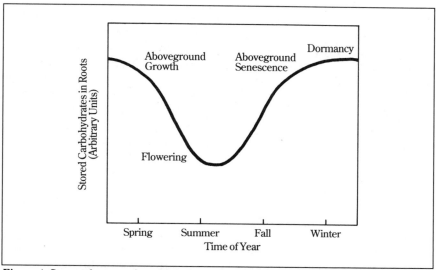

Figure 4. Seasonal progression of stored carbohydrates in roots of perennial plants.

Transport of Carbohydrates

After carbohydrates have been produced, they must be transported to zones of either use or storage. If use occurs within the leaf cell, transport occurs in the cell cytoplasm and is of relatively short distance. However, if use or storage occurs to other parts than the leaf of production, long-distance transport, called translocation, is necessary. Translocation occurs in the symplastic portion of the plant, which is a continuous system of living plant cells connected by phloem tissue (fig. 3).

The translocation of carbohydrates within plants is explained by the source-to-sink theory, in which 'sources' are areas of production (photosynthetically active leaves), while 'sinks' are areas of use (e.g., actively growing shoot tips, actively respiring roots, underground storage structures). The driving force for phloem transport is the mass flow of solutes dissolved in water from regions of high concentration to regions of low concentration. Foliar-applied herbicides that are able to penetrate the plant cuticle, such as glyphosate and 2,4-D, must enter the symplast by passing into the cytoplasm of epidermal cells; from there they may be translocated throughout the plant by way of the phloem. Information on the relative mobility and primary transport pathways for a number of herbicides is provided in table 1 of Chapter 7.

Storage organs present an interesting case in transport because they may act as either sources or sinks, depending on the physiological state of the plant (fig. 4). In early spring, when new shoots are being produced from perennial roots systems, underground organs may act as a source, as food substances are translocated to actively growing parts of the plant. During flowering, which requires large amounts of energy, stored underground carbohydrate reserves are generally at their lowest point. Later in the year, when leaves are producing carbohydrates for storage, the same organs may act as a translocation sink. Winter dormant periods are when stored reserves are highest (fig. 4). This seasonal cycling of translocation and stored food reserves is important to consider in weed control, for it regulates both movement of herbicides throughout a perennial plant and regeneration of shoots following damage to roots.

Transport and Evaporation of Water

The need to keep stomata open for CO_2 uptake allows loss of water vapor. This process, called transpiration, regulates the temperature of the transpiring organ, which is cooled as water evaporates. However, as more and more water is lost through open stomata, guard cells become less turgid, and stomata are closed (fig. 3). Although wilting can occur as water is lost, the regulation of guard cells by turgor reduces the chance of plant death from water loss. The amount of water used by some species in transpiration can be very large. For example, many herbaceous crops and weeds can transpire 1 or 2 gallons of water per day. Thus, plants are obviously in a position of compromise for survival. The need for CO_2 for photosynthesis must be balanced with the loss of H_2O through transpiration. As a result, relatively large amounts of water must be supplied to plants for maximum productivity.

Long distance transport of water, mineral nutrients, and other substances in plants occurs in response to water-potential gradients produced by transpiration. As water evaporates from a plant surface, more water moves to that surface to fill the deficit, effectively pulling water and dissolved substances through the plant from the soil to the leaves. The movement of water in plants occurs in the apoplast, a continuous system of cell walls, intercellular spaces, and xylem tissue (fig. 3).

Water and nutrients enter roots through root hairs and move towards the vascular cylinder largely through apoplastic walls and spaces. At the endodermis, however, movement of any water solution through cell walls is restricted by the Casparian strip (fig. 3), and therefore, must move into the symplast at the cytoplasm of the endodermal cells in order to reach the xylem. Thus, everything entering the vascular tissue, including soil-applied herbicides such as the triazines and ureas, must first pass through the filtering process of the plasma membrane of the endodermis before it can be transported throughout the plant. Once past the endodermal cells, water and nutrients move into the xylem tissue and are transported apoplastically upward through the plant. Although water is used by plants to conduct metabolic processes for growth, and for storage, most of the water that moves through plants is lost through transpiration.

PLANT GROWTH AND DEVELOPMENT

Plant growth occurs when cells divide and enlarge at the meristematic regions of the plant. As described above, plant meristems are located at the shoot and root tips, in buds, and in various internal tissues (e.g., pericycle). Differentiation of cells into tissues also occurs near meristems. Thus, any method of weed control that affects meristems may prevent normal growth and differentiation of plant cells. Plant development is the pattern in which cells become organized into tissues and organs to result in the mature form of the plant. Basic differences in seeds and seedling development occur between dicots and monocots, which are important both in weed identification and in selecting weed control methods.

Seeds and Germination

Even during storage, a seed is a living unit composed of three basic parts: an embryo, a source of food, and an external covering, or seed coat (fig. 5). Food is usually stored in cotyledons of dicots and the endosperm of monocots. As long as the seed is relatively dehydrated, it remains dormant. It is alive, but all metabolic processes are occurring at very slow rates. To activate the plant embryo, seeds of most species need only to be saturated with water and placed in a suitable environment. This process is called germination and occurs in the soil. Most weed seeds, in contrast to crop seeds, also require light for germination, which therefore occurs at or near the soil surface. Once the microenvironmental conditions that allow germination to proceed are met, further events occur within the seed that allow the seedling to develop.

Since the plant embryo relies on its own food reserves, a mechanism is required to mobilize those reserves for use during germination. Very soon after the seed begins to absorb water (imbibition), the activated embryo produces a plant hormone called gibberellin (GA). Gibberellin diffuses from the embryo to the aleurone layer underneath the seed coat. The presence of GA signals the aleurone layer to produce and secrete an enzyme, α-amylase, which converts the starchy cotyledons or endosperm to sugars. Usually by the third or fourth day after imbibition, the embryo has grown in size, since it is now able to utilize carbohydrates and minerals from the digested food. After about a week, the stored food is completely converted and used, but the embryo usually is no longer dependent on its reserves since the seedling plant has emerged from the soil. The first true leaves derive energy from the

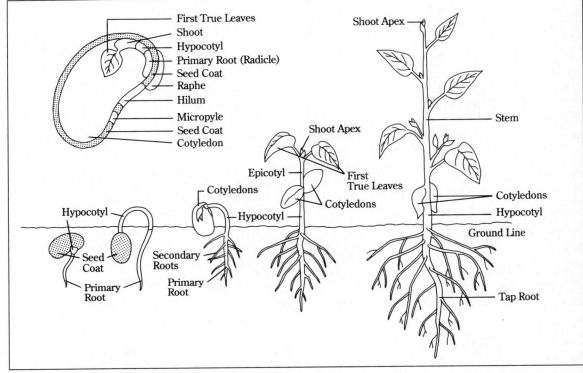

Figure 5. Seed, germination, and emergence of bean, a typical dicot.

environment by photosynthesis, and the roots absorb water and minerals from the soil.

While dry seeds in the soil are difficult to kill, there are many steps in the process of germination that may be disrupted (see Chapter 3). Furthermore, the seedling is considered the most vulnerable stage of a plant's life and is generally the easiest to control by physical or chemical means.

Growth

As the seed germinates, the emergence of the primary root, or radicle, from the seed usually occurs first in both dicots and monocots, followed by the expansion of the seedling shoot. Both organs grow rapidly. Both the root tip and the shoot tip have meristems where new cells are continually produced by cell division. Rapid growth of both the root and the shoot of a seedling occurs with the elongation of newly produced cells from the meristem in a process called primary growth. As the plant grows, specific zones develop immediately behind the meristems that are physi-

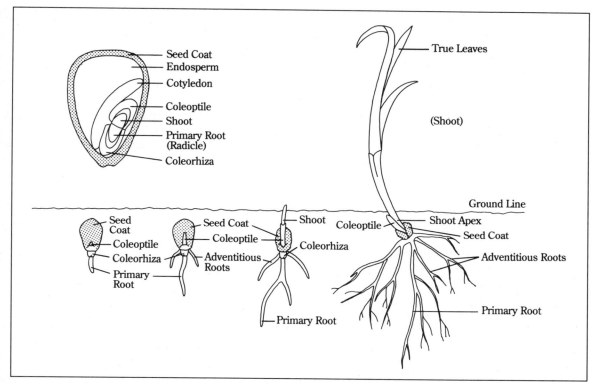

Figure 6. Seed, germination, and emergence of corn, a typical monocot.

cally and physiologically different, in a process called differentiation. The cells in these zones become specialized into tissues and organs to perform specific functions. Throughout the life of the plant, primary growth continues by means of cells that are continually produced in the meristems. Following primary growth, additional cells are produced in many dicot plants from the vascular cambium, a cell layer between the xylem and phloem, resulting in an increase in diameter of roots and stems. This type of growth, called secondary growth, is characteristic of perennial plants, especially woody ones. Examples of woody perennials include tanoak, a tree, and Scotch broom, a shrub, two common weeds in areas where the desired crop is also woody, e.g., Douglas fir trees. Stems of monocots are primarily herbaceous, while those of dicots may be either herbaceous or woody.

Emergence and Establishment

Shoot emergence patterns from the soil are of two principal types. Epigeal emergence, typical of many dicots, occurs when cotyledons are carried above the soil surface during emergence, while hypogeal emergence, typical of grass plants, occurs when cotyledons remain below the soil surface during emergence. In most dicots, within a short time after germination the shoot apex is elevated completely above the soil surface (fig. 5). In monocots, the shoot emerges from the soil with the apex and surrounding leaves encased in a sheath, called a coleoptile. Unlike dicots, the internodal regions do not elongate immediately, and the shoot apex remains close to the ground (fig. 6). The shoot apex of monocots typically lengthens just before flowering. Thus, at the seedling stage, the meristems of most dicots are exposed above the soil surface, while those of monocots are well protected at the base of the plant. These characteristics are important to consider in weed control, particularly herbicide placement decisions.

Mineral Nutrition

Mineral elements are essential in plant nutrition. A deficiency of any particular element may make it impossible for a plant to complete its life cycle. The elements needed in large quantities for plant growth are called macronutrients and include carbon, hydrogen, oxygen, nitrogen, phosphorus, potassium, sulfur, calcium, and magnesium. These elements are the basic materials from which cytoplasm, membranes, and cell walls are maintained. In addition, many other elements are required in lesser or trace amounts yet are essential to plant growth. These micronutrients include boron, chlorine, cobalt, copper, iron, manganese, molybdenum, and zinc. Symptoms of nutrient deficiency can include loss of green color (chlorosis), stunting and malformation, or death (necrosis) of plant parts. Many of these symptoms may also result from herbicide injury (see the plant diagnosis section of Chapter 7); thus, it is important to be able to recognize them.

Most of the essential elements plants need are obtained from the soil. Minerals are also commonly added to soils in commercial fertilizers. Leaf, or foliar, analysis is widely used as a means of detecting nutritional deficiencies, excesses, and imbalances in plants. To be available for plants, mineral elements in the soil must be present in solution. They can then move by diffusion through the soil solution to roots and be taken up by roots with water.

ENVIRONMENT AND PLANT GROWTH

The environment of a plant is the summation of all living (biotic) and nonliving (abiotic) factors that affect the growth, development, and distribution of the plant. The biotic portion of the environment includes microbes, animals, and other plants, whereas the abiotic components include soil, water, nutrients, and climatic conditions. The environment is often divided into the macroenvironment and the microenvironment. The macroenvironment is the broad-scale regional environment, which includes many aspects of soil and climate such as overall light intensity, precipitation patterns, and temperature. The microenvironment is the smaller-scale aspect of the environment that is influenced by the presence of objects (rocks, soils, other vegetation) and by topography.

Factors in the environment that influence plant growth are usually divided into two categories, resources and conditions. Environmental resources are consumable and include light, CO_2, water, nutrients, and oxygen. In contrast, environmental conditions such as temperature, soil pH, and soil bulk density (compaction) are not directly consumed. Plants respond directly to the resources and conditions in their surrounding microenvironment. Thus, the physiological and morphological characteristics of plants will vary according to the specific microenvironments in which they occur. Even though the macroenvironment may be relatively constant from year to year, the microenvironment often is not; thus, plant responses can be expected to vary from growing season to growing season. This phenomenon must be kept in mind, especially when considering weed management practices, since these also must be tailored to the microenvironment and the desired plant response.

REFERENCES

Anderson, W.P. 1983. *Weed Science: Principles.* 2nd ed. West Publishing Co., St. Paul. 655 pp.
Barden, J.A., R.G. Halfacre, and D.J. Parrish. 1987. *Plant Science.* McGraw-Hill Book Co., New York. 551 pp.
Esau, K. 1977. *Anatomy of Seed Plants.* 2nd ed. John Wiley and Sons, Inc., New York. 550 pp.
Radosevich, S.R. and J.S. Holt. 1984. *Weed Ecology. Implications for Vegetation Management.* John Wiley and Sons, Inc., New York. 265 pp.
Ross, M.A. and C.A. Lembi. 1985. *Applied Weed Science.* Burgess Publishing Co., Minneapolis. 340 pp.
Salisbury, F.B. and C.W. Ross. 1978. *Plant Physiology.* 2nd ed. Wadsworth Publishing Co., Inc., Belmont, CA. 422 pp.
Weier, T.E., C.R. Stocking, M.G. Barbour, and T.L. Rost. 1982. *Botany: An Introduction to Plant Biology.* John Wiley and Sons, Inc., New York. 720 pp.

2

WEEDS

by Howard Rhoads[1], George Gowgani[2], Gerald Croissant[3], and Larry W. Mitich[4]

By one simple definition, a weed is a plant out of place. But any agriculturally valid definition of a weed must take into account that a weed is also a plant which is doing or is capable of doing economic harm. This harmful aspect is overlooked by two other views that may be valid under some conditions but seldom are from the farmer's perspective. One of these allows that one person's weed is another's wildflower. The other sees a weed as a plant whose virtues have not yet been discovered (for instance, some validity as a potential source of plant breeder's germ plasm for disease resistance in crops). One of the best definitions of a weed, which permits inclusion of the other views, is that a weed is a plant that does more harm than good and has a habit of encroaching where it is not wanted.

Sources of germ plasm have yet to be eliminated by centuries of weed control efforts, and some flowering weeds will always survive for the enjoyment of those who are inclined to appreciate their beauty. Cover for wildlife and game will continue to exist no matter how intense the efforts at weed control. Weeds are not without some virtues, at least insofar as they do carry on photosynthesis and return some oxygen to the air, and their roots and vegetation may help prevent soil erosion caused by wind or water. But in agricultural situations, crop plants of various kinds could accomplish the same things and present fewer problems in the process.

There are at least 350,000 species of plants in the world. About 250,000 of those are flowering, seed-bearing plants called angiosperms. Almost

1, 2. California Polytechnic State University, San Luis Obispo, CA. 3. California State Polytechnic University, Pomona, CA. 4. University of California Cooperative Extension, Davis, CA.

all of the weedy plants are in this group. Weed identification is the first important step in any weed-control program. Anyone with some understanding of botanical terms could, with practice, learn to use one of the various plant-identification keys that have been compiled for individual states or regions. These keys (e.g., *A California Flora* by P.A. Munz) are usually quite detailed and use many scientific terms to describe plants and plant parts. Although these keys include descriptions of weeds, it is more convenient for weed-control purposes to have an identification handbook that describes *only* species that tend to cause problems as weeds. Many such weed-identification guides have been published, and some of them are included in the references. Nearly every state has at least one guide or handbook to aid the weed-control specialist in identifying the most common weed pests. Although convenient and easy in principle, using a picture guide to identify an unknown weed specimen may be time-consuming given that, in a state like California, more than 500 species may occur as weeds. Therefore, it will be helpful to learn some basic principles of weed identification, even when referring primarily to picture guides.

METHODS OF CLASSIFICATION

Plant classification is the arranging in groups of similar plants according to established criteria. Taxonomists use a system based on morphological similarities of groups of plants. One or more characteristics can be chosen which can be found in one group but not in another. The extremely large group of flowering seed plants can be easily distinguished from nonflowering plants such as algae, fungi, mosses, and liverworts. The taxonomist continues looking for less and less obvious traits as the groups of plants are narrowed down to smaller numbers until eventually there is only one species with one particular combination of characteristics not found in any other species. The basic botanical characteristics of plants and associated terminology are discussed in Chapter 1.

Botanical (Binomial) Classification

The general principles of classifying plants will also help to clarify how plants are named scientifically. The scientific or botanical name of a weed is used mainly in technical journals in which recommendations for control may be given. The botanical system of classification has many other advantages: it is a universal language, shows genetic relationship to other plants, and sometimes partially describes the plant. Common names alone can be very confusing because of the lack of uniformity of such names from one location to another. The weed 'black medic,' for example, is also called 'hop medic,' 'black clover,' 'trefoil,' 'nonesuch,' and 'blackseed' in different places. There is, however, only one scientific name for black medic: *Medicago lupulina.*

One common method of classifying plants is illustrated by the following outline, which provides alternative sets of characteristics from kingdom to subclass. Additional and more detailed assistance in classification from subclass to species follows the outline.

Kingdom	**Plant**
Sub Kingdom I	Plants with an embryo; includes algae, fungi, and lichens. No weed problems, except some aquatics. ...... Thallophyta
Sub Kingdom II	Plants with an embryo; includes chiefly land plants. ...... Embryophyta
Division A	Plants without vascular system; mainly mosses and liverworts. ...... Bryophyta
Division AA	Plants with vascular system; includes all flowering and seed plants and ferns. ...... Tracheophyta
Class B	Cone-bearing plants with exposed seeds; pines, spruces, firs, cedars, redwoods, and cycads. ...... Gymnospermae
Class BB	Flowering plants with enclosed seeds. ...... Angiospermae
Subclass C	Plants with one cotyledon in the seed; long, narrow leaves with parallel veins; a fibrous root system; and flower parts mostly in three or multiples of three. ...... Monocotyledonae
Subclass CC	Plants with two cotyledons; broad leaves with net venation; taproot or fibrous roots; flower parts usually in fours or fives. ...... Dicotyledonae

After a plant has been classified into one of the two subclass categories, it is placed in a specific order according to the plant key used. Dicots are comprised of 56 orders, monocots have 13. The orders are divided into families. An order, like a family, is made up of plants whose similarities are greater than their differences. Many of the similarities are usually rather obvious and easy to determine. Table 1 gives a listing of a few important "weed families" with one or more prominent identifying characteristics.

TABLE 1. IDENTIFYING CHARACTERISTICS OF SOME COMMON WEED FAMILIES

Common Name	Scientific Name	Main Feature
Lambsquarters	*Chenopodiaceae*	Flower is non-showy; leaf often shaped like a goose foot.
Grass	*Gramineae*	Long, narrow leaves; non-showy flowers.
Legume	*Leguminosae*	Fruit is a long or coiled pod; flower is butterflylike.
Mallow	*Malvaceae*	Roundish leaves, palmately lobed; disc-like fruit.
Milkweed	*Asclepiadaceae*	Milky sap; opposite leaves.
Nightshade	*Solanaceae*	Flower is star-shaped; fruit is a berry.
Mustard	*Cruciferae*	The four petals narrow to a claw below the wide or blade part, which spreads in the form of a cross, hence cruciform.
Pigweed	*Amaranthaceae*	Small, dry flowers in dense clusters; tiny, one-seeded, inflated fruit.
Sedge	*Cyperaceae*	Triangular stems; grasslike.
Sunflower (thistle)	*Compositae*	Flowers in heads, many with thistles.

Each family is further subdivided into a specific genus, which is further subdivided into species. The genus and species designations are then combined to give the scientific name of a particular plant. Since two category names are used, this plant-classification system is referred to as a binomial system of nomenclature. For easy recognition the scientific name is always italicized, and the initial letter of the genus only is always capitalized.

Life-Habit Classification

Another system of classifying weeds is according to their growth habits. There are three principal groups: annuals, biennials, and perennials.

Annuals

Weeds that complete their growth, reproduce, and die in one year or less are classed as annuals. These weeds pose the most common problems in many cultivated fields because of their large number and their ability to reproduce in crops that are planted annually. Annual weeds normally reproduce only by seed, and they are heavy seed producers. Frequently, their seeds can remain dormant for up to several years. Annuals may be classified as either summer annuals or winter annuals, depending on the time of year they begin growth. Most summer annuals grow actively during the summer, produce seeds, and die by the end of summer or early fall (table 2).

Winter annuals may germinate before winter but produce very little growth until the temperature starts to rise towards the end of winter or early spring. In a mild, warm climate (such as that of Southern California), winter annuals may begin growth much earlier, and some summer annuals may live through the winter (table 2).

TABLE 2. SOME COMMON SUMMER ANNUAL AND WINTER ANNUAL WEEDS

Summer Annuals	Winter Annuals
Pigweed	Common chickweed
Lambsquarters	Common yellow mustard
Purslane	Shepherdspurse
Prostrate spurge	Prickly lettuce
Crabgrass	Ripgut brome
Russian thistle	Common foxtail
Barnyardgrass	Annual bluegrass
Knotweed	Fiddleneck
Wild turnip	Wild radish
Puncturevine	Burclover
Annual sunflower	Redstem filaree

Biennials

Biennial plants require 14 to 24 months to complete their cycle of growth and reproduction. Because of this growth habit, they are sometimes confused with winter annuals. However, they usually begin growth in the spring and produce only vegetative growth (often just a short rosette or clump of leaves) the first year, followed by flower stalks and seeds after the winter season. After producing seeds, the biennial dies. Biennials are typically rather large plants when mature and have thick, fleshy roots. It is not a very large group of plants, and they generally cause problems only in pastures or other permanent-type plantings. Some common biennials are listed in table 3. Note also that some of the species listed may act as either annuals or biennials, depending on the climatic conditions, and a few may react as short-lived perennials in mild climates.

TABLE 3. SOME COMMON BIENNIAL WEEDS

Strict Biennials	Biennials That May Act As Annuals
Bullthistle	Horseweed
Common mullein	Little mallow
Wild parsnip	Henbit
Burdock	Filaree
Houndstongue	Pepperweed
Wild carrot	Fieldcress
Poison hemlock	Wild pennycress

Perennials

Plants that live for three years or longer are classed as perennials and may reproduce several times before dying. These plants appear as annuals in their first year of growth and can be rather easily controlled while they still maintain their annual habits. However, if they are allowed to go into a second year of growth, their underground structures become thick or enlarged with stored food, and they are difficult to control.

A few perennial weeds reproduce almost entirely by seed and are called *simple perennials.* Examples include dandelion, curly dock, plantain, chicory, and pokeweed. Most perennials, however, are *creeping perennials.* They have aboveground and underground vegetative structures that can readily propagate new plants asexually, although most of them also have seeds. The creeping structures may be rhizomes, which are underground modified stems, growing horizontally and forming roots and shoots at the nodes (joints); or stolons (runners), which are aboveground, horizontally creeping stems that reproduce much the same as rhizomes but are usually easier to control due to accessibility. Bermudagrass has both stolons and rhizomes, which results in its being a rather persistent plant.

A few perennials have other, specialized underground reproductive systems called tubers or nutlets. The tuber or nutlet is somewhat like a compressed rhizome. Yellow nutsedge (nutgrass), called by some "the world's most troublesome weed," reproduces from tiny nutlets less than ¾ inch long that are easily dragged from one spot to another in the process of growing a crop. This weed is very hard to control when well established.

Some perennials have an unusual creeping or horizontal root called a rootstock. This is a true root, but it can produce shoots at any point. It may also grow downward to great depths. Field bindweed rootstocks have been found as deep as 20 feet. Some other very persistent weeds with rootstocks include Canada thistle, leafy spurge, whitetop, Russian knapweed, silverleaf povertyweed, western ragweed, white horsenettle, and poison oak.

Since some translocated herbicides are more likely to affect stems and leaves while others affect roots, it is important to know which plants have rootstocks and which have rhizomes, stolons, or tubers.

Other vegetative reproduction occurs in weeds with bulbs (wild garlic), corms (basal stem of certain grasses), and apomictic seeds (certain grasses).

Seeds, however, are the most common mode of transportation of a weed species from one area to another. The seed has been described as "a small plant packaged for easy shipment." On the other hand, vegetative reproduction may account for localized spreading of weeds as a result of the reproductive parts being dragged throughout a field by farm implements.

TABLE 4. NUMBER OF SEEDS PRODUCED PER PLANT
FOR SOME WEEDS

Weed Species	Seeds per Plant
Wormwood	1,075,000
Mullein	223,200
Redroot pigweed	117,400
Purslane	52,300
Shepherdspurse	38,500
Curly dock	29,500
Field dodder	16,000
Kochia	14,600
Sunflower	7200
Barnyardgrass	7160
Common ragweed	3380
Canada thistle	680
Wild oat	250

Source: Stevens, O.A. 1932. Amer. J. Bot. 19:784–794.

Stevens' classic work in North Dakota (table 4) showed that, of the 101 annuals, 19 biennials, and 61 perennials he observed, the weeds had an average of 20,832, 26,600, and 16,629 seeds per plant, respectively. Unfortunately, we seldom deal with an individual plant but, rather, a population. It has been reported that a dense stand of rushes produced more than five billion seeds per acre with a density of over eight million per square yard. Such large production from a single weed population is indeed cause for concern.

Weeds such as dodder and nightshade are becoming increasingly serious pests in tomatoes. Due partly to their resistance to herbicides labeled for use on tomatoes and their high production of seed (16,000+ and 170,000+ per plant for dodder and nightshade, respectively), it is imperative that even single plants, let alone populations, be removed prior to their setting of seed. Should these weeds become as prevalent as many other common annuals, it would quickly make tomato production in infested fields uneconomical if not impossible. It is as easy today to come to the same conclusion as Muenscher in 1924, that a single plant of one of the worst weeds can, if left to produce seed, develop enough seed in one season to cover an entire area of ground the next season.

Regulatory Classification

The federal government and most states have one or more lists of noxious weeds for the purpose of preventing, restricting, or eradicating certain species that either are extremely difficult to control (such as the creeping perennials) or cause difficult problems in crops (such as yellow starthistle in cereals, quackgrass in potatoes, and dodder in alfalfa seed crops). The presence of primary (or prohibited) noxious weed seeds in agricultural seeds prevents the legal sale or distribution of such seed for planting purposes. Thus, 'noxious weed' means any species of plant which is or is liable to be detrimental or destructive and difficult to control or eradicate. A list of these primary and secondary noxious weeds can be found in the state agricultural code for most states.

At present, the California Seed Law designates two categories of noxious weeds: prohibited and restricted. Prohibited noxious weeds are so designated because:

- They are not known to occur in California or are of limited distribution; or
- They are not widely distributed in California and reproduce by seeds and/or underground root systems; or
- They are currently under eradication measures in the state.

Restricted noxious weeds are simply those not designated as 'prohibited.' The objective of the seed law is to prevent specific weeds from becoming established in, or being transported into, new areas as a contaminant of planting seed.

Some states, California among them, have regulatory laws that provide for intensive control or eradication of noxious weeds. The California weed law is administered by the director of the state's Department of Food and Agriculture and enforced by county agriculture commissioners or their deputies and inspectors. The weed law classifies weed plants when found growing in the state according to degrees of noxiousness that, by law, require certain treatment. This method of classification involves an "ABC" listing. "A" weeds must be eradicated, quarantined, or otherwise "held" at the state-county level; "B" weeds must be intensively controlled and eradicated (if possible) at the county level; and "C" weeds require control, intensive control, or eradication, as local conditions warrant, also at the county level. Weed laws often provide for the formation of control districts that frequently match county boundaries.

By contrast, common weeds are plants that are easier to control by normal cultural practices. They are usually annual weeds and reproduce only by seed, but because of their prevalence, they cause most of the agricultural damage and yield loss, and prevention of them is deemed nearly impossible.

Habitat Classification

A habitat is simply "a place to live." Many weeds can grow almost anywhere—infesting crops and thriving equally well along roadsides, in lawns and gardens, and in wastelands or waterways. However, there are some weeds that usually infest only a certain kind of crop or grow and develop best under special environmental conditions or in preferred locations. The weeds of cultivated land constitute a fairly large group, as do those of lawns and golf courses, and of wastelands and pastures.

A complete list of weeds that associate with certain crops or that grow under special conditions can be found in such publications as *Weeds of California* and others included in the references.

Plant-Type Classification

This method of classification groups weeds according to their morphological characteristics. Four distinct types of weeds are recognized: (1) grasses such as johnsongrass and wild oat, (2) broadleaves such as field bindweed and mustard, (3) brushes such as coyote brush and California sage, and (4) woody plants such as willow and tree tobacco. Plant-type classification is very useful where selective control of one type in a given situation is desired, e.g., broadleaf weed control in cereal crops.

Daylength Classification

Daylength classification is based on the photoperiodic responses of plants that account for the effect of daylength on flowering and reproduction. There are three distinct groups: (1) short-day weeds, (2) long-day weeds, and (3) day-neutral weeds. Short-day weeds, such as cocklebur and lambsquarters, are stimulated to vegetative growth, with delayed flowering and maturity when the days are long, and produce flowers and fruits when the days are relatively short. Long-day weeds, such as henbane and dog fennel, require a relatively long day for the formation of inflorescences, but they increase in vegetative growth when the days are short. Day-neutral weeds, such as nightshade, will flower under any photoperiodic conditions. Due to insufficient studies, this method of classification is not used for weeds to any large extent.

Thermal Classification

Thermal classification is based on the temperatures at which particular weeds make their best growth. This method is not used much due to the lack of sufficient study. In practice, when it is used, thermal classification depends on knowing which crops are affected. Warm-season crops such as corn and tomatoes associate with warm-season weeds such as barnyardgrass and nightshade. Cool-season crops, such as cole crops, have cool-season weeds such as mustard and wild oat. When crop rotations using warm- and cool-season crops are employed, the general level of weed populations may be lower than when monoculture is practiced.

Use Classification

Weeds are also grouped according to their uses. Some weeds are edible and can be used for human consumption, e.g., watercress, dandelion, and purslane (Mexican lettuce). Others, such as filaree, burclover, and sandlove grass, are highly desirable for livestock feed. These weeds are just as high, or even higher, in total digestible nutrients (TDN) than some cultivated forages. Many weeds, however, are not fit for human use or livestock feed. These weeds are known as poisonous weeds. The list of poisonous weeds is extensive; some are included in table 5.

TABLE 5. SOME IMPORTANT POISONOUS WEEDS

Milkweed (many species)	Halogeton
Locoweed	Klamathweed
Poison hemlock	Lupine
Flixweed	Tree tobacco
Jimsonweed	Cocklebur
Larkspur	Spiny clotbur
Common horsetail	Nightshade

Photosynthetic Pathway Classification

In recent years plant physiologists have discovered that not all plants have the same photosynthetic pathway. Some plants using the Calvin-Benson pathway are exclusively termed C_3 *plants*, because the first stable product of photosynthesis in such plants, PGA (phosphoglyceric acid), has three carbon atoms. In other plants, the first stable photosynthetic products are 4-carbon compounds including such organic acids as oxaloacetate, malate, and aspartate, which are therefore called C_4 *plants.* Some C_3 and C_4 weeds are listed in table 6. For a practical weed-control specialist this difference may seem to be insignificant, but for a weed-and-herbicide physiologist it is of utmost importance because there are several variations in the physiology, biochemistry, and morphology of C_3 and C_4 weeds. Because of these variations, C_4 weeds are more efficient than C_3 weeds as far as photosynthesis is concerned, and they are better competitors, particularly when the temperature is high.

TABLE 6. SOME C_3 AND C_4 WEEDS

C_3 Weeds	C_4 Weeds
Little mallow	Prostrate spurge
Redstem filaree	Puncturevine
Klamathweed	Common purslane
Black mustard	Russian thistle
Shepherdspurse	Redroot pigweed
Common chickweed	Saltbush
Curly dock	Purple nutsedge
Lambsquarters	Bermudagrass
Broadleaf plantain	Johnsongrass
Jimsonweed	Barnyardgrass
Common mullein	Large crabgrass

LOSSES CAUSED BY WEEDS

Weeds are the most persistent of all crop pests. Considerable reduction in crop yield results from competition between weeds and crops for water, soil nutrients, space, and light. When the supply of all or any of these essentials is not adequate for the optimum growth of both crop and weed, competition occurs. Considerable variation exists among species of crops and weeds in their competitive abilities. A strong plant competitor—either crop or weed—retards the growth of other plants growing in association with it. Annual losses in crop yield and quality due to weeds, combined with the costs of weed control, are greater in the United States than those due to insects, plant diseases, and nematodes combined. While maximum yield losses can exceed 90% of the potential yield in many crops, the actual losses in farmers' fields are generally much lower.

McWhorter and Patterson made a survey of various lists of important agronomic weeds and found that such weeds have many characteristics in common. Of the worst 37 soybean weeds in the United States, they determined that 38% are monocots, 32% are perennials, 35% have some form of vegetative reproduction, 19% produce rhizomes, 38% have the C_4 photosynthetic pathway, and 55% are exotic to the United States. In another study, Wax found that 55% of the 37 worst soybean weeds have allelopathic properties.

In *The World's Worst Weeds,* Holm et al report that of the world's 18 worst weeds 72% are monocots, 44% are perennials, 61% reproduce vegetatively, and 33% produce rhizomes. McWhorter and Patterson found that 78% of these same weeds have the C_4 pathway. Patterson also points out "the tremendous overrepresentation of C_4 plants and monocots as important agronomic weeds in proportion to their occurrence in the world's flora."

Pavlychenko did many of the classic studies in plant competition. In a 1935 study of root development of weeds and crops in competition under dry farming, he and Harrington observed that competition for water begins in the soil when root systems overlap in their search for water and nutrients. Weeds were discovered to be strong competitors for water. The amount of water used by a plant during its seasonal growth is called the *water requirement.* The water requirement for the aerial parts of a plant is the number of pounds of water needed to produce a pound of dry matter. Shaw reported that a plant of wild mustard requires four times as much water as a well-developed oat plant, and a plant of common ragweed requires three times as much water as a corn plant.

As early as 1927, researchers in Akron, Colorado, determining the water requirement for crops and weeds, reported that any measure of water requirement is exact only for the environment under which the plant is grown. The plant is affected by soil fertility, parasites, humidity, the cropping history, and other climatic and soil conditions. The data in table 7 were obtained in Colorado and so would not be precise for other areas.

TABLE 7. THE WATER REQUIREMENTS OF CERTAIN CROPS AND WEEDS, AKRON, COLORADO, 1927

Crop	Water Requirement[1]	Weed	Water Requirement[1]
Alfalfa	844	Cocklebur	415
Barley	518	Gumweed	585
Bromegrass	977	Knotweed	678
Buckwheat	540	Lambsquarters	658
Corn	349	Nightshade	487
Flax	783	Pigweed, prostrate	260
Millet	285	Pigweed, redroot	305
Oats	583	Purslane	281
Potatoes	575	Ragweed	912
Red clover	759	Russian thistle	314
Rye	634	Wild sunflower	577
Sorghum	305		
Soybeans	646		
Sugar beets	377		
Sweetclover	731		
Wheat	545		

1. *Pounds of water per pound of dry matter produced.*

The water requirement per acre of any plant can be determined by multiplying the production of the plant in pounds of dry matter per acre by the plant's water requirement.

In an Iowa study, moisture was found to influence plant growth both before and after dry periods. The authors concluded that a shortage of water in the spring may decrease competition by restricting the germination and growth of seeds to a point where they do not reduce yields. On the other hand, a wet spring with lush growth followed by a dry period can increase the detrimental effect of weeds on a crop.

The dominance of a plant is determined also by its success in competing for light. Light becomes a factor when the crop plant or weed is tall, the population is high, and one plant shades another.

In *Shading Effects on Annual Weeds in Soybeans,* Bush and Staniforth reported that "shading was responsible for a significant but not excessive fraction of the total yield reductions." The differences in light intensities measured at the sides of the rows affected the soybean yield, while the differences measured at the top of the plants had no direct effect on yields. Some weeds such as green foxtail and redroot pigweed are intolerant of shade, but others such as field bindweed, common milkweed, spotted spurge, and Arkansas rose are shade-tolerant. Shading suppresses the growth of several weeds, including common lambsquarters, common ragweed, and wild buckwheat.

Some weeds have an allelopathic effect on crop plants by synthesizing and releasing toxic or inhibitory substances that interfere with germination of crop seeds or subsequently retard growth of the plants. Patterson states that allelopathy is clearly related to competition "because competition-induced stress may increase the production of allelopathic substances, and growth inhibition caused by allelopathy may reduce the competitive ability of the affected plant."

Working with barley in England in the 1930s, Blackman and Templeman observed that by adding nitrogen to plots infested with wild mustard, corn chrysanthemum, and wild radish, the yield of the crop was raised to that of the weed-free check plots. When high levels of nitrogen were added, competition occurred for other factors, because in the weed-free crop there was a linear response to additional nitrogen, and in the weedy crop there was a leveling-off of response to higher rates of application. Blackman and Templeman concluded: "In a year of normal rainfall, competition between the crop and the weed is primarily for nitrogen and light. The light factor, however, is only operative when the weed species is tall and the density is high. In the majority of cases, competition is solely for nitrogen, while the critical period is confined to the early stage in the development of cereal."

In the 1960s, Rademacher conducted experiments with oats containing wild mustard and grew the infested crop at various nutrient levels. At the early tillering stage, the yield losses in oats were 11.4%; they increased to 25.85% at the end of tillering and reached 30% to 40% at harvest. Rademacher commented, "Competition for nutrients, especially nitrogen, starts at the time of germination and can assume quite dramatic proportions among young plants."

Vengris, Colby, and Drake studied plant nutrient competition between weeds and corn and reported that "even at high rates of fertilization with nitrogen, phosphorus, and potassium fertilizers, weeds competed strongly for essential nutrients, suppressed the growth of corn, and resulted in decreased yields of corn." When grown with weeds and fertilized with 200 pounds of P_2O_5 per acre, corn yields were lower than those of corn grown alone with no phosphorus fertilization. Because all plots had been liberally fertilized with nitrogen and potassium, these results clearly indicate the impracticability of maintaining yields in weedy corn fields by simply increasing the rate of fertilization.

Shaw reported that one wild mustard plant takes up twice as much nitrogen and phosphorus and four times as much potassium as a well-developed oat plant. Dodder, a parasitic weed, absorbs all of its food directly from the crop host.

Research in North Dakota has indicated that barley competes with weeds for nutrients more vigorously than does wheat. While wild oat prevented barley crops from fully utilizing soil fertility, it did not affect crop quality. Densities of 70 and 160 wild oat plants per square yard reduced wheat yield 22.1% and 39.1% respectively, compared to a crop with a weed-free control.

The extent to which competition from weeds can reduce crop yields depends on species, density, and duration. Naturally, species of crops and weeds differ in their competitive abilities. Working with cereal crops, Canadian researchers Shebeski and Friesen found that 600 green foxtail plants per square yard caused less damage than 200 wild oat, wild mustard, or wild buckwheat plants.

Likewise, in a competition comparison of pale smartweed and barley, single barley plants were found surrounded by varying numbers of smartweed and vice versa. While the barley was not affected by the presence or absence of the smartweed, the growth of the smartweed was greatly affected by the presence of the barley. The smartweed did not affect adjacent plants of its own species.

According to Pavlychenko and various other researchers, strong competitors dominate because of their faster and taller growth, early emergence, and larger embryos.

In studying the responses of corn hybrids to yellow foxtail competition, Staniforth reported a consistent and significant difference in tolerance of foxtail competition between a late-maturing and an early-maturing hybrid. Results from a two-year study indicated that the bushel production per hundredweight of foxtail for the late-maturing hybrid may have been subjected to severe foxtail competition at a critical or vulnerable period in its growth pattern, while the early-maturing hybrid was past a critical period in its growth before the onset of severe competition from foxtail.

In a Canadian study, green foxtail reduced corn yields a minimum of 5.9% and a maximum of 17.5% at varying densities. Green foxtail was less competitive than common lambsquarters, which reduced yields 12.6% and 38.1% at varying densities. Loss in crop yield virtually equalled the weed-yield increase.

Smith et al. reported 35%-to-74% yield losses in rice in the United States due to weeds. Barnyardgrass is the world's worst rice weed. A linear relationship was found between rice yield and barnyardgrass density in Japan. When barnyardgrass yielded 100 grams per square meter (dry weight), rice yield decreased by 80%.

Crops can tolerate some weed competition before yields are affected. According to the Canadian study, 10 wild mustard plants per square yard in flax, 25 in oats, and 50 in wheat and barley were sufficient to cause significant crop losses. Once the weed population reached 100 to 200 plants per square yard, any further increase was relatively insignificant.

Various densities of common ragweed were established in rows of sugar beets in Michigan. One-half, one, and two ragweeds per sugar beet reduced yields 15% compared to yields from check plots with no weeds present from emergence of the sugar beets until harvest. In Illinois, an increase in the yield of weeds was offset by a decrease in yield of shelled corn, cobs, and stalks.

It is readily apparent that weed competition is capable of reducing yield and frequently the quality of almost any crop. Research currently under way may reveal the levels of weed populations required to constitute an "economic threshold." More likely, however, an economic threshold, if determined, will only apply to a specific crop containing specific weeds under a specific set of growing and cost/income conditions. Thus, the "acceptable" level of weed competition will probably continue to be a matter of individual judgment, and the number of weeds acceptable to one grower may be totally unacceptable to another.

EFFECTS OF WEEDS ON MAN AND HIS ENVIRONMENT

While the immediate economic effect of weeds as competitors with their crops, and their effect as general nuisances in other areas, are well known and have been experimentally documented, some may fail to realize the significance of weeds and weed control in our daily lives. Weed costs to agriculture in the United States, including both those of control and loss of yield, presently exceed $6 billion annually. If intangible losses could somehow be assigned a value, the U.S. total would probably exceed $10 billion. Consumer prices for agriculturally produced foods, feeds, and fibers are higher due to losses caused by weeds. But how much more are the consumers paying?

In a 1977 letter to the then U.S. secretary of agriculture, C.A. Black explained that although hand-weeding experiments in Minnesota corn proved to be more productive "energywise" than chemical control, they were a disaster economically. Using a farm-labor price of $2.65 per hour for 1976, a net loss of $66 per hand-weeded acre resulted, while the net profit due to the use of a herbicide was $78 per acre.

Further, wrote Black, "If all the corn in the United States were to be weeded by hand labor in a period of six weeks, 17.7 million people working 40 hours per week would be required." The specter of moving that many workers into the rural corn-growing areas of the United States boggles the imagination. Even the most untutored would surely realize that it could not be done, even for just this one crop, without ruinous effects on the rural environment. What would be the effects if such maneuvers were extended to all the crops presently grown in this country?

Dramatic deaths, such as that of 1200 sheep in Utah in 1971 due to eating the poisonous plant halogeton, occur throughout the world every year on larger or smaller scales. Larkspur (sometimes called "cow poison") is particularly troublesome in some cattle-producing regions, while lupine is often poisonous to sheep. Livestock sickness or death may occur due to photosensitization of animals' skin by Klamathweed, burclover, puncturevine, or wild buckwheat; selenium poisoning from locoweed, woody aster, or goldenrod; molybdenum poisoning from legumes; nitrate poisoning from pigweed, fiddleneck, buckthorn, milk thistle, and many more. Mechanical injuries from starthistles, cocklebur, brome (foxtails), needlegrass, and puncturevine also contribute to the total loss.

Besides direct poisoning or injury of livestock, animal products such as off-flavored milk from wild onions and frenchweed, wool contaminants (burs), and general animal unthriftiness also contribute to economic losses. Likewise, crop quality may be reduced by such factors as planting seed contaminated with weed seeds.

Weeds are known to serve as off-season hosts for a number of crop diseases and insects that directly attack a later-growing crop and act as vectors in the transmission of virus diseases. They reduce the value of farmland to the extent that soils are contaminated with weed seed and make nonagricultural lands less useful. (For example, poison oak preventing fishing along a streambank.) They serve as fuel sources for wildfires along highways and railroads and in mountainous terrain. They contribute to highway accidents by obstructing a driver's line of vision or the visibility of precautionary road signs.

Although the role weeds play in impairing human health with hay fever (ragweed, goldenrod), stinging nettles, and poison oak is well known, monetary values are hard to assign to these effects because full documentation of days lost from work due to illness does not exist, and the value of individual suffering is unassignable. Some weeds are directly responsible for loss of human life. Children have died from eating poison hemlock by thinking the plant was carrots. Jimsonweed seeds are poisonous, as are the berries of certain nightshade plants.

Other losses of human life or productivity may occur due to weeds. Teratogens, substances that cause birth defects in humans and livestock, are passed directly to humans by accidental ingestion and through secondary sources such as milk from animals that have eaten weeds containing teratogens. In California in 1980, a deformed baby was born of a mother who had consumed local goat's milk during her pregnancy. Circumstantial evidence and prior experiments with animal-feeding indicated that a connection might have existed between the browse plants (lupine) eaten by the goat and the birth defects. "Milk sickness" in the nineteenth century may have resulted from drinking milk from cows that foraged on snakeroot. Other weeds that are known to carry teratogens include wild tobacco, poison hemlock, and skunkcabbage.

GENERAL WEED-CONTROL MEASURES

Since specific weed-control measures will be discussed in detail in later chapters, only a general overview will be offered here. There are four major methods of weed control—five, if prevention is included—and every specific form of control will fall under the heading of one of these general methods. Sometimes, a grey area appears when a specific control procedure has attributes of more than one of the major control methods. The major methods of weed control are: cultural, physical and mechanical, biological, and chemical.

Cultural or ecological weed control in its simplest form is the modification of the weed's immediate environment so that either crop competition is improved or weed competition is depressed or both. This method of weed control includes crop rotations, fertilizer use to favor a crop, preparation of good seedbeds for planting, correct seeding rates, irrigation and preirrigation, and utilization of clean seed of highly adapted, competitive crop varieties.

Physical and mechanical weed control includes anything that is done physically to destroy the weed: hand pulling, hoeing, mowing, plowing, cultivation, burial, smothering. Flooding and burning are special types of physical control measures.

Biological weed control is based on the principle that most organisms have natural enemies that can be used to destroy them. Grazing animals and plant parasites are most frequently employed against weeds, provided suitable agents can be found. In other cases, plant pathogens and viruses have been tried. While the method has considerable appeal, it is not, by any means, a perfect solution to weed control since every biological agent must be managed selectively or the effects of control may be worse than those of the weed. Furthermore, except for the use of grazing animals, the control is too slow to be economically feasible for most farmers. Individuals should not use parasites or pathogens unless such use is approved by appropriate agencies such as the California Department of Food and Agriculture.

Chemical control is the fourth and most recent major method of combating weeds. Spectacular progress in the use of chemicals to supplement the other methods has been made since World War II. Properly handled, both selective and nonselective chemicals can be used without great risk to people, animals, or the general environment. Chemicals kill plants either by direct contact or as a result of translocation. Some are foliar-applied, while others are applied to soil or injected into roots. Early-stage chemical weed controls frequently result in nearly weed-free crops at harvest time, with corresponding benefits in yield and quality. Labels and other sources of information should always be consulted to determine the legality of use and the conditions under which the herbicide will perform as intended.

In agriculture, it is rare that only one major control method will be employed in a given situation. Almost always, at least two methods will be required. Chemical control is generally less desirable for homeowners than for those treating commercially sized non-crop or agricultural areas because of the tendency towards overapplying by homeowners who are unfamiliar with techniques of safe application and rate control. Nevertheless, at least one acceptable procedure for weed control should be available for almost any situation.

REFERENCES

Agamalian, H. 1980. *Weed control strategies in vegetable crops. Proc. Calif. Weed Conf.*

Aspinwall, D. and F.L. Milthorpe. 1959. *An analysis of competition between barley and white pericaria. The effects on growth. Ann. Appl. Biol.* 47:156–172.

Bibliography of weed control publications of North America. 1978. WSSA publication.

Black, C.A. 1977. *A "Comment from CAST" to Secretary Bergland. Oct. 12 letter.*

Blackman, G.E. and W.G. Templeman. 1938. *The nature of the competition between cereal crops and annual weeds. J. Agri. Sci.* 28:247–271.

Bush, L.B. and D.W. Staniforth. 1962. *Shading effects on annual weeds in soybeans. Proc. North Cent. Weed Control Conf.* 19:46–47.

Carlson, H., J. Hill and K. Baghott. 1981. *Wild oat competition in spring wheat. Proc. Calif. Weed. Conf.*

Chisaka, H. 1966. *Competition between rice plants and weeds. Weed Res. J. Weed Soc. of Japan.* 5:16–22.

Colbert, F.O. 1981. *Weed competition in tree and vine crops. Proc. Calif. Weed Conf.*

Cudney, D.W. 1981. *Weed competition in agronomic crops. Proc. Calif. Weed Conf.*

Editorial. Nov. 1971. *Pollution from herbicides or weeds. Crops and Soils Magazine.*

Elmore, C.L. 1981. *Weed competition in turf and ornamentals. Proc. Calif. Weed Conf.*

Ennis, W.B., Jr. 1976. In *World Soybean Research.* L.D. Hill, ed., pp. 375–386. Interstate Printers and Publishers, Inc., Danville, IL.

Growers Weed Identification Handbook. #4030. Coop. Ext., Univ. of Calif.

Hewson, R.T., H.A. Roberts, and W. Bond. 1973. *Weed competition in spring sown broad beans. Hort. Res.* 13:25–32.

Hill, J. 1974. *Methods of analyzing competition with special reference to herbage plants. III. Monocultures vs. binary mixtures. J. Agri. Sci., Camb.* 83:57–65.

Holm, L.G., D.L. Plucknett, J.W. Pancho, and J.P. Herberger. 1977. *The World's Worst Weeds: Distribution and Biology.* Univ. Press of Hawaii.

Kempen, H.M. and J. Graf. 1980. *Cotton weed control—today and tomorrow. Proc. Calif. Weed Conf.*

Kilgore, W.W., D.G. Crosby, A.L. Graigmill, and N.K. Poppen. 1981. *Toxic plants as possible human teratogens. Vol. 35. Calif. Agriculture.*

Klingman, G.C., F.M. Ashton and L.J. Noordhoff. 1982. *Weed Science, Principles and Practices, 2nd Ed.* John Wiley & Sons.

Knake, E.L. 1962. *Losses caused by weeds. Proc. North Cent. Weed Control Conf.* 19:1.

Lange, A.H. 1974. *Weeds destroy more crops than pests and diseases. Sept. 24 Santa Maria Times, Santa Maria, CA.*

Martin, P. and B. Rademacher. 1960. *Studies on the mutual influences of weeds and crops.* In *The Biology of Weeds.* Blackwell Scientific Publications, Oxford.

McWhorter, C.G. and D.T. Patterson. 1980. In *Proc. World Soybean Res. Conf. II.* F.T. Corbin, ed., pp. 371–392. Westview Press, Boulder, CO.

Miller, G.R. and W.F. Meggitt. 1962. *Competition of weeds and sugar beets. Proc. North Cent. Weed Control Conf.* 19:21.

Mitich, L.W. 1981. *Zero-till—is it for California? Proc. Calif. Weed Conf.*

Mulvihill, J.J. 1972. *Congenital and genetic disease in domestic animals. Vol. 176, Science.*

Muenscher, W.C. 1955. *Weeds. 2nd Ed.* MacMillan, New York.

Munz, P.A. 1968. *A California Flora.* Univ. of Calif. Press.

Murphy, A.H., R.M. Love and L.J. Berry. 1954. *Improving Klamathweed ranges. Calif. Ag. Exp. Sta.— Ext. Ser. Cir.* 437.

Nalewaja, J.D. and W.E. Arnold. 1970. *Weed control methods, losses and costs due to weeds, and benefits of weed control in wheat and other small grains.* In *FAO Int. Conf. on Weed Control, Davis, CA.*, pp. 48–64.

Nelson, D.C. and R.E. Nylund. 1962. *Competition between peas grown for processing and weeds. Weeds.* 10:224–229.

Noggle, R.G. and G.J. Fritz. 1976. *Introductory Plant Physiology.* Prentice-Hall, New Jersey.

Norris, E.L. 1939. *Competing ability of different plants. Univ. of Nebraska Studies XXXIX* (2).

Norris, R.F. 1981. *Zero tolerance for weeds? Proc. Calif. Weed Conf.*

Patterson, D.T. 1982. *Effects of light and temperature on weedcrop growth and competition.* In *Biometerology in Integrated Pest Management,* J.L. Hatfield and I.J. Thomason, eds., Academic Press, NY, pp. 407–420.

Pavlychenko, T.K. and J.B. Harrington. 1934. *Competitive efficiency of weeds and cereal crops. Can. J. Res.* 10:77–94.

Pavlychenko, T.K. and J.B. Harrington. 1935. *Root development of weeds and crops in competition under dry farming. Sci. Agri. 6:151–160.*

Perrier, G.K., W.A. Williams, and S.R. Radosevich. 1981. *Managing range and pasture to suppress tarweed. Vol. 35. Calif. Agriculture.*

Rademacher, B. 1961. *Fragen der unkrautkonkurrenz. 40 Jahne Int. fur Phytopathologie Aschersleben. Deutsche Akademie der Landwirtschaftswissenschaften zu Berlin. Tagungsberichte Nr. 33:151–179.*

Robbins, W.W., M.K. Bellue, and W.S. Ball. 1970. *Weeds of California. CDFA publication.*

Selected weeds of the United States. 1970. *#AH366. USDA.*

Shantz, H.L. and L.N. Piemeisel. 1927. *The water requirement of plants at Akron, CO. J. Agri. Res. 34:1093–1190.*

Shaw, W.C. (no date). *How weeds can reduce yields and quality. Know your limiting factors in crop production. American Potash Institute, Washington, D.C.*

Shaw, W.C. 1978. *Herbicides: the cost/benefit ratio—the public view. Proc. Southern Weed Sci. Soc. 31:28–47.*

Shebeski, L.H. and G. Friesen. 1959. *Recent developments in chemical weed control. Agric. Inst. Review. 14:26–30.*

Sibuga, K.P. and J.D. Bandeen. 1978. *An evaluation of green foxtail (Setaria viridis L.) Beauv. and common lambsquarters (Chenopodium album L.) competition in corn. Weed Sci. Soc. Amer. Abstr. No. 142.*

Smith, R.J., W.T. Flinchum, and D.E. Seaman. 1977. *Weed control in U.S. rice production. U.S. Dept. Agri. Handbook No. 497. 78 pp.*

Staniforth, D.W. 1961. *Responses of corn hybrids to yellow foxtail competition. Weeds. 9:132–137.*

Staniforth, D.W., W.G. Lovely, and C.R. Weber. 1963. *Role of herbicides in soybean production. Weeds. 11:96–98.*

Stevens, O.A. 1932. *The number and weight of seeds produced by weeds. Amer. J. Bot. 19:784–794.*

Vengris, J., W.G. Colby, and M. Drake. 1955. *Plant nutrient competition between weeds and corn. Agron. J. 47:213–216.*

Wax, L.M. 1976. In *World Soybean Research, L.D. Hill, ed., pp. 420–425. Interstate Printers and Publishers, Inc., Danville, IL.*

Weakley, C.V. 1980. *Competition of fiddleneck in wheat. Proc. Calif. Weed Conf.*

Zimdahl, R.L. 1980. *The case for weed science. Agrichemical Age.*

Zimdahl, R.L. 1980. *Weed-crop competition, a review. International Plant Protection Center, Oregon State Univ., Corvallis. 196 pp.*

3

CULTURAL AND PHYSICAL CONTROL METHODS

by John T. Schlesselman[1], Gary L. Ritenour,[2] and Mahlon M.S. Hile[3]

CULTURAL WEED CONTROL

With man's change from nomadic hunter or herder to cultivator of crops some 10,000–12,000 years ago came the desire to modify his environment to meet specific needs. Early cultivators found that certain plant species had the uncanny ability to resist their increasing efforts to control them and were either inconvenient, poisonous, or otherwise harmful, or competitive with the species they were trying to cultivate. The more man disturbed the environment, the greater became his problem with unwanted vegetation. Many weed species are never found in the wild state and have apparently evolved with man. Zohary has described field bindweed, wild radish, and darnel, among many others, as obligate weeds since their natural or wild habitats are unknown. Many weeds sustain themselves in both wild and cultivated habitats and have been referred to by Muzik as facultative weeds.

Man quickly learned in his management of the land that unwanted vegetation or weeds tend to be very competitive, widely adaptable, capable of rapid germination and high seed production, and possessing dormancy periods and extreme longevities. They are therefore capable of building up large reservoirs of seeds in the soil, which, when a given site is disturbed, are capable of rapid reinfestation.

WEED SEED POPULATIONS

A high population of weed seeds in any given soil may be the result of (1) accumulation of weed seeds from plants allowed to reach maturity;

1. Rohm and Haas Company, Reedley, CA. 2,3. California State University, Fresno, CA.

(2) dissemination of weed seeds into an area by wind, water, or livestock; or (3) seeds dispersed by man as contaminants in crop seed or through poor equipment sanitation. A low population may result from (1) loss due to the biotic factors of the environment, such as natural decay; (2) loss of seeds' viability in the soil; or (3) losses due to production pressures of man such as applications of preemergence herbicides and cultural management including preirrigation and tillage.

Brenchley and Warington reported that the soils of the Rothamsted Experiment Station in England were infested with up to 113 million wild poppy seeds per acre. During a two-month period, Muenscher, studying the effects of weeds plowed-under on an area of 100 square feet in an old clover field in New York, found 4000 individual weeds from 28 families, 65 genera, and 82 species. Harper cites the viable weed seed populations of three soils under varying cropping patterns in Great Britain (table 1).

TABLE 1. TYPICAL BURIED WEED SEED POPULATION EXPRESSED IN TERMS OF VIABLE SEEDS PER SQUARE FOOT (FROM HARPER, 1960)

(a) A sandy soil; 8 years' cropping, 7 cereal, 1 root crop plus 1-year at Wellesbourne; cited by Roberts, 1958

Species	No. seed	Species	No. seed
Annual bluegrass	2,948	Pineapple weed	262
Prostrate knotweed	563	Scarlet pimpernel	234
Shepherdspurse	480	Birdseye speedwell	232
Thale cress	302		

(b) Rothamsted heavy clay; continuous wheat; cited by Brenchley and Warington, 1933

Species	No. seed	Species	No. seed
Cornpoppy	2,122	Prostrate knotweed	54
Lady's mantle	269	Ivyleaf speedwell	44
Foxtail	259	Thymeleaf sandwort	18
Corn speedwell	153	Shepherdspurse	10
Byzantine speedwell	56		

(c) Woburn light sand; continuous wheat; by Brenchley and Warington, 1933

Species	No. seed	Species	No. seed
Lady's mantle	215	Annual bluegrass	138
Corn spurry	404	Prostrate knotweed	50
False chamomile	152		

Harper also noted that the type of cultivation employed and the subsequent cropping pattern were important in the population dynamics of the soil. But cultivation is not the only way in which seeds become buried in a soil. Some species such as wild oat and filaree have mois-ture-sensitive appendages that bend and twist in response to changes in humidity, thereby twisting and turning their way into the soil. Seeds can fall down cracks that extend into the subsoil. Rodents and earth-worms are also responsible for burying seeds as they burrow and move the soil surface. Muenscher reported that, in soils infested with wild carrot and left undisturbed for from three to 10 years, viable wild carrot seeds could be obtained 4 inches below the surface.

GERMINATION

Germination is ordinarily thought of as a series of steps resulting in ac-tivation of a quiescent embryo and its subsequent emergence from the seed. For this process to occur, seeds require an environment that pro-vides moisture, oxygen, and a suitable temperature regime. Germina-tion normally begins with the imbibition of water, which is a physical process of the hydroscopic components of the seed. As the seed coat, embryo, and storage components of the seed imbibe and rehydrate themselves, the seed coat softens, and the membrane becomes more permeable. Enzymes that were formed during seed maturation are ac-tivated as they become hydrated in the seed. Mitochondria, which fur-ther energize metabolism, are then formed. Storage components, such as lipids, protein, and carbohydrates, are solubilized and used anaboli-cally or catabolically. The increase in solubilization of stored reserves and production of additional enzymes results in an osmotic gradient pulling more water into the seed. Embryo growth is then notable as ri-bonucleic acid (RNA) and deoxyribonucleic acid (DNA) increase, and storage products are utilized for new structural needs. Turgor pressure increases, and continued metabolism results in the emergence of the radicle from the seed coat followed soon after by the plumule and the further development of the seedling. The establishment of a seedling upon germination depends more upon the vigor of the seed and its rela-tive placement in the germination zone and subsequent environmental conditions than upon the germination percentage. Germination is nor-mally considered irreversible after the emergence of the radicle from the seed coat, and the success or failure of the germination event often depends on its rapidity. In general, weed species germinate much more rapidly than cultivated species under a wider range of environmental conditions.

Some seeds show a sensitivity to light, and their germinations are enhanced after only a short exposure to light of the imbibed seed. Other seeds germinate only in the dark. Most crop seeds germinate independ-ently of light or darkness. Some enhancement of weed-seed germina-tion from soil disturbance can be attributed to this light sensitivity even if the exposure is only for a short period. It can be shown that imbibed redroot pigweed seed can be enhanced to higher germination percentages by as little as a five-second flash of red or polychromatic light even though many of its seeds germinate in the dark.

Periodicity of Germination

Relatively few weed species will germinate equally well throughout the year. Conditions for germination are sometimes best or are only met during specific seasons of the year. Though often associated with the tillage practices of man, some seeds germinate predominantly in the fall or spring, regardless of human disturbance.

The periodicities of germination of many important weed pests have led to their classification as either summer or winter annuals. Barnyardgrass is seldom a problem in winter-planted cereals or lettuce, though major problems are found in spring-planted melons and sorghum. The reverse is true of fiddleneck and filaree, which germinate in the winter and become major problems in spring management.

Greater knowledge of the periodicity of the weed population in an area will allow better timing and selection of herbicides and tillage.

DORMANCY

Seeds missing one or more requirements for germination often experience a period of quiescence and will germinate once these requirements are met. If the requirements for germination are met and the seed remains ungerminated but alive, it becomes dormant.

Dormancy is a marvelous mechanism for ensuring survival of a species, as it will prevent the entire population from being exposed to the same set of growing conditions, no matter how inviting, at any one time. Preirrigation, droughts, and unsuitable weather do not have as adverse an effect on the survival of weeds with dormancy since such weeds are often prevented from germination for extended periods of time and are subsequently guaranteed the viability of some seed for seasons to come.

Dormancy can be either genetically controlled (innate) or induced or enforced by environmental conditions to which the seed is exposed.

Innate Dormancy

Seed coats of some species are either impermeable to water or oxygen or both. Seeds with waterproof seed coats are often called hard seeds. Pigweed, annual morningglory, clovers, vetch, mustards, and even shepherdspurse have this type of dormancy. Cocklebur, lettuce, and many grasses have seed coats which are impermeable to the movement of gases, most notably that of oxygen. Scarification, i.e., abrasion due to tillage or chemical weathering of the seed coat, is often required to initiate germination.

Several species possess seed coats that are mechanically resistant to the swelling and rupture which occur during germination. Pepperweed, mustard, shepherdspurse, and pigweed exhibit this type of dormancy and may attain up to 1000 psi within the seed coat. Chemical or mechanical injury and high-temperature drying may be required to break this type of dormancy.

Another type of dormancy is achieved by a rudimentary or under-developed embryo that requires a period of further development after seed dissemination before it will germinate. Smartweed displays this type of dormancy. Smartweed may further require a series of physiological changes in the seed involving the breakdown or synthesis of substances which can affect germination. This period of physiological-biochemical changes occurring after dissemination is called after-ripening. Several members of the grass and mustard families may require varying periods of after-ripening.

Studies have shown that endogenous inhibitors can prevent germination when all other conditions are favorable. The ecological significance of inhibitors is unknown, though they do ensure dissemination and provide reservoirs of viable seed to promote survival. Compounds such as coumarin, abscisic, cafferic, and ferulic acids, mustard oils (mainly found in the crucifers), numerous aldehydes, and phenols have been shown to be responsible, either directly or indirectly, for dormancy. Many of these are either leached from the seed or metabolized eventually to a point where they no longer interfere with germination. Many herbicides mimic this response by inhibiting germination of a seed or the growing point of a vegetative organ (e.g., EPTC inhibits the growth of nutsedge tubers).

Induced or Enforced Dormancy

Seeds that would germinate immediately after dissemination are thrown into dormancy by subjection to unfavorable conditions during maturation or germination. Many are induced into a period of thermal dormancy when exposed to high temperatures during maturation. Seeds that have been buried deep in the soil and exposed to high CO_2 and low oxygen pressures may not germinate immediately upon being brought to the surface.

Enforced dormancy can result from removal of the seed from environmental conditions favorable to germination, e.g., exposure to excessive moisture or deep tillage. The seed in such cases will remain dormant until favorable germination conditions are restored.

SEED LONGEVITY

The subject of seed longevity is extensive and must take into account the condition of seeds at maturity and conditions under which seeds have been stored. There are seeds that cannot survive much longer than a month under ideal conditions. Citrus seeds, which have a germination potential for up to four years under refrigeration, will die if allowed to dry. In contrast, Odum has shown with archaeological evidence that lambsquarters seeds 1700 years old have survived to germinate in the cool, moist climate of Denmark.

Darlington and Steinbauer report of a weed-burial study by Beal in 1879 in which 20 weed species were buried in uncorked bottles. With periodic sampling it was noted that 10 species—redroot pigweed, prostrate pigweed, common ragweed, black mustard, Virginia pepperweed, evening primrose, broadleaf plantain, purslane, moth mullein, and curly dock—were still alive after 20 years. Eighty years after burial, moth mullein still germinated at a rate of over 70%, and a few seeds each of evening primrose and curly dock were still germinating. Toole and Brown reported a burial study in which Duvel placed 107 species of weed seed in porous clay pots at depths of 8, 11, and 42 inches in the soil. When these seeds had been sampled periodically over time, it was shown that 36 species did not germinate after one year, and another 36 species were still viable after 38 years. It was also noted that depth of burial resulted in little variation in longevity because all depths were below that normally associated with emergence.

Obviously, we cannot wait for the weed population in the soil to die or disappear. Repeated shallow cultivation over several years, preventing reseeding, can effectively reduce the surface weed seed population of a given area. But any deep tillage in the next 20 years or more will result in the appearance of much the same set of weed species, though possibly not in the same numbers. Any period of neglect allowing reinfestation marks the start of a new survival period.

VEGETATIVE PROPAGATION

Though most weeds reproduce sexually in the formation of a seed, many of the most serious and persistent perennial weeds can also multiply by asexual or vegetative means. A distinct competitive advantage exists in terms of food reserves for a vegetative organ over a seed, and this results in more rapid initial establishment. Vegetative organs are more resistant to herbicides; they can develop under a wider range of environmental conditions and have a greater base from which to establish themselves. Further confounding the efforts to control such weeds is the fact that these weeds quite often have periods of vegetative dormancy.

The structure of vegetative propagation may be a rhizome, stolon, tuber, root, bulb, bulblet, or a corm, or some combination of two or more of these structures.

Purple nutsedge has a combination of these structures that further complicates control. This weed has a corm—a short, vertical, fleshy stem with aerial leaves and adventitious roots—which is located near the soil surface, as well as a chain of tubers connected by a rhizome. When repeatedly disturbed by tillage, the tubers tend to be formed at progressively greater depths and, with increasing dormancy, can often resist intensive tillage programs. It has been shown that, in areas where dry fallow can be practiced, purple nutsedge can be killed by subsequent desiccation. Yellow nutsedge, on the other hand, produces hard, drought-resistant tubers that are not easily controlled by tillage. Combining varying periods of tuber dormancy and prolific seed production, nutsedges are becoming one of the most serious pests in the world.

The depth of tillage often affects the extent to which control is achieved, as does the effective regeneration depth of the type of vegetative structure present. Yellow woodsorrel and many of the stoloniferous grasses spread dry stems that grow along the soil surface. Quackgrass and johnsongrass spread vegetatively by rhizomes. Pammel and King buried quackgrass rhizomes at 4, 6, 8, 12, and 24 inches. Few shoots were able to regenerate from 8 inches, and none were observed from 12 inches or deeper. Generally, most regeneration is within 2–4 inches of the surface. Deep plowing can be successful in the partial control of quackgrass, johnsongrass, and many stoloniferous grasses by placing the regenerative structures below their effective zone. Root segments of such weeds as field bindweed and Canada thistle can regenerate from any place on the root provided it is placed near the surface, and, therefore, deep plowing may move more regenerative tissue into a position to grow.

The age or phenological stage of development of the plant can be very important in determining its relative susceptibility to tillage. Arny has shown that quackgrass seedlings under six to eight weeks of age are as easily killed by tillage as most annual grasses. Johnsongrass and bermudagrass both start out as annuals but upon development and maturation of rhizomes become perennials.

Vegetative propagation normally results in a very slow spread of a single plant. Tillage and other cultural practices have resulted in more rapid spreading by segmentation or transport to new locations.

PREVENTIVE WEED CONTROL

Preventive weed-control measures include anything done to prevent the introduction of a new species into any specific geographical area.

When one observes a large number of weed species infesting any parcel of land, one may feel that land has "every weed in the world." Actually, an average land parcel contains only 30–50 species of plants that could be considered significant weeds. Rogers states that there are 30,000 species in the world that can be considered significant weeds, with about 1800 of them being major pests. Of the latter 1800, it is estimated that over 1400 species are not now found in the United States. Extensive efforts are being made to keep these weeds from being introduced into the United States. The federal Noxious Weed Act and the Federal Seed Act were passed to assist in attaining this goal. These laws are enforced by various government agencies. However, everyone in agriculture can help keep unwanted species out of the United States by cautioning those who travel out of the country not to "sneak" any plant or plant parts past U.S. Customs officials when returning.

Over one-half of the major weed species now found in the United States are not native. Most of the nonnative species were introduced from other countries as contaminants of planting seeds brought by immigrants from many parts of the world during the early settlement of this country. The settlers were unaware of the weed problems they were creating. Since then, new species of weeds have continued to be introduced into the United States from other countries. Johnsongrass was brought from Turkey in the 1830s for its potential value as a forage crop. Russian thistle seed apparently was introduced from Russia in a shipment of flax seed circa 1873. Williams lists 36 species of weeds that have been purposefully introduced into the United States for various reasons, which later developed into problem weeds. Among them is waterhyacinth, which is now a major aquatic weed problem in the southeastern United States and in some areas of California. Also included on the list is hydrilla, which was originally introduced into Florida from Africa in the late 1950s as an aquarium plant. It was first found in California in 1977 and has since been identified in several locations in the state. Hydrilla can be a problem by impeding waterways and is an aggressive competitor in rice culture.

Preventive weed control is also being practiced at the state and local levels. All states in the United States have seed laws that restrict the movement of seeds from other states. At the local level, individual landowners can practice preventive weed control by at least two methods. One is to use only crop seed that is free of weed seeds; another is to understand and combat the natural abilities of many weeds for effective dissemination.

Dissemination often occurs through certain biological capabilities of the weed, and it may also result from the action of other organisms. Weeds can be spread from one location to another by movements of seeds, asexual plant parts (such as tubers), or, on occasion, of the entire plants.

Biological capabilities of weeds that assist in their dissemination include forceful dehiscence and utilization of wind, water, and wild animals. Mature seeds of several weed species, including yellow woodsorrel and teasel, are forcefully ejected from the mature plant. The distance these seeds travel is not great, but when repeated, ejections over a number of generations lead to significant spreading. For longer distances of spread, many species have evolved specialized characteristics that take advantage of various components of the environment.

Many use wind to disseminate seeds. Dandelion and groundsel are two members of the Compositae family in which a modified calyx forms a parachute-like structure that carries the seed quite long distances in the wind. In other species, a part of the mature shoot breaks off and is blown by the wind. Witchgrass stems become brittle as the seed matures and the open-panicle-type seed head breaks off and is blown along the soil surface spreading seed. At maturity, the entire aboveground shoot of Russian thistle is broken off by wind and moved around as a tumbleweed, spreading seeds and often becoming a traffic hazard in the process. The only practical way of stopping seeds that disseminate by forceful dehiscence or wind from utilizing these biological mechanisms is to eliminate the plants before they mature.

Many other weed seeds are disseminated long distances in moving water. This is a problem especially in irrigated agricultural areas. Studies in California and Washington verify that a large number of seeds of many species can be spread this way. Preventive weed control practiced along the ditchbanks of the delivery ditches in irrigation districts greatly reduces this problem.

Dissemination of weeds by animals is common, much of it spread by wild animals over which agriculturists have little control. The spread of wild asparagus by birds carrying the fruit away to eat and of small mistletoe via the sticky seeds that adhere to the feet of birds are examples of such dissemination in the wild. Several rangeland weeds, including mesquite, are spread from site to site by the seeds' surviving passage through the digestive tracts of cattle. Cattlemen can prevent this type of dissemination by confining animals long enough for seeds to be excreted before releasing the animals into uninfested rangeland.

Equipment sanitation is another important means of preventing the spread of weeds from one location to another. Both seeds and asexual parts of weeds are frequently carried into new areas on agricultural and road-building equipment that has not been properly cleaned.

CROP ROTATION

Crop rotation, the practice of growing different species of crops from one year to the next in a given field, is a major cultural weed-control technique in all annual and short-lived perennial crops (e.g., alfalfa). Whenever any one crop is grown year after year (monoculture) in the same field, the population of certain weed species will tend to increase. This happens because the same environmental and cultural conditions that favor the crop also favor those weed species—for example, the buildup of wild oat in fields continuously planted to wheat or barley, or the increase in nightshade in California tomato fields when tomatoes are planted several years in a row. If the farmer persists in planting the same crop in such situations, he must either tolerate the yield and/or quality loss due to increased weed densities or be prepared to meet increased weed-control costs.

Walker points out that, in the United States prior to 1945, crop rotations and tillage were the major methods of weed control. In terms of weed control, the main reason for using crop rotation is not to control the weeds directly but to allow the use of alternative weed-control techniques. Starting in the 1940s, with the development of selective herbicides, agriculturists could take advantage of alternate herbicides in conjunction with crop rotation. For instance, with the currently available herbicides it is difficult to control nutsedges in cotton. Consequently, nutsedge has become a prevalent weed in cotton fields. If such a field were to be rotated to field corn, selective herbicides could be used to control the nutsedge problem. In essence, crop rotation allows herbicide rotation.

It should be pointed out that crop rotation fits well into an overall, integrated pest-management program since crop rotation, as well as aiding in weed control, can also be used to help control many insect, disease, and nematode problems.

One problem associated with crop rotation is the plantback problem following herbicide use. Most herbicide labels carry restrictions on crops that can follow the previous herbicide application. Some restrictions are based on potential crop injury, while others are based on the potential for the carryover of residues from the previous application. Examples of information taken from individual herbicide labels are as follows:

- Do not rotate with any crops other than cotton, onions, soybeans, or spearmint/peppermint within a 10-month period after treatment with this product.
- Land treated with this herbicide may be planted to other crops the following year. To avoid crop injury, do not plant sugar beets, red beets, or spinach for 12 months following an application. Land should be plowed to a depth of 12 inches prior to planting these crops.
- Replanting crops other than those shown on this label in treated soil within eight months of application may result in crop injury. However, all crops on this label may be planted following harvest of a crop treated with this herbicides.

COMPETITION

The competitive effects that weeds have on crops are discussed in Chapter 2. In view of those effects, one weed-control technique that should be used whenever possible is that of growing the crop so as to maximize its competitiveness with weeds. Methods of such control-via-competition to be considered below include general crop culture, smother crops, and plant breeding.

General Crop Culture

Anything that can be done to get a good, uniform crop stand off to a fast, vigorous start and then to maintain it in full vigor will greatly reduce weed problems. An informed choice of optimum planting dates is one such measure. In California, alfalfa is commonly planted in late fall or early spring. However, when seeded in the fall, young alfalfa seedlings are exposed to several months of cool weather during which they exhibit little growth, while winter annual weeds grow vigorously unless herbicides are used to control them. Alfalfa planted in the spring will grow more quickly and thus be more competitive with weeds in a shorter time.

In row crops, decreasing row width and/or increasing seeding rates can sometimes help reduce weed problems. Rogers found that when cotton was grown in rows 42 inches apart, 14 weeks of weed control was required if no yield loss was to be incurred. However, when row width was reduced to 31 inches, then the weed-control period was shortened to 10 weeks for no yield loss. The control period was further shortened to six weeks when the rows were 21 inches apart.

Precision planting of row crops also provides a means of reducing competition and allows easier management of cultural practices that follow planting. For example, the precision placement of vegetable seeds such as lettuce, broccoli, or cauliflower allows the thinning operation to be done in a manner that provides maximum weed removal with minimum crop (plant) injury. Likewise, clump planting of crops such as tomatoes provides the potential for complete stands and also allows for easier removal of troublesome weeds with minimal crop damage.

As row crops grow during the season, their increased leaf areas make them more competitive with any weed seedlings that may emerge. An experiment on silverleaf nightshade showed that, as levels of shading increased, not only was the growth of this weed reduced but its seed production was stopped.

Obviously, crops can only compete adequately with weeds when there is a uniform stand of a sufficient population of healthy crop plants. Weed control is always much more difficult to achieve where a poor crop stand is obtained.

Smother Crops

Some crops have an inherent ability to grow quickly and thus out-compete many weed species. These are referred to as smother crops. Field corn and domestic sunflowers are two such crops. To control more prostrate species of weeds, shorter crop species such as alfalfa and wheat can serve as smother crops.

Plant Breeding

Plant breeders are constantly striving to develop varieties of crops that are more vigorous in their growth habits. More vigorous plants tend to produce higher yields. One major reason for this is that the more vigorous the crop, the more effectively it can compete with weeds. Studies with rice have shown that cultivars with the most vigor in early stages of growth produced higher yields.

In coming years, plant breeders will be asked not only to breed even more competitive crop varieties but also to develop ones that produce allelopathic chemicals to reduce weed growth. They may further be asked to develop varieties that can tolerate certain herbicides to which that crop was originally susceptible. Additional information on the use of these techniques may be found in Chapter 6.

PHYSICAL WEED CONTROL

This section deals strictly with methods of physical weed control, including the use of fire, water management, mulching, and solarization. Mechanical weed control is covered in Chapter 4.

Fire

Fire has been used for centuries as a method of destroying unwanted vegetation in non-crop areas as well as in cropping situations. The heat from flames causes the cell sap of plants to expand, rupturing the cell walls. A coagulation of protoplasm and inactivation of enzymes also result from the high temperatures. The thermal death point for most plant cells is between 113° and 131°F. Most dry seeds, however, are more tolerant of high temperatures than are plant tissues, and they most often require prolonged exposures to effectively limit their successful germination.

As a method of weed control, fire has the advantages of eliminating dead vegetation and reducing the density of the next season's weeds, with none of the "carry-over" that some herbicides have. Its drawbacks include the inability to kill subsurface weed seeds, possible crop injury, and air pollution. The use of fire is probably most practical in conjunction with other methods of weed control.

Nonselective Burning

With this method of weed control, all plants contacted are killed. Field burning is one kind of nonselective burning. Nonselective burning of crop refuse (e.g., stubble, chaff, etc.) in crops such as rice and cereals is regulated and requires that specific conditions be met prior to the initiation of the burning process.

Burning of stubble from previously grown cereal crops greatly reduces the potential for seed germination and therefore reduces the likelihood of the cereal becoming a weed in the following crop. Burning followed by irrigation and deep tillage further reduces the potential for cereal crops to become weeds. In grass seed production, field burning removes the straw and stubble where diseases flourish and kills 95–99% of the weed seeds at the soil surface.

Rangelands can be modified with fire to reduce certain weed pests and encourage more palatable types of vegetation. For example, a controlled burn reduced an infestation of common goldenweed by 85–91%. During the growing season immediately following the burn, forage production was improved by 730 lbs/A (oven-dried weight), primarily as a result of increased buffalograss.

Control burns in forestlands have also been somewhat successful in eliminating the understory and reducing the threat of uncontrolled fire from excess combustible fuel. However, elimination of certain shrub understories by fire have sometimes been erratic and less effective than chemical control.

The parasitic weed dodder in alfalfa serves as an exemplary situation for nonselective burning. In this case, some alfalfa would also be eliminated along with the dodder.

Selective Burning

A directed flame or a hooded burner is used where the crop is to be protected from injury. Crops in which this technique is used include cotton, corn, soybeans, grain sorghum, castor beans, and sesame.

Proper timing is essential for greatest weed control and minimal injury to the crop. Generally, the best weed control is obtained when the weeds are 1–2 inches tall. In cotton, flaming can begin when the stems are $3/16$ inch in diameter at ground level. By this time, the cotton plant is about 8 inches tall.

Timing is also critical for selective burning in corn, which should not be flamed when the crop is between 2 and 12 inches high. Corn less than 2 inches tall can be flamed, since the growing point is still underground. Corn taller than 12 inches tall will not be injured by flaming small weeds at the base of the plants.

Water Management

Proper use of water will have a definite impact on many weeds, both annual and perennial. Like agricultural crops, weeds require a given set of conditions for optimum growth and development. Water management can play a vital role in reducing specific weed problems.

Preirrigation

The use of irrigation prior to the planting of row crops is an established practice that aids in reducing clods and preparing the land for subsequent tillage operations, providing soil moisture for subsequent crop germination and/or production, and also germinating weed seeds prior to planting. Weeds that are germinated can then be removed by either physical or chemical methods.

Flooding

Flooding will control only weeds that are completely immersed and thus denied oxygen for their roots and leaves. This method of weed control had its beginnings in the cultivation of rice. It was found that flooding the land with 6 to 10 inches of water for three to eight weeks during the summer controlled weeds such as barnyardgrass, signalgrass, sprangletop, hemp sesbania, and northern jointvetch. Flooding also controls such common perennials as camelthorn, hoarycress, and horse nettle. In one study conducted in California, a 13-acre area of Russian knapweed was flooded for 60 days. One hundred percent of the knapweed was killed.

Some weed species react differently to flooding, depending on their stages of development. For example, field bindweed plants are satisfactorily controlled by flooding, while field bindweed seed can remain immersed for many years and still be capable of germinating.

Studies have also shown weed control by flooding to be more effective in coarse soils than in fine soils.

Draining

This method is used to control aquatic weeds growing in drainage ditches and irrigation canals. Drainage is an inexpensive and effective way to control cattail, bulrush, and reed canarygrass.

Mulching

The purpose of mulching is to exclude light from weeds, thereby eliminating the photosynthetic process within them. The most commonly used mulches are hay, manure, grass clippings, straw, sawdust, wood chips, rice hulls, black paper, and black plastic film. For perennial weeds, the layer of hay, manure, etc., on the soil must be thicker (2–4 feet and more) than for control of annual weeds. The most effective mulching material is the kind applied as a continuous sheet, i.e., black paper or black plastic. Particle mulches cannot prevent all the weeds from breaking through. Crops in which mulches mainly are used are strawberries, sugarcane, and pineapple. Unfortunately, mulching materials and application are quite expensive and therefore limited to small areas or high-value crops.

Soil Solarization

One of the most difficult tasks of weed control has been the killing of ungerminated weed seeds in the soil. To date, soil fumigants, mainly methyl bromide, have been the most prominent means available for killing these seeds. But a new nonchemical technique called soil solarization has been developed in Israel.

Soil solarization involves placing a clear polyethylene plastic sheet over soil that is moist and well tilled. The plastic sheet needs to be kept in place for at least four weeks. Soil solarization should be practiced during periods of high solar radiation to be most effective in the shortest period of time. Incoming radiation is trapped under the clear plastic by the "greenhouse effect," which increases the soil temperature.

The mechanisms by which soil solarization leads to the death of weed seeds are not yet completely understood. Some seed death may be directly due to the high soil temperature achieved. However, it is quite likely that there are some secondary effects such as high soil temperatures weakening the seeds, making them more vulnerable to pathogen attack. Soil solarization is also showing promise as a control technique for soilborne diseases and nematodes.

REFERENCES

Anderson, W.P. 1983. *Weed Science: Principles.* 2nd ed. West Publishing Co., St. Paul.

Arny, A.C. 1927. *Successful Eradication of Perennial Weeds.* Ontario Dept. Agr., Agr. and Expt. Union Ann. Rpt. 48:58–63.

Boyd, J.W. and D.S. Murray. 1982. *Effects of shade on silverleaf nightshade.* Weed Sci. 30:264–269.

Brenchley, W.E. and K. Warington. 1930. *The weed seed population of arable soil. I. Numerical estimation of viable seeds and observations on their natural dormancy.* J. Ecol. 18:235–272.

British Crop Protection Council. 1968. *Weed Control Handbook.* Vol. I: Principles. 5th ed. Fryer, J.D. and S.A. Evans, eds. Blackwell Scientific Publications, Ltd., Oxford.

Coble, H.D. 1980. *Crop rotation vs. monoculture: Weed control.* Crops Soils, 32:8–9.

Crafts, A.S. 1975. *Modern Weed Control.* Univ. of Calif. Press. Los Angeles.

Darlington, H.T. and E.P. Steinbauer. 1960. *The eighty-year period for Dr. Beal's seed viability experiment.* Amer. J. Bot. 48:321–325.

Day, B.E. and R.C. Russell. 1955. *The effect of drying on the survival of nutgrass tubers.* Calif. Agr. Expt. Sta. Bull. 751.

Hardison, J.R. 1981. *Field burning and the environment.* Agricultural Research USDA. 30(3):12.

Harper, J.L. 1960. *Factors controlling plant numbers.* In: The Biology of Weeds. A symposium of the British Ecology Society, pp. 119–132. Blackwell Scientific Publications, Ltd., Oxford.

Katan, J. 1981. *Solar heating (solarization) of soil for control of soilborne pests.* Ann. Rev. Phytopathol. 19:211–236.

Kawano, K., H. Gonzalez and M. Lucena. 1974. *Intraspecific competition, competition with weeds, and spacing in rice.* Crop Sci. 14:841–845.

Kelley, A.D. and V.F. Burns. 1975. *Dissemination of weed seeds by irrigation water.* Weed Sci. 23:486–493.

Mayeaux, H.S. and W.T. Hamilton. 1980. *Fire fights common goldenweed. Agricultural Research USDA* 28(12):16.

Muenscher, W.C. 1955. *Weeds. 2nd Ed. MacMillan, New York.*

Muzik. T.J. 1970. *Weed Biology and Control. McGraw-Hill Book Co., New York.*

National Academy of Sciences. 1968. *Principles of Plant and Animal Pest Control. Vol. 2: Weed Control. Public. 1597. Washington, D.C.*

Newcomer, J.L. 1976. *Field crops and seed. The Agronomist (newsletter). Univ. Maryland.*

Odum, S. 1965. *Germination of ancient seeds. Floristical observations and experiments with archaeologically dated soil samples. Dan. Bot. Ark.* 24:1–70.

Pammel, L.H. and C.M. King. 1909. *Notes on the eradication of weeds, with experiments made in 1907 and 1908. Iowa Agr. Expt. Sta. Bull.* 105:265–300.

Rodgers, E.G. 1974. *Weed prevention is the best control. Weeds Today, p. 8.*

Rogers, N.K., G.A. Buchanan and W.C. Johnson. 1976. *Influence of row spacing on weed competition with cotton. Weed Sci.* 24:410–413.

Shull, H. 1962. *Weed seed in irrigation water. Weeds* 10:248–249.

Smith, R.H., Jr. and C.W. Shaw. 1966. *Weeds and their control in rice production. USDA Bull. 292.* 64 pp.

Tappeneiner, J.C. II. 1979. *Effect of fire and 2,4-D on the early stages of beaked hazel* (Corylus cornuta) *understories. Weed Sci.* 27:162–166.

Toole, E.H. and E. Brown. 1946. *Final results of the Duvel buried seed experiment. J. Agr. Res.* 72:201–210.

Walker, R.H. and G.A. Buchanan. 1982. *Crop manipulation in integrated weed management systems. Weed Sci.* 30 supplmnt:17–24.

Williams, M.C. 1980. *Purposefully introduced plants that have become noxious or poisonous weeds. Weed Sci.* 28:300–305.

Zohary, M. 1962. *Plant Life of Palestine. Roland Press Co., New York.*

4

MECHANICAL CONTROL METHODS

by Harold M. Kempen[1] and James Greil[2]

Since the arrival of chemical herbicides on the farming scene, progressively less attention has been directed toward older, proven mechanical weed-control techniques. In fact, both the skills needed to set up implements properly and the management experience required to arrange farming operations in sequences for successful weed control are disappearing. One has only to remember that before 1960, herbicide usage hardly existed; yet farmers generally succeeded in growing crops without excessive losses from weeds. Today's farmer generally combines mechanical and chemical methods to obtain the desired economic means of elimination or suppression of weed populations.

Mechanical weeding techniques are sometimes less expensive than chemical control methods. For successful control, a weed manager must know the capabilities and limits of mechanical techniques so that integration with chemical controls can be made. One must also recognize that every program has its shortcomings. Solving one problem can induce another.

For the greatest success with mechanical weed control techniques in irrigated areas, good land preparation is a necessity. Land leveling on surface-irrigated fields allows subsequent preplant cultivation, bed-listing and shaping, and postplant precision tillage to be made with greater ease. The laser method of leveling land has simplified this previously difficult task (fig. 1).

In row crops, orchards, and vineyards, close tillage can reduce any necessary hand-weeding costs. For example, hand-weeding a 4-inch band

1. University of California Cooperative Extension, Kern County, CA. 2. California Polytechnic State University, San Luis Obispo, CA.

Figure 1. Laser-beam land leveling enhances mechanical tillage in crops. Photo courtesy H.M. Kempen.

of weeds might cost $75 or more per acre, but a 2-inch band could reduce that cost to $50 per acre, a substantial savings.

Mechanical techniques eliminate weeds by burial or uprooting. In row crops and grapes, soil can be thrown over small weeds that emerge after an irrigation or rain, burying them. Of course, the row crop must be taller than the weeds to permit burial. Uprooting is accomplished by various tools that slice, cut, or turn the soil in which the root system grows. The roots and shoots will desiccate before weed reestablishment. In wet periods, winter annual weeds may re-root. Certain succulents, such as purslane, and rhizomes of perennial weeds, such as johnsongrass and bermudagrass, can regrow if the soil is slightly moist.

Mechanical tillage or mowing is often done during the earlier periods until crop competition is adequate to shade out later emerging weeds. Knowing the proper time for tillage or mowing, as well as the possible impact on soil structure, is critical for successful control.

IMPLEMENTS

The terminology of farm equipment has only recently been standardized. Considerable regional variation exists in the names farm people use to describe their tools.

Disc Harrow

This common implement has circular blades 20 to 36 inches in diameter that are spaced 7 to 15 inches apart, which cut 3 to 12 inches into the soil (fig. 2).

Figure 2. Disc harrows are most widely used for land preparation and herbicide incorporation. Photo courtesy E.A. Kurtz.

The offset disc is the most commonly used disc in irrigated agriculture for primary tillage. Depth control is obtained either by changing the angle of the disc gangs or adjusting the gauge-wheel height (if applicable). Use of these discs is often required for optimum soil preparation before herbicide incorporation.

The tandem disc is widely used on loam soils and is usually a lighter-duty disc for secondary tillage. Depth is controlled by gauge wheels.

Disc harrows are more expensive to operate than spring-tooth harrows. They compact soil more under certain circumstances and require more horsepower than spring-tooth harrows.

Spring-Tooth Harrows

These harrows have spring loaded, circular shanks with variously shaped sweeps or shanks on the tips. Shanks are usually at least 7 inches apart to avoid trash buildup during tillage. Other harrows are designed for one-pass tillage before planting and often have behind them spike-tooth harrows, a chopper, or a rolling metal basket to smooth soil. They are more common in the Midwest where growers often prepare seedbeds and incorporate herbicides shallowly (sometimes called "surface blending"). Generally, they are used for secondary tillage.

In California, spring-tooth harrows are often used in dryland grain seedbed preparation or fallow-ground maintenance. Low organic matter or compaction often causes cloddy soils on which spring-tooth harrows do less well than discs.

These tools work best on friable and coarse-textured soils (sands, sandy loams). Spring-tooth harrows are the best for uprooting perennial weeds.

Figure 3. Plowing is used primarily to turn under plant residue. Photo courtesy H.S. Agamalian.

Plows

Because plows have a higher power requirement than the disc or harrow and are more expensive to operate, their use is reserved for covering crop and weed debris, what engineers call "primary tillage." A "plow sole"—or compacted layer—can develop from repeated plowings unless some chiseling or ripping is also done. Types of plows include the moldboard, chisel, disc, wide-sweep, and bedder (fig. 3).

Can moldboard plows bury weed seeds and tubers? They can reduce populations by 50% or more, but probably not by 90%. The use of a jointer to tip the surface 6 inches of soil down to a 12-to-16–inch furrow will increase the percentage of reduction. But with prolific seed producers, weeds may have produced 40 million seeds or nutsedge tubers to an acre. Reducing that population by 90% may only provide the spacing between weeds that will permit robust weed growth. Weed seeds that have considerable inherent dormancy can be returned after a second plowing and become problems in subsequent years.

Miscellaneous Tillage Equipment

Spike-tooth harrows are used with and without discs in soil preparation. "Blind" harrowing in some crops can effectively remove percentages of weeds (and crop plants) effectively. Rod weeders, often used on fallow ground in the Great Plains areas, are rarely used in California. Rotary,

Figure 4. Listing is done on row crops to prepare flat land into rough, preshaped beds prior to final bed shaping. The operator is following the mark made by the marker arm on the previous pass (arrow A). The marker arm (arrow B) indicates where the center of the tractor should be on the next pass. Photo courtesy E.A. Kurtz.

ground-driven cultivators are widely used in row crops. Lister shovels are sometimes used after cereal crops to list beds and then split them in order to desiccate perennial grassy weeds during the rainless California summers.

ROW-CROP CULTIVATION

For the most precise row-crop cultivations, one should use a line diagram in the shop in conjunction with accurate field measurements for accurate row spacings. Lines drawn on a slab of concrete in or near the shop should give exact dimensions on furrow and crop spacings and the exact spacings for the tractor wheels, the furrows, and crop rows. Then bed-lister shovels and the marker arm can be placed exactly where intended. Later, the planter can be set up on the line diagram at the exact spacing. Following planting, cultivator sweeps can also be placed for precision cultivation. Vertical and other minor adjustments are made in the field. These are very important, too, because unless the soil volume is uniformly displaced by bed-lister shovels, later cultivations will be affected. Tractor wheel furrows are always compacted, and vertical adjustments must compensate for this. Tractor wheels should remain in certain furrows all season so that compaction is minimized. Four-row (used in most vegetable crops) and six-row (used in cotton and some other field crops) equipment is often favored for just this reason.

Figure 5. Powered rotary tillers are used to eliminate residues from previous plantings and to incorporate herbicides and provide a uniform bed for planting and cultivation. Photo left shows use on the flat to eliminate crop and weed residues, while photo right is of four-bed equipment showing beds being formed and herbicide being applied and incorporated. Photos courtesy L.H. Miner and E.A. Kurtz.

Listing

The most important operation prior to bed shaping and planting is listing, which usually involves the application of preplant fertilizers during the preparation of rough, preshaped beds. For the most efficient operations, one should list beds in the same direction and order in which they will be planted and cultivated. If a four-row planter or cultivator is to be used, the beds should be listed four rows at a time. It is essential not to straddle a "guess row" during cultivation as this will disrupt precision cultivation and result in missing some weeds or destroying crop plants. The guess row is that furrow which is between passes (rows) of the lister. For example, four-bed listers (fig. 4) are equipped with marker arms and five shovels (bottoms). The marker arm (in the unlisted area) marks the center line of the next tractor pass. If the marker arm is not accurately positioned, then the guess row (bed) will be either too narrow or too wide, which can create serious problems with subsequent operations (e.g., cultivation). Rows can also be aligned by measuring the field ends in advance and marking across the ends and middle of the field with white paper sacks, filling them with soil to keep them in place.

Powered Rotary Tillers

Power take-off (PTO) units on tractors permit rotary tillers to eliminate existing vegetation and pulverize clay loam or cloddy soils for row-crop seedbed preparation. They till soils for 2-to-5–inch depths and are often combined with bed shapers to give a precise row-crop bed. Weed kill is thorough, but power requirements are high. Powered rotary tillers are

Figure 6. Row-crop cultivators may include reversed-disc hillers and various bed knives to dislodge small weeds. Photo courtesy J.K. Clark.

often used for vegetables and other small-seeded crops to ensure uniformity in herbicide incorporation, planting, and irrigation (fig. 5).

These implements are often called bed mulchers, rototillers, or rotovators. Most of them till vertically, but one type utilizes horizontally turning tines. Tines can have straight rectangular teeth, angled teeth (L- or C-shaped), or round teeth. Additional information on methods of herbicide incorporation may be found in the Soil Incorporation section of Chapter 7.

Sled Cultivators

Sled-mounted cultivators can give very accurate control in row plantings. Sleds require more tractor power to pull them than gauge-wheel cultivators but provide the greater precision desirable for vegetable row-crop production (fig. 6). Guide wheels (cone wheels, rubber guide wheels, etc.) also can improve the precision of cultivations if set up exactly.

Rotary Ground-Driven Cultivators

A cultivation technique that has become very popular in recent years is the rolling cultivator unit, often called a Lilliston (fig. 7). Such a rotary ground-driven cultivator is used in many instances for the first two to four cultivations after planting row crops. It is guided by the shapes of the beds. Guidance can be improved by also having a guide marker at the front of the tractor.

Figure 7. Cultivators often use high-speed rotary ground-driven gangs. Photo courtesy J.K. Clark.

The rotary cultivator unit comes on a rear-mounted, three-point-hitch toolbar. For close cultivation of row crops, a dual-disc weeder can be attached for each row. Reversed disc-hillers cut soil away from the row. Behind them are flat-bed knives (also called beet hoe, bed sweeps, etc.) that run flat under the soil, cutting off weed roots and reforming the furrows and beds.

Spring-Tooth Cultivators

Another type of cultivation implement for row crops also mounted on a hydraulically operated three-point hitch is the spring-tooth cultivator shown in figure. 8. It usually has a cone guide wheel that follows the side of the furrow and guides the rear toolbar assembly. The gauge wheels provide vertical control. To use it, the planter must place V-marks in the soil made with 4-inch "duckfeet" on the end of cultivator shanks. The duckfeet are placed behind planter gauge wheels and also in the furrows where the tractor tires run. This then permits cultivating, before or shortly after crop emergence, at speeds near 5 mph. The tunnel shields protect the row crop from flowing dirt.

The points attached to the base of each spring-harrow tine can be changed from 1 to 3 inches in width. These tear up the weeds and leave them on the soil surface. A minimum speed of 3.5 mph is required. The unit works well except on clay soils that are too dry and break up into

Figure 8. On small cotton, shields keep clods out of the seed row when spring-tooth harrow cultivators are being used. Photo courtesy J.K. Clark.

clods. They are favored for use in heavy thatch, such as bermudagrass, field bindweed, and nutsedges.

Cultivator Tillage Tools

Cultivator sweeps are used to make a furrow and to return soil against the crop to cover seedling weeds and enhance harvest operations. The names of cultivator tillage tools vary. Names such as 'plant hoe,' 'V-sweep,' 'cultivator knife,' 'bed knives,' 'square-turned knives' (right and left), 'shovels,' 'vegetable knives,' 'Alabama sweeps,' 'chisel plow sweeps,' 'cultivator sweeps,' 'duckfoot sweeps,' and 'listers' refer to different tillage tools that can be attached to tool shanks to do different tillage jobs. Some are used just for weed removal, others are used for moving soil, and still others for both. Students may wish to refer to the *Agricultural Engineers Yearbook* for standardized soil-tillage and tool nomenclature, which was published in 1981.

SPECIAL CULTIVATOR TOOLS

A spring-hoe weeder (fig. 9) aids in closer cultivation and removes small weeds after an irrigation. It works very well on medium soils but not quite as well on fine ones. Crops must be well rooted to withstand it. It squeezes

Figure 9. In established crops, row-weeders can remove seedling weeds or bury them. Photo courtesy B.B Fischer.

the soil in the crop drill row, lifting the soil and snapping off small-rooted weeds.

A sequence of three cultivations often will clean up large or small weeds in a well-rooted crop such as sugar beets or cotton. Rotating blades mounted ahead of rotary spinners will remove most grassy weeds in the drill row, thereby greatly reducing the need for hand weeding. Spring-hoe cultivators can then cover many other weeds. Where thinning is needed, running beet rows twice in opposite directions with rotary spring-wheel thinners will take out tall weeds. The rotary spinners catch remaining weeds and deposit them in the furrow (fig. 10).

The Texas rod-weeder is probably the ultimate in simplicity and cost-effectiveness for what it can do (fig. 11). Spring steel ⅛-inch rods extending from a single coil and attached to cultivation shovels or sweeps, one on each side of a row and directly opposite, run just below the soil line of the drill row. As the rods are pulled through the soil, they remove seedling weeds emerging after irrigation of a firmly rooted crop. Major usage has been in 8-to-36–inch tall cotton (annual morningglory, especially), 4-to-16–inch sugar beets, and 6-to-12–inch cole crops. It works well on poorly rooted weeds.

Cultivation is used in orchards, vineyards, and row crops, while mowing is used primarily in orchards, vineyards, and non-crop areas. One of the most widely used mechanical tools is the spring-hoe weeder. It will till previously shaped conical berms in the vineyard row quite

Figure 10. Specialty equipment such as these rotary spinners can remove a high percentage of weeds in crop rows. Photo courtesy B.B Fischer.

aggressively, removing fairly large weeds. Caster wheels at the end of the springs aid in reducing damage to vine trunks and trellis stakes. This weeder often is attached to narrow vineyard discs.

The hoe (or French) plow is used in vineyards to remove winter weeds from the berm. In the spring, the soil is disked and returned to the vine row, usually after a deep irrigation. In-row tillage is possible with the advent of hydraulic motors and sensors.

Besides affecting weed control, tillage can reduce such insects in grapes as overwintering omnivorous leafroller. Disking is used to incorporate volatile dinitroaniline herbicides. In-row drip or fan-jet plastic emitter systems are attached a foot above the soil in order to permit in-row tillage in grapes and other crops.

Tillage in trees is limited where sprinkler or drip emitter systems are used. In trees under furrow irrigation, normal disking or harrowing is usually done, with berms left undisturbed and treated with herbicides. Tillage too close to trees can induce wound diseases such as crown gall and Ceratocystis.

Mechanical mowing is widely practiced in orchard middles, especially in almonds. A vegetative cover has a number of advantages, including better water penetration, erosion control, and early orchard entry for insecticide spraying. It keeps the orchard cooler and freer of dust (which enhances spider mite populations). However, mowed vegetation requires about one-third more water and nitrogenous fertilization. Mowing in the tree row is possible but requires that no obstacles be present to interfere with equipment.

Figure 11. The Texas rod-weeder uses spring-loaded tines to remove seedling weeds in crop rows. Photo courtesy H.M. Kempen.

HAND WEEDING

Precision cultivation and herbicide use will not eliminate all weeds. Therefore, hand weeding is a necessity in row-crop production and in some orchard and vineyard situations. Hand weeding removes those last few weeds which, if allowed to go to seed, will reinfest the field. As mentioned earlier, prevention of weed seed production is desired, especially of those which are aggressive competitors. Hoeing or shoveling out occasional johnsongrass plants is often more practical than spraying them.

Weeds need to be about 4 inches tall to be effectively hoed; smaller weeds are usually missed. Precision planting or the use of a synchronous or random thinner prior to hoeing will cut hoeing costs markedly. Electronic or mechanical thinners cannot distinguish between plants. Some weeds look like the crop (e.g., nightshade in tomatoes). Proper timing can aid in visual separation of weeds from crop plants. Good hoeing-crew supervision is critical under these circumstances.

Weeds should not be allowed to get too large because they are much more competitive with crops when they are bigger. Additionally, the removal of larger weeds often results in either plant (crop) injury and/or yield losses during the weeding operation. Pulling large weeds is a salvage job, but it can be done more easily after an irrigation.

In orchards and vineyards, hoeing is often needed during the first year of establishment. Excessive competition may kill some crop rootings, usually due to drought. As a result, a two-year-old crop could require first-year management techniques. Trees or vines should not be planted in a sod turf or weed cover, as growth is severely reduced in such situations. Supervision, monitoring, and incentives all are needed to get optimum results from hoe crews.

REFERENCES

Anonymous 1982. Terminology and definitions for soil tillage and soil-tool relationships. Agricultural Engineers Yearbook. pp. 247–249.

Anonymous 1982. Terminology and definitions for agricultural implements. Agricultural Engineers Yearbook. pp. 232–241.

Anonymous 1983. Catalog of CPI Agricultural Equipment Tillage Tools. CPI, 243 Orange Ave., P.O. Box 1087, Patterson, CA.

Burnside, O.C., C.R. Fenster, LL. Evetts and R.F. Mumm 1981. Germination of exhumed weed seed in Nebraska. Weed Sci. 29:577–586.

Donaldson, T.W. and G.R. Code 1981. Effect of cultural treatments on wild radish density in wheat. Proc. 6th Austr. Weeds Conf. 1:79–80.

Flaherty, D.L., et. al 1981. Grape Pest Management. Univ. of Calif. Publ. 4105 pp. 276–277.

Kempen, H.M. 1980. Johnsongrass. Proc. West. Cotton Prod. Conf. Fresno, CA.

Koch, W. and M. Hess 1980. Weeds in wheat; Documenta Ciba-Geigy pp. 33–40.

Roberts, H.A. Viable weed seeds in cultivated soils. 1970. Rept. Nat. Veg. Res. Sta. (1969) Wellesbourne, Warwickshire, U.K. pp. 25–38.

Schroch, W.A., L.A. Thompson, Jr. and E.O. Beasley 1981. Pesticide incorporation: Distribution of Dye by Tillage Implements. North Carolina AES, Raleigh. 31 pp.

5

BIOLOGICAL CONTROL METHODS

by Sara S. Rosenthal[1], Donald M. Maddox[2], and Kathy Brunetti[3]

There are aphids for roses and weevils for corn,
There are worms for tomatoes and beans;
The farmer grows weary, the gardener worn
From the battle of growing the greens.
There are sprays for controlling each ornery pest,
But the thing that the world really needs—
A miracle cure for the grower's unrest—
Is a bug that would eat only weeds.

While the bug that eats only weeds may seem a miracle to the rancher or gardener whose crops are plagued by pests, such "bugs" are really quite common. All plants have herbivores, diseases, and other parasitic or competitive plants that influence their abundance. Weeds are no exception. Discovering such natural enemies and using appropriate ones for biological control is what this chapter is all about.

Biological control of a weed, then, is simply using the plant's natural enemies to lower its population to the level where the plant is no longer an economic problem. It involves the application of ecology, particularly the principles of population dynamics and of herbivore-host plant relations, to weed control.

1, 2. United States Department of Agriculture, Albany, CA. 3. California Department of Food and Agriculture, Sacramento, CA.

Figure 1. A pad of the prickly pear cactus opened to show larvae of the moth, Cactoblastis cactorum. *Photo courtesy D.M. Maddox.*

HISTORY

Biological weed control is very old. Probably the first effort was the spread of a cochineal insect, *Dactylopius ceylonicus* Green, in southern India during the 1860s to control the prickly pear cactus. Both plant and insect had come originally from Brazil. The insect had been first introduced into India in 1795 because it was mistaken for the cochineal insect of commerce, *D. coceus* Costa, the dried body of which is used to make a crimson dye. When it was found to be so destructive to the prickly pear, infested cactus segments were distributed in India and Ceylon to suppress this plant pest.

In 1902 there was an attempt to control lantana in Hawaii by biological means. Albert Koebele, an entomologist, went to Mexico to study the insects attacking the plant in its home of origin and brought 18 species back to the islands. However, due to slow transportation, few of the insects reached Hawaii alive, and only eight species became established. While some weed reduction was achieved with these, a greater degree of control was desired. With the development of air transportation, work on biological controls for lantana was resumed in the 1950s. Now this pest is successfully controlled in drier parts of Hawaii by a complex of insects made up of the lantana lacebug, *Teleonemia scrupulosa* Stål, and three leaf-feeding moths, *Catabena esula* (Druce), *Hypena strigata* F, and *Syngamia haemorrhoidalis* Guenee. In wetter areas they are aided by three beetles: a stem-borer, *Plagiohammus spinipennis* (Thom), and two leaf-feeders, *Octotoma scabripennis* Guer. and *Uroplata girandi* Pic.

During the 1920s, Australia became active in biological weed-control research. The most famous result of this work was the reduction of prickly pear infestation by the moth, *Cactoblastis cactorum* (Berg). The larvae of this moth mine within the cactus pads (fig. 1). It is a very valuable biocontrol agent for prickly pear, not only in Australia but also in South Africa, New Caledonia, Hawaii, the West Indies, and Mauritius.

Another famous example of the success of this method is the suppression of Klamathweed in California. Between 1945 and 1950, initial releases of two leaf-feeding beetles, *Chrysolina hyperici* (Forst.) and *C. quadrigemina* (Suffrian), a root-boring beetle, *Agrilus hyperici* (Creutzer), and a gall fly, *Zeuxidiplosis giardi* (Kieffer), were made against this weed. *C. quadrigemina,* known as the Klamathweed beetle, was by far the most important and successful biological control agent. Because of the remarkable control of Klamathweed by *C. quadrigemina,* the Humboldt County Wool Grower's and the Humboldt County Cattlemen's associations together erected a monument to show their gratitude for the beetle that saved their rangelands.

The tremendous successes with control of prickly pear and Klamathweed stimulated the more recent, greatly increased research efforts in this field. Biological controls are now used against weeds all over the world, but primarily in the United States, Canada, Australia, and other member countries of the British Commonwealth. There have been 192 organisms established in different countries on 86 introduced weeds, and 33 organisms established for the control of 25 native weeds.

ECOLOGICAL FOUNDATION

Detailed explanations of the population dynamics theory basic to biological control may be found in textbooks and review articles on this subject. Each organism, plant, or animal has a population size that fluctuates around some characteristic "equilibrium" level or long-term mean density. This mean level of abundance depends on the natural controls limiting the population. Such natural controls include limited resources, climate, competitors in the same or different species, and natural enemies. Some of these controls, like climate, are density independent, i.e., their actions do not depend on population size. If the climate is too cold or the soil too acidic, for example, the plant cannot exist in that area and population size is irrelevant. Other natural controls, like some natural enemies, act in a density-dependent manner. These natural enemies are said to have density-dependent action if, as the plant population increases, the intensity of impact of the natural enemies increases while relatively little damage or mortality is caused by these enemies when plant populations are low.

Many weeds are introduced plants that became pests because they have entered new areas without density-dependent natural enemies. In the area of introduction they may grow in solid stands, while in their native home they may be abundant but are often able to exist only as scattered plants. At home their natural enemies may or may not play an important role in determining their abundance since herbivores, theoretically, are under natural control themselves. Lack of natural checks in their new homes has allowed the plants' populations to increase to levels that bring them into conflict with man's interests. In the area of introduction, the weeds' numbers may be lowered by introducing their natural enemies. The same ecological principles apply to the population sizes of herbivores. In order to be effective -control agents, they must be imported into the target area without *their* parasites and predators.

Good discussions of the influence of herbivores on plant populations are found in books on plant ecology by Harper and by Barbour et al. Herbivores consume, on the average, about 15% of all living plant material. The relationship between phytophagous (plant-feeding) organisms and their food plants may be very complex. In some circumstances such destruction of tissues may even stimulate plant growth. However, in general, this feeding has an overall negative impact on a plant's growth, reproduction, and survival. Plant feeders have been known to affect natural plant distribution patterns. For example, seed predators may be very important in regulating tropical tree populations. Most examples of herbivores regulating their hosts come from research on biological control of weeds.

For biological control of weeds, host specificity is so important that there is special interest in the way phytophagous organisms choose their plants. Host selection by plant feeders, like that of natural enemies used to control insect pests, depends on habitat selection by the herbivore, the finding of the plant within the habitat, its acceptance as a food or breeding place, and suitability of the plant as a host. For instance, the Klamathweed beetle, ordinarily a major biological control agent for Klamathweed, is a poor control of this plant where it is growing in the shade of other plants. The herbivore may only recognize or accept its host and find it suitable if the plant has the proper size, shape, color, hairiness, or chemical content. The specificity of a number of species of seed head flies whose larvae live in the flower heads of different species of thistles is related to the relative sizes of their ovipositors and the diameters of the flowerheads. If an otherwise appropriate thistle head is too large or too small, the fly cannot position the egg properly for larval development. Thus, that thistle species escapes attack by the fly. Insects associated with *Hypericum* spp. are stimulated by the chemical compound hypericin and may use that to locate their hosts. The phosphate, nitrogen, and carbohydrate content of alligatorweed is important to its use by the alligatorweed flea beetle.

For expediency, it is necessary to test the host specificity of a potential biological control agent in the artificial conditions of the laboratory and field cages where the clues normally used by the herbivore to select its host are distorted. Under such circumstances, an insect may seem to have a wider host range than it would really have in nature. Where possible, an attempt is made to find the basis of host specificity to better predict what plants would really be hosts under natural conditions.

Whether the biological control agent actually has an impact on the weed depends on its population and the amount of stress it puts on the individual plants. Plants may appear to produce excess foliage, yet defoliators can be damaging if their activity takes place at a time of year when the plant is particularly vulnerable. A stem feeder able to destroy the vascular tissue, the vital plant tissue used to conduct nutrients and water, destroys its host.

COMPARISON WITH OTHER METHODS OF PEST CONTROL

The theoretical basis of biological control of weeds is similar to that of biological control of insects. Yet there is a very important difference. In the case of insect parasitism or predation, the natural enemy kills its host outright. While it is beneficial if the weed's natural enemy kills its host, this is not necessary for it to be a successful control agent. If it can decrease an annual plant's reproductive rate by destroying the seeds or reduce a weed's ability to compete with other plants by slowing its growth, this may be enough for the pest population to be sufficiently lowered.

Biological control is slower acting than other control methods used against weeds. It should not be tried when the destruction of the weed is needed immediately. Control may not be achieved until one to 10 years after natural enemies are released. It commonly takes about 12 years from the beginning of a biological control project until some suppression is achieved. It may take 20 years. Nevertheless, biological control is a relatively inexpensive solution to weed problems. By the most recent estimate, a biological control program may cost $1.8 million or more but still be the most cost-effective solution. It is far less than the $15–20 million now needed for development of a chemical herbicide plus the cost of its repeated application.

Another difference from other control methods involves selectivity. Biological weed-control agents must be very host specific so as to prevent damage to commercially valuable crop plants and ecologically valuable native plants. For example, insects released to control thistles in the genera *Cirsium* and *Carduus,* some of the most important range weeds, must damage neither artichokes nor closely related, rare, native plants in the genera *Cirsium* and *Saussurea.* They must be even more limited in their food habits than the parasites and predators used to suppress insect pests. Herbicides, or the manner in which they are used, may be selective, but for biological control, where the agent will disperse and spread beyond our control, selectivity is a necessity. Because of their

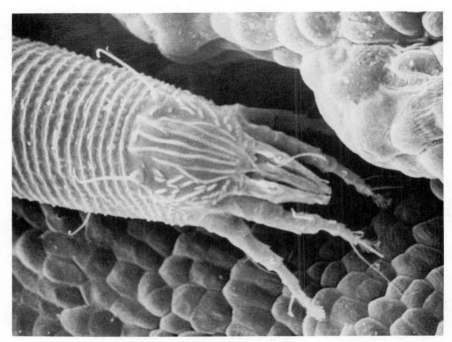

Figure 2. The gall mite, Aceria chondrillae, *that galls the buds of its host, rush skeleton-weed. Photo courtesy C. Hunter.*

high host specificity these biological control agents should cause no harmful side effects, such as residue problems or ecosystem disturbance. Such selectivity is of course an advantage where only one weed is important or very difficult to control, but a disadvantage where several weeds must be suppressed at the same time.

The object of biological control is not to eradicate the weed, but to reduce its numbers to the point where the plant is no longer an economic problem. Eradication is contrary to the theoretical ecological basis of biological control. Ideally, biological control is self-perpetuating. Therefore, some of the pest problems should always be present to maintain at least a small population of the natural enemy able to increase in numbers and prevent any future increase by the weed. Such control is permanent; there is no need to apply it again and again like a chemical.

DIVERSITY OF BIOLOGICAL CONTROL AGENTS

Most of the biological control agents used against weeds are insects. When the number of damaging insect pests is considered, it seems natural to concentrate on this taxonomic group when seeking plant-destroy-

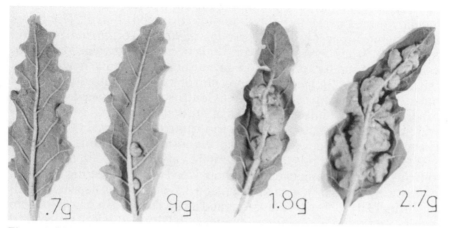

Figure 3. Sizes and weights of various silverleaf nightshade leaves galled by the nematode Nothanguina phyllobia. *Photo courtesy C.C. Orr.*

ing organisms. A wide variety of insects, members of seven different orders, are successful biological control agents for weeds. So far, examples from four orders have been mentioned. A thrips, *Amynothrips andersoni* O'Neill, was released for control of alligatorweed. Some other examples from different insect groups include the seed-feeding wasp *Eurytoma attiva* Burks, which along with a leaf-feeding beetle, *Schematiza cordiae* Barber, gives complete control of black sage in Mauritius. The gall-forming fly *Procecidochares utilis* (Stone) gives complete control of pamakani or Crofton weed in Hawaii.

Another group of arthropods that can be very damaging to plants is the Acari, or mites. The best example of a biological control agent from this group is the gall mite *Aceria chondrillae* (G. Canestrini) (fig. 2) being used successfully for the suppression of rush skeletonweed in Australia and recently reported for that use into the United States. This mite forms galls in vegetative and flower buds. It damages its host plant by reducing plant production, blocking shoot development, and weakening the whole plant.

Other invertebrates employed as biological control agents include snails and nematodes. The fresh water snail *Marisa cornuarietis* L. not only feeds on a variety of submersed aquatic weeds in Florida but is known to eat the eggs of disease-carrying snails in Puerto Rico. While controlling water weeds it reduces snail- and mosquito-borne diseases. The use of this snail is limited because it also attacks young rice plants. The nematode *Nothanguina phyllobia* Thorne feeds and reproduces in the actively growing leaves and stems of silverleaf nightshade (fig. 3). In Texas, Orr has shown the nematode to be an effective biological control for this weed.

Vertebrates may be good biological control agents also. There is special interest in the use of fish for aquatic weed control. The grass carp or white amur, *Ctenopharyngodon idella* Val., originated in China but since 1960 has been spread worldwide because of its value for aquatic weed control and fish production. In southern California, herbivorous fish in the genus *Tilapia* are able to control weeds in both quiet waters and in rapidly flowing canal systems. Control of aquatic weeds by these fish lowers the maintenance costs of the waterways and reduces the available breeding habitats for the mosquito *Culex tarsalis* Coquillett. The manatee or sea cow, *Trichecchus manatus* L., a mammal that may weigh over 2000 pounds, has been studied in Florida and in the tropics with the hope that its giant appetite would lead to rapid clearing of weeds from waterways. The use of the manatee is restricted by its slow breeding, its inability to live in cold water, and a need to protect it from poaching due to the good quality of its meat. In China, ducks are used to control crop insect and weed pests on land. The ducks furnish meat and income as well. In the United States, geese, which like to eat narrow-leaved plants, are used in several states for weeding crops such as cotton, strawberries, corn, orchards, and vineyards. Goats are well known for their value in clearing brush from pastures.

Another active area of biological weed control is plant pathology. Plant diseases may be caused by fungi, bacteria, viruses, mycoplasmas, or nematodes. Additionally, nutrient deficiencies, chemical and air-pollution damage, and other environmental problems such as sun scald are also considered plant diseases. Although an understanding of these noninfectious diseases can be used to suppress weeds, it is the infectious diseases, particularly those caused by fungi, that have been used in biological control. Before plant disease can occur there must be a susceptible host, a virulent pathogen, and a suitable environment. Each of these elements of the "disease triangle" influences plant disease development in different ways.

The susceptibility of the host is very important. Many fungi are host specific; they will attack only one or a few species of plants. They may be so specialized that particular strains of one fungus species may only attack certain forms of the host species. The *Chondrilla* rust, *Puccinia chondrillina* Bubak & Syd, which attacks rush skeletonweed, is one such specialized fungus. The most common form of rush skeletonweed in Australia is not infected by rust strains from France, northern Italy, or Spain, but the fungus strain from Vieste, in southeastern Italy, is highly virulent against it. Even if the correct host species is present, a fungus may be unable to infect unless the plant is at the correct stage of development during its infective stage. Plants alter physiologically and biochemically as they grow and may be susceptible to different diseases at different times. Weeds that can be infected in their early stages are good prospects for control by fungi.

The causal agent is the plant pathogen itself. Most fungi spread by means of spores, i.e., small reproductive structures which germinate into strands of fungus able to attack the plant. Whether infection occurs depends on the quality and quantity of spores. Not all spores germinate, and not all germinating spores are capable of infecting. A good candidate for a biological control agent, then, is a fungus that needs only a few spores to infect or from which massive amounts of spores can easily be obtained.

Getting the host and the fungus together is not enough. If the environment is not suitable, no disease can occur. Many fungal spores require free water from rain, dew, or irrigation before they can germinate. Some, like powdery mildews, are inhibited by too much water. Temperature can also be critical; fungi may be killed by extremely high or low temperatures, and they usually grow best at an optimum temperature range. The maximum, minimum, and optimum temperatures differ for different diseases. For a fungus to be effective as a biological control agent, the environment must be suitable at the time of year it is to be applied. Spores of the *Chondrilla* rust germinate at a wide range of temperatures and this fungus has a wide geographical range. It was expected to be well adapted to Australian conditions because it is damaging to rush skeletonweed in similar climates. Because of the success with this fungus in Australia as a classical biological control, it has now been released for control of that weed in the United States as well.

Besides animals and microorganisms, biological control agents can be other plants that are either parasitic, competitive, or allelopathic. A particularly imaginative example of the use of plants is the control of water weeds using spike rushes. The spike rushes are only ¾–2⅓ inches tall, yet they were found by Yeo to form a sod on the bottom of waterways and prevent the establishment of larger, rooted, submersed weeds that would otherwise interfere with the flow of water. Frank and Dechoretz have shown that they are allelopathic against pondweeds.

PROCEDURE

The process in developing a biological control project consists of (1) determining the suitability of the weed problem for biological control, (2) surveying the weed for natural enemies in both its naturalized and native homes, (3) studying the biologies and host relations of the natural enemies to determine how they may be used to solve the problem, (4) implementing control, and (5) evaluating the effectiveness of the natural enemies.

The selection of an appropriate weed is influenced by a number of economic and ecological factors. The economic losses caused by the weed plus the cost of other controls must be greater than the cost of the biological control project. Where current control methods are inadequate to achieve the degree of suppression desired or are not feasible because the land is of low value, biological methods may be very useful. By understanding the causes of the weed problem one can determine the possibility of biological control providing a solution. For instance, biological control may not solve problems caused by poor land management. To prevent conflicts of interest, the weed should have no close relatives of economic or ecological importance and it should not be of value in some other area. For this reason, little biological control has been attempted against grasses in spite of their being some of the worst weeds in the world. Many are closely related to important grain crops. Others are weeds in one area, but important as lawn covers or as forage somewhere else. There appears to be a greater probability of success with biological control if it is targeted against neutralized biennial or perennial weeds growing in areas of low disturbance, such as rangeland, and where one weed dominates the plant community.

In conducting surveys of natural enemies and studying their ecology it can be difficult to judge what organisms would be the best biocontrol agents. To be effective they must be damaging to the weed and able to survive in the area of introduction. Emphasis should be placed on natural enemies attacking vital plant parts and those parts not already damaged by herbivores in the area where control is wanted. Host specificity of feeding, development, and reproduction of potential biological control agents must be shown. A system of rating the value of different natural enemies for biological control was developed by Harris.

When selecting a target weed or the kinds of plants to use in host-specificity testing to determine whether an organism can be introduced into the United States for further research in a quarantine facility or release in the field, advice is solicited from the federal Working Group, Biological Control of Weeds (WGBCW). The WGBCW is made up of representatives of the United States Department of Agriculture (USDA), the United States Department of the Interior (USDI), the Environmental Protection Agency (EPA), and the U.S. Army Corps of Engineers (ACE). The recommendations of the WGBCW are sent on to the Animal and Plant Health Inspection Service (APHIS) of the USDA, and APHIS gives the final approval for the importation and release of the biological control agent. Approval must also be obtained from the particular states involved.

There are several methods of implementing biological control. The one most commonly used is classical biological control. This method relies on the utilization of exotic herbivores or pathogens with narrow host ranges which are usually sought in the weed's home or origin, the geographical area where the plant-herbivore or plant-pathogen interactions have coevolved. It has been the most effective against naturalized weeds as they do not have a full complement of natural enemies. How-

Figure 4. Alligatorweed infesting the Ortega River in Florida before (left) *and after* (right) *its control by the flea beetle,* Agasicles hygrophilla. *Photo courtesy C.F. Zeiger.*

ever, there are also examples of its value against native weeds. One such instance, in California, is the control of prickly pear cacti on Santa Cruz Island using a cochineal insect, *Dactylopius* spp., that was introduced from the mainland without its own natural enemies. The efficacy of an introduced natural enemy varies from site to site depending on its preadaptation to the new environments and how it complements existing stresses on the plant. Another method is to increase the effectiveness of an introduced organism or one already present by manipulation. For example, in South Africa the control of prickly pear with another cochineal insect can be improved if the cacti are sprayed with DDT at a dosage low enough to keep from harming the insect yet high enough to kill its ladybird beetle predators. A third way of accomplishing biological control is by augmentation. In this method the natural enemies are mass reared and released at appropriate times and places.

The simplest and most dramatic way of showing the value of a biological control agent is with a series of photographs taken of the weed infested area before and after the natural enemies are released (fig. 4). The effect of such a project may also be evaluated using an ecological study to show the reduction of the weed population in the release area. Using surveys of the number of musk thistle plants per plots and of the recent musk thistle plants infested by the seed head weevil, *Rhinocyllus conicus* Froel., Kok and Surles, proved that the weevil gave control of the weed in Virginia within six years of its release. By conducting large-scale surveys, reduction of weed infestation due to natural enemies may be shown over a wider area. As discussed below, reduction of California land infested with puncturevine was demonstrated from a survey of the county agricultural commissioners. There have been substantial monetary benefits from biological control of weeds, but accurate cost-benefit analyses have seldom been made. Examples of two cases where such an evaluation was made are the control of black sage in Mauritius where the total cost of the program was $25,000 by 1952 compared to the annual benefit of $250,000 saved since then, and the control of a prickly pear in South Africa where the cost of biological control was $42,500 up to 1950 with a saving of $237,000 per year since then.

CONTROL METHODS AND APPLICATION: CLASSICAL BIOLOGICAL CONTROL

In this section, detailed descriptions of two successful biological control projects on two specific weeds will be used to exemplify the use of the classical method in the United States. One of these is a project dealing with an aquatic weed, and the second is one dealing with a terrestrial weed. The different phases pursued in classical biological control are discussed in relation to each of the weed projects described. Other examples and more information on biological weed control may be found in the review articles and monographs listed at the end of this chapter.

Waterhyacinth

History and Suitability for Biological Control
Waterhyacinth is a free-floating aquatic plant that is believed to have been introduced into the United States from South America at the Cotton Exposition in New Orleans in 1884. Specimens of the plant were carried home by visitors to the exposition, and it consequently became a serious weed problem in the southeastern United States due to its high reproductive rate and its lack of effective natural enemies. Waterhyacinth completely covers slow-moving streams, canals, and small lakes; interferes with fishing and water transportation; causes excessive water loss through evapotranspiration; is responsible for oxygen deficiencies that kill fish in aquatic habitats; and usurps water areas used for rice culture. Waterhyacinth is also a major aquatic weed problem in Africa, India, Southeast Asia, and Australia. It is ranked as the eighth most important weed in the world. The plant propagates itself both vegetatively (daughter plants) and by seeds. Waterhyacinth can be controlled by herbicides, but the plant's high rate of reproduction results in rapid reinfestation. Perkins presented a recent review of the biological-control efforts against waterhyacinth.

Foreign Exploration for Natural Enemies
Research on the biological control of waterhyacinth was conducted by the Agricultural Research Service (ARS) in Argentina, fully sponsored by the Army Corps of Engineers. Aquiles Silveira Guido had initiated a

study of insects attacking alligatorweed and waterhyacinth between 1961 and 1965 at Montevideo, Uruguay.

With the success of the alligatorweed project there was great interest in similar work on waterhyacinth. Research on it began in 1967 when B.D. Perkins went to Argentina. He studied natural enemies of waterhyacinth until 1971, from which time the research was continued by C.J. DeLoach until June 1974 and by H.A. Cordo after that.

Exploration for natural enemies of waterhyacinth was carried out by several workers in the United States, Central America, northern South America, and India. More than 70 species of arthropods were found to feed on waterhyacinth. Six species of arthropods have been given serious consideration as candidates for introduction, and one other potential biological control agent is native to the United States.

Biology and Host Specificity of Candidate Organisms

Perkins has pointed out that damage to waterhyacinth resulting from an attack by arthropods can occur in two ways: by the direct removal of tissue and by the decomposition of tissue that surrounds the feeding area. If such damage is severe enough, the reproduction of the plant may be slowed or halted. Reproduction by vegetative means greatly surpasses reproduction by seeds in any area where the plant is established. Seeds are important in the distribution of the plant to other areas (via the feet of waterbirds), and for survival during adverse periods. Perkins divides the biological agents responsible for direct removal of plant tissue into four categories: (1) defoliators and external leaf feeders; (2) petiole borers; (3) leaf tunnel producers; and (4) scavenger species that enhance the effect of attack by other species. Samples of these categories are given below.

- Defoliators and external leaf feeders:

A grasshopper, *Cornops aquaticum* (Bruner), is found throughout South America, causing heavy damage in some localities. The eggs are deposited inside the petioles, and the nymphs and adults feed on the leaves of waterhyacinth. Silveira Guido and Perkins determined its host-plant specificity and found that oviposition and development occurred only on waterhyacinth and *Eichornia,* although some feeding occurred on pickerelweed in the field.

The most important natural enemies found were two species of weevils of the genus *Neochetina,* tribe Bagoini, that attack waterhyacinth in South America. The weevils, *N. bruchi* Hustache and *N. eichhorniae* Warner, strongly prefer waterhyacinth, and their host-plant specificity was tested extensively at the ARS laboratories in Argentina and Albany, California. Their biologies and effects on the host plant are similar. The adults feed on the surface of the leaves and petioles and lay their eggs inside the petiole. The larvae tunnel downward inside the petioles and the crown, causing extensive damage, and pupate on the roots.

- Petiole borers:

The larvae of *N. bruchi* and *N. eichhorniae* as indicated above tunnel downward inside the petiole. Larval tunneling tends to weaken the petioles so that they break or blacken as a result of fungal attack.

The larvae of the pyralid moth *Acigona infusella* Walker enter the petiole and tunnel inside during their development, finally forming naked pupae inside the petiole. They cause heavy damage to the host plant; a single larva is capable of damaging several plants during its development. Saprophytic fungi entering the damaged tissues subsequently increase the effect. While *A. infusella* is considered the most damaging arthropod found on waterhyacinth in Argentina, it may have too wide a host range to allow its introduction into the United States.

Another pyralid, *Sameodes albiguttalis* (Warren), is similar to *A. infusella* and does similar damage to the plant. It spins a white cocoon before pupating in the petiole. Host-plant testing completed at the ARS laboratory in Argentina indicates that this moth is safe to use.

Larvae of the native moth *Arzama densa* (Walker) inflict considerable damage to waterhyacinth plants by feeding on tender leaves and apical buds when they are young and then, as they become older, burrowing into the petiole and, eventually, the rhizome. This species transferred to waterhyacinth after its introduction into the United States from the closely related pickerelweed.

- Leaf-tunnel producers:

The waterhyacinth mite *Orthogalumna terebrantis* Wallwork feeds in wounds on the leaves or petioles of waterhyacinth. The larvae and nymphs make tunnels in the leaf epidermis. They can reach high populations and cause severe damage to the host plant. As many as 20,000 mites may occur in a square foot of waterhyacinth. The tunneled leaves are often dried by the sun, which kills them. This mite occurs on waterhyacinth throughout South America, Jamaica, and in the southeastern United States. It is believed to have been introduced into the United States along with its host.

- Scavengers that enhance the effect of attack by other species:

Perkins has reported that several insect scavenger species, such as scarab beetles, tend to enhance the effect of attack by other insects, notably *Neochetina*. In Argentina, however, none are specific to waterhyacinth. Although it is impossible to introduce them from another country as biological control agents, they already exist in many locations where waterhyacinth is found and can become significant because they increase the stress on the plant. Feeding and deposition of feces inside the petioles or crown, or externally, cause the plants to putrefy.

Introduction, Establishment, and Evaluation
After due consideration was given to the research data presented on host specificity, the WGBCW gave approval for introduction of *Neochetina*

eichhorniae, and subsequently *N. bruchi,* into the ARS quarantine laboratory at Albany. Following completion of testing, final approval was given for release of these weevils by the WGBCW with subsequent approval by authorities in Florida, Mississippi, and Louisiana. *N. eichhorniae* and *N. bruchi* were initially released in Florida in 1972 and 1974, respectively. *N. bruchi* was released in California in 1982. *N. bruchi* is established at release sites in Florida but is often dominated by *N. eichhorniae* moving in from other areas. *N. eichhorniae* is established throughout Florida and is also well established in Mississippi and Louisiana.

The effect of *N. eichhorniae* has been rather spectacular. The weevil causes a gradual attrition and reduction of waterhyacinth in many areas, thus reducing the plant's competitive ability which often results in a shift in the plant community. Center reported that the effects of weevil damage are rather subtle and are difficult to observe over the short term. Such damage may be expressed as a decrease in the size of the plants. Plants at his study site in Florida went from an average of 40 inches or more, at the time of weevil release in 1974, to an average height of 25 inches in 1978. As the weevil populations increased, the plants became progressively smaller. He also noted an inhibition of the growth of the mat. Areas that were cleared remained clear longer. The peak standing crop declined from 5 pounds to about 3 pounds (dry weight)/square foot. Waterhyacinth coverage of this study site declined from over 90% in 1974 to about 25% in 1980.

More dramatic changes have occurred in other areas. Perkins was able to demonstrate that waterhyacinth had disappeared at some sites in southern Florida by 1976. In Australia, Wright reported that *N. eichhorniae* has caused the death of plants and collapse of the floating mats subsequent to the establishment of the weevil in several parts of Queensland and that the amount of damage is increasing. Dr. Al Cofrancesco of the ACE Aquatic Plant Control Research Program reported that a substantial reduction of waterhyacinth acreage has occurred in Louisiana. Waterhyacinth in the state averaged about 1.2 million acres prior to the 1974 releases of *N. eichhorniae.* About four years after the release of the weevils there was a decline in acreage, and in 1979 and 1980 it had declined to less than 350,000 acres. Also, Goyer and Stark reported that *N. eichhorniae* has brought about a considerable reduction in waterhyacinth in the "Bayou Morgan City Area" in Assumption Parish, Louisiana. There *N. eichhorniae* has caused reductions in plant height, weight, root length, and the number of daughter plants produced.

The moth, *Sameodes albiguttalis,* was released in Florida in 1977 at several sites. Significant levels of damage are now becoming apparent in some places, and there is a noticeable reduction in the growth rate of mats. At present, the damage is rather sporadic because of emigration of the moth population away from the sites. *S. albiguttalis* was released in California in 1983.

While *Arzama densa* can be very damaging to individual plants it is not an effective biological control agent. It begins feeding on waterhyacinth too late in the growing season, and it suffers a high mortality rate from parasites and pathogens.

The waterhyacinth mite's ability to stress its host has been underestimated. While it can be damaging where it is found, this mite's populations are sporadic. However, its tunnels are conducive to the fungus *Acremonium zonotum* (Saw.) Gams. and the mite has a synergistic relationship with the weevil *N. eichhorniae*. Both the fungus and the weevil increase the indirect effect of the mite on its host. The weevils feed and reproduce more in the presence of the mites.

Puncturevine

History and Suitability for Biological Control

Puncturevine, a member of the caltrop family, is an herbaceous summer annual which thrives in semi-arid and Mediterranean climates. In Mediterranean climates puncturevine germinates in spring following winter rains. The stems grow in a radial fashion and are procumbent. Seed production is prolific, the seed exhibiting a variable dormancy that ensures seed supplies during unfavorable times.

Puncturevine is cosmopolitan in its geographic distribution. Its native range is believed to be primarily North Africa and the Mediterranean region between 30 and 50 degrees N latitude. Records show that the plant is naturalized in southern Russia, South Africa, New Zealand, India, the United States, and Australia.

The first records of puncturevine as an alien plant in California were made in the early 1900s. The plant is believed to have gained entry into the United States via importation of livestock from the Mediterranean area. It has since spread throughout most of the United States although the northern states are uninfested except for eastern Washington and Idaho. The most severe infestations occur in the Southwest.

There are a host of problems associated with puncturevine. Most importantly the spiny seed pods tend to repel animals when the plant is fruiting. The spiny seed pods disturb the grazing of cattle and sheep and cause toxic symptoms and acute photosensitization in livestock in Australia. Moreover, the spines of the fruits cause extreme soreness to the hooves of grazing animals, and, when ingested, are capable of puncturing the stomach linings of sheep and cattle, thus the name puncturevine. The other common name, goat head, also comes from the seed pods which break into five spiny burs, each looking like a goat's head. Studies by Dr. Marius van Tonder et al. in South Africa showed that the disease *Tribulus ovis* of sheep and cattle was caused by *T. terrestris,* and it was postulated that the possible etiological factor could be a plant-metabolite or a fungus associated with the plant.

Figure 5. A puncturevine seed weevil on puncturevine seed. Photo courtesy J.K. Clark.

Foreign Exploration for Natural Enemies

In California, puncturevine became abundant enough to attract attention as a pest around 1912–1915 and was so troublesome by 1925 that the California Department of Agriculture developed a basic plan for its control. The counties adopted the plan and expended more than $500,000 from 1927 to 1930 for its chemical control. Substantial money was still being spent by the counties to control the plant with herbicides during the early 1950s. In 1956, the California Agricultural Commissioners Association passed a resolution requesting research on the possibilities of biological control.

Puncturevine was considered a good candidate for biological control because it is difficult to suppress chemically and may occur extensively on low-value land. Chemical or mechanical methods under such conditions are uneconomical and in some cases unfeasible. A survey for natural enemies of puncturevine was initiated in 1957 by G.W. Angalet, an ARS entomologist. He surveyed the areas of the Rajasthan Desert, Bangalore, and New Delhi, as well as the coastal and interior areas of southern France and Italy. Angalet discovered several insects feeding on puncturevine, but elected to concentrate on two species of weevils since they were consistently present and causing damage to the plant in 90% of the locations where the plant was found in India and the Mediterranean. One of the candidate natural enemies is a pod-infesting weevil, *Microlarinus lareynii* Jacquelin du Val, and the other a stem-infesting weevil, *M. lypriformis* Wollaston.

Biology and Host Specificity of Candidate Organisms

The female puncturevine seed weevil is attracted to the young, developing puncturevine seed pod for oviposition. She chews a small hole in one section of the pod, deposits her egg in the excavated hole, then seals it with black fecal cement (fig. 5). The seed pod is made up of five sections, each section usually containing three seeds. The chewed excavation normally penetrates the seed chamber, allowing the hatching larva direct access, and larval feeding generally destroys the seeds in two or more sections. Pupation occurs in the pod, and the adult chews its way out. A single pod may serve as the food source for one to three developing weevils. The life cycle from egg to adult in the field usually requires about 25–30 days at 68°–86°F.

The life cycle of the puncturevine stem weevil is similar to that of the seed weevil, although the female oviposits in the root crowns, stems, and occasionally the pedicels of a developing plant. The younger, more tender tissues are preferred. The female, as before, chews a small hole in the stem, deposits an egg, then covers the excavated hole containing the egg with black fecal cement. The larva, on hatching, usually tunnels 3–5 inches inside the stem and completes its development. Pupation occurs at the end of the tunnel, and the imago exits from the stem by cutting a small circular exit hole. Andres and Angalet reported that one large plant in India yielded over 400 weevils, the stems of which were completely hollowed. The life cycle of the stem weevil from egg to adult requires about 49–51 days.

Studies of the weevils' seasonal history and host specificity carried out by Andres and Angalet in Italy demonstrated that the biology of these insects is very closely bound to that of their host plant. They reported that adult weevils are present in varying numbers throughout the year although their host plant is not present during the cooler months. The weevils overwinter in ground cover, debris, and around adjacent plants. These adults do not reproduce, but are semi-active, obtaining some food and moisture from various plants when needed. When their host plant reappears in the spring, the overwintering weevils congregated under the young seedlings. Stem weevil oviposition occurs immediately, eggs being deposited at the juncture of the cotyledons and stem. At Catania, Italy, Andres and Angalet observed 84% of the puncturevine seedlings being attacked. The seed weevil adults feed on the young plant stems but do not oviposit until seeds are formed. Seed weevil feeding and oviposition peak in July, then gradually decline until October and November, being directly influenced by temperature. The number of weevil generations varies, but one to three generations occur annually in most areas of Italy.

To determine the host specificity of the weevils, Andres and Angalet tested 39 species of plants belonging to 21 families. The weevils develop eggs and oviposit only after they have fed on puncturevine or closely related Zygophyllaceae. However, in the absence of puncturevine, both weevil species accept other plants as food and survive for different lengths of time. When female weevils are removed from puncturevine to feed on nonrelated plants, their oocytes retrogress, and egg-laying by ovipositing females ceases. Under forced conditions weevils damage some other plants, but when these same plants are offered with puncturevine no damage results. In field populations adults emerging in late August and September enter reproductive diapause and do not develop eggs until the reappearance of puncturevine in the spring. Furthermore, Andres and Angalet surveyed 88 other plant species growing adjacent to puncturevine in India. Of these, 22 were of economic value. They found no weevils feeding in them. Huffaker et al. also reported additional feeding tests that showed the weevils are specific to puncturevine and closely related Zygophyllaceae.

Introduction, Establishment, and Evaluation

Test data on the host specificity of the seed and stem weevils was reviewed by the WGBCW. It concurred that the weevils are sufficiently host specific and approved their introduction. During July 1961 the first seed and stem weevils, collected in Catania, Sicily, by Andres were received and screened in the quarantine facility of the University of California at Albany. The first releases of the seed weevil in the United States were made on July 12, 1961 in Nevada by D.M. Maddox and Nevada cooperators, followed by releases in California on July 13 by Professor C.B. Huffaker of the University of California. Subsequent releases were made in Arizona, California, Colorado, Utah, and Washington by Maddox in cooperation with state and university personnel. The stem weevil was first released in Arizona on July 27 by Maddox and Arizona cooperators, followed by other releases in California, Colorado, Nevada, and Washington.

Both seed and stem weevils became established in Arizona, California, and Nevada, but failed to establish in Colorado (initially) and Washington. The seed weevil also established in Utah. Both weevils have since become established in Colorado from cold-hardy populations in Kansas and Texas. A history of the weevils' introduction, release and movement in the United States is given by Maddox.

Puncturevine has been either partially or nearly controlled in most areas where weevil establishment has occurred, although indigenous parasitoids, predators, and cold weather affect weevil densities. There is good evidence now that over the years cold-hardy strains of the weevils have developed in the Panhandle of Texas, in Oklahoma, Kansas, and Colorado. Dispersal of cold-hard stock should enhance establishment in the northern range of the host plant. Maddox and Andres report on the status of the weevils in California. Of the 58 counties in California, 57 have puncturevine present; 32 stated that the weed has decreased as a direct result of the weevils; 13 reported an increase in the weed; and 12 said the weed population remains unchanged. Furthermore, they estimated that if the weevils are credited with 25% of the overall reduction of the weed reported by agricultural commissioners in the survey (a conservative estimate), then the weevils have brought about an annual savings of up to $1.7 million in spray costs.

In a field experiment, Maddox evaluated the impact on their host plant of two weevil species separately by measuring various physiological, morphological, and histological plant parameters over time. The stem weevil caused the greater impact, significantly affecting all parameters by destroying vascular tissues. The seed weevils, on the other hand, caused significant reductions in the percent of seed germinating by affecting the plant systemically.

A 15-year census plus a two-year comparison of weevil-infested plots and plots kept relatively weevil-free by use of insecticide were conducted by Huffaker, Hamai, and Nowierski. They showed quantitatively that the combined activity of the two weevils substantially reduces the amount of viable puncturevine seed produced and the amount of ground covered by the weed. Therefore, the weevils provide a continued stress on their host plant and are contributing to a significant lessening of the puncturevine problem.

Thus, in conclusion, suppression of waterhyacinth and puncturevine demonstrates the successful use of the classical method of biological control. As mentioned above, there have been many such cases in the United States and in other parts of the world. The development of classical biological controls for such problem weeds as leafy spurge, ragwort, knapweeds, and others is continuing in this country.

SUMMARY AND CONCLUSIONS

Biological control of weeds is the use of living organisms to lower plant pest populations to the point where the plants are no longer economic problems. It is an ecological approach to weed management. Plant and arthropod population dynamics and the herbivore-host plant relations involved are aspects of ecology particularly applicable to biological control. It differs from other methods of control in that it (1) does not necessarily kill the pest outright, but may only lower its competitive ability; (2) may be slow-acting; (3) is relatively inexpensive; (4) is very selective; (5) causes no harmful side effects; and (6) can be permanent.

The use of biological control of weeds dates back to the 1860s but it was little used until the 1920s. Some success with lantana and spectacular successes with the control of prickly pear and St. Johnswort, or Klamathweed, have more recently stimulated increased research efforts in biological weed control all over the world. Most of the biological control agents used against weeds have been insects, but mites, snails, nematodes, fish, mammals, birds, plant pathogens, and even other plants can also be effective.

The procedure in developing a biological control project consists of (1) determining the suitability of the weed problem for biological control, (2) surveying the weed for natural enemies in both its naturalized and native homes, (3) studying the biologies and host relations of the natural enemies to determine if and how they may be used to solve the problem, (4) implementing their use in weed control, and (5) evaluating their effectiveness. The most common method of implementing biological control has been the classical one, i.e., through the introduction of new natural enemies. Other ways of implementation are by the manipulation or augmentation of already existing natural enemies and by the use of allelopathy.

Biological control of waterhyacinth demonstrates the successful use of the classical approach against aquatic weeds. This pest is a native of South America. It rapidly reproduces vegetatively, making it difficult to control by conventional means. The most important biological control agents used against waterhyacinths are weevils that feed externally as adults and tunnel in the petioles as larvae; moths that burrow in the petioles as larvae; and mites that feed within the leaves and petioles. All these organisms are from South America.

Among many others, a terrestrial weed effectively controlled biologically is puncturevine. It originated in Europe and the Mediterranean area, as did many of our agricultural weeds. Puncturevine is not only difficult to control by usual procedures, but occurs extensively on low-value land, where it is not feasible to use other control methods, as well as on cropland. The natural enemies used against it are the seed weevil and the stem weevil, imported from Italy.

Classical biological control is most applicable to dominant, perennial, introduced weeds in undisturbed environments. It is especially suitable on low-value, inaccessible rangeland or in aquatic situations where other control methods may be too expensive or unfeasible.

Augmenting the action of existing natural enemies may be utilized for the management of weed species that are natives, annuals, or are pests of cultivated crops, i.e., situations where classical biological control is limited. Northern jointvetch is an example of a weed that may be controlled using an anthracnose caused by a fungus.

The possibility of using allelopathy in weed control is a tempting area of research. Allelopathy is the reason smother crops, such as barley, are able to prevent weed growth and germination. By screening the known germ plasm of crop species, allelopathic individuals may be recognized. Thus far, the world's collections of cucumbers and oats have been screened in this way and accessions with greater ability to release allelopathic chemicals have been found.

Biological weed control is particularly valuable because it is ecologically sound. Even though it can be very effective and have a high cost:benefit ratio, biological control should not be thought of as a panacea. In many situations, biological control cannot solve problems caused by overgrazing or other poor land-management practices; it can only alleviate them. Biological control is not any more appropriate than is any other method to suppress all weeds in all situations, but should be considered as an option wherever possible. Biological control of weeds should be as much a part of integrated pest-management systems as is the biological control of arthropods.

ACKNOWLEDGEMENTS

We are sincerely grateful to Allan Krueger and Jon Skilman for commenting on this manuscript and giving it students' criticism, the most relevant kind it could receive. We also thank C.B. Huffaker, L.E. Ehler, R. Charudattan, L. Sonder, and L.W. Mitich for reviewing the text.

REFERENCES

Andres, L.A. 1981. Insects in the biological control of weeds. pp. 337–344 in Pimental, D., ed., CRC Handbook of Pest Management in Agriculture, Vol. II, CRC Press, Boca Raton, FL. 501 pp.

Andres, L.A. 1982. Integrating weed biological control agents into a pest management program. Weed Sci. 30:25–30.

Andres, L.A. and G.W. Angalet. 1963. Notes on the ecology and host specificity of Microlarinus lareynii and M. lypriformis (Coleoptera: Curculionidae) and the biological control of puncturevine, Tribulus terrestris. J. Econ. Entomol. 56(3):333–340.

Andres, L.A., C.J. Davis, P. Harris, and A.J. Wapshere. 1976 Biological control of weeds, pp. 481–99 in C.B. Huffaker and P.S. Messenger, eds., Theory and Practice of Biological Control. Academic Press, New York. 788 pp.

Barbour, M.G., J.H. Burk and W.D. Pitts. 1980. Terrestrial Plant Ecology. Benjamin/Cummings, Menlo Park, CA. 604 pp.

Casida, J.E. 1979. Pesticide research to maintain and improve plant protection. Part I, pp 45–53 in Geissbuehler, H., ed., Advances in pesticide science, New York. 3 parts.

Charudattan, R., D.E. McKinney and K.T. Hepting. 1981. Production, storage, germination, and infectivity or uredospores of Uredo eichhorniae and Uromyces pontederiae. Phytopathol. 71(11):1203–1207.

Charudattan, R. and H.L. Walker, eds., 1982. Biological Control of weeds with Plant Pathogens. John Wiley & Sons, Inc., New York. 293 pp.

Commonwealth Inst. Biol. Control. 1978. Screening organisms for biological control of weeds. Commonwealth Agric. Bureaux, Farnham Royal, England.

DeBach, P., ed. 1964. Biological Control of Insect Pests and Weeds. Chapman and Hall, London. 844 pp.

DeBach, P. 1974. Biological Control by Natural Enemies. Cambridge Univ. Press, Cambridge. 323 pp.

DeLoach, C.J. and H.A. Cordo. 1976. Life cycle and biology of Neochetina bruchi a weevil attacking waterhyacinth in Argentina, with notes on N. eichhorniae. Ann. Entomol. Soc. Am. 69:643–652.

Fay, P.K. and W.B. Duke. An assessment of allelopathic potential in Avena germ-plasm. Weed Sci. 25:224–29

Frank, P.A. and N. Dechoretz. 1980. Allelopathy in dwarf spikerush Eleocharis coloradoensis. Weed Sci. 28:499–505.

Freeman, T.E. 1977. Biological control of aquatic weeds with plant pathogens. Aquatic Biology. 3:175–184.

Frick, K.E. and J.M. Chandler, 1978. Augmenting the moth (Bactra verutana) in field plots for early-season suppression of purple nutsedge (Cyperus rotundus). Weed Sci. 26:703–10.

Goeden, R.D. 1978. Part II: Biological Control of Weeds. pp. 357–414 in Clausen, C.P. ed. Introduced parasites and predators of arthropod pests and weeds: a world review. USDA Agricultural

Handbook No. 480. 545 pp.

Goyer, R.A., and J.D. Stark. 1981. *Suppressing waterhyacinth with an imported weevil. Louisiana Agriculture 24(4):4–5.*

Harper, J.L. 1977. *Population Biology of Plants. Academic Press, New York. 892 pp.*

Harris, P. and R. Cranston. 1979. *An economic evaluation of control methods for diffuse and spotted knapweeds in western Canada. Can. J. Plant Sci. 59:375–382.*

Hasan, S. and A.J. Wapshere. 1973. *The biology of* Puccinia chondrillina, *a potential biological control agent of skeletonweed. Ann. Appl. Biol. 74:325–332.*

Huffaker, C.B. 1959. *Biological control of weeds with insects. Ann. Rev. Entomol. 4:251–76.*

Huffaker, C.B., J. Hamai and R.M. Nowierski. *Biological control of puncturevine* Tribulus terrestris L. *in California after twenty years of activity of introduced weevils. Entomophaga 28:387–400.*

Huffaker, C.B. and P.S. Messenger, eds. 1976. *Theory and Practice of Biological Control. Academic Press, New York. 788 pp.*

Julien, M.H., ed. 1982. *Biological control of weeds; a world catalogue of agents and their target weeds. Commonw. Inst. Biol. Control. 108 pp.*

Klingman, D.L. and J.R. Coulson. 1982. *Guidelines for introducing foreign organisms into the United States for biological control of weeds. Weed Sci. 30:661–7.*

Kok, L.T. and W.W. Surles. 1975. *Successful biocontrol of musk thistle by an introduced weevil,* Rhinocyllus conicus. *Environ. Entomol. 4:1025–1027.*

Maddox, D.M. 1976. *History of weevils on puncturevine in and near the United States. Weed Sci. 24:414–419.*

Maddox, D.M. 1980. *Seed and stem weevils of puncturevine: a comparative study of impact, interaction, and insect strategy. Proc. V Int. Symp. Biol. Contr. Weeds, Brisbane, Australia, 1980:447–67.*

Maddox, D.M., and L.A. Andres. 1979. *Status of puncturevine weevils and their host plant in California. Calif. Agric. 33(6):7–9.*

Maddox, D.M. and M. Rhyne. 1975. *Effects of induced host-plant mineral deficiencies on attraction, feeding, and fecundity of the alligatorweed flea beetle. Environ. Entomol. 4(5):682–86.*

Perkins, B.D. 1974. *Arthropods that stress waterhyacinth. PANS 20(3):304–314.*

Perkins, B.D., and D.M. Maddox. 1976. *Host specificity of* Neochetina bruchi Hustache (Coleoptera Curculionidae), *a biological control agent for waterhyacinth. J. of Aquatic Plant Mang. 1:59–64.*

Putnam, A.R. and W.B. Duke. 1974. *Biological suppression of weeds: evidence for allelopathy in accessions of cucumber. Science 185:370–372.*

Rosenthal, S.S., D.M. Maddox and K. Brunetti. 1984. *Biological methods of weed control. Thomson Publ. Fresno, CA. 88 pp.*

van den Bosch, R. and P.S. Messenger. 1973. *Biological Control. Intext Educational Publishers, New York, 180 pp.*

Wilson, F. 1964. *The biological control of weeds. An. Rev. Entomol. 9:225–44.*

Zwoelfer, H. 1973. *Possibilities and limitations in biological control of weeds. OEPP/EPPO Bull. 3:19–30.*

Zwoelfer, H. and P. Harris. 1971. *Host specificity determination of insects for biological control of weeds. Ann. Rev. Entomol. 16:159–78.*

6

BIOCHEMICAL CONTROL METHODS

by Jack Kiser[1]

INTRODUCTION

The control measures discussed in this chapter use our increasing knowledge about the biological systems within the environment to develop a more effective and environmentally safe integrated weed control system. I use the phrase integrated weed control system because no single control method can cure all the existing weed problems, and agriculture must use all the tools at its disposal in an integrated fashion to manage weeds.

Biological control of weeds is not new, and in fact predates chemical control. The first known biological control measure was in India in the 1860s. However, classical biological control (see Chapter 5) is limited by the nature of the environment and the length of time required to provide economically effective control. As our knowledge of the environment and the interactions between organisms within the environment grows, new possibilities for using these interactions are becoming known, and new methods, such as augmentative biological control, allelopathy, and bioherbicides, are being pursued as additional tools in the management of weeds.

Biotechnology

Another area, which is related to biological control in that it uses biology or organisms to develop new tools for weed control, is biotechnology. Biotechnology has been used to develop crop plants tolerant to

1. Calgene, Davis, CA.

herbicides. The development of herbicides involves the production of novel chemicals and the subsequent screening of plants, both weeds and crops, to determine the usefulness of the chemical. A chemical's ability to kill weeds and not the target crops determines the chemical's use. This is a very effective method for the development of herbicides, but it limits our uses to the selectivity that can be achieved by chemical modification. Some herbicidal compounds, which are most useful in terms of selectivity, have had detrimental effects on the environment and humans. On the other hand, some very effective herbicidal compounds, which are also very safe because they specifically inhibit biochemical processes unique to plants, lack the required selectivity to make them useful as products. The ability to select the herbicide and then make the crop tolerant to that herbicide gives added dimension to our flexibility in the herbicides we choose for different uses. We can choose herbicides that are more ecologically sound and kill a wider range of weed species and then, using the tools of biotechnology, make the crop tolerant to the herbicide.

METHODS OF CONTROL

Alternative Biological Control

Classical biological weed control has been described as discovering natural enemies to weeds and using them to lower the weed population to a level where it is no longer an economic problem. The essential ingredients are knowledge about the economic thresholds of weed-caused crop losses and a pest that attacks only the weed and is able to survive in large enough populations to be of economic benefit in weed control. As new techniques and increased knowledge about our environment are developed, new definitions of biological control have emerged. One is the use of natural or modified organisms, genes, or gene products to reduce the effects of undesirable organisms (pests), and to favor desirable organisms. This broader definition would include the production of bioherbicides, the production of herbicides derived from natural products, or breeding for allelopathy.

Augmentative Control

Classical biological control is best adapted to perennial weeds in undisturbed environments such as pastures, rangeland, roadsides, and aquatic situations. Natural enemies can build a population with a constant supply of weeds for survival, and no pesticides or cultural practices (e.g., irrigation) interfere with the population under these situations. This type of control is limiting and not applicable to a large portion of agricultural uses where more than one weed species needs to be controlled and an immediate control level is necessary.

Augmentation may be used to overcome some of the limitations of classical biological control. Augmentation is the inundative release of the control agent during the time when control is most needed. Several limitations can be overcome by this approach. In crop situations where a population of control agents are needed early in the crop season but the agent has not had any source of food or proper environment for survival, an inundative release can bring populations up to an effective control level. In situations where pesticide use for the control of other pests interferes with population establishment of the biological control agent, a release could potentially be timed with pesticide applications, which could harm the control agent, to give adequate population levels for control.

Examples of augmentative control for insects include the use of *Dactylopius* sp. for control of prickly pear in New South Wales. The temperatures are too cool there for adequate control populations to survive, so systematic distribution of the insect is done every season. In Mississippi, the native moth *Bactra verutana* Zeller attacks purple nutsedge, but the population size is too small after winter to give adequate control. Mass reared larvae and adults are released in cotton fields at the beginning of the season, which can give adequate control for the growth of the cotton to surpass that of the nutsedge.

When compared to the development of classical control, augmentation has most of the same requirements for success. Additional requirements include the ability to rear, transport, and distribute the agent in an economical fashion. Often this is not cost effective when insect agents are considered. However, the use of plant pathogens as augmentative agents may be very promising.

Plant Pathogens

Plant pathogens hold promise as augmentative agents because many can be easily cultured in laboratories, can be stored in resting stage forms which are relatively compact for a large amount of innoculum, and can be applied with commercial herbicide application equipment. Plant pathogens often are very host-specific and may be affected by fungicide applications but not by insecticides or herbicides used for other pest control. Pathogens used in this fashion are called bioherbicides.

Good bioherbicides generally have the following qualities: (1) they are unable to produce an epidemic without the interference of man, (2) are easily cultured in a laboratory, (3) produce large amounts of collectible innoculum, (4) are highly virulent, (5) are host-specific, and (6) are not hazardous to man, animals, or the environment.

The additional requirements for development of a bioherbicide above those needed for insect augmentation are determination of the natural constraints preventing a candidate from becoming epidemic, development of application procedures and rates, and Environmental Protection Agency (EPA) registration for use.

Examples of bioherbicides include the use of northern jointvetch anthracnose, a fungal pathogen, for control of northern jointvetch in rice. This disease is normally occurring on jointvetch in the problem areas; however, low, early season spore production and poor spore dispersal under natural conditions result in inadequate control. Both of these deficiencies are easily overcome by the pathogen's use as a bioherbicide, and this agent is being marketed in Arkansas. Another example is the first bioherbicide registered for use in the United States, *Phytophthora palmivora,* a fungus infecting milkweed vine. It is used in Florida citrus groves for control of milkweed vine. It is applied to the soil around the trees, where it infects the vines and kills or severely stunts the vines' growth. It has been used since 1981.

Allelopathy as Biological Control

The concept of allelopathy is the excretion of organic or inorganic compounds by one plant which have a detrimental or beneficial effect on neighboring plants. The neighboring plants can be of the same or different species in various cases. These excreted compounds are generally secondary metabolites or compounds not involved in primary plant metabolism. The production of these compounds is influenced by the environment around the plant, such as stresses, availability of nutrients, and overall physiological condition. In order for a secondary metabolite to be effective as an allelopathic agent, it must be released from the plant and made available to the neighboring plants. This can happen as a constant release from a plant tissue which is leached by water into the surrounding soil area or during decomposition of dead plant material. There must either be a constant supply of the compound, or the compound must accumulate in the soil.

Determining whether plant interactions are due to competition or if allelopathic responses are present is a complicated process. Utilization of cover crops of various species, such as barley, rye, sorghum, oats, and sweet clover has been a common practice. It was thought that this inhibited weed growth through competition. Experiments with leachates of many cover crops has shown that allelopathic compounds are involved.

Germ plasm collections of several crops have been studied and shown to have varying levels of allelopathy. This indicates that there is potential for breeding crop plants for greater allelopathic response.

Other than the use of cover crops, few examples of the utilization of allelopathy exist. Allelopathy is hard to separate from other responses due to environment and competition between plants under field conditions. The effects of allelopathy observed under more controlled greenhouse conditions may not transfer to practical field conditions because of the presence in the field of soil microbes, other plants, and varying weather and other environmental conditions. There is potential for the use of natural phytotoxins, but more research will be needed before practical applications will be realized.

Herbicide Tolerance

Herbicide tolerance in plants is the fundamental concept behind herbicide use. The ability of a herbicide to kill weeds while leaving the crop intact is what determines that herbicide's usefulness. Herbicide tolerance through biotechnology offers the ability to select safer herbicides and produce crop plants tolerant to these herbicides. There are several herbicides, such as glyphosate or phosphinothricin (a herbicide used in Japan and other countries but not registered in the United States), which have little or no selectivity and kill almost all plants. These herbicides have use under crop situations only where the herbicide can be applied without contact with the crop as in wick applications or some directed sprays. Tolerance to these herbicides would give broad spectrum weed control to crops in an inexpensive postemergence broadcast spray system.

HISTORY

Biotechnology is a new field. It has emerged through the development of cell culture and molecular biology or DNA manipulation techniques. The use of selection pressure in a plant cell culture system to develop a herbicide-tolerant line was shown in the late 1970s. The ability to transform (take DNA from one organism and integrate it into another unrelated organism) plants was first reported in 1983. Herbicide tolerance in tobacco through the insertion and expression of a bacterial gene was reported in 1985.

Several examples of crop plants manipulated to be tolerant to a herbicide exist. Tissue culture selection has been used to develop tolerance to picloram in tobacco, to glyphosate in carrot and alfalfa, and to imidazolinones and sulfonylureas in corn. Examples of tolerance to herbicides created through molecular biology include glyphosate and bromoxynil tolerance in tobacco, and tomato and phosphinothricin tolerance in potato, tomato, and tobacco. Sulphonylurea tolerance was isolated by mutagenizing seed of *Arabidopsis thaliana,* a small plant, and screening seedlings in the presence of the herbicide. A gene for tolerance isolated from these mutants was transferred to tobacco using genetic engineering.

MECHANISMS

A wide variety of mechanisms for tolerance to herbicides exist in nature. The uptake of the herbicide can be inhibited, so that it is not absorbed into the plant. The transport to the active site can be inhibited, so that the herbicide does not reach its target. The site of action can be altered. If there is one specific metabolic or structural protein affected by the herbicide (the site of action), that protein can be overproduced so that all the herbicide is absorbed, leaving functional protein available. The protein at the site of action can also be altered structurally, so that the herbicide will not cause inhibition. The herbicide can be detoxified by conjugation, hydrolysis, or degradation to a nontoxic form.

In the selection of herbicide tolerance through cell biology, any of these mechanisms may be found; however, it is likely that uptake inhibition would be related to the structural components of the plant and thus would not be manifested in cell cultures. The two strategies which have been used predominantly in genetic engineering for herbicide tolerance have been an altered site of action or the detoxification of the herbicide. These two mechanisms of tolerance are often controlled by a single gene. If the site of action or metabolism of the herbicide is known, development of a good selection system for the isolation of the gene is possible.

METHODS OF DEVELOPMENT

There are three methods which have been used to develop herbicide tolerance in crop plants. Classical breeding can be used to transfer herbicide tolerance between closely related species. For example, atrazine tolerance, found in a mutant from a wild mustard, was transferred into the crop rapeseed. The ability to transfer a tolerance trait or any other trait by this method requires the ability to make a viable cross between the two species. This mandates the use of closely related species.

Tissue culture can be used to select mutant cell lines of a crop with herbicide tolerance. This is a form of mutation breeding (the selection of desired characteristics from a population which has been subjected to some agent causing extreme frequencies of DNA mutation). Mutational changes arising from culturing plant tissues are called somaclonal variation. Sometimes, additional mutation pressure will be applied by the use of a chemical mutagen in the culture. In selection for herbicide tolerance through tissue culture, cells of the target crop are cultured in the presence of the herbicide. Any cell lines that grow are tolerant. This process allows millions of cells to be screened at one time in a petri plate. Under a classical mutation breeding program an acre of land is needed to screen a few thousand plants.

Tissue culture selection has limitations. The ability to regenerate whole plants from a cell line must be present before this process can be used. Regeneration of cell lines from culture has been successful in a limited number of species, and where it has been successful, it is not always practical as a routine procedure. Cell lines derived from this process may exhibit transient expression (the cell line has tolerance but the plants derived from those lines do not). No morphological evaluation of the cell lines with tolerance can be done in culture, so many cell lines may need to be regenerated before a plant with tolerance and normal morphology is found.

Molecular biology offers an advantage over the other two techniques in that there are no limitations on the source of tolerance. If the mode of action of the herbicide or degradation metabolism for a herbicide are known, then a source for tolerance can be found or selected, and a gene can be taken from any organism and transferred to the target crop. The majority of the tolerances developed by this technique have been isolated from bacteria. Bacteria are easy to use for selection of tolerance and for the isolation of the tolerance gene. They are often good sources for degradation mechanisms, and species can be found that contain the same metabolic pathways as plants; for instance, photosynthesis and aromatic amino acid production. Bacteria with a degradation system for the herbicide or the metabolic pathway the herbicide affects in plants can be grown on enrichment cultures containing the herbicide, and mutant lines can then be selected which possess the desired system of tolerance.

Genetic Engineering

There are three basic steps involved in genetic engineering for herbicide tolerance, assuming the target herbicide and crop have been chosen: (1) Selection of a genetic source for tolerance. This can include mutagenizing a source and selecting a tolerant line or screening potential source species for tolerance or for the ability to degrade the herbicide. Sources for tolerance used thus far have been either bacteria or plant cell lines. The more that is known about the herbicides' mode of action in plants and degradation in the environment, the better a choice can be made of a source species for the tolerance trait. The metabolic process a herbicide acts on or the degradation metabolism for the herbicide must be present in the source. (2) Isolation of the tolerance gene. This step requires a knowledge of the tolerance mechanism, so that a proper selection system for the gene can be used. (3) Transformation of the target crop species. Currently, this has been done by a process called cocultivation. In this process, a bacteria called *Agrobacterium tumefaciens* is engineered to contain the gene for tolerance. *A. tumefaciens* causes a disease in a wide range of plant species known as crown gall. During the infection process, DNA, called the t-DNA, from *A. tumefaciens* is transferred and integrated into the plant's DNA. By inserting the gene for tolerance in place of some of the t-DNA, the gene for tolerance can be transferred to the plant. Cells from the target crop species are cultured in the presence of *A. tumefaciens,* and then plants containing the tolerance gene are selected. These plants are then regenerated. Cocultivation has not been successful with all crop species, and new techniques for transfer of the tolerance genes are being developed with some success.

Techniques such as ballistics or microinjection, where a larger plant part can be exposed to the DNA, can avoid the need for regeneration from cells or callus tissue. This will allow the transformation of species which are hard to regenerate. Microinjection involves the insertion of DNA into a plant part using a microscopic needle. The DNA can be inserted into the nucleus of a cell. Ballistics involves the transport of microscopic beads coated with DNA into a cell by propulsion from an explosive charge. Both of these techniques can be used on intact plant parts, where limited culturing under lab conditions and no regeneration is needed.

ADVANTAGES, DISADVANTAGES, AND RISKS

Advantages

The advantages of biochemical weed control methods are:

(1) Allows the choice of herbicides. This means herbicides with lower mammalian toxicity, less damaging effects in the environment (such as groundwater contamination), broad spectrum weed control, and high potency to reduce amounts of chemicals released into the environment can be selected. Selective response in plants will be less of a criteria for the selection of potential herbicides.

(2) Use of postemergence herbicides allows for analysis of the weed problem before application and judicious timing of applications which should result in lower herbicide use and reduced costs.

(3) There are weed problems now present in many crop practices which cannot be controlled that could be solved through herbicide tolerance; for instance, nightshade control in tomatoes. Tomatoes and nightshades are closely related, and no known herbicide gives effective control of nightshade without damage to tomatoes.

(4) Increased ability for postemergence weed control can be of value in areas where reduced tillage is desirable to reduce erosion.

(5) The use of bacteria or other organisms as sources of genetic material for tolerance is possible through genetic engineering. The use of bacteria as a system to screen and design new herbicides is possible

as a result of knowledge gained through their use in the development of herbicide tolerance.

(6) Allows for greater elucidation of plant metabolic pathways. By separating genes for tolerance, a greater dissection of the metabolic pathways of plants is possible, and this will lead to the better understanding of these pathways. Also, the understanding of a herbicide's action in the plant or its degradation in the environment is needed in order to achieve herbicide tolerance. This will lead to further characterization of herbicides.

Disadvantages and Risks

The disadvantages and risks associated with biochemical control are:

(1) There is potential for herbicide tolerance to cause the tolerant crop to become a serious weed problem in other crops or for the transfer of the tolerance genes to related weedy species to occur. Both of these potential risks can be predicted and monitored. Weed competition studies with the tolerant plants can be performed and the outcrossing of the tolerant plant to weeds predicted from the wealth of knowledge available on this subject. The potential for a crop becoming a serious weed problem due to the transfer of a single gene for herbicide tolerance is low. Many factors are involved in a plant's ability to outcompete crop species under natural conditions, and most of these traits are multigenic. Crop species have been bred for yielding a particular desirable product. The selective pressure put on crop plants to produce the desired product has led to decreased adaptive ability in the environment and thus ability to become a serious weed. The breeding process has involved the change in many characteristics of the originator of the crop species, and a single gene change is unlikely to overcome these changes.

Pest control, through chemicals or breeding (as in disease resistance), continually risks the development of resistance to chemicals or to pest resistant varieties developed through breeding because of the high level of selection pressure imposed by the extremely effective reduction of pest population sizes from these methods of control. Weed tolerance to herbicides has been relatively slow. Most herbicides affect primary metabolic pathways in plants, and these pathways are highly evolved and not very amenable to mutational changes. Selection pressure for herbicide tolerance in weeds is less than that seen in insect pests or pathogens because of several factors. The life cycle of plants is generally longer than that for other pests or pathogens, so fewer generations occur during any period of selection. Crops are rotated, and this allows for the growth of susceptible weeds in the alternate seasons. Weed seed is known to overwinter and last for several years, so new sources of susceptible weeds are present to compete with tolerant lines. Also, weeds have a level of plasticity in growth; if the competition of neighboring weeds is low, the remaining weeds will produce significantly greater amounts of seed, thus allowing susceptible escaped weeds to compete well with tolerant lines. All of these factors would affect a tolerant outcross as well as a natural selection.

Additional factors in the case of genetically engineered herbicide tolerance are that many of the herbicides being targeted for tolerance are those that do not have a long soil residual effect, so escape weeds later in the growing season when the weeds do not have a great economic impact is likely, and this adds to the susceptible weed supply. A wide cross between a crop plant and a related weed species generally has a lower competitive ability than other weeds, and this would affect the natural selection potential of the tolerant weed. However, some instances of this type of weed tolerance may occur over time. It has occurred with classical chemical weed control. If it occurs, a broad spectrum of relatively safe herbicides are available as alternatives.

(2) The metabolites of the herbicide or products from engineered genes may have unexpected effects on plants, with the results that plants become an unsatisfactory food source. This can be analyzed using similar means as those used for conventional herbicide regulatory clearance and food safety practices. Also, when detoxification strategies are used, bacterial genes that mimic known natural plant detoxifications, which have already been studied extensively and have a record for safety, can be used. One of the goals of genetically engineering herbicide tolerance is to shift to compounds with more favorable mammalian toxicities.

(3) Genetic engineering for tolerance to a few exceptional herbicides might lead to widespread use of these few with a reduction in the development of new compounds due to exorbitant costs. This would lead to fewer and fewer compounds being used over a large area and increasing the chances for weed tolerance and vulnerability to this tolerance due to lack of alternative control compounds. This problem has been brought up regarding the use of herbicide tolerance in rotation crops such as atrazine-tolerant soybeans, so that soybeans can be easily rotated with corn. However, there has been a shift in the genetic engineering goals to the production of tolerance to more favorable compounds rather than increasing tolerances for crop rotation purposes. Also, the large number of modes of action of herbicides is some assurance that this will not happen. Some of the techniques involved in biotechnology and herbicide tolerance should add flexibility to the selectivity requirements in herbicide development, allow for the development of new types of herbicides, such as naturally occurring compounds, and possibly reduce some of the costs of herbicide development.

Each of these problems has a counterpart in nonbiotechnological weed control, and awareness and the ability to deal with these problems in a rational manner are increasing. Control of crop pests is an ongoing interaction with a changing ecosystem, and as each control measure is used, selection pressure is put on the myriad of genetic diversity within the ecosystem to counteract the control. Thus, pest control is not a win or lose situation but a continuous process in which all means of control must be utilized and coordinated.

STAGE OF DEVELOPMENT

The practical use of herbicide tolerance in agriculture has not yet been realized, with the exception of atrazine tolerance in a few crops, such as rapeseed as discussed earlier. This tolerance is known to reduce crop yields by 10% and yet is used commercially. This illustrates the potential of herbicide tolerance traits. Yield reduction from herbicide tolerance developed through genetic engineering is not expected. As stated earlier, biotechnology is a new field, and the first products from this field are now going through preliminary field testing. Several potential herbicide tolerance products are among those being tested. Examples are glyphosate tolerance in tobacco, tomato, and rapeseed; bromoxynil tolerance in tomato and tobacco; and phosphinothricin tolerance in potato and tobacco.

There are also several regulatory concerns which must be satisfied before herbicide tolerance will be used in the field. Assurance that no pest problem is being created must be shown in order to get United States Department of Agriculture (USDA) and EPA clearance for growing the crop. Herbicide residue and toxicity data on the tolerant crop must clear the EPA for label registration of the herbicide for this use. Assurance of no significant changes to the quality or health and safety of food and feed crops must be supplied to EPA and Food and Drug Administration (FDA) before use.

Products from this technology are expected to reach the market in the early 1990s.

HERBICIDES DERIVED FROM NATURAL PRODUCTS

The use of natural compounds as herbicides fits under the heading of biological control with our broadened definition. However, I chose to discuss them here because this is an area where genetic engineering for herbicide tolerance and herbicide development can join together to produce more effective and environmentally sound control methods. One of the major problems in the development of herbicides from natural products is that many of the potential compounds are not selective. A good example of this is a compound with the common name bialophos. This compound is a registered herbicide in Japan with almost no plant selectivity. Bialophos is the first naturally occurring compound to be isolated in quantity as an herbicide. This compound rapidly degrades to phosphinothricin, which is the active herbicide. Synthetically produced phosphinothricin has also been patented for use as a herbicide. As mentioned earlier, herbicide tolerance to this compound has been developed in tobacco, tomato, and potato. Thus, a naturally occurring compound which would only be available for limited crop use can be used as a broadcast herbicide in crops. There are other naturally occurring compounds which provide the chemical basis for new herbicides that are produced synthetically. One such compound is anisomycin, which was used to develop the synthetic herbicide methoxyphenone (a herbicide used in other countries but not registered in the United States).

CONCLUSIONS

Biological control and biotechnology offer new tools for the control of weeds. Although biological control is not a new field, increased knowledge about the interactions between organisms in our environment and new ways of thinking about potential means of biological control is leading to more effective and useful ways of using organisms to combat weed problems, as in augmentative biological control.

Biotechnology will enable more flexibility in the use of herbicides and their development. Herbicides will be selected more on the basis of their effectiveness and environmental safety and less on their plant selectivity.

All of these techniques should lead to a more economic, environmentally sound, and efficient, integrated system of weed control.

ACKNOWLEDGEMENT
I am very grateful to Robert M. Goodman for valuable review of this manuscript.

REFERENCES

Charudattum, R., D.E. McKinney, and K.T. Hepting. 1981. Production, storage, germination, and infectivity of uredospores of Uredo eichorniae and Uromyces pontederiae. Phytopathol. 71(11): 1203–1207.

Comai, L., D. Facciotti, W.R. Hiatt, G. Thompson, R.E. Rose, and D.M. Stalker. 1985. Expression in plants of a mutant aro A gene from Salmonella typhimurium confers tolerance to glyphosate. Nature 317(6039): 741–44.

Comai, L. and D. Stalker. 1986. Mechanism of action of herbicides and their molecular manipulation. Oxford Surveys of Plant Molecular and Cell Biology, 3:167–195.

DeBlock, M., J. Botterman, M. Vandewiele, J. Dockx, C. Thoen, V. Gossele, N. Rao Movva, C. Thompson, M. Van Montagu, and J. Leemans. 1987. Engineering herbicide resistance in plants by expression of a detoxifying enzyme. EMBO, 6(9): 2513–2518.

Duke, S.O. 1986. Naturally occurring chemical compounds as herbicides. Rev. of Weed Sci. 2:15–44.

Fay, P.K. and W.B. Duke. An assessment of allelopathic potential in Avena germplasm. Weed Sci. 25:224–28.

Fillatti, J.J., J. Kiser, R. Rose, and L. Comai. 1987. Efficient transfer of a glyphosate tolerance gene into tomato using a binary Agrobacterium tumefaciens vector. Bio/tech. 5:726–30.

Frank, P.A. and N. Dechoretz. 1980. *Allelopathy in dwarf spikerush* (Eleocharis coloradoensis). *Weed Sci.* 28:499–505.

Frick, K.E. and J.M. Chandler. 1978. *Augmenting the moth* (Bactra verutana) *in field plots for early season suppression of purple nutsedge* (Cyperus rotundus). *Weed Sci.* 26:703–10.

Goloubinoff, P.M. Edelman, and R.B. Hallick. *Chloroplast-coded atrazine resistance in* Solanum nigrum: psb A *loci from susceptible and resistant biotypes are isogenic except for a single codon change. Nuc. Acids Res.* 12(24): 9489–9496.

Goodman, R.M. 1987. *Future potential, problems, and practicalities of herbicide-tolerant crops from genetic engineering. Weed Sci.* 35(suppl. 1):28–31.

Gressel, J. and L.A. Segel. 1978. *The paucity of plants evolving genetic resistance to herbicides: possible reasons and implications. J. Theor. Biol.* 75:349–371.

Haughn, G.W., J. Smith, B. Mazur, and C. Somerville. 1988. *Transformation with a mutant* Arabidopsis acetolactate *synthase gene renders tobacco resistant to sulfonylurea herbicides. Mol. Gen. Genet,* 211:266–71.

Hauptmann, R.M., G. della-Cioppa, A.G. Smith, G.M. Kishore, and J.M. Widholm. 1988. *Expression of glyphosate resistance in carrot somatic hybrid cells through the transfer of an amplified 5-enolpyruvylshikimic acid-3-phosphate synthase gene. Mol. Gen. Genet.*

Horsch, R.B., R.T. Fraley, S.G. Rogers, P.R. Sanders, A. Lloyd, and N. Hoffmann. 1983. *Inheritance of functional foreign genes in plants. Science,* 223:496–498, 211:357–63.

Lockerman, R.H. and A.R. Putnam. 1979. *Evaluation of allelopathic cucumbers* (Cucumis sativum) *as an aid to weed control. Weed Sci.* 27: 54–57.

Putnam, A.R. and W.B. Duke. 1978. *Allelopathy in ecosystems. Ann. Rev. Phytopatholl.* 16:431–51.

Quimby, P.C. Jr. and H.L. Walker. 1982. *Pathogens as mechanisms for integrated weed management. Weed Sci.* 30:30–34.

Rice, E.L.1974. *Allelopathy. Academic Press, New York.* 35 pp.

Rice, E.L.1979. *Allelopathy—an update. Bot. Rev.* 45:15–109.

Schroth, M.N. and J.G. Hancock. 1981. *Selected topics in biological control. Ann. Rev. Microbiol.* 35:453–76.

Templeton, G.E. 1982. *Biological Herbicides: discovery, development, deployment. Weed Sci.* 39:430–33.

Templeton, G.E. , D.O. TeBeest, and R.J. Smith Jr. 1979. *Biological weed control with mycoherbicides. Ann. Rev. Phytopathol.* 17:301–310.

Yeo, R.R. 1980. *Spikerush may help to control waterweeds. Calif. Agric.* 34:12–13.

7

CHEMICAL CONTROL METHODS

INTRODUCTION

by Floyd M. Ashton[1], Alden S. Crafts[2], and Harry S. Agamalian[3]

In the last half-century, weed control has become one of the principal technologies responsible for the increased agricultural production characteristic of this period. The USDA reported that U.S. farmers were expected to have used $3.5–4 billion worth of pesticides in 1984. This usage represents 550 million pounds of active ingredients, 450 million pounds of which are herbicides. Given that every arable acre of land in the world has a potential infestation of weeds that may interfere with crops, it is not surprising that growers are becoming increasingly aware of the role of weeds in limiting production. Herbicides are also used on noncropland to control vegetation.

It is of paramount importance to understand that chemical weed control is only one method of controlling weeds which often must be integrated with other methods for optimum results. Such combinations of methods result in the various systems approaches to vegetation management discussed in Chapter 10.

COMPONENTS

A successful chemical weed-control program depends on the appropriate interaction of the plant, the herbicide, and the environment. When one considers the complexity of the many diverse species of crops and weeds, the great array of herbicides, and the infinitely variable environment, it becomes apparent that any discussion of chemical weed con-

1, 2. University of California, Davis, CA. 3. University of California Cooperative Extension, Monterey County, CA.

trol must be developed from an initial understanding of these three components.

Plant

Both crops and weeds have specific characteristics that must be considered in developing a successful chemical weed-control procedure. These include form, growth, and function. Since these aspects are discussed in Chapters 1 and 2, only those most relevant to chemical weed control will be mentioned briefly here. In order to select the proper herbicide and the method of application, one needs to know: (1) whether the crop and/or weed is an annual, biennial, or perennial; (2) the stage of growth of each (e.g., germinating seed, seedling, or established plant); and (3) the growth form (e.g., upright or horizontal leaves, deep or shallow root system, etc.).

In general, annual weeds are easier to control than established perennial weeds. Germinating seeds and young seedlings of perennial weeds are as easy to control as annual weeds up to the time they develop their perennial characteristics. In general, young weeds are easier to control than older weeds. Germinating seeds can usually be controlled with an appropriate soil-applied herbicide. Emerged seedlings can usually be controlled with an appropriate foliar-applied herbicide; these may be translocatable (systemic) or have only contact action. Although established annual weeds may be controlled by a contact herbicide, better control is usually obtained with a translocatable herbicide. With a contact herbicide, dormant lateral buds of broadleaf weeds or the growing points of grasses may develop to reestablish the plant. Established perennial weeds are the most difficult to control. Their control requires a translocatable herbicide, usually with repeat treatments. Sometimes, when herbicides are used to control annual weeds in a perennial crop (e.g., in orchards), perennial weeds may subsequently invade the area and present a much more difficult weed-control problem.

Herbicides

In a recent issue of *Weed Science* over 150 herbicides were listed, many of which are formulated in more than one way, providing a great array of commercial products.

Every herbicide has its specific chemical, physical, and biological properties. Of primary concern here is their movement and degradation in plants and soils. Information regarding such properties allows one to predict how they may be used in the field. The translocation pattern of a given herbicide often determines how it is used, whether it is applied to leaves or roots via the soil. Herbicides translocated in the symplastic system (phloem transport) are usually applied to the leaves,

TABLE 1. RELATIVE MOBILITY AND PRIMARY TRANSLOCATION PATHWAY(S) OF HERBICIDES[1,2]

Good Mobility			Limited Mobility			Little or No Mobility
In apoplast	**In symplast**	**In both**	**In apoplast**	**In symplast**	**In both**	
amides	glufosinate	AMA	bromoxynil	oxadiazon	AMS	bensulide
bentazon	glyphosate	amitrole	chloroxuron	phenoxys	chloramben	DCPA
carbamates[3]	sulfosate	arsenicals[4]	difenzoquat		endothall	diclofop
diclobenil		asulam	diquat		fenac	dinitroanilines
diphenamid		dalapon	fluridone		fenoxaprop	diphenylethers
ethofumesate		dicamba	paraquat		fluazifop-P	
methazole		fosamine			haloxyfop	
napropamide		sethoxydim			naptalam	
norflurazon					propanil	
pyrazon					quizalofop	
TCA					sulfonylureas	
thiocarbamates						
triazines						
uracils						
ureas[5]						

1. *Translocation rate may vary considerably in different species. Some herbicides may also move from the symplast to the apoplast and vice versa.*
2. *When a class of herbicides is given see Chapter 8, Herbicides, for the individual herbicides included.*
3. *Except asulam, which has good mobility in both the symplast and the apoplast.*
4. *Organic arsenicals.*
5. *Except chloroxuron, which has limited mobility in the apoplast.*

and those translocated in the apoplastic system (xylem transport) are usually applied to the soil. A few herbicides (amitrole, for example) are readily translocated in both systems. The general translocation pattern is usually specific for a given herbicide; however, the extent to which it is translocated may vary in different species. Translocation patterns for many herbicide families or individual herbicides, some of which are registered for use in California and some of which are not, are provided in table 1.

A herbicide that is not translocated and/or that is degraded rapidly in plants will not control perennial weeds. The degradation of a herbicide usually makes it essentially nonphytotoxic. Paraquat and trifluralin are not translocated, whereas amitrole and glyphosate are. Glyphosate is not readily degraded in plants, whereas chlorpropham is degraded rapidly. In soils, a herbicide that is rapidly degraded (e.g., propham) is not effective for perennial weeds or industrial sites but may be quite suitable in short-season crops. A herbicide that is degraded slowly in soils (e.g., prometon) is ideal for industrial sites. Herbicides that are bound tightly to soils and are not subject to downward movement with rainfall are not effective for the control of deep-rooted species.

Environment

Various aspects of the environment can have profound effects on the success of a given herbicide application. These aspects include soil type, soil microflora, water (rainfall or type of irrigation), temperature, and sunlight. A given herbicide may or may not be bound significantly to soil particles. The major components of the soil responsible for this binding are organic matter and clay. In addition to its effect on the movement of herbicides in soil, this binding may also reduce their phytotoxicity. Many product labels indicate that higher application rates of the herbicide should be used on soils containing considerable clay and/or organic matter to be effective. Some herbicides (e.g., paraquat, glyphosate) are bound so tightly that they are essentially nonphytotoxic in most soils. Most herbicides are mainly degraded by soil microorganisms; therefore, environmental conditions favorable for their growth (warm temperatures and adequate moisture) accelerate herbicide decomposition. Excessive rainfall shortly after a foliar application may remove the herbicide before it is taken up by the plant or leach it below the appropriate horizon after a soil application. The influence of the type of irrigation will be discussed later. In general, temperature influences the effectiveness of foliar-applied herbicides more than soil-applied herbicides. For example, a postemergence application of dinoseb, a herbicide once widely used on peas but no longer registered, was found to be most effective when the temperatures after application were expected to be between 70 and 85°F. Lower temperatures were found to not always provide adequate weed control, while higher temperatures sometimes resulted in crop injury. Several herbicides (e.g., paraquat) require sunlight to be effective; under low light or cloudy conditions they may be less effective and/or the appearance of phytotoxic symptoms may be delayed.

SELECTIVITY

Selectivity is a term used to indicate that one plant species (the weed) is injured by a given herbicide while another species (the crop) is not. The uninjured species is considered to be tolerant and the injured species susceptible. This is an extremely important concept, because it means that weeds can be controlled by a herbicide without injuring the crop.

Selectivity is relative, not absolute, because excessive rates of any herbicide or extreme environmental conditions can obliterate the difference between tolerant and susceptible species, and both may be injured. It is desirable to have herbicides recommended for use in crops with at least a '2×' safety factor—that is, applications at twice the recommended rate will not injure the crop. However, in some cases this de-

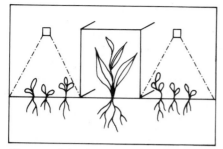 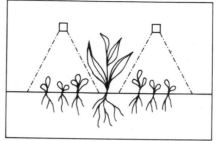

Figure 1. Selective placement of herbicides applied after crop emergence accomplished with a shield protecting the crop (left), *and a directed application* (right) *in which spray is directed towards the base of crop plant, favoring minimum crop coverage and maximum weed coverage.*

gree of selectivity is not achieved, and extreme care should be taken to make certain the proper rate is applied.

Occasionally a tolerant weed not controlled by the herbicides used in the crop will become a problem. This usually occurs when crop rotation is not practiced and/or there are a limited number of herbicides available for the crop. Sometimes a combination or sequential application of two or more herbicides is required to control all the weeds. Selectivity is more difficult to obtain for weeds that are closely related to the crop (e.g., nightshades in tomatoes).

The mode of selectivity for an individual herbicide between a given weed and the crop is usually very specific. The basis of selectivity may be a differential growth pattern, depth of rooting, location of growing point, leaf cuticle, etc., or a physiological, biochemical, biophysical difference. Perhaps the most common basis of selectivity between two species is their relative ability to change the herbicide molecule to a nonphytotoxic form. For example, atrazine is rapidly degraded in corn but not in most weeds. Other reported differences in selectivity include absorption and translocation.

Selectivity can also be obtained with relatively nonselective herbicides by using application methods that maximize weed exposure and minimize crop exposure to the herbicide. These include directed and shielded sprays (fig. 1), recirculating sprayers, roller applicators, and wick/wiper applicators.

Resistance

Resistance may be considered a unique type of selectivity in which the two plants involved are different biotypes of the same species. The resistant biotype survives and grows normally at the usual effective dose of the herbicide. The resistant and susceptible biotypes are identical in appearance. The resistant biotype occurs in very low numbers in the native population. It is only with the continuous use of the same herbicide for several years that the resistance becomes apparent. Triazine resistance is the most extensively studied example. The triazine molecule binds to a protein of the photosynthetic electron transport system and blocks photosynthesis in the susceptible biotype but not in the resistant biotype. By 1982, triazine resistance had been confirmed in at least 18 genera and 30 species located in at least 23 states (USA), four provinces of Canada, and seven countries of Europe. Additional information on resistance is available in the monograph on this subject edited by LeBaron and Gressel (1982).

SOIL APPLICATIONS

Most soil-applied herbicides are used to control annual weeds. They interfere primarily with weed growth at the stage of seed germination or seedling establishment. They usually have little, if any, effect on mature weeds. Often the seedlings never emerge from the soil; and if they do emerge, they are usually stunted and misshapen. Therefore, these herbicides must be present in the soil horizon occupied by the germinating weed seeds. This placement is accomplished by soil-incorporation or preemergence application followed by rainfall or overhead irrigation. Normal furrow irrigation following a preemergence treatment does not usually place the herbicide in the soil horizon where weed seeds germinate.

A few soil-applied herbicides control established annual weeds, as well as herbaceous and woody perennial weeds. They are usually nonselective and used on noncropland. They require sufficient rainfall or irrigation to leach them into the absorbing root zone of the weed. This is necessary because they are mainly photosynthetic inhibitors and must be absorbed by the roots and translocated to the leaves via the apoplastic transport system (xylem) to be effective.

Herbicides are applied to the soil as preemergence- or preplant-incorporated treatments, and they may be selective or nonselective. Selectivity is essential in crops but undesirable in noncrop situations where all vegetation must be controlled (fig. 2).

Preemergence Herbicides

These herbicides are applied to the soil surface after the crop is planted but before the crop or weeds emerge. Rainfall has to occur or overhead irrigation must be applied within several days after application for them to be effective. In areas of frequent rainfall, this is probably the most common method used for the control of annual weeds in crops.

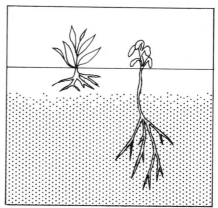

░░░░ Herbicide

Figure 2. The position of the herbicide in the soil profile influences control of shallow- or deep-rooted crops and/or weeds. When herbicide remains near the surface, deep-rooted crop is not affected, while weed is controlled (left). When the herbicide is leached deeper in the soil profile, shallow-rooted crop is not affected, while deep-rooted weed is controlled (right).

Occasionally 'preemergence' is used to refer to a situation where the crop has not emerged but the weeds have. In this case, one should be more specific and indicate that the herbicide is applied preemergence to the crop and postemergence to the weeds. Contact-type herbicides can frequently be used this way in crops that emerge later than most of the weeds, e.g., paraquat in peppers.

Preplant Soil-incorporated Herbicides

These herbicides are incorporated into the soil before planting the crop. Methods of incorporation are discussed later in this chapter. This technique was initially developed to minimize the loss of volatile herbicides (e.g., EPTC) from the soil surface. However, shortly thereafter it was found that many herbicides that proved ineffective in the arid southwest as preemergence treatments with furrow irrigation were effective when incorporated into the soil.

Herbicide Persistence in Soils

Persistence of herbicides in the soil is a critical factor. On an industrial site, long persistence is desirable; however, on cropland, it should last just long enough to give season-long weed control but not long enough to injure the following crop. Atrazine is interesting in this regard, because it is relatively persistent. It is used at high rates on noncropland for total vegetation control, and at low rates in corn and sorghum for

TABLE 2. PERSISTENCE OF BIOLOGICAL ACTIVITY AT THE USUAL RATE OF HERBI-CIDE APPLICATION IN MOIST-FERTILE SOILS, SUMMER TEMPERATURES, IN A TEM-PERATE CLIMATE[1,2]

1 month or less	1–3 months	3–12 months	Over 12 months
acrolein	AMS	ametryn	arsenic
amitrole	amides	atrazine	borate
arsenicals[3]	bentazon	bensulide	bromacil
asulam	bromoxynil	clopyralid	chlorate
dalapon	chloramben	chlorimuron	chlorsulfuron
dazomet	chloroxuron	DCPA	fenac
desmedipham	chlorpropham	dichlobenil	fluridone (in soil)
dinoseb	dicamba	difenzoquat	hexaflurate
diquat[4]	diphenylethers	dinitroanilines	picloram
endothall	dipropetryn	diphenamid	prometon
fluazifop-P	linuron	diuron	tebuthiuron
fosamine	methazole	ethofumesate	terbacil
glyphosate	metribuzin	fluometuron	
metham	naptalam	fluridone (in water)	
methyl bromide	oxyfluorfen	hexazinone	
paraquat[4]	prometryn	isoxaben	
phenmedipham	pyrazon	metsulfuron	
phenoxys	siduron	napropamide	
propanil	TCA	norflurazon	
propham	terbutryn	pronamide	
sethoxydim	thiocarbamates	propazine	
		simazine	
		sulfometuron	
		triameturon	
		triclopyr	

1. *These are approximate values and may vary with application rate and environmental conditions.*
2. *When a class of herbicides is given see Chapter 8 for the individual herbicides included.*
3. *Organic arsenicals.*
4. *Diquat and paraquat are irreversibly bound to the soil but are biologically unavailable.*

the control of most annual grasses and broadleaf weeds. It is selective because it is rapidly degraded in these crops but not in most weeds. However, even at low rates it can persist long enough to injure other crops planted the following year. The relative persistence of many herbicide families or individual herbicides, some of which are registered for use in California and some of which are not, is provided in table 2. Herbicides are inactivated in soils by biological, chemical, and physical means. Inactivation by biological and chemical means usually involves a degradation of the molecule, whereas physical means involve its tight binding to other substances. For most herbicides, biological inactivation is probably the most important, and this primarily involves microorganisms. Therefore, conditions favorable to the growth of microorganisms accelerate herbicide degradation in soils. These factors include warm temperatures, adequate moisture, and sufficient aeration. Excessively high or low temperatures, high or low soil moisture, and compacted soils decrease their biological inactivation.

FOLIAR APPLICATIONS

Herbicides applied to the leaves are considered to be of two types, contact or translocated. In general, the contact-type herbicides are non-selective, but the translocated herbicides may be either selective or non-selective.

Contact Herbicides

Contact herbicides have their action on that part of the plant to which they are applied, usually the leaf. Since they do not move to untreated parts of the plant, they are relatively ineffective on perennial weeds with regenerative rhizomes and stolons. Such perennials rapidly recover from a contact-herbicide treatment. However, these contact herbicides are very effective on a broad spectrum of young annual weeds because they are relatively nonselective. Paraquat is a good example of this type of herbicide.

Translocated Herbicides

Translocated herbicides applied to the leaves move from the treated leaves to other parts of the plant and may act primarily at these distant sites. They tend to accumulate in such areas of rapid growth as growing points, root tips, and areas of rapidly elongating shoots and roots. They are effective on both annual and perennial weeds. The degree of movement of the translocatable herbicides varies considerably. Amitrole and glyphosate are very mobile, whereas 2,4-D has limited mobility. The relative mobility and primary translocation pathway of many herbicides are provided in table 1. This table includes both foliar- and soil-applied translocated herbicides.

FATE IN THE ENVIRONMENT

Scientists and the general public are becoming increasingly concerned about the fate of pesticides in the environment. Most herbicides are relatively nontoxic to man; they are designed to injure plants, not animals. The toxicological properties of herbicides are given in the *Herbicide Handbook* (1983) of the Weed Science Society of America.

Figure. 3 illustrates the great diversity of processes that lead to the detoxification, degradation, and disappearance of herbicides from the

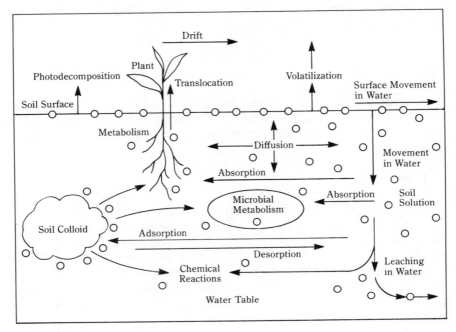

O Herbicide Molecule

Figure 3. Diagrammatical sketch of the interrelations of processes that lead to detoxification, degradation, and disappearance of herbicides. (Courtesy Sheets and Kaufman, 1970.)

site of application. Some may be lost by drift during the application, but this can be minimized by not spraying when the wind exceeds 5 mph and avoiding small droplets in the spray. Some may be subject to photodecomposition in the air and on plant or soil surfaces. Herbicides with a high vapor pressure (e.g., EPTC) are lost by volatilization unless they are incorporated into the soil soon after application. Some may be lost by the runoff of surface water. Such losses are minimized under good agricultural practices.

Herbicides that enter the plant via leaves or roots are subject to degradation within the plant. Herbicides that enter the soil from a direct application or plant residues undergo numerous fates, as shown in fig. 3. Some can be leached downward and ultimately reach the water table; however, this is not common and usually only occurs in relatively coarse, sandy soils with excessive rainfall or irrigation. Most herbicides remain in the upper soil profile where they are subject to biological and nonbiological degradation. Such processes usually involve a relatively rapid breakdown of the herbicide molecule; however, a few herbicides (e.g., glyphosate and paraquat) are inactivated by being strongly bound to clay and organic matter.

ADDITIONAL READING

Anderson, W.P. 1983. Weed Science: Principles, 2nd ed. West Publishing Co., St. Paul. 655 pp.
Ashton, F.M. and A.S. Crafts. 1981. Mode of Action of Herbicides, 2nd ed. John Wiley & Sons, Inc., New York. 525 pp.
Ashton, F.M. and W.A. Harvey. 1971. Selective Chemical Weed Control. Univ. of Calif. Cir. 558. 17 pp.
Beste, E.E., ed. 1983. Herbicide Handbook of the Weed Science Society of America, Urbana, Ill.
Brown, A.W.A. 1978. Ecology of Pesticides. John Wiley & Sons, Inc., New York. 525 pp.
Crafts, A.S. 1975. Modern Weed Control. Univ. of Calif. Press, Berkeley. 440 pp.
Klingman, G.C. and F.M. Ashton. 1982. Weed Science: Principle and Practices, 2nd ed. John Wiley & Sons, Inc., New York. 449 pp.
LeBaron, H.M. and J. Gressel, eds. 1982. Herbicide Resistance in Plants. John Wiley & Sons, Inc., New York. 401 pp.
Matsumura, F. and C.R. Krishna Murti, eds. 1982. Biodegradation of Pesticides. Plenum Press, New York. 312 pp.
McEwin, F.L. and G.R. Stephenson. 1979. The Use and Significance of Pesticides in the Environment. John Wiley & Sons, Inc., New York. 538 pp.
Sheets, T.J. and D.D. Kaufman. 1970. Degradation and effects of herbicides in soils. In: FAO International Conference on Weed Control (T.J. Holstun, Jr., ed.). pp. 513–538. Weed Science Society of America, Urbana, Ill.

ADJUVANTS AND FORMULATIONS

by Gary Ritenour[1]

ADJUVANTS

Nearly all herbicides are made of molecules that have physical and/or chemical properties that would make it impossible to apply the pure technical grade active ingredient in the field in a uniform, effective manner. Adjuvants are organic chemicals that have been developed to aid in some way the physical or chemical properties of a pesticide when it is applied. There are several types of adjuvants. The major ones used with herbicides are surfactants (dispersants), spreaders or stickers (wetting agents), and oil concentrates. Adjuvants are used to increase the activity of foliar applied herbicides. Most adjuvants, and in particular spreader-stickers (wetters), increase the contact surface area between spray droplets and leaf surfaces by reducing the surface tension of water. Oil concentrates, on the other hand, are a blend of petroleum or vegetable based oils and emulsifiers that are used mostly when leaf or tissue penetration is desired. Drift control agents are another type of adjuvant used with some herbicides particularly when they are applied by aircraft. Thousands of different adjuvants have been synthesized, and any one of them may be better at performing a particular adjuvant function, such as being a surfactant. In addition, they could have some other adjuvant characteristic such as a spreader-sticker. It is common for adjuvants to

1. *California State University, Fresno, CA.*

possess overlapping characteristic (i.e., be able to partially function as more than one type of adjuvant).

Surfactants

Surfactants (dispersants or surface active agents) affect the surface properties of molecules and particles they contact. As such, they can alter the emulsifying, wetting, and suspension properties of herbicides. Surfactants possess both an oil-soluble (lipophilic) end and a water-soluble (hydrophilic) end. This property of one molecule having differential solubilities allows surfactants to act as a chemical bridge that interfaces between solutions and/or surfaces where the constituents are not of like solubilities. The lipophilic end is always a long-chain hydrocarbon. The electrons forming the bonds in that hydrocarbon chain are essentially equally shared between the carbon and hydrogen atoms. Thus, the hydrocarbon chain is nonpolar and is soluble in other nonpolar substances such as the leaf cuticle and many herbicides and organic solvents. The other end of the surfactant molecule is polar and therefore soluble in water, which is made up of polar molecules. Water molecules are polar because the electrons forming the bonds between the two hydrogen atoms and the one oxygen atom are not equally shared. The oxygen has a greater affinity for the electrons than the hydrogen. Therefore, within a water molecule, the oxygen has a partial negative charge, and the hydrogen has a partial positive charge in spite of the fact that the overall molecule is electrically neutral.

The method by which the water soluble end of surfactants obtain polarity forms the basis for classifying them. The three most common types are: cationic, anionic, and nonionic. Cationic adjuvants ionize in water to leave a residual positive charge on the surfactant molecule. The positive charge is often found on a quaternary nitrogen atom. Anionic adjuvants ionize in water with a negative charge on the adjuvant. Many anionic surfactants are sulfonates. Both cationic and anionic adjuvants are used only on a limited basis with herbicides because the ionic component of these products can react with some herbicides and minerals found in some waters and can inactivate the herbicides. By far, the most popular type of adjuvant is comprised of nonionic components.

Nonionic Adjuvants

Nonionic adjuvants are able to contain a polar end using the same concept discussed above for the water molecule (i.e., unequal sharing of electrons). Many nonionic surfactants use repeating units of oxyethylene $[-(CH_2-CH_2-O)-]$ to obtain polarity without having an ionized electrical charge. The generalized structure of an alkylphenol polyoxyethylene nonionic surfactant is:

$$CH_3(CH_2)_x \quad \text{---} \quad \bigcirc \quad \text{---} \quad O(CH_2\text{-}CH_2\text{-}O)_y$$

In each of the oxyethylene units electrons are more tightly held by the oxygen than the carbon or hydrogen. Thus, the oxygen has a partial negative charge, and the remainder of the unit has a partial positive charge. When several of the oxyethylene units are attached end to end, that portion of the surfactant molecule becomes water soluble. The larger the number of oxyethylene units used (i.e., y increases), the greater will be the hydrophilic nature of that end of the surfactant molecule. Likewise, the longer the hydrocarbon chain (i.e., x increases), the more oil-soluble will become the lipophilic side of the surfactant molecule. By varying both y (number of oxyethylene groups) and x (number of methyl groups), many surfactants can be created, each with unique solubility characteristics. In surfactant terminology, this is referred to as the hydrophilic-lipophilic balance or HLB. However, using the HLB system to predict adjuvant solubilities is only effective when relating the HLB to nonionic molecules.

Commercial brands of adjuvants are often blends of chemicals with more than one structure; e.g., one chemical that is a particularly good emulsifier may be mixed with another that is a good wetting agent.

Always read the herbicide label regarding the potential use of adjuvants. Some foliar applied herbicides are sold with the surfactant premixed in the commercial product, while others may require or prohibit the addition of a surfactant or other adjuvant when the herbicide is mixed in the sprayer. In some cases, the use of additional adjuvant is optional depending on the species and size of the weeds to be controlled and the amount of spray solution used. Some herbicides do not require the addition of an adjuvant when applied alone but may require one when applied in combination with certain other herbicides and/or other agricultural chemicals. If an adjuvant addition is needed, the herbicide label should supply information on the types and/or brand(s) to use and indicate what concentration of surfactant in the spray solution is needed.

FORMULATIONS

The technical grade active ingredient of herbicides is usually processed before being made available for use. This is referred to as formulating the herbicide. Creating the commercial formulation may involve physical processes, such as grinding, and the use of one or more additives. Herbicides are formulated to improve any of several properties relating to their use. These properties include storage life, safety to the user, mixing characteristics, stability in spray solution, and herbicidal activity and use patterns. There are many possible formulations. Physical properties of the technical grade active ingredient normally determine which formulation will be used for a particular herbicide. Two key physical factors are: type of technical material (i.e., liquid or dry); and solubility (i.e., in organic solvents or water). However, other factors previously mentioned are also considered.

Some herbicide active ingredients are sufficiently water soluble that they can be dissolved in water to form a true solution. Such herbicides tend to be easy to formulate. These formulations can be either a water-soluble powder (SP) or a water-soluble liquid (S). Water-soluble liquids require less initial mixing (agitation) than powders in the spray tank. Once dissolved, both form true solutions, and the active ingredients will neither sink to the bottom nor float to the top of the spray solution.

Most herbicides are so low in water solubility that the required amount cannot be dissolved in the volume of water normally used in herbicide application. Thus, several formulation types have been created in which the active ingredient is suspended in water or another carrier during application. Since it is a suspension and not a true solution, the active ingredient can separate from the water if not handled properly. If this occurs, it will sink to the bottom or rise to the top of the spray solution, depending on its density, and will not be uniformly mixed or applied. To prevent this, the spray solution should be continually agitated.

Wettable powders (WP or W) are created by grinding the active ingredient into fine particles, usually in combination with an inert clay, adding a wetting agent to aid in dispersion of the powder, and a dry surfactant or dispersant to help keep the herbicide particles suspended in the spray solution. However, even with the surfactant present, the herbicide particles tend to settle out rapidly if the agitation of the spray mixture is not adequate. Several herbicides are formulated as pelletized wettable powder called water-dispersible granules (WDG) or dry flowables (DF). Aqueous suspension (AS) formulations have also been developed which are essentially a wettable powder suspended in a viscous liquid. One problem associated with AS formulations is that they have a relatively short shelf life. This is due, in part, to the inability to remain in one phase for any length of time following the formulation process. The WDG, DF, and AS formulations are safer than WP for the person mixing the spray solution because these formulations greatly reduce any dust associated with opening and pouring containers of wettable powders. Additionally, WP and other similar products can be formulated in water soluble packages, which further reduces the potential dust hazard during the mixing process. In a spray solution, particles of WDG, DF, and AS formulations have settling properties similar to wettable powders and should be agitated continuously.

The emulsifiable or emulsible concentrate (E or EC) formulations are used in situations where the herbicide is low in water solubility and/ or a liquid formulation is desired. The basic components of this formulation are the herbicide dissolved in an organic solvent with a surfactant or dispersant added. When this formulation is added to water in the spray tank, the organic solvent droplets containing the herbicide become emulsified into the water. This formulation mixes easily with water. However, the herbicide is in suspension (i.e., not a true solution) and over time the emulsion can break down, allowing for nonuniform distribution of the herbicide in the spray solution. Although most EC formulations remain in suspension easier than WPs, keeping the agitator operating helps ensure a uniform mixture in the spray tank. Care should be taken, however, not to over-agitate EC formulations, as this can result in excessive foaming and uneven application.

Granular (G) formulations are designed to be applied dry. They can be made by impregnating or coating the herbicide into or onto an inert ingredient (carrier) such as clay, and by coating onto an inert ingredient such as sand. Pelletized granular products have also been developed using modified WP formulations and compressing them into various shapes and sizes. Granular formulations offer another method of application that meet the needs of specific products (e.g., reduce mammalian toxicity) and/or use patterns (e.g., reduce plant phytotoxicity and/ or drift). Granular formulations have also been shown to delay photo-decomposition and/or volatility of some soil-active herbicides.

REFERENCES

Anderson, W.P. 1983. Weed Science Principles. 2nd ed. West Publishing Co. St. Paul. 665 pp.
Helena Chemical Co. 1988. Your Guide to Spray Adjuvants. 30 pp.
Mathews, G.A. 1979. Pesticide Application Methods. Longman Group Ltd. London. 334 pp.
McHenry, W.B., and R.F. Norris. Study Guide for Agricultural Pest Control Advisers on Weed Control. 64 pp.
Ware, G.W. 1983. Pesticides Theory and Application. W.H. Freeman. San Francisco. 308 pp.
Weed Science Society of America. Adjuvants for Herbicides. 144 pp.

CHEMICAL APPLICATION METHODS

GROUND

by Janet Rose Blume[1] and Gary Ritenour[2]

Application Equipment

Ground application is the most common method of applying herbicides. With the use of ground applicators, a herbicide may be applied either

1. Pacific Gas and Electric Company, Stockton, CA. 2. California State University, Fresno, CA.

Figure 4. Example of a postemergence herbicide application by ground to a row crop, in this case a bedtop treatment to onions. Photo courtesy E.A. Kurtz.

broadcast, in narrow bands, as individual spot treatments, or as a shielded or directed spray to or away from a specific part of the plant or area.

Spraying with hydraulically regulated, boom-type field sprayers is the most common method of applying all types of herbicides (fig. 4), except granular formulations. Ground sprayers vary greatly in size, structure, and application method but are made up of the same components: the boom, pump, tank, filters or strainers, pressure regulators, hoses, and nozzles.

Booms

Horizontal booms with directly attached nozzles, or nozzles attached to vertical drop pipes, are used on ground sprayers. Drop pipes are employed for between-the-row spraying of row crops.

Boom length can vary from a few feet to over 70 feet, depending upon the type of use.

Height adjustment should be provided to suit varying weed and crop conditions. Nozzle spacing should provide complete, even coverage of the sprayed area.

Pumps

The pump provides the pressure to force the spray mixture through the nozzles with sufficient velocity to obtain droplet formation. Pump size is determined by the size of the boom and number of nozzles, the pressure required to deliver a determined gallonage or rate per acre, and the speed of travel. Five of the most frequently utilized pumps are the piston, centrifugal, gear, roller-impeller, and diaphragm.

Piston pumps afford a variety of uses with a wide pressure range. Their flow is low and requires mechanical agitation. They are very dependable and resistant to wear from abrasive materials. They are expensive but easily repaired.

Centrifugal pumps deliver high volumes at low pressure but do not provide high pressure unless they are operated at high speed. They are generally not self-priming, but they are resistant to abrasive materials and relatively inexpensive.

Gear pumps have high-pressure capabilities and will provide both pressure and suction. They are inexpensive but have a limited life with extensive use of abrasive or corrosive materials.

Roller-impeller–type pumps provide adequate flow and volume for most uses but will not withstand abrasive materials. The pumps are moderately priced, and worn parts are easily replaced.

Diaphragm pumps are expensive to purchase and repair but will give a long service life. They provide very high pressure and high volume and are often used for ultrafine atomization of sprayed materials.

Tanks

Tanks are made of a variety of corrosion-resistant material such as stainless steel, mild steel with rust resistant interiors, fiberglass, or reinforced plastic. To ensure homogeneity of a solution, hydraulic or mechanical agitation is used in sprayer tanks. The size of a tank depends upon boom size, average size of the field, the number of gallons applied per acre, and the type of carriage, which is determined by ground conditions.

Filters and Strainers

Filters or strainers may be part of the nozzle, installed as an in-line filter, or placed on the intake from the spray tank. The size of the strainer openings is regulated by the size of the nozzle orifices. Screens should not be finer than 50 mesh for wettable powders but can be 100 mesh for emulsions and true solutions.

Pressure Regulators

The pressure regulator is essential for keeping the spray pressure at a constant level and providing a uniform gallonage per acre at any given speed. The pressure is usually regulated by a screw-adjusted spring pressurizing a ball. A downstream pressure gauge is helpful in determining and setting actual pressure.

Hoses

Hoses should not react with the chemicals to be used and should withstand the pressure or vacuum developed by the pump. They should not crimp, and their size should be determined by the maximum pressure at which it will be used.

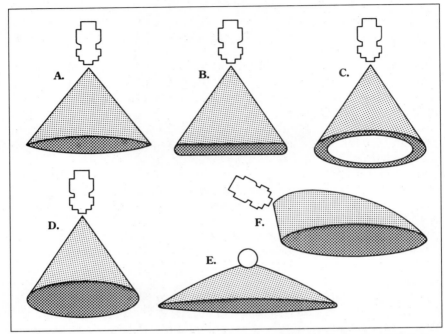

Figure 5. Examples of nozzle types and spray patterns: a) flat fan, b) even fan, c) hollow cone, d) solid cone, e) flood, f) offset.

Nozzles

Selection of the appropriate nozzle is one of the most critical steps in the accurate application of any liquid. The nozzle converts the liquid into spray droplets and specific patterns. Orifice design and condition of their operation influence uniformity of application, rate of application, and spray drift. Nozzles are made of brass, aluminum, stainless steel, nylon, rubber, plastic, or ceramic materials. Precautions should be made to avoid damaging the nozzle during cleaning and general handling.

Several factors are important in determining the best nozzle for a particular operation. Four basic types of nozzles used for ground applications of herbicides are: fan, cone, flood, and offset (fig. 5).

Fan nozzles are the most commonly used for both band and broadcast applications due to their uniformity of coverage. Uniform coverage is achieved by spacing the flat-fan nozzle so that each spray pattern overlaps the other by 30–50%. To achieve this overlap, properly aligned nozzles are commonly spaced along the boom at 18-to-24–inch centers, with the nozzle spray angle between 65 and 80 degrees. Nozzle height is also critical to proper overlap. Information on the correct nozzle height and spacing for uniform coverage is provided in table 3 and figure 6.

Even-fan nozzles are designed to give a uniform application over a

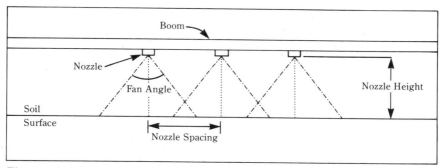

Figure 6. Example of proper nozzle spacing and overlap to obtain uniform coverage.

TABLE 3. NOZZLE HEIGHT FOR UNIFORM COVERAGE

Nozzle type	Nozzle height 18" spacing	Nozzle height 20" spacing	Nozzle height 24" spacing
65° fan	19" to 21"	21" to 23"	25" to 27"
73° fan	16" to 18"	20" to 22"	22" to 24"
80° fan	14" to 16"	17" to 19"	19" to 21"

wider strip than flat-fan types and are used when making band applications of herbicides in row crops.

Flood nozzles operate at low pressures and produce large droplets in a wide angle spray pattern. They are used more to apply soil-active herbicides than foliar-active ones.

Cone nozzles are normally operated at higher pressures. They produce smaller droplets than other nozzle types; therefore, they give excellent coverage of plant surfaces, but the drift potential is also greater. Consequently, cone nozzles are used more with fungicides and insecticides than in herbicide applications.

Offset nozzles do not apply the spray as uniformly as fan nozzles; however, they are useful when it is not practical to position the nozzle directly over the sprayed area. Such situations are often found in tree and vine crops and most noncrop areas (e.g., roadsides, ditchbanks, fencerows, etc.).

Sprayer Calibration

Before a herbicide is applied, it is essential that the sprayer be checked and calibrated. Check the nozzles to see that they are the type and orifice size desired. In most herbicide applications by ground, all nozzles will be the same type and size. In certain applications such as band applications in tree and vine crops, a mixture of types and/or sizes may be used. Inspect the tank and screens to make sure they are clean. Add water to the tank. Start the sprayer. With it running in a stationary position, check the operating pressure, shut-off valve, agitation system, spray pattern of each nozzle, and output of each nozzle. Any nozzles with significantly different delivery rates should be replaced. However, as a set of nozzles becomes worn, better uniformity of application is obtained if the entire set of nozzles is replaced at once rather than replacing the set nozzle by nozzle over time. The operating pressure should be set within the range recommended for the nozzle type being used.

Sprayer calibration involves determining how many gallons of spray solution are being applied to each sprayed acre. Sprayers should be calibrated in the field, as soil conditions can affect the speed of travel. Also, check that the boom height is correct while in the field. The sprayer should be calibrated with only water in the tank. Do not add herbicide to the tank yet as it is impossible to know how much to add until the sprayer is calibrated. Most herbicides do not significantly affect the rate of output from the sprayer when mixed with water. However, if a particularly thick or viscous solution results when the herbicide is added, one should recheck the delivery rate of spray from the nozzles and recalibrate if necessary.

There are many satisfactory ways to calibrate a sprayer. One of the most common and accurate techniques involves determining the amount of spray solution applied to a small test area as follows:

1. Measure the length of the test distance. Any distance can be used, but for most calibrations 100 feet is satisfactory.

2. With the sprayer traveling at the intended operating speed, time the number of seconds it takes to travel the test distance.

3. With the sprayer stopped, operate it at the desired pressure, collect and measure the number of fluid ounces or milliliters of spray being delivered from three to four nozzles to obtain an average for the number of seconds it took to travel the test distance.

4. Measure the width (in feet) sprayed by all nozzles.

5. Use the following formula to calculate gallons of spray per acre. Note: for this and other formulas, values can be expressed in pounds or grams (454 grams = 1 pound) and also in ounces or milliliters (3785 milliliters = 1 gallon). Metric measurements will be the most accurate when small amounts of herbicide or liquid are used in a formula.

$$\text{gal spray/A} =$$
$$(\text{number test areas to make 1 acre}) \ (\text{gal spray applied in test area}) =$$

$$\left[\frac{43{,}560 \text{ sq ft/A}}{(\text{test distance in ft.}) \ (\text{sprayed width in ft.})} \right] \left[\frac{(\text{fl oz/noz. for test distance}) \ (\text{number noz. on sprayer})}{128 \text{ fl. oz./gal.}} \right]$$

If all the nozzles on the sprayer are not the same size, one needs to calculate the gallons sprayed in the test areas (right hand portion of formula) from the combined output of whatever nozzles were used.

There are other ways that sprayers can be accurately calibrated. However, a word of caution about the dangers of using any short-cut calibration technique. It is not uncommon for a sprayer operator to have a short-cut way to calibrate a sprayer. However, the operator's system works because the same nozzle size, nozzle spacing, speed of travel, pressure, etc., are used continuously each time the operator uses the equipment. If someone else tries to use that same short-cut method and any of the potential variables are different from those used by the other person, the resulting calibration will be in error.

Most ground application equipment can apply 20–100 gallons of finished spray per acre. Most herbicides are equally effective at these rates as long as the proper amount of herbicide is applied. However, some herbicide labels state specifically the gallons of spray per acre that should be used. If one wants to change the gallons of spray per acre being applied, it may be done by changing the operating pressure and/ or altering the speed of travel. If larger changes in delivery rate are required, it is best to change nozzles with a different size orifice. Whenever any changes are made in nozzle type or size, the sprayer should be recalibrated.

In applying herbicides, one does not normally mix enough spray solution to spray just 1 acre. Rather, a tankful of solution is mixed. To know how much of the formulated herbicide to put in each tankful of spray solution, one must first determine the number of acres each tankful will spray. The following formula is useful:

$$\text{acres sprayed/tankful} = \frac{\text{tank capacity in gal}}{\text{gal spray/A}}$$

Herbicide labels tell how much of that formulated product should be applied to each sprayed acre. With that information, one can determine how much of the formulated product to use in each tankful of spray.

$$\text{amount of formulated herbicide/tankful} =$$
$$(\text{acres sprayed/tankful}) \ (\text{amount formulated product per acre})$$

In the case of liquid formulations, the amount per tankful will be in some unit volume such as pints or gallons, while powder formulations will be in units of weight (normally pounds, but with some very active herbicides, labels use weight ounces, i.e., 1 wt. oz. = $\frac{1}{16}$ of a pound or 28.4 grams).

Special note on potential error of using ounces as a unit of measure in herbicide application: One pint of water is 16 ounces and weighs about 1 pound. Therefore, the weight of 1 ounce of water is approximately $\frac{1}{16}$ pound. However, remember that a pint is a unit of volume and that ¹⁄₁₆ of this volume (i.e., 1 fluid ounce) will weigh ¹⁄₁₆ pound (i.e., 1 weight ounce) only if the substance being measured has the same density as water. This is seldom the case with either liquid or dry formulations of herbicides. Standard containers calibrated in ounces are really fluid ounces (a unit of volume). Therefore, *never* use the ounce measurements on those containers to measure out a weight of herbicide because each fluid ounce may weigh considerably less or more than ¹⁄₁₆ of a pound, and large errors in the rate of herbicide application will result.

Often the person who operates the sprayer in the field is not the one who sets up and calibrates the sprayer. Problems with misapplication of herbicides could be greatly reduced if a little more time were invested in making sure the sprayer operator knows the importance of all facets of the operation being performed.

The following checklist summarizes the steps involved in calibrating a sprayer. It is also useful as a record of each application.

EXAMPLE OF A HERBICIDE APPLICATION CHECKLIST

Location _____ Date _____

Crop and Stage of Growth _____ Herbicide _____

Herbicide Formulation: Powder _____ % ai or Liquid _____ lb ai/gal.

Recommended Rate of Formulation/Acre: Powder _____ lb Liquid _____ gal.

Type _____ and number designation of nozzles _____

Number of nozzles _____ to provide width of spray pattern _____ ft.

Sprayer speed _____ ft. in _____ seconds Operating pressure _____ psi

Individual nozzle output _____ fluid oz. or ml. in _____ seconds

Spray tank capacity _____ gallons

Calculate:
- Gallons of spray solution being applied per acre
- Number of acres to be treated with each tankful
- Amount of formulated herbicide to be added to each tankful

Example: A broadcast boom-type sprayer has 18 nozzles and sprays a width of 27 feet. It takes 12 seconds for the sprayer to travel 100 feet. When operated at a pressure of 35 psi, each nozzle delivers 11 fluid ounces or 325 milliliters of spray solution in 12 seconds. The sprayer has a tank capacity of 225 gallons. The hypothetical herbicide "Klout" is formulated as a wettable powder that is 75% active ingredient by weight. The "Klout" label states that 1.5 pounds of the formulated product is to be applied per acre.

Question 1. How many gallons of solution are being applied per acre?

$$\text{gal/A} = \left[\frac{43,560 \text{ sq. ft.}}{(100 \text{ ft.}) \ (27 \text{ ft.})}\right] \ \left[\frac{(11 \text{ fl. oz. or } 325 \text{ ml./noz.}) \ (18 \text{ noz.})}{128 \text{ fl. oz. or } 3785 \text{ ml./gal.}}\right] = 25$$

Question 2. How many acres will each tankful spray?

$$\text{A/tankful} = \frac{\text{gal/tankful}}{\text{gal spray/A}} = \frac{225}{25} = 9$$

Question 3. How many pounds of "Klout" should be added to each tankful?

$$\text{lb/tankful} = (\text{acres sprayed/tankful}) \ (\text{lb. product/A}) = (9) \ (1.5)$$
$$= 13.5 \text{ lb. of formulated product.}$$

Amount Active Ingredient vs. Amount Formulated Product

Herbicide labels tell what rate of formulated product to use. However, other sources such as Extension service newsletters and research journals often discuss the rate in terms of pounds of active ingredient per acre (lb ai/A). To convert back and forth between amount of formulated product per acre and lb ai/A, the following two formulas are useful.

For any dry formulation (soluble powder, wettable powder, dispersible granules, granules, etc.):

$$\text{pounds formulated product/A} = \frac{\text{lb ai/A}}{\text{decimal equivalent of \% ai in formulated product}}$$

Example: A wettable powder herbicide is to be applied at the rate of 2.0 pounds product/A. The commercial product is 75% ai (note—the percent ai by weight has to be stated on all herbicide labels). How many lb ai/A are to be applied?

$$2.0 \text{ lb. product} = \frac{\text{lb ai/A}}{0.75}$$

or lb ai/A = (2.0) (.75) = 1.5

The weight of the formulated product will *always* be larger than the weight of ai.

For any liquid formulation (emulsible concentrate, soluble, aqueous suspension, etc.):

$$\text{gallons of formulated product/A} = \frac{\text{lb ai/A}}{\text{lb ai/gal. of formulated product}}$$

Example: A herbicide is formulated as an emulsible concentrate that contains 4.0 lb ai/gal. How much of the formulated product should be applied per acre if one wants to apply 0.5 lb ai/A?

$$\text{gal. formulated product/A} = \frac{0.5}{4.0} = 0.125 \text{ gal. (which} = 1 \text{ pint or } 473 \text{ ml/A)}$$

All manufacturers of herbicides formulated as liquids print on the label what weight of herbicide is contained in some unit of volume. The vast majority of labels indicate how many pounds of ai are contained in each gallon of formulated product. However, read the label closely as occasionally some other unit of volume, such as quart, will be used. For such products one must convert the amount of ai to a per-gallon basis before using the aforementioned formula.

Most herbicides formulated as liquids require less than 1 gallon of the formulated product per acre. The fraction of a gallon answer usually obtained when using the aforementioned formula can be converted to a more useful unit of volume using one of the following equivalents:

1 gallon = 4 quarts = 8 pints = 16 cups = 128 fluid ounces = 3785 milliliters

Calculations for Lawn and Garden Areas

When herbicides are applied to lawns or gardens, the area involved is measured in square feet. Consequently, the labels of herbicides marketed for those uses often tell how much of the formulated product to use per 1000 square feet of area.

The sprayer most often used is a hand-pump type with a capacity of 1 to 2 gallons. It is difficult to apply herbicide uniformly with this type of sprayer. These types of sprayers do not have pressure regulators or agitation systems. To minimize problems associated with the lack of these items, it is best to fill the sprayer only half full and to pump up and shake the sprayer often. Also, the sprayer usually operates with only one nozzle which makes it difficult to apply the spray uniformly.

To calibrate this equipment and obtain some visual evaluation of the evenness of the spray application, first measure out an area 10 feet × 10 feet on a dry concrete surface. Place the sprayer on a flat surface and fill it with a known volume of water (e.g., 1 gallon or 3785 milliliters). Spray the 10 × 10 foot area. Place the sprayer in the exact position it was when first filled. Determine how many cups, fluid ounces, or milliliters of water were applied to the 100 square feet.

Example: The hand pump sprayer to be used has a total capacity of

2 gallons. However, to improve the uniformity of application, only 1 gallon of solution will be used at a time. When calibrating the sprayer it is determined that 2 cups (16 fluid ounces or 473 milliliters) of water were required to spray 100 square feet. The herbicide to be used is a liquid, and the label directs that 4 fluid ounces of 118 milliliters of the formulated liquid be applied per 1000 square feet. How many fluid ounces or milliliters of the formulated liquid should be used for each 1 gallon of spray solution?

- If 2 cups (16 fluid ounces or 473 milliliters) of water sprays 100 square feet, then 1 gallon (16 cups) of water will spray:

$$\frac{16 \text{ cups}}{2 \text{ cups}} \times 100 \text{ square feet} = 800 \text{ square feet}$$

- If 4 fluid ounces or 118 milliliters of formulated herbicide is to treat 1000 square feet, then the amount of formulated herbicide needed for 1 gallon of spray solution is:

$$\frac{800 \text{ square feet}}{1000 \text{ square feet}} \times 4 \text{ fluid ounces or } 118 \text{ milliliters} = 3.2 \text{ fluid ounces or } 95 \text{ milliliters}$$

REFERENCES

1971. *Weed Control, vol. 2, National Academy of Sciences.* Washington, D.C.

Anderson, W.P. 1983. *Weed Science Principles.* 2nd ed. West Publishing Company, St. Paul. 655 pp.

Brazelton, R.W., N.B. Akesson and W.E. Yates. 1972. *Study guide for agricultural pest control advisers on the safe application of agricultural chemicals equipment and calibration.* Univ. of Calif., Div. of Ag. Sci.

Brazleton, R.W. and W.B. McHenry. 1976. *How much chemical do you put in the tank?* Univ. of Calif. Div. of Ag. Sci.

Crafts, A.S. 1975. *Modern Weed Control.* Univ. of Calif. Press. Berkeley.

Crafts, A.S. and W.W. Robbins. 1962. *Weed Control, 3rd ed.* McGraw-Hill, New York.

Delavan. *Choosing the Best Pump.* Delavan Manufacturing Co. West Des Moines, Iowa. 1983.

Fischer, B.B. 1971. *Herbicide sprayer calibration.* Univ. of Calif., Div. of Ag. Sci.

Kepner, R.A., R. Bainer and E.L. Barger. 1978. *Principles of Farm Machinery, 3rd ed.* AVI Publishing Co., Inc., Westport, Conn.

Klingman, G.C. 1961. *Weed Control.* John Wiley & Sons, Inc., New York.

Spraying Systems Co. *TeeJet agricultural spray nozzles and accessories.* Spray Manual Catalog 39. Wheaton, Ill.

SOIL INCORPORATION

by Lauren M. Burtch[1] and Tad H. Gantenbein[2]

Most herbicides require soil incorporation to provide weed control as the crop emerges. In humid regions, rainfall is often sufficient to pro-

1. *Amstar Corporation, Spreckels Sugar Division, Mendota, CA.* 2. *John Taylor Fertilizers, Sacramento, CA.*

vide adequate soil incorporation. In the arid parts of the western United States, however, when rainfall patterns are not dependable, some system for incorporation must be provided.

Four systems of incorporation may be used for row-crop production in California. These are: (1) power incorporation, (2) disc incorporation, (3) sprinkler or rainfall, and (4) ground-driven rolling cultivators.

Each method has advantages and disadvantages, and each can be adversely affected by the condition of the seedbed. A firm, well-tilled seedbed that promotes rapid seed germination on a given soil type also favors adequate incorporation and is favorable for the performance of herbicides. Extreme deviations from the ideal seedbed can result in poor herbicide performance. Large clods prevent uniform distribution of water and herbicide. Conversely, a too-fine, powdery seedbed also prevents uniform incorporation. Thus, proper seedbed preparation becomes the keystone for each method of incorporation.

Some herbicides incorporated with rolling-cultivator equipment lose much of their effectiveness if irrigation water is allowed to go over the tops of the beds. This situation is difficult to correct once the crop has emerged. Rebuilding beds and deepening furrows create mechanical problems and make cultivating the weeds difficult. Furrows should be made deep enough and beds packed firmly to withstand irrigations. These problems are more prevalent in coarse, sandy soils but occur also in finer clay loam soils.

Power Incorporation

Power incorporation is generally considered the optimum method of incorporating herbicides in bands because it can result in uniform distribution of the herbicide to a predetermined depth (fig. 7). The method is expensive and can cause problems if the incorporator is not correctly adjusted and maintained. The incorporator should be equipped with a bed shaper that is adjusted to ensure an adequate volume of soil between the properly calibrated and adjusted nozzle and the power-driven incorporator teeth, or tines. Rollers or pressure plates are generally required to firm the bed behind the incorporator and ahead of the planter. The arrangement and condition of the teeth on the drum are most important, for worn, broken, or improperly arranged teeth can result in poor herbicide distribution. Incorporation to an improper depth and at too-fast forward speeds are factors that can adversely affect results. Soil moisture is also very important, for too dry, finely tilled soil will not form a uniform bed. Too much moisture in the soil can cause equally serious problems, because moist soil tends to build up on the inside of the incorporator shield, limiting herbicide incorporation and resulting in poor soil tilth.

One step that is consistently overlooked by growers is the construc-

Figure 7. Front view of one bed of a four-bed power incorporation unit applying an herbicide prior to planting a row crop. Photo courtesy E.A. Kurtz.

tion of the incorporator with regard to nozzle placement. The nozzle openings may be too small for the spray pattern or the nozzle may be too close to the incorporator hood. Either situation causes soil to build up on the walls of the spray opening, thus reducing the pattern to less than the desired band width. This is particularly common when conditions are dry and the mechanical incorporation creates dust. Reduced rates and poor weed control result from uneven herbicide distribution.

To prevent such problems, the nozzle should be mounted low enough so that the spray pattern does not hit the side walls of the shaper or incorporator housing. To prevent soil from building up on the hood, the spray nozzle should be directed toward the front. Periodic visual inspections are needed to ensure that the problem is corrected.

Knowledge of both the expected weed infestation and the characteristic of the herbicide to be used is also important. Some herbicides perform best when incorporated to depths of 2½–3 inches, while others require shallower incorporation. The water solubility of the herbicide can adversely influence performance. For example, a highly soluble herbicide should be incorporated at a shallow depth, since it could be displaced by subsequent rainfall or sprinkler irrigation, resulting in poor weed control. The leaching characteristics of a herbicide can also adversely influence performance. For example, pyrazon, which performs well under shallow incorporation, can be displaced by sprinkler irrigation where more than 2 inches is applied during an irrigation, resulting in injury to the crop.

Disc Incorporation

Disc incorporation of herbicides has considerable merit. It can be economical, fast, and efficient for some herbicides and soil conditions. Problems associated with this method include overlapping, resulting in excessive rates of application, or, where gaps occur in a spray pattern, skips or excessive rates. Careful nozzle placement and calibration are important considerations, as are the size and condition of disc blades and the condition of the soil. The soil should be uniformly tilled so that the disc can operate at a constant speed, and the incorporation depth must be sufficient to prevent the lister from placing untreated soil on the beds. Rates should be adjusted to take into consideration the concentration of herbicide thrown into the crop row by the lister. It is always advisable to use crowder- or pusher-type listing shovels rather than pointed shovels that may penetrate below the depth of herbicide incorporation. There are basically two sizes of crowders, one for single-row beds and one for double-row beds. Beds should be high enough to prevent flooding but low enough to provide for complete wetting in furrow-irrigated fields.

Rolling Cultivators

Rolling cultivators are useful for incorporating herbicides in some situations. Seedbed preparation is very important for this method since the ground-driven rolling cultivators usually provide shallower and less-thorough incorporation than other methods. Excessive clods will often limit the use of this method which is usually best suited for nonvolatile herbicides requiring shallow rather than deep incorporation. The rolling-cultivator gangs must be properly aligned so that the herbicide is incorporated only in the desired band. The method works best when more than two gangs are used in tandem, with each gang offset slightly in opposite directions to facilitate incorporation. Using a roller is advisable to smooth and firm the bed ahead of the planter.

Sprinkler or Rainfall Incorporation

Sprinkler or rainfall incorporation can be effective with nonvolatile herbicides. The solubility and rate of application are important considerations, and the amount of subsequent rain or sprinkler irrigation can directly affect herbicide performance. Too much or too little water can result in too-deep or too-shallow incorporation, adversely affecting herbicide performance and crop safety. The condition of the seedbed, including the extent of its soluble-salts content, can be important in this as in other methods. Wind velocity and direction can be of more significance with sprinkler incorporation after herbicide application than with other methods because wind can influence water distribution and encourage crusting, which can limit crop emergence.

The importance of effective soil incorporation of herbicides cannot be overemphasized. Careful selection of an incorporation method and awareness of its performance can result in excellent weed control and crop safety. Conversely, a lack of understanding and improper mounting and adjustment can render any herbicide program a failure.

SOIL FUMIGATION

by Robert J. McKeand[1]

True soil fumigants are volatile, organic chemicals which have a relatively high vapor pressure and low solubility in water. Included are materials such as chloropicrin, methyl bromide, and dichloropropene. Other commercially important volatile soil pesticides not usually regarded as true soil fumigants include metham and dazomet. For the purpose of this discussion, all of these materials will be considered as fumigants. Table 4 lists these chemicals by common name and use.

TABLE 4. CHEMICALS USED AS SOIL FUMIGANTS

Chemical	Effective against		
	Fungi	**Nematodes**	**Weeds**
1,3-D		X	X[1]
chloropicrin	X	X	X
methyl bromide	X	X	X
dazomet	X	X	X
metham	X	X	X
1,3-D + methyl isothiocyanate	X	X	X

1. Perennial weeds

Although not all fumigants are widely used as herbicides, some (e.g., metham and methyl bromide) are effective tools that may be utilized in specific situations to provide weed control.

The mode of activity of all fumigants is similar. Volatilization takes place in the soil, and the vapors diffuse through the soil to contact the organism to be controlled.

The overall effectiveness of any fumigant is determined by the dosage delivered to the pest and is a function of the concentration and the time of exposure. This is referred to as the *CT factor* (concentration/time factor). Other important factors that bear heavily on the success

1. Great Lakes Chemical Corporation, Fresno, CA.

or failure of fumigation are soil temperature, soil moisture, soil preparation, organic-matter content, application method, and surface seal.

Optimum soil temperature for application of most soil fumigants is between 65° and 75°F at a depth of 6 inches. Low soil temperature slows volatilization, which results in less adequate concentration, and therefore poor control. Low soil temperature also allows the fumigant to remain in the soil for long periods and may result in phytotoxicity to the next crop planted. If soil temperatures are too high, the fumigant may diffuse too rapidly or escape before providing adequate concentration for good control.

Adequate soil moisture is necessary to achieve good weed control by fumigation. Moisture softens weed seed coats to facilitate penetration of the fumigant. It is also necessary for proper fumigant diffusion. Too much water in the soil will retard diffusion while too little will allow the fumigant to diffuse too rapidly. Coarse-textured soils (sands) can be fumigated at higher moisture levels than fine-textured soils (clays). Soil moisture should be in the range of 15–75% of field capacity depending on soil type. Proper moisture content can be determined by squeezing a handful of soil into a ball. If it will not form a ball, it is too dry. If the ball will not break apart easily when touched with a finger, it is too wet. If moisture can be squeezed from the ball, it is also too wet.

Soils to be fumigated should be in good tilth, free of large clods which may protect weed seeds from adequate exposure to the fumigant or prevent a good seal. Organic matter should be well decomposed before treatment. Undecayed plant material is not penetrated readily, and soils high in organic content absorb fumigant, necessitating higher dosages. Undecomposed crop residue can also form chimneys through which fumigants may escape from the soil surface.

Most fumigants are applied by chisel injections with chisels spaced 8–12 inches apart to a depth of 6–10 inches. Metham, however, may also be applied through sprinkler and drip irrigation systems.

Once placed in the soil, a seal must be formed on the soil surface in order to retain fumigant vapors. The type of sealing will vary with the volatility of the chemical being used. Usual methods include the use of water seals, plastic covers, or packing the soil surface with rollers or drags. Due to its high volatility, methyl bromide must be sealed by plastic covers. Plastic seals may also be used on the less volatile fumigants to increase herbicidal activity, especially if the fumigant is injected near the surface of the soil.

Although not usually used as a herbicide, 1,3-D may be used for control of underground vegetative portions of perennial weeds such as field bindweed. It is not generally effective on weed seeds. Another fumigant, chloropicrin, is toxic to most weeds, but it is mostly used as a soil fungicide either alone or in combination with methyl bromide.

Metham can be applied in water as a sprinkling can drench. It can

Figure 8. Application of methyl bromide and/or chloropicrin, in which the fumigants are injected into the soil and immediately covered with polyethylene. Photo courtesy E.A. Kurtz.

be injected or applied as a soil drench through hose proportioners or through irrigation systems. It is registered for weed control in both ornamentals and crop plantings. To treat soil, inject or apply metham to the soil surface in sufficient water to drench the soil. The material should be evenly distributed and then the soil packed and a water seal applied. A gas-tight plastic seal can be used if water is not applied. If injected, a water seal is not necessary, but better results can be expected if a seal is used. After application, soil should not be disturbed for three to four days; it should then be cultivated. Three weeks or more should be allowed between treatment and planting, depending on soil and weather conditions, to avoid damage to the subsequent crop.

Dazomet is a granular material which is applied to the soil surface and sealed with a water drench. Because it is not immediately water soluble, it cannot be applied as a drench or through irrigation systems. After an exposure period of three to four days, it should be aerated for two weeks before planting or until the odor of the fumigant is no longer present. If there is doubt about completeness of aeration of either product, a simple germination test can be used.

Methyl bromide may be applied either by soil injection or as a topical application. In either case, it must be covered by a polyethylene cover to prevent loss to the atmosphere. The topical application or "raised-tarp" method is accomplished by first covering the surface of the soil with plastic tarp and sealing all edges by burying them. The cover must be held above the soil surface 4–6 inches. This can be done by using crumpled fertilizer bags, burlap bags stuffed with straw, inverted flower pots, or wooden supports. Then after the cover is in place, methyl bromide is injected under the cover into an evaporating pan. The cover should remain in place for 24–48 hours after application.

Methyl bromide is applied to large areas by means of tractor-drawn applicators which automatically inject the fumigant, lay down the polyethylene sheets, and seal them together by gluing (fig. 8). Following the exposure period, the cover is removed to aerate the soil. Seeding may be done after seven days, but aeration should continue for 14 days before setting out vegetative material.

ULTRA-LOW-VOLUME APPLICATION

by Harold M. Kempen[1]

The advantage of ultra-low-volume (ULV) spraying is lower cost because less water is needed to distribute the herbicide. When applying herbicides by airplane, cost is greater as volumes increase from 1 to 3 gal/A, volumes normally used to apply 2,4-D in cereals, to 10 gal/A for most other herbicides. If water is distant, cost escalates rapidly. Helicopters, which settle upon the nurse truck, can apply rates of 50 gal/A with acceptable cost in certain situations.

Introduction of the rotary atomizer (often called spinning disc) to commercial agriculture in 1977 has resulted in major research thrusts on ultra-low-volume ground application. This research has concentrated primarily on controlled droplet application or 'CDA.'

CDA implies that all droplets delivered by the atomizer are of uniform size. The first commercial units did come close to doing that, producing mostly 250-micron-diameter droplets. (One hundred microns is about the diameter of a human hair.) The tractor-operated units did not produce droplets as uniformly, but the spectrum of droplet size was much narrower than when hydraulic conventional nozzle orifices (such as 8002s) were used.

The rationale for wanting uniform droplet size is that more area can be covered if all droplets are equally sized. Therefore, lower volumes of uniform droplets can provide equal coverage of plants as higher volumes would with conventional equipment.

Research on the engineering aspects of CDA applicators has continued since the introduction of commercial models. Such results are reflected in manufacturers' operating instructions as well as in the upgraded equipment itself. Research on field usage of ultra-low-volume applications has shown that ULV is a feasible, but often not better, substitute for conventional spraying. Uniformity of application is no problem if guidelines on flow-rates, atomizer speeds, spacing, etc., are followed. Some drawbacks with CDA tractor-mounted systems presently exist, such as monitoring of flow rates and atomizer speeds. Problems

1. University of California Cooperative Extension, Kern County, CA.

associated with using more highly concentrated spray solutions need consideration by users. Using the CDA systems is more complex and costly. It also restricts the user to ULV application only.

Field-usage evaluations have shown that foliar, systemic herbicides, which translocate well in plants (e.g., glyphosate), perform better at ULV 3–5 gal/A than at 30–100 gal/A through conventional nozzles. Residual herbicides such as simazine, can be applied equally well. Foliar-contact herbicides such as bentazon, oxyfluorfen, and acifluorfen require thorough weed coverage and therefore must be applied in very small droplets to ensure coverage. While the ULV rotary atomizers are capable of doing that, drift and swath displacement become more of a problem, being greater with the finest droplets produced by such equipment than from conventional 8001 spray tips. When the smallest droplets are used, winds of about 5 mph or more would induce considerable displacement, an amount that would be unacceptable in smaller fields.

A major shortcoming of CDA units in field usage can be canopy penetration. Large weeds will intercept spray when they move laterally off of the atomizer, and if too large, will not permit penetration. Of course, if emerged weeds are sprayed when they are small, no problems with CDA units occur.

In California, early commercial usage of CDAs was primarily in orchards. After a decade, use continues to be primarily in orchards, and especially where wind is not common. With better use of fine screens to prevent nozzle plugging of 8001 spray tips, growers have been able to use regular boom setups as well. This permits applications with small four-wheel high flotation all-terrain vehicles (ATV) so that field entry can occur in the winter when soils are wet, to enable treatment of small weeds. Such ATV equipment setups can also be used for spot-treatment, field end sprays, and general farm use. Its use (with rotary atomizers) for row crops is limited due to spray band limitations. Additionally, the use of ULV or low volume applications are not permitted by many herbicide labels.

Considerable research was done on computer-monitored injection of formulated pesticide concentrates into sprayers, electrostatic applicators, or applicators using air as a carrier instead of water. Regulatory requirements by state and federal agencies have largely stopped such research. But private research on conventional hydraulic nozzles has improved application technology to where water volumes and pressures needed to apply herbicides have been reduced.

Pedestrian units are used on roadsides, ditches, around transformers, on farmsteads, small-acreage farms, forests, range sites, and steep-terrain areas. These units apply about 1 gallon of water diluent per acre in one or two 48-inch circles and therefore are limited to small areas of application. Wettable-powder formulations do not flow adequately through some CDA units, but emulsifiable and water-soluble formulations do.

Water-dispersible granules and flowable formulations usually require at least a 50 percent dilution with water.

REFERENCES

Akesson, N.B. et al. 1984. Spray applications technology. California Weed Conference pp. 17–46.
Ambach, R.M. and R. Ashford. 1982. Effects of variations in drop makeup of the phytotoxicity of glyphosate. Weed Science 30:221-224.
Kempen, H.M. 1981. Evaluation of CDA for use in annual and perennial California crops. Abstracts: Weed Science Society of America, Las Vegas, NV, pp. 74.
Merritt, C.R. and W.A. Taylor. 1978. Effects of volume rate and drop size on the retention of aqueous solution by Avena fatua L. Symposium on Controlled Droplet Application, pp. 12-13, April 1978. Monograph, British Crop Protection, 1978. pp. 22.
McWhorter, C.G. and M.R. Gebhardt. 1987. Methods of applying herbicides WSSA Monograph 4. Weed Science Society of America, Champaign, IL, p. 358.
Pearson, S.L., L.E. Bode and B.J. Butler. 1981. Characteristics of controlled droplet applications. No. Cent. Weed Cont. Conf. 36:1-2.

WICK/WIPER

by Dennis Stroud[1] and Harold M. Kempen[2]

History and Philosophy

The application of herbicides using a wick/wiper applicator was devised in the mid-1950s for applying phenoxy herbicides in areas where spray drift could cause injury to adjacent vegetation.

In the late 1970s, the use of wick/wiper applicators again became a popular tool for weed control. Renewed interest for these applicators came about because of their usefulness in applying glyphosate, a nonselective, foliar-applied, translocated herbicide.

The process is very simple. The effectiveness of a wick or wiper applicator relies on the height differential between the weed and the desirable vegetation (fig. 9). By adjusting the height of the applicator properly, it is possible to wipe the herbicide on the leaf surface of the weed and, because of the crop's lesser height, avoid contact with it. For most uses, it is recommended that a height differential between the weed and the desirable vegetation be present prior to application. This height differential will allow for maximum results and minimal damage to non-target plants.

When using a wick/wiper applicator, the amount of actual herbicide solution applied per acre can be 0.25–0.50 gal/A. This ultra-low-volume application is effective due to the high concentration of the solution being applied. In most instances, a 25–50 percent herbicide solution is used. These highly concentrated solutions are wiped over the weeds extending above the crop area. The systemic action of the herbi-

1. *Barber-Rowland Inc., Geyserville, CA.* 2. *University of California Cooperative Extension, Kern County, CA.*

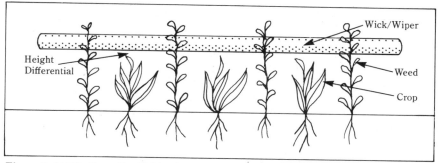

Figure 9. Application of herbicides through a wick/wiper requires a sufficient height differential between crop and weed to allow the herbicide to contact the weed without damaging the crop.

cides used for these applications enables this small amount of highly concentrated herbicide solution to be translocated throughout the weed. Once the herbicide has been translocated in the weed, death or suppression occurs. It is often recommended that this type of application be made over the area two times in opposite directions to allow for maximum coverage.

A major disadvantage of relying on wick/wiper applicators is that extreme competition to the crop from the weeds has usually already occurred, which makes the application a "salvage" operation and not a good weed management technique. Also, usage is crop-specific and must be described on the product label in order to be legally used. Some crops, especially vegetables and sugar beets, are too sensitive to herbicides such as glyphosate to permit usage.

Equipment

The equipment used for this type of application is varied. The only component that the different types of equipment have in common is some sort of absorptive material to act as the wick/wiper surface, which is generally made up of multi-filament, synthetic rope, sponge, paint-roller covers, carpet, burlap, etc. They all "wick" (or absorb) the herbicide solution and "wipe" it on the weed.

Wick and wiper applicators come in all shapes and sizes. Landscape-gardeners most commonly use a hand-held applicator. When used in row-crops, they are mounted on tractors; for ditchbanks, they can be mounted on trucks. Although the size of these applicators varies, their construction is similar. The majority use PVC pipe as the reservoir of the system. Attached to this reservoir is the wick/wiper surface. Some systems are pressurized to ensure even flow. Those units that are not pressurized rely on gravity. In all types, it is essential that the wiping surface be constantly saturated with herbicide solution to ensure maximum weed control.

Costs

The cost of the equipment can vary greatly, depending upon the implement used. A hand-held wick/wiper is relatively inexpensive, but large tractor-mounted units can be considerable investments.

The chemical cost per treated acre will vary greatly depending on the density of the weed population.

Potential Problems and Precautions

A major problem with the use of these systems is the dripping of excess herbicide due to the oversaturation of the wiping surface. The dripping solution contacting the desirable vegetation can cause severe injury. Good equipment and its proper adjustments can minimize this problem.

The ground speed of the tractor-truck-mounted wick/wiper should not exceed 5 miles per hour. In areas of higher weed density, a slower speed should be used to allow adequate coverage and proper feeding of the solution to keep the wick saturated.

It is especially important to keep the wick/wiper clean and free of foreign matter (e.g., dirt, dust, organic matter, etc.) which can reduce effectiveness.

Weed control obtained by this method is acceptable but often not as good as conventional spraying. In most instances, retreatment is necessary.

REFERENCES

Dale, J.E. 1978. *The rope-wick applicator—a new method of applying glyphosate. Proceedings Southern Weed Science Society* 31:332.
Derting, C.W. 1987. *Methods of applying herbicides, WSSA Monograph 4. Weed Science Society of America, Champaign, IL.*

IRRIGATION

by Paul J. Carey[1] and Warren E. Bendixen[2]

The application of herbicides through irrigation systems (often referred to as chemigation) has increased during the last 15 years in surface (flood, furrow, and basin), drip, and sprinkler-irrigation systems.

1. *Formerly Stauffer Chemical Company, Fresno, CA.* 2. *University of California Cooperative Extension, Santa Barbara County, CA.*

The advantages of this method of herbicide application are:
- Increased effectiveness
- Uniform application
- Immediate incorporation and activation
- Timely applications
- Economical
- Maximum use of irrigation systems

Application of herbicides requires good water management. The irrigation system should be designed to apply the water and incorporate the herbicide uniformly.

Initially, there was concern about the uniformity of herbicide applications through irrigation systems. However, it has been demonstrated that herbicides can be applied through irrigation systems as uniformly as with other methods. Ground-sprayer equipment has a coefficient of uniformity of 60–90 percent; properly designed surface-irrigation systems, 70–90 percent; and sprinkler-irrigation systems, 75–95 percent.

Irrigation systems should be checked before applying the herbicides to assure a uniform application. Before herbicides are injected into sprinkler systems, the systems should be checked for uniform pressure throughout the pipeline, sprinkler-head uniformity and size of orifice, and leaky gaskets and holes in the pipeline. In surface-irrigation systems, efficiency requires level fields, and, in furrow-irrigated fields, uniform bed configuration.

This technique has the advantage of incorporating herbicides as they are applied. Downward and lateral movement is influenced by the chemical properties of the herbicide, the amount of organic matter in the soil, the amount and type of clay, and the amount of water applied.

The placement of the herbicide, in the case of a preemergence application, should coincide with the depth of the germinating weeds. Most small-seeded weeds germinate in the upper 2 inches of the soil.

Some herbicides have greater soil mobility than others. The chemical properties of the herbicide that influence movement include water solubility, volatility, and the absorption capacity of the clay and organic matter. To obtain the best herbicide effectiveness, the correct amount of water should be applied for each herbicide, the intended use, and soil type. The following herbicides have shown excellent results but require different water-management practices: metham, metribuzin, and EPTC. These move easily through the soil profile with water solution and should be applied in small amounts of water. Ethalfluralin and oryzalin are strongly absorbed, and the amount of water applied has less influence on their movement. The movements of alachlor, metolachlor, chlorpropham, and pronamide are intermediate compared to those of the other herbicides.

This technique has the advantage of lower application costs, especially when timed to coincide with irrigation. Otherwise, the cost is

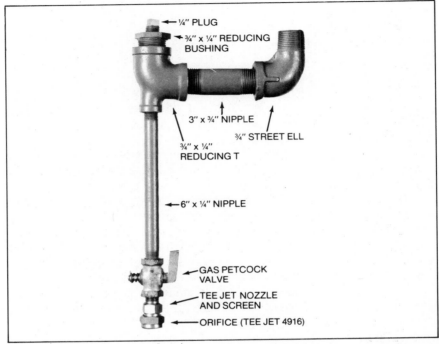

Figure 10. Typical constant-head siphon device to be attached to 5- or 30-gallon drums of herbicide formulations to ensure uniform application through an irrigation system.

influenced by the cost of water and the irrigation expenses, which are one-half those typically for conventional spraying and mechanical incorporation.

The following problems associated with this method should be considered before proceeding:

- Poorly designed or maintained irrigation systems should not be used for herbicide application.
- Most herbicides may require agitation in the nurse tank during the time of application.
- Variations in soil texture within the same field affect preemergent applications and herbicide movement and the weed control obtained.
- Both the size of the crop and the size of the weed influence postemergent herbicide applications.
- Some herbicides are volatile, and high temperatures and windy conditions can adversely affect their efficiency. This problem can be minimized by nighttime application.
- With surface-gravity systems, irrigation water containing herbicides must be confined to the treated area by keeping it in the field and using recirculation systems.

Application in Flood, Furrow, Border, or Basin Systems

In gravity-flow, surface-irrigation systems, a constant-head siphon device can ensure uniform application. Simple application devices that can be attached to any 5- or 30-gallon drums are available (fig. 10). Without a constant-flow device, uniform application cannot be achieved.

The length of time required for application can vary considerably from one irrigation to the next. The flow rate of the herbicide should be monitored throughout the irrigation cycle because it may change with variations in temperature. Herbicide application should be started as soon as the irrigation begins. When the herbicide is applied through a stand pipe, a vented tube should be attached to the flow meter carrying the material to the main irrigation pipeline.

An example of a typical 12-hour application follows:

$$\frac{\text{Pt of herbicide per acre} \times (\text{ml per gal} \div \text{pt per gal}) \times \text{acres}}{\text{minutes for irrigation}} = \text{ml per minute}$$

Example: 10 acres of sugar beets are to be treated in a 12-hour irrigation at 3 pounds of active ingredient (3½ pints of a 7 pound per gallon EC) per acre.

$$\frac{3.5 \times (3785 \div 8) \times 10 \text{ acres}}{720} = 23 \text{ ml per minute}$$

By referring to the flow rate chart on the manufacturer's label, the correct orifice size for this example can be determined. The indicated orifice size for this flow rate is 0.022. The actual flow rate in the field may vary, and the correct orifice must be determined by actual measurement because the flow rate of a given herbicide may also vary with temperature. The flow rate should be rechecked occasionally during application.

Application in Sprinkler-irrigation Systems

The simplest injection system consists of adapting a hose from the herbicide tank with an orifice to the suction side of a centrifugal pump. The amount of material drawn into the water line during irrigation is determined by the orifice size. If it is necessary to inject into pressurized irrigation pipelines, there are several types of injector pumps that can be adapted to the irrigation system.

A portable injector system can be attached to pressure irrigation lines using pressurized herbicide tanks and carbon dioxide cylinders. A coupler with an orifice (TeeJet 4916 series) should be installed between the herbicide tank and the pipeline. Maintaining a higher pressure (5 psi) in the herbicide tank forces the herbicide into the irrigation line.

To apply the herbicide through a sprinkler system, it is essential to:

- Determine the acres irrigated during a set and multiply this by the required chemical rate to find total gallons of chemical.
- Determine the time required to apply the correct amount of water.
- Divide the total gallons of either formulated or diluted chemical by the set time to find the injection rate.
- Adjust the injection pump or pressure to deliver the calculated rate.

An example of a typical sprinkler application follows:

- 10 acres to be treated with 3 pounds of active ingredient
- (3½ pints of a 7-pound-per-gallon EC) per acre
- 10 acres × 3½ pints = 35 pints formulated herbicide
- 35 pints ÷ 12-hour irrigation = 2.9 pints per hour

The 35 pints of formulated product should be placed in the herbicide tank and the injector pump set to deliver 2.9 pints/hour.

When herbicide wettable powders are used through sprinkler systems, they must be mixed with water and the diluted formulation injected in the same manner as above.

Other items to consider in the application of herbicides through sprinkler systems are:

- Allow the sprinkler system to operate with clean water for a period of time to flush lines and individual nozzles prior to the injection of the herbicide.
- Inject the herbicide at the proper period during the irrigation cycle according to labeled instructions.
- Allow the sprinkler system to operate for a period of time after the herbicide has been injected to flush (clean) the lines and nozzles prior to turning the system off.

Safety Equipment

Safety-check or vacuum-relief valves are essential to prevent back flows into the main water source. Local regulations should be observed for the specific equipment required. Solenoid valves or water-pressure valves should be installed so that the injection equipment stops when the irrigation water stops.

REFERENCES

Ogg, Alex and Clarence Dowler. 1987. Methods of applying herbicides, WSSA Monograph 4. Weed Science Society of America, Champaign, IL.

AIRCRAFT

by Norman B. Akesson[1] and Stanley V. Walton, Jr.[2]

Agricultural aircraft provide a wide range of services which have become indispensable to the highly mechanized agriculture in California and in the United States in general. The earliest use of aircraft was for spreading insecticides as dusts on cotton in the southeastern United States. World War I military aircraft (Curtis JN6) were adapted to this work by simply placing a dust hopper in the rear cockpit of the two-seat "Jenny."

While considerable insecticide dust application acreage was developed in the 1930s, and by 1935 some liquid spraying was done in California, the development of herbicide application by aircraft had to wait for (1) development of highly effective synthetic herbicides such as the phenoxy acetic acids and (2) economically productive aircraft and reliable spray distribution systems. Herbicide dusts enjoyed a brief period of use, but due to the very high drift hazard associated with small dust particles (90% customarily less than 20 microns diameter), the use of herbicide dust formulations quickly came under strict regulation and in some cases, such as that of the phenoxy herbicides, a prompt ban was imposed circa 1947 by the Civil Aviation Administration (now the Federal Aviation Administration).

Herbicides, therefore, have been largely formulated and applied as water-base sprays with some minor use of large-granular-type materials (1–2 mm diameter). For example, the forms of materials applied by air and ground equipment in the United States in 1978 were distributed as follows:

Sprays	Granulars	Fertilizers	Baits & seeds	Dusts
78%	7%	6%	5%	4%

The specific crops and percentage of each treated by aircraft were:

	Cotton	Rice	Wheat	Vegetables	Corn	Soybeans	Sorghum
Acres (mil)	46,500	14,000	18,000	8700	11,800	8500	8800
Flight hrs (thou)	645	316	265	174	166	163	109
% of total crop treated by air	60	95	15	40	10	10	40

and the type of pesticide or application as a percent of total aircraft use (includes fertilizer and seeding operations) was:

Insecticide	Herbicide	Fertilizer	Fungicide	Seed	Defoliant
54%	22%	11%	7%	4%	4%

1. University of California, Davis, CA. 2. Farm Air Flying Service, Inc., El Macero, CA.

The total number of aircraft in use for agriculture in the United States moved from around 4000 in the 1950s to 5000 in the 1960s followed by a rapid rise in the 1970s to around 8600 total aircraft. The farm recession of the early 1980s restricted further growth with a peak of around 9000 aircraft in 1980 which has changed only slightly during the mid 1980s. In California there are about 1400 agricultural aircraft, including those used part-time for agriculture and for other activities. Texas has an equal number, while the next closest—Arkansas—has about half of this number. Fixed-wing aircraft with a load capacity of 1400–2000 lb are most common among the types used, which range from 1000-to-3500-lb load capability.

Rotary-wing (helicopter) aircraft were used nationwide on something under 10% of the treated acres in 1978. California helicopter use is estimated at approximately this same level, although it may have increased with insecticides and fungicides in the mid-1980s.

The primary advantages of aircraft over ground equipment lie in their ability to cover large areas in a short time, flying over tall crops and irrigation structures and providing a competitive cost structure. Aircraft are another element in the rapid mechanization of agricultural production which now finds one production agricultural worker providing food and fiber for some 50 others in the United States. Aircraft have contributed to this shift in the working force and have helped to make possible the increased production per acre that the use of pesticides and fertilizers have occasioned throughout the world.

Herbicide Dispersal Equipment

The hopper for granular and dust application is located above a slide gate which meters the flow of materials into the ramair spreader. Air at 125–150 mph from the propeller slipstream enters the spreader from the front and picks up the materials, discharging them at the left. The vanes in the spreader deflect the granules outward into the vortex created by the aircraft wing, which helps to spread the granules over a swath approximately equal to the wingspan of the aircraft. Figure 11 shows a typical pattern of granules spread by a ramair device mounted on a Cessna AgWagon aircraft. This graph was produced from data taken from tests made by flying aircraft over a fixed area and measuring the granules' distribution.

The vertical scale at the left shows the collection rate in lb/A. The useful swath width is primarily a function of the aircraft wingspan and gross weight, increasing as weight and wingspan are increased. The flight height of the aircraft will also affect the useful swath, but practical considerations limit the height to 20–30 feet, and little additional swath width can be gained by flying any higher than this. As the rate of discharge through the spreader is increased, the pattern tends to concentrate at

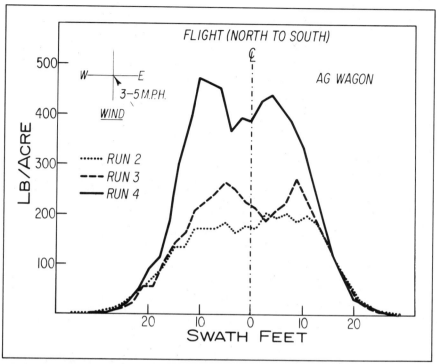

Figure 11. Typical pattern of a granular application involving the use of a ramair device on a Cessna AgWagon.

the center. In order to obtain a relatively uniform pattern across a field, the swaths for successive passes must be carefully matched by using an optimum flagged swath width and careful flagging, usually from both sides of the field being treated.

Liquid spray applications of herbicides are the most widely used form and provide flexibility in application rates, both by altering the concentration in the spray solution as well as the total volume applied. In a typical spray system mounted on fixed-wing aircraft, the hopper or tank is located centrally over the wing, its capacity ranging from 200 to as much as 500 gallons, depending on the size of the aircraft. The spray pump is powered by a windmill, and its discharge is controlled by a valve, which not only controls the flow to the spray boom but also directs it through a venturi device when the boom is shut off. This provides a vacuum on the boom which aids in closing the diaphragm check valves at each nozzle and reduces the losses from dripping or leaking nozzles during turns and while ferrying.

Rotary-wing aircraft are usually operated at speeds much lower than fixed wing or 60–70 mph compared with 100–120 mph. At the lower

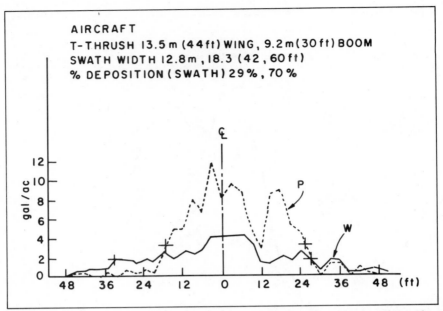

Figure 12. Typical pattern of a liquid application involving a fixed-wing aircraft, a turbo-powered Thrush.

speed the ramair spreader will not function adequately and thus other devices must be used to obtain the swath spread. Rotary disc spreaders similar to the old end-gate seeders on ground applicators may be used. These may be an integral part of the helicopter or may be a separate hopper-spreader device slung by cable from the helicopter. The rotary spreaders have also been used on fixed-wing aircraft but have the disadvantage of requiring a powered drive, either windmill, electric, or hydraulic. Patterns from these devices are equal to or better than the ramair types, but initial cost and maintenance requirements have prevented widespread adoption of these on fixed-wing aircraft.

Loading may also be accomplished by a 'quick-couple' connection at either end of the spray boom or by pouring in from the top opening in the hopper. The boom-and-nozzle distribution system is attached to the wing structure. Controls in the cockpit include windmill brake and a boom control valve. A 'quick-dump' gate in the bottom of the hopper is provided and controlled from the cockpit in an emergency. Rotary wing aircraft systems are typically similar to those for fixed-wing aircraft. However, power for the spray pump comes from electric or hydraulic motors.

Figure 12 shows a typical spray pattern for a fixed-wing aircraft, a turbine-powered Thrush, which has a 44-foot wingspan and a 30-foot boom length and which is operated at 115 mph. The lower scale shows the swath width, and the vertical scale shows gal/A applied. Two curves are shown identified as P (dashed lines) and W (solid line). These indicate two different drop sizes, the P at about 1200 microns, a very large, low-drift-type spray, and W at around 500 microns for better plant coverage. While the larger-drop-size spray P tends to reduce the amount of material available to drift, (i.e. the percentage by volume of drops less than 122 microns), the total amount of active chemical available to drift is small, but the loss in biological efficacy can be serious due to poor coverage of the target plants. Also the effect on the usable flagged swath width is serious, reducing the swath from 60 feet for the smaller-drop-size spray to 42 feet for the larger one. The percentage recovered—i.e., the amount of the released spray collected in the swath—is increased with the large drops from 30% to 70%. But this also intensifies the spray pattern variability and reduces swath overlap which is desirable in smoothing out the spray pattern.

The alteration in drop size as shown in figure 12 is best obtained by using different type nozzles—for example, straight jet stream orifices for large drops and use of whirl plates such as numbers 56, 46, 45, etc., placed back of the orifice plates for smaller-drop-size spray. Increasing the pressure at the nozzles and directing the discharge at sharper angles to the air stream, i.e. directly across, will also make smaller drop size sprays. Yet another technique is that of using certain water-soluble polymer spray additives, but these have limited capabilities for drift-loss control and changing nozzles and angle to the air stream offers the best means to change drop size.

Rotary-wing aircraft, operating at lower air speeds, have less ability to alter drop size by changing nozzle angle to the air stream. Thus, changing nozzle whirl plates offers the best means to change drop size, with less change in size occurring as the pressure is raised or lowered. It should be noted that when selecting nozzles for the aircraft the choice of drop size needs to be made first, and then the number of nozzles and flow rate along with swath width are chosen in order to provide the gal/A coverage desired.

The pattern of spray coverage laid down by the aircraft is shown in figure 13. Here the flagged swath width of the spray release is shown at far left. A typical crosswind is shown at 3–5 mph which displaces the swath downwind and also tends to cause (not shown) a higher peak on the upwind side of the spray pattern. The released spray drop size range was from 30 to 600 microns with a volume median size (50% above and 50% by volume above and below this size) of around 350 microns. The flagged swath tends to collect only drops above 200 microns diameter, but the extended or displaced swath collects drops from around 100 to 200 microns. The importance of using this extended swath needs emphasis. The extended swath provides much needed coverage provided by smaller spray drops and helps to fill in the normal peaks and valleys

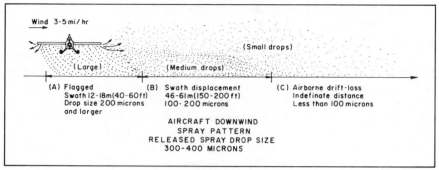

Figure 13. Effect of drop size and wind conditions on aircraft swath displacement.

of the aircraft pattern. This extended swath will go downwind from the flagged swath to 200 or more feet, depending on drop size, flight height, and strength of the crosswind. But it is important to remember that the largest portion of the spray will fall in the flagged and extended swath with the true drift-loss portion (under 100 microns) being only that which goes into the air and which can be carried for considerable distances downwind.

In order to obtain a measure of the amounts collected in the flagged and extended swaths, as well as the drift losses downwind, spray-recovery graphs such as those in figure 14 are constructed.

Here the spray was collected on plastic sheets laid under the aircraft and downwind to 660 feet and beyond. Five different deposit curves are shown, flown under similar weather conditions and at similar heights. The topmost curve A is for a helicopter and microfoil boom applying a very-large-drop-size spray of nearly all one constant size. This gives a very high recovery in the 50-foot swath of 90%, with 99% of the spray accounted for in a distance of 164 feet downwind. But this drop size of 900–1200 microns volume median diameter (vmd) gives very poor plant coverage and should only be used with high-potency, high-risk herbicides such as phenoxys, propanil, paraquat, and other restricted herbicides. Curve B is for a fixed-wing aircraft with ⁶⁄₆₄-in. orifice straight jets for a 900–1000 micron vmd. Recovery is not quite as high for the microfoil, but 96% is recovered in the extended swath to 164 feet. Similarly, with this system poor plant coverage occurs, and use should be limited to restricted herbicides.

When the #46 whirl plate is used with the cone nozzle directed with the air stream, a drop size of around 450 microns vmd results. The recovery curve C shows 75% caught in the flagged swath, and a total of 94% in the flagged and extended swath or out to 164 feet. At a 330-foot distance, 95.6% is recovered and 97.2% out to 660 feet. Curve D is for a fixed-wing aircraft applying drops of around 200 microns vmd, customarily used for insecticides, but giving good plant coverage and useful

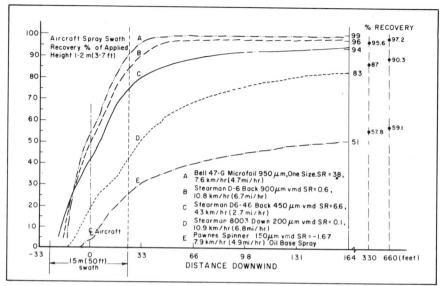

Figure 14. Effects of various aircraft and nozzle types and sizes on swath displacement under similar weather conditions.

for herbicides where no potential hazard exists. The recovery in the flagged swath now drops to around 40%, with 83% collected out to 164 feet, 87% at 330 feet, and 90.3% at 660 feet downwind. The remainder of the spray beyond 660 feet is the airborne drift loss and is dispersed in the atmosphere. Under low wind and temperature inversion (warm overhead air) this airborne spray can be transported for many miles downwind.

The final curve E is used for insecticides and fungicides and results in significant quantities of spray being carried out of the treatment area. As long as the spray is not highly toxic, or where no potential downwind damages are likely to occur, the use of fine drop size sprays of 150 microns vmd are highly successful particularly with nonvolatile oil carriers such as those with pyrethroid sprays.

These very small drop sizes have a remarkable biological magnification effect, and although the tests would show that 25–40% of the spray is lost out of the treatment area, the remaining spray has tremendous covering and contact capabilities. However, they are not suitable for even the most innocuous herbicides where damage to nontarget plantings must be of first consideration.

In summary, aircraft use for applying herbicides provides a rapid, accurate, and cost-effective procedure. Significant care must be exercised to keep drop size large, not to apply with wind drift toward a known susceptible planting, and to avoid applications of restricted herbicides under temperature-inversion-type weather. A great variation in drop size is possible and is the most important consideration when setting out to do the specific job. Nozzle manufacturers and university and federal research teams are currently providing much-needed information on drop-size capabilities and proper nozzles to be used under differing conditions. Aircraft operators have field-proven information available to them to enable safe and highly effective herbicide applications by air.

ADDITIONAL READING

Akesson, N.B., W.E. Yates, R.W. Brazelton and E.T. Natwick, 1983. *Laboratory and field studies on vegetable oil-base spray applications, ASAE Paper 83-1510, St. Joseph, MI.*

Akesson, N.B. and W.E. Yates, 1984. *Physical parameters affecting aircraft spray applications. Am. Chem. Soc. Symposium Series #238, Washington, D.C.*

Akesson, N.B. and W.E. Yates, 1976. *The use of aircraft in agriculture, FAO Manual #94, Agr. Engr. Dept., Univ. of Calif., Davis.*

Akesson, N.B. and W.E. Yates, 1979. *Pesticide application equipment and techniques, FAO Agr. Services Bull. 38, Agr. Engr. Dept., Univ. of Calif., Davis.*

Tayler, J.E., et al. 1984. *Professional standards for aerial application of pesticides in California, Vols. 1–2, Technical Appendix, Calif. Agr. Aircraft Assoc., Inc., Sacramento.*

Ware, G.W., et al. 1983. *Reducing pesticide application drift losses, Coop. Ext. Ser., Univ. of Ariz., Tucson.*

Yates, W.E., R.E. Cowden and N.B. Akesson, 1983. *Nozzle orientation, air speed and spray formulation effects on drop size spectrums. Trans. ASAE 26(6):1638–43, St. Joseph, MI.*

AQUATIC

by Nathan Dechoretz[1]

The selection of a proper aquatic herbicide and its formulation is influenced by many factors, notably the growth habits of weeds and the location, nature, and use of the aquatic site. Generally, aquatic herbicides are applied in liquid or granular form. Liquid formulations are applied as solutions, suspensions, or emulsions. The various types of granules available are: (1) granulated pure chemical such as crystalline copper sulfate, (2) granules or large-size pellets of clay and other materials impregnated with the herbicide, and (3) controlled-release granules or pellets designed to free the active material in the desired amounts over an extended period of time.

Once the appropriate herbicide and formulation are selected, the application technique utilized will very often determine whether or not the chemical will be effective in controlling the weeds. Proper application technique depends upon several factors, all of which should be considered when deciding how to solve a particular problem. These factors include the nature of the herbicide, type of weed, nature of the area to be treated, the area surrounding the application site, and stage

1. *California Department of Food and Agriculture, Sacramento, CA.*

of plant growth at time of application. The following brief discussion summarizes various application techniques in current use and draws attention to the advantages and disadvantages associated with each of them. Since the techniques used in irrigation canals are generally quite different from those used in static or limited-flow systems, they will be discussed separately.

Flowing Water Systems

Acrolein, copper sulfate, and the dimethyl-alkylamine salt of endothall are the only herbicides presently recommended for aquatic weed control in irrigation canals. These herbicides are usually introduced below the water surface at a given site on the canal. The duration of the herbicide application depends on the phytotoxicity of the chemical, the volume of water flow, the biomass of weeds present, water quality, and water temperature. The type of equipment required depends on the nature of the compound and the amount of material to be applied. Generally, endothall is pumped into the canal from holding tanks; however, any system, including gravity flow, that maintains the desired application rate can be used.

Acrolein, a highly volatile and reactive compound (a lachrymator) has been used successfully for weed control in irrigation systems since 1960. Special precautions should be taken when applying this material. Acrolein is injected into the water from closed tanks held under constant pressure by nitrogen gas. The flow rate is metered to maintain the desired application rate.

During the last 50 years copper sulfate has been used almost exclusively for control of algae in water. The techniques employed to apply the copper crystals to flowing water are quite diverse. In large canals with high volumes of water flow, large quantities of copper sulfate may be applied by the 'slug' method. This simple treatment is made by backing a dump truck or similar device up to the application site and applying the algicide en masse.

Aerial applications of copper sulfate to large conveyance systems such as the California Aqueduct have proven to be very efficient and economical. This method permits treatment of large sections of canal in a relatively short period of time. If the canal meanders appreciably, however, the limits on aircraft maneuverability may prohibit use of this method.

Another common technique is to place the copper crystals in a cloth bag and suspend the bag in the canal until the copper sulfate crystals have dissolved. The bags are usually suspended from a structure that crosses the canal, such as a foot bridge. This simple method can be very effective when the algicide is applied at a number of locations along small canals.

At times, a constant application of copper sulfate, not exceeding 1.0 ppm of copper ion, is applied for extended periods in order to provide adequate control of algae. This is usually the case in canals which supply water for human consumption. Under these conditions, the suspended bag and slug method described previously are generally unacceptable. Various types of automatic intermittent or continuous feeding devices are available and have been tested and proven to be very effective for these situations.

Static Water Systems

Static water is usually defined as water in ponds, lakes, or reservoirs in which comparatively little or no inflow or outflow occurs. Sloughs and drains are generally thought of as flowing systems; however, the amount of flow in these systems is often very limited. Weed-control practices in sloughs and drains are similar to those used in static water, and they are included in this section.

In static or limited-flow situations, herbicides are usually applied over the surface of the water or injected at various depths below the water surface. Water-surface applications are almost always recommended for control of immersed or floating weeds. Liquid formulations can be applied (1) by aircraft, (2) with ground equipment for small ponds or when the weeds occur only around the margins and (3) by boat, using various types of booms or spray guns. Surface spraying is also utilized for submersed weed control; however, in water of considerable depth, other techniques are being developed which permit treating only that portion of the water column containing the weed growth.

Aquatic herbicides are frequently applied over the water surface in granular or pellet forms. These sink quickly to the bottom soil where much of the herbicide is released. In small areas the materials may be broadcast from a boat by hand or manually operated spreaders. For moderate-sized areas of several acres, the granules can be applied from a boat equipped with a motor-driven spreader. Coordinating boat speed with a uniform output of the spreader ensures a constant application rate. Aerial applications are usually more efficient when large areas are to be treated. Application rates are based on the surface area or volume of water to be treated.

There are several advantages in making surface applications with granular materials. Herbicide drift is often a problem when chemicals are sprayed in liquid form. This is especially true with aerial applications. This problem may be reduced significantly when good-quality, dust-free granular formulations are used. Furthermore, since water is not needed to apply granular materials, it is often possible to use less costly application equipment.

Disadvantages associated with the application of herbicides in granular form are: (1) large amounts of bulky materials are often needed, creating a handling and transportation problem; (2) application is seldom as uniform as it is with sprays; and (3) granular forms of a herbicide are usually more costly than the liquid.

The most common technique for subsurface application of liquid formulations of herbicides is injection through hoses or pipes that extend a short distance into the water. The herbicide solution is pumped to a boom mounted on the bow or stern of a boat. The boom is fitted with a series of short, vertically mounted hoses that trail in the water. In shallow water or in water of moderate depth, weed control usually depends upon good dispersion of the chemical in the water.

In many situations, treatment of the entire water column is not necessary or desirable. Some weeds may be controlled by treating only the bottom 1–3 feet of water. By using this method, the amount of herbicide and the cost of treatment can be lowered significantly. Consequently, the possibility of detrimental effects on the aquatic environment is also reduced. This technique is especially applicable where weed growth is present only near the soil-water interface. Bottom treatments are generally made by attaching several long, flexible hoses to a boat-mounted boom at intervals of 3–5 feet. The ends of the hoses are usually weighted so they remain near the bottom, and they are equipped with some type of nozzle. The length of hose and speed of the boat can be adjusted to obtain the desired depth of treatment.

The application of herbicides to water in special emulsion-type formulations has been found recently to be advantageous for control of some weeds. These relatively new formulations are called 'double invert' or 'bivert emulsion' systems. In contrast to a simple invert emulsion (droplets of water surrounded by oil), each spray droplet of a bivert emulsion has three layers: an inner oil core, middle water layer, and an outer oil layer. The toxicant may be included in the oil phase, the water phase, or both phases. The emulsions are injected below the water surface through suspended hoses as with the other injection equipment. Upon injection into the water, the droplets of mayonnaise-like emulsion descend through the water column, land on and adhere to the submersed vegetation. The herbicide is then released in close proximity to the plants. The major disadvantage inherent in this technique is the need for more sophisticated equipment than is necessary with other methods of application, and the fact that the various components must be mixed and applied with extreme care. All chemical components must be measured accurately, and the pressure and vacuum hoses on the machinery must be securely attached and air tight.

The use of herbicides has proven to be a valuable and necessary tool for managing various aquatic systems. For optimum results, the application technique selected can often be as important as selection of the proper herbicide.

PLANT DIAGNOSIS

by David W. Cudney[1]

Herbicides, applied properly, result in large increases in production efficiency. However, sometimes our best intentions go awry and herbicides end up in nontarget areas. Hence, it is important to be able to diagnose in the field whether problems encountered are indeed due to misuse of herbicides or to other causes.

The present section will be divided into two subsections. The first discusses the overall process of diagnosing plant symptoms in the field. It not only deals with herbicides but touches on other causes of plant maladies as well. The second subsection deals with the types of herbicide-related symptoms shown by plants and some individual herbicides or herbicide families which can cause these symptoms. The reader should note that references to herbicides or herbicide families in table 5 include some that may not be registered for use in California.

Plant Symptoms

Investigating possible herbicide-injury symptoms in the field is both a science and an art. The science involves gathering relevant information and making observations. The art enters when the observations and information are analyzed to arrive at a logical conclusion as to the cause or causes of a problem.

As one's experience increases in the field, the ability to diagnose problems should increase. This will not occur if one fails to keep an open mind, ask the right questions, and make good observations.

When asked to diagnose a problem in the field, whether one's expertise is in entomology, plant pathology, weed science, or any other discipline, the problem should be approached in three steps:
- Information gathering
- Taking careful notes of patterns in affected areas
- Carefully recording individual plant symptoms

Only after taking these steps will one have enough information to draw valid conclusions.

Information Gathering

Before entering a field, inquire about the cultural operations that have been performed in the field. What variety is planted in the field? How was the field prepared for this crop and how was it planted? What previous crops were grown in the field and what procedures and pesticides were used in them? What pesticides were applied to the existing crop

1. *University of California Cooperative Extension, Riverside, CA.*

and when? Have there been any unusual weather conditions which might account for the problem?

One can never have too much background information, and it is hazardous to try to diagnose a problem with too little information.

Field Pattern

Row Effects: Row effects can be due to herbicide residues but also can be due to machinery operations, poor planting practices, excesses or deficiencies of fertilizers, root pathogens spread by equipment, spray patterns, or problems associated with irrigation.

Scattered Abnormal Plants: The presences of scattered abnormal plants can be due to seed problems such as genetic mutations or insect-borne pathogens, or bird or rodent injury.

Irregular Patterns Related to Soil Differences: There are many possible reasons for irregular patterns, including herbicide residues. (Most residual herbicides will show greater injury in coarse-textured soils low in organic matter.) Other problems associated with irregular plant growth are variations in soil type, nutrition deficiencies, salinity, nematodes, soil compaction, excess or deficient soil moisture, and plant diseases associated with high soil moisture.

Irregular Patterns Not Related to Soil: Herbicide drift is a likely cause of this type of field pattern; however, other likely causes can be: faulty irrigation practices, soilborne insects, nematodes, fungi, foliar insect damage, insect-borne viruses, poor leveling and/or flooding, erosion of treated soil into an area, and mechanical injury.

Seasonal Effects: These types of effects are seen on a broad scale, affecting rather large areas. They include: frost damage, seasonal nutrient deficiencies, effects of high temperature, high wind, and atmospheric pollution.

Plant Pattern

The final step of the information-gathering process is to look at individual plant symptoms. These symptoms may appear not only at the tops of the plants but at the roots as well. It may also be necessary to examine various external as well as internal structures under some magnification. (A hand lens may be helpful.) Plant symptoms can include: stunting, chlorosis, necrosis, discoloration of internal tissue, discoloration and overgrowth resulting from surface injury, shortened internodes, and malformation of leaves and/or stems. Such symptoms can vary in severity depending on the extent of the injury. Sometimes, combinations of problems can cause symptoms that can make diagnosis very difficult. The following are general plant symptoms and some of the likely causes of these symptoms. It should be noted that herbicide injury is only one of many causes that can produce these symptoms.

Stunting: Herbicides which affect cell division and elongation often produce stunting. Other causes include: excess or deficiency of soil moisture, soil compaction, salinity, root diseases, insects, injury from other pesticides, nematodes, and root insects.

Chlorosis—Necrosis: Several herbicides can produce these symp-

TABLE 5. CLASSIFICATION OF PLANT SYMPTOMS ASSOCIATED WITH HERBICIDES

SYMPTOM	HERBICIDE GROUP	COMMENTS
CHLOROSIS: abnormal yellowing of green plant tissue; usually starts in the leaves, and as chlorosis increases, necrosis or death of the yellowed plant tissue can follow.	FOLIAR APPLIED: amitrole dalapon glyphosate DSMA, MSMA	Foliar-applied herbicides are absorbed and translocated through plant tissue and can cause destruction or interference with the photosynthetic mechanisms.
	SOIL APPLIED: triazines (atrazine, hexazinone, metribuzin, prometryn, simazine) substituted ureas (diuron, linuron, tebuthiuron) uracils (bromacil, terbacil) norflurazon	These soil-applied herbicides move into the plant with the transpiration stream and concentrate in the leaves where they affect the photosynthetic mechanisms of the plant and cause yellowing and eventually necrosis of the tissue.
STUNTING: a reduced growth in plants. Plants do not germinate or show poor growth. Often root systems will be dramatically reduced.	FOLIAR APPLIED: carbamate (barban, desmedipham, phenmedipham) glyphosate grass herbicides (fluazifop-P, sethoxydim) sulfonylureas (chlorsulfuron, trimeturon)	These herbicides produce stunting or complete lack of germination in susceptible species as a result of interference with cell division or elongation, or affect the plants' metabolic processes in such a way as to eventually cause reduced growth.
	SOIL APPLIED: thiocarbamate (EPTC, molinate) carbamate (chlorpropham, propham) dinitroaniline (benefin, oryzalin, pendimethalin, prodiamine, trifluralin) phthalic acid (DCPA, endothall) amides (alachlor, metalochlor, naproamide, pronamide) sulfonylureas (chlorsulfuron, trimeturon)	

SYMPTOM	HERBICIDE GROUP	COMMENTS
DESICCATION OF PLANT TISSUE: a collapse of plant tissue at or very near the point of application. The tissue desiccates soon after application. If application is light, e.g., a few drops on a leaf, symptoms may be less severe, resulting only in necrotic spots at the point of application.	FOLIAR APPLIED: sulfuric acid weed oils dinitrophenols (dinoseb) bipyridylums (paraquat, diquat) benzonitrile (bromoxynil) diphenylether (acifluorfen, oxyfluorfen)	These herbicides do not move much within plants; they have their effects at the site of application. High dosage rates affect cell-membrane integrity, causing a leakage of materials from various organelles and a rapid desiccation of tissue. The bipyridylums affect electron transport in photosynthesis. The dinitrophenols act as uncoupling agents in respiration.
MALFORMATION OF STEMS AND LEAVES: Symptoms include elongation and cupping of leaves. Twisting of stems and petioles is also common. Stems may show swelling and splitting near the soil line. Grasses may show reduced growth, lodging, or multiple heading.	FOLIAR APPLIED: phenoxy herbicides (2,4-D, MCPA, MCPP) dicamba picloram triclopyr glyphosate	A common effect is on DNA and RNA, affecting both cell division and protein synthesis. Many of these herbicides are referred to as 'hormone' or 'hormonal' herbicides in that they produce symptoms at very low rates of application. Drift injury is common with phenoxy herbicides. Glyphosate can result in the production of multiple growing points at shoot tips subsequent to sublethal dosages.
	SOIL APPLIED: DCPA thiocarbamates (cycloate, EPTC, pebulate) dicamba picloram triclopyr	DCPA and the thiocarbamates result in stunting and a less severe malformation of the leaves. The thiocarbamates often cause leaves to stick together.

toms. However, other causes of chlorosis and necrosis include nutrient deficiencies, ion toxicities, viruses, other plant diseases, insect injury, and spray damage from other pesticides.

Discoloration of Internal Tissue: Probable causes of internal tissue discoloration include disease organisms, nematodes, nutrient deficiencies, insects, and uptake of excess chemicals from the soil.

Discoloration—Overgrowth from Surface Injury: Agents responsible for this type of injury include disease organisms, nematodes, nutrient deficiencies, mechanical injury, wind, and rodent damage.

Malformation of Leaves and Stem: Growth regulator-like herbicides are often blamed for this type of injury; however, other causes include viruses, abnormal growing conditions (wind, cold, etc.), genetic variations, insect feeding responses, or mechanical injury to growing points.

Herbicide Symptoms

The information in table 5 is intended as a general guide to symptoms caused by herbicides. Some herbicides produce more than one type of plant symptom. For example, glyphosate can produce chlorosis, stunting, and malformation, and EPTC and alachlor can produce malformation and stunting. Few herbicides affect just one plant mechanism. This is particularly true of those herbicides which affect protein synthesis. Many of these proteins are enzymes that can alter or affect the various plant metabolic pathways, thus having a multiple effect on the plant.

Rates of herbicide exposure, the age of the affected plant, and the environmental conditions also affect the speed and severity of plant reaction to herbicides. Older plants may recover from exposure to light dosages, seedling plants may not. Under warm growing conditions with high light intensity, plant response may be much faster than during cool winter conditions. Soil type has a varied effect on the activity of soil-applied herbicides. Herbicides show low activity on fine-textured organic soils and maximum activity on coarse, sandy soils low in organic matter.

All these factors should be taken into account when evaluating plants for herbicide symptoms.

8

HERBICIDES

by George Gowgani[1], F.A. Holmes[2], and Floyd O. Colbert[3]

Herbicides are chemicals used to control or inhibit plant growth. An ideal herbicide is characterized as one that is easy to apply, effective, safe, cost-effective, and causes no harm to the public health or the environment. Most weed scientists consider selectivity also to be a desirable characteristic.

Discovering and developing an organic herbicide is a time-consuming process. It begins with the synthesis of thousands of chemicals in the manufacturers' laboratories. Chemicals are ultimately tested on plants or, more recently, using tissue culture bioassay techniques. If the chemical shows any potential for the intended use, the next step is greenhouse trials. From the greenhouse, the chemical is taken to manufacturers or university field research stations. It is tested for weed control and/or crop tolerance. Reaching this development stage takes anywhere from a few months to several years.

Once the potential suitability of a herbicide is determined, toxicological testing begins. This is one of the most complex and involved parts of herbicide development. Throughout the development process, data are collected and records kept for the purpose of eventual registration through the Environmental Protection Agency (EPA) and the California Department of Food and Agriculture (CDFA). Following the laboratory and limited field trial portion of development, the CDFA can issue a Research Authorization (RA) to allow small scale field trials. These tests are conducted under the scrutiny of both CDFA and the local agriculture commissioner and usually require that the treated crop be de-

1, 3. California Polytechnic State University, San Luis Obispo, CA. 2. E.I. DuPont Company, Los Gatos, CA.

stroyed. These types of experiments are commonly followed by issuance of a Federal Experimental Use Permit (EUP), granted by the EPA and the CDFA which allows for large scale field testing, most often under a temporary tolerance. When a temporary tolerance is issued under an EUP, then the treated crop may be marketed. These carefully monitored trials allow for data to be obtained under a wide range of climatic conditions, soil types, and application techniques. After many years of experimentation and expenditures of millions of dollars, a tolerance and label are approved by the EPA and CDFA. Details of the registration process can be found in the Regulatory and Registration section of Chapter 9.

The registration of herbicides (and other pesticides), especially in California, is an ever-changing process with constantly changing laws, rules, and regulations. Every attempt has been made to provide the most up-to-date registration information within individual sections of this text. Herbicides, other than those included for historical or educational purposes, cited in this and other chapters were, to the best of the authors' knowledge, registered for use in California at the time this revision was being prepared (table 1).

A number of regulatory decisions and/or economic considerations have affected the registration of herbicides since the publication of the initial text. The following herbicides referred to the original text are, under one or more regulatory processes (e.g., voluntarily cancellation or removal from an individual label), no longer registered for use in California. The authors recognize that individual herbicides may continue to be marketed for a period of time during one or more of the aforementioned processes, and therefore make no implications as to the continued use of the following materials.

- Agronomic crops: dalapon, dinoseb, propham, and terbacil
- Vegetable crops: chloramben, chloroxuron, dalapon, dinoseb, diphenamid, propham, and terbacil
- Horticultural crops: chloroxuron, dinoseb, diphenamid, and terbacil
- Ornamentals and turf: dinoseb and diphenamid
- Forest, rangeland, and Christmas trees: fosamine, siduron, silvex, and 2,4,5-T
- Noncropland and aquatics: fosamine

Due to regulatory changes now being enacted and/or economic considerations, it is expected that additional herbicides will either lose registration status or that the label amendments will not include all uses cited in this text. Under these conditions it is imperative that the user read and note all label instructions prior to selecting any herbicide and that all labeled precautions and directions be adhered to during the course of any application.

Also, herbicide manufacturers named in this chapter may be different in this revised text version, due to company acquisitions, joint ventures, sales licensing agreements, etc. Examples of companies that fit

into one or more of the aforementioned categories are:
- ICI's acquisition of Stauffer agricultural products
- ICI's acquiring the licensing agreement for paraquat from Chevron
- DuPont's acquisition of Shell's agricultural products
- Rhône-Poulenc's acquisition of Union Carbide's products
- The formation of Valent U.S.A. Corporation, which includes products from Chevron, Sumitomo, and PPG.

GENERAL INFORMATION

As with weeds that are classified into selected groups (e.g., life habitat, thermal requirements, plant family) for easier study of these pests, chemical herbicides can also be grouped. For quick access to pertinent information, herbicides are grouped together based upon the following: usage, contact or translocated; method of application, selective or nonselective; time of application; plant injury symptoms; mode of action; and toxicity (table 2).

Usage

Crop use provides one way of classifying herbicides. There are herbicides for aquatics, crops (e.g., agronomic, vegetable, and horticultural), and more specifically for individual crops or other uses such as corn, lettuce, peaches, turf, and ornamental shrubs.

Contact or Translocated

Contact herbicides control vegetation primarily by coming in contact with the plant tissue (e.g., paraquat) rather than as a result of translocation. Translocated herbicides are compounds that move within the plant and have effects throughout the entire plant system (e.g., glyphosate).

Method of Application

Herbicides can be grouped together according to the way in which they are used, such as soil applied, foliar applied, soil or stem injection, and through water.

Selective or Nonselective Herbicides

A selective herbicide is one that is more toxic to some plant species than to others at the normal rate of application (e.g., bromoxynil being selective for broadleaves and fluazifop-P for grasses). Nonselective herbicides are effective on all weed species (e.g., glyphosate and paraquat).

Time of Application

The timing of a herbicide application will depend upon many factors, such as crop, existing weeds, growth stage of crop and/or weed, herbicide used, and environmental conditions, particularly rainfall. In addition, herbicide labels will have specific directions regarding when and how to apply the product. These directions are usually provided in such terms as preplant, preemergence, and postemergence to crop and/or weeds. Examples for these types of herbicide applications include:

Crop
- (PPI) Preplant herbicides are soil incorporated prior to planting the crop, usually in the final stages of seedbed preparation (e.g., trifluralin in cotton and EPTC in beans).
- (PRE) Preemergence herbicides are applied prior to or at seeding; just prior to crop emergence or at the time of transplanting (e.g., alachlor in corn and DCPA in onions); or to established crops (e.g., simazine in almonds). Preemergence products may also be applied at lay-by (e.g., DCPA in onions and pendimethalin in garlic).
- (POE) Postemergence applications are made after crop emergence (e.g., bromoxynil in barley and diuron to established alfalfa). In some cases the herbicide is applied post-directed to the crop (e.g., oxyfluorfen in cotton and sethoxydim in sugar beets).

Weed
- (PRE) Herbicides are applied prior to weed emergence (e.g., alachlor in corn, simazine in peach orchards and along roadsides, and trifluralin soil incorporated in dry beans). They may also be applied at lay-by (e.g., DCPA in onions and pendimethalin in garlic).
- (POE) Herbicides are applied to emerged weeds (e.g., 2,4,-D to broadleaf weeds in barley, glyphosate to weeds in grape vineyards and along roadsides, and fluazifop-P to grasses in garlic and onions).

Plant Injury Symptoms

Most herbicides, regardless of chemical family, can be classified into stunting, chlorosis and necrosis, and growth regulating-type injuries. Examples of herbicides demonstrating these effects on plants for the above mentioned classes are trifluralin, atrazine, and 2,4,-D, respectively. Additional information regarding injury symptoms can be found in the Plant Diagnosis section of Chapter 7.

Mode of Action

Herbicide mode of action is the chemical interaction that interrupts a biological process necessary for plant growth and development. The modes of action for most herbicides are well understood, and several excellent texts have been published covering each individual herbicide or family of chemicals. For example, it has been established that triazine and substituted urea compounds inhibit plant photosynthesis and that carbamate-type herbicides inhibit plant cell division. Additional information on herbicide mode of action, relative mobility in plants, and general soil persistence can be found in the introduction portion of Chapter 7.

Toxicity Classification

Every herbicide has an assigned LD_{50} value (lethal dose of a herbicide which will kill 50% of the test animals based on mg of chemical per kg of body weight). If the tested LD_{50} value is less than 50, the chemical is classified as highly toxic. A value higher than 50 but less than 500 is considered moderately toxic. LD_{50} values over 500 are classified at lower toxicity or comparatively free from danger. The majority of herbicides fall into the last category. Additional information regarding pesticide toxicity can be found in the Regulatory and Registration Section of Chapter 9.

CHEMICAL CLASSIFICATION

The previous section illustrates the many ways herbicides can be grouped for information. The purpose of this section is to provide general and specific information regarding herbicide chemical classification. General information will be provided for each family of herbicides on chemical structure, principal mode(s) of action, or activity and degradation. General information on the primary use and formulations available, with specific information on toxicity and water solubility, for chemicals within each individual family is also included. Where water solubility of a chemical is greater than 100,000 ppm, it has been listed as soluble.

It should be noted that no attempt has been made to list all registered uses, and no references have been made to combination uses for these chemicals. Emphasis has been placed on those herbicides used on crops produced in California. The reader should refer to labels for specific information on usage and weeds controlled.

Organic Herbicides

These are chemical compounds which contain carbon atoms. Carbon atoms differ from other element atoms in that *they can bond with one another and form straight chains or closed ring structures* (e.g., benzene).

Hydrogen is the most common element bonded to the carbon atom, followed by oxygen. Other elements occurring in organic herbicides include phosphorus, nitrogen, sulfur, and halogens (e.g., bromine and chlorine). Discovery chemists use this knowledge regarding elements required and their arrangement to find new organic compounds which have herbicidal activity.

Most organic herbicides have one common advantage: they are biodegradable. This assures that these herbicidal chemicals will not remain for an extended period in the environment without being broken down into smaller molecules and/or to elements.

There are many possible designations that can be given to a chemical family (Anderson 1983); therefore, the authors have selected a classification nomenclature for its ease of understanding; they are listed alphabetically as follows and in table 3:

Aliphatics

Dalapon   Cacodylic acid   Glyphosate

Aliphatic herbicides have open chains or are without rings in their structural formulas. Aliphatic herbicides are subgrouped into the following three categories:

Chlorinated aliphatics (dalapon) are particularly effective in controlling grass species. Growth inhibition and leaf chlorosis and necrosis are the common phytotoxic systems of this group. No chlorinated aliphatic herbicides are registered for use in California.

Organic arsenicals have been used as herbicides for many years and presently are primarily used as plant desiccants.

Other aliphatics form a very diverse group of chemicals. Acrolein is used in aquatic weed control, methyl bromide as a soil fumigant, and glyphosate, which is nonselective, as a foliar-applied herbicide that interferes with synthesis of chlorophyll and aromatic amino acids, which are essential to plant life.

The behavior of aliphatic herbicides in or on soils is varied; generally they are not persistent in soil at the normal rate of application. Microbiological degradation is the major cause of decomposition for most aliphatics, except that organic arsenicals are inactivated in soil by surface adsorption and ion exchange.

Amides

R₂ ... N — C — R₁ ... R₃

Amide structure

Amides are a very diverse group of herbicides. Most are used selectively during the preplant or preemergent period. They control grasses better than broadleaves. Uptake can occur through seeds, roots, and shoots. These herbicides do not translocate. Their mode of action is to inhibit growth in terminal leaf, shoot, and meristems. They interfere with normal cell division and elongation and protein synthesis.

Microorganisms play a major role in degradation of amides, but some amides are inactive against common soil microorganisms. Loss from photodecomposition and/or volatilization is relatively low.

Benzoics

— C — O — H

Benzoic acid

These herbicides are derivatives of benzoic acid. Their basic chemical structure is composed of a benzene ring and a carboxyl group. They are one of the group of herbicides described as growth hormone herbicides. Benzoics may move from leaves to the meristems and also in the transpiration stream so they may be soil applied. They are thought to interfere with nucleic acid metabolism and disruption of the transport system in plants due to induced cellular proliferation.

Benzoics are relatively mobile in soil. Degradation by soil microorganisms is the major pathway of loss under most conditions.

Bipyridiliums

These herbicides are for the most part nonselective. Because there is little or no translocation, complete coverage is necessary for favorable results. They destroy the cell membranes and interfere with photosynthesis in treated plants. They have no soil activity and are not significantly metabolized by soil microorganisms.

Carbamates

Carbamic acid   General structure of the carbamic acid ester

Carbamate herbicides are generally classified into two groups. These herbicides derive their basic chemical structure from carbamic acid.

Phenylcarbamates or carbanilates are esters of carbamic acid. Some of the herbicides in this group are applied as preemergence materials; however, most are applied postemergence. The mode of action is inhibition of meristematic development. Soil application of some members of this group results in uptake by seeds, shoots, and roots.

Thiocarbamates contain sulfur in their basic structure. They are quite volatile which makes it very important to incorporate them into soil or water-in soon after application. They can also be applied in irrigation water. Thiocarbamates inhibit meristematic development, both by reducing cell division and causing cell elongation.

Dinitroanilines

Aniline   Dinitroaniline

Dinitroanilines are composed of the chemical aniline with two nitro groups attached to its phenyl ring.

Dinitroanilines are generally volatile and susceptible to photodecomposition. Some must be incorporated in the soil shortly after application to prevent chemical breakdown and/or loss. They are used prior to planting for annual weed control and are most effective against grass weeds. They are absorbed by roots and shoots as they pass through the treated soil and cause inhibition of growth.

The mode of action of the dinitroanilines is as a mitotic poison. They inhibit both root and shoot development, apparently by interfering with cell division and adversely affecting the development of cell wall and membrane during mitosis. The most typical symptom of affected plants is the inhibition of lateral root formation. Growth reduction in roots and shoots and swelling and irregularities in various tissues also result.

Dinitroanilines are strongly adsorbed in soil and show negligible leaching. Microorganisms are believed to contribute to the degradation and disappearance of dinitroanilines from soil.

Diphenyl Ethers

Nitro-diphenylether

Diphenyl ether herbicides have as a common nucleus two phenyl rings joined by an ether bond with a nitro group attached to one of them.

The principal uses of this group of herbicides are preemergence or early postemergence to the crop for the control of annual weeds. They are foliar applied and do not translocate. The mode of action of diphenyl ethers appears to be interference with photosynthesis and inhibition of meristematic activity.

Diphenyl ethers do not have a uniform pattern of degradation. Some are broken down rapidly by the soil microorganisms while others disappear due to photodecomposition.

Nitriles

General structure — nitriles

Nitriles, also called benzonitriles, have a phenyl ring with a nitrile as the nucleus. There are only two herbicides in the group. The first, bromoxynil, is a contact herbicide primarily effective on broadleaf weeds. The second, dichlobenil, is a very volatile chemical and should be incorporated in the soil to prevent damage to desirable vegetation. It is also an inhibitor of germination.

Bromoxynil inhibits both photosynthesis and respiration, while dichlobenil inhibits the activity of dividing meristems, acting primarily on growing points and root tips.

While microbial breakdown and volatilization are believed to be responsible for the disappearance of dichlobenil from the soil, the degradation process is not well understood.

Phenoxys

General structure — phenoxys

2,4-D (2,4-dichlorophenoxy acetic acid)

Phenoxy herbicides have a general molecular structure composed of a phenyl ring attached to an oxygen, which in turn is bonded to an acid. The most widely recognized herbicide in this family is 2,4-D.

The phenoxys are a type of growth hormone. They were among the first of the organic herbicides to be developed. Phenoxys are generally foliar applied and are translocated throughout the plant in both the photosynthesis and transpiration streams.

In practice, the acid form of the phenoxy herbicides is rarely used. Most phenoxy herbicides are formulated for use as salts and esters of their parent acids. The common salt forms of the phenoxy herbicides are the amine, sodium, and ammonium salts; less common salts include potassium and lithium. The amine salts of the phenoxy herbicides dissolve readily in water, forming a true solution.

Esters of the phenoxy herbicides are soluble in oils and insoluble in water. For field use, they commonly are formulated as emulsifiable concentrates for application in either oil or water carriers. Esters of the phenoxy herbicides are formed by the reaction of their acid form with an alcohol. The reaction replaces the hydroxy (-OH) of the carboxyl group with the respective alcohol.

A given ester of the phenoxy herbicides is identified by the alcohol reacting to replace the hydroxyl of the carboxyl group of the parent-acid herbicide. For example, the methyl ester is formed when the alcohol is methanol. The short-chain esters are highly volatile and present a real hazard to susceptible desirable plants.

At the normal rate of application, phenoxy herbicides persist from one to four weeks in soil. Their decomposition in soils is attributed primarily to microbial attack.

The mode of action of the phenoxy herbicides is believed to include interference with nucleic acid metabolism, disruption of the translocation system, inhibition of photosynthesis and oxidative phosphorylation, and effect on cell division. The primary mode of action of phenoxy herbicides has not been clearly established.

Sulfonylureas

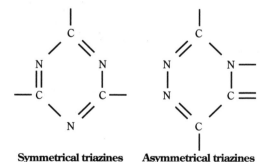

General structure — sulfonylureas

This herbicide class has been discovered and individual chemicals registered since the initial publication of this text. These herbicides are active at very low rates, e.g., chlorsulfuron is used in wheat in terms of grams per acre. The sulfonylureas are more effective on broadleaf weed species and are absorbed and translocated through both plant foliage and roots. Plant injury symptoms are slow to appear and include slight chlorosis and purpling in the youngest tissue followed by necrosis, thus resulting in plant death.

The behavior of sulfonylureas in western agricultural soils, especially high pH soils, may persist into the next crop. The user must follow the label carefully regarding plant-back crops.

Triazines

Symmetrical triazines   **Asymmetrical triazines**

The triazines constitute a large group of herbicides. Various substitutions on the nucleus yield compounds of different chemical and biological properties. Based on the substitution in the 2-position of the molecule, three subgroups are formed. With chlorine (Cl) in this position, the compounds are known as the chloro group, and the generic name 'azine.' When a -OCH$_3$ group is in the 2-position, the methoxy group with common names ending in '-ton' results. When a -SCH$_3$ is substituted in the 2-position, methylthio or methylmercapto compounds with common names ending in '-tryn' are formed.

Asymmetrical triazines differ from the symmetrical triazines in that the carbon and nitrogen atoms in the basic ring structure are not symmetrical; that is they are arranged alternately as shown.

The principal use of this large group is the selective preemergence and postemergence control of seedling grasses and broadleaf weeds in crops and with some of them, the nonselective control of vegetation in noncrop areas. They are more effective on broadleaf weeds and do not control established annual or perennial weeds at selective rates. They are readily absorbed in soil and resist leaching. Triazines are absorbed by roots, translocated upward in the transpiration stream, and accumulated in leaves. They are nonmobile in phloem. Some are foliar absorbed, but translocation out of the leaves is very minor. Triazines affect several biochemical reactions in plants but are known for their powerful effects on inhibiting photosynthesis by interfering with the CO$_2$ fixation and the splitting of water (Hill reaction). The ability of plants to degrade the herbicide is the basis of selectivity. Tolerant plants inactivate or detoxify the herbicides to a greater extent than sensitive plants.

Microbial breakdown is one of several processes involved in the degradation of simazine. In soils, microbial activity accounts for decomposition of a significant amount of triazines. Under normal climatic conditions, loss of triazines from soil by photodecomposition and/or volatilization is considered insignificant.

Uracils

General structure — uracil

In this group, bromacil is the only registered herbicide for use in California. Bromacil is used for selective control of a wide range of annual and perennial weeds in cropland and for nonselective weed control in noncrop areas.

Its mode of action is inhibition of photosynthesis. Microbiological degradation apparently is a mode of disappearance from soils. Soil diphtheroids are among the organisms involved in the breakdown of this uracil.

Ureas

$$H - N - C - N - H$$

Urea

Urea herbicides have as their common chemical skeleton a basic structure as shown.

The urea herbicides are generally nonselective when used at high rates. They are effective on grasses and broadleaves. Any selectivity depends on herbicide placement and plant tolerance. They do not inhibit seed germination. The mode of action is very similar to the triazines and uracils as they also inhibit photosynthesis. Monuron was the first of the urea herbicides in general use, but it is no longer manufactured for use in the United States.

Microbes are the primary factor in the disappearance of ureas from soils and in the aquatic environment. Losses by photodecomposition or volatilization probably are insignificant except when the urea compounds are left exposed on the soil surface for several weeks under hot, dry conditions.

Unclassified Organic Herbicides
This section includes those organic herbicides that do not fall into any of the other organic and inorganic chemical groups covered in previous discussions.

Inorganic Herbicides

Inorganic herbicides were the first chemicals used in weed control. These are herbicides that contain no carbon. Inorganic herbicides were widely used in crop- and noncropland before the discovery of the organic herbicides. Some of the most commonly used inorganic herbicides are listed in table 3.

TABLE 1. COMMON, CHEMICAL, AND TRADE NAMES AND MANUFACTURERS OF HERBICIDES

Common name Chemical name	Trade name	Manufacturer
acifluorfen 5-[2-chloro-4-(trifluoromethyl)phenoxy]-2-nitrobenzoic acid	Blazer/Tackle	Rohm and Haas/Rhône-Poulenc
acrolein 2-propenal	Magnacide H	Magna
alachlor 2-chloro-*N*-(2,6-diethylphenyl)-*N*-(methoxymethyl)acetamide	Lasso	Monsanto
ametryn *N*-ethyl-*N'*-(1-methylethyl)-6-(methylthio)-1,3,5-triazine-2,4-diamine	Evik	Ciba-Geigy
amitrole 1*H*-1,2,4-triazol-3-amine	Amitrole	Rhône-Poulenc
AMS ammonium sulfamate	Ammate X-NI	DuPont
asulam methyl[(4-aminopheynl)sulfonyl]carbamate	Asulox	Rhône-Poulenc
atrazine 6-chloro-*N*-ethyl-*N'*-(1-methylethyl)-1,3,5-triazine-2,4-diamine	several	several
barban 4-chloro-2-butynyl 3-chlorophenylcarbamate	Carbyne	United Agri-Products
benefin *N*-butyl-*N*-ethyl-2,6-dinitro-4-(trifluoromethyl)benzenamine	Balan	Elanco
bensulide *O,O*-bis(1-methylethyl) *S*-[2-[(phenylsulfonyl)amino]ethyl] phosphorodithioate	Prefar/Betasan	ICI Americas
bentazon 3-(1-methylethyl)-(1*H*)-2,1,3-benzothiadiazin-4(3*H*)-one 2,2-dioxide	Basagran	BASF
bifenox methyl 5-(2,4-dichlorophenoxy)-2-nitrobenzoate	Modown	Rhône-Poulenc
borax sodium tetraborate decahydrate	several	several
bromacil 5-bromo-6-methyl-3-(1-methylpropyl)-2,4(1*H*,3*H*)pyrimidinedione	Hyvar	DuPont
bromoxynil 3,5-dibromo-4-hydroxybenzonitrile	Buctril	Rhône-Poulenc

butylate   Sutan   ICI Americas
S-ethyl bis(2-methylpropyl)carbamothioate

cacodylic acid   several   several
dimethyl arsinic acid

chlorpropham   Furloe   Valent
1-methylethyl 3-chlorophenylcarbamate

chlorsulfuron   Glean   DuPont
2-chloro-N-[[(4-methoxy-6-methyl-1,3,5-triazin-2-yl)amino]carbonyl]benzenesulfonamide

copper chelate   several   several
alkanolamine or ethylene diamine complex

copper sulfate   several   several
cupric sulfate pentahydrate or triethanolamine

cyanazine   Bladex   DuPont
2-[[4-chloro-6-(ethylamino)-1,3,5-triazin-2yl]amino]-2-methylpropanenitrile

cycloate   Ro-Neet   ICI Americas
S-ethyl cyclohexylethylcarbamothioate

dalapon   several   several
2,2-dichloropropanoic acid

DCPA   Dachtal   Fermenta
dimethyl 2,3,5,6-tetrachloro-1,4-benzenedicarboxylate

desmedipham   Betanex   Nor-Am
ethyl [3-[[(phenylamino)carbonyl]oxy]phenyl]carbamate

diallate   Avadex   Monsanto
S-(2,3-dichloro-2-propenyl) bis(1-methylethyl)carbamothioate

dicamba   Banvel   Sandoz
3,6-dichloro-2-methoxybenzoic acid

dichlobenil   Casoron   Uniroyal
2,6-dichlorobenzonitrile

dichlorprop   Weedone   Rhône-Poulenc
(±)-2-(2,4-dichlorophenoxy)propanoic acid

diclofop   Hoelon   Hoechst-Roussel
(±)-2-[4-(2,4-dichlorophenoxy)phenoxy]propanoic acid

diethatyl   Antor   Nor-Am
N-(chloroacetyl)-N-(2,6-diethylphenyl)glycine

difenzoquat   Avenge   American Cyanamid
1,2-dimethyl-3,5-diphenyl-1H-pyrazolium

dinoseb   several   several
2-(1-methylpropyl)-4,6-dinitrophenol

diquat   Diquat   Valent
6,7-dihydrodipyrido[1,2-α:2',1'-c]pyrazinediium ion

diuron   several   several
N'-(3,4-dichlorophenyl)-N,N-dimethylurea

DSMA   several   several
disodium salt of MAA

endothall   Endothal   Pennwalt
7-oxabicyclo[2,2,1]heptane-2,3-dicarboxylic acid

EPTC   Eptam   ICI Americas
S-ethyl dipropyl carbamothioate

ethalfluralin   Sonalan   Elanco
N-ethyl-N-(2-methyl-2-propenyl)-2,6-dinitro-4-(trifluoromethyl)benzenamine

ethofumesate   Nortron   Nor-Am
(±)-2-ethoxy-2,3-dihydro-3,3-dimethyl-5-benzofuranyl methanesulfonate

fluazifop-P   Fusilade   ICI Americas
(R)-2-[4-[[5-(trifluoromethyl)-2-pyridinyl]oxy]phenoxy]propanoic acid

fluometuron   Cotoran   Ciba-Geigy
N,N-dimethyl-N'-[3-(trifluoromethyl)phenyl] urea

glyphosate   Roundup/Rodeo   Monsanto
N-(phosphonomethyl)glycine

hexazinone   Velpar   DuPont
3-cyclohexyl-6-(dimethylamino)-1-methyl-1,3,5-triazine-2,4(1H,3H)-dione

linuron   Lorox   DuPont
N'-(3,4-dichlorophenyl)-N-methoxy-N-methylurea

MCPA   several   several
(4-chloro-2-methylphenoxy)acetic acid

MSMA   several   several
monosodium salt of MAA

mecoprop   several   several
2-(4-chloro-2-methylphenoxy)propanoic acid

metham   several   several
methylcarbamodithioic acid

methyl bromide   several   several
bromomethane

metolachlor   Dual   Ciba-Geigy
2-chloro-*N*-(2-ethyl-6-methylphenyl)-*N*-(2-methoxy-1-methylethyl)acetamide

metribuzin   Lexone/Sencor   DuPont/Mobay
4-amino-6-(1,1-dimethylethyl)-3-(methylthio)-1,2,4-triazin-5(4*H*)-one

molinate   Ordram   ICI Americas
S-ethyl hexahydro-1*H*-azepine-1-carbothioate

napropamide   Devrinol   ICI Americas
N,N-diethyl-2-(1-naphtalenyloxy)propanamide

naptalam   Alanap   Uniroyal
2-[(1-naphthalenylamino)carbonyl]benzoic acid

norflurazon   Solicam/Zorial   Sandoz
4-chloro-5-(methylamino)-2-(3-(trifluoromethyl)phenyl)-3(2H)-pyridazinone

oryzalin   Surflan   Elanco
4-(dipropylamino)-3,5-dinitrobenzenesulfonamide

oxadiazon   Ronstar   Rhône-Poulenc
3-[2,4-dichloro-5-(1-methylethoxy)phenyl]-5-(1,1-dimethylethyl)-1,3,4-oxadiazol-2-(3*H*)-one

oxyfluorfen   Goal   Rohm and Haas
2-chloro-1-(3-ethoxy-4-nitrophenoxy)-4-(trifluoromethyl)benzene

paraquat   Gramoxone   ICI Americas
1,1'-dimethyl-4,4'-bipyridinium ion

pebulate   Tillam   ICI Americas
S-propyl butylethylcarbamothioate

pendimethalin   Prowl   American Cyanamid
N-(1-ethylpropyl)-3,4-dimethyl-2,-6-dinitrobenzenamine

phenmedipham   Betanal   Nor-Am
3-[(methoxycarbonyl)amino]phenyl (3-methylphenyl)carbamate

prometon   Pramitol   Ciba-Geigy
6-methoxy-*N,N'*-bis(1-methylethyl)-1,3,5-triazine-2,4-diamine

prometryn   Caparol   Ciba-Geigy
N,N'-bis(1-methylethyl)-6-(methylthio)-1,3,5-triazine-2,4-diamine

pronamide   Kerb   Rohm and Haas
3,5-dichloro(*N*-1,1-dimethyl-2-propynyl)benzamide

propachlor   Ramrod   Monsanto
2-chloro-*N*-(1-methylethyl)-N-phenylacetamide

propanil   Stam   Rohm and Haas
N-(3,4-dichlorophenyl)propanamide

propazine   Milogard   Ciba-Geigy
6-chloro-*N*,*N'*-bis(1-methylethyl)-1,3,5-triazine-2,4-diamine

pyrazon   Pyramin   BASF
5-amino-4-chloro-2-phenyl-3(2*H*)-pyridazinone

sethoxydim   Poast   BASF
2-[1-(ethoxyimino)butyl]-5-[2-(ethylthio)propyl]-3-hydroxy-2-cyclohexen-1-one

simazine   several   several
6-chloro-*N*,*N'*-diethyl-1,3,5-triazine-2,4-diamine

sodium chlorate   several   several
$NaClO_3$

sulfometuron   Oust   DuPont
2-[[[[(4,6-dimethyl-2-pyrimidinyl)amino]carbonyl]amino]sulfonyl]benzoic acid

sulfuric acid   several   several
H_2SO_4

TCA   several   several
trichloroacetic acid

tebuthiuron   Spike   Elanco
N-[5-(1,1-dimethylethyl)-1,3,4-thiadiazol-2-yl]-*N*,*N'*-dimethylurea

thiobencarb   Bolero   Valent
S-[(4-chlorophenyl)methyl] diethatylcarbamothioate

triallate   Far-go   Monsanto
S-(2,3,3-trichloro-2-propenyl) bis(1-methylethyl)carbamothioate

triclopyr   Garlon   Dow
[(3,5,6-trichloro-2-pyridinyl)oxy]acetic acid

trifluralin   Treflan   Elanco
2,6-dinitro-*N*,*N*-dipropyl-4-(trifluoromethyl)benzenamine

2,4-D   several   several
(2,4-dichlorophenoxy)acetic acid

2,4-DB   Butoxone   Rhône-Poulenc
4-(2,4-dichlorophenoxy)butanoic acid

2,4,5-T   several   several
(2,4,5-trichlorophenoxy) acetic acid

vernolate   Vernam   ICI Americas
S-propyl dipropylcarbamothioate

weed oil   several   several
aromatic petroleum derivatives

TABLE 2. HERBICIDES CLASSIFIED BY METHOD OF APPLICATION AND LISTED BY
COMMON NAME

Aquatic herbicides

acrolein	diquat	2,4-D
copper chelate	diuron	simazine
copper sulfate	endothall	
dichlobenil	glyphosate	

Contact herbicides

acifluorfen	desmedipham	paraquat
AMS	diclofop	phenmedipham
barban	difenzoquat	propanil
bentazon	dinoseb	sulfuric acid
bifenox	diquat	weed oil
bromoxynil	endothall	
cacodylic acid	oxyfluorfen	

Foliar translocated herbicides

amitrole	dicamba	mecoprop
asulam	dichlorprop	molinate
2,4-D	DSMA	MSMA
2,4-DB	fluazifop-P	sethoxydim
2,4,5-T	glyphosate	thiobencarb
dalapon	MCPA	triclopyr

Soil-applied herbicides

alachlor	EPTC	pebulate
ametryne	ethalfluralin	pendimethalin
atrazine	ethofumesate	prometon
benefin	fluometuron	prometryn
bensulide	hexazinone	pronamide
borax	linuron	propachlor
bromacil	metham	propazine
butylate	methyl bromide	pyrazon
chlorpropham	metolachlor	simazine
chlorsulfuron	metribuzin	sodium chlorate
cyanazine	molinate	sulfometuron
cycloate	napropamide	TCA
DCPA	naptalam	tebuthiuron
diallate	norflurazon	thiobencarb
dichlobenil	oryzalin	triallate
diethatyl	oxadiazon	trifluralin
diuron	oxyfluorfen	vernolate

TABLE 3. SELECTED INFORMATION FOR HERBICIDE FAMILIES

Family/ Common name	Acute oral Toxicity LD_{50} (mg/kg)	Water Solubility (ppm)[1]	Formulation[2]	Use	Type of Application[3]	Weeds Controlled
ALIPHATICS						
acrolein	46	soluble	S	aquatic	POE	floating/submerged weeds and algae
cacodylic acid	830	soluble	S	noncrop	POE	general control
dalapon	9330	soluble	SP	no longer registered	POE	annual/perennial grasses
DSMA	2800	soluble	SP, S	agronomic turf noncrop	POE	annual/perennial grasses
glyphosate	4320	10,000	S	agronomic vegetable horticultural ornamental forest noncrop aquatic	POE	general nonselective control
methyl bromide	vapor toxicity 200 ppm	soluble	gas	vegetable horticultural	PRE	general weed control
MSMA	700	soluble	S	agronomic horticultural turf noncrop	POE	annual/perennial grasses
TCA	5000	soluble	SP	no longer registered	PRE, POE	annual/perennial grasses
AMIDES						
alachlor	1800	148	EC, G	agronomic ornamental	PPI, PRE	annual grasses some broadleaves yellow nutsedge
metolachlor	2780	530	EC	agronomic horticultural	PPI, PRE	annual grasses some broadleaves
napropamide	5000	73	WP, EC, G	agronomic vegetable horticultural ornamental	PPI, PRE	annual grasses broadleaves
naptalam	1770	200	EC, G	vegetable ornamental	PPI, PRE	annual grasses broadleaves
pronamide	8350	15	WP	agronomic vegetable horticultural ornamental turf	PPI, PRE	annual grasses broadleaves

propachlor	710	700	WP, G	agronomic	PPI, PRE	annual grasses broadleaves
propanil	1384	500	EC	agronomic	POE	annual grasses, especially barnyardgrass
BENZOIC						
dicamba	1028	4500	EC, G	agronomic vegetable turf	POE	broadleaf and woody plants tolerant to phenoxy herbicides
BIPYRIDILIUMS						
diquat	230	soluble	S	noncrop aquatic	POE	general nonselective control
paraquat	157	soluble	S	agronomic vegetable horticultural noncrop	POE	general nonselective control
CARBAMATES						
Phenylcarbamates						
barban	1350	11	EC	agronomic	POE	selective wild oat control
chlorpropham	3800	88	EC, G	agronomic vegetable	PPI, PRE	annual grasses some broadleaves dodder
desmedipham	10,250	7	EC	agronomic	POE	annual broadleaves
phenmedipham	8000	1	EC	agronomic	POE	annual broadleaves, less effective on pigweed than desmedipham
Thiocarbamates						
butylate	4659	45	EC, G	agronomic	PPI	annual grasses some broadleaves
cycloate	2000	85	EC	agronomic vegetable	PPI	annual grasses some broadleaves
diallate	395	14	EC	agronomic	POE	annual grasses (wild oat)
EPTC	1630	375	EC, G	agronomic vegetable ornamental	PPI	annual grasses some broadleaves
metham	820	soluble	S	agronomic vegetable horticultural ornamental turf	PRE	general weed control
molinate	720	1000	EC, G	agronomic	PPI, POE	annual grasses
pebulate	921	30	EC	agronomic vegetable	PPI	annual grasses some broadleaves

Family/ Common name	Acute oral Toxicity LD_{50} (mg/kg)	Water Solubility (ppm)[1]	Formulation[2]	Use	Type of Application[3]	Weeds Controlled
thiobencarb	1903	30	EC, G	agronomic	PRE	annual grasses
triallate	1675	4	EC, G	agronomic	PRE	annual grasses wild oat
vernolate	1780	109	EC, G	agronomic vegetable	PPI	annual grasses some broadleaves
Miscellaneous carbamates						
asulam	8000	soluble	S	noncrop	PRE	annual grasses some broadleaves
DINITROANILINES						
benefin	5000	0.1	DF, G	agronomic vegetable turf	PPI, PRE	annual grasses some broadleaves
ethalfluralin	10,000	0.3	EC	agronomic	PPI	annual grasses some broadleaves
oryzalin	10,000	2.5	AS, WP	horticultural ornamental	PRE	annual grasses some broadleaves
pendimethalin	1250	0.5	EC, G	agronomic vegetable horticultural ornamental turf	PPI, PRE	annual grasses some broadleaves
trifluralin	5000	0.3	EC, G	agronomic vegetable horticultural ornamental	PPI, PRE	annual grasses some broadleaves
DIPHENYLETHERS						
acifluorfen	3330	soluble	S	agronomic	POE	broadleaves some grasses
bifenox	6400	0.35	WP, EC, AS	ornamental	PRE, POE	broadleaves
oxyfluorfen	5000	1	EC	agronomic vegetable horticultural ornamental	PRE, POE	broadleaves some grasses
NITRILES						
bromoxynil	190	200	EC	agronomic vegetable turf noncrop	POE	broadleaves
dichlobenil	2460	18	WP, G	horticultural ornamental	PRE, POE	grasses broadleaves

PHENOXYS

2,4-D	375	600	EC, S	agronomic horticultural ornamental turf forest/rang land	POE	annual/perennial broadleaves
2,4-DB	1960	insoluble	EC, S	agronomic	POE	broadleaves
2,4,5-T	485	238	EC, S	no longer registered	POE	woody plants
dichlorprop	800	710	EC, S	noncrop	POE	broadleaves
MCPA	800	insoluble	EC, S	agronomic turf	POE	broadleaves
mecoprop	930	620	EC, S	turf	POE	broadleaves

SULFONYLUREAS

chlorsulfuron	5545	pH 5/30	WDG, G	agronomic	POE	annual grasses broadleaves
sulfometuron	5000	pH 5/<10	WDG, G	noncrop	PRE, POE	annual/perennial grasses broadleaves

TRIAZINES

atrazine	1780	70	WP, AS, G	agronomic ornamental forest noncrop	PRE, POE	annual grasses broadleaves
cyanazine	334	160	WP, AS, G	agronomic noncrop	PRE, POE	annual grasses broadleaves
propazine	5000	8.6	WP, AS, G	agronomic	PRE	broadleaves
simazine	5000	5	WP, AS, G	agronomic vegetable horticultural ornamental turf forest noncrop aquatic	PRE	annual grasses broadleaves
ametryn	1150	165	WP	agronomic horticultural	PRE, POE	annual grasses broadleaves
metribuzin	1937	1200	WP, AS, G	agronomic vegetable	PRE, POE	annual grasses broadleaves
prometon	2755	750	WP, EC	noncrop	PRE, POE	broadleaves
prometryn	3750	48	WP, AS	agronomic vegetable	PRE, POE	annual grasses many broadleaves

URACILS

bromacil	5200	815	WP	horticultural noncrop	PRE, POE	annual/perennial grasses broadleaves

Family/ Common name	Acute oral Toxicity LD$_{50}$ (mg/kg)	Water Solubility (ppm)[1]	Formulation[2]	Use	Type of Application[3]	Weeds Controlled
UREAS						
diuron	3400	42	WP	agronomic vegetable horticultural noncrop aquatic	PRE, POE	grasses, broadleaves
fluometuron	8900	90	WP	agronomic	PPI, POE, PRE	grasses, broadleaves
linuron	1500	75	WP, AS	agronomic vegetable noncrop	PRE, POE	grasses, broadleaves
tebuthiuron	644	2300	WP, G	noncrop	PRE	brush, woody plants, annual/perennial general weed control
UNCLASSIFIED ORGANIC HERBICIDES						
amitrole	24,000	soluble	SP, S	noncrop	POE	annual/perennial grasses, broadleaves
bensulide	770	25	EC, G	agronomic vegetable ornamental	PPI, PRE	annual grasses some broadleaves
bentazon	2063	500	EC	agronomic vegetable turf	POE	annual broadleaves
DCPA	3000	1	WP, G	agronomic vegetable ornamental turf	PPI, PRE	annual grasses some broadleaves
diclofop	2176	50	EC	agronomic	POE	grasses
diethatyl	2300	100	EC	agronomic vegetable	PPI, PRE	annual grasses some broadleaves
difenzoquat	270	soluble	S	agronomic	POE	selective wild oat control
dinoseb	58	soluble	EC, S	no longer registered	POE	annual grasses broadleaves
endothall	38	soluble	S, G	agronomic aquatic	PRE, POE	annual grasses broadleaves
ethofumesate	5650	110	EC, AS	agronomic	PPI, PRE	annual grasses broadleaves
fluazifop-P	3000	2	EC	agronomic vegetable horticultural	POE	annual/perennial grasses
hexazinone	5278	33,000	WP, S	agronomic forest noncrop	PRE, POE	annual/perennial grasses broadleaves

norflurazon	8000	38,000	WP, AS, G	agronomic horticultural	PRE	grasses
oxadiazon	8000	0.7	EC, G	ornamental turf	PRE, POE	annual grasses broadleaves
pyrazon	3030	300	WP	agronomic vegetable	PRE, POE	annual broadleaves
sethoxydim	2676	4800	EC	agronomic vegetable horticultural	POE	annual/perennial grasses
triclopyr	630	430	EC	turf forest noncrop	POE	annual broadleaves, brush, woody plants
weed oil	variable	insoluble	S	no longer registered	POE	annual grasses broadleaves

INORGANIC HERBICIDES

AMS	3900	soluble	S	noncrop	POE	woody plants
borax	2660	soluble	G	noncrop	PRE	general weed control
copper chelate (alkanolamine complex)	0.65–2.42 g/kg	soluble	S, G	aquatic	POE	algae
copper chelate (ethylene diamine complex)	0.75 ml form./kg	soluble	S	aquatic	POE	algae
copper sulfate (cupric sulfate pentahydrate)	470	soluble	SP	aquatic	POE	algae
copper sulfate (triethanolamine)	8 ml form./kg	soluble	SP	aquatic	POE	algae
sodium chlorate	1200	soluble	S	noncrop	POE	general weed control
sulfuric acid	1 mg/cubic meter	soluble	S	vegetable	POE	grasses, broadleaves

1. *Where water solubility is greater than 100,000 ppm, it is listed as soluble.*
2. *AS   = Aqueous suspension*
   DF   = Dry flowable
   EC   = Emulsifiable concentrate
   G   = Granular
   S   = Soluble concentrate
   SP   = Soluble powder
   WDG = Water dispersible granule
   WP   = Wettable powder
3. *PPI   = Preplant incorporated*
   PRE = Preemergence
   POE = Postemergence

9

SAFETY AND REGULATION

INTRODUCTION

by Robert W. Brazelton[1] and Norman B. Akesson[2]

Most laws and regulations are developed to fill particular needs, and in cases involving a history of accidents or damage from pesticides, it is highly likely that an unfortunate type of incident or oversight leading to injury, especially when repeated numerous times, will result in regulatory action designed to eliminate the incidence of risk.

The overall extent of such laws and regulations is overwhelming, but this text will deal only with some most likely to concern weed-control personnel and associated management.

Origin and Relationships of Laws and Regulations

Within the governmental system, laws, regulations, ordinances, administrative rulings, and interpretations occur from the federal, state, and county levels down to ordinances of local governments. The requirements and effects can vary in detail and may sometimes even conflict with each other. The history of regulatory activities in California in recent years has shown that state regulations often are more comprehensive and restrictive than federal ones.

In the field of chemical weed control, pesticides in use are both subject to federal regulation and also closely monitored and controlled by the California Department of Food and Agriculture under which, not infrequently, controls are more restrictive or detailed than under federal ones. At the same time, regional, county, or local variations may exist to meet special problems.

1. University of California Cooperative Extension, Davis, CA. 2. University of California, Davis, CA.

Regulations/Variations

An excellent material for control of weeds in rice is propanil. Unfortunately, when applied to large acreages at a specific time of year, highly susceptible prune trees growing nearby may be damaged. The problem is complex, involving timing, crop relationships, weather patterns, etc., and because of this combination of factors, it became necessary to restrict the use of propanil in one geographic area. In another part of the state, propanil was allowed because such restrictive conditions do not exist there. As another example, 2,4-D may be used successfully to control broadleaf weeds in remote and extensive grain fields in one area while similar use elsewhere in the state may be restricted due to the close proximity of sensitive crops such as grapes.

The ultimate point of enforcement of pesticide regulations is the county agricultural commissioner's office, and, at the county level, special local conditions may lead one commissioner to enforce regulations somewhat differently from his counterparts elsewhere in the state.

Anyone involved in weed-control work over a widespread geographic area must be aware of these variations and adjust accordingly.

Public Reactions

While the use of agricultural weed-control methods may be very successful in the field, changing agricultural/urban interfaces can lead to differences of opinion and even outright conflict. For instance, a material that has been determined safe by the regulators on the basis of thorough scientific analysis can become a source of contention as a result of changes in drinking-water flavors, odors in the air, or allergic effects. While the complaints may be irritating to the weed controller at times, he or she must recognize the legitimacy of certain complaints and be prepared to alter treatment methods or even entire cultural practices.

Crop Rotations

Crop rotations often introduce practical problems that can be anticipated when the label is carefully studied and related to long-term crop-rotation planning. For example, a herbicide can be applied to a tolerant crop one year, but, if long-lasting characteristics or excessive use effects are carried over into the next year, a subsequently planted susceptible crop may be severely damaged. Other elements are involved as well, hence the need for regulation and extensive, detailed label recommendations.

Civil vs. Criminal Violations

Generally, in cases of nonconformance to weed-control regulations, civil-court actions result. However, in some cases, laws other than pesticide or operational regulations may have been violated. In cases where severe worker injury or death results, or where negligence is proved, it is entirely possible that the violator may face criminal action and severe penalties established for conviction in such cases. One example is the use of spray equipment closer than a specified distance from a high tension power line. This might occur where retractable spray booms are elevated for turnaround or transport where power lines are present.

Applicability of Regulations

In general, regulations are applicable to employees and places of employment. For example, an employer who wishes to use a Category I toxic material must require his employees to observe the regulations established by the Department of Food and Agriculture for handling that material.

If a piece of equipment or material or operational procedure is covered by a regulation, the regulation may apply to employees but not to private operations. If only a private owner is involved and the particular regulation exempts those working, the person involved is well advised to be aware of potential hazards and the consequences of any accident which may occur.

The point to be kept in mind with regard to regulations, whether they are chemical- or machine-oriented, is that the employer is responsible whenever personal injury results to the employee in the course of work. Where the violation relates to crop damage, assignment of responsibility may often have to be determined by the courts. The best defense for those involved in weed-control procedures lies in maintaining a thorough knowledge of label requirements, operational regulations, and general safety orders and standards. This is a tall order, but today it is a necessity.

Rules and regulations as they apply to the activities of the California Department of Food and Agriculture will be discussed in more detail elsewhere in this text.

Perspective of Pesticide Safety

For a good many years, the word 'pesticides' has raised the red flag and at times raised emotions to a fever pitch. But comparison of the incidence of pesticide injury relative to agricultural injuries is instructive. From 1972 through 1981, there were no confirmed deaths attributed to agricultural pesticide injury in California. However, within the same time period but considering only 1976 through 1981, more than 150 persons died in tractor accidents alone, and they included some spray-rig operators (classified as tractor drivers). There are, then, safety orders of several types and safe operational procedures other than pesticide regulations with which weed-control personnel should be acquainted. In fact, these should be so well implanted as to be "second nature" in the daily operations of both managers and workers.

DIVISION OF OCCUPATIONAL SAFETY AND HEALTH

For over half a century, regulation of safety in industry has been in existence in California. The Division of Occupational Safety and Health (DOSH) developed the so-called 'Cal/OSHA' program. For many years this agency has based its regulatory functions on safety standards referred to in California as *safety orders*. Generally these safety orders relate to mechanical or electrical devices and related work procedures, but when chemicals are involved, the agency may join the Department of Food and Agriculture in enforcement in accordance with pre-established cooperative agreements. The legal implications of regulations may change from time to time, so the employer or private operator must be aware of responsibilities that apply and respond accordingly.

Safety Orders

The most basic safety order of significance to employers is a relatively recent one which is brief (only three sentences) and easy to understand. It provides the basis upon which weed-control operators can establish their safety programs. While the legal implications of this order may change as a result of regulatory or legislative interpretation, the concepts are basic to safe operations and can form the basis for any safety program. It simply reads:

ACCIDENT PREVENTION PROGRAM. Effective October 1, 1977, every employer shall inaugurate and maintain an accident-prevention program which shall include, but not be limited to the following:

- *A training program designed to instruct employees in general safe work practices and specific instructions with respect to hazards unique to the employee's job assignment.*
- *Scheduled periodic inspections to identify and correct unsafe conditions and work practices which may be found.*

This order involves both the machine and the worker. Machine safety is covered by the number of safety orders, and worker training is spelled out in others which will be discussed in more detail next.

Tractor Operation

The tractor accident is the most common cause of death in agricultural field operations. The hazard of severe injury has existed since tractors first came into use. Investigations of thousands of tractor-related deaths and injuries over several decades have shown the majority to have been cause by violation of well-defined rules. Causes call for prevention, and extensive worldwide research proved conclusively that the single most effective form of protection would be the development of a satisfactory rollover-protection device for tractors similar to those which have been saving the lives of racing car drivers for years. That device called ROPS (rollover protective structure), combined with the use of a seatbelt to hold the operator in the "zone of safety," has been highly successful and is now required by law.

This history has led to the development of nine rules for tractor operation—one regarding ROPS and the other eight based on the major causes of accidents.

California Safety Orders and federal OSHA regulations require that the *employer* must train each new tractor driver (or spray-rig operator where a tractor is used) in these rules when the driver is hired and once per year thereafter.

These rules are:

1. Securely fasten your seatbelt if the tractor has a ROPS. (Many large field boom sprayers may be exempt from this rule by reason of their structures.)

2. Where possible, avoid operating the tractor near ditches, embankments, and holes.

3. Reduce speed when turning, crossing slopes, and on rough, slick, or muddy surfaces.

4. Stay off slopes too steep for safe operation.

5. Watch where you are going, especially at row ends, on roads, and around trees.

6. Do not permit others to ride on the tractor.

7. Operate the tractor smoothly— no jerky turns, starts, or stops.

8. Hitch only to the drawbar and hitch points recommended by the tractor manufacturer.

9. When tractor is stopped, set brakes securely and use park lock if available.

Forklifts

The handling of herbicides in quantity often involves the use of forklifts to lift pallet loads of containers. This is a specialized area, and the safe operation of forklifts is given rather special attention in California's safety orders, which are too lengthy to include here. Because the safety requirements related to forklifts are extensive, it is advisable that anyone responsible for such operations become well acquainted with these requirements.

Guarding

Spray equipment often involves the use of power-take-off shafts, gear drives, vee belts, or chain drives. Through the years these have been involved in many cases of laceration, amputation, and death. Therefore, the guarding of these drives has been a high priority in safety-order enforcement. Most commonly, home-built spray equipment will have a sheet metal guard below such a drive to keep it from entangling plant material, though the top, which is accessible to the operator, often may be open and unguarded. Regulations detailing requirements for guarding equipment because of the high degree of hazard involved are too extensive to be covered in detail here.

Very simply, the gist of the orders is that if a part rotates in transmitting power, it shall be completely enclosed and the guard itself, if made of material with openings such as expanded metal or grating, shall be spaced far enough away from the moving parts to protect fingers from contact. The wise manager will specify on purchase orders that the equipment being purchased should be designed and manufactured to meet safety standards. Or, if it is absolutely necessary to purchase equipment that does not meet safety standards when delivered, the employer would be wise to take steps to modify the equipment to bring it into conformance.

Power-take-off tractor drive shafts are particularly hazardous. Often these shafts are correctly supplied with free-rotating shield tubes but, upon installation, the connecting universal joints are unguarded. Loose clothing commonly comes in contact with such a part rotating at some 540 rpm and results can be disastrous. If the shaft itself is unguarded, the injury potential is substantially higher.

Electrical Hazards

Basically, all electrical equipment and wiring in weed-control operations must meet existing safety regulations, as well as local building-code requirements. Proper grounding and protection of wiring from physical damage is important, and selection of properly sized wiring to meet electrical load-carrying requirements is essential. Weed-control personnel normally may encounter the greatest hazard on field jobs working near high-voltage overhead power lines. Training should emphasize the motto "Look Up and Live."

Such power lines are often found along the edge of a field or running to irrigation pumping stations. The most common cause of electrocution in agriculture is raising aluminum irrigation pipe so that it touches the power line, or driving under a line with equipment such as a long spray boom raised vertically for transport.

Operators should be trained to avoid such contacts, and to realize that, if they are on a mobile unit that makes such contact and they are initially unharmed, they are probably protected from grounding by the insulation provided by the unit's rubber tires. The best action in such a case is probably to remain in the safe position until rescued, or, if they attempt to get off, to make certain that neither they nor the machine touch the ground with any part. If they jump off, the jump should be completely clear, not touching any part and not allowing anyone to come in contact with the machine until the power company has shut off power and given the word that it can be moved safely.

NOTE: This overhead-power-line hazard has led to one of the most severe enforcement policies. Not maintaining 10 or more feet of clearance between upraised equipment and the power line is not only contrary to safety orders, but may also involve criminal charges under the Labor Code. Every employer and employee should be well informed of the requirements.

Employee Exposure and Medical Records

Regulations provide for employee access to personal medical records and exposure cards. The complexity of applying these regulations in practice is a matter which the employer should investigate thoroughly and perhaps request assistance in interpreting.

CHEMICAL DRIFT AND ITS CONTROL

The safety aspects of chemical drift have long presented problems in weed-control operations. These problems have ranged from damaged roses in the garden adjacent to a vacant lot where city workers applied a herbicide, to major losses and consequent lawsuits due to the drift of herbicides onto grape vineyards, cotton fields, and prune orchards. Some of these cases have been severe enough to cause serious financial damage to those involved or to lead to the banning or severe restriction of the use of the particular herbicide.

Drift-control Factors

Given that the safety of an operation may be impaired by numerous factors, among which may be the production of undesirable drift, a few practical application rules should be noted. The possibility of drift may be related to:

- type of application equipment and the droplet size produced
- chemical formulation
- microclimate
- size of area to be treated
- the operator's technique and skill.

Drift

When spray applications are made, the larger spray droplets of perhaps 100–200 microns in diameter and larger fall below the applicator (aircraft or ground sprayer) or may be carried a short distance downwind as swath displacement. The smaller droplets (under 100 microns), however, may be carried downwind great distances before reaching the ground, or lofted upward and carried even greater distances. If such a cloud of tiny droplets remains concentrated enough upon reaching the ground, economic damage may be done to the crop on which it descends. Such a situation is normally found when there is severe temperature inversion and little wind velocity. On the other hand, if air-mixing and lofting of the material to higher altitudes occur, it is entirely possible that the particles will be sufficiently scattered and degraded to pose no economic hazard. Drift may involve:

Tiny droplets: These can be carried in the air and deposited as noted above to cause damage.

Vapor: Volatile herbicides, once deposited, may volatilize and the vapor may cause damage to downwind sensitive crops on contact; or the vapor may collect on dust or plant particles in the air and thus be transported in the air.

Crystals and dust: Once a herbicide is in place on the target crop and the ground beneath the crop, the material may adhere to dust particles or the water may just evaporate to leave tiny crystals of the active materials. Then mechanical agitation created by passing vehicles or by the force of winds may cause these crystals or contaminated dust particles to once again become airborne only to be deposited downwind on sensitive crops.

NOTE: If the weed-control person is aware of such problems, the distinction between slight visual damage and economic damage should be kept in mind. If only a small spot is detected here and there on plants or tree leaves, the damage may be insignificant; no real commercial damage has been done. However, if widespread discoloration, defoliation, or some other form of plant damage occurs, seriously affecting the sensitive crop, the drift may then be considered a serious problem.

It is this latter kind of drift damage that causes deep concern and that may result in legal actions to recover losses. Drawing the fine line between two kinds of damage is difficult, considering both the emotions and the profit motives likely to be involved. So it should be clear that in herbicide application, every precaution must be taken to avoid any form of material transfer to sensitive areas.

Swath Displacement

A rather widespread misconception has led to viewing as 'drift' the movement of offending material across a fence line and into an adjacent sensitive crop when the wind is blowing in the direction of the crop. Usually, movement of this kind involved damage for a distance of only perhaps 150–200 feet. A classic example of such short-distance movement caused severe damage to grape vineyards adjoining a railroad right-of-way some years ago when railroad workers sprayed weeds along the right-of-way. Such short-distance movement of rather high concentrations of active material is not properly the same 'drift' that may do damage at substantial distance. In such cases, the wind has merely moved the swath application downwind a short distance, and this can be more accurately defined as *swath displacement,* essentially a mechanical process of literally moving the normal spray droplets with the wind. Classic drift, on the other hand, depends largely upon a different mechanism involving smaller droplets.

Microweather

From the above descriptions, it will be seen that one prime element controlling drift is air. Hence, microweather—or the precise air movement, temperature, and humidity at the plant level and above the crop in the immediate application area and in nearby areas likely to be affected—is the controlling factor. The overall weather pattern for a county or larger area of a state may actually be substantially different from the immediate environment at crop level. Hence, the applicator must examine these extremely localized conditions and not be led astray by the more general weather report that would be given for the region.

Temperature and Relative Humidity

Temperature and relative humidity have significant effects on the evaporation rates of water mixes, but, as a practical matter where application work to be done is extensive and the time element critical, these factors may not normally be considered, even though temperature limits may be specified. Other factors affecting spray-droplet movement have more immediate effects, which in turn may be modified by temperature.

Temperature Inversion

This condition of the immediate atmosphere in the crop area can present the greatest drift hazard to nearby sensitive crops. A typical inversion occurs early in the morning although it can also occur at other times. During the night, especially on a clear night, the ground radiates warmth to the cooler sky. The air above, however, may retain a large portion of its daytime heat. As dawn approaches, the air at ground level will be cool and as the air temperature is measured progressively upward, it will prove progressively warmer and then, further upward, will decline continually to higher altitudes. This, in effect, creates a warm-air blanket or barrier above the crop, effectively holding the lower air and its spray-droplet load near the ground and below the level of highest temperature. This spray-contaminated air can move laterally at a low level allowing the small spray droplets in relatively high concentration to drop slowly and to eventually be deposited on some sensitive crop. This condition can produce the most severe drift damage.

Lapse

The opposite of inversion is a condition called 'lapse.' It can be most easily described by referring to the same early morning field condition that generated an inversion. As the day progresses, the sun warms the ground, raising its temperature until it is warmer than the air above it. From that time on, the highest temperature in the system is at the ground, and, progressing upward, the temperature is found to decline with increase in altitude. This situation allows droplets light enough to float in the air to be lofted upward. As they move upward with warm air rising from the ground, horizontal wind movement may cause mixing, and the droplets may finally fall to earth, but because of the wide scattering during the lapse, they will probably be so widely dispersed as to cause no visual or economic damage.

Sensitive Area Considerations

Considering the effects of microweather, it becomes clear that whenever sensitive crops exist nearby, the wise chemical applicator will make the effort to analyze the microweather situation in order to determine an appropriate spray time. An adverse application condition at 7:00 a.m. can suddenly yield to ideal conditions a short time later. Smoke layers have commonly been used as excellent indicators, and where environmental controls permit, they can be used to identify an inversion. An alternative method would be to identify the nature of time, temperature, and wind conditions.

Spray Nozzles

The previous discussion of chemical drift points toward a critical factor that may have a major influence on drift. That factor is droplet size. Ideally, of course, applications would be made with all droplets the same size, small enough for good coverage yet large enough to minimize drift. Much research and development have gone into making nozzles or other droplet generators that can do this. Substantial progress has been made, but unfortunately, the commercially available single-drop-size generator remains to be developed.

Some nozzles do a better job than others. Typical fan, offset, and cone nozzles disperse a wide range of droplet sizes. Newer developments such as the "raindrop" and the "low pressure" (LP) nozzles have narrowed the range of drop size. The applicator must be alert and not drawn into a web of wishful thinking that he is now using a "drift-proof" nozzle. Some rotary devices are advertised as producing a very narrow range of droplet sizes, which they can do under very specific conditions of fluid flow and velocity, but the fact remains that even these release a percentage of droplet sizes smaller than desirable minimums.

Wind-shear Effect

While a great deal of attention is given to the selection of nozzles to obtain proper droplet size, the manner of installation of those nozzles on an aircraft can substantially change the desired droplet diameter. If the nozzle discharges parallel to air flow as the aircraft moves forward, most droplets will be the size intended unless aircraft speed is too great. If the nozzle is rotated downward so that the angle of the discharge stream to the airflow approaches 90 degrees, the air will shear off the stream, effectively breaking it up to produce a much smaller droplet spectrum, thus increasing the potential for drift.

Spray-nozzle Wear

In general, the applicator must be aware that the flow of chemicals through nozzles wears them out. Nozzle life varies, depending upon the hardness and other physical characteristics of the nozzle material and upon the abrasiveness of the chemical flowing through the nozzle. Sooner or later, however, the orifice size will become enlarged and misshapen, and at that point an increased material flow can seriously affect sprayer calibration, and, as the size of the orifice increases, the amount of material being applied may surpass the safety limits. The result may be over-application with the possibility of residue problems, costly waste of spray material, and assorted crop damage.

The applicator must recognize the vital need for periodic inspection and calibration to assure that the material is applied uniformly and in the right amount. It is important to know that nozzles of different materials and spraying different formulations wear at different rates, but that eventual wear is inevitable. One cannot go merrily on his way expecting to get by without periodic calibration simply because he believes the nozzles are hardened stainless and therefore could "never wear out."

SAFETY IN AERIAL CONDITIONS

Weed-control personnel may have various assignments that involve them in aerial operations. Some may work full time in this area while others, as advisers or chemical-company representatives, only become involved occasionally. The "full-timer" may be well-trained, but the occasional visitor may be more subject to hazard. Some basic rules apply for both safety and good relations with aerial operators.

Rotors and Propellers

Helicopter rotors and airplane propellers rotate at such high speeds that they may be invisible. When working near such aircraft, the greatest danger lies in lack of attention. Anyone concentrating on a problem or involved in conversation may be momentarily distracted and, in the process, inadvertently step into a turning rotor or propeller. The main helicopter rotor can turn close enough to the ground to strike a person; it has happened. The power generated by such blades is hard to believe. The small tail rotor, even though most are guarded, spins at a speed that makes it invisible.

These dangers are so deadly that one simply must remember that, when an engine is running, the responsibility for personal safety lies strictly with those on the ground. Everyone should *stay clear,* maintain awareness of the rotating part above all other matters, and not permit any discussion, argument, or technical matter to result in any form of distraction that could lead to a serious accident.

There is one variation on these rules that is equally important: *Never turn your back on an approaching aircraft.* The typical agricultural aircraft moves on the ground in the tail-down position. This substantially reduces the pilot's vision directly in front of the plane, and it is up to people on the ground to consider that the pilot cannot see anyone in front of the plane and to stay clear.

Aircraft Crashes

A person nearby when such a disaster occurs may be in a position to save the pilot's life with proper action. On the other hand, ignorance and improper action on the part of those present at a crash scene have been known to contribute to the pilot's death. The right procedures to follow are those outlined in the California Agricultural Aircraft Association's manual, *Ground Crew—This Is Your Life;* they are adapted as follows:

1. *Do not panic.* You can't think clearly or help the pilot unless you are calm.

2. Get the fire extinguisher out of your truck and go immediately to the plane.

3. If the plane is on fire:
- Try to get the pilot out and move him to a safe distance.
- Put out the fire with your extinguisher unless it is too dangerous to do so.

4. Check the pilot's clothing to see if he has been splashed with pesticides. If so, and he isn't seriously injured, help him to the nearest water and wash him several times with soap.

5. If the pilot isn't seriously injured, take him to a hospital or a doctor. *Be sure* to tell them if he has been exposed to pesticides and the name of that pesticide. Take a label with you if it is available. The doctor can use its instructions.

6. If the pilot is seriously injured or unconscious, *do not move him* from the plane except to save his life from fire.

7. Check to see if he is strangling or choking; check for bleeding. When there is severe bleeding, make a pad out of a clean cloth and hold it very firmly with your hand directly over the cut. Keep pressure on the cut , and raise the wounded area if you can. As soon as practical, go or have someone go to the nearest phone to call for an ambulance or a doctor. Be sure to tell them where you are.

8. If you can't get an ambulance, phone your company immediately and tell them what has happened and *exactly* where the injured pilot is.

9. Follow the ambulance to the hospital or doctor's office to make certain they know the pilot has been exposed to pesticides. If they give him a shot of morphine for pain and he has phosphate poisoning it could kill him.

Good Manners

Anyone working around or visiting an agricultural aircraft should know that a pilot depends on the proper functioning of his aircraft for his work and his life. Most pilots take great pride in their aircraft and may deeply resent the actions of any visitor who mars or damages them.

There is very little reason for a casual visitor to climb on the plane. If it is necessary to do so, the proper walkways are clearly marked (usually, a black, non-slip surface). The area outside of the walkway is strictly off-limits and not intended to support the weight of a person. Also, contact with or damage to any other part of the aircraft must be avoided. The pilot will appreciate attention to such correct procedures which may prevent future problems or accidents.

Cleaning and Rinsing

During normal flight operations it is easiest to flush the aircraft tank, to fill it partially with clean water, and then fly back over the treated area to spray the rinse water on the crop. This technique reduces the problem of disposal of rinse water at the landing strip. Of course, it will be more economical to dump at the strip, and therein lies a problem.

Disposal of rinse water and possible spilled chemical must be done in a manner that meets state regulations, and, in particular, must be done so that there is no possibility of contamination of groundwater. This always requires good judgment, respect for regulations, and a good understanding of the possibility of severe consequences of improper dumping.

Waste disposal is the concern of regulating agencies. The regulations that apply essentially require the system to be capable of preventing contamination of groundwater and streams. Because of the great variety of soil conditions and operation requirements, no further details will be gone into here. Anyone involved in such rinse-water disposal should contact the local county agricultural commissioner for assistance.

When Cleaning Aircraft or Equipment Remember:
- That it is contaminated from the use of chemicals.
- To wear chemical-resistant boots and gloves, and other protective clothing.
- To be sure to have plenty of ventilation.
- That it can be dangerous to steam-clean equipment because steam can change chemicals into vapor that can be absorbed and inhaled more readily.
- To keep clear of steam, splash, and vapor.
- After washing equipment—bathe.
- To use plenty of soap and water, or solvent.
- After washing equipment—change clothes. Do not wear clothing that may be contaminated.

Maintenance Hazards

Spray systems normally have plugged or worn nozzles at some time. Since such systems have been carrying chemicals, the person working on one should consider that a chemical may be present and should, therefore, take the necessary precautions to avoid contact with it when removing parts. The temptation to blow backward through a plugged nozzle should be overcome, since, naturally, any part which has been in contact with a poison should not be put to one's lips. Nozzles are delicate with finely machined orifices and so must be cleaned with something soft, a wooden toothpick, or soft brass wire—not a pocketknife!

If for some reason welding must be done, the system must be absolutely clean to prevent the formation of dangerous gases. Any welder should also be aware of the dangers of welding on galvanized material and the consequent dangerous fumes.

Wear Protective Equipment When You Handle Chemicals

The correct procedures for handling chemicals are covered in detail in regulations too extensive to include here. Also, from time to time, new developments make it necessary to revise the regulations. If agricultural chemicals are to be handled, the county agricultural commissioner should be contacted for copies of the latest regulations and any other instructions he may wish to give regarding such activities.

Special Rules for Flagmen

1. Wear protective clothing and equipment: Coveralls, hard hat, and respirator when exposed to vapors, spray mist, or dust.

2. Know what chemical is being used. Read the label before going to the field.

3. Keep as much spray and dust off yourself as possible. *Always* start flagging on downwind side and flag into the wind—never into the drift.

4. If possible, never flag under power lines or near fences. If the plane should cut the wires or snag the fence, the trailing wires could hurt you.

5. In applying Category I materials, where possible flag in the field adjacent to the one you are treating.

6. When you arrive at the field to be treated, warn people who are in or around that field that an aircraft is going to treat the field. Ask them to stay out of the field and away from the drift.

7. Park vehicles off the highway or road in such a manner that they will not block traffic.

8. Watch the airplane at all times—but especially when it is approaching you. Do not turn away, or you won't be able to tell how close it is.

9. After the airplane is lined up in your position, move at least the distance of the next pass, but *do not turn your back* on an approaching airplane.

10. Stay at the field location until the pilot has *completed* the job. In case of an accident, you may be able to help the pilot.

REFERENCES

Akesson, N.B., and W.E. Yates. Pesticide application—equipment and techniques. FAO Serv. Bull. No. 38, Univ. of Calif., Davis, 1979.

Akesson, N.B., and W.E. Yates. The use of Aircraft in Agriculture. FAO Agricultural Series No. 2, FAO Ag. Dev. Paper No. 94, Univ. of Calif., Davis, 1974.

Akesson, N.B., W.E. Yates, and R.W. Brazelton. Guidelines for improving insecticide, herbicide, and crop defoliant application efficiency. Ag. Eng. Dept., Univ. of Calif., Davis

Akesson, N.B., W.E. Yates, and R.W. Brazelton. Monitoring airborne pesticide chemical levels and their effects on workers mixing, loading and applying or entering treated fields. ASAE Paper No. 78-3565, 1978.

Akesson, N.B., and W.E. Yates. Drift loss control: Anything new? Aerial Applicator, Nov./Dec., 1981, pp. 4–5.

Brazelton, Robert W. Calibration of herbicide sprayers, Leaflet No. 2710, Coop. Ext., Univ. of Calif., 1975.

Brazelton, Robert W., and W.B. McHenry. How much chemical do you put in the tank? Leaflet No. 2718, Coop. Ext., Univ. of Calif., 1975

Doll, S.D., E.L. Knake, and B.J. Butler, Effects of wear on nozzle tips. Ill. Res., Vol. 8, No. 2, pp. 10–11, Ill. Ag. Exp. Stn., 1966.

Yates, W.E., R.E. Cowden, and N.B. Akesson. Effect of nozzle design on uniformity of droplet size from agricultural aircraft. ASAE Paper AA-81-002, 1981.

REGULATION AND REGISTRATION

by Keith T. Maddy[1], Frank Schneider,[2] and Sue Edmiston[3]

Two federal statutes provide the authority to regulate pesticides: the Federal Insecticide, Fungicide, and Rodenticide Act (FIFRA), and several sections of the Food, Drug, and Cosmetic Act (FDCA). FDCA establishes tolerances of pesticides in food. FIFRA, enacted in 1947 and amended several times, most recently in 1988, states that health and environmental concerns are to be balanced against the benefits of use. It provides for control of pesticides, creates a restricted-use classification for selected pesticides, and permits states to regulate pesticides in a manner consistent with federal requirements.

The regulations for the enforcement of FIFRA are in the Code of Federal Regulations, Protection of Environment, Title 40, Parts 150 to 189. It is the responsibility of the Environmental Protection Agency (EPA) to administer these regulations.

Pesticides cannot be distributed or offered for sale by any person or state unless registered with the EPA. A pesticide is classified for general or restricted use by the EPA. Restricted-use pesticides require more precautions during application than do general-use pesticides.

Changing pest-control needs and increased environmental concerns in different states have increased the states' legislative role in pesticide regulation.

California has adopted additional regulations to meet environmental and safety concerns and needs of the public, farm employees, and farmers. The state has also developed its own restricted-materials list using the following criteria: (1) danger to or impairment of public health; and (2) hazard to farmworkers, crops, and domestic animals and/or subsequent plantings from persistent residues in the soil.

Most herbicides are not as acutely toxic as such insecticides as the organophosphates, but, in laboratory animal studies, a number of them have shown the potential for causing chronic effects if exposure is sufficient. Herbicides are legally classified as pesticides and are subject to federal registration and use requirements.

California also has pesticide worker-safety and restricted-materials regulations to specify safe work practices for employees who mix, load, apply, store, or otherwise handle pesticides or enter treated areas. The work practice regulations are designed to reduce risk during exposure.

It is the responsibility of employers to provide safe workplaces for employees and to ensure that employees follow safe work practices. Employees are required to be aware of pesticide-worker safety hazards and pesticide safety regulations applicable to all activities they perform.

1, 2, 3. California Department of Food and Agriculture, Sacramento, CA.

The California Department of Food and Agriculture (CDFA) is the lead agency for enforcing federal and state pesticide laws and regulations. The county agricultural commissioner is responsible for enforcing all federal, state, and county regulations and is the local source of information on these regulations. For example, prior to obtaining a permit to use any restricted pesticide, applicants must contact the agricultural commissioner in the county where use is anticipated and confirm with the commissioner that the applicants have knowledge of regulations and safety precautions, and answer any additional questions pertaining to the proposed use.

LABEL REQUIREMENTS AND INTERPRETATION

All labels are required to contain information specified by FIFRA and the regulations in Title 40 (Section 162.10). The label must clearly show the following: the product trade name; the name of the registrant; net weight or measure of contents; the EPA registration number; the registration number of the formulation plant; an ingredient statement giving the name and percentage by weight of the active ingredient and the percentage of inert ingredients; the use-classification (general or restricted); directions for use; warnings or precautionary statement.

The warnings and precautionary statements deal with questions of toxicology and environmental, physical, or chemical hazards. A toxicity category is assigned to every pesticide product according to the criteria in the following table of possible acute effects:

Toxicity categories

Hazard indicators	I	II	III	IV
Oral LD_{50}	Up to and including 50 mg/kg	From 50 thru 500 mg/kg	From 500 thru 5000 mg/kg	Greater than 5000 mg/kg
Inhalation LC_{50}	Up to and including 0.2 mg/liter	From 0.2 thru 2 mg/liter	From 2 thru 20 mg/liter	Greater than 20 mg/liter
Dermal LD_{50}	Up to and including 200 mg/kg	From 200 thru 2000 mg/kg	From 2000 thru 20,000 mg/kg	Greater than 20,000 mg/kg
Eye effects	Corrosive, corneal opacity; not reversible within 7 days	Corneal opacity; reversible within 7 days; irritation persisting for 7 days	No corneal opacity; irritation reversible within 7 days	No irritation
Skin effects	Corrosive	Severe irritation at 72 hours	Moderate irritation at 72 hours	Mild or slight irritation at 72 hours

LD_{50} or LC_{50} is the dose or concentration required to kill 50% of the test animal population.

The signal word DANGER is required for any pesticide meeting one or more of the criteria under Toxicity Category I. Toxicity Category II materials require the signal WARNING, while Categories III and IV use the signal word CAUTION.

Both federal and state laws and regulations require that pesticides be used in accordance with the labeling, and this includes following the safety precautions on the label. However, it is impossible to include detailed instructions necessary for adequate safety procedures for all of the combinations of circumstances that may occur. For example, one might assume that the most hazardous vapors or spray mist occur in confined spaces indoors, but hazardous conditions may occur in open areas if there is no wind.

The period of greatest hazard in any pesticide-applications procedure is usually during pouring and mixing operations in which splashing and spilling may occur on either skin or clothing. To protect the eyes from splashes or spills when handling liquid pesticides, a face shield is superior to goggles because of the personal comfort and complete face protection afforded. However, when handling powders or dusts, goggles are preferred since particles will rise under a face shield. Respiratory protection is needed whenever volatile, toxic liquid pesticides or toxic dusts and powders are handled.

Skin protection for workers is the most difficult problem associated with the application of pesticides. In hot weather, the use of clothing impervious to pesticides may create a hazard of heat prostration greater than that of pesticide exposure. Recent innovations in designing protective clothing with new porous fibers may alleviate this problem in the future.

CDFA regulations require an employer to base the training for employees on information given on the label, in the regulations, and in appropriate Pesticide Safety Information leaflets available through the county agricultural commissioner's office. They also require that employees be provided with protective clothing and devices to mitigate exposure hazards shown on the labeling. Protective-device requirements found on a label must be interpreted relative to the real or potential hazard of the situation. For example, if the hazard has been mitigated by such measures as enclosed cockpit, boom location, remote-control operation, or closed pumping system, the operator is not required to take the protective measures stated on the label. The CDFA publishes "Guidelines for Interpreting Pesticide Label Statements for Protective Device Requirements," pertaining to their interpretation of labels and protective device requirements. This information may be obtained from the CDFA or your agricultural commissioner.

Closed Systems

Hand pouring has been found to be the most hazardous activity involved in the handling of highly toxic liquid pesticides and has resulted in serious human illnesses. A "closed system" removes a pesticide from its original container, rinses the emptied container, and transfers the pesticide and rinsate through connecting hoses, pipes, and couplings that are sufficiently tight to prevent exposure of any person to the pesticide or rinse solution. Some closed systems also measure the amount of chemical needed, completely eliminating human exposure to the chemical. Use of such systems is required when using Toxicity Category I liquid pesticides.

Respiratory Protection

One requirement of a respiratory-protection program is to first assess the inhalation hazards to which workers will be exposed. The assessment process involves first gathering information concerning the toxicity of the pesticide(s); determining whether it will be a gas, dust, vapor, or mist exposure; accurately estimating the concentrations around the worker; and noting any special precautionary requirements determined through the latest research.

When hazardous concentrations of pesticides cannot be removed from the worker's breathing zone, or when emergency protection against occasional or brief exposure is needed, the employer must provide, and the employee must use, approved respiratory equipment.

Each employee must be instructed and trained by management in the need, use, sanitary care, and limitations of any respiratory equipment he may have to use.

Several organizations and individuals are available to answer questions arising from specific instances. Among them are:
- Safety equipment retailers (see local telephone directory Yellow Pages).
- California Department of Food and Agriculture.
- County Agricultural Commissioner.

Worker Health and Safety

There are both state and federal laws and regulations pertaining to worker health and safety. California has had laws and regulations in place for agricultural workers since the mid-1970s. These regulations, titled "The California Code for Regulations Pertaining to Worker Safety," are updated as required to ensure a safe agricultural working environment in California. California's existing regulations specify that when there is a conflict between state and federal law, the most restrictive requirement applies. In addition to providing information pertaining to safe work practices and associated responsibility, California's regulations include recommendations for re-entry intervals to ensure that workers are not exposed to toxic concentrations of pesticides. All Toxicity Category I pesticides require one-day re-entry periods, while other individual pesticides carry intervals appropriate to their toxicity, residual properties, and crop/use patterns. With the exception of Toxicity Category I materials, there are currently no re-entry intervals listed for herbicides.

First Aid and Decontamination Procedures

A person who becomes ill while working with pesticides should stop work immediately, notify the supervisor or a fellow employee of the situation, and take whatever measures are necessary to eliminate continued pesticide exposure. The ill person should go to a source of fresh air, remove work clothing, shower completely (including washing the hair), and change into clean clothing. (If shower facilities are not immediately available, the person should remove all clothing immediately and use whatever water source is available to clean the body.) If the person collapses suddenly while working with pesticides, he or she should be removed from the pesticide use area immediately and given whatever resuscitation may be necessary.

Persons caring for the ill worker should be aware that a sudden collapse may be due to a heart attack or other medical emergencies not related to pesticide exposure. Rescuers should also be careful not to contaminate themselves while caring for a victim whose skin and clothing may be saturated with pesticide chemicals. Once the ill person has been resuscitated (if necessary) and decontaminated, he should be transported immediately to the nearest emergency-medical-care facility. It is very important to supply the physician or emergency room personnel where the victim is taken with as much information as possible regarding the circumstances under which the illness began. It is also useful to provide the examining physician with the name of the product or products the victim was handling or was exposed to, and pertinent information about it/them, including labels and antidotes if known.

REGISTRATION OF HERBICIDES IN CALIFORNIA

Products submitted to the California Department of Food and Agriculture for possible registration must also hold current federal (EPA) registration or be in an EPA review process. Prior to federal registration, the registrant must submit data according to Title 40, Section 162.8 of the federal regulations. These data requirements include, but are not limited to, the following:

- Efficacy
- General chemistry (composition and analytical method for the technical and formulated products)
- Environmental chemistry (field stability, degradation data, etc.)

- Hazard to humans and domestic animals (acute toxicity, subacute and chronic toxicity, first-aid and diagnostic information, foliar residue, and exposure information)
- Hazard to nontarget organisms (toxicity to fish and avian species)

The data submitted determine the registerability and the use-classification (signal word and necessity, if any, for restricted material). Requirements of some or all of these data may be waived if the registrant submits evidence that the properties of the product are fundamentally different from those considered by the EPA in establishing data requirements.

Before the state of California registers a herbicide for use, it must have a federal registration as a pesticide. California requires at least the same data as that submitted to the EPA. California may also require additional data if the properties of the product warrant such action under the state's unique use-conditions or laws. Exact data requirements may be found in the California Administrative Code, Title 3, Chapter 4. The following is a list of some of the pertinent "California-only" data requirements:

- **Dermal Absorption** (To assess the rate and extent of absorption through the skin as well as the chemical's effect once it enters the body.)
- **Mixer/Loader/Applicator Exposure** (To determine the extent of exposure and the necessity for additional use-precautions.)
- **Medical Management Data** (This information, backed by experimental data, is needed in order to inform physicians of the methods of treatment for overexposure.)
- **Field Re-entry Information** (Dislodgeable-foliar and soil-residue data under California conditions.)
- **Spray Adjuvants—Acute Toxicity** (To assess the potential hazards of use.)
- **Residue-Test Methods** (To have the best possible, fastest method to assure foods comply with residue tolerances.)
- **Efficacy** (Required for all label claims to ensure that the user will get a useful product.)
- **Hazard to Bees** (For products likely to contact apiaries or pollinating bees.)
- **Closed-System Compatibility** (Viscosity information required on all Toxicity Category I pesticides.)
- **Effects on Pest-management Systems** (Required for addition of new crops to label.)
- **Inert-ingredient Hazards** (To assess chronic toxicity of more hazardous inert ingredients.)
- **Volatile Organic Materials** (To evaluate ambient air-quality standards of these materials.)

- **Other Data Upon Request** (This includes, but is not limited to, data on pesticide drift, phytotoxicity, environmental effects, analytical and environmental chemistry, effects from use of two or more products in combination, and contaminants in products.)

In addition, products may be used in California under a Section 5 (experimental use permit) registration, a Section 24(c) (special local need) registration, and/or a Section 18 (emergency) exemption registration. Experimental use permits allow for the development of data. If a pesticide registered for experimental use is applied on food crops, the crop will be destroyed if no food tolerance has been established. A Section 18 exemption may allow the use of an unregistered pesticide when emergency conditions exist. Emergencies can be a pest outbreak with no pesticides registered for that use or alternative method of control available, and where significant economic or health problems will occur. A Section 24(c) registration can allow for the minor use of a particular pesticide when this use is not registered on the label. No pesticide which has been canceled or suspended may be used under a 24(c) registration.

PESTICIDE STORAGE, TRANSPORTATION, AND DISPOSAL

All storage areas should be clean, dry, and well-lighted during use. Storage areas containing pesticides with the signal words DANGER or WARNING on the label must have warning signs posted at all probable directions of approach. These signs should say: "DANGER POISON STORAGE AREA," or some similar warning, and be readable from a distance of 25 feet. Pesticides should be stored only in properly labeled original containers, never in food or beverage containers.

All pesticides should be transported in a secure, upright position, with the opening closed to prevent spillage. All containers must have some form of labeling attached, which should be either the original labeling or with service container labeling as specified by regulations.

Empty unrinsed pesticide containers are considered hazardous waste and must be disposed of in an approved manner. Each emptied container that held less than 28 gallons must be triple-rinsed upon emptying. This rinse solution should be added to the mix tank. Some empty containers may be reconditioned by recyclers approved by the California Department of Health Services. Containers that cannot be reconditioned must be disposed of at a disposal site approved by the Water Resources Control Board. Emptied pesticide containers awaiting disposal or reconditioning should be stored in a locked enclosure and under control of a responsible person.

Storage of pesticide waste products (old materials, unused tank mixes) or emptied containers may require a hazardous waste facility permit. The Department of Health Services provides information concerning specific requirements.

Outer shipping containers not contaminated with pesticide residues and containers that held dry pesticide formulations shall be disposed of as permitted by state and local regulations. If regulations permit, these containers may be disposed of by burning at the use site. (Always stand upwind from the smoke while burning bags or outer containers.)

Finally, users should contact the county agricultural commissioner who will be familiar with all local requirements pertaining to disposal of pesticide containers.

RECOMMENDATIONS

Of the many regulations that apply to the use of pesticides in California, one of the most important deals with who can give what advice on what chemical to apply and under what circumstances.

In California it is unlawful for any person to act or offer to act as an agricultural pest control adviser without first having secured an agricultural pest control adviser's (PCA) license from the CDFA. Additional information pertaining to the responsibilities of the PCA may be found in Chapter 10. An appropriate B.S. or B.A. degree or applicable college course work plus suitable experience is required of applicants.

Applicants for licensing must elect to be examined for certification in one or more of the following categories:
- Control of insects, mites, and other invertebrates.
- Control of plant pathogens.
- Control of nematodes.
- Control of vertebrate pests.
- Control of weeds.
- Defoliation.
- Plant growth regulation.

Agricultural pest control advisers must put all recommendations concerning any agricultural use in writing. One copy of each written recommendation must be signed, dated, and furnished to the grower. Where a pesticide use is recommended, a copy must also be furnished to the dealer and the applicator. Each written recommendation must include, when applicable, the following:
- The name and dosage of each pesticide to be used or description of method recommended.
- The identity of each pest to be controlled.
- The owner or operator, location, and acreage to be treated.
- The commodity, crop, or site to be treated.
- The suggested schedule, time, or conditions for the pesticide application or other control method.

- A warning of the possibility of damages by the pesticide application that are known to exist.
- The signature and address of the person making the recommendation, the date, and the name of the business that the person represents.

  Any other information the CDFA may require such as:
- Total acreage or units to be treated;
- Concentration and volume per acre or other units;
- Worker re-entry interval, if one has been established; preharvest or preslaughter interval; and label restrictions on use or disposition of the treated commodity, by-products, or treated area;
- Criteria used for determining the need for the recommended treatment; and
- Certification that alternatives and mitigation measures that would substantially lessen any significant adverse impact on the environment have been considered, and, if feasible, adopted.

  In addition, the recommendation should designate the pest by accepted common name.

LEGISLATIVE CHANGES

In the past few years, a series of administrative and regulatory actions concerning pesticides have been taken by the federal government, and a number of pieces of state and federal legislation and one state initiative have been enacted. These are now having a major impact on which pesticides will be used in California, as well as when and where they will be used. In the mid-to-late 1980s these were being implemented simultaneously; they will significantly affect pesticide use in the 1990s. Several of these are summarized below.

Pesticide Contamination Prevention Act of 1985

The stated purpose of the Pesticide Contamination Prevention Act, enacted by the California Legislature, is to prevent further pesticide contamination of California groundwater which may be used for drinking water. The act requires the CDFA to:

- Collect and analyze environmental fate data on all pesticides registered for agricultural use in California to determine groundwater data gaps and identify and monitor potential contaminants;
- Review any pesticide or related chemical found in groundwater or in soil under certain conditions to determine if that chemical pollutes or threatens to pollute groundwater as a result of legal agricultural use, and take appropriate corrective action when necessary; and

- Compile and maintain a statewide data base of wells sampled for pesticide active ingredients.

  Examples of herbicides that are currently being reviewed under this act include atrazine, bromacil, diuron, prometon, and simazine.

Birth Defects Prevention Act of 1984

This required the CDFA to acquire complete study data developed in accord with 1984 EPA federal regulations for general chronic effects, cancer, reproductive effects, teratology, neurotoxicity, and mutagenicity for each of the more than 600 pesticide active ingredients registered. It also required risk assessments that could lead to restrictions or cancellations in accordance with the severity of adverse effects found.

A number of herbicides have had assessment notices to fill data requirements under this legislation. The cost of filling the initial data requirements for each individual pesticide has been estimated at approximately $3 million. Examples of individual herbicides that have had assessment notices in the range of the aforementioned amount include chloramben, chlorsulfuron, DCPA, oxyfluorfen, and terbacil.

Toxic Air Contaminants Act of 1983

This act requires, among other things, that the Director of Food and Agriculture, in consultation with other agencies and groups, determines the appropriate degree of control measures for pesticides identified as toxic air contaminants. Pesticides, including a number of herbicides (e.g., 2,4-D, bromoxynil, diquat, methyl bromide, and paraquat) are currently under review. Suggested practicable control techniques to prevent an endangerment to the public health include, but are not limited to, the following: label amendments, applicator training, restrictions on use patterns or locations, changes in application procedures, reclassification as a restricted material, and cancellation.

The Safe Drinking Water and Toxic Enforcement Act of 1986 (Proposition 65)

This act is a result of a ballot initiative passed by the people of California. It provides that "no person in the course of doing business shall knowingly and intentionally expose any individual to a chemical known to the state to cause cancer or reproductive toxicity without first giving clear and reasonable warning to such individual," (Health and Safety Code Section 25249.6). Three key issues associated with this act relate to warning, labeling, and discharge requirements. This act also requires the governor to publish each year a current list of chemicals known to the state to cause cancer or reproductive toxicity. A number of pesticides have been listed, many of which are no longer registered for use in California. The only herbicide currently listed is amitrole.

Endangered Species Protection

The EPA is required by current law to regulate the use of pesticides so that a hazard to endangered species (including weeds) is avoided. The EPA has experienced great difficulty in implementing this law. The EPA proposes to make significant progress in this area in the next few years. The first proposals on restriction or non-use of chemicals to accomplish this would have significantly reduced the number of chemicals (including some herbicides) and the areas where they could have been used. As label changes are made and regulations are put into place, the locales and the time of year when some herbicides can be used will be affected by this program.

People who have an interest in continued use of chemical pesticides would do well to become actively involved in supporting enactment and enforcement of laws and regulations that allow continued use of pesticides. Along with this, of course, should go careful attention, so that the environment and the public's health are not adversely affected.

INDIVIDUAL HERBICIDES

There are a number of herbicides that are registered for use in California that have special problems associated with either their toxicity or use. It is not the intent of this section to single out individual products or formulations, but to provide *examples* of individual herbicides that fall into one or more of the aforementioned categories.

Toxicity Related

Toxicity Category I
- Acifluorfen, acrolein, alachlor, benefin, difenzoquat, fluazifop-P, metolachlor, paraquat, and sulfuric acid.

It should be noted that inclusion in Toxicity Category I may be made on the basis of either the actual toxicity of the herbicide, or the toxicity of the inert ingredients included in the formulation (e.g., solvents), or both.

Use Related

Spray and/or Vapor Drift
- 2,4-D, dicamba, and MCPA—drift to sensitive broadleaved row, vegetable, tree, and vine crops.

- Chlorsulfuron and sulfometuron—drift to sensitive tree and vine crops.
- Glyphosate and paraquat—drift to young (emerging) seedlings, especially vegetable crops, and also drift to established, sensitive broadleaved and grassy species.
- Propanil—drift to sensitive tree crops (e.g., prunes).

Soil Contamination

- Bromacil—off-site problems associated with tree roots extending into treated areas (e.g., walnuts).
- Crop rotation—label restrictions regarding the planting back of crops following registered applications (e.g., simazine and trifluralin).
- Noncrop herbicides (e.g., bromacil, chlorsulfuron, dicamba, prometon, sulfometuron, and tebuthiuron)—off-site movement to sensitive crops and carryover (residues) in soil.

Surface Water Contamination

- Rice herbicides (e.g., bentazon, molinate, and thiobencarb)—use in relation to residue levels in surface water.

10

VEGETATION MANAGEMENT SYSTEMS

by Bill B. Fischer[1], Edward A. Yeary,[2] and John E. Marcroft[3]

Agriculturists in the United States are setting phenomenal records in the production of food, feed, fiber, and fuel crops. Most consumers appreciate the increasing need for efficient and economical production of these agricultural commodities, but only agriculturists are aware of the significant role effective, economical weed control plays in the optimum production of these crops.

The benefits of effective, economical control of unwanted, competing vegetation are numerous. The more obvious ones are:

- Reduction in crop losses caused by weeds.
- Reduction in the cost of crop production.
- Reduction in the energy (including fuel) requirements to produce crops.
- More efficient use of the available water.
- Increased crop yields.
- Increase in the efficiency of fertilizers and other essential micronutrients.
- Increase in the efficiency of harvest.
- Potential reduction in the need for insect and disease control.
- Reduced fire hazards.
- Improvement of recreational areas and facilities.
- Improvement in human and animal health.
- Improvement in the aesthetic value of our environment.

The economic losses caused by weeds, and the cost of their control in the United States, have been estimated to exceed $16.2 billion a

1. University of California Cooperative Extension, Fresno County, CA. 2. University of California Cooperative Extension, Parlier, CA. 3. Agricultural consultant, Salinas, CA.

year. There are approximately 1800 weed species that can cause serious economic losses. In cultivated crops, about 200 species of weeds are found to be troublesome, but rarely do more than 15 to 20 different species require management attention in a single crop. The weed species infesting an area on any one farm vary in their germination times, rates of growth, and life cycles. However, significant technological advances have been made in the past two decades that enable growers to control all unwanted, competing vegetation with integrated systems of vegetation management.

VEGETATION MANAGEMENT

The need to control unwanted, competing vegetation was appreciated as early as 15,000 years ago when man learned that he could grow certain plants in preference to others. Since that time, first through trial and error and more recently through research and education, the cultivation of plants has changed dramatically, but not uniformly, throughout the world. It is significant that none of the tools and methods of weed control used in the past have been completely abandoned. Even the most primitive ones are still used at times in the most technologically advanced systems of crop production.

In this text, weeds, herbicide-application techniques, and various methods of weed control in specific crops and groups of crops are discussed in detail. Effective, economical methods of weed control on any one farm hinge on a systematic, integrated approach to vegetation management that encompasses all crops grown there. All cultural operations in the production of crops on a farm can significantly affect weed populations, their distribution, and the development of effective methods for their control. Therefore, weed control on a farm can be more suitably characterized as *vegetation management,* which is defined as: an environmentally sound system of farming, using all available knowledge and tools, to produce crops free of economically damaging, competitive vegetation. Effective vegetation management can be characterized as Integrated Pest Management, or IPM. It provides a long term management strategy for minimizing losses caused by weeds (pests), with as little cost as possible and minimal disruption of the environment.

In the past, when mechanical devices and hand hoeing were the main methods of controlling weeds, there was a limited need for accurately identifying them and for keeping records of their distribution on the farm. Today, with chemical compounds (herbicides) being used extensively to control weeds, and especially with the increasing use of selective herbicides, proper identification of weeds and knowledge of their distribution on the farm are essential for the development of an economically and agronomically sound weed-control program.

The Ideal Selective Herbicide

The ideal selective herbicide would be a chemical compound that could be applied preplant, preemergence, or postemergence and prevent the growth of all unwanted vegetation without causing injury to any crop. It would have residual properties that would ensure its disappearance from the field by the time the crop is harvested. Such a herbicide is not available, and it is doubtful that one will be developed in the foreseeable future. Therefore, agriculturists will continue to depend on combinations and sequential applications of herbicides and other vegetation-management practices to achieve and maintain effective weed control.

Although complete reliance on herbicides alone for seasonal control of weeds is possible, in many crops the most effective, economical control will combine the use of herbicides and cultivations in an integrated, approach to vegetation management on the entire farm.

The need for weed control is universally recognized, but there is no agreement as to the best or most effective method. There are good reasons for this. One weed-control practice may be well suited to one field or crop, but the same method in another area or in another field growing the same crop may be ineffective and even damaging.

Every management decision made in the production of a crop can significantly affect every other necessary operation or event occurring in the field. In weed control, advanced planning is essential and can be very profitable, but plans must be flexible enough to allow for the many unforeseen and unpredictable events that can occur during the growing season and that are beyond the control of even the best manager. In crop production, we are dealing with biological systems that are dynamically interacting and continuously changing.

In an integrated vegetation-management system, a farm manager must try to create or enhance conditions that are: (1) favorable for the growth of desirable vegetation (crops), (2) unfavorable for the growth of unwanted, competing vegetation (weeds), and (3) unfavorable to the presence of destructive insects and disease-causing organisms. To accomplish this, all available knowledge and tools—mechanical, chemical, or biological—must be used in the right combinations.

The essential components of a viable, integrated vegetation-management system are numerous; the more important ones include field selection, a carefully planned cropping sequence, adequate seedbed preparation, timely irrigations (including preirrigations), sanitation, weed identification, proper fertilization, and effective insect and disease control.

Field Selection

Crops differ significantly in their tolerance to salinity and in their vigor of growth. The application of herbicides, preplant or preemergence, on saline soil can adversely affect the establishment of a crop. Therefore, through proper field selection, a manager can control the emergence and growth of the crop.

Selective herbicides may be available to control a specific weed in one crop effectively and at a reasonable cost, but the same weed species in another crop can be controlled only with repeated cultivations and hand hoeings. For example, black nightshade cannot be controlled in tomatoes with preplant-incorporated herbicides, except with fumigants such as metham, but it can be controlled effectively in cotton or sugar beets with readily available selective herbicides. Numerous examples such as these can be cited. Therefore, a farmer with knowledge of the weed infestation can significantly reduce the cost of weed control through field selection.

The presences of perennial and parasitic weeds should also be considered in field selection. Fields infested with dodder, for instance, should be planted with crops that are not hosts to this parasitic weed. Perennial weeds are generally less expensive to control in fallow fields, and certain crops are able to compete more effectively with them than others. Field bindweed can be more readily controlled in cotton than in melons, peppers, or tomatoes. Alfalfa and sugar beets, when planted in the fall, can compete more effectively with field bindweed than many other crops.

Cropping Sequence

Selective herbicides are widely used in the production of crops. They differ greatly in their residual properties. Small quantities of a herbicide used in one crop may remain in the soil and adversely affect the growth of a crop planted sequentially.

Available information about the residual properties of a herbicide should be carefully considered before using it and when planning the cropping sequence.

Land and Seedbed Preparation

Proper land leveling promotes the efficient application and uniform distribution of irrigation water. This in turn can influence the effectiveness and persistence of herbicides. Many herbicides degrade more rapidly in areas of fields where water collects, resulting in poor weed control or shorter residual control. Poor water distribution can adversely affect the crop growth and reduce its ability to compete with weeds.

Good seedbed preparation can enhance the uniform germination of crop seeds and the rapid growth of the seedling. In a well-prepared seedbed the performance of preplant incorporated, or preemergence-applied herbicides is enhanced.

Preirrigation and Timely Crop Irrigations

Irrigation of the field prior to planting is desirable. It can germinate weed seeds and seeds of crops (volunteers) previously planted in the field. This will not eliminate the potential weed problem, but it can significantly reduce the population.

Preirrigation enhances the final seedbed preparation and the performance of herbicides by eliminating or minimizing cloddy conditions. Neither preplant-incorporated nor preemergence-applied herbicides will provide adequate weed control in cloddy seed beds.

Sanitation

Even when farmers control weeds adequately in the crop, they often ignore weeds around the perimeters of fields and along fence rows, ditchbanks, and roadsides. They should be controlled by herbicides or cultivations before they produce their seeds.

Weeds can serve as hosts to many organisms such as nematodes, insects, viruses, and other disease-causing agents, and to parasitic plants such as dodder. These organisms can survive on the weeds, and their

Weed Infestation Record

Field _____ Current crop _____ Date planted _____

Herbicide _____ Rate _____ Date applied _____

Previous crop _____ Date of this survey _____

ANNUAL GRASSES						NIGHTSHADE FAMILY					
Annual bluegrass	1	2	3	4	5	Black nightshade	1	2	3	4	5
Barnyardgrass	1	2	3	4	5	Hairy nightshade	1	2	3	4	5
Volunteer grains	1	2	3	4	5	_____	1	2	3	4	5
_____	1	2	3	4	5	SUNFLOWER FAMILY					
GOOSEFOOT FAMILY						Common groundsel	1	2	3	4	5
Lambsquarters	1	2	3	4	5	Prickly lettuce	1	2	3	4	5
Nettleleaf goosefoot	1	2	3	4	5	_____	1	2	3	4	5
_____	1	2	3	4	5	OTHER BROADLEAF ANNUALS					
MUSTARD FAMILY						_____	1	2	3	4	5
Brassica species (mustards)	1	2	3	4	5	PERENNIAL WEEDS					
Shepherdspurse	1	2	3	4	5	Field bindweed	1	2	3	4	5
Wild radish	1	2	3	4	5	Nutsedge	1	2	3	4	5
_____	1	2	3	4	5	_____	1	2	3	4	5

Figure 1. Example of weed identification and distribution form. Circle the appropriate number to indicate the degree of infestation: 1 = very few; 2 = light; 3 = moderate; 4 = heavy; 5 = very heavy.

Weed Infestation Record

Orchard Location _____ Crop _____

Control methods and dates _____

	Nov _____		Feb _____		May _____	
	% of total weeds		% of total weeds		% of total weeds	
Annual Grasses	treated	untreated	treated	untreated	treated	untreated
Annual bluegrass						
Barnyardgrass						
Volunteer grains						
Annual Broadleaves						
Groundsel						
Filaree						
Lambsquarters						
Mustards						
Puncturevine						
Perennials						
Bermudagrass						
Johnsongrass						
Field bindweed						
Nutsedge						

Figure 2. Example of weed identification and distribution form. Monitor three times a year and note the percentage of each weed in relation to the total weed population. If you have treated and untreated areas, such as in strip weed control, record the weed species in each area separately.

populations increase. Such organisms can migrate or be transmitted by vectors to crops. Sanitation and the use of weed-free planting seed are very important methods of preventive weed control, as well as control of many other harmful organisms.

Weed Identification and Distribution

Weed identification is essential in planning a vegetation-management program, but it is only the first step. Records must be kept of weed distribution to enable proper field selection and the selection of preemergence herbicides or herbicide combinations. The importance of proper weed identification and keeping records of their distribution cannot be overemphasized. Records of weed infestations in individual fields can be documented in various formats. Two examples of methods used in recording this information are provided in figures 1 and 2. Similar forms can be developed to meet the needs of individual crops or for specific areas.

Records of weed infestations enable one to select a cropping sequence that can minimize weed-control costs, and to select the most effective tools, whether mechanical or chemical, for control.

Fertilization

Proper fertilization is an integral component of an effective weed-control program. Vigorously growing crops provide better competition with weeds and are more resistant to damage by insects and diseases. They are less adversely affected by herbicides, whether applied preplant, preemergence, or postemergence.

Insect and Disease Control

Adequate insect and disease controls are rarely considered to be parts of a good weed-control program. However, judicious use of insecticides and fungicides can ensure the vigorous growth of the crop, thereby increasing its competitive ability. Also, insect- and disease-damaged weeds are not as effectively controlled with certain herbicides as those that are growing vigorously.

Factors Influencing Herbicide Performance

In planning and developing an effective vegetation-management program, it is essential to know of factors that can affect the performance and selectivity of herbicides. These factors include:

Timing
Timing of the application relative to the growth of weeds and crop.

Soil Type
For instance, coarse soils may require lower rates than fine soils.

Moisture
Weeds stressed for moisture may not be effectively controlled with postemergence herbicides.

Temperature
Air and soil temperature can influence both the effectiveness and selectivity of herbicides.

Vigor
Seedling weeds growing vigorously are most susceptible to postemer-

gence herbicides. Conversely, vigorously growing crops are less susceptible to selective herbicides.

Rate and Accuracy

The rate of application and accuracy of calibration are extremely important factors that influence the performance and selectivity of herbicides. *Only the applicator can make a herbicide effective and safe to use.*

Some of these factors can be controlled by growers, others are subject to conditions beyond their control. Some can't be predicted or anticipated, and certain unforeseen conditions may require employing alternative methods of control that may have been considered less effective and less economical in earlier planning. For example, unfavorable weather conditions could prevent accessibility to the field for the timely application of herbicides by ground or air; by the time the field can be entered, the weeds have grown beyond their susceptible stage. In such a case, cultivation and hand hoeing, although more costly, might prove the most economical methods of control.

There is often a tendency to apply a herbicide in the hope that it will do some good, even though the weeds are beyond their most susceptible stage of growth. In most situations, this is wishful thinking and the money, time, and energy spent to buy and apply the herbicide would have been better spent in cultivation and hand weeding.

The least expensive herbicide may be the least economical if it fails to provide the expected control. Conversely, the most expensive method of control may be the most economical to use. Poor herbicide performance and crop injury are often caused by factors that growers or applicators can control or manipulate. They often result from improper selection of herbicides, improper timing of application, improper adjustment of the application rate of incorporation devices, or improper calibration of the sprayer.

Is There a Best Strategy?

Can a best strategy or model be devised for the control of unwanted vegetation in specific crops and used in all areas where they are produced? Unfortunately, the answer is *"No."* To illustrate the difficulty, let us consider weed-control problems in sugar beets.

In many areas of California, sugar beets are overwintered; therefore, a specific field can be infested with winter annual broadleaf weeds and grasses at the time of planting, and summer annuals can be troublesome in the same field in later stages of crop growth. In the same area, perhaps a few miles away, sugar beets may be planted in the spring or summer months and harvested the following year. The weed infestations in these latter fields will be significantly different from those planted in the fall or winter months because of the difference in planting sequence and climatic conditions. Therefore a strategy that is effective in one field may be ineffective or even damaging to the beets in another field under a different set of conditions. Economical methods must be developed for individual fields.

Weed-susceptibility charts and summary statements relating to the use and performance of herbicides have been developed; among them, the ones illustrated in this chapter. Such charts can serve as useful guides in developing effective weed-control strategies and especially in the selection of herbicides. But we cannot overemphasize the fact that the weed-control program in any one crop has to be an integrated part of the total vegetation-management system on the individual farm.

Strategies in Perennial Crops

The development of strategies of vegetation management in orchards and vineyards might be an easier task. As opposed to annual crops, introduction of weed seeds in orchards and vineyards is not a problem. We need not worry about the effect of the residual properties of the herbicides on a crop that may be planted sequentially within a few weeks or months. The cultural practices followed in the management of the orchard and vineyard floors do not vary from year to year. Soil and irrigation management can be manipulated to enable growers to use herbicides safely and effectively.

Over 80% of the citrus orchards in California are under complete nontillage management, and unwanted vegetation in them is controlled with one or two applications of soil-persistent herbicides. Growers are able to maintain very effective weed control by using herbicides singly or in combination. With simazine, diuron, and bromacil, most of the weeds can be controlled.

Herbicides recently registered for use in vineyards and deciduous orchards will enable horticulturists to use complete nontillage or strip (partial) nontillage management. However, to prevent the buildup of annual or perennial weeds that may be resistant to specific herbicides, they will need to select and rotate the use of herbicides carefully.

Susceptibility of Weeds to Herbicides

A significant amount of information has been gathered regarding the susceptibility of weeds to herbicides. Some of this information appears on the labels of specific herbicides. However, more useful to farmers and pest control advisers are weed-susceptibility charts that list the herbicides registered for use in a specific crop and the susceptibility of commonly occurring weeds to those herbicides.

Weed-susceptibility charts have been developed by numerous applied-research workers. Three examples of methods used in the prepa-

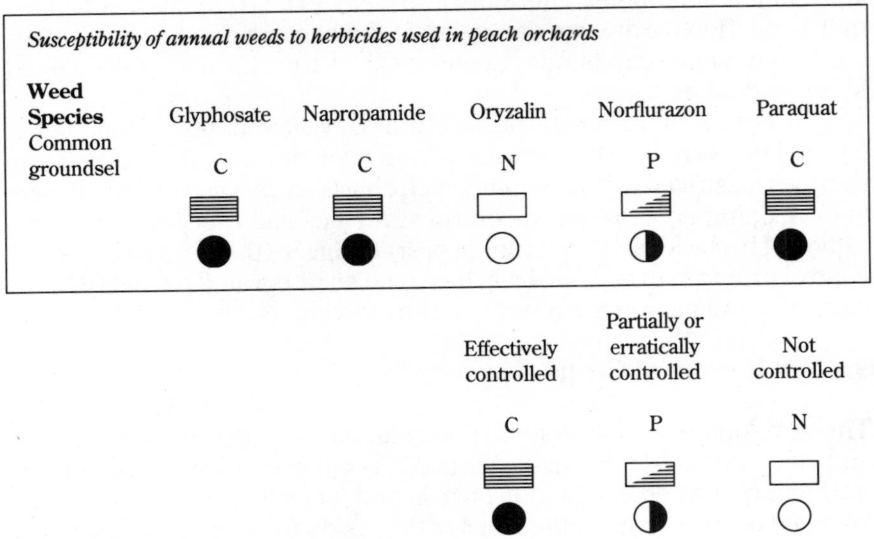

Susceptibility of annual weeds to herbicides used in peach orchards

Weed Species Common groundsel	Glyphosate C	Napropamide C	Oryzalin N	Norflurazon P	Paraquat C

	Effectively controlled	Partially or erratically controlled	Not controlled
	C	P	N

Figure 3. Three methods of indicating weed susceptibility to herbicides.

ration of charts are shown in figure 3. They are included in integrated pest-control manuals, pamphlets published by the University of California Agricultural Sciences publications, and more recently by commercial companies selling specific herbicides. Computer programs are being developed that will enable anyone to obtain information about the relative susceptibility of weeds to herbicides and the registration of herbicides for specific crops.

The performances of herbicides are influenced by many factors, some of them enumerated in this chapter and discussed in other sections of this book. Observations relating to the performance of herbicides and summarized in an abbreviated form can be very useful. They can be prepared for every crop grown on any one farm and can serve as guides in the effective, economical selection and use of herbicides. An example of this method is shown in table 1.

Model Development of Vegetation-Management Systems

Development of models that afford flexibility for the effective, economical control of unwanted vegetation is desirable. The task seems formidable, however, because we are dealing with many species of plants that occur in mixed populations. Even though the development of models with reliable predictability may be remote, the information needed for the construction of models can be very helpful in developing effective vegetation-management systems.

TABLE 1. EXAMPLE OF HERBICIDE PERFORMANCE IN SUGAR BEET TRIALS CONDUCTED IN THE CENTRAL SAN JOAQUIN VALLEY

Method of application	Herbicide	Conditions favoring most effective weed control	Conditions resulting in poor control or injury	Application period
Preplant Incorporated Only	cycloate or pebulate	Summer annual broadleaf weeds and grasses in well-prepared seedbeds in nutsedge-infested fields. Requires thorough incorporation.	Where winter broadleaf weeds are expected, or where cloddy seed-bed conditions are expected.	March through September
Preemergence or Preplant Incorporated	pyrazon	Winter broadleaf weeds, mild temperatures with good growing conditions.	Cold temperatures with poor growing conditions. When grasses or volunteer cereals are expected. Under sprinkler irrigation where more than 2" are applied per set.	October through February
	ethofumesate	When volunteer barley, wheat, and wild oat are expected. Annual grasses except ryegrass.	When winter weeds other than volunteer cereals are expected.	October through February
	diethatyl	For winter and summer annual grasses other than volunteer cereals and wild oat. When pigweeds are present.	When winter broadleaf or volunteer cereals are present. When broadleaf weeds other than pigweed are expected.	All planting periods
Postemergence	desmedipham + phenmedipham	When vigorously growing winter and summer annual broadleaf weeds in their seedling stage are present.	When grasses, knotweed, or swamp smartweed are present. When other weeds are beyond their seedling stage of growth. Delay application after 3 p.m. when temperature exceeds 80° F to reduce injury. Do not apply to weeds that are under moisture stress.	All planting periods
	endothall	When fiddleneck, knotweed, or swamp smartweed predominate.	When weeds other than fiddle-neck and/or swamp smartweed are present.	October through February
	sethoxydim fluazifop-P	Vigorously growing summer and winter annual grasses before tillering, except annual bluegrass. Irrigation following treatment.	When grasses are moisture-stressed and in late tillering stage. Not irrigated following treatment.	All planting periods
Post-thinning Soil incorporated (Lay-by)	trifluralin	Summer annual grasses, pigweed, and lambsquarters with thorough soil incorporation into clean fields.	When resistant weed species predominate. When poor soil incorporation is obtained. Where established weeds are present.	February through August
Post-thinning Injected into Irrigation water	EPTC	Injected into irrigation water for control of summer annual grasses and broadleaf weeds before or immediately after germination. Where trifluralin-resistant species including nutsedge are expected, repeat application may be required.	Where poor subbing or water distribution occur. Where large or resistant weeds including sunflower and cocklebur predominate. Where follow-up treatment is not provided for.	February through August

The study of the biology of weeds has received limited attention until fairly recently. Information is sorely needed on:

- Dormancy and the influence of temperature, moisture, and depth in the soil on weed seed germination.
- Growth and development of weeds—especially about their relative susceptibilities to herbicides at different stages of growth.
- Competition among weed species.
- Environmental influence on the growth, development, and reproduction of weeds.
- The influence of natural enemies on the weed population.
- The effect of allelopathy among plants.

These are some of the areas that need further study. Only the availability of this information will enable agriculturists to develop models. But, more importantly, this information will enable them to develop more effective vegetation-management systems.

Integrated Vegetation-Management Systems

There is no prescription for the development of an effective vegetation-management system that will meet the needs of all farmers, landscape managers, recreational managers, and forest managers. The most economical strategy for the control of unwanted competing vegetation will be influenced by the following factors:

- The skill of the manager.
- The availability of tools and equipment, custom applicators, labor and its skill, and financial resources.
- In crop production, the number of different crops grown on the farm.

The first step in the development of an effective weed-control program is the definition of the problem present or anticipated. To do so in crop production, the prerequisites are: (1) knowledge of the particular weed infestation or the proper identification of the weed species present, and (2) a record of their distribution. Another requirement is knowledge about the susceptibility of weeds to the registered herbicides and information about the herbicides' residual properties.

With this information, a farm manager can begin to assign fields for specific crop production. It is important to keep in mind that the objective should not be the production of optimum yields but maximum net returns. A specific field may have the potential to yield the highest tonnage of tomatoes per acre, but if it is heavily infested with weeds of the nightshade family it may be more profitable to plant in a field free of these weed species even though that field may yield 2 or 3 tons less per acre. There are numerous other crops that can be planted in nightshade-infested fields and in which selective herbicides can be used to control the weeds effectively at a much lower cost than in tomatoes. This is illustrated in table 2.

TABLE 2. EXAMPLES OF THE EFFECTIVENESS OF HERBICIDES TO CONTROL NIGHTSHADES IN SELECTED CROPS

Crop	Herbicide	Application technique*
Alfalfa— Established Seed crop	diuron	POE
	EPTC	POC
	hexazinone	POE
	pronamide	POE
Beans—snap	alachlor	PPI & PRE
	EPTC	PPI
	ethalfluralin	PPI
	metolachlor	PPI & PRE
Carrots	linuron	POE
	Stoddard solvent (carrot oil)	POE
Corn	alachlor	PPI & PRE
	bromoxynil	POE
	butylate	PPI
	cyanazine	PPI & POE
	dicamba	POE
	EPTC	PPI
	metolachlor	PPI & PRE
Cotton	cyanazine	PPI & POE
	fluometuron	PPI & POE
	oxyfluorfen	POE
	prometryn	PPI & POE
Garlic	bromoxynil	POE
	DCPA	PRE & POC
Lettuce	pronamide	PPI & PRE
Melons	naptalam	PPI & POC
Onions— Dry bulb	bromoxynil	POE
	DCPA	PRE & POC
	oxyfluorfen	POE
	sulfuric acid or n. phuric (Enquik)	POE
Sugar beets	cycloate	PPI
	EPTC	POC
	ethofumesate	PPI & PRE
	pebulate	PPI
	phenmedipham + desmedipham	POE
	pyrazon	PPI, PRE & POE
Tomatoes	DCPA	POC
	metham	PPI
	pebulate	PPI & POC

* PPI = Preplant incorporated
  PRE = Preemergence
  POE = Postemergence to crop and weeds
  POC = Postemergence to crop, preemergence to weeds

Information presented is a summary developed from applied research trials. Before using herbicides in any crop, consult the label and make sure it is registered for the specific crop and follow directions carefully.

There are very few farms in California where, through intelligent selection, the cost of weed control could not be significantly reduced. Planting some crops in fields infested with certain species of weeds that can be controlled only with repeated hand hoeings is asking for extra expense. Numerous charts listing the susceptibility of weeds to specific herbicides are available, and from them, one can derive guidelines such as the following.

Avoid planting the crops listed in the column on the left if the field is infested with weeds listed in the right column.

Crops	**Weeds**
alfalfa	dodder
cantaloupe, peppers, tomatoes	dodder, nightshade species
onions, garlic, peppers	purple and yellow nutsedge
lettuce	annual sowthistle, prickly lettuce, common groundsel, horseweed, flaxleaf fleabane
cole crops	mustard species
safflower	wild sunflower
sugar beets	wild beet
cantaloupe, onions, garlic	field bindweed
corn, sorghum	johnsongrass

Information is available for the development of effective and economical vegetation-management systems for farms, forests, recreational, and noncrop areas. Such development is an attainable goal when pursued cooperatively among research, extension, and industry personnel.

ECONOMIC CONSIDERATIONS

Farm managers bear the responsibility of using all the resources available to them, singly and in combination, to earn maximum net income. Implements are chosen in this manner to perform work at the lowest cost. Similarly, methods and materials for vegetation management should be selected and used to accomplish this task in a way that will do its part to maximize net income over time. Short- and long-range effects must be considered, since an immediate solution to one problem may create long-range problems that would subsequently reduce earnings.

Economic problems caused by weeds include nonproductive use of water and nutrients, lower product quality, and diminished yields. Weeds add to harvest and cleaning costs and are a continuing source of reinfestation, in some cases they also serve as hosts to insects and plant diseases.

Availability and costs of materials change over time, often very rapidly. Rising costs of machines and labor are also anticipated. It is only possible to prepare budgets for vegetation-management alternatives at one point in time, and the time of usefulness of these budgets is very brief.

Once it is determined that a weed problem is present, management is challenged to assemble all available information about methods that can be used to solve the problem. Costs of chemical, mechanical, and hand-labor solutions, as well as of combinations of methods, must be determined. Knowing the costs of available treatment options, together with the longer-range benefits and adverse consequences, will lead to selecting the most economical plan.

Methods of control may differ greatly for managers of large field- and row-crop farms; small-scale, diversified farms; and farms made up of long-lived plantings such as trees and vines, even though they are all combatting the same weed. The unit cost of hand labor to combat equal weed infestations will not differ much from one farm to another, but options of field and crop rotation and mechanical and chemical control will be very different in numbers and in unit costs.

Managers of large-scale farms planted to field and row crops usually have the most methods and combinations of methods available. Field selection and crop rotation alone or in combination with chemicals applied during normal cultural operations usually represent the lowest-cost approach to weed control. If special equipment such as spray rigs are needed, their fixed costs will be spread over large acreage and will add very little to the cultural costs of crop production. Hand labor, specifically for weed control, may be used to a limited extent. Custom applications of materials, except by air, are not often required; however, these services are available and can be used very effectively when needed on large-scale farms.

Managers of farms planted to long-lived crops such as orchards and vineyards do not have the rotation method of control available to them. Chemical and mechanical options are much more restricted than on large farms growing a number of different annual crops. Special equipment for chemical and mechanical weed control may be needed, along with the skilled labor required to operate it safely and successfully. In many cases, the use of custom services may be the lowest-cost approach. Careful budgeting and planning will develop the lowest-cost procedures.

Small-scale farms present a wide range of problems in weed control. Hand labor is very often the method of choice on all types of small farms. Where trees and vines are in the cropping pattern, hand application of chemicals may be combined with hand labor and tillage to achieve the lowest-cost control. Where annual crops are grown, some rotation programs can be used together with hand labor, mechanical methods, and solarization. It is seldom cost-efficient to purchase specialized equipment for weed control. Custom services can be used together with whatever options the manager has available to minimize economic losses caused by weeds.

THE ROLE OF THE PEST CONTROL ADVISER

Whether the grower depends on his own staff or on a commercial adviser, the role of the pest control adviser (PCA) is of utmost importance in the systems approach to pest management. It is indeed the PCA who will represent and use the various technological disciplines that collectively influence agricultural production.

The modern PCA is a product of the highest level of pest management technology. PCAs must be generalists, willing and able to manage the control of those insects, diseases, vertebrates, nematodes, and weeds that would otherwise compete with efficient crop production. Successful pest control must be interrelated with all aspects of crop production, including irrigation and nutrition.

The PCA must be an active participant in the production of a crop. While some growers pursue the same practices followed by their fathers or neighbors over many years, the changing economy of agriculture requires the application of all available skills in order to be successful. Hence, the role of PCA is one of teacher, scientist, psychologist, and diplomat.

PCAs have the opportunity and responsibility to learn as much about crop production in general as about the pest to be controlled and the various alternative methods of control. The application of such appropriate practices has been termed integrated pest management (IPM). To avoid an overly lengthy definition of IPM, let us merely state that integrated pest management is the *systems* approach to managing pests. After careful evaluation of the crop environment and economy, the decision for biological, cultural, and/or chemical treatment should be made on the basis of overall technical considerations.

Of all the pests that infest crops, weeds often account for the greatest cost during the culture of the crop. The adequate control of weeds allows the crop to grow without competition for sunlight, water, and essential nutrients. Uncontrolled, weeds can become hosts of virus diseases, shelters for vertebrate pests, and ultimately, through their seed production, for increased weed infestation, thereby decreasing the value of the land and increasing subsequent farming costs.

Annual Crops

The potential for annual weed infestation in an annual crop will depend on the degree of seed development that may have occurred as a function of the previous crops. Obviously, it is advisable to destroy surviving weeds as soon after harvest as possible. However, it is at that time as well that the PCA should take the opportunity to record the various weed species to determine their population density within the field.

Growers of annual crops often rotate two or three crops or as many as a dozen unrelated crops. In some areas, this involves two to three crops on the same parcel of land during a one-year period. Under these conditions, the PCA's recommendations for weed control should take into account the varieties of weed species observed earlier. In planning crop rotations, growers should consider planting specific crops on parcels in which selective herbicides can be used to control a weed potential that may not be anticipated in an alternative location. This method of planning follows the concept of "herbicide rotation."

A registered herbicide is considered for use in a particular crop because of the tolerance of that crop to that specific herbicide. However, the herbicide may not control all potential weeds in the crop, a fact that argues for selecting another crop for planting if possible.

One of the hazards in the rotation of annual crops is the possibility of crop injury or a plantback restriction from a pesticide (e.g., a residual herbicide) applied to the previous crop. The degree of hazard may depend on any of the following conditions:

- Rate of herbicide applied per farmed acre.
- Soil texture. (Coarse soils represent a longer residual effect.)
- Degree of organic matter. (High organic matter may represent a shorter residual effect.)
- Rates of irrigation (or rainfall) since herbicide treatment.
- Label (plantback) restrictions.

PCAs must be well versed in use conditions on herbicide labels to give the user sufficient warning of problems that follow from the misuse of herbicides. Such a warning should be clearly stated on the grower's copy of the adviser's written recommendation for treatment.

Perennial Crops

In many ways, the control of weeds within a perennial crop culture is easier than in an annual crop; the control is even easier under conditions of minimum tillage or nontillage due to the reduction of annual weeds being introduced.

The control of weeds under perennial conditions will facilitate harvest, reduce the shelter for vertebrate pests, and minimize plant populations serving as hosts for such potential insects as lygus, thrips, etc.

In perennial crops, especially in orchards and vineyards, the use of herbicides takes advantage of a "positional tolerance" of the crop to the chemical. The herbicide will not leach significantly into the soil profile so that the crop roots will avoid exposure while the weeds in the upper inch or so are controlled. This type of tolerance obviously may depend on soil texture and/or irrigation practice and is clearly one reason for the PCA to understand all aspects of product use.

Application

After having considered all the various factors of registered herbicide use under specific agronomic conditions, the final and generally most important consideration is that of the manner of product delivery. Often it may be up to the pest control adviser to decide between application by air or by ground. Given these choices, the PCA must consider at least the following:

- Relative effectiveness of the two systems.
- Need for complete coverage of the foliage.
- Potential for drift.
- Adjacent areas intolerant to drift.
- Labeled approval for either system of delivery.

When application is by ground rig, it is the responsibility of the PCA to confirm the accuracy of the calibration. The PCA's recommendation should be written clearly enough so that the equipment operator can understand the volume(s) of product(s) per treated acre. As an added precaution against error, it is advisable that the PCA also designate the volume(s) of product(s) per tankload and the total area a single tankload should cover.

In the event that the application is to be accomplished through the grower's equipment, it is recommended that the PCA communicate directly with the driver and regularly confirm the continuing calibration of the spray unit. Among the checkpoints to consider are the following:

- Uniform delivery of solution from all nozzles.
- A full width of delivery from each nozzle.
- Nozzles should be checked regularly for wear, and screens checked for plugging.
- The delivery system should have an active agitation (paddle and/ or bypass) to maintain good product suspension in the tank.
- The operating pressure should be adequate enough to allow the fan to provide droplets generally uniform in size.
- If herbicides are being delivered to a banded area, i.e., a treated area less than the broadcast area, the application should be confined to treat no more or less of the band than is intended by the proportionate use over the broadcast acre allowed on the product label.

Regulations

To the PCA in the field it must seem that no activity could be more regulated than the recommendation and use of pesticides in California; many of these are discussed in Chapter 9 of this text. While these regulatory requirements may seem unduly restrictive, there is a reason for them. Even if the individual PCA may not fully agree with this last statement, the fact is that these statutes collectively represent the agricultural laws of California; it is imperative that each PCA is familiar with such laws with special reference to their application and to his or her professional activities.

It is also important to realize that many counties in California have special ordinances which address local needs in the regulation of pesticide use. Such needs may represent the protection of bee pollinators in one crop during the period of insecticide use in another, the termination of phenoxy applications in grain prior to the period of sensitivity to phenoxy drift to adjacent crops, and so on. The authority for such ordinances can be found in Section 11503 (California Food and Agriculture Code).

After having evaluated the pest potential in a specific parcel and determined the need for treatment with a restricted use pesticide, the regulations (Section 6434, Code of California Regulations) require that the county agricultural commissioner receive a Notice of Intent (NOI) to Apply Restricted Materials; a sample of this NOI is found as figure 4. From the information contained on this document, the commissioner will confirm that the intended use of pesticide(s) is allowed by label(s) registered with the state and will further be applied in an area which will not represent an off-target hazard. Following the approval by the office of the agricultural commissioner, the application may then proceed.

The pesticide label is written to advise two categories of activity. The first category is clearly written to guide the adviser in his or her need to interpret product use, e.g., crop, method and time of treatment, rate per acre, etc. The other category of advice is directed toward the pest control operator/applicator (PCO), e.g., possibly involving the sequence of mixing products, the dilution with water, timing and/or conditions of product delivery, etc. Although the PCO is often an independent contractor, his interests are obviously quite similar to those of the adviser; there should indeed be a mutual interest in the success of a pesticide application. It is for these reasons, for instance, that an aerial application should not be set up for a field too small or irregularly shaped to fly or that the presence of a sensitive adjacent crop be properly considered and identified by the adviser, i.e., in spite of the obligation by the applicator to substantially limit drift to the target area.

Liability

Much of the exposure to liability in the use of herbicides can be reduced through a thorough and continuous communication between the grower and the community, attention to labeled cautions and directions, as well

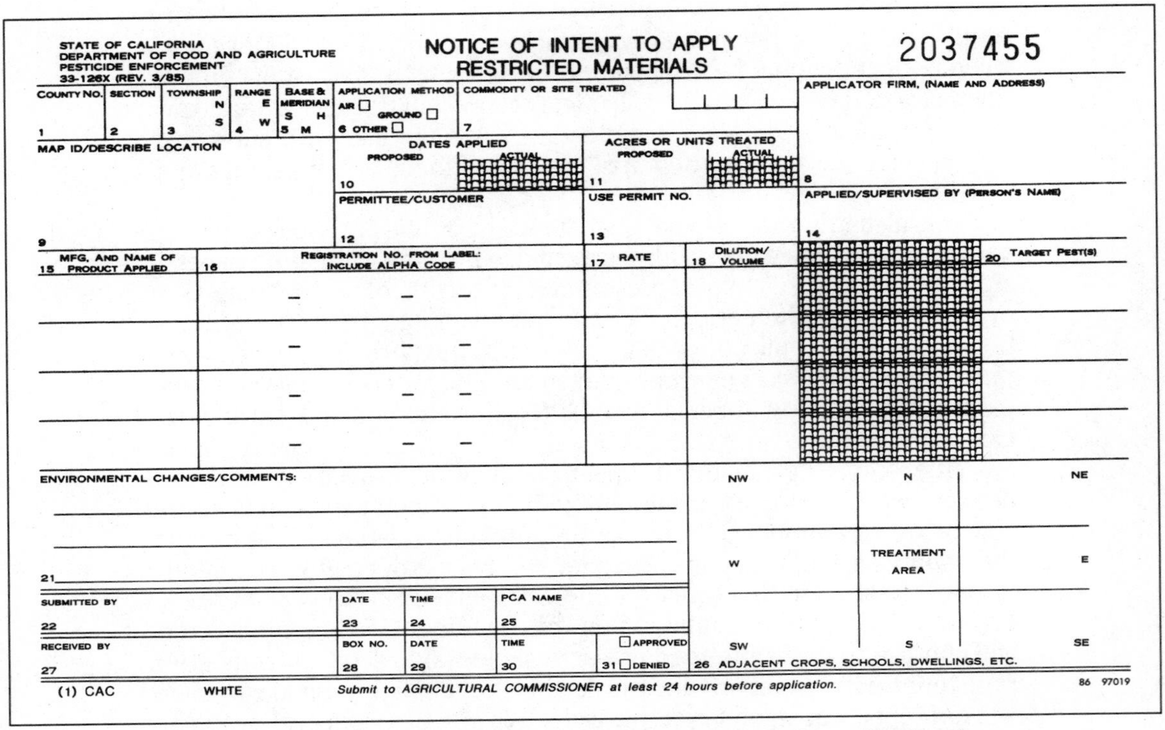

STATE OF CALIFORNIA
DEPARTMENT OF FOOD AND AGRICULTURE
PESTICIDE ENFORCEMENT
33-126X (REV. 3/85)

NOTICE OF INTENT TO APPLY
RESTRICTED MATERIALS

2037455

1 COUNTY NO. | 2 SECTION | 3 TOWNSHIP N S | 4 RANGE E W | 5 BASE & MERIDIAN S H M | 6 APPLICATION METHOD AIR ☐ GROUND ☐ OTHER ☐ | 7 COMMODITY OR SITE TREATED | 8 APPLICATOR FIRM, (NAME AND ADDRESS)

9 MAP ID/DESCRIBE LOCATION | 10 DATES APPLIED PROPOSED ACTUAL | 11 ACRES OR UNITS TREATED PROPOSED ACTUAL

12 PERMITTEE/CUSTOMER | 13 USE PERMIT NO. | 14 APPLIED/SUPERVISED BY (PERSON'S NAME)

15 MFG. AND NAME OF PRODUCT APPLIED | 16 REGISTRATION NO. FROM LABEL: INCLUDE ALPHA CODE | 17 RATE | 18 DILUTION/VOLUME | 20 TARGET PEST(S)

21 ENVIRONMENTAL CHANGES/COMMENTS:

22 SUBMITTED BY | 23 DATE | 24 TIME | 25 PCA NAME

27 RECEIVED BY | 28 BOX NO. | 29 DATE | 30 TIME | 31 ☐ APPROVED ☐ DENIED

NW N NE
W TREATMENT AREA E
SW S SE
26 ADJACENT CROPS, SCHOOLS, DWELLINGS, ETC.

(1) CAC WHITE *Submit to AGRICULTURAL COMMISSIONER at least 24 hours before application.* 86 97019

Figure 4. Example of Notice of Intent form to be completed prior to the application of restricted materials.

as to good application techniques. All of these areas of professional involvement collectively represent opportunities for the pest control adviser to fill a real need in the agricultural community.

SUGGESTED READING

Allee, D. 1967. American agriculture—its resources for the coming years. Daedalus, fall 1967:1071–1081.

Anders, L.A. 1982. Integrating weed biological control agents into a pest management program. Weed Sci. 30 Suppl. 1:25–30.

Anderson, W.P. 1977. Weed Science: Principles. West Publishing Co., St. Paul.

Bell, D. 1967. The year 2000—the trajectory of an idea. Daedalus, summer 1967:639–655.

Crittendon, A. 1983. Hunger: the last word. RF Illustrated, June 1983:8.

Gunther, F.A. and Gunther, J.D. 1970. Residue Reviews, Springer-Verlag, Vol. 32.

Hatzios, K.K. 1982. Metabolism of herbicides in higher plants, CEPCO Division Burgess Publishing Co.

Hill, G.D. 1982. Herbicide technology for integrated weed management systems. Weed Sci. 30 Suppl. 1:13–16.

Kempen, H.M. 1981. Weed management consulting in California. Proc. Sixth Australian Weed Conf. 1981:5–8.

Schreiber, M.M. 1982. Modeling the biology of weeds for integrated weed management. Weed Sci. 30 Suppl. 1:2–12.

Shaw, W.C. 1982. Integrated weed management system technology for pest management. Weed Sci. 30 Suppl. 1:2–12.

The World Food Problem, Vol. I & II. A Report of the President's Science Advisory Committee. May 1967.

Thomas, B. and Pratt, D. 1982. Herbicide tolerance. *Calif. Agric.* 36–8:33.

Wolff, A. 1982. How plants protect themselves. *RF Illustrated,* June 1982:9–11.

Zimdahl, R.L. 1982. Weed-crop competition, a review. *International Plant Protection Center, Corvallis. Ore.*

ENVIRONMENTAL RELATIONSHIPS

by Boysie E. Day[1] and Robert Meeks[2]

A dictionary defines the environment as our "external conditions in their totality," that is, everything outside ourselves, whether physical, biological, social, aesthetic, or other. The environment is infinitely complex. Certainly one of its important components is the earth's vegetation, including crops, ranges, forests, and other land plants, as well as those in water. We manage the plant environment by suppressing some plants and cultivating others. Thus weed control is a major part of environmental management. Its aims include the enhanced capacity of the environment to produce plant products and the suppression of vegetation in various situations to create better conditions for a wide range of human activities. Obviously, the achievement of such ends cannot be universally beneficial and please everyone or be entirely free of risks. Although the aims and accomplishment of weed control are to modify the environment, when one speaks of its environmental impact one is usually referring to negative effects.

When the forester kills unwanted hardwoods, or the rancher converts brushland to pasture, or a farmer sprays or plows his wheat field, the results are modified environments that produce more lumber, beef, and grain. These are positive achievements contributing to the general welfare. Other results may be soil erosion, silting of streams, lower populations of wildlife, reduced opportunities for outdoor recreation, altered natural beauty, etc.—effects that may be judged harmful depending upon one's point of view. The responsible manager takes into account as many of these factors as can be anticipated, and tries to accomplish objectives with a minimum of harm. Weed-control workers are responsible for environmental changes affecting not only themselves but others as well.

Some undesirable environmental changes are the result of methods employed, while others are direct consequences of accomplishing intended objectives. For example, soil erosion of grain lands caused by tillage for weed control can be virtually eliminated by switching to no-

1. University of California, Berkeley, CA. 2. Orange County Public Works, Anaheim, CA.

till farming. The problem in this case is the method used for weed control rather than the fact that weeds were controlled. On the other hand, if a noxious legume is eliminated from a pasture, its benefits as a nitrogen fixer are lost, regardless of the method used to get rid of it. There are unwanted or inadvertent effects inherent in all such undertakings and in all methods, no matter how carefully planned and executed. There are also accidents, misjudgments, unusual conditions, changes in the weather, and other unpredictable circumstances that affect results and add hazards. Dry weather can delay the breakdown of herbicides in the soil, causing injury or loss of subsequent crops. Unwanted effects can also extend past the area being treated to neighboring properties and beyond.

Environmental changes resulting from vegetation management may cause economic losses, degrade natural resources, and lead to social disturbances. For example, the plowing and planting of large areas of the Great Plains not suited to conventional farming contributed to the dust bowl, a costly disaster that degraded resources and caused much human suffering. Weed control can also lead to conditions that are not of great economic importance but affect personal enjoyment and quality of life. These include changes in wildlife habitat and positive or negative effects on fishing, hunting, camping, and other outdoor recreation.

Weed-control activities can generate social, aesthetic, and even moral trauma. Concerns focus sharply on the use of herbicides rather than upon traditional practices. The fact that there may be traces of herbicides in food is disquieting to many, and the notion that this endangers health is widespread. Ethical arguments are often raised. There is much interest nowadays in "natural" foods, cosmetics, and other products and processes. Herbicides do not qualify as "natural," and food produced by their use may be viewed as less nutritious or aesthetically inferior to food produced by handwork and tillage or by "organic" methods. Some oppose herbicides on the grounds that poisoning anything, whether plant or animal, is morally wrong. Such concerns, whether rational or not, enter the political arena and become reflected in restrictive regulations. Conflicting aesthetic and moral values, public anxiety, and complex regulations are as much a part of the working environment of the weed-control practitioner as the crops and weeds themselves.

The objectives, methods, and environmental effects of vegetation management differ greatly for agriculture, range management, forestry, industry, and other endeavors. These categories are examined separately below.

Farming

In annual crops the aim is to suppress all weeds. In orchards and vineyards the need is either to control all weeds or prevent tall and rampant growth. The technology of attacking all kinds of plants and leaving only one is inherently hazardous. The environmental component most at risk is the crop itself, and it is the farmer, not the consumer nor the public at large, whose welfare is most in jeopardy. The hazard is not from herbicides alone but from other methods as well. Tillage can damage the root systems of crops and cause indirect injury by compacting the soil. Attempts to clean too close to trees and vines with machinery can injure these crops. Some herbicides have such narrow margins of selectivity that variations in soil conditions or unusual weather can lead to crop losses. Herbicides sometimes carry over in the soil to affect subsequent crops.

One potential environmental hazard is that of spray drift: the movement of vapors or droplets of herbicides from treated areas. Drift from spraying by ground rigs is rarely significant, but there have been cases of extensive damage to crops from aerial applications, particularly of the phenoxy herbicides. With proper use of current technology, injurious drift need never extend more than a few yards off target. Greater drift is clear evidence of negligence. Herbicide movement in runoff water rarely extends more than a few inches or feet. Leaching of herbicides into the water table has been limited to treatments applied to very sandy soils. Well water in farming areas can be freely used to irrigate crops and for other uses without fear of herbicide injury.

Herbicides are rarely toxic to farm animals and wildlife. Their effects on animals are substantial but indirect through changes in habitat. Chemicals make it easier to control plant growth in orchards, along fence rows, and in waste places. This is done to reduce nearby sources of weed seeds, plant diseases, rodents, and insect pests. It is also detrimental to an already-sparse wildlife habitat. In other cases, however, herbicides can have the reverse effect. The no-till production of grains, a system retaining either crop cover or crop trash throughout the year, provides an improved animal habitat over the prior practice of summer fallow by plowing. Increased populations of rodents, birds, and other animals, including reptiles, hawks, and other predators, develop in no-till fields.

Contrary to all evidence, a common belief holds that the farm use of herbicides causes chemical residues at toxic, or at subtoxic but chronically hazardous, levels in food and water. Extensive toxicological research and careful monitoring of food supplies fail to substantiate these fears. The ability of modern chemistry to detect infinitesimal levels of chemicals in commodities gives reassurance that the very low levels of herbicide residues found are well within safety limits. This is also a basis for alarm. The news media and the public find it difficult to deal realistically with trace residues often expressed in parts per billion or trillion, the one in units equivalent to a quarter of an inch in the radius of the earth and the other to the thickness of a spider web in that distance.

It is also said that the widespread use of herbicides is exhausting the soil. The fact is that herbicides are powerful tools for soil conservation. Herbicides reduce the need for plowing, a practice contributing to wind and water erosion and other harmful effects, but have few benefits beyond weed control. No-till farming greatly reduces soil erosion and provides for a more productive farmland.

Ranges and Pastures

Pastures are sites of artificial vegetation while ranges are modified natural environments. Both are harvested by grazing, a destructive practice that suppresses forage species and allows unpalatable weeds to take over. This is the central and critical problem in range and pasture management. Large areas of native western grassland have been converted to brushland as the result of grazing by domestic animals. Herbicides, mechanical brush removal, fire, and, for pastures, plowing and replanting are the principal means of combatting this. The better California ranges were originally brushlands or open woodlands. Initial clearing and maintenance is by machinery, fire, chemicals, or combinations of these. Some critics object to range improvements as excessively destructive for little gain, and done at much cost to natural beauty and wildlife habitat. Others object to the methods—fire for its smoke and hazard to wildlife, and herbicides for the many objections raised against chemicals. Public belief that rangelands are often misused or neglected has led to distrust of the rancher as a custodian of wildlands and has created doubts about the wisdom of whatever management practices he undertakes, including highly effective programs of range improvement.

Forests

There are strong opinions about many aspects of forest management, not the least of which is the use of herbicides. Herbicides are mainly used in conjunction with other operations in site preparation for reproduction or replanting, and for so-called 'release' from competition in the early stages of a production cycle to allow the preferred species to become dominant. Other methods may be used, but herbicides are often more efficient and are less conducive to soil erosion and other environmental harms. Handwork for timber release, using axes and power saws, is more expensive and is also exceptionally dangerous to workers. Nevertheless, the use of chemicals in forests has generated vocal opposition and restrictive regulations. The claim is that herbicides poison people and wildlife, ruin the soil, pollute streams, kill fish, and cause many other problems.

Actually, herbicides are used only once or twice in a forest cycle of a half century or more and could not do the dire things claimed. Probably the underlying basis for the opposition is not the direct hazards of chemicals but dislike for the changes being made in forest conditions. There is a common feeling that forests should be left to go their own way as natural habitats, and not be made into tree farms.

Urban and Industrial Weed Control

Vegetation can be a nuisance and a hazard around factories, refineries, parking lots, lumber yards, airfields, highways, railroads, transformer yards, and utility rights of way. Soil sterilants are employed where the need is to eliminate all vegetation. Selective herbicides and mowing are used where the aim is to allow only low-growing plants. Mowing favors the sod grasses, the preferred vegetation for playgrounds, athletic fields, home lawns, cemeteries, and the open areas of parks. Turf is periodically weeded with herbicides to suppress unwanted broadleaved plants and weedy grasses. Herbicides are widely used in the management of other ground covers and to maintain landscape plantings generally.

The general public observes these weed-control practices more than any others. Areas treated with herbicides are rarely out of sight of the urban dweller. Yet, despite the prevalent concern of city people over the use of chemicals on farm or forest, these uses of herbicides close at hand are seldom challenged or even recognized. A likely reason for this is that the urban resident understands his own environment and recognizes that vigorous management including weed control is essential to it. On the contrary, he does not know firsthand what farmers and foresters are doing and is likely to give credence to rumors of dangerous or negligent practices.

Fire Protection

Fire prevention codes in California require that each spring vacant lots be cleared of the dry trash from winter weeds. This is commonly done by disking, but there is increasing use of soil-residual herbicides prior to or during the growing season to prevent trash buildup. The result is a safer environment for humans at the minor cost of a few wildflowers and a reduced habitat for insects and, to some extent, for birds.

Fire lanes, called fire breaks or fuel breaks, are maintained in brushlands near cities by mechanical and chemical means. The preferred vegetation on the lanes is grass to hold the soil. In addition to their primary purpose, the lanes enhance wildlife habitat by diversifying available feed and plant cover, and by creating open areas suitable for larger animals. The strips of grass make brushlands accessible for hunting, hiking, photography, and wildlife observation. They also form routes of escape from wildfires for people and animals. However there are some objections to the lanes on aesthetic grounds. The brown stripes on hills compromise the viewing pleasures of purists who prefer their brushlands undisturbed.

Aquatic Weeds

Few environmental disturbances are so upsetting to the public as the invasion of water weeds into lakes, streams, and reservoirs. Weed growth can choke canals and drains, threaten irrigation and domestic water supplies, and interfere with boating, fishing, swimming, and commercial navigation. In such cases, there is general alarm and clamor for corrective action. Mechanical, chemical, and biological control measures can be employed with more or less success, but usually at high cost. Public emotion often makes cost a secondary consideration in the choice of method to environmental propriety as the public and interest groups see it. Differing views may make rational actions impossible. Controversy is commonplace in public activities, but it is particularly acute in matters related to water and wetlands. Economic, health, recreational, and aesthetic interests in public waters are often conflicting, and whatever is done gives legitimate offense to one group or another. Aquatic weed control is greatly limited by these constraints.

Wilderness and Wildlife Management

There is an important place for herbicides in the management of game habitat, nature preserves, and even designated wilderness areas. Management of wildlife habitat is particularly aided by the wise use of herbicides. Herbicides have the unique capacity to alter plant species' composition without involving the massive disturbance of the ax, bulldozer, or dragline. This provides mild and discriminating means to improve plant communities in ways suitable to wildlife. Overgrown duck marshes can be improved by the use of herbicides to open up avenues for birds to land and take flight. Emerged plants such as cattails, mats of floating weeds, and massive blooms of algae can be thinned or removed by aquatic herbicides to improve fish and waterfowl habitat. Another, more extreme example is the use of herbicides for large-scale production of grain crops that provide feed for waterfowl along the main migration flyways. Wildlife habitat management involves maintaining or carefully changing the structure and species mix of plant communities, tasks for which herbicides are uniquely suited.

The management objective for nature preserves and wilderness areas is to retain the native fauna and flora in as close as is reasonably possible to their original conditions. This objective appears simple but is actually the most difficult resources-management goal to achieve. The problem is the invasion of aggressive alien plants that displace native species. Some western landscapes have been so completely altered by the invasion of foreign plants that the nature of the original plant community is no longer known and is beyond all prospect of reconstruction. Examples are the overwhelming encroachment of the blue gum eucalyptus into California woodlands, brushlands, and forests, and the spread of the poisonous halogeton into the great basin desert. Eucalyptus has become so dominant in some situations as to leave hardly a trace of the native vegetation.

It is public policy to protect national parks and designated wilderness areas from such invasions using both preventive and eradicative methods. To actually do so, however, would require an effort far more strenuous than any now applied. It is a challenging problem in weed control as well as in public policy. Action against non-native species is supported by some environmentalists and opposed by others.

Summary

We feed, clothe, and house ourselves in ever larger numbers by new technology, of which herbicides are a component. The contribution of herbicides toward a safer and more productive environment is very great, and the negative effects are few. However, the increasing use of weed-control chemicals alarms environmental groups and other segments of the public. Their fears are expressed over the real or supposed side-effects of chemicals on human health and the well-being of other nontarget organisms. Yet controversy about weed control existed before the era of herbicides. Fifty years ago there was as great a public outcry against plowing as the present one about chemicals. A popular book titled *Plowman's Folly* focused attention on this means of weed control as being highly destructive to the soil. Plowing was the environmental issue of the "dust bowl" era. Nowadays, concern over plowing has subsided and indeed critics of herbicides advocate returning to tillage as preferable to chemicals. Yet as the tractor replaced the horse against a storm of opposition, so are herbicides replacing the plow, and in the face of equal furor.

Herbicides have become as much an integral part of farming as the hoe or cultivator, and have been accepted with equal enthusiasm by all parties including industrial and urban land managers and homeowners. The result is a better environment. Nevertheless, errors and setbacks have occurred in the past, and others are sure to come. There are individuals and groups who oppose the use of herbicides and who persist in their efforts to bring legal action to restrict their use. They perceive herbicides as degrading the environment. Whether the perception is rational or not is immaterial. In politics it is perception that counts.

Most arguments against herbicides emphasize the possible health effects of chemical residues in food or fears of poisoning animals in treated areas. There is every evidence that neither is the case, but no amount of research or direct experience has been able to quiet these fears entirely, and indeed ultimate proof is not possible. However, as the era of large-scale use of herbicides approaches the half-century mark, the passage of time has brought a more balanced view. In practice, responsibility for the safety of herbicides falls primarily, if not entirely, on the manufacturers, handlers, and applicators of herbicide concentrates. Poisonings are known to have occurred from consuming concentrates, either by mistaking them for beverages or from suicidal intent. Health studies of workers reveal no ill effects from the normal handling and application of herbicides. Unlike the health and accident exposure of workers with traditional methods, herbicide workers command low occupational insurance premiums. The occupational risks are less than those for the operators of the tractors, plows, mowing machines, chain saws, and other machinery replaced by herbicides.

There are significant environmental hazards in the use of herbicides, but these are seldom noted by critics. There are failures of selectivity, delayed breakdown, and errors of application that affect crops in treated areas. These result from imperfect technology, carelessness, accidents, and unusual weather or soil conditions. That such events have been commonplace is indicated by the numerous lawsuits involving landholders, their neighbors, and their applicators, suppliers, and manufacturers. The only important hazard away from the treated site is that of spray drift, which is preventable by good practice, although good practice is tedious and expensive and not always followed.

There are concerns that drift might lead to the buildup of herbicides at distant places without anyone knowing about it, and that this might affect animal and human health. The answer is that herbicides are many times more toxic to plants than to animals, and such drift or accumulation would be clearly evident from plant-injury symptoms that would occur at rates far below levels that are toxic to other organisms. Herbicides are not insidious but announce their presence unmistakably. There can be no secret drift. In cases of suspected drift one needs only to investigate the plants in the affected area and in the supposed path of movement. Plant-injury patterns will not only establish the fact of drift but will unerringly point the finger to the source.

The effect of better weed control is environmental improvement on a vast scale. However, herbicides have come along at a time of general alarm over the real or imagined dangers of chemicals of all sorts in the environment and must share that onus.

11

AGRONOMIC CROPS

INTRODUCTION

by Jack P. Orr[1]

Agronomic crop production extends over a wide range of cultural and environmental variables in California, extending from the cooler, short seasons of Tule Lake to the warmer climate of the Imperial Valley, with many variations in between. Weed species, crop and weed populations, and cultural practices vary immensely. Good management of weed populations while producing agronomic crops is a primary requirement of a successful farming operation. The aim of all producers of agronomic crops should be to create favorable conditions for crops while creating unfavorable ones for weeds.

Ten major agronomic crops have been selected for discussion in this chapter. The chapter chairman expresses appreciation to each crop author for his contribution.

In presenting this information, an attempt is made to outline weed problems and to educate the reader on programs available for control. A good management system requires a combination of methods, including cultural and physical, mechanical, biological, and chemical methods. Such a system should be designed to economically reduce weed populations without impairing crop development.

The crop statistics used in this section are based on 1987 information as provided in the *California Field Crop Statistics 1983–1987,* published by the California Agricultural Statistics Service.

Because many mechanical and chemical weed-control methods are common to more than one agronomic crop, we have provided photographs illustrating specific examples of the use of these methods on individual crops.

---

1. University of California Cooperative Extension, Sacramento County, CA.

ALFALFA *(Medicago sativa)*

by Larry W. Mitich[1]

Alfalfa is a crop of major importance in California. In 1987, there were 1,150,000 acres of alfalfa hay which produced an average yield of 6.7 tons per acre. Additionally, there were 67,000 acres of alfalfa seed which produced an average yield of 605 pounds per acre.

Total agronomic yield losses due to weeds in California have been estimated by the USDA to be $200,100,000 annually. Alfalfa producers share in this tremendous loss.

A variety of broadleaf and grassy weeds infest alfalfa fields. The following list of the 10 most common weeds in California alfalfa fields is from a 1987 survey.

Yellow foxtail	London rocket
Barnyardgrass	Common chickweed
Shepherdspurse	Common sowthistle
Common groundsel	Dodder species
Coast fiddleneck	Annual bluegrass

An additional eight species of weeds have been indicated as being troublesome in California alfalfa fields under certain conditions.

In California, alfalfa has two distinct weed populations: the winter annual weeds which germinate with winter rains, and the summer annual weeds (usually grasses) which germinate in early spring and exist through summer. Dodder, the parasitic plant, also grows in the summer, but it is a special problem not related to the others.

Losses Caused by Weeds

Weeds compete with the alfalfa for water, nutrients, and light. They may also affect quality. When downy brome or wild barley are in hay, livestock may develop serious mouth and throat abrasions that often become infected. Dairymen are concerned about flixweed in hay grown in certain regions because it causes off-flavors in milk. Coast fiddleneck and common groundsel are toxic if heavily infested fields are cut and the hay is fed to livestock.

Research on alfalfa grown for hay indicates that first-cutting hay yields are often highest when winter annual weeds are present. However, the quality of the hay is reduced drastically. Protein content as low as 9% has been measured in hay containing 80% weeds. When the weeds were controlled with herbicides, the protein content rose to over 20%. A good

1. University of California Cooperative Extension, Davis, CA.

weed-control program, then, can more than double the nutritive value of the hay and vastly improve the quality. First-cutting alfalfa hay sometimes has to be sold for pelleting because it is so weedy.

Weed-control Methods

Any successful weed-control practice must interfere with the growth of the weed intended for control or enhance the growth of the crop relative to the weeds. Cultural practices which help maintain a vigorous stand of alfalfa are essential.

Weed Control in Seedling Alfalfa

Weeds frequently cause a major problem in establishing alfalfa. The presence of a heavy stand of weeds can result in loss of the crop, as seedling alfalfa generally is a poor competitor with weeds. Light to moderate weed infestations will not reduce the alfalfa stand but can weaken the young alfalfa, retard growth, and delay the first cutting.

Tillage
A good uniform tillage operation during seedbed preparation will control many weeds, allowing, where possible, greatly reduced seed germination of several common winter annual weeds.

Timing of Planting
Alfalfa should be sown at the proper time so that a vigorous stand is obtained. In the Central Valley, good stands have been established throughout most of the year. Best results, however, have been obtained with October or March plantings. Fall plantings, in particular, provide the young stands with an opportunity to become well established prior to the germination of summer grasses. Spring and late summer are ideal for establishing alfalfa in northeastern California. At elevations higher than 5000 feet, alfalfa should be seeded in May or June but no later than August 15. The best planting period in the Imperial Valley is October, with the first week being optimum. However, the period from the last few days in September through all of November is also suitable. October plantings make rapid growth, compete well with weeds, and develop sturdy plants before onset of cool weather.

Plantings that are established without a companion crop are more vigorous and competitive with weeds than when a companion crop is used. Crop competition is the best method of long-term weed control in alfalfa. Weed-free seeds should always be used, and an alfalfa variety recommended for the area and soil type should be planted. Mowing established weeds above the alfalfa seedlings inhibits their growth, freeing the alfalfa from considerable competition. Insect control is also essential as insect attacks can reduce the competitive ability of alfalfa and provide conditions favorable for the invasion of weeds.

Cultural Controls

Weed problems may be reduced by establishing a vigorous stand of seedling alfalfa. Seedlings that germinate and grow rapidly due to warm temperature, adequate soil moisture, and shallow plantings generally result in a relatively weed-free stand. Adequate soil fertility, especially phosphorus, is essential for good seedling establishment and competition with weeds.

Preirrigation or rainfall will germinate many weed seeds which can be removed by cultivation. However, several cultivations may be required to sufficiently deplete the weed-seed population.

Chemical Control

Herbicides should be used in combination with good management practices to control weeds during alfalfa establishment. Herbicides are valuable in establishing a vigorous alfalfa stand, which reduces weed contamination of the first cutting of hay. The herbicides cleared for use in seedling alfalfa differ in types of weeds controlled and in soil persistence. Be sure to read the entire label first and follow the instructions carefully when using any herbicides.

Preplant and Preemergence. Preplant incorporated treatments of EPTC effectively control some annual broadleaf and most annual grass weeds in alfalfa sown without a grass or a combination crop. Incorporate EPTC into the soil immediately after application to prevent herbicide loss by volatilization.

Benefin has effectively controlled annual grasses, pigweed species, common lambsquarters, and some other broadleaf weeds when applied preplant and incorporated just before seeding.

Postemergence. Use postemergence treatments of 2,4-DB amine or 2,4-DB ester to control broadleaf weeds in seedling alfalfa when sown alone. Apply 2,4-DB when weeds are less than 3 inches tall and when legumes have one to four trifoliate leaves. A trifoliate leaf is composed of three leaflets attached to one petiole. Wild mustard is not effectively controlled by 2,4-DB. For 2,4-DB to work properly, the alfalfa should not be under drought stress, and air temperature at the time of spraying should not exceed 90°F or fall below 50°F.

Other herbicides used in alfalfa establishment include pronamide and paraquat.

Weed Control in Established Alfalfa

Weeds are often a serious problem in established stands of alfalfa. Yield and quality of the hay will be impaired if the weeds are not controlled.

Weeds can also substantially reduce the number of alfalfa plants in a stand.

Tillage
In established alfalfa, winter annual weeds can be controlled sometimes by cultivations, but injury to alfalfa crowns also occurs, causing a delayed first cutting or increased loss of stand from crown disease.

Cultural Control
Alfalfa is weakened by moisture stress, disease, improper cutting, and soil compaction which contributes to weed problems in established stands. Proper management keeps most weed problems in established alfalfa to a minimum. Improper cutting schedules often mean weedy hay.

Weed infestations also can result from improper timing of irrigations, particularly during summer months. Barnyardgrass and yellow foxtail will become readily established when alfalfa is stressed before or during harvest, and water is applied when there is scant alfalfa growth to shade the ground. Adjusting the irrigation schedule to provide water near the cutting date and allowing alfalfa plants to continue growth during the harvest period will usually reduce weed infestations.

Weed problems are often aggravated by fall and winter grazing in the mountain areas. However, if grazing is conducted so that the animals are in the field for a limited time (similar to that of a cutting), good alfalfa vigor and competitiveness during the winter will be maintained. Never graze livestock repeatedly or continuously on wet fields, or before there are 10–12 inches of alfalfa regrowth.

Chemical Control
Herbicides also may be used to control weeds in combination with good crop management. Several herbicides are registered for use in established alfalfa. These herbicides differ in types of weeds controlled and in soil persistence.

Preemergence. In areas where alfalfa is dormant during the winter, the wettable-powder formulations of simazine may be used on pure alfalfa stands established for a year or more to control seedlings of wild mustard, London rocket, shepherdspurse, and other species. Established weeds are not consistently controlled. Application should be made after the last cutting in the fall and before the ground freezes. Grasses in the alfalfa will be injured or killed. Simazine should not be used on sands, loamy sands, gravelly soil, or on soils where soil pH is above 7.5; it is used only in northern counties.

The wettable-powder formulation of metribuzin may be applied on alfalfa or alfalfa-grass mixtures to control certain grass and broadleaf weeds when the alfalfa is dormant in fall or spring. Use of metribuzin is restricted to north of Interstate 80.

Pronamide is used on pure stands of alfalfa to suppress perennial grasses. Pronamide will also control many annual grasses and some annual broadleaf weeds but will not control perennial broadleaf weeds. Apply pronamide in the fall when soil temperatures are below 60° F but before the ground freezes. Applications may be made in the fall of the seeding year. Best results are obtained when annual grasses are treated when they are 1–2 inches tall.

Hexazinone is used to control some annual grasses and broadleaf weeds when applied preemergence. It also controls seedlings present at the time of application. On dormant varieties, apply hexazinone after the alfalfa becomes dormant and before new growth begins in the spring. Apply the herbicide to nondormant and semidormant varieties during winter months when alfalfa plants are least actively growing. Rate selection is based on soil texture and organic matter content.

Trifluralin is applied from December to mid-February in most counties, before germination of summer grasses. Trifluralin controls foxtails and other annual grasses and some broadleaf weeds, including knotweed. High rates of granular trifluralin are used to control dodder (a repeat application may be required in spring). Trifluralin must be incorporated by ½ inch of rainfall or sprinkler irrigation within three days after application; nongranular formulations can also be water-run.

Diuron controls many seedling annual grass and broadleaf weeds when applied preemergence or early postemergence to the weeds. Treat only stands established one year or more. Do not apply to seedling alfalfa or alfalfa-grass mixtures. Use where alfalfa becomes winter dormant and in areas of California (north of the Tehachapi Mountains) where alfalfa becomes semidormant.

Postemergence. In established alfalfa, apply the amine salt or the ester of 2,4-DB to control annual broadleaf weeds. Apply when the weed seedlings are 1–3 inches tall (two-to-five-leaf stage). Do not apply when extremes of temperature or moisture are expected within a few days following application. Crop injury is likely to occur if applied after growth has started.

EPTC is metered postemergence into irrigation water to control weeds prior to emergence in established alfalfa. This treatment controls many species of annual grassy and broadleaf weeds.

Chloropropham also is applied postemergence through irrigation water in late fall or winter to established stands of alfalfa or when the crop has six or more true leaves. Weeds controlled are chickweed, downy brome, and other annual grasses and broadleaf weeds. Chloropropham also can be applied postemergence to established alfalfa stands by spray application.

Sethoxydim effectively controls many grass weeds except annual bluegrass. It is applied to emerged weeds before grasses become large; May to June is an appropriate time for application in the Central Valley and the low desert. Sethoxydim should be applied after bales are removed from the field but before alfalfa regrowth can interfere with spray coverage. Application should be followed by an irrigation. A non-herbicidal crop oil adjuvant must be used.

Paraquat is registered for use in dormant alfalfa. Paraquat should be applied to established stands after the last fall cutting when the crop is dormant but before spring growth starts. The application should be made when broadleaf weeds and grasses are succulent and growth is 1–6 inches tall. Paraquat should not be applied following the last cutting if the alfalfa is more than 2 inches tall. Animals should not be pastured in treated fields prior to the first cutting.

REFERENCES

Guenther, H.R., and H.P. Cords. 1975. *Winter annual weeds in alfalfa in western and northern Nevada.* Univ. of Nevada, Coop. Ext. Ser., Leaflet C-169. 4 pp.

Lehman, W.F. 1979. *Alfalfa production in the low desert valley areas of California.* Univ. of Calif., Div. of Agri. Sci., Leaflet 21097. 22 pp.

Norris, R.F., W.Y. Isom, V.L. Marble, and S.R. Radosevich. 1977. *Weed control in seedling alfalfa.* Univ. of Calif., Div. of Agri. Sci., Leaflet 2917. 6 pp.

Radosevich, S.R., R.F. Norris, W.H. Isom, and V.W. Marble. 1975. *Weed control in established alfalfa.* Univ. of Calif., Div. of Agri. Sci., Leaflet 2766.

CEREALS (Wheat, Barley, and Oats)

by Jack P. Orr[1]

Wheat, barley, and oats are California's most important grain crops. Acreage and values for these crops vary from year to year. For example, the planted acreage of wheat has declined from 885,000 acres in 1985 to 590,000 in 1987, and barley from 500,000 to 400,000, while oat acreage has increased from 340,000 to 380,000 over that period. In 1987 there were 590,000 acres of wheat planted with a harvested value of $117,249,000; 400,000 acres of barley planted with a harvested value of $32,895,000; and 380,000 acres of oats planted with a harvested value of $5,040,000. Wheat varieties grown are predominantly hard red wheats planted in the fall. They grow in the spring and are erroneously referred to as winter wheats. Because certain varieties are sensitive to herbicides, labels should be checked before an application is made.

The most common broadleaf and grassy weeds that infest cereals include black mustard, common yellow mustard, turnip mustard, wild radish, fiddleneck, minerslettuce, chickweed, Italian ryegrass, wild oat, field bindweed, canarygrass, smartweed, johnsongrass, and yellow starthistle.

1. *University of California Cooperative Extension, Sacramento County, CA.*

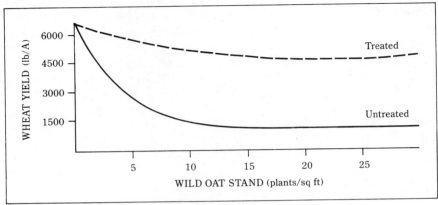

Figure 1. Influence of wild oat populations on wheat yield.

Since cereals are grown across such diversified conditions, a wide spectrum or single weed species may be present in light to heavy infestations. These variable factors affect the cereal yield. A properly planned, integrated weed-management system will control or minimize weed populations.

Weed Competition

As few as seven wild oat plants/sq ft can reduce wheat yields by 3000 lb/A in comparison to a 6000 lb/A yield potential where no wild oat exists (fig. 1).

Other studies show that barley is more competitive than wheat with wild oat; however, 14 wild oat plants/sq ft can amount to a 27.2% yield reduction in barley and 39% reduction in wheat.

Studies by Appleby, Olson, and Colbert at Oregon State University show Italian ryegrass to be a serious weed problem in grain fields. As ryegrass densities increased, wheat grain yields decreased. The percentage of yield reduction tended to be higher in short wheat cultivars compared to tall cultivars (table 1).

Cultural Practices

Seedbed Preparation and Planting

A properly prepared seedbed can have a direct influence on yield. The soil should be plowed or disked as deeply as possible to break up soil compaction and reduce risk of herbicide carryover if cereals are planted after sugar beets, tomatoes, field corn, or other crops. Planting depth is especially important to wheat. Physiology of semi-dwarf Mexican wheat dictates the planting depth no deeper than 2 inches. A depth greater

TABLE 1. GRAIN YIELDS OF FOUR WHEAT CULTIVARS GROWN UNDER THREE RYEGRASS DENSITIES

Cultivar	Ryegrass Density	Wheat Grain yield	Grain yield Reduction
	Plants/sq ft	lb/A	%
Druchamp (tall)	0	3096	0
	4.4	2520	19
	11.0	2232	28
Yamhill (tall)	0	3924	0
	4.4	2925	26
	12.0	2709	31
Nugaines (semi-dwarf)	0	3042	0
	4.4	2214	24
	10.6	1908	37
Hyslop (semi-dwarf)	0	3465	0
	4.9	2565	26
	11.0	2115	39

than this could result in a low plant population; it is very important to use high-quality seed. Certified seed assures the grower of weed-free seed. The use of non-certified seed risks the introduction of new weed infestations.

An integrated weed management system combines fertilization, irrigation, tillage, herbicide applications, and high plant populations. Studies in the delta have shown that higher plant populations are very effective in reducing competition of smartweed, johnsongrass, mustard, wild oat, canarygrass, and chickweed.

Good field sanitation is a prerequisite for weed control. Fields free from hard-to-control weeds should be selected. When problem fields must be planted, plans for weed control should be made in advance. The use of clean planting and harvesting machinery and clean tillage implements is essential. Perimeters of fields should be kept free of ryegrass, wild oat, johnsongrass, and smartweed because they serve as an initial reservoir for seed to infest the field.

Fertilization

Fertilization is very important in cereal production to keep the grain vigorous and healthy for maximum weed competition. Starter fertilizer containing adequate levels of phosphorus is necessary in irrigated and upland areas. Starter fertilizer should be placed near the seed to provide early availability to the crop and not the weeds. Broadcast fertilization may enhance weed growth, especially of wild oat and canarygrass.

Irrigation

Irrigation and drainage of cereals is very important for high yields. They should be planted on raised beds 2.5 to 5 feet apart. Good irrigation and drainage practices keep cereals in a vigorous growth condition for maximum competition with weeds.

Under dryland conditions, it is advisable to fallow fields every other year to prevent weed seed buildup. No weeds should be permitted to escape the fallowing operations. It is advantageous to let the fall rains germinate the first flush of weeds before tillage operations for planting are started. The weeds can be destroyed by tillage before planting, thus reducing later weed competition. Vigorous stands make chemical control programs more effective.

Fields should be rotated to cultivated crops to reduce infestations of johnsongrass, wild oat, ryegrass, and certain other weed species. Crop rotations permit weed populations to be reduced chemically, mechanically, and physically in the alternative crop.

Chemical Control

Since cereals are slow-growing in the winter, they do not compete well with weeds. Under most conditions, chemical weed control in cereals is necessary during this time.

The success of a herbicide application is dependent upon weed species present, the timeliness and thoroughness of herbicide application, conditions at the time of application, herbicide rate, and crop management after the application. After a herbicide has been applied, weeds may again become a problem if late winter rains cause additional weed seeds to germinate. Also, drought-stressed weeds are very difficult to control, especially if they are beyond the seedling stage.

Postemergence Broadleaf Weed Control

Postemergence herbicides are applied to the weeds after the crop is up. Bromoxynil, 2,4-D amine and low-volatile ester, and MCPA amine and ester are effective herbicides for controlling certain broadleaf species. Figure 2 illustrates the proper application timing of these herbicides to the crop. Figure 3 illustrates a typical application.

The best control is obtained when weeds are small, and before the crop has reached the jointing stage and created an impenetrable canopy over the weeds. Bromoxynil, a contact herbicide, is most effective on young seedling weeds with no more than two to four leaves. Good coverage is more important than with phenoxy herbicides. Bromoxynil is less effective than phenoxy herbicides on older weeds. Bromoxynil drift is considerably less hazardous to other crops than drift from phe-

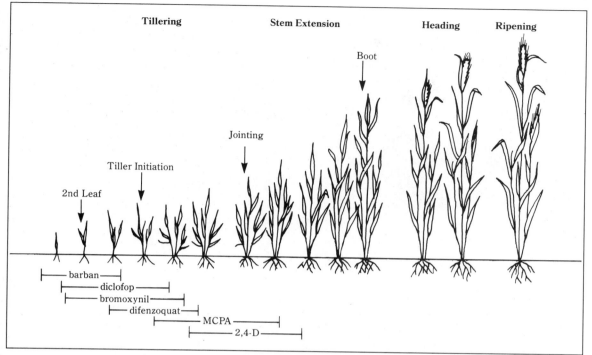

Figure 2. Growth stages in cereals and timing of weed-control herbicides.

noxy herbicides. Bromoxynil successfully controls fiddleneck at the early stages of growth, whereas the phenoxy herbicides have only partial control. However, fiddleneck that has reached the flowering stages will not be controlled.

The phenoxy herbicides (hormone type), 2,4-D ester and MCPA amine and ester, are most effective when applied to small and succulent weeds. The ester form is generally more effective than the amine form. The prime time for applying 2,4-D amine and 2,4-D ester is after the cereals are well established and tillered, but before they reach the boot stage. Serious yield reductions can occur if application is made before tillering or at boot stage. Older and larger weeds are more difficult to control than young, small ones. Dense weed populations require a more thorough application with a greater spray volume to ensure that weeds are contacted by the herbicide.

MCPA does not give as effective weed control as 2,4-D amine and 2,4-D ester herbicides, but it is more selective to the cereals when they are at the early stages of growth.

Dicamba is effective for broadleaf weed control; however, cereals are more sensitive to it than to 2,4-D. Dicamba cannot be used on fall-seeded barley. The combination of bromoxynil and MCPA is a very ef-

Figure 3. One of the most common methods of controlling such weeds as mustard in cereal crops (left) *is by aircraft application of herbicide* (right). *Photos courtesy J.P. Orr and H.S. Agamalian.*

fective one for increasing the weed-control spectrum.

Chlorsulfuron is registered for use on wheat which is followed by fallow and is not in a crop rotation.

Grass Weed Control with Postemergence Herbicides

Grassy weeds causing yield reductions in cereals include wild oat and annual ryegrass. Difenzoquat is an effective herbicide for controlling wild oat, and best results are obtained when application is made to the cereals just prior to the stage of tiller initiation through fully tillered (fig. 2). The application rate should be adjusted to the wild oat population. Maximum wild oat control is obtained when temperature, moisture, fertility, and cultural practices provide favorable conditions for plant growth. If applied when plants are under stress (e.g., cold, wet, or hot, dry weather or low soil fertility), difenzoquat can produce yellowing or tip burn on the wheat and barley. Difenzoquat cannot be used on varieties Probrand 771, Klassic, or any Durham varieties, due to phytotoxic effects. Difenzoquat can be combined with bromoxynil or 2,4-D for control of broadleaf weeds.

Barban is a postemergence herbicide for control of annual ryegrass and wild oat. Fair-to-good control can be obtained when the ryegrass is very small (seedling stage). Application to the wheat can be made from the two-leaf stage to tiller initiation (fig. 2). Best results are obtained at the highest label rate. The grain should not be covered with dew when application is made to ensure best selectivity in cold weather. Crop injury may occur if the crop is under stress due to drought, low fertility, or extended cold, foggy weather at the time of application.

Preemergence Grass Weed Control

Triallate is a preemergence herbicide for control of wild oat in barley. It is applied before or after seeding and must be incorporated. Results can be erratic if the zone of treatment does not have good moisture.

REFERENCES

Appleby, A., P. Olson, and D. Colbert. *Winter wheat yield reduction from interference by Italian ryegrass.* Agron. Jour., 1976.

Carlson, Hill, and Bagghot. *Wild oat competition in spring wheat.* Calif. Weed Conf., 33rd Annual Proc.

Clement, L.D., L.F. Jackson, T.E. Kearney, J.P. Orr, R.L. Sailsbery, and J.F. Williams. 1982. *Wheat production in the Sacramento Valley.* Univ. of Calif., Coop. Ext. Ser.

Hill, J.E., W.H. Isom. 1980. *Broadleaf weed control in wheat and barley.* Div. of Agric. Sci., Univ. of Calif., Leaflet 21012.

Wheat. Documenta Ciba-Geigy.

CORN *(Zea mays)*

by David L. Bruce[1]

Corn is produced in California for grain, silage, and forage. The largest acreage is associated with the grain crop, and in 1987 there were 425,000 planted acres with a harvested value of $69,825,000. The greatest concentration of field corn in California is in or adjacent to the Sacramento–San Joaquin Delta areas. California produces less feed grain, including corn, than is required for feeding livestock in the state. As a result of the state demand and shipping costs from other producing states, California growers receive a higher price for corn.

Weeds compete with corn for light, nutrients, and water, especially during the first three-to-five weeks of corn growth. Research has shown that when weeds are not controlled before they are 6–8 inches in height, yields of corn are reduced. Weeds germinating late in the corn-growth period do not reduce yields as much as early infestation. However, weeds can slow harvest and provide a seed source for the infestation of subsequent crops.

Weeds that are problems in California corn production vary from one area to another. Annual broadleaf weeds that commonly cause problems in corn include pigweed, lambsquarters, purslane, nightshades, and velvetleaf. Perennial broadleaf weeds such as field bindweed also compete and reduce yields in corn. Annual grasses that plague corn growers are barnyardgrass, crabgrass, fall panicum, and proso millet. Perennial problem grasses are johnsongrass and bermudagrass. Purple

1. *Formerly Stauffer Chemical Company, Goleta, CA.*

Figure 4. Control of broadleaved and grassy weeds in corn (left) *is essential to reduce competition and can be accomplished through a combination of herbicides and tillage* (right). *Photos courtesy J.P. Orr.*

and yellow nutsedge are perennial sedges that also compete with corn, especially early in the growing phase.

A grower should keep a record of weed infestations and soil types in his fields to help in the design of an integrated weed-control program using field selection, herbicides, crop rotation, cultivation, and crop competition.

Cultural Practices

Certain cultural practices can control weeds prior to planting. Selection of a relatively weed-free field greatly enhances the economics of growing corn.

A well-prepared seedbed free of large clods provides favorable conditions for corn seed germination and early growth as well as improves weed control of preplant herbicides.

In California, corn is commonly planted flat to preirrigated beds or planted on dry beds and irrigated up. A flush of weeds germinates with the emerging corn with either of these methods of planting.

It is important to select a vigorously growing variety that will compete favorably with weeds. Certain corn plantings at correct row spacings and population density can also discourage late-season weed growth by shading.

Cultivation is an effective method used to control weeds in corn. Tools used for early cultivation are the rotary hoe and the rotary cultivator. Corn should be cultivated as the weeds are emerging; shallow cultivation can kill weeds without disturbing the crop if proper soil conditions exist. Shovel or sweep-type cultivators can be used later in the season if necessary. Sweeps following irrigations can significantly reduce weeds between rows, but weeds in the crop row may require further control. Yellow nutsedge and johnsongrass growth can be suppressed by cultivation that throws soil to the back of the corn plant.

Chemical Control

Herbicides also may be used in combination with good crop management and tillage to control weeds (fig. 4). Preplant, preemergence, or postemergence herbicides are available that will selectively control most species of weeds in corn. Herbicides should be selected on the basis of weeds present, stage of corn growth, soil type, geographic area, and succeeding rotation crop.

Preplant, preemergence herbicides are applied to the soil surface and mechanically mixed in the soil before the crop is planted. A herbicide application made prior to corn emergence offers the advantage of controlling weeds before they can compete with corn seedlings. Preplant herbicides are applied broadcast when corn is planted on flat ground and incorporated by disking before beds are formed, or applied in a band on preformed beds, then incorporated with a bye-hoe, rolling cultivator, or roterra (table 2).

TABLE 2. HERBICIDES COMMONLY USED ON CALIFORNIA CORN

Preplant, preemergence	alachlor
	atrazine
	butylate + safener
	cyanazine
	EPTC + safener
	metolachlor + safener
	vernolate + safener
Postemergence	atrazine
	dicamba
	2,4-D

Butylate and vernolate formulated with safeners are preplant-incorporated herbicides. These herbicides control most grasses and certain broadleaf weeds. If the soil is adequately disked prior to the herbicide application, rhizomatous johnsongrass and nutsedge can be suppressed. Butylate and vernolate are short-lived in the soil lasting from six to 10 weeks under cropping conditions.

EPTC plus safener is more active on broadleaf species and some difficult-to-control weeds such as wild cane, nutsedge, and johnsongrass. EPTC is also a short-lived herbicide lasting six to 10 weeks.

Metolachlor plus safener is applied preplant-incorporated. It is most active against annual grasses and certain broadleaf weeds. If the herbicide application is preceded by adequate disking, it can suppress rhizomatous johnsongrass and nutsedge. Metolachlor is relatively short-lived in soil, lasting from eight to 10 weeks under cropping conditions.

Alachlor, similar to metolachlor, is applied preplant-incorporated and controls a wide variety of annual grasses and certain broadleaf weeds. Its persistence is similar to metolachlor. Soil moisture is important for the activity of these two herbicides; under dry soil conditions their performance may be reduced.

Postemergence herbicides are used to control emerged seedling weeds. An over-the-top spray can be used until corn is 6–10 inches high; on larger corn a directed spray should be used to minimize risk of corn injury. Widely used postemergence herbicides include 2,4-D amine, dicamba, and atrazine plus oil. The addition of a nontoxic oil enhances postemergence activity of some herbicides such as atrazine.

Atrazine is used for control of most broadleaf and certain grassy weeds in corn. Atrazine can be applied preplant-incorporated or postemergence, but before weed seedlings are more than 1.5 inches high. Postemergence in combination with oil is generally the preferred method of application. The main disadvantage of atrazine is that it may persist in soils for 12–18 months after application. Crops such as tomatoes and sugar beets following a corn crop treated with atrazine may be injured. Band applications and deep tillage will reduce problems of carryover. Crops other than corn or sorghum should not be planted within 18 months after application of atrazine.

The postemergence herbicide 2,4-D amine is used for broadleaf weed control on corn 2–8 inches high. After corn is 10 inches in height, a directed spray utilizing drop nozzles is used. Corn should not be sprayed from tassel to dough stage of growth. Applications of 2,4-D amine are restricted in California. Spray drift to sensitive broadleaf crops such as small-seeded legumes, beans and other vegetables, ornamental plants, and fruit crops should be avoided.

Dicamba is also a restricted-use postemergence herbicide in California. It can be used for control of broadleaf weeds until corn is 24 inches high, but it is best timed from the spike stage until corn is 5 inches high. Seedling weeds are easier to kill at early stages of growth, and weed competition with corn is less severe. Dicamba controls pigweed, field bindweed, nightshade, and velvetleaf. As with 2,4-D amine, spray drift to sensitive plants should be prevented.

REFERENCES

California at a glance. July 1984. California Crop Year 1983. Calif. Farmer Publ. Co.
California crop activity charts. 1981. Calif. Farmer Publ. Co.
Calif. Field Crop. Rev. April 1981. Vol. 2, No. 2. USDA. Calif. Dept. of Food and Agric.
Chapman, Stephen R., and Lark P. Carter. 1976. Crop Production, Principles and Practices. W.H. Freeman and Co. pp. 258–279.

Crafts, Alden S. 1975. Modern Weed Control. Univ. of Calif. Press, Berkeley. pp. 262–283.
Herbicide Handbook. 4th ed. Weed Sci. Soc. of Amer. Champaign, Ill. 479 pp.
Kearney, T.E., F.R. Kegel, J.P. Orr, J.D. Smith, and K.H. Ingebretsen. 1980. Field corn production in California. Coop. Agric. Ext. Univ. of Calif. Leaflet 21163.
Martin, John H., Warren H. Leonard, and David L. Stamp. 1976. Principles of Field Crop Production. 3rd ed. MacMillan Publ. Co. Inc. pp. 323–382.
Metcalfe, Darrel S., and Donald M. Elkens. 1980. Crop Production, Principles and Practices. 4th ed. New York: MacMillan Publ. Co. Inc. pp.333–365.
Orr, Jack P. 1981. Weed control in field corn—Res. Rpt. Coop. Agric. Ext. Univ. of Calif.
Weed control in corn. 1974. Div. of Agric. Sci. Univ. of Calif. Leaflet 6001.
Western Fertilizer Handbook. 5th ed. 1975. Danville, IL: Interstate Printers and Publishers, Inc. 250 pp.

COTTON *(Gossypium hirsutum)*

by Harold M. Kempen[1]

Cotton has been the major field crop in California for many years. In 1987, 1,140,000 acres of upland cotton with a value of $991,392,000 were harvested in California. Yields of lint over the last four-year period were 2.1–2.6 bales (480 pounds net per bale) per acre. Because yields are so high, California often ranks as the second most productive state in the United States, behind Mississippi, or third after Mississippi and Texas.

Cost of production varies from $600 to $900/A. Weed-management costs are about $60/A. However, costs vary widely, depending on weed species present, how well herbicides work, and which crops cotton is rotated behind. Usually, California growers hoe and hand pull weeds not controlled by herbicides in young cotton. This practice reduces weed seed production and removes herbicide-resistant weeds which otherwise would become much more numerous in one to three seasons. Also, occasional weeds can seriously impede mechanical harvest.

Problem weeds are: (1) those winter annuals which germinate after soils are irrigated before planting, (2) those germinating with the seeded cotton, and (3) those growing when irrigations are made after cotton emergence.

Winter annuals include many mustard family species, especially London rocket, shepherdspurse, black mustard, composite species such as sowthistle, chickweeds, lambsquarters, little mallow, and grass family species such as annual bluegrass, canarygrass, and wild oat. Volunteer cereals also are often a problem (fig. 5).

Weeds that germinate with cotton include several grasses, especially barnyardgrass, several pigweeds, lambsquarters, and recently two nightshades, black and hairy. Several perennial weeds also germinate in plantings: the sedges (yellow and purple), johnsongrass, bermudagrass, and field bindweed.

Weeds which germinate after irrigations are applied to emerged

1. University of California Cooperative Extension, Kern County, CA.

Figure 5. Control of grassy weeds in young cotton (left) *is essential to reduce competition and other problems associated with weeds and weed seed at harvest* (right). *Photos courtesy H.M. Kempen and F.O. Colbert.*

cotton in early May to mid-June include annual morningglory and ground-cherry. These two weeds plus green amaranth can cause severe harvesting problems if not carefully managed.

Cultural and Physical Control

Two major regions of production occur in California, the San Joaquin Valley and the Imperial Valley. Ninety percent of the acreage is north of the Tehachapi Mountains, where a one-quality cottonseed district limits varieties to Acala selections. SJ2, GC10, and SJ5 are the preferred varieties. They are planted from mid-March to mid-April into moist, preirrigated soils. This practice greatly reduces annual weed seed emergence since rains within two weeks after planting occur only 50% of the time.

In the Imperial Valley, cotton is usually planted into dry soils and then furrow-irrigated to obtain germination. Acreage is limited due to insect problems.

Most plantings are spaced 38 inches apart to facilitate cultivations and harvest, although there is a trend towards plantings as close as 30 inches. A population of 20,000 to 60,000 plants per acre usually permits maximum yields, but normally it should be 40,000 to 50,000. Except for problem soil-crusting areas, cotton is planted to a stand. Seeds are placed ¾ to 1¾ inches deep into moist soil, or slightly shallower if irrigated up.

Cotton is grown on many types of soil, from moderately alkaline clay loam soils to loamy sands.

San Joaquin Valley growers list (bed up) fields from October immediately after harvest until late February. Exact spacing is required to permit close cultivation later. Irrigation follows from November (on fine-textured soils) to March (on coarse soils). Beds are harrowed, rototilled, or cultivated just prior to planting. Bed tops are removed during planting to plant seed into optimum soil moisture. A ring-roller is often run over planted fields a day or two after planting to prevent a crust. If rains occur soon after planting, a mild spike-tooth harrowing is done to break the resulting crust. Later, growers close-cultivate. When cotton is about 6 inches tall or more, soil is thrown against the woody stems to permit furrow irrigation. The soil covers weeds coming after early irrigations and forms a peaked bed for harvesting with spindle pickers. Usually four cultivations are needed to do this. A side-dress of fertilizer is done on sandier soils about mid- to late May. The final cultivation should be done as cotton is closing the furrows. Most weeds emerging after this are unable to compete with cotton if stands are good and cotton grows 5 feet tall or more.

Harvest is entirely mechanical, beginning in late September and continuing up to January. Use of field storage (in modules) permits rapid harvest and enables early soil preparation for subsequent crops before winter rains become frequent.

Crop Rotation

Rotation commonly is used on California farms, more for disease control and maximum production than for weed control. Certain weeds are worse after less competitive vegetable crops. An example is nutsedge after onions or peppers. Corn and cereals are favored preceding cotton, but volunteer cereals can be weed, in winter-irrigated cotton ground.

Dry fallowing in the summer preceding cotton allows excellent control of johnsongrass, bermudagrass, and purple nutsedge. Lack of summer rainfall in the San Joaquin Valley allows for desiccation of perennial rootstocks or tubers if five spring-tooth harrowings or repeated listings are made. However, some soils have perched water tables or are excessively cloddy and do not permit thorough desiccation. Glyphosate controls johnsongrass or bermudagrass where dry fallowing is not possible and permits shorter turnaround times between crops.

Biological Control

Biological control of grassy weeds, especially johnsongrass and bermudagrass, is logical and economical, using weeder geese. Most growers, however, do not use geese because of management difficulties.

Chemical Control

Herbicides are used preplant, postemergence, and at lay-by (table 3). Most are soil-active residual herbicides, but others (foliar herbicides) control emerged weeds. Spot treatments, wick/wiper, and hooded sprayers permit selective control of perennial weeds with nonselective, translocated herbicides.

TABLE 3. HERBICIDES COMMONLY USED ON CALIFORNIA COTTON

Preplant/preemergence	Residuals:	DCPA, fluometuron, pendimethalin, prometryn, trifluralin, oxyfluorfen
	Contacts:	glyphosate, paraquat, oxyfluorfen
Postemergence	Grass control:	fluazifop-P, sethoxydim
Postemergence	Directed spray:	MSMA (to bloom) cyanazine, diuron, fluometuron, oxyfluorfen, prometryn
Lay-by–directed sprays	As rows close:	cyanazine, diuron, fluometuron, oxyfluorfen, prometryn, trifluralin
Perennial weeds	All perennials:	Spot treat with glyphosate
	Johnsongrass and bermudagrass:	fluazifop-P, sethoxydim
	Field bindweed:	Hooded spray at lay-by or pre-harvest spray with glyphosate

Preplant

A common practice in California cotton is to use a dinitroaniline herbicide—pendimethalin or trifluralin—well in advance of planting. The herbicide is incorporated into soil after fields are smooth, taking care to keep the herbicide shallow. Then San Joaquin Valley growers list and preirrigate. When planting in moist soil, beds are knocked down to permit cotton seed placement near the base of the treated soil. Cotton roots are retarded by deeply placed dinitroanilines (e.g., pendimethalin or trifluralin). Fluometuron or prometryn are sometimes combined with a dinitroaniline if nightshade is common. Imperial Valley growers often use DCPA, which is very safe on cotton, plus prometryn (which controls nightshade species), before irrigating up cotton. These residual herbicides, plus three to five cultivations, control most weeds after cotton is planted.

Many growers use contact herbicides before cotton is planted to kill winter weeds emerging after preirrigation or from winter rains.

Postemergence—Topical

After cotton emergence MSMA may be needed for heavy nutsedge populations. However, repeated close cultivations, an earlier irrigation, and bedding controls moderate populations without crop yield losses. Fluometuron plus surfactant is a possible salvage treatment for nightshade or pigweed populations without crop-yield losses. Postemergence, selective grass-control herbicides such as sethoxydim or fluazifop-P, can be used to control escaped annual and perennial grasses. For annuals, very early treatments are best, as drought-stressed grass is not controlled well. For perennials, two treatments are usually needed to get the degree of control desired.

Postemergence—Directed Spray

Some growers utilize cyanazine, prometryn, diuron, or fluometuron for nightshade and nutsedge control (sometimes with MSMA), applying the herbicide as a directed spray at the base of the 3.5–6-inch cotton plants.

Lay-by Directed Sprays

For certain competitive weeds such as annual morningglory or green amaranth, and where cotton is short or stands do not shade well, use of a lay-by herbicide may be warranted. Several choices are possible. Some such as cyanazine and fluometuron work best on fine-textured soils; whereas diuron and prometryn do better on coarse-textured soils, and oxyfluorfen does best on emerged weeds, cyanazine, oxyfluorfen, and prometryn are not as persistent and may be favored for certain crops planted after cotton.

Because dinitroanilines are usually used preplant, a second lay-by treatment is not recommended. Soil persistence of these products is additive, and the spectrum of weeds controlled by each of them is quite similar. An exception may be for johnsongrass seedlings which can germinate as late as September and form rhizomes.

Perennial Weeds

All perennial weeds should be kept off of all farms (fig. 6), but, when present in cotton, they must be controlled completely. Selective grass herbicides such as fluazifop-P will reduce johnsongrass and bermudagrass greatly, but eradication is needed. Spot-treatment with herbicides is effective. Occasional plants can be removed better by hoeing. Slightly higher rates of dinitroanilines are needed to prevent late-season seedling reinfestation of johnsongrass.

Field bindweed, Russian knapweed, or silverleaf nightshade are perennial broadleaved weeds that must be controlled or eradicated. Hooded sprayers at lay-by or pre-harvest applications permit control with glyphosate if treatment is carefully planned. These broadleaved perennial weeds all have seeds, so long-term monitoring is needed to prevent reinfestations should perennial rootstocks be killed.

Figure 6. Control of perennial weeds such as bermudagrass along the edges of fields (in this case, cotton) is essential to reduce in-field encroachment and problems in present and subsequent crops. Photo courtesy H.M. Kempen.

Control with herbicides such as glyphosate is often possible between crop plantings. For example, weeds can be irrigated to cause germination and treated at the optimum stage of growth, giving excellent control prior to cotton planting.

REFERENCES

Abernathy, J.R. 1980. Recirculating sprayers and rope applications. West. Cotton Prod. Conf. pp 44–45.
Elliott, F.C., M. Hoover and W.K. Porter, Jr. 1968. Cotton: Principles and Practices. 532 pp.
Fischer, B.B. and A.H. Lange. 1975. Eleven dinitroaniline herbicides: their residual properties and crop tolerance. Fresno Co. bull. Runcina Vol. 2. 5 pp. and tables.
Fischer, B.B. 1980. Strategies for field bindweed control. Proc. West. Cotton Prod. Conf. pp 41–44.
Integrated pest management for cotton in the western region of the United States. Univ. of Calif. State-wide integrated pest management project. Div. of Ag. and Nat. Res. Pub. 3305, 1984.
Keeley, P.E. 1980. Weed control strategies—Yellow nutsedge. Proc. West. Cotton Prod. Conf. pp 40–41.
Keeley, P.E., J.H. Miller and H.M. Kempen. 1975. A survey of weeds on cotton farms in the San Joaquin Valley. Proc. Cal. Weed Conf. pp 39–47.
Kempen, H.M. 1981. The place of the weed manager in today's crop management systems. Proc. West. Soc. Weed Sci. 33: 193–199.
Kempen, H.M. 1981. Weed seed production. Proc. West. Soc. Weed Sci. 34:78–81.
Kempen, H.M. 1980. Weed management consulting and its interaction with IPM. Proc. Beltwide Cotton Conf. pp 180–181.
Kempen, H.M. 1980. Progress with new equipment for application. Proc. 32nd Cal. Weed Conf. pp 135–138.
Kempen, H.M. and J. Graf. 1980. Weed control strategies—johnsongrass. Proc. West. Cotton Prod. Conf. pp 74–75.
Kempen, H.M. 1987. Growers weed management guide. Thomson Pub., Fresno, CA.
Miller, J.H., H.M. Kempen, D.W. Cudney, B.B. Fischer, and P.E. Keeley. 1981. Weed control in cotton, Lf. 2991, 18 pp.
Miller, J.H., P.E. Keeley, R.J. Thullen and C.H. Carter. 1978. Persistence and movement of ten herbicides in soil. Weed Sci. 26:20–27.
Nuckton, C.F. and C.O. McCorkle. 1980. A statistical picture of California's agriculture. LF. 2992.

Roberts, H.A. 1970. *Viable weed seeds in cultivated soils. Report, National Veg. Res. Sta. for 1969.*
Thullen, R.J. and P.E. Keeley. 1981. *Longevity of buried yellow nutsedge tubers. Proc. West. Soc. Weed Sci. p 81–86.*

DRY BEANS *(Phaseolus* spp.*)*

by Lawrence Clement[1]

The production of dry beans has been well established in the economic base of California agriculture. In 1987, 168,000 acres of dry beans with a value of $84,186,000 were harvested in California. There are a number of varieties that contribute to this acreage, with blackeyes having the largest acreage followed by light red kidneys, large limas, small limas, and others.

The cost of production varies from $300 to $400/A, depending on the variety, cultural practices, and whether it is single- or double-cropped. Weed-control costs are also variable for the same reasons. Generally, weed control costs the grower $20–25/A for a single preplant herbicide application. Growers who apply postemergence herbicides spend an additional $10–15/A.

Weed Spectrum in Dry Beans

Each production district in California has unique weed problems. Although the spectrum can be diverse, there are several common weed species that are troublesome in every district. Black nightshade, hairy nightshade, yellow nutsedge, and barnyardgrass present most problems for weed control. In all districts there are also problems with the control of field bindweed, velvetleaf, groundcherry, johnsongrass, jimsonweed, purslane, pigweed, and bermudagrass. Where dry beans are double-cropped behind cereals, volunteer barley and wheat present problems to growers.

Each production district and areas within each district present unique weed problems to growers that can be associated with culture, irrigation, soil type, variety, and microclimates. In each case, growers and their pest control advisers should be aware of individual field variations and the growers' personal experiences.

Cultural Practices

Not only does the weed spectrum vary from district to district, but so do the growers' cultural practices. It would be difficult to completely present the diversity of cultural practices conducted by California dry

1. *University of California Cooperative Extension, Solano County, CA.*

Figure 7. Dry beans require a weed-free environment for maximum yields (left). *Perennial weeds such as nutsedge* (right) *can cause reduced yields and increased harvest costs. Photos courtesy J.P. Orr.*

bean growers as they relate to weed control. The approach here is to present a summary of the more common practices.

In most cases, dry beans are planted to moisture following a preirrigation. After the preirrigation, the beds are listed and the crop planted 3–4 inches deep into moisture. This allows for a 1–2-inch dry mulch of soil over the planted crop, reducing weed seed germination until the first irrigation when the crop is established. Dry mulching also has a secondary beneficial effect for the crop in reducing the incidence of *Rhizoctonia* root rot and allowing for a more vigorous seedling. Beans that are irrigated up tend to be less vigorous and less competitive with weeds.

Although the most common method is by furrow irrigation, a significant portion of the state's acreage is under sprinkler irrigation. Sprinkler irrigation can be advantageous by allowing the grower to better control a germination irrigation and uniformly activate preplant herbicide applications.

Except in the coastal districts, dry beans are usually double-cropped following winter cereals. In this situation, the crop is planted between June 1 and July 1. Plantings after July are generally discouraged in areas where early fall rains present harvest problems. In the crop-rotation pattern, the previous herbicide program must be carefully considered before planting beans. Certain varieties are more sensitive to herbicide residues than others, and growers must consider the potential for crop damage. For example, limas and other flat-podded varieties are sensitive to EPTC or alachlor which can delay maturity of red kidneys when wet, cool soil conditions are present.

Following winter cereals, the grower has a limited time in which to plant beans. Once the cereal crop is harvested, growers usually burn the stubble, cultivate, preirrigate, apply a herbicide, and plant. Stubble burning removes excess organic material, destroys a portion of the weed seeds, and facilitates a uniform herbicide application.

Soil temperatures at planting can be critical for the crop as well as for optimum weed control. Most bean cultivars have their highest germination and emergence rates at soil temperatures between 60° and 80°F. Temperatures above 95°F will delay or otherwise reduce the stand population. A less vigorous crop with a reduced plant population will be less competitive with any weed population. With a final stand population of between 65,000 to 70,000 plants per acre (one plant per 4 inches on 30-inch centers), most vine-type bean varieties are able to outcompete many weed species, especially when combined with an effective preplant herbicide.

Growers are encouraged to clean harvesters before and after each harvested field. This will prevent the spread of troublesome weeds to other fields and production areas. Nightshade is a particularly troublesome weed in dry beans, and the berries are commonly mixed in with harvester trash.

Chemical Control

A problem with dry bean weed control in California is that the majority of registered herbicides are limited to preplant incorporation or preemergence application. Hence, weed escapes pose problems to growers when their herbicide selection does not match the weed spectrum. This is especially true of grassy weeds and nutsedge (fig. 7). Given the wide spectrum of dry bean varieties planted in California, it is necessary for growers to match, as closely as possible, the variety, the herbicide, and the target weed spectrum.

Preplant-Incorporated and Preemergence

Trifluralin

The most commonly used herbicide for all dry bean varieties is trifluralin. Trifluralin is a broad-spectrum material that has activity on most weed species found in dry beans. The fact that trifluralin does not have activity on weeds in the nightshade family or the nutsedges creates an increased problem with these weeds in dry beans and many other crops. The best way to apply trifluralin is by broadcast followed by immediate disking for incorporation. Incorporation of 2–4 inches has proven to be most effective. Power incorporation to preformed beds is also a common practice in dry beans. Moisture is not necessary for activation, as trifluralin kills weeds as they germinate. Some growers apply trifluralin as a lay-by treatment, although this causes some problems with placement due to the common 30-inch bed culture. Trifluralin is considered a very safe material, but some injury has occurred when the crop has been stressed. Growers must consider carryover to sensitive crops in the rotation patterns, especially when considering a lay-by treatment.

EPTC

Another commonly used herbicide for dry beans is EPTC. It has broad-spectrum weed control and must be incorporated into the soil immediately. Generally, EPTC is applied broadcast and disc incorporated. Most effective control is obtained by crossdisking 4–6 inches deep before bed listing. This is especially true for control of nutsedge. Power incorporation is also a common practice and provides excellent control when incorporated 2–4 inches deep in the bed tops. EPTC can be easily lost from the soil surface by volatilization when moisture is present during application. If a grower intends to preirrigate before planting, a different product should be chosen, as moisture will reduce effectiveness of this herbicide. Several dry bean varieties are sensitive to EPTC, namely the flat-podded varieties such as blackeyes and limas. EPTC may also be used as a lay-by treatment prior to pod formation.

Alachlor

Another commonly used preplant herbicide for dry beans is alachlor. The moisture necessary for activation of alachlor should occur by either rainfall or irrigation within 10 days of application. One-third to ¾ inch is usually sufficient for activation. Excessive water after application may reduce activity. Some growers, preferring to preirrigate, will apply alachlor 2 inches deep; however, weed control can be sporadic without moisture activation. Alachlor has activity on nightshade, nutsedge, and other weeds by contact during germination. Flood irrigation following application will result in failure of adequate weed control. Alachlor is broadcast and disc incorporated thoroughly 2 inches into the soil surface. Discs and disc harrows should be set to work the soil no deeper than 4 inches. Shallow and uniform incorporation is essential for optimum control. Alachlor is registered for use in all production areas of California except Kern County. Alachlor alone or in combination with other materials such as trifluralin may delay maturity if wet, cool soil conditions occur after the application is made.

Metolachlor

Metolachlor controls a wide spectrum of weeds including barnyardgrass, crabgrass, foxtails, yellow nutsedge, pigweed, and smartweed. Partial control of common purslane, hairy nightshade, seedling johnsongrass, and volunteer sorghum is attainable. Tank mixes with EPTC or trifluralin will increase the weed-control spectrum.

Metolachlor can be applied preplant-incorporated (2 inches) or preemergence followed by sprinklers or rainfall within seven days. Cultivation or supplemental tillage after preplant application must not exceed the depth of incorporation, or loss of weed control can occur. Some crop injury may occur under high moisture conditions during the seedling and early growth stages of the crop.

Glyphosate

Glyphosate, a nonselective herbicide, is labeled for use on all dry, edible beans for preplant or pre-crop-emergence application. For the control of such troublesome weeds as morningglory, nutsedge, and nightshade, glyphosate has proven to be an effective material. Application to young plants is usually more effective than on fully matured plants. The target weed must be growing actively in order to translocate the glyphosate throughout the plant for complete control.

Pendimethalin

Pendimethalin, a dinitroaniline herbicide, can be applied preplant immediately before planting or up to 60 days prior to planting. Incorporation should take place prior to planting and within seven days of application. Pendimethalin will control a broad spectrum of grasses and broadleaf weeds.

Ethalfluralin

Ethalfluralin can be used preplant incorporated. Incorporation must be made with a power tiller 2 to 3 inches in depth. A broad spectrum of annual grasses and broadleaved weeds can be controlled. Ethalfluralin can be expected to give fair to good control of nightshade.

Bentazon

Currently, bentazon is the only material labeled for postemergence application in California. It is mainly used for control of morningglory, nutsedge, hairy nightshade, and smartweed in the delta. Target weeds are best controlled within the 2-to-10-leaf stage. Dry beans should be in the first trifoliate stage with leaves fully extended. Rainfall or sprinkler irrigation within eight to 10 hours can reduce effectiveness. Bentazon does not control black nightshade. Higher temperatures increase activity, and nutsedge can be controlled more effectively with split applications.

Nonphytotoxic crop oil must be added to bentazon for effective weed control. This treatment is the only one that has been shown to control velvetleaf in beans.

Metolachlor, ethalfluralin, alachlor, and EPTC can be expected to give control of nightshade. Trifluralin and pendimethalin are longer lasting but will not control nightshade.

Tank-Mix Applications

There are several tank mixes of materials for use on dry beans. Combinations can increase the spectrum of weed control; however, mixes can change the chemistry of the products and add to the label precautions.

Other Considerations

Most preplant-incorporated herbicides need adequate soil moisture for activation. Incorporation into dry soils generally results in poor weed control. This is particularly true of alachlor which, until the first irrigation, remains inactive. Subsequent irrigation may cause injury to young bean seedlings. The herbicide must be placed in the zone where weeds are coming from. Nightshade usually germinates in the top 2 inches, while nutsedge comes from much deeper—up to 6 inches or more.

Most of the newer herbicides have shorter residual periods of weed control; consequently, we do not get some of the weeds which germinate with later irrigations. The use of these shorter-lived herbicides in combination with one of the longer-lived dinitroanilines increases the length and spectrum of weed control.

Between two of our more troublesome weeds, hairy and black nightshade, hairy nightshade is the easier to control. Alachlor, metolachlor, and ethalfluralin have shown activity on black nightshade preplant, and bentazon is available for postemergence applications, provided the weeds are relatively small.

EPTC and alachlor are probably the best herbicides available for nutsedge control. EPTC causes crop injury in blackeyes and limas. Alachlor performance has sometimes been erratic, depending upon the soil moisture, but by using a subsurface layering method (spray blade), excellent nutsedge control has been obtained without crop injury.

SAFFLOWER *(Carthamus tinctorius L)*

by *Thomas E. Kearney*[1]

There were 106,000 acres of safflower harvested in 1987 with a value of $26,962,000. Safflower is considered a relatively new crop in California, with the first commercial production in 1950. Weed competition is a major problem in the production of safflower. Winter-planted safflower will remain in the prostrate or rosette stage until spring. Early-spring-planted safflower will remain in a rosette stage before elongation. This prostrate growth habit of safflower makes it a poor weed competitor. The weed

---

1. *University of California Cooperative Extension, Yolo County, CA.*

species which are most serious competitors with safflower are lambs-quarters, pigweeds, mustards, wild oat, and volunteer cereals.

Cultural Control

After extensive testing, it was found that spring plantings were the most desirable for safflower. With spring plantings, the fall and winter weeds which have germinated can be eliminated prior to planting. Safflower has a deep taproot system. It was found that safflower could be drilled or planted into moisture and would germinate and grow normally with no surface moisture being applied. This root system enables safflower to germinate and grow while the soil surface remains dry. A dry soil surface helps prevent the germination of shallow weed seeds. In close-drilled safflower, shallow harrowing is effective in controlling shallow-rooted seedling weeds when the safflower is 3–6 inches high. The shallow cultivation should be made crosswise or diagonally across the drill rows. Wide-row-planted safflower, 20 inches or more, can be cultivated like conventional row crops for weeds between the rows. Normally, safflower is not irrigated in the Sacramento Valley; however, it is often irrigated in the San Joaquin Valley. Irrigations are usually applied after the plants are well established and have used some of the available moisture.

The fertilization method used for safflower is advantageous for weed control. The main fertilizer element used is nitrogen, which is injected as aqua or anhydrous ammonia. This deep placement does not stimulate the growth of undesirable weeds on the surface of the ground such as is the case with topdressing of cereals. Marketed safflower seed contains no weed seeds. Therefore, the introduction of weeds in the field does not occur with the planting seeds.

Chemical Control

Chemical weed control in safflower is accomplished by using preplant herbicides. Commonly used preplant incorporated herbicides for weed control in safflower include trifluralin, EPTC, and metolachlor. Another herbicide registered for use on safflower is chloropropham.

Trifluralin is the most commonly used herbicide due to its residual activity and broad spectrum weed control. It is quite effective on a broad range of weeds. However, its prolonged use has created a new spectrum of weed problems. The main weed problems that are developing in fields where this chemical has been used are the mustards, velvetleaf, and wild sunflower.

EPTC is more active on broadleaf species and some difficult-to-control weeds such as wild cane, nutsedge, and johnsongrass. EPTC is also a short-lived herbicide, lasting six to eight weeks. EPTC does not create problems for following crops.

Metolachlor is applied preplant-incorporated. It is most active against annual grasses and certain broadleaf weeds. If the herbicide application is preceded by adequate disking, it can suppress rhizomatous johnsongrass and nutsedge. Metolachlor is relatively short-lived in soil, lasting from eight to 10 weeks under cropping conditions.

GRAIN SORGHUM *(Sorghum bicolor)*

by James M. Gaggero[1]

Sorghum is produced in California for grain, silage, and forage. The largest acreage is associated with the grain crop, and in 1987 there were 25,000 planted acres with a harvested value of $3,629,000. Yields of grain sorghum average 4500–5000 pounds per acre. The crop can be produced with late spring plantings on soils with salt, sodium, and boron problems and on poorly drained soils. Grain sorghum is commonly used in double-cropping systems following barley and wheat. Cost of production averages $300 per acre, with weed-management costs averaging $20 per acre.

Unmanaged weeds can reduce yields, promote lodging, and increase harvest costs. Early-season weed competition may reduce yields in grain sorghum greater than late-season weed competition. However, late-season weeds may interfere with harvest and provide a seed source to infest subsequent crops. A weed-management program must be based on the weed-infestation history of the field and must integrate cultural and chemical control methods for optimum production (fig. 8).

The major broadleaf weed problems in grain sorghum production areas of California are lambsquarters, pigweeds, groundcherry, annual morningglory, and purslane. Barnyardgrass is the most widespread grass weed pest in grain sorghum. Other major grass weed pests are sprangletop and johnsongrass. Fields heavily infested with johnsongrass or nutsedge should not be planted to grain sorghum.

Cultural Control

Effective seedbed-tillage practices in preirrigated soils, before seeding, can remove many germinated seedling weeds. Cultivation of emerged grain sorghum in row plantings will control annual weeds, except for weeds growing in the plant row. Conventional cultivating tools should be set only as deep and as close to the grain sorghum as necessary to control weeds but not so deep or so close as to injure the grain sorghum roots. Rotary hoes and tine-tooth or spike-tooth harrows can be used

1. Zoecon Corporation, Citrus Heights, CA.

Figure 8. Weeds in grain sorghum (left) *can promote lodging, reduce yields, and increase harvest costs, while maximum yields are attainable through the use of a well-managed program involving cultural and chemical control methods* (right). *Photos courtesy J.P. Orr.*

on close row plantings for removing seedling johnsongrass. Use of tillage equipment should be avoided when the soil is too wet, as soil compaction may result which can reduce grain sorghum root development, rate of growth, and yields. Hand hoeing of weeds is normally not done because of high cost and ineffectiveness. However, small areas of johnsongrass and sorghum-johnsongrass outcrosses should be removed to prevent further spreading. Both rhizomes and seedheads should be removed from the field.

A well-prepared seedbed, free of large clods, promotes uniform and vigorous sorghum emergence, which will allow the grain sorghum to compete better with weeds. It also facilitates cultivation and improves weed control from preplant-incorporated and preemergence herbicides. Planting of grain sorghum is most commonly done in preirrigated soils; however, grain sorghum may be planted in dry soils and irrigated up. Preirrigation may germinate many weed seeds, and these weeds can be removed by shallow tillage prior to planting. Grain sorghum planted in preirrigated fields usually competes well with later emerging weeds. Grain sorghum planted in dry soil and irrigated up may result in the simultaneous emergence of the crop and weeds. Barnyardgrass can be a serious problem when irrigating up the crop. Fields with high weed or weed-seed infestation levels should be avoided as they may not produce economically regardless of the control methods used.

Chemical Control

Herbicides available for use in grain sorghum may be divided into three groups: Preplant-incorporated, preemergence, and postemergence.

Preplant-incorporated herbicides are applied before planting and mixed into the soil to a shallow depth. Weed control is influenced by several factors, such as the seedbed condition, amount of crop residue on the soil surface, depth and type of incorporation, rate of herbicide used, and weed species. Crop residue on the soil surface can intercept the herbicide, so such residue should be worked thoroughly into the soil before applying a preplant herbicide. Propachlor, a preplant or preemergence herbicide lasting four to eight weeks, should be incorporated to a 2-inch depth or to moisture. Do not incorporate propachlor to a depth greater than 4 inches or dilution of the herbicide will occur, resulting in a lack of weed control. When planting on flat ground, broadcast propachlor preplant and incorporate by shallow disking, or apply to the soil surface after planting and incorporate with sprinkler irrigation. For bed plantings, apply propachlor in a band on preformed beds and incorporate with a power-driven rotary tiller or rolling cultivator. Propachlor should not be used where the crop is flood irrigated within the first six to eight weeks of growth, because the herbicide is very soluble and will be leached below the weed seed zone. Propachlor usually gives good control of crabgrass, sprangletop, sandbur, purslane, pigweed, knotweed, and nightshade; partial control of barnyardgrass and lambsquarters; and no control of cocklebur.

Preemergence herbicides are applied at planting or immediately after planting, but before the crop or weeds emerge. Preemergence treatments require mechanical incorporation or an irrigation (or rainfall) to leach the herbicide into the zone of germinating weed seeds for control. Preemergence weed control is influenced by the same factors as those for preplant-incorporated herbicides. In addition, the time of application is important and should be done either at or immediately after planting. Propazine, a preemergence herbicide lasting 12 to 18 months, should be applied at or immediately after planting and incorporated by irrigation to ensure herbicide activity. Propazine usually gives good control of purslane, lambsquarters, pigweed, knotweed, and cocklebur; partial control of nightshade; and no control of barnyardgrass, crabgrass, sprangletop, and sandbur. Propazine is a triazine herbicide and may carry over in the soil and harm sensitive, subsequent crops. Atrazine is a preemergence herbicide only for use on furrow-irrigated grain sorghum, or it can be used postemergence. Atrazine used as a preemergence herbicide must be incorporated into moist soil or irrigated after application by sprinkler or flooding. Atrazine should not be used on sand or loamy sand soils or on grain sorghum planted in the furrow. Atrazine usually gives good control of purslane, lambsquarters, pigweeds, knotweed, and cocklebur; partial control of barnyardgrass and nightshade; and no control of crabgrass, sprangletop, and sandbur. Atrazine will persist in the soil for 12 to 18 months, so carryover may be a problem on sensitive subsequent crops.

Postemergence herbicides are applied to the leaves of both the crop and weeds. The degree of weed control is influenced by weed species present, soil moisture, stage of weed growth, and rate of weed growth. Weeds should be small and growing well under favorable soil-moisture conditions. Atrazine can be used postemergence before weeds reach a height of 1 inch. 2,4-D is also used postemergence to control broadleaved weeds. This herbicide usually gives good control of purslane, lambsquarters, pigweed, cocklebur, and nightshade; partial control of knotweed; and no control of barnyardgrass, crabgrass, sprangletop, or sandbur. To avoid injury to the crop, 2,4-D should be applied as a directed spray rather than broadcast, preferably with drop nozzles, after the grain sorghum is 4 to 6 inches in height, but before the crop reaches the boot stage. Do not spray 2,4-D at the boot stage or later stages. Care must be taken to avoid drift with 2,4-D to sensitive crops. 2,4-D is a restricted herbicide requiring a permit from the county agricultural commissioner.

REFERENCES

California agriculture in 1982. USDA, Stat. Rpt. Ser., Agric. Statistician.
Irrigated grain sorghum production in California. Univ. of Calif., Div. of Agric. Sci., Leaflet #2873, February 1976.
Weed control in grain sorghum. Univ. of Calif., Div. of Agric. Sci., Leaflet #21030, July 1978. Univ. of Calif. Ag. Ext. Ser.

RICE *(Oryza sativa)*

by D.E. Bayer[1], J.E. Hill[2], and Donald E. Seaman[3]

Rice is grown on approximately 400,000–500,000 acres in California, second to Arkansas and about equal to Louisiana and Texas. There were 367,000 acres of rice harvested in California in 1987. The value of this production has not yet been estimated; however, values for the previous four-year period have ranged from $88,172,000 to $206,146,000 on 328,000 to 450,000 acres. About one-half of this production is on very heavy clay soils best suited economically for rice. Consequently, fields have been in continuous rice production for many years. Rice production since the introduction of short-statured varieties in 1979 has ranged from 68 to 77 cwt (6800 to 7700 lbs) per acre, the highest in the United States. Production costs vary from $600 to $800 per acre of which $40 to $80 may be weed-management costs.

Weed control has been a major concern of the rice grower since the beginning of rice production in California. The system of seeding rice into continuously flooded fields was developed as a cultural method

1, 2, 3. University of California, Davis, CA.

of controlling barnyardgrass. Although this method was initially effective, its continued use encouraged the spread of aquatic biotypes of barnyardgrass (watergrasses), as well as many other aquatic weeds. Most of these other major weed problems infesting rice fields are marsh plants that thrive and compete effectively with rice under continuous flooding.

Virtually all rice-production management practices affect the competitive abilities of both the rice plant and the weeds. Previous crops, seedbed preparation, soil fertility, time of planting, choice of cultivar, stand density, water management, and pest control all interact to determine the vigor and competitive abilities of both the rice and weeds. Weeds may contribute to insect problems by serving as alternate hosts and/or creating stagnant water for breeding sites.

Cultural Methods

Cultural methods for the control of specific rice weeds, such as tillage and drying for perennial weeds, and water depth for watergrass control, have been effective as have selective rice herbicides. Selective herbicides are not always available for all rice weeds. Cultural methods remain an integral part of a successful integrated weed-control program in water-sown rice. Specific cultural practices are important in improving the effectiveness of currently available chemicals for rice weed control. Fortunately, many of these methods are those most beneficial to rice stand establishment and development.

Seedbed Preparation
The rice seedbed should be tilled 6 to 8 inches deep as soon as it is dry enough to allow field tillage without excessive soil compaction. Disking, chiseling, or plowing in fall, winter, or early spring will increase soil aeration, temperature, and rate of drying in the spring. Rice seedbeds should be worked as early as possible to hasten crop-residue decomposition and to decrease the incidence of algae (scum) and various common weed problems.

The rice seedbed should be worked into a cloddy condition in which most clods are relatively small (1–2 inches in diameter). A cloddy seedbed facilitates anchorage of rice seeds and seedlings, which favors more uniform rice stands. Finer seedbeds may require "V-grooving" or "creasing" with a roller to facilitate anchorage. Large clods not broken or worked down in tillage operations provide a favorable environment for rapid weed seedling growth and establishment. Clods so large that they are exposed above the water surface provide an excellent condition for growth and survival of grassy weeds, even with the use of currently available herbicides. A land-smoothing implement (triplane) is useful for clod-size reduction and eliminating seedbed high spots, which are favorable for weed infestations.

Fertilizer Management

Nitrogen and phosphate fertilizers should be incorporated into the soil 2–5 inches deep to reduce their availability to weed seedlings that germinate near the soil surface. Submersed aquatic weeds such as southern naiad, chara, and algae grow more vigorously and may become well established when high rates of nitrogen and phosphorus are left on the soil surface. Topdressed applications of nitrogen and phosphorus into the water also encourage rapid growth of weeds.

Weed-Free Rice Seed

Good-quality rice seed free of weed seed and red rice should be used to prevent weed infestations. The use of certified rice seed will minimize this source of weeds. Certified rice seed can have a maximum of 0.10% weed seeds and only 22 barnyardgrass (watergrass) seeds per kilogram of rice seeds. It can have no red rice or noxious weed seeds. The certification process is designed to minimize the transfer of weed seed in seed sources. The planting of contaminated seed will be costly to a weed-management program for many years.

Special Cultural Practices for Specific Rice Weeds

Deep plowing and crop rotation are two methods frequently used to reduce perennial infestation of American pondweed, cattail, and river bulrush populations. Plowing 8 to 14 inches deep to expose underground stems of cattails and tubers of river bulrush and winter buds of American pondweed will usually reduce populations of these perennial weeds if sufficient drying of reproductive plant parts is attained in the spring. To facilitate soil desiccation rotation to a nonirrigated crop in conjunction with this practice will be even more effective in controlling these weeds than when rice is grown continuously. Good drainage of rotated fields is necessary because a water table near the soil surface will keep these perennial weeds alive. Efforts should be made to prevent transfer of stems, tubers, and buds to noninfested areas of fields by tillage operations.

Water Management

Proper water management is the most important factor in successful weed control in water-sown rice. A continuous water depth of 3–6 inches is important in improving effectiveness of currently used rice herbicides and reducing severity of weed competition. Lowering the flood of water or complete draining favors weed growth and intensifies weed competition with rice even when currently available herbicides are used. Exposure of soil to air as a result of draining a rice field greatly increases the diffusion of oxygen into the soil profile. This increase in oxygen concentration initiates the germination of weed seeds distributed throughout the soil profile and favors establishment and growth of most weeds.

A permanent flood restricts oxygen diffusion into the soil profile and thereby decreases weed seed germination and growth. For example, sprangletop usually does not germinate and emerge through a depth of 4 or more inches of water; but if the soil is drained, sprangletop seeds germinate rapidly and subsequent plant growth is virtually uncontrolled by submergence. Barnyardgrass establishment also is greatly encouraged by field draining. Exposure of soil long enough to allow secondary root development in barnyardgrass seedlings greatly reduces the effectiveness of currently used barnyardgrass herbicides. Sedges and broadleaf weeds are favored also by extremely shallow water and/or field draining. These weeds usually appear earlier and are of a broader age-range in drained fields. The lack of uniform weed development may reduce the effectiveness of broadleaf herbicides due to differential emergence from the water at the time of herbicide application. Timing of herbicide applications in orr to obtain optimum weed control may then be difficult.

Water maintained at a depth of 6–8 inches for 21–28 days after planting will provide partial control of most barnyardgrass species if conditions are favorable. A well-leveled field without numerous soil depressions or elevations is essential for acceptable control by this method. Ambient temperatures of 77–86°F and subsequent elevation of water temperatures greatly enhances barnyardgrass control by this method. However, climatic conditions are not always favorable during the early stand establishment period of rice, and often only sporadic control is observed. Factors such as low temperatures, overcast skies, seedling diseases, and strong winds that move water off fields at this early plant-growth stage make this method of barnyardgrass control less reliable.

Chemical Control

Herbicides should be used in combination with good crop management to control weeds (table 4). Competition from weeds is most limiting to rice yields during the early stages of growth and development of the rice plant (approximately the first 30 days following seeding). Weed removal when the rice plant is still in the early vegetative stage allows more time for the rice plant to maximize the use of resources released to it as a result of removing the weeds.

In California, rice is grown under a continuously flooded system, which restricts application of a herbicide to: (1) preplant, which may include soil incorporation; (2) postplant, before the weeds and/or rice plant emerge above the water; and (3) postplant, after the rice and weeds have emerged above the water.

The herbicides most commonly used in California rice production are all phytotoxic to the rice plant when used at excessive rates or applied to weak, severely stressed plants or during adverse weather conditions. High temperatures increase the phytotoxicity, while cool temperatures limit the effectiveness of these herbicides.

TABLE 4. INFLUENCE OF APPLICATION ON HERBICIDE ACTIVITY

Herbicide	Application time	Water depth
molinate	Preplant or preflood incorporation or postflood either pre- or post-emergence	Preflood—the sooner you flood the better; then keep the field flooded. Postflood—deepen water at time of application to cover weed foliage; then lower water after 4–6 days. Do not expose soil surface after treatment.
thiobencarb	Postemergence (2-leaf rice)	Prior to application, water should be shallow. Following application raise water to cover high spots. Do not expose soil surface after treatment.
propanil	Postemergence	Water depth must be lowered at time of application to expose maximum weed foliage. Raise water following application.
MCPA	Postemergence	Early application requires lowering water to expose foliage of small plants, but care should be taken to avoid letting soil dry.
bentazon	Postemergence	Weed foliage must be exposed at time of application. Water may have to be lowered, but do not drain field completely.
endothall	Postemergence	Flood water must be held static for 3–5 days.

The choice of which herbicide to use should be based on previous years' records and on correct identification of seedlings present in the current year's crop. Schedule herbicide applications to coincide with the developmental stages of the crop and weed (figs. 9, 10, 11). Scheduling these applications on a calendar basis following planting is unreliable, as stages of development will vary from year to year, depending on cultural and environmental factors. When the developmental stages of the crop and weed do not coincide for a particular herbicide, it should not be used, as either injury to the rice or less than optimum weed control will result.

Most rice soils contain relatively high amounts of clay and frequently have an impervious subsoil that restricts the percolation of water. Since movement of water through these soils is limited, movement of soil-

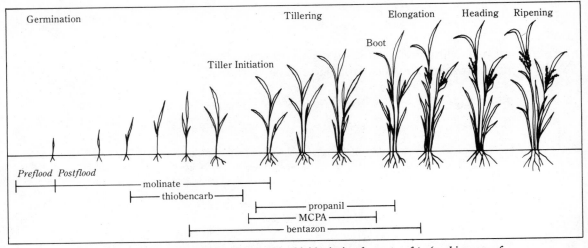

Figure 9. Stages in rice development and herbicide timing for crop safety (and in range for normal weed control).

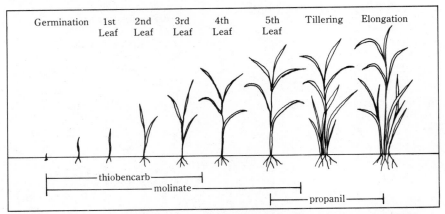

Figure 10. Stages in barnyardgrass development and herbicide timing for most effective control.

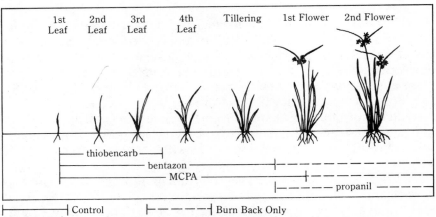

Figure 11. Activity of herbicides on smallflower umbrellaplant at various life stages.

applied (soil-active) herbicides will also be limited. Significant movement of herbicides into these soils will only occur when the soil profile is dry, prior to flooding the field. When moisture in the soil profile increases through rainfall or incomplete drying, depth of leaching or movement of the herbicide into the soil profile will be reduced. Even when the herbicide is readily adsorbed out of the flood water to the soil, it will be concentrated on the surface of the soil. Thus, both placement of the herbicide in the soil (where in the soil profile the herbicide is concentrated) and site of uptake by the rice plant and weeds are important considerations when selecting the proper herbicide and type of application method.

Proper water management is essential for optimum herbicide performance and should be based on the herbicide to be used. The strategy should be to encourage rapid, uniform emergence of the crop and to maintain a healthy, vigorous, fast-growing seedling. Best results have been obtained when weed emergence and growth have been uniform. When weed emergence occurs over an extended period of time, it becomes difficult and frequently impossible to apply the herbicide at a time when all the weeds will be controlled.

When using foliar-applied herbicides such as MCPA, bentazon, and propanil, it is essential that the weed foliage be exposed to the herbicide at the time of application. Small weeds submerged in the water or seedlings that have not emerged from the soil at time of application will not be controlled. Following application, the weed foliage must remain exposed for 24 to 48 hours to allow sufficient uptake of the herbicide before weed foliage can be covered with water. In the case of propanil, it is essential that the weed foliage be submerged following application to obtain optimum control. The water level should always be reestablished as soon as possible following application of any foliar-applied herbicide to aid in controlling of sprayed plants, reduce germination of other weeds, and to avoid undue stress to the rice plants.

Applications made to flooded fields with ground equipment may provide unsatisfactory control if splashing results or if sprayed foliage is forced under water; this is because the herbicide will be washed off the weed foliage before it can penetrate.

Many herbicides leave residues in the flood water following label usage. Holding of treated water to prevent herbicide residues from polluting downstream, untreated water is a recommended practice especially when using molinate, thiobencarb, and bentazon. For precise water holding requirements, consult the local agricultural commissioner.

Extreme caution should be used when applying herbicides late in the growing season to avoid interfering with panicle initiation, formation of the pollen, and pollination. After pollination of the rice plant has been completed, some herbicides can be safely applied. Remember, any use of a herbicide must be in compliance with the label. Application of herbicides late in the development of the rice plant will not benefit the grower by reducing competition from the weeds but may benefit him by reducing lodging of the rice plant or by reducing the green plant material that would increase harvesting and drying costs.

Use caution when applying combinations or sequential applications of pesticides, as they may damage the rice plant. For example, propanil will adversely affect rice plants if improperly applied with either a carbamate or an organophosphate insecticide.

SUGAR BEETS *(Beta vulgaris)*

by Lauren M. Burtch[1]

Sugar beet acreage varies somewhat from year to year depending upon projected gross revenues from alternate crops. In 1987 there were 215,000 acres harvested with a value of $172,502,000 and an average yield of 27.7 tons per acre.

Sugar beets are grown from the southern tip of the Imperial Valley to the northern portion of the Sacramento Valley. The crop is regularly planted by geographic location beginning in early September in the Imperial Valley, and terminating the following June in specific areas designated for harvest the following spring. This planting season, unique to California, permits scheduling processing operations over a long calendar period with a minimum risk from disease problems caused by overlapping crop patterns. Cost of production varies from $700 to $1000 per acre depending on planting and harvest dates, water costs, and weed populations. Weed costs vary widely depending on planting season, weed species present, and effectiveness of the herbicide program on beets as well as other crops in the rotation. The crop is usually seeded at high rates, and excess beets and escape weeds are removed by mechanical means, or by hand, as part of the thinning operation. Usually one additional hoeing is budgeted to remove weed escapes, or new weed emergence after planting.

The wide range of planting and harvesting dates results in crop exposure to a broad range of weed problems including summer or winter annual, biennial, or perennial weeds. Most perennial types are difficult to control, and sugar beet growers are advised not to plant in fields where field bindweed, johnsongrass, or bermudagrass are expected to be competitive. Other weed pests to be avoided are common cocklebur, common sunflower, little mallow, and Russian thistle (fig. 12).

Since sugar beets are not strong competitors with weeds, many common annuals as well as volunteer crops can infest the crop and re-

1. Amstar Corporation, Spreckels Sugar Division, Mendota, CA.

Figure 12. Control of Russian thistle is an important component in the sugar beet curly top virus management program as it is the host plant for beet leafhopper, which is the vector for this virus disease. Photo courtesy J.K. Clark.

quire control through appropriate chemical and mechanical methods. Weed species vary widely with geographic location and growing season. Common winter annuals are black mustard, shepherdspurse, coast fiddleneck, volunteer cereals, and winter annual grasses. Barnyardgrass, redroot pigweed, and lambsquarters are examples of common summer annual weeds.

Cultural Methods

Sugar beets are grown under irrigation as a part of a rotation program designed to minimize risk from weeds, soilborne diseases, nematodes, and other soil pests. The rotation sequence must consider the possibility of residual herbicides, which could be damaging to emerging seedlings. Seedbed preparation should be deep and thorough to encourage maximum field emergence and subsequent growth. A well-prepared seedbed is also an integral part of an effective weed-control program. Preirrigation is often used in the absence of rainfall as a weed-control tool as well as to assist in seedbed preparation.

Sugar beets are adapted to a number of soil types ranging from coarse sands to fine clay loams, and herbicide rates must be fine-tuned to soil type to allow for maximum crop safety without losing herbicide activity. Emerging seedlings can also be damaged by salt toxicity, and herbicide activity is generally intensified when salt concentrations are high. Varieties have been developed that are adapted to specific geographic areas. Commercially processed seed is nearly weed free.

Nitrogen and phosphorus fertilizers are judiciously applied to maximize sugar production and to better enable the crop to compete with weeds.

Weed Control

Since sugar beets are planted and harvested over much of the calendar year, no single herbicide, or combination, is able to provide season-long weed control. The key to a successful weed-control program is field selection and knowledge of the weed spectrum as well as knowledge of the herbicide's ability to control expected weeds. The herbicide choices for the planting season beginning in October and ending in March are listed in table 5.

TABLE 5. HERBICIDE CHOICES FOR THE FALL AND WINTER PLANTING SEASON (OCTOBER TO MARCH)

Preemergence or Shallow incorporated	Postemergence Pre-thinning	Lay-by Post-thinning
pyrazon BW	pyrazon BW	trifluralin B
ethofumesate B	phenmedipham +	pyrazon BW
diethatyl GA	desmedipham BW	sethoxydim G
	endothall B	
	sethoxydim G	

GA = Winter grasses
  G = Volunteer cereals and winter annual grasses
BW = Winter broadleaf weeds
  B = Winter broadleaf and winter annual weeds

Pyrazon is the most widely used herbicide for control of winter annual broadleaf weeds. Since volunteer cereals and annual grasses are almost universally present with broadleaf species, ethofumesate is widely used in combination with pyrazon. Diethatyl can be substituted where desired for annual grass control.

Incorporation can be mechanical before planting, or preemergence with rainfall or sprinkler irrigation where appropriate.

Sugar beets grow slowly during the winter months, and postemergence treatments are sometimes necessary to provide supplementary control or to replace pyrazon on soil types where beet seedling injury occurs. A 50-50 mixture of phenmedipham plus desmedipham is effective against small broadleaf weeds, but applications must be timed carefully to avoid beet injury and to obtain maximum weed control. Split applications at reduced rates are very effective for controlling weeds and reducing sugar beet injury. Endothall or sethoxydim can be used against volunteer cereals and wild oat. Trifluralin is widely used as a lay-by treatment and is designed to control summer annual weeds that emerge after cultivation normally ceases.

TABLE 6. HERBICIDE CHOICES FOR THE SPRING AND LATE-SUMMER PLANTING SEASON (FEBRUARY TO OCTOBER)

Preemergence or Shallow incorporated	Postemergence Pre-thinning	Lay-by Post-thinning
diethatyl B	desmedipham +	EPTC B
ethofumesate B	phenmedipham BW	trifluralin B
pebulate B	desmedipham +	sethoxydim G
cycloate B	phenmedipham +	
	ethofumesate BW	
	sethoxydim G	

BW = Summer annual broadleaf weeds
B = Summer annual grasses and/or broadleaf weeds
G = Summer annual grasses

A different program is required for fields planted in the period beginning in February and ending in October (table 6). Pebulate and cycloate have filled this need for many years. These herbicides behave in a similar manner and require thorough incorporation before planting. Ethofumesate and diethatyl can be used either singly or in combination. Both are stable and require less incorporation than pebulate or cycloate and can be used under sprinkler irrigation. A postemergence application of the desmedipham-plus-phenmedipham combination is effective against most broadleaf escapes. The combination of desmedipham-plus-phenmedipham-plus-ethofumesate is very effective for controlling difficult broadleaf species, such as knotweed. Sethoxydim is an excellent postemergence grass herbicide for use in sugar beets, with the exception of annual bluegrass. Sethoxydim cannot be combined with the desmedipham-plus-phenmedipham due to antagonism. Trifluralin and EPTC are often used as lay-by treatments for control of late-emerging summer annual grasses and broadleaf species.

The present-day California sugar beet grower is fortunate in having a long list of effective herbicides for weed control. Nevertheless, weed-control success depends on careful field selection, knowledge of weeds expected, and the characteristics of the herbicides available.

REFERENCES

Calif. Beet Growers Assoc. Annual Rpt. 1982.
Fischer, B.B., L.M. Burtch, and R. Smith. 1972. The science and art of weed control in sugar beets. A prog. rpt. Runcina: 7 UCCE, Fresno.
Fischer, B.B., L.M. Burtch, and L.M. Brown. 1980. Sugar beet applied research studies—weed control—mildew control. A prog. rpt. Runcina: 21 UCCE.

IRRIGATED PASTURES

by W.B. McHenry[1] and Melvin R. George[2]

Irrigated pasture, like alfalfa and other solid-seeded crops, has a distinct potential advantage of out-competing most of the 800 or so weed species reported in California. Irrigated pasture and hay and annual forage crops are solid seeded and thus are potentially better able to "smother" or shade out unwanted plants more effectively than are row crops. Any management influence that reduces pasture plant vigor and density also reduces the competitive dominance of the pasture plants (annual or perennial forages). Pasture thinning permits weeds to capture light, moisture, and nutrients intended for the desired forage plants.

Weed control in irrigated pastures can be accomplished through a combination of cultural and management practices. Practices that maximize forage yields by sustaining high forage crop vigor will simultaneously reduce weed establishment. Specific weed-reducing practices are important during land preparation, at seeding time, during seedling establishment, and periodically after establishment (fig. 13).

Weed Control Before Pasture Seeding

Existing weeds, particularly difficult perennials, on a field scheduled for pasture seeding should be controlled prior to surface grading. Bermudagrass, johnsongrass, and Canadian thistle are prime examples. Underground rhizomes of these species are readily spread by leveling and cultivation operations. Curly dock can also be a problem, particularly on fine textured, moisture-holding soils. Biennial weed species such as tansy ragwort and bristly oxtongue can be treated with 2,4-D or controlled through dry cultivation prior to land preparation. Weed seed dormancy precludes obtaining complete weed eradication.

Proper land leveling needs to be accomplished to prevent high spots (spots that dry), and poorly drained low areas. Both conditions reduce pasture populations, thereby reducing competition of weeds. Poorly drained areas at the low or drain end of pastures are common. Good drainage will also reduce the incidence of soil compaction by livestock and farm equipment. Unfortunately, there are numerous dry- and wet-ground weed species to capture resources where forage plants fade from areas due to poor irrigation practices. Establishment of a uniform slope is highly recommended prior to committing a field to pasture seeding.

Annual weed populations can be reduced after land leveling and prior to seeding by irrigating the field to germinate weeds and then following with cultivation. Two cycles of irrigation and cultivation will reduce

1, 2. University of California Cooperative Extension, Davis, CA.

Figure 13. Poisonous weeds, such as tansy ragwort, can reduce forage production in irrigated pastures and increase the potential for animal poisoning. Photo courtesy W.B. McHenry.

weediness and develop a good seedbed for the drilling of pasture species. Raising a "smother crop" like a grain or hay crop (sudangrass, etc.), the summer preceding pasture seeding is an alternative to weed germination and cultivation. Smother cropping should be practiced only to suppress annual weed populations. Herbicides recommended for the specific grain or hay crop will further reduce weeds as well as enhance the quality of the smother crop. Soil-active herbicides that characteristically break down slowly and that might jeopardize establishment of the pasture seeding should be avoided.

Establishing the New Pasture

Annual or perennial pasture seedlings are sensitive to drying or excessively muddy conditions. The pasture manager should appreciate that, at this stage, light, moisture, and nutrients are amply available to both the pasture plants and to weed species. Many weeds have an adaptive ability to survive alternate wetting and drying of the soil.

The young pasture should be given every opportunity for competing successfully in the early phase of growth. Selection of adapted grass and legume varieties, legume inoculation, appropriate fertilizer, proper seeding depth, and time (spring or fall, depending on the region) are examples of practices that encourage a good start.

During the spring and early summer, clipping of permanent pasture can be practiced, when the soil surface is dry, onto the grass canopy to allow more light to reach shorter-statured legumes. Effort should be made to avoid compaction of wet soils by operating tractors over a wet pasture. Clipping should be continued as needed even after grazing commences. Grazing of new pastures should be delayed until late spring or summer to ensure complete establishment; and initial grazing should be light. Young pastures are more susceptible to grazing and, if over-utilized, the forage plants will be thinned and open the new planting to weed invasion.

Weed Control in Established Pastures

Maintenance of a productive, established pasture includes cultural practices similar to those required for rapid pasture establishment. Irrigation frequency and rates that minimize moisture stress, particularly of shallow-rooted legumes, are essential to maintain high forage production and quality. Prolonged stress reduces plant vigor and eventually leads to thinning of pasture plants. Soil compaction by livestock can be a problem on heavier soils when they are muddy due to irrigation or rain. Compacted soils will reduce vigor quickly and lead to weed establishment. Compaction is a direct cause of weed invasion. Appropriate fertilization with nitrogen, phosphorus, or sulfur, or blends of them, helps retain a productive grass-legume balance and keeps the pasture in a vigorous condition. Livestock stocking rates must be adjusted with the seasons to avoid overgrazing and soil compaction.

Mowing permanent pastures at least annually promotes a more even balance of forage species by increasing light for the lower legume canopy. It also improves the chances of uniform utilization by stock by removing mature, less palatable, and lower-quality growth. Clipping is an additional pasture-management aid in removing the upright flower stalks of thistles and other tall-statured weeds, thereby reducing seed dispersal. Clipping is usually not effective in killing weeds. Some problem weed species—bermudagrass and pennyroyal, for example—grow below usual mowing heights and are benefited by the increased light made available by clipping (or grazing).

Very intensive grazing for a few days, practiced on a rotational basis—called *mob stocking,* or short-duration, high-intensity grazing—is a management system widely adopted in New Zealand and other countries. This system is intensively utilized for a few (commonly one to four) days and then allowed to recover for 30 or more days before grazing is repeated. Proponents of mob stocking indicate that more uniform and complete forage and weed utilization occurs. These systems frequently make extensive use of electric fencing. The additional fencing required for mob stocking and rotational grazing offers additional management flexibility such as avoidance of soil compaction following irrigations.

The appearance and continued expansion of weeds in a pasture is a biological indicator to stockmen that the livestock-carrying capacity of the pasture is decreasing. The vigor, and thus the competitive advantage, of the forage plants has been allowed to decline, perhaps by overgrazing, and the ever-present weeds have captured the light, moisture, and nutrient resources.

If weeds do appear and persist, a very direct control measure should be adopted and, at the same time, pasture-management deficiencies should be identified and corrected. The use of a mower to prevent annual weeds from flowering and developing seed has been mentioned. The hoe and shovel are time-honored weed-control tools for early, small infestations and should not be overlooked. Alternatively, registered herbicides such as 2,4-D for broadleaved weeds may be selected to spot out early and small infestations and halt their spread. It should be emphasized that 2,4-D can reduce productivity of legumes such as strawberry clover and ladino clover for several weeks. This effect is reduced by timing 2,4-D applications in the first day or two following an irrigation. By contrast, clovers undergoing moisture stress at the end of an irrigation cycle are most seriously retarded.

If, after several years of well-intentioned but less-than-adequate management, weeds become dominant and forage species have become sparse and virtually noncompetitive, the only practical recourse is to plow, control difficult perennial weeds, and reseed. Introducing a competitive smother crop prior to pasture reseeding should be given strong consideration to reduce annual weeds.

Sometimes herbicides and minimum-till sod seeding can be used to control weeds and rejuvenate pastures. This is a less costly means of rejuvenating a pasture if there are herbicides registered to control the problem weeds and if sufficient density of old, but vigorous, pasture plants still remain. Minimum-till sod seeders are available for lease from some seed companies in California.

12

VEGETABLE CROPS

INTRODUCTION

by Edward A. Kurtz[1]

Vegetable production in California extends over a wide range of areas with extreme variables in cultural and environmental factors that influence production. Careful management of weed populations during the production of vegetable crops is necessary for a successful farming operation.

Fifteen vegetable crops, representing a variety of cultural, environmental, and production conditions, have been selected for discussion in this chapter. All references to acreage and value were obtained from the California Agricultural Statistics Service for 1987.

In presenting this information, no attempt has been made to include mention of all the variables associated with weed management systems, species of weeds present, or all the factors that go into the day-to-day decision-making processes aimed at a successful weed-management program. What has been presented are outlines of problems and programs that will help the reader determine what systems are available.

One necessity in a vegetable-crop weed management system is a basic knowledge of the cultural problems associated with the production of the crop. Most relationships between cultural systems involved in crop production and weed management are rather easily discernible. Some, however, are subtle and require regular observations and decisions to assure maximum rewards consistent with the costs involved.

Mechanical and hand tillage have been the traditional means of controlling weeds. Current emphasis, however, is on the use of chemicals designed to selectively suppress or eliminate weed populations without impairing crop development. Examples of the most common methods of applying chemicals to vegetable crops are provided in figure

---

1. Agricultural consultant, Salinas, CA.

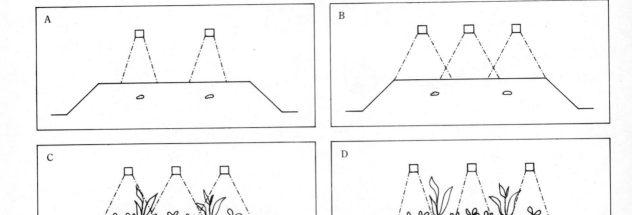

Figure 1. Four of the most common methods of applying herbicides to vegetable crops are: (A) Preemergence to crop and weeds as a banded bedtop treatment; (B) preemergence to crop and weeds as a total bedtop treatment; (C) postemergence to crop and weeds as a total bedtop treatment; (D) postemergence to crop and weeds as a bedtop, directed treatment.

1. Since no individual chemical or combination of chemicals will provide control of all weed species, the combination of mechanical and chemical systems usually provides the best weed control during the production of vegetable crops in California. Many of the mechanical and chemical weed control methods are common to more than one vegetable crop; photographs illustrating specific examples are included.

The aim of all vegetable producers should be to create favorable conditions for crop production while providing unfavorable ones for weeds. Selection of weed management systems must depend upon many factors, some of which are controllable and some of which are not. The key to a successful weed management program in vegetable crops is to be able to anticipate the known and adapt to the unexpected.

ARTICHOKES (*Cynara scolymus*)

by Harry S. Agamalian[1]

Artichokes are grown commercially in several coastal counties of California. Principal production areas are Monterey, San Mateo, Santa Cruz,

1. University of California Cooperative Extension, Monterey County, CA.

and Santa Barbara counties. In 1987, this crop was grown on 11,126 acres with a crop value of $36,716,421.

The crop is grown primarily as a perennial plant propagated from vegetative shoots. In certain regions, however, direct seeding for bearing artichokes is being used. It is favored by mild winter temperatures as it is susceptible to frost. A plant usually requires one season of vegetative growth prior to the production of artichokes. Once the plant is established, vegetative growth is removed in early summer. Subsequent irrigation stimulates new growth. In early fall, with the advent of short days, flower initiation results in the development of the edible buds.

Most weed problems in artichokes are related to crop competition for nutrients and moisture. Weed management in this crop is classified in two areas: (1) plant establishment and (2) bearing artichokes. Also, certain weeds (especially mustard types) that are attractive to honeybees in the blooming periods must be controlled before applications of insecticides harmful to honeybees are made.

A second biological interaction is important to consider for optimum weed control. The control of meadow mouse, another pest of artichokes, is highly dependent upon the absence of weeds, and weed management is generally correlated with bait treatments for this pest.

Other broadleaf weeds that are a problem in artichokes are burning nettle, sowthistle, common groundsel, little mallow, and chickweed. Wild oat may be a problem in certain production areas; however, one perennial, Bermuda buttercup, has become an increasingly important weed. Its bulblike seed makes for easy distribution throughout certain production areas.

The establishment of newly planted artichokes is preceded by thorough soil preparation. This is accomplished mainly by using disc and chisel implements. Rows are marked in two directions as the plants are planted on a grid usually 10-by-4-foot intervals. Soils are generally of good water-holding capacity, of fine to medium texture. After transplanting or direct seeding, pronamide may be applied followed by sprinkler irrigation. Annual weed control in newly planted fields may be accomplished using a combination of mechanical methods and herbicides. In the early phase of crop development, cultivation in two directions may be used. This practice is followed by hand weeding around the individual plant. Several cultivations may be made, but once the plant develops maximum vegetative growth, cultivation is made in only one direction.

The treatment of established artichoke plants usually involves applications of herbicides in a split or two-stage program. Initial applications are made with preemergence herbicides applied as band treatments to the artichoke plants shortly after new vegetative growth appears in midsummer. Herbicides registered for use are pronamide, napropamide, and simazine. Sprinkler irrigation is essential following this application to activate these chemicals.

Weed control between the rows during the summer and early fall periods is usually accomplished by cultivation. In the late fall period, deep winter drains are established between rows to ensure optimum plant growth during periods of inclement weather. Following the establishment of these ditches, a herbicide treatment is made in the area between the plant rows. Oxyfluorfen is usually applied as a directed spray between the plant rows. This herbicide has preemergence and postemergence activity, and it is effective on Bermuda buttercup. Combination treatments of oxyfluorfen and simazine or pronamide will enhance winter weed control. Thus, the total soil surface area may ultimately be treated in this split or two-stage program.

It is important to keep the field free of weed growth during the winter harvesting periods. Artichokes are handpicked; consequently, weed-free fields are essential for ease of harvesting operations.

Since the artichoke plant is a perennial, there is no concern for residual herbicides because there are no crop rotations. Most plantings are maintained for eight to 10 years. During the last year of production, residual herbicides should not be used, thus reducing crop rotation restrictions. Pronamide provides the highest degree of crop tolerance, followed by napropamide, oxyfluorfen, and simazine. In using these herbicides, it is essential to adjust rates to weed species and the soil texture. Any effective weed control program should include herbicides and cultural practices as the weed species or soil texture dictates.

ASPARAGUS *(Asparagus officinalis)*

by Robert J. Mullen[1]

There were 39,700 acres of asparagus harvested in California during 1987, with an average yield of 3000 pounds per acre for a total crop value of $74,746,000. California produces 71% of the fresh-market asparagus grown in the United States and 24% of the processed product (frozen or canned). Total state acreage is increasing at a modest rate.

Asparagus is grown on a wide range of soils and in a number of geographic areas in California. The primary production areas are the San Joaquin-Sacramento deltas (approximately 23,000 acres), the Salinas Valley, the southern San Joaquin Valley, the Southern California desert region, and the south coast area (Orange County).

Asparagus is produced for three primary markets: fresh, frozen, and canned. Eighty-seven percent of California's asparagus production in 1987 was marketed as fresh spears, 8% of production was frozen, and 5% went into canned spears and soups.

1. *University of California Cooperative Extension, San Joaquin County, CA.*

Figure 2. Harvesting by hand in a crop such as asparagus, under a dense population of a perennial weed such as field bindweed, can be difficult and time consuming, reduces harvest efficiency, and increases costs. Photo courtesy H.S. Agamalian.

The majority of California's asparagus is grown in the highly organic peat (muck) soils of the San Joaquin–Sacramento deltas, but the crop also does quite well in sandy soils, loams, and even clay loam soils. Coarse, sandy soils produce asparagus earlier in the spring.

Asparagus prefers a moderate-to-warm environment during harvest (cutting) with optimum soil temperatures between 65° and 85°F.

Commercial asparagus plantings are established by three methods: traditional planting of one-year-old crowns, transplanting 10-to-12-week-old seedlings, and direct seeding. In all three methods furrows are used and light cultivation is practiced so that soil is thrown into the furrows over the course of the growing season, keeping weed competition to a minimum but allowing the young asparagus to develop.

Each year, in late winter, the cutting beds are reshaped, throwing up soil on each side of the bed from the furrows. This practice also provides some control of winter weeds that have emerged, particularly where preemergence herbicides have not been used or applications have been delayed by weather conditions. Reshaping the beds also allows drying of rain-soaked fields by loosening the soil surface and permitting oxygen to enter into the beds.

Normally, established asparagus beds are not cultivated very often. Shallow cultivation for weed control or to allow "airing out" of the beds is sometimes practiced; this also allows better water penetration during furrow irrigation. Frequent and/or deep cultivation may cause some root injury and decrease yields, particularly if done during cutting.

Asparagus harvesting is still primarily accomplished by hand with long-handled knives (fig. 2). Many fields are cut every day or every other day, and weeds present at this time can create severe problems in terms of both competition and reduced harvest efficiency.

Crop rotation plays an important role in asparagus production. Asparagus is a perennial crop which will occupy the same ground for 10 to 12 years, and, over that period, weeds that are difficult to control such as yellow nutsedge, bermudagrass, johnsongrass, field bindweed, Russian thistle, common groundsel, and barnyardgrass tend to build up in fields. Serious soilborne disease organisms like Fusarium decline *(Fusarium oxysporum)* and Phytophthora crown spear rot *(Phytophthora megasperma)* also cause severe losses in asparagus fields. To surmount these difficulties, growers, at the end of a field's productive life, must rotate out of asparagus for a period of years substituting such crops as field corn, cereals, etc., to dry out the soil and act as efficient competitors with many weeds. Also, a number of herbicides registered for such crops as corn, beans, cereals, and other vegetables can be used to greatly reduce the population of problem weeds following an asparagus planting. In some fields, perennial weeds such as yellow nutsedge, bermudagrass, field bindweed, and johnsongrass may have become so prevalent that, following removal of the asparagus crop, the fields may have to be left fallow for at least a year.

A combination of tillage and a herbicide program involving a translocated, postemergence chemical like glyphosate may be necessary to return the fields to a condition suitable for other crops. In addition to crop rotation, field selection is of prime importance before planting an asparagus crop. In fields with serious weed problems (particularly bermudagrass, yellow nutsedge, field bindweed, and johnsongrass), or ones that have had a series of equipment-intensive crops such as tomatoes, alfalfa, sugar beets, etc., the potential for diseases due to soil compaction and poor drainage is great, and such fields should be avoided. An asparagus crop is a long-term, expensive investment, and care must be taken wherever adequate preplant preparation cannot be properly achieved.

Weeds create problems in asparagus production throughout the normal growing season (late winter to late summer). Winter annuals and summer annuals are problems, as are perennial weeds from spring through late summer and early fall.

Some of the most troublesome winter annuals are common groundsel, shepherdspurse, annual sowthistle, mustard, common chickweed, knotweed, and annual bluegrass. The principal summer annuals are barnyardgrass, common purslane, lambsquarters, pigweed, and nightshade. Perennial weed species, besides those previously mentioned, include swamp smartweed and kelp. Some geographic areas have weed problems that are particularly prevalent in them. In the Imperial Valley, for instance, Mexican sprangletop and fivehook bassia are especially troublesome, while the Salinas Valley has some buildup of Russian thistle and burning nettle, and the Delta has problems with swamp smartweed.

A number of herbicides are now available for use on asparagus in California. Given the diversity of weed species present in the crop and the number of soil types and use patterns that occur in various production areas, not all materials can be used with success and/or with complete safety to the crop. Producers must design a weed management program in which a combination of cultural practices and herbicide selection will result in the most effective, economical, and safest weed control. Modifications to selected weed programs each year, through accurate record keeping and detailing of weed species that have not been controlled, are a must. Following are general comments on weed control with regard to types of planting and timings of application.

Direct-Seeded Asparagus (practiced on a limited scale in Southern California)

Preemergence
Such contact herbicides as paraquat and glyphosate are used to control emerged weeds after seeding of the crop but at least a week before crop emergence. To prevent injury to germinating crop seedlings, do not apply paraquat preplant or preemergence to soils lacking clay minerals. Linuron as a preemergence treatment is registered for use on direct-seeded asparagus, with considerable restrictions to ensure successful results.

Postemergence
Linuron is registered for use on direct-seeded asparagus when the ferns are 6–18 inches tall. The weeds should not be over 4 inches tall, and the spray volume should be sufficient for thorough coverage of weeds.

Transplant Seedlings (10–12 weeks old)

Postemergence
Linuron is registered for use in transplant seedlings with the same restrictions as for direct-seeded asparagus. Fluazifop-P and sethoxydim are registered on nonbearing asparagus for control of annual and perennial grasses, but application cannot be made to spears that will be harvested within one year of treatment.

Newly Planted Crowns

Preemergence
Generally, no herbicide is currently used preemergence on newly planted crowns except in the San Joaquin Delta where diuron can be used.

Postemergence

Linuron is applied when the fern growing from newly planted crowns is 6–18 inches tall and weeds are not more than 4 inches in height. Fluazifop-P and sethoxydim are registered on nonbearing asparagus for control of annual and perennial grasses but with the same treatment restrictions on spears to be harvested within one year of treatment as for transplant seedlings.

Established Beds

Preemergence

As previously mentioned, linuron is labeled for preemergence use on established beds. Metribuzin can be used in early spring before spear emergence. Prior to crop emergence, metribuzin also has excellent postemergence activity should weeds emerge early. It can also be applied postharvest after the last cutting day of the season but prior to fern emergence. Contact herbicides such as paraquat or glyphosate are used to control emerged weeds prior to crop emergence in late winter to early spring.

Diuron is one of the most widely used preemergence herbicides in established asparagus because of its safety to the crop. Application should be made before weeds become established but no earlier than four weeks before spear emergence and no later than the early cutting period. If weeds are controlled into the cutting period by cultural practices, application may be delayed until immediately after the last cultivation. Common groundsel is somewhat tolerant of diuron, and its continued use in certain areas has created a buildup of this weed.

Simazine is also available for preemergence use in established asparagus but it is not quite as safe to the crop as diuron. Care should be taken in using it in California on light-textured soils. A new biotype of common groundsel is showing resistance to triazine herbicides in some production areas.

Napropamide is now labeled for use in established asparagus as a soil application from winter to early spring prior to weed emergence. It has given good control of many annual grasses and is quite effective on triazine-resistant common groundsel. Consequently, combinations of napropamide and diuron (or simazine) are being used.

Trifluralin is used as a soil-incorporated treatment in established asparagus from winter to early spring before spear emergence or after harvest is completed in late spring or early summer and before ferning begins. Adequate sprinkler irrigation or rainfall are needed to activate trifluralin applied in late spring to early summer prior to ferning. Continued use of trifluralin gives excellent suppression and eventual control of field bindweed. Combinations with diuron or simazine are also being used.

Postemergence

Linuron is registered for use on established asparagus beds either as a postemergence application before the cutting season or immediately after a cutting. Linuron can also be used as a directed postemergence spray to the fern stage of growth for dudain melon control. The spray should be directed to the base of the fern.

Glyphosate can be used on established beds prior to crop emergence for control of emerged annual and perennial weeds. Application should not be made in the week before the first spears emerge. Glyphosate is also registered for use on established asparagus as a postharvest treatment. Application should be made after the last harvest and after all spears have been removed (clean cutting of the beds). Direct contact of the spray with the asparagus may result in serious crop injury. Glyphosate has excellent activity on perennial weed species such as bermudagrass, field bindweed, swamp smartweed, and johnsongrass when used as directed.

2,4-D is also registered for use in established asparagus beds for control of many broadleaf weeds. If spears are present, treatment should be made immediately after cutting.

Dicamba can be applied during the cutting season to emerged and actively growing weeds immediately after the field has been cut, but at least 24 hours before the next cutting. If spray contacts emerged spears, twisting or crooking of spears may result. If such crooking occurs, discard the affected spears. Dicamba can also be combined with 2,4-D to achieve improved control of field bindweed, but caution should be exercised to prevent crop injury.

A number of herbicides are available to asparagus producers for the management of most weed problems, but some problem weed species still remain. It is hoped that ongoing public and private research will develop solutions, which, combined with existing chemical, cultural, and application technology, will enable growers to stay ahead of weed infestations. At a time of high production costs, high interest rates, and limited returns on investment, today's asparagus grower cannot afford to have weed competition in his crop, whether it is during stand establishment, the cutting season, or the ferning season. A prudent, well-thought-out weed-management program will benefit both producer and consumer.

REFERENCES

Sims, William, Robert Mullen, Frank Souther, 1984. *Growing Asparagus in California. Div. of Agric. Sci., Univ. of Calif.*

Mullen, Robert J., 1986. *The asparagus industry in San Joaquin County. Div. of Agric. Sci., Univ. of Calif. Coop. Ext.*

Takatori, Frank H., Sims, William L., et al. 1980. *Establishing the commercial asparagus plantation. Div. of Agric. Sci., Univ. of Calif.*

Kempen, Harold M. 1987. *Growers Weed Management Guide, Thomson Publications.*

BELLPEPPER *(Capsicium annuum* var. annuum*)*

by Bob Scheuerman[1]

The acreage of bell peppers in California has varied between 10,000 and 16,000 acres during the past few years. California ranks second in the nation in the production of bell peppers. There were 16,550 acres grown in 1987 at a value of $70,695,904.

Peppers are harvested in California over a long period of time, from April in the Coachella Valley to December in the south coast counties. San Joaquin, Fresno, Santa Clara, San Benito, Merced, and Ventura counties have been the major producing areas of the state. Peppers are produced for the fresh market and for processors, such as dehydrators, freezers, and canners.

Peppers are a warm-season crop and need a long growing season for maximum production. They are both transplanted and direct-seeded, depending on the production area, season, and when the crop is to be harvested for a specific market.

Row spacing and plant spacing vary with almost every production area. Some use single rows spaced anywhere from 30 to 42 inches apart, with plants 12–14 inches apart. Some areas plant twin rows on a bed, with beds 40–60 inches apart and plants spaced 16–18 inches apart, and twin rows 14–18 inches apart. Approximately 13,000 bell pepper plants per acre are needed for a 40-inch single-row spacing with plants 12 inches apart.

Irrigation is usually by the furrow or sprinkler methods. Drip irrigation is being used in San Diego County. Methods of irrigation will depend on soil type, water costs, water availability, and personal preference.

Bell peppers are harvested by hand and usually taken to a packing shed where they are washed, graded, and bulk packed into cartons. The presence of weeds at harvest can interfere with the selection of desirable peppers.

Weeds are a problem in both direct-seeded and transplanted bell peppers. In some areas, beds are preformed during the winter months and planted in the spring. These beds get very weedy prior to planting. Cool weather during the early planting season results in slow emergence of direct-seeded pepper seedlings and competition from weeds. Weeds in transplanted peppers can be cultivated more easily for control, but can also become a problem after harvest begins in the late season. Peppers are cultivated quite often for weed control, but care must be taken not to disturb the root system or compact the soil. Crews are often used to hand hoe weeds between the plants. Weed control can become quite

---

1. *University of California Cooperative Extension, Merced County, CA.*

expensive with the amount of handhoeing that is done. Peppers are rather slow growing and do not shade the soil surface as fast as some other crops. This allows the weeds to compete more with the peppers. Annual grasses and broadleaf weeds are most troublesome.

Proper field selection, cropping sequence, plant-bed and seedbed preparation, planting times, preirrigation, knowledge of the weed infestation, and a vigorously growing crop are some factors that can influence weed control.

Through proper field selection and rotation of crops, a grower can avoid fields infested with perennial weeds and annuals that cannot be controlled with available herbicides. The residual properties of herbicides that were used in the preceding crop should also be considered.

Proper land and seedbed preparation will be more conducive for rapid germination of pepper seeds and rapid growth of transplants, and will enhance the performance of the herbicide.

Planting too early under cold temperatures will slow germination of the pepper seed and growth of transplants, thus allowing weeds to take over or compete more with the crop. Preirrigation can enable a grower to prepare a better seedbed. It can also germinate weed seeds that can be destroyed prior to planting. Preirrigation can favor uniform planting and emergence of peppers. This, in turn, favors the performance of herbicides.

Knowing the weeds that have been previously growing in the field year after year is necessary for the proper selection of a herbicide.

A vigorous and healthy growing crop is a great competitor of the weeds. Proper fertilization, irrigation, good soil, and insect and disease control are integral parts of a good weed-control program.

Chemical Control

The following herbicides are registered for use in California:

Bensulide
Preemergence. For use on direct-seeded bell peppers. Limited to use on bell peppers in Southern California.

DCPA
Preemergence. For use four to six weeks after transplanting or on direct-seeded plants 4–6 inches in height.

Glyphosate
Apply only prior to planting to established weed populations.

Napropamide
Preemergence. For use on direct-seeded plants and transplants.

Paraquat

Postemergence of weeds. For use on emerged annual broadleaf weeds and grasses, and for top kill and suppression of perennials prior to planting of peppers. Used widely on overwintered preformed beds, prior to planting crop.

Sethoxydim

Postemergence treatment for grass control. For use on bell peppers only.

Trifluralin

Preplant incorporated. For use on transplants only. To be used prior to transplanting. Do not use after transplanting.

The control of weeds throughout the season is necessary in this crop, especially during the early season due to the long, slow emergence period of direct-seeded peppers.

SUGGESTED READING

Sims, William L., Paul G. Smith. 1976. Growing peppers in California. Div. of Agric. Sci., Univ. of Calif.

Runcina Vol. 8. Evaluation of herbicides in the production of peppers. Fischer, B.B., et. al. 1975–76. Univ. of Calif. Coop. Ext.

Johnson, Hunter, Jr., et al. Vegetable crops: planting and harvesting periods for California. Div. of Agric. Sci., Univ. of Calif.

Runcina Vo. 29, Peppers, weed control studies, Fischer, B.B., 1983–85. Univ. of Calif. Coop. Ext.

BROCCOLI *(Brassica oleracea* var. botrytis*)*

by Roy L. Hale[1]

There were 107,600 acres of broccoli produced in 1987 with a value of $212,562,000. In terms of importance in the market, California produces approximately 97% of the nation's available supply of fresh-market and frozen broccoli.

Production in California occurs primarily in the cool areas with moist climates. The central coast area (Monterey and San Luis Obispo counties) produced over 56% of the total harvested acres in California in 1987. The other growing areas, in order of harvested acreage, are the south coast, desert, and San Joaquin Valley. The latter two areas produce only during the cool months (November through February), using certain selected varieties for production, and account for only about 10% of the total produced in California.

1. *Agricultural consultant, Santa Maria, CA.*

Figure 3. Weeds such as little mallow (left) *interfere with hand harvesting and the selection of individual heads* (right). *Photos courtesy J.K. Clark.*

Soil condition is important for broccoli production, but less critical than the climate. Most soil types can be used, but all should be well drained, provide adequate soil moisture, and be rich in nutrients.

Broccoli is produced for two primary markets: fresh and freezer. Approximately 79% of the broccoli produced in the state is for fresh market.

Broccoli is primarily produced on two rows on 38–40 inch beds (13,756–13,068 row-feet per acre) and is direct-seeded at rates ranging from ½ to ¾ pound of seed per acre. Precision planting is usually 1½–3 inches apart. At the present time, transplants are not used except in isolated instances of small acreage. Broccoli seed germinates rather easily at 55–75°F, but without a preemergence herbicide it is very susceptible to competition from weeds during the germination and early-growth stages. The average distance between plants after thinning is 6–10 inches.

Following crop emergence, cultural methods remain quite similar throughout the production areas. There are slight differences in cultivation intensity and frequency between summer and winter plantings, between areas, and between growers.

Broccoli is harvested on a semi-mechanical basis by cutting the stalk to the desired length by hand and mechanically transporting the stalk to bins in the field. This method of harvesting is used for both the fresh and freezer markets. Fresh-market broccoli is also packed directly in the field. Weeds can present a problem at harvest by covering the stalks and heads and by interfering with the selection of desirable heads (fig. 3). Weed seeds also can present problems by contaminating the broccoli heads.

Crop rotation is a concern when a persistent herbicide not registered, or to which broccoli is sensitive, has been used on the previous crop. Crop rotation must also be taken into consideration in deciding which crop and which weed species to avoid prior to planting. Fields in which cereal grains were previously grown and in which adequate pre-plant preparation (e.g., burning of stubble, irrigation, and deep tillage) cannot be done should be avoided because of the lack of available herbicides that provide good grass control. Also, fields with past histories of heavy infestations of annual grasses should be avoided. Areas with known infestations of perennial weeds should always be avoided, as there are no available chemicals to control these weeds in broccoli.

In broccoli production, weeds can be a problem throughout the growing season. The problems differ from area to area and at different time periods; they include winter annuals, summer annuals, and perennials. Some weed species are unique to individual areas, but many are found in all areas. Generally, though, the most serious weed problems occur during the preemergence, pre-thinning, and harvest stages of growth.

Some of the most troublesome year-round weeds are: annual sowthistle, chickweed, common groundsel, lambsquarters, London rocket, little mallow, mustard, shepherdspurse, and burning nettle.

During the summer periods, the following weed species are generally a problem: common purslane, black nightshade, hairy nightshade, nutsedge, and redroot pigweed.

Weed-control programs must be closely coordinated with cultural conditions to provide maximum control of problem weed species and minimum crop injury. General comments relating to weed control and timings of application follow:

Preplant

DCPA, bensulide, and trifluralin can be used as preplant incorporated herbicides. Glyphosate and paraquat can be used on listed or preformed beds. During inclement weather when fields are too wet to cultivate, these two chemicals have provided an acceptable level of control on established weed populations. Trifluralin can be used as a pretransplant soil incorporation or as a preplant soil incorporation for direct-seeded fields; for best results, incorporate thoroughly. Trifluralin can be used in all production areas, but rates should be adjusted according to soil types because direct-seeded cole crops have been known to have a marginal tolerance to trifluralin at recommended rates.

Preemergence

DCPA or napropamide can be used in all the broccoli production areas and in all types of soil except muck and peat. They are usually applied after seeding or transplanting and before the initial irrigation. If applied after transplanting, the treated area must be weed free. Neither DCPA nor napropamide controls all weed species, and both are more effective in some areas than in others, depending on the time of year and general climatic and soil conditions.

Bensulide is also used in all the broccoli production areas and is not limited to any particular soil type, but it can be more effective in any one type over another under some conditions. Bensulide does not control a high percentage of problem weeds. It can be applied either preplant or preemergence after seeding. Any crop on which bensulide is not registered should not be planted for 18 months following its use on broccoli.

Postemergence

There are currently no herbicides registered for use as postemergence applications. However, the postemergent use of liquid nitrogen as a surface (banded) application has been shown to be an effective treatment for controlling weeds. Although not registered as a herbicide, the secondary benefits of this fertilization practice have resulted in effectively reducing weed populations and associated costs. When applied at the proper time, liquid nitrogen controls several broadleaf weeds that are tolerant to the commonly used preemergent herbicides with minimal crop damage. A delay of irrigation for two to three days is necessary to get maximum weed control from the solution.

Alternative Methods

Mulch planting, a program that requires no herbicides and relies entirely on cultivation for weed control, has been successfully used in the Salinas Valley. If ideal weather conditions exist, the procedure includes thorough plowing and disking, bed formation, preirrigation, germination of weeds, and light tilling to remove weeds with conjunctive planting of crop at ½ to ¾ inch depth.

Cultivation and weeding crews are other methods of controlling weeds in broccoli during the postemergence period, but if the weeds are not controlled early (preemergence and pre-thinning), this can be an extremely repetitive and costly procedure. Cultivation and weeding crews require close supervision to reduce the potential for yield reductions resulting from plant and root damage or the actual loss of plants.

In summary, weeds present serious problems during all stages of broccoli production, but they are far more serious during both the germination and early postemergence period. If weeds are not controlled early in the season, they cannot be tolerated during the crop production period.

INDIVIDUAL CONTRIBUTIONS

Chism, William (Bill). *Weed technologist, vegetable crops, University of California, Cooperative Extension.*
Snyder, Marvin. *University of California, Cooperative Extension, Santa Barbara County, CA.*

REFERENCES

Integrated pest management for cole crops and lettuce, University of California, Statewide integrated pest management project, Division of Agriculture and Natural Resources, Publication 3307, 1985.

BRUSSELS SPROUTS *(Brassica oleracea* var. gemmifera*)*

by *Norman C. Welch*[1]

There were 3,517 acres of Brussels sprouts produced in California in 1987 with a value of $11,519,800. Brussels sprouts are ranked as a minor vegetable crop in California and in the United States generally. Eighty-five percent of Brussels sprout tonnage in the United States is produced in California.

Production in California occurs mainly along the coast in Santa Cruz, Monterey, and San Mateo counties. The cool, moderate temperatures near the ocean are required to produce large tonnages of high-quality sprouts.

Brussels sprouts are produced for the fresh and frozen markets. Approximately two-thirds of the state tonnage of Brussels sprouts is produced for processing.

Four hybrid varieties of Brussels sprouts account for 90% of production in California: Lunet, Prince Marvel, Valiant, and Dolomic.

Brussels sprouts are mostly planted as transplants on 36-inch beds with 16–20-inch spacings between plants in the row. Transplants are grown in nursery beds that have been fumigated with methyl bromide and chloropicrin for weed and disease control.

Single-harvested plants have their terminal growing points removed about six to eight weeks before harvest. This helps produce a more uniform size of sprouts and results in higher yield for single harvested crops. At harvest the leaves are removed by hand, using a large knife. The stalks are cut either by hand or machine, then hand-fed into a rotary knife, stripping the sprouts in a single pass. The sprouts are then loaded into a bulk trailer and hauled to a central shed, cleaned (using roller cages or drums), and hand sorted.

Crop rotation is not normally practiced, as there is a limited amount of land suitable for Brussels sprouts production. Field sanitation is practiced to avoid certain diseases. This consists of disking under crop resi-

---

1. *University of California Cooperative Extension, Santa Cruz County, CA.*

due and allowing much of it to decay before replanting. Soil pH above 7.2 is required for control of club root, a serious disease. Soil fumigation for cyst nematodes is also essential for good production.

Weeds present problems in Brussels sprout production primarily in the early part of the season. Proper planting and cultivating techniques usually eliminate most weed problems. Brussels sprout plants are planted into a shallow V, then soil is cultivated into this small furrow around the base of the plants as they grow. With proper timing of cultivation, herbicides are not normally used on most soil types. However, on a few sandy soils found in wind-belt areas near the ocean, chemical weed control is used in place of cultivation to help prevent wind and soil erosion from loose soil.

Some of the weeds most troublesome to Brussels sprouts are: mustard, nightshade, common lambsquarters, pigweed, burning nettle, little mallow, common groundsel, henbit, pineappleweed, and purslane.

Only a few herbicides registered for use on Brussels sprouts are now available in California. No individual herbicide or combination of materials now registered will control all weed species in this crop. The following herbicides are registered for use on Brussels sprouts in California: bensulide, DCPA, napropamide, and trifluralin.

Trifluralin is occasionally used at transplanting time. This material must be incorporated immediately after application. When crop rotation is practiced, care must be taken to avoid crops sensitive to trifluralin.

REFERENCES

Integrated pest management for cole crops and lettuce, University of California, Statewide integrated pest management project, Division of Agriculture and Natural Resources, Publication 3307, 1985.

CARROTS *(Daucus carota* var. sativa*)*

by L.H. Miner[1]

Carrots are an important vegetable crop in California. Although they are grown in many of the 50 states, California, Arizona, Texas, and New York account for about three-fourths of the commercial production. Carrots were grown on 43,000 acres in California in 1987 with a value of $125,952,000.

The two main outlets for carrots are fresh market and processing. The principal production areas in California are the San Joaquin Valley (Kern County, especially), the central coast, the south coast, and the desert areas of Imperial and Riverside counties. Production occurs in

1. Soilserv, Inc., Salinas, CA.

areas with a wide range of climatic conditions and over a wide range of soil types. Carrots grow best at mean temperatures between 60° and 70°F, but nevertheless they have adapted to both the cool coastal areas and winter plantings in the desert region. Carrots are grown somewhere in California during each of the four seasons of the year.

In selecting fields for carrot production one should choose soils suitable for good growth. Soils with known nematode infestations should be avoided or treated with soil nematicides prior to planting. Fields with known infestations of perennial weeds and fields last planted to cereals also should be avoided, because herbicides used in carrots are not very effective on perennial weeds and volunteer grain.

Deep sandy loam soils are most desirable for carrot production, but carrots are also grown successfully on soils coarser and finer than sandy loams. Where water can be controlled, silt loams and even clay loams produce high yields of high-quality carrots. Cultural practices such as irrigation, cultivation, and fertilization are quite similar in all production areas. Good water management is extremely important.

Carrots are grown usually on 40-inch beds (13,068 row-feet per acre). The number of seed lines per bed and subsequent plant populations may vary within individual areas, but there are generally six seed lines per bed with the plants spaced at approximately 1-inch intervals in each seed line. Carrots do not allow for close mechanical cultivation.

In harvesting commercial plantings, the roots are loosened with a carrot lifter or plow. If the roots are to be marketed with the tops on, they are bunched in the fields. They are then hauled to packing sheds where they are washed and iced. To an increasing extent, however, the tops of fresh carrots are being removed in the fields and the roots then harvested mechanically, loaded in bulk, and transported to packing sheds for washing and packaging. Weeds can be particularly troublesome at harvesttime as they can become entangled in both the crop and the harvest equipment.

Weeds in carrots mean the difference between profit and loss. A group of Wisconsin scientists carried out a research program in which they allowed 15% of an existing weed stand to remain in carrots for the first five and one-half weeks before removing the weeds. This treatment reduced the yield of carrots by 78%. A 50% weed population reduced carrot yield by 91%. The researchers concluded that controlling weeds during the first four weeks of crop growth was critical. It is especially important that the weed program approach 100% control. A few scattered weeds allowed to survive may grow so rapidly and so large that they may be nearly as harmful as a thick weed infestation. Weeds present problems in carrot production throughout the growing season. The prevalent ones occur at different times and can be categorized as follows: winter annuals, summer annuals, and perennials. Many weed species are found under all production conditions, while some are unique to individual areas.

Some of the most troublesome winter weeds are London rocket, mustard, pineappleweed, common groundsel, shepherdspurse, little mallow, annual sowthistle, canarygrass, and volunteer cereals.

Weeds that present problems during the summer periods include barnyardgrass, lambsquarters, pigweed, nightshade, common purslane, Russian thistle, and little mallow.

Herbicides registered for use in carrots include bensulide, fluazifop-P, glyphosate, paraquat, linuron, selective petroleum oil, and trifluralin. Some application methods registered elsewhere are not registered for use on carrots in California. The limited number of available herbicides and the diversity of weeds make it difficult to maintain adequate control throughout the growing season. No individual herbicide is available that will control all weed species under all production conditions.

Any weed-control program in carrots must be selected after considering such factors as cultural practices, including water management, soil types, weed infestation, etc. Generally, more than one herbicide will be needed for effective control. Common practice is to use either a preplant or preemergence herbicide application followed by one or more postemergence treatments.

Trifluralin is often used in preplant applications as a preemergence treatment. Glyphosate and paraquat are used to kill weeds on preformed beds prior to planting, as well as post-plant preemergent to the crop. Linuron can also be used prior to crop emergence in Monterey County under a 24(c) registration.

Herbicides that can be used after crop emergence include petroleum oils (carrot oil), fluazifop-P, and linuron.

The single most accepted program is a preplant incorporation of trifluralin into moist soil, followed by a postemergence application of linuron or fluazifop-P. Carrot oil can then be used to control weeds and grasses missed.

More detailed discussions of the registered herbicides follow.

Fluazifop-P

Fluazifop-P is a selective postemergence herbicide for control of annual and perennial grass weeds. Special precautions must be observed in the harvest date following application and in the selection of crops following carrots treated with fluazifop-P.

Glyphosate

Glyphosate may be applied on preformed beds or prior to the emergence of carrots for the control of emerged annual weeds. Glyphosate may be applied using conventional booms or with controlled droplet applicators (CDAs). Special precautions must be observed in the selection of crops following a glyphosate application because of long crop rotation restrictions on the label.

Linuron

As mentioned earlier, linuron is registered for both preemergence and postemergence use. Its registration for preemergence use in California is limited to Monterey County. Linuron is applied postemergence when weeds are in the one-to-two-leaf stage and when the crop is 3–6 inches tall. To avoid crop injury, it is suggested that linuron not be applied within two weeks of an application of carrot oil.

Paraquat

Paraquat may be used preplant or preemergence to kill emerged annual broadleaf weeds and grasses and for top kill and suppression of perennials. Application may be made before, during, or after planting. Crop plants emerged at time of application will be eliminated.

Selective Weed Oil (Carrot Oil)

Petroleum distillates, such as Stoddard solvent, used for selective weed control in carrots are normally clear and have a gravity API of 42°F or above, a minimum flashpoint of 100°F, and an aromatic content of 10–20%.

The tolerance of young carrots for certain petroleum oils is probably physiological. Although the carrot plants are wetted by the oil, they are not appreciably affected.

Carrot oil is applied in postemergence applications after the carrots have at least two true leaves and before the root is ¼ inch in diameter. Carrots should not be sprayed with selective weed oil under conditions of high temperature or high relative humidity or when foliage is wet with dew or rain. To reduce injury, carrot oil is often applied during the night or early morning, and the crop is irrigated within 48 hours.

Trifluralin

Trifluralin is used for preemergence control of annual broadleaf weeds and grasses in carrots and must be applied and incorporated prior to planting. Rates vary depending on soil type. Special precautions must be observed when selecting crops to follow carrots treated with trifluralin because of its extended residual life.

ACKNOWLEDGEMENTS

The author expresses appreciation to Harry Agamalian, Carl Bell, and Harold Kempen, University of California Cooperative Extension, for their technical assistance.

REFERENCES

Boswell, Victor R. 1954. Commercial growing of carrots. USDA, ARS, leaflet No. 353 (3–8).
Klingman, G.C. Weed Control As a Science. John Wiley & Sons, Inc. pp. 269–270.
Crafts, A.S. 1947. Oil sprays for weeding carrots and related crops. Calif. Agric. Ext. Circ. 136, (2).
Robbins, W.W., A.S. Crafts, and R.N. Raymor. 1942. Weed Control. McGraw-Hill Book Co. p 171.

CAULIFLOWER *(Brassica oleracea* var. italica*)*

by Elaine A. Hale[1]

There were 51,100 acres of cauliflower produced in California in 1987 with a value of $147,156,000.

Production in California occurs over a limited range of areas because the plant is a cool-season crop. The central coast area (Monterey and San Luis Obispo counties) produced the largest amount of cauliflower (over 50%) in 1987. The other main production areas are the south coast, desert, and San Joaquin Valley. The latter two areas produce only from November through February, using selected varieties for production, and they account for a small percentage of the total grown in California.

The soil condition is less critical than the climate. Most soil types can be used, but all should have good drainage, fertility, and adequate moisture.

Cauliflower is produced for two markets: fresh and frozen. Approximately 90% of the cauliflower grown in California is for fresh market production.

Cauliflower is usually produced on a single-row, 38- or 40-inch bed (13,756–13,068 row-feet per acre) and can be direct-seeded or transplanted. The average distance between plants after thinning is 12–16 inches. Normally, cauliflower seed germinates readily at 55–75°F. The germination period is very critical because, during it, the competition from weeds is extremely severe.

Following crop emergence, cultural methods remain practically the same throughout all production areas. There will be slight alterations in cultivation intensity and frequency between winter and summer plantings, regions, and growers.

Cauliflower is harvested both by hand and by a semi-mechanical method. Processing cauliflower is harvested by hand and transported to the processing plant in large, portable bins. Cauliflower harvested for fresh market is almost always packaged in the fields. Mechanical harvesting and field wrapping are becoming more popular as economical time- and labor-saving devices. Weeds can present serious problems at harvest by covering individual cauliflower plants and interfering with selection of desirable heads.

1. Agricultural consultant, Santa Maria, CA.

The immediate problem weeds present to the cauliflower crop is that of competition. This is especially important during germination and early postemergence. If weeds are not controlled early, they can also be a serious problem during harvest in areas where mechanical-harvesting methods are used.

Crop rotation is important when a persistent herbicide to which cauliflower is sensitive has been used on the previous crop, and also in terms of which crop and weed species to avoid prior to planting. Fields in which cereal grains were previously grown, and in which adequate preplant preparation (e.g., burning of stubble, irrigation, and deep tillage) cannot be doneproperly , should be avoided because of the lack of available herbicides that provide good grass control. Also, fields with past histories of heavy infestations of annual grasses should be avoided. Areas with known infestations of perennial weeds should always be avoided as there is no chemical available to control these weeds in cauliflower.

Weeds can be a problem in cauliflower production throughout the growing season. The problems differ from area to area and at different time periods and include winter annuals, summer annuals, and perennials. Some weed species are unique to individual areas, but many are found in all areas under all production conditions. Even though the most serious weed problems occur early in production, there can be critical times at harvest in those areas where mechanical harvesting is used. This is especially true when weeds are not adequately controlled during the early growth of the crop.

Some of the most troublesome year-round weeds are: annual sowthistle, chickweed, common groundsel, lambsquarters, London rocket, little mallow, mustard, shepherdspurse, and burning nettle.

During the summer the following weed species are generally a problem: common purslane, black nightshade, hairy nightshade, nutsedge, and redroot pigweed.

There are very few available herbicides for use on cauliflower in California, and no individual herbicide or combination of materials now registered will control all weed species under all production conditions.

Weed control programs should be closely linked to cultural conditions to provide a maximum control of problem weed species and minimum crop injury. General comments relating to weed control in relation to timing of application follows.

Preplant

DCPA, bensulide, and trifluralin can be used as preplant incorporated herbicides. Glyphosate or paraquat can be used on listed or preformed beds. During inclement weather when fields are too wet to cultivate, these two chemicals have provided acceptable control of established weed populations. Trifluralin can be used as a pretransplant soil incorporation or as a preplant soil incorporation for direct-seeded fields; for best results, incorporate thoroughly.

Preemergence

DCPA or napropamide can be used in all cauliflower areas and in all types of soil except muck and peat. They are usually applied after seeding and prior to the initial irrigation. Neither DCPA nor napropamide control all weed species, and both are more effective in some areas than in others, depending on the time of year and general climatic and soil conditions. DCPA has been observed to be more effective on weeds of winter rotations vs. summer or spring, suggesting a direct correlation to the amount of water vs. degree of control.

Bensulide is also used in all the cauliflower production areas and is not limited to any particular soil type; but it can be more effective in any one type than in another under certain conditions. Bensulide does not control a high percentage of problem weeds. It can be applied either preplant or preemergence after seeding.

Postemergence

DCPA or napropamide can be applied when cauliflower is transplanted. They must be applied immediately after transplanting to a bed free of weeds. This treatment should be sprinkled following application.

In addition to the use of preemergent herbicides applied in the postemergent crop period, the postemergent use of liquid nitrogen as a surface (banded) application has been shown to be an effective treatment for controlling weeds. Although not registered as a herbicide, the secondary benefits of this fertilization practice have resulted in effectively reducing weed populations and associated costs. When applied at the proper time, liquid nitrogen controls several broadleaf weeds that are tolerant to the commonly used preemergent herbicides with minimal crop damage. A delay of irrigation for two to three days is necessary to get maximum weed control from the solution.

Alternative Methods

Mulch planting, a program that requires no herbicides and relies entirely on cultivation for weed control, has been used with success in the Salinas Valley. If weather conditions are ideal, the procedure is preceeded by thorough plowing and disking, bed formation, preirrigation, germination of weed seeds, and light tilling to remove weeds with conjunctive planting of crop at ½ to ¾ inch depth.

Cultivation and hand weeding are other methods of controlling weeds in cauliflower during the postemergence period; but if the weeds are not controlled early (preemergence and prethinning) this can be an extremely repetitive and costly procedure. Cultivation and hand weeding require close supervision to reduce the potential for yield reductions resulting from plant and root damage or the actual loss of plants.

In summary, weeds present serious problems during all stages of cauliflower production, but they are far more serious during both germination and early postemergence because weed infestations during this period set the stage for critical infestations during harvest.

INDIVIDUAL CONTRIBUTIONS

Chism, William (Bill). Weed technologist, vegetable crops, University of California, Cooperative Extension. Snyder, Marvin. University of California, Cooperative Extension, Santa Barbara County, CA.

REFERENCES

Integrated pest management for cole crops and lettuce, University of California, Statewide integrated pest management project. Division of Agriculture and Natural Resources, Publication 3307, 1985.

CELERY *(Apium graveolens* var. dulce*)*

by R.A. Brendler[1]

Celery is produced in California all year. In 1987 there were 21,300 acres produced with a value of $136,348,000. The principal production areas are Ventura County (10,300 acres), Salinas-Watsonville (6,200 acres), and Santa Maria-Oceano (3,600 acres).

Because celery harvesting is a once-over operation and the optimum time for harvesting spans only a few days, transplanting and planting are continuous and often scheduled so that some specified acreage will be ready to harvest each week. Planting schedules have been developed to allow for differences in growing time at different times of the year. In Ventura County all celery is transplanted. In the Salinas-Watsonville and the Santa Maria-Oceano areas more than 70% is transplanted. Transplanting in Ventura County begins the first week in August and continues through the second week in April for a harvest season beginning the first of November and continuing to the middle of July. In Salinas-Watsonville and Santa Maria-Oceano, planting or transplanting is from February through August for harvest in June through December.

Celery thrives in a wide range of soil textures and types, provided they are all well drained. Medium-textured soils without compaction problems are preferred.

1. University of California Cooperative Extension, Ventura County, CA.

Preparation of soil for a celery crop begins with ripping to a depth of 18 inches, or plowing to a depth of 12 inches, or both, followed by disking and rolling, land-leveling, fertilization with manure or mineral fertilizer, and bed formation. Cultivation following planting or transplanting controls most weeds and maintains bed shape. These cultivations must be shallow because of the abundance of celery roots near the surface. Weeds in the celery row are controlled by herbicides, hoeing, or pulling.

For field-seeded celery, several irrigations, preferably by sprinkler, are required to assure germination and emergence. Following transplanting, the soil surface is kept moist for about two weeks by repeated sprinkler or furrow irrigation. The need for repeated applications of water directly affects the use and availability of herbicides during the period immediately following transplanting.

Although at least one celery-harvesting machine has been developed and used successfully, almost all the celery in California, except that harvested for processing, is hand-harvested. Most celery harvested for the fresh market is now packed in the field, while some is hauled in bins to packing sheds. Packers in the fields are provided with packing platforms on wheels that are pushed through the field as celery is cut and placed on them. Celery is graded for size as it is packed. The presence of weeds at harvesttime can seriously affect the speed, and thus the cost, of the harvesting operation. Such weeds as burning nettle can be particularly troublesome at this time.

Without herbicides, the cost of weed control in transplanted celery can often exceed $200 an acre. By spending about $50 an acre on chemical weed control, the total cost of weed control beyond routine cultivation can be kept well below $100 an acre. Cropping history, time of year, location of the field, and other environmental conditions determine the kinds of weeds that will be found in a celery field.

One or more of the following weeds are likely to require control: little mallow, chickweed, nettleleaf goosefoot, lambsquarters, common groundsel, London rocket, burning nettle, redroot pigweed, tumble pigweed, purslane, shepherdspurse, and annual sowthistle. A few species of annual weeds often dominate the weed population, making it feasible to adjust postemergence treatments according to species. Perennial weeds are seldom a problem in the intensively farmed land used for celery.

For field-seeded celery, prometryn is applied on the soil surface immediately after planting and activated by the sprinkler- or furrow-irrigation water applied for germination.

The most common weed-control practice in transplanted celery is a postemergence application of prometryn in the third or fourth week after transplanting. At this time most of the weeds have emerged, and there will be some control of weed seeds that germinate after this application. The label and the local agricultural commissioner need to be consulted regarding plantback restrictions for prometryn.

When prometryn is not to be used because of restrictions or failure to control some weeds, it is advisable to try selective weed oil (carrot oil or Stoddard's solvent) or linuron for postemergence applications.

Glyphosate can be used to control small weeds that have emerged before transplanting or field seeding or weeds that have emerged between field seeding and emergence of the crop.

Where summer planted celery is grown, grassy weeds may be a problem. The use of trifluralin as a preplant application for either direct-seeded or transplants is effective on grasses and several broadleaf weeds. The sequential use of prometryn or linuron as a postemergence application will enhance the weed-control program.

Weed control in celery is necessary to ensure a high-quality crop at harvest. Weeds in direct-seeded celery can produce serious competition during the seedling stage, while any weeds present at harvest tend to interfere with harvesting operations.

ACKNOWLEDGEMENTS

The author expresses appreciation to Harry Agamalian, University of California Cooperative Extension, for technical assistance.

GARLIC *(Allium sativum)*

by Edward A. Kurtz[1]

There were 16,177 acres of garlic produced in California in 1987 with a value of $49,831,000.

Garlic production in California occurs in three primary production areas and on many soil types. The primary production area is the San Joaquin Valley (Fresno and Kern counties), while the two other producing areas are the desert (Imperial County), and the central coast (Monterey and San Benito counties). The only soil types not conducive to garlic production are those with a high clay content, which tend to impede harvesting operations.

Garlic is produced for the fresh market and for dehydration. Bulbs from approximately two-thirds of the state's acreage are processed into various forms of dehydrated garlic.

There are many varieties of garlic, but the most prevalent in California are California Early and California Late.

1. Agricultural consultant, Salinas, CA.

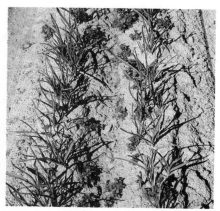

Figure 4. Although complete control of weeds is always desirable, suppression of individual weed species is also important to reduce competition for water, nutrients, and light during production of vegetable crops. Photo right shows effect of suppressing burning nettle in garlic following application of a postemergence herbicide, while photo left shows an adjacent bed on which no herbicide was applied. Photos courtesy E.A. Kurtz.

Garlic is mostly produced on 40-inch beds (13,068 row-feet per acre) and reproduced vegetatively by replanting cloves saved from the previous crop year. Most garlic seed is produced in Oregon, Nevada, or northern California and is not normally taken from the production areas previously described. Garlic cloves produce vigorously growing plants, but nevertheless, garlic is susceptible after emergence to plant stunting from weed competition (fig. 4).

Garlic is planted to reach the final desirable plant population at harvest and does not require thinning during production. Garlic for both processing and fresh market is grown on two seed lines per bed with populations ranging from 183,000 to 261,000 plants per acre.

Such cultural practices as irrigation, cultivation, and fertilization are quite similar in all production areas, except that in the desert, generally more acreage is irrigated by the furrow method rather than with sprinklers as in other areas.

Garlic grown for fresh market is harvested on a semi-mechanical basis or by hand labor into either sacks or bins. Garlic grown for processing is harvested by mechanical means into bulk trailers and transported directly to processing facilities. Weeds such as little mallow, prostrate knotweed, barnyardgrass, field bindweed, and nutsedge present serious problems at harvest where mechanical equipment is involved.

Crop rotation is extremely important both in terms of which crops and weed species to avoid prior to planting and which crops should not follow garlic. Fields that were previously grown in cereal grains and in which adequate preplant preparation (e.g., burning of stubble, preplant irrigation, and deep tillage) cannot be done properly should be avoided.

Fields with known histories of infestations of such perennial weeds as field bindweed, johnsongrass, yellow nutsedge, and quackgrass should also be avoided. Such crops as spinach, parsley, and alfalfa are not recommended to be planted following garlic because of potential off-flavor problems associated with volunteer garlic during harvest.

Weeds present problems in garlic production throughout the growing season. They occur in different time periods and can be categorized as follows: winter annuals, summer annuals, and perennials. Many weed species are found under all production conditions, while some are unique to individual areas.

Some of the most troublesome winter weeds are London rocket, mustard, pineappleweed, common groundsel, shepherdspurse, little mallow, annual sowthistle, canarygrass, and volunteer cereals.

During the summer, the following weed species are generally troublesome: barnyardgrass, common lambsquarters, pigweed, nightshade, common purslane, Russian thistle, and little mallow.

Examples of weeds that are particularly troublesome in individual production areas are: canarygrass (desert); barnyardgrass (San Joaquin Valley); and little mallow (central coast).

There are a number of herbicides available for use on garlic in California. However, the wide range of production areas and the extreme diversity of weed species allow for many problems in maintaining adequate control during the production season. No individual herbicide or combination of materials now registered will control all weed species under all production conditions.

Weed-control programs are closely tied to cultural conditions to provide maximum control of problem weed species and minimum crop injury. General comments relating to weed control in relation to timing of application follow:

Preplant

Weeds can become especially troublesome prior to planting on listed or preformed beds in years during periods of inclement weather. When such beds are too wet to allow cultivation, applications of glyphosate or paraquat can provide an acceptable means of controlling weeds.

Preemergence

DCPA and pendimethalin may be used where garlic is grown under sprinkler irrigation, while chlorpropham is primarily used in the central coast area on the fine-textured (clay and silty clay) soil types there. All materials are applied after planting and prior to the first irrigation.

Occasionally, no preemergence materials are used, and an application of weed oil or paraquat is made to germinated weeds prior to crop emergence. Any crop emerged at the time of this treatment will be damaged, but the timing of the treatment, in terms of potential stand reduction, is not as critical on garlic as it is on onions.

Postemergence

In general, garlic has a greater degree of crop tolerance to registered postemergence herbicides than do onions. Therefore, timing of early-season treatments is not as critical on garlic as it is on onions. Crop injury at any time, but especially just prior to or during the bulbing process, should be avoided or reduced crop yields may result.

The following materials are registered for use during this period with the indicated restrictions:

Bromoxynil
Primary activity is on broadleaf weeds. Minimum restrictions.

Fluazifop-P
Primary activity is on grassy weeds. Minimum restrictions.

Cultivation and weeding are other means of controlling weeds in garlic during this period. During the early season, cultivation can be made both on the bed top and in the furrows. However, as harvest approaches, this operation is restricted to the furrow areas. Both cultivation and weeding crews must be carefully managed to reduce the potential for yield reductions resulting from the loss of bulbs during these operations. Under normal plant-population conditions, losses of 2–3 grams per bulb, or the loss of one bulb per bed-foot, can result in yield reductions of approximately 1000 pounds per acre.

The results of experiments conducted by Agamalian illustrate the effects of weeds on garlic production. In the trials, a preemergence application of DCPA + chlorpropham provided excellent season-long weed control with no stand reduction or crop injury. The physical removal of weeds by hoeing at various intervals after garlic emergence resulted in moderate to severe stand (plant) reduction and subsequent yield losses. Yields following the herbicide treatment were 11.1 tons per acre, while removal of weeds starting at 60 days after garlic emergence was 9.7 tons per acre. Removing weeds at 90 and 120 days after emergence resulted in yields of 7.5 and 5.7 tons per acre respectively, while weed removal just prior to harvest provided a yield of 5.2 tons per acre.

Lay-by

Herbicide applications at lay-by are determined somewhat by the type of irrigation available and its activity in relation to the herbicide. Lay-by applications are made primarily in hopes of maintaining low levels of weed populations between this period and harvest. DCPA and pendimethalin are the materials most used during this time. However, neither controls weeds that are already emerged, nor is either effective on all species. Chlorpropham is also available for use during lay-by on certain soil types in individual production areas.

Preharvest

The relatively long interval between final irrigation and harvest, combined with reduced competition from the garlic crop as it dries, makes weed control during this period extremely critical.

The common method of weed control in garlic for those weeds established prior to harvest is undercutting. This technique is used to reduce established weed populations and to dry tops prior to harvest.

In summary, weeds present serious problems during all stages of garlic production. The combination of high plant populations, no thinning requirements, extended growing season, and mechanical harvesting creates a situation where competition from weeds during the germination, production, or harvesting periods cannot be tolerated.

REFERENCES

Growing garlic in California. Rev. Dec. 1976. Div. of Agric. Sci., Univ. of Calif. leaflet 2948.
Personal communication: Harry S. Agamalian, Univ. of Calif. Coop. Ext.
Fischer, B.B. 1983. Evaluation of herbicides for weed control in onion & garlic, A progress report, Runcina, Vol. 25, University of California Cooperative Extension, Fresno County.
Fischer, B.B. 1985. Weed control studies in onions & garlic, A progress report of applied research, University of California, Cooperative Extension, Fresno, County.

IRISH POTATOES *(Solanum tuberosum* L)

by Harold M. Kempen[1]

California produced 51,300 acres of Irish potatoes in 1987 with a value of $161,972,000. California ranks fourth behind Idaho, Maine, and Washington in potato acreage.

Kern County is the main production area (55%) in California for fresh-market potatoes. Tule Lake growers store russet production for late-winter sale. Monterey County grows mainly Kennebecs, the variety most used for potato chips. Potatoes are also grown in the Riverside, Santa Maria, and Stockton areas.

Widespread plantings make weed problems as well as production systems quite varied. Varieties also differ in how competitive they are

1. *University of California Cooperative Extension, Kern County, CA.*

with weeds. For example, Kennebec is a vigorous variety and is harvested while plants are green. White Rose, a thin-skinned, fresh-market potato, while also vigorous, must be allowed to mature before harvest, thus allowing late-season weed growth and weed seed production. Red La Soda is also grown for fresh market. More recent varieties, Centennial and Norkotah, are variable in growth habit, so weeds often compete better with these species.

Ground storage is widely practiced with Kennebecs in coastal regions, until potato chip factories need the tubers. Likewise, July plantings of fresh-market potatoes are kept in the ground during the winter until good market prices occur. Potatoes stored in the field require specific weed-control measures.

Potato tuber pieces are usually planted in 32-inch beds. After planting about 3–5 inches deep, beds are peaked using rolling cultivators and sometimes rotary corrugators so that cut seed is ultimately 6–8 inches deep. In some regions, beds are "dragged off" before emergence and rebedded, this being largely a weed-control practice. While growers formerly cultivated potatoes after emergence, most prefer not to because of root pruning, soil compaction, and the hazard of a sudden temperature rise when sprinkling is needed.

Nearly all harvesting is done mechanically. Weeds can interfere with harvesting, and, in the case of nutsedge, tuber penetration can prevent sale. Late-season weeds, especially the taller ones—black nightshade, barnyardgrass, several mustards, common lambsquarters, and wild oat— greatly reduce tuber size because of competition for light.

Crop rotation is probably of less importance in potato production than in any other vegetable crop. Potatoes are good competitors. They are a short-season crop, thus they permit fallow periods before or after, and are thoroughly cultivated prior to planting. When controlled by certain herbicides, perennial weeds offer little problem. After potato harvest, some crops such as onions, garlic, and carrots can be plagued by volunteer potatoes from small tubers. Also, if herbicides fail to control certain weeds such as nutsedge, black nightshade, or mustards, these weeds can become very dense in rotational crops. Many Kern County growers regularly dry-fallow potato fields and replant the next year and do not rotate to other crops.

Herbicides are used on most potato acreages, but, because of regional differences, seasonal plantings, soil, and previous crop-loss histories, use patterns vary widely in different regions.

For example, in Kern County a grower may plant before Christmas and only treat weeds on formed beds in early February before potato emergence, using paraquat or glyphosate. A February planting often calls for one application of EPTC before planting, a second treatment within a month (usually through sprinklers), and often a third if nutsedge is a problem. A July planting may call for a trifluralin or pendimethalin plus

EPTC combination incorporated after planting with a ground-driven rotary cultivator to control nutsedge and purslane.

In northern California regions, metribuzin and metolachlor are used more frequently. Finer-textured soils or those high in organic matter and with lower transpiration rates make them safer in those areas than in Kern County. Weeds present—mustards, kochia, common groundsel, and little mallow—make them a better choice. Centennials are sensitive to metribuzin; varietal tolerance varies. Metribuzin is not registered for use in Kern County.

Chemigation (applying herbicides through sprinklers) was first introduced in the United States in the 1960s with EPTC on potatoes. This method saves application costs, avoids soil compaction, and permits more accurate timing of application even when soils are wet. With wind not often a problem in Kern County (but common in most other California potato-growing areas), sprinkler application is more accurate than aerial application. Sequential applications of EPTC four to six weeks apart are often used for the most troublesome weed, yellow nutsedge. Care must be taken to avoid well contamination as well as damage to sensitive crops. EPTC applications should not be made immediately before or after applying fertilizers or fungicides. A good way to monitor when it is necessary to retreat for nutsedge is to observe regrowth at sprinkler lines, which is where herbicide breakdown and nutsedge regrowth first occur.

Nutsedge can be a problem at harvest despite earlier EPTC treatments and excellent potato competition. Desiccation of nutsedge shoots with paraquat or diquat after potatoes reach maturity will prevent further entry of nutsedge roots or rhizomes into tubers. Glyphosate spray or drift onto mature potato foliage can result in tuber breakdown, which will induce in-transit soft rot.

Where potatoes are ground-stored for later harvest in Monterey County, diquat is used to reduce and/or eliminate weed problems during the ground-storage period.

REFERENCES

Anonymous. 1981. Vegetable production guide. Ministry of Agric. and Food, Prov. of Br. Col. 89 pp.
Blake, G.R., K.H. Boetter, E.P. Adams, and J.K. Aase. 1960. Soil compaction and potato growth. Amer. Potato J. 37:409–413.
Flocker, W.J., H. Timm, and J.A. Vomacil. 1960. Effect of soil compaction on tomato and potato yield. Agron. J. 52:345–348.
Integrated pest management for potatoes, University of California, statewide integrated pest management project, Division of Agriculture and Natural Resources, Publication 3316, 1986. pp. 117–138.
Kempen, H.M., C.L. Elmore, J. Bishop, and R.E. Voss. 1976. Evaluation of herbicides for weed control in potatoes. Kern Co. Prog. Rpt. 188 pp.
Kempen, H.M. 1987. Growers weed management guide. Thomson Publications, Fresno, California, pp. 131–137.
Page, B.G. and W.T. Thomson. 1981. The insecticide, herbicide and fungicide quick guide. 130 pp.
Pusateri, F.D. 1977. Annual Rpt. Calif. Potato Res. Advisory Board. pp. 123–124.
Thornton, R.E. and J.B. Sieczka 1980. Commercial Potato Production in North America. Potato Assoc. of Amer. Handbook. 36 pp.

Young, J.R. 1981. Proceedings National Symposium on Chemigation.
Zimdahl, R.L. 1976. Deferential susceptibility of potato cultivars to four herbicides. Amer. Potato J.
53:211–219.
Zimdahl, R.L. 1971. Weed control research in Colorado potatoes—a review. Amer. Potato J. 48:423–427.

LETTUCE *(Lactuca sativa)*

by Harry S. Agamalian[1]

In 1987, California lettuce was produced on 149,500 acres with a crop value of $598,232,000. Other major production areas in western irrigated regions include Arizona, Colorado, and New Mexico.

Lettuce represents an important vegetable crop to several California counties. Monterey and Imperial counties provide approximately 90% of the summer and winter production of iceberg-type lettuce in the United States. Lettuce cultivars are mainly of the iceberg (head) and leaf lettuce types.

Being a cool-season vegetable, it requires even-to-moderate temperatures of 55–70°F for optimum growth. It also requires exacting cultural practices of good seedbed preparation; nutrition; irrigation; disease, insect, and weed control; and timely harvesting.

The major production regions of California lettuce are the central coastal counties, low deserts of Imperial Valley, and the central San Joaquin Valley.

Lettuce plantings in the coastal valley extend from winter to mid-summer; Imperial Valley plantings are made late summer to late winter; San Joaquin plantings encompass two brief periods, late summer and early winter.

Although these periods represent generally cool temperatures, the weed spectrum will often include both summer and winter annual weeds. Consequently, weed-management systems, including the use of herbicides, must allow for weed shifts during the cropping season.

The major lettuce plantings are direct-seeded with optimum plant populations requiring thinning at a later stage of development. Weed problems are greatest at time of lettuce emergence (fig. 5) or after transplanting. A second flush of weeds may occur following thinning and cultivation.

The types of weeds in the three major environmental areas will vary. Grassy weeds are found in the lower deserts and central San Joaquin Valley and normally are not a problem in coastal valleys. Broadleaf weeds are common to all districts, but specific types will vary according to season.

1. *University of California Cooperative Extension, Monterey County, CA.*

Figure 5. Control of weeds during early stages of crop development is essential to reduce competition and increase crop vigor. In crops such as lettuce, weed control is necessary to reduce thinning costs and crop injury associated with thinning under weedy conditions. The lettuce bed on left received a preemergence application of herbicide, while the untreated bed on right is heavily infested with common purslane. Photo courtesy H.S. Agamalian.

Several broadleaf weeds common to all regions (fig. 6) include: pigweed, purslane, common groundsel, annual sowthistle, shepherdspurse, mustard, burning nettle, nightshade, and lambsquarters. Some of the grassy weeds are barnyardgrass, canarygrass, and volunteer cereals.

Planting periods in the three major districts are as follows: central coastal valleys, December to August; lower deserts, August to February; and central San Joaquin Valley, August to December. These periods are mainly associated with iceberg-type lettuce; leaf lettuce planting periods may be extended in some districts.

Transplanting of lettuce to shorten the growing season is practiced to some extent. It has other advantages as well, such as earlier harvest. Weed management is also enhanced, with greater options being available to the grower using this method of production.

Seedbed preparations include plowing, disking, and chiseling. Plowing as a means of disease and weed control has proved beneficial. Land leveling is necessary to ensure adequate water management and enhance weed management as well.

Following seedling emergence, the crop is cultivated four to five times for weed control and other cultural benefits. Precision seeding with sled-type equipment will allow for close cultivation providing good weed control between the seed lines. This method of seeding also allows for more efficient hand (hoe) thinning and associated weed control with minimal crop damage. Lettuce grown in California must be irrigated. Both sprinkler and furrow irrigation methods are used. Sprin-

Figure 6. Many weeds are in the same families as crops and thus are difficult to control with herbicides. Examples are common groundsel in lettuce (left), *annual sowthistle in lettuce* (center), *and mustard in broccoli* (right). *Photos courtesy J.K. Clark.*

klers are often used from planting to thinning. After thinning, furrow irrigation is commonly used.

Almost all lettuce is field-packed, either with wrapper leaves or wrapped with film. Boxes are then transported to cooling facilities for later transportation to markets. Most lettuce fields require two harvests to obtain maximum yields. Weeds at harvesttime can interfere with crop quality and harvester efficiency (fig. 7).

In the coastal valleys, lettuce is usually grown in rotation with other vegetable crops. In the lower desert and the San Joaquin Valley, rotation with agronomic crops such as small grains may be common. In most situations, lettuce is grown as a single crop per season.

Methods of weed control are closely related to the planting season. With winter plantings, it is often difficult to carry out tillage operations for weed removal and incorporation of herbicides.

A well-designed weed-control program will include good cultural methods and selective herbicides. Wherever possible, it is advisable to preirrigate to stimulate weed seed germination. A subsequent tillage can reduce some weed competition. Postplant, preemergence herbicides are more commonly used in winter plantings than preplant, incorporated applications.

In order to avoid weed-crop competition, herbicides and cultural methods must be used prior to seeding.

Herbicides registered for use in lettuce production include: benefin, bensulide, glyphosate, paraquat, and pronamide. Benefin must be preplant incorporated. Pronamide and bensulide may be applied either preplant incorporated or postplant preemergence. Make all preemergence applications while the crop is under sprinkler irrigation.

The use of nonselective herbicides such as glyphosate or paraquat

Figure 7. Weeds interfere with harvests of many vegetable crops, and individual species such as burning nettle (left) can be particularly troublesome in lettuce, which requires that each head be picked by hand (right). Photos courtesy H.S. Agamalian and E.A. Kurtz.

are effective when weeds emerge prior to lettuce. This practice is also effective on established seedbeds prior to planting when inclement weather limits mechanical control of emerged weeds. Both chemicals are classified as nonresidual herbicides.

Preplant Incorporation

For best results, proper depth of incorporation is important. Benefin should be mixed into the top 2–3-inches of soil. Excessive depths will dilute the herbicide, resulting in poor performance. Too shallow mixing may reduce lettuce tolerance. Soil tilth with minimum clods will provide best results for preemergence herbicides.

Avoid applying preplant, incorporated herbicides in wet soils, which may cause mechanical "soil pans" to develop. Such soil pans interfere with seedling tap roots and growth and may also cause the herbicide to be layered, reducing crop selectivity.

Seeding can be done immediately following treatment with any preplant incorporated herbicide. Irrigation should be applied within two to three days, so as to minimize volatility loss from the soil. There are many types of soil applicators. The ones with L-shaped teeth usually provide better mixing than those with straight teeth. For shallow incorporation, the straight tooth is effective. Ground speed of 2–3 miles per hour is acceptable for mixing. Excessive speed may reduce the mixing process.

Preemergence

Oftentimes, postplant, preemergence applications of either pronamide or bensulide are made at time of seeding. This method allows for combining seeding and herbicide application in one operation. Sprinkler irrigation must follow one to two days after treatment. This time interval may vary with the herbicide and air temperature. With lettuce herbicides, an irrigation of 1 inch of water is considered adequate for herbicide movement into the zone of weed seed germination.

Postemergence

The application of postemergence herbicides is not a general practice with lettuce. Because of limited herbicide availability and the relatively short growing season, weed management is not enhanced with postemergence herbicides. In transplanted lettuce, with rooted plants, a herbicide may be applied preplant or immediately after planting. Under these conditions, a preemergence herbicide such as pronamide is used. Once a lettuce plant has developed eight to 10 leaves, weed competition becomes less likely to affect development of lettuce quality.

Hoeing of lettuce fields for weed control at the time of thinning is another method of removing undesirable weed species. This operation must be carefully supervised to avoid crop loss, as the damage or elimination of one lettuce plant per 6 bed-feet can result in the potential loss of 181 cartons of lettuce per acre at harvest. Precision seeding reduces the likelihood of crop damage during the thinning operation.

Although herbicide persistence may not be a factor with the growing crop, several lettuce herbicides have relatively long soil persistence. Pronamide, benefin, and bensulide will persist past the normal crop-growing season. With these properties in mind, crops that are tolerant to these chemicals should be selected to follow lettuce.

Weed control in lettuce is necessary to assure a high-quality crop at harvest. Weeds in direct-seeded lettuce can produce serious competition during the seedling stage, while any weeds present at harvest tend to interfere with the harvesting operations.

REFERENCES

Integrated pest management for cole crops and lettuce, University of California, statewide integrated pest management project, Division of Agriculture and Natural Resources, Publication 3307, 1985.

MUSKMELONS *(Cucumis melo)* AND WATERMELONS *(Citrullus melo)*

by Carl E. Bell[1]

The term *muskmelon* describes several types of melons grown in California. The principal type by acreage is cantaloupe. Next is honeydew,

1. *University of California Cooperative Extension, Imperial County, CA.*

followed by others melons such as casaba, crenshaw, Persian, Santa Claus, and Juan Canari. Watermelons are a related but separate species.

In 1987, California produced 85,100 acres of cantaloupes, valued at $146,798,000. This amounted to 52% of the total U.S. production, making California the principal cantaloupe-producing state.

Honeydew production in the United States was also concentrated in California during 1987, with $43,754,000 worth of melons produced on 20,600 acres.

The largest melon acreage in California is located in the San Joaquin Valley, followed by the desert and the Sacramento Valley, respectively. Large-scale production is limited to these areas because of the climatic requirements of melons.

San Joaquin and Sacramento Valley melons are planted in the spring for summer harvest. After preplant operations such as plowing, ripping, and disking, 40-inch or 80-inch beds are listed. These beds are preirrigated once or twice to achieve deep, even, soil moisture. Forty-inch beds are preirrigated with furrow irrigation and 80-inch beds by sprinklers.

After the beds are dry enough for tillage, they are cultivated to a depth of 3–6 inches, using rolling cultivators or harrows. When the surface is dry, seeds are planted down into the moisture in a mulch. The beds are not irrigated until the stand is established.

In the desert valleys, two crops are grown each year. A fall crop is planted in the summer (July and August), and a spring crop is planted in the late winter (January and February). The fall crop is planted on alternate 40-inch beds in much the same manner as the San Joaquin Valley, except that the melons are planted in dry soil and irrigated up by furrow or sprinkler systems.

The spring crop is planted on 80-inch slant beds. The beds are peaked to a height of 24–30 inches and run east to west. The crop is seeded on the south-facing slope to receive the most solar radiation and warmth. Hotcaps are used by some watermelon growers. Asphalt mulch may be sprayed in a 4–6-inch-wide band over the seed lines as an alternate method of heat enhancement. The crop is germinated by using furrow irrigation. After emergence, the melons are thinned by hand. Cultivation serves the purpose of removing weeds and altering the peaked beds to flat 80-inch beds with the seed line repositioned in the center.

Melon harvest in all areas of the state is by hand, although mechanical harvesting methods are being researched. Modern operations use conveyors to speed picking and reduce damage losses, particularly for watermelons. In the desert area, harvest in the summer is only in the early morning or at night under artificial lights. Weeds can present problems at harvest by covering desirable melons and increasing the time required to select mature, marketable melons.

Crop rotation is important to melon production for several reasons. Among them are the possibility of herbicide residues and the levels of weed populations in previous crops. The number of available herbicides for melons is limited, and therefore, a field with high weed pressures, particularly from broadleaves, will require a lot of expensive cultivation and hand labor. Also, melons are quite sensitive to the residues of such herbicides as triazines, and fields treated with these herbicides should be avoided.

Most melons originated in warm climates, such as that of the Mediterranean region; therefore, they grow best during the warm seasons of the year. Weed problems are most severe when melons are started during cool periods. In the desert, spring melons germinate slowly and compete poorly against weeds. Conversely, fall melons germinate in less than five days and outgrow most weeds.

Any annual or perennial weed can be a problem in melons, but a few are particularly troublesome. Field bindweed, pigweed, common lambsquarters, common purslane, and barnyardgrass are typical problem weeds.

Herbicides can reduce other weed-control requirements if properly used, but it should be remembered that an integrated program is desirable. Some notes on registered herbicides follow.

Preplant/Preemergence

Weeds can be especially troublesome prior to planting on listed or pre-formed beds in years during periods of inclement weather. When such beds are too wet to allow cultivation, preplant applications of glyphosate or paraquat can provide an acceptable means of controlling established weed populations.

Bensulide is used throughout the state, providing good control of annual grasses and some broadleaves. Incorporation from 1½ to 2½ inches mechanically or by rainfall is necessary for best results. This herbicide resists leaching and is quite persistent (up to 12 months). Sensitive rotational crops are: corn, sorghum, sudangrass, and sugar beets.

Naptalam provides excellent control of broadleaf weeds, particularly those in the nightshade family. Preplant incorporation to a depth of 1½–2½ inches results in the best activity. Naptalam leaches readily in coarse soils and is not recommended for use in the desert area on coarse soils because of previous experience with crop injury.

A combination treatment of bensulide and naptalam provides excellent broad-spectrum weed control.

Lay-by

DCPA is used at the four-to-five-true-leaf stage for control of annual grasses and some broadleaf weeds. This herbicide is effective only prior to weed emergence and should be applied following weeding or cultivation. Soil incorporation is not recommended.

Trifluralin is applied at the three-to-four-leaf stage. This herbicide is effective on annual grasses and several broadleaf weeds. Soil incorporation is necessary for activity. This is best accomplished with two passes perpendicular to each other with a rolling cultivator. Care should be taken during application to avoid contacting the crop foliage, particularly the youngest leaves. Trifluralin is persistent in the soil up to 12 months, and rotations to corn, sorghum, sudangrass, and sugar beets should be avoided.

Proper weed control is essential for high yields of quality melons. An integrated approach combining good cultural practices, cultivation, and herbicide use is the best way to achieve your goals.

REFERENCES

Tyler, K.B., et al. 1981. *Muskmelon production in California. Div. of Agric. Sci., Univ. of Calif., Leaflet 2671.*
Schweers, V.H. and W.L. Sims. 1977. *Watermelon production. Div. of Agric. Sci., Univ. of Calif., Leaflet 2672.*
Fischer, B.B. 1981. *Weed control studies in cucurbits. Runcina Vol. 22, Coop. Ext., Fresno County.*

ONIONS *(Allium cepa)*

by Edward A. Kurtz[1]

There were 37,200 acres of dry bulb onions produced in California in 1987 with a value of $129,125,000.

Production in California occurs over a wide range of areas and soil types. The four main production areas are San Joaquin Valley (Fresno, Kern, and San Joaquin counties), the desert (Imperial and Riverside counties), central coast (Monterey County), and the northern areas (Siskiyou and Modoc counties).

Onions are produced for three primary markets: green bunching, dry bulb for the fresh market, and dry bulb for processing (dehydration). Approximately 65% of the state's onion acreage is produced for processing.

Onions are mostly produced on 40-inch beds (13,068 row-feet per acre). As a small, hard-seeded crop, it is difficult to germinate and very susceptible to competition from weeds, especially during the germination and early growth stages.

Onion seed is planted to reach the final, desirable plant population at harvest and does not require thinning during production. The number of seed lines per bed and subsequent plant populations vary within

---

1. *Agricultural consultant, Salinas, CA.*

individual production areas and intended uses (green bunching, fresh market, or processing).

Onions are usually grown with four to six seed lines per bed for processing and four to seven seed lines for the fresh market. The different numbers of seed lines per bed relate to "salt problems" inherent in the desert areas and the specific local need to plant fewer seed lines in other areas to either allow more space for cultivation and weed control or to obtain larger bulbs for the fresh market.

Cultural practices such as irrigation, cultivation, and fertilizing are quite similar in all production areas, except that more acreage is generally irrigated up by the furrow method in the desert as compared with sprinkler irrigation in the other production areas.

Green bunching onions are harvested by hand or by semi-mechanical means into bins. Dry bulb onions grown for the fresh market are harvested by semi-mechanical means into either sacks or bins. Onions grown for processing are harvested mechanically into bulk trailers and transported directly to processing facilities. Weeds such as little mallow, prostrate knotweed, barnyardgrass, and field bindweed present serious problems at harvest where mechanical equipment is involved.

Crop rotation is extremely important both in terms of which crops and weed species to avoid prior to planting and which crops should not follow onions. Fields previously grown in cereal grains and in which adequate preplant preparations (e.g., burning of stubble, preplant irrigation, and deep tillage) cannot be properly done should be avoided. Fields with known histories of infestations of perennial weeds such as field bindweed, johnsongrass, yellow nutsedge, and quackgrass should also be avoided. Crops such as spinach, parsley, and alfalfa are not recommended for planting following onions because of potential off-flavor problems associated with volunteer onions during harvest.

Weeds present problems in onion production throughout the growing season. They occur at different time periods and can be categorized as follows: winter annuals, summer annuals, and perennials. Many weed species are found under all production conditions, while some are unique to individual areas.

Some of the most troublesome winter species are London rocket, mustard, pineappleweed, common groundsel, shepherdspurse, little mallow, annual sowthistle, and volunteer cereals.

During the summer periods, the following species are generally a problem: barnyardgrass, common lambsquarters, pigweed, Russian thistle, and little mallow.

Weeds that are particularly troublesome within individual production areas are as follows: canarygrass (desert); barnyardgrass (San Joaquin Valley); and little mallow (central coast).

A number of herbicides are available for use on onions in California. However, the wide range of production areas and the extreme diversity in weed species allow for many problems in maintaining adequate control during the production season. No individual herbicide or combination of materials now registered will control all weed species under all production conditions.

Weed-control programs are closely tied to cultural conditions to provide maximum control of problem weed species and minimum crop injury. General comments on weed control in relation to timing of application follows.

Preplant

Weeds can be especially troublesome prior to planting on listed or preformed beds in years during periods of inclement weather. When such beds are too wet to allow cultivation, preplant applications of glyphosate or paraquat can provide an acceptable means of controlling established weed populations.

Preemergence

DCPA is used in all areas and is primarily applied after planting and prior to the first irrigation. DCPA does not provide control of all weed species but is extremely important in reducing weed competition during the critical early stage of crop establishment.

Occasionally, in place of a preemergence application of DCPA, an application of a nonselective herbicide (e.g., glyphosate, paraquat, or weed oil) is made to germinated weeds prior to crop emergence. The timing of this treatment is extremely critical, in that any crop emerged will be either damaged or eliminated if contacted by the herbicide.

Postemergence

Timing of postemergence treatments in relation to weed and crop size is also extremely critical. For the most part, weeds are much more susceptible in the early-growth stages while most of the available herbicides cannot be used prior to the two-true-leaf crop stage. In certain circumstances, trade-offs occur in which some crop damage and plant losses become acceptable in light of the need to prevent complete crop loss from weed competition. Crop injury just prior to or during the bulbing process, however, should be avoided to assure that crop yields will not be reduced.

The following materials are registered for postemergence use with indicated restrictions:

Acid
Sulfuric acid and Enquik/N-TAC (sulfuric acid from urea-sulfuric) are

two types of acid available. Both materials are hazardous to handle. Primary use is during the early-season production phase (one to four crop leaves). Usually phytotoxic to crop.

Bromoxynil
Limited to application between the two-to-five-true-leaf crop stage. Usually causes some leaf curling to crop. Should not be applied to onions with any foliar damage (e.g., thrips, sand, etc.).

Fluazifop-P
Primary activity is on grassy weeds. Minimum restrictions.

Oxyfluorfen
Should not be used before the two-true-leaf crop stage. Should not be applied to onions under stress (e.g., drought, wind injury, frost damage, etc.).

In addition to these herbicides, the postemergent use of surface (banded) treatments of liquid nitrogen have been shown to be effective in reducing weed populations. Although not registered as a herbicide, the secondary benefits of this fertilization practice, when applied under the proper conditions, have resulted in the control of several broadleaf weeds with minimal crop damage.

Cultivation and weeding crews are other methods of controlling weeds in onions during this period. High plant populations require that cultivation be restricted mainly to the furrow areas and that weeding crews be carefully supervised to reduce the potential for yield reductions resulting from root or bulb damage or the loss of bulbs during these operations (fig. 8). The results of experiments by Agamalian illustrate the effects of weeds on onion production. In the trials, preemergence applications of DCPA reduced numbers of weeds by 55% and reduced the need for hand-weeding hours per acre from 199.7 to 44.0 as compared to an untreated control. Postemergence applications of bromoxynil reduced weeds by 87%, reduced the number of onion bulbs lost due to weeding from 9760 to 523, and increased yield per acre from 8.1 to 12.8 tons as compared to the untreated control.

Lay-by

Herbicide applications at lay-by are somewhat restricted by the type of irrigation available and its relationship to the herbicide. DCPA is the material of choice for use during this time period. Although it gives control only of weeds not yet emerged and does not control all species, DCPA plays an important role in maintaining weed populations at acceptable levels between lay-by and harvest.

Figure 8. Removal of weeds by hoeing is common practice in many vegetable crops. Photo left shows a weeding crew removing undesirable vegetation (weeds) and excessive crop plants in lettuce. Photo right shows damage that can occur on crops such as onions, which are planted close together on the bed and subject to injury when weeds in close proximity to the crop are removed. Photos courtesy L.H. Miner and E.A. Kurtz.

Preharvest

The final method of control in onions of those weeds that become established prior to harvest is undercutting. This technique is used primarily to reduce established weed populations and also to dry the onion tops before harvest begins.

In summary, weeds present serious problems during all stages of onion production. The combination of high plant populations, problems in stand establishment, no thinning requirements, and semi-mechanical or mechanical harvesting creates a situation where competition from weeds during the germination, production, or harvesting periods cannot be tolerated.

REFERENCES

Fischer, B.B. 1983. Evaluation of herbicides for weed control in onion & garlic, A progress report, Runcina, Vol. 25, University of California, Cooperative Extension, Fresno County.
Fischer, B.B. 1985. Weed control studies in onions & garlic, A progress report of applied research, University of California, Cooperative Extension, Fresno County.
Personal communication: Harry S. Agamalian.
Voss, Ronald E. Onion production in California. Div. of Agric. Sci., Univ. of Calif.

SPINACH *(Spinacia oleracea)*

by Philip P. Osterli[1]

There were 9,790 acres of spinach produced in California in 1987 with a value of $18,949,695. Spinach is ranked fifteenth in California on a scale of importance as a vegetable crop and fifty-eighth of all commodities grown in California.

California leads the nation in spinach production, accounting for approximately 47% of the U.S. fresh-market production and 50% of the processed product. Approximately three-quarters of the state acreage is devoted to processing while accounting for only 45% of the value. The leading counties for processing are Stanislaus, Monterey, Ventura, and Yolo, while Monterey, Ventura, and Santa Barbara pace the state's fresh-market production.

The crop requires a cool climate, preferring an average monthly temperature of 60° to 65°F, but it will grow at 50° to 60°F. Spinach for processing is planted from October through January and harvested from March through early May. The fresh-market crop is grown year-round in the cool coastal regions.

Spinach is grown two rows to a standard vegetable bed with 40-inch centers (13,068 row-feet per acre). The seed is usually planted in dry soil and irrigated up with either furrow or sprinkler irrigation. Spinach seed is planted to reach the final desirable plant population at harvest and, consequently, the plants are not thinned during production. All operations, except hoeing and weeding, are highly mechanized.

Following irrigation for germination, spinach is irrigated frequently enough to keep it growing vigorously until harvested. If there is no rain during the growing season, the crop may be irrigated three or four times.

Spinach is usually grown under contract with a processor who does the harvesting. A mechanical harvester cuts spinach from two beds and elevates it into trailers pulled alongside the harvester. Spinach sold for fresh consumption is mechanically cut and hauled to a central packing shed for washing, sorting, and typing into consumer-sized bundles, or bunched and boxed in the field.

As the crop is not thinned, and because of the general lack of available herbicides that provide adequate weed control, spinach should be planted in relatively weed-free fields. Most of the weed control in spinach consists of between two and four careful, shallow, close cultivations while the crop is small, and hand-pulling of weeds prior to harvest.

Weeds present problems in spinach production throughout the growing season. Numerous winter annual broadleaf weeds and grasses naturally infest the fields, and spinach growers encounter major prob-

1. *University of California Cooperative Extension, Stanislaus County, CA.*

lems in attempting to control them. Some of the most troublesome winter annuals are shepherdspurse, mustard, London rocket, chickweed, common groundsel, burning nettle, annual bluegrass, and volunteer cereals. Chickweed is especially objectionable because it bleaches to whitish yellow in processing, and even small pieces cannot, therefore, be tolerated in the final product. Chickweed grows vigorously during the cool winter and early spring months. It has long, weak stems that are difficult to remove from the rows of spinach with cultivators and too costly to remove by hand. Burning nettle is also an extremely bothersome weed at harvest and creates problems during the grading operation and in processing.

The effective use of herbicides for weed control in spinach has been demonstrated by numerous field trials. Cycloate, diethatyl, glyphosate, and phenmedipham are registered in California for use on spinach.

Preplant

Cycloate requires mechanical soil incorporation and exhibits limited effectiveness on winter annual weeds and marginal spinach selectivity.

Preemergence

Diethatyl can be used as a preplant incorporated application but is primarily applied as a preemergence treatment. This herbicide will provide good weed control if rainfall or sprinkler irrigation follows the preemergence application. It is primarily effective on annual grasses and will also control some broadleaf weed species.

Postemergence

Phenmedipham provides excellent control of broadleaf weeds up to the four-true-leaf stage of growth. Seedling spinach as young as the cotyledon stage of growth exhibits good tolerance. Phenmedipham does not control grasses or volunteer cereals. Phenmedipham has no residual soil activity germination of weed seeds can occur following treatment.

In summary, weeds present serious problems during all stages of spinach production. The combination of high plant populations, difficulties in stand establishment, no thinning requirements, and mechanical harvesting create a situation where competition from weeds during either the germination, production, or harvesting periods cannot be tolerated.

REFERENCES

Agamalian, Harry. 1978. Spinach weed control progress report. Univ. of Calif. Coop. Ext., Monterey County.

Brendler, Robert A. and Robert C. Rock. 1975. *Costs and practices for row crops.* Univ. of Calif. Coop. Ext., Ventura County.

Fischer, Bill B. 1981. *Runcina Vo. 24, Evaluation of herbicides for weed control in spinach.* A progress report. Univ. of Calif. Coop. Ext., Fresno County.

Lorenz, Oscar A. and Donald N. Maynard. 1980. *Knott's Handbook for Vegetable Growers.* 2nd ed. John Wiley & Sons, Inc. New York.

MacGillvray, John H. 1948. *Western Vegetable Production.* Revised ed. Assoc. Students Store, Univ. of Calif., Davis.

TOMATOES *(Lycopersicium exculentus)*

by Arthur H. Lange[1] and Jack P. Orr[2]

In 1987 there were 28,600 acres of fresh-market tomatoes and 214,000 acres of processing tomatoes grown in California with a total value of $560,728,000. Most of the early-spring, fresh-market tomatoes are grown in San Diego and Imperial counties, and the summer and fall tomatoes in Fresno, Merced, Stanislaus, San Joaquin, and Monterey counties.

Processing tomatoes are grown throughout the San Joaquin and Sacramento valleys, with Fresno, Yolo, and San Joaquin counties accounting for the major acreage.

Good land preparation is the first step in weed control. Fields taken out of row crops and allowed to develop high populations of difficult-to-control weeds should be avoided for most row crops, including tomatoes. If it becomes necessary to use a heavily infested field, then preirrigation and two to three diskings or a plowing and disking will aid significantly in the control of weeds. Addition of animal manures heavily laden with weed seed should be avoided. Where manure is to be used, it should be well composted or fumigated to prevent the increase of herbicide-tolerant weed species. Fall bedding for early spring tomatoes is often preferred, especially in areas with long, wet springs.

Tomatoes are mostly grown on single or double rows on 60–66-inch beds. In fields with difficult weed problems, some growers continue to use one row per bed. These are often planted in the center of a 30-inch bed, with every other bed left unseeded. After the stand is irrigated up and well established, the unplanted beds are split down the center, and half the soil is thrown to the shoulders of the planted beds, producing 60-inch beds with a single seed line in the center. Other tomato growers plant double rows 14–20 inches apart on established beds.

The successful production of processing tomatoes for machine harvest is dependent on weed control, especially in the seed lines.

The most troublesome annual weeds are those in the tomato family: black nightshade, hairy nightshade, and groundcherry species. Other

1. University of California Cooperative Extension, Parlier, CA. 2. University of California Cooperative Extension, Sacramento, CA.

Figure 9. Weeds interfere with mechanical harvesting in a number of vegetable crops. Photo left shows a clean tomato field and a normal harvest. Photo right shows a tomato field heavily infested with field bindweed which will cause a reduction in yield and make harvest difficult and costly. Photos courtesy B.B. Fischer and J.K. Clark.

important annual weeds are shepherdspurse, wartcress, pigweed species, common lambsquarters, barnyardgrass, and common purslane. Many other annual broadleaf and grass weed species can occur in tomato fields and present problems. Most are controlled by the herbicides registered for use on tomatoes or a combination of herbicides and mechanical methods.

Of the perennials, yellow nutsedge is the most prevalent and most difficult to control. Johnsongrass and field bindweed (fig. 9) are perennial weed problems that should be avoided in field selection, but there are some control measures, including deep cultivation and fumigation, which will give the tomatoes some help if it becomes necessary to utilize fields with perennial weed problems.

For general selective weed control, a number of herbicides are available in California. No single herbicide or combination of materials will control all weed species under all production conditions. The following practices are used to control weeds in tomatoes at the indicated period. General conditions are provided followed by specific references to individual herbicides.

Fall Bedding

One of the most efficient ways of controlling weeds in tomatoes is to practice fall bedding, treating the seed line with a fumigant material such as 1,3-D fumigants or metham in a single band treatment 4–6 inches wide down the seed line, and the rest of the bed with a residual combination of herbicides such as napropamide or bensulide plus metribuzin.

By such practice, the beds are kept clean during the winter, and winter rains are used to incorporate the herbicides. With proper timing, this practice not only controls the early weed problems but also allows for earlier planting, which is often an advantage in meeting cannery quotas for early processing tomatoes.

Napropamide
Napropamide is a long residual herbicide for use preplant incorporated in the control of most annual grasses and broadleaf species. Incorporation should be in the 1–2-inch range.

Bensulide
Bensulide is a long residual preplant incorporated herbicide mainly for control of grasses. Do not plant to any crop not specified on the label for 18 months.

Metribuzin
Applied in the fall after the beds are formed, it is incorporated by means of winter rainfall. In combination with napropamide, metribuzin will give winter weed control. Metribuzin is most effective for control of mustards. Note, however, that tomatoes cannot be planted for 100 days after an application of metribuzin.

Glyphosate or Paraquat
Weather conditions sometimes do not allow applications of residual herbicides to provide effective control of weeds during this period. Under these conditions, foliar herbicides such as glyphosate or paraquat are used. When applied either postbedding or postplanting to seedling weeds, either of these herbicides will eliminate the first flush and allow tomatoes to have a vigorous start. Care must be taken with postplant applications, as any emerged tomatoes will be eliminated.

Preplant Fumigation

Metham
For control of nightshade species apply metham with a spray blade, as a water band, or through a sprinkler system. A soil cap must be formed over the band and left for 14 days. At the end of this period, the cap is removed with a V-shaped blade down to the original bed top surface and tomatoes are planted.

Preplant Incorporation

Cultural practices after soil preparation are similar in most areas. Herbicides are usually power incorporated into preformed beds or incorporated into listed beds. The width of the band will depend on how close the cultivation can be accomplished.

A number of good, preplant-incorporated herbicides have been developed over the years for annual broadleaf and grass weed control. The herbicides commonly used in California are selected on the basis of the expected weed population. If nutsedge and hairy nightshade are the most common species present, pebulate can give good results. An effective method is to broadcast the pebulate and incorporate with a disc; two-thirds of the pebulate should be applied prior to disking and one-third to the bed top and incorporated with a power tiller. If hairy nightshade is the only problem, then shallow incorporation (1.75–2 inches) is essential. If black nightshade is the major species, then plug planting using chlorpropham preemergence can be very effective.

Pebulate
Pebulate is a volatile herbicide, lasting approximately eight weeks, that must be immediately incorporated either preplant or lay-by. It is effective for control of annual grasses and broadleaves. It is the only herbicide that will control yellow nutsedge and hairy nightshade when applied preplant. Partial dodder control can be obtained. Incorporation must be 1.75–2 inches for effective hairy nightshade control. Tomatoes may show elongation and thickening.

Napropamide
Napropamide is a long residual herbicide for use preplant incorporated in the control of most annual grasses and broadleaf species. Incorporation should be in the 1–2-inch range.

Bensulide
Bensulide is a long residual preplant-incorporated herbicide mainly for control of grasses. Do not plant to any crop not specified on the label for 18 months.

The combination of pebulate and napropamide is the most common in California for broad-spectrum weed control.

Post-thinning/Lay-by

Following emergence and stand establishment, trifluralin, EPTC, or pebulate is often applied on the bed between double rows and on the bed shoulder, and incorporated to control weeds. Weedy furrows can be cultivated and the shoulders knived, but a well-timed lay-by application gives excellent season-long weed control at a reasonable cost.

Trifluralin
A volatile herbicide for season-long annual grass and broadleaf control,

trifluralin must be incorporated immediately after application with a power tiller. Do not apply directly over the tomatoes. Trifluralin is an apical dominance inhibitor, and reduced yields will occur.

EPTC
A volatile, short-lived herbicide for control of nightshade, yellow nutsedge, johnsongrass seedlings, annual grasses, and broadleaves. Do not use on sandy soils, and do not irrigate for five days after application. EPTC must be incorporated immediately with a power tiller.

Pebulate
A volatile, short-lived herbicide for control of hairy nightshade, yellow nutsedge, annual grasses, and broadleaves. Pebulate must be incorporated immediately with a power tiller.

Postemergence

Sethoxydim
Labeled and effective only on grassy weeds except for annual bluegrass The rate needed for perennial johnsongrass control is not labeled for tomatoes.

Metribuzin
May be applied as a directed spray on established tomatoes in the 5–6-leaf stage for postemergence control of broadleaf species. Do not apply under cloudy conditions.

Post-transplant

Pebulate
Apply before or after transplanting. Hot caps, if used, should be vented. Pebulate must be incorporated with a power tiller at lay-by.

   DCPA is also registered post-transplant and post-thinning lay-by but may be injurious to tomatoes.

Cultural Practices

Cultural practices, such as irrigation, cultivation, and fertilization, are quite similar in most fresh market and processing tomato production areas.

   Cultivation (fig. 10) and hand weeding can be used to reduce weed populations during the germination and postemergence period; but if the weeds are not controlled early (preemergence and prethinning), this can be an extremely repetitive and costly procedure. Cultivation and hand weeding require close supervision to reduce the potential for yield re-

Figure 10. Cultivation is common practice in many vegetable crops to remove weeds, aerate the soil, and improve irrigation efficiency. Examples of two types of cultivation: a rotary-powered unit removing weeds on the bedtop in tomatoes (left) *and a tool-bar-mounted unit, equipped with various types of knives, removing weeds on the bedtop and in the furrow in broccoli* (right). *Photos courtesy J.K. Clark and E.A. Kurtz.*

ductions resulting from plant and root damage or the actual loss of plants.

In summary, weeds present serious problems during all stages of tomato production, but they are far more serious during both germination and early postemergence because weed infestations at the later stages of production can interfere with mechanical harvesting (fig. 9).

Specific Weed Problems

Nutsedge

Two of the fiercest competitors with tomatoes are yellow and purple nutsedge. These weeds compete readily for early moisture and can often outgrow the young, struggling tomato plant. While the nutsedges do well in the sandy soils, they also do well and are extremely vigorous in the high organic soil of the delta and appear to be on the increase throughout the tomato-growing production areas. Tomatoes can be competitive when pebulate is properly incorporated. Low label rates are adequate in the light soils, but these rates, and even the top of the label, are not adequate for the heavy (fine), highly organic soils of the delta. EPTC is effective as a lay-by application.

Nightshade

Nightshade species are probably the most widespread and competitive weeds in California processing tomatoes. The most prominent species are black and hairy nightshade. These weed species germinate primarily in the top inch of soil, with about the same temperature requirements as tomatoes.

Metham has been shown to be an effective agent for controlling nightshade species. It can be applied with one or more of the following systems: spray blade, water banded (drench), or sprinkler and/or drip irrigation. It is essential to have adequate moisture for weed seedlings to germinate.

Hairy nightshade can be controlled with a shallow incorporation of pebulate (1.75–2 inches). Metribuzin is labeled for use as a post-directed application when tomatoes are in the five-leaf stage. Another is to plug plant, using activated carbon (5%) in the plug media and applying chlorpropham preemergence under sprinkler irrigation. Even so, some care must be taken in coarse soils to incorporate the chlorpropham with the proper amount of water to avoid excessive amounts in the root zone in the newly planted tomatoes.

One way to reduce populations of these species is to alternate crops which allow the use of herbicides that will effectively reduce nightshade populations (see table 2, Chapter 10).

Dodder

Fields infested with dodder should not be selected for the culture of tomatoes because there is currently no labeled herbicide for control of this problem. The best control measure is spot treatment with flaming to destroy both the dodder and tomato and thereby prevent spreading and seed production. Hand hoeing can also be effective, but dodder must be buried or carried out of the field.

Broomrape

Branched broomrape is not widespread in California. Most of the outbreaks have occurred in the Bay Area, mostly in Alameda and Santa Clara counties in the heavier soils. Tarped methyl bromide plus chloropicrin has kept this problem from becoming a serious hindrance to the production of tomatoes in California. Growers and/or pest control advisers observing broomrape in tomato fields should report it to the county agricultural commissioner's office.

REFERENCES

Integrated pest management for tomatoes, University of California, Statewide integrated pest management project, Division of Agriculture and Natural Resources, Publication 3274, 1985.

13

HORTICULTURAL CROPS

INTRODUCTION

by Edwin E. Sieckert[1], Clyde L. Elmore[2], and Arthur H. Lange[3]

Deciduous fruit and nut orchards, vineyards, citrus, and soft fruits are grown on approximately 2 million acres in California. Information published by the California Department of Food and Agriculture in 1986 indicated over 90% of the U.S. production of almonds, apricots, figs, grapes, kiwifruit, nectarines, olives, pistachios, plums, prunes, and walnuts and over 75% of the avocados, lemons, and strawberries were produced in California.

Vegetation management in fruit, nut, and citrus orchards, vineyards, and soft fruits is a major factor in growing and harvesting a crop. The vegetation is managed many different ways, depending upon the crop, location, and grower. Growers will set up cultural and other weed control operations for their crops that best fit their time, machinery, and economic resources.

Insect, mite, disease, and vertebrate pest control is generally better implemented when weeds are controlled or carefully managed. Crop losses from these pests are thus substantially reduced.

Applications of pesticides, growth hormones, and foliar and soil nutrients are also made easier where vegetation is managed. Most cultural operations are easier when tall weeds are not present to slow or hinder workers during irrigation, thinning, pruning, or harvest. When weeds are allowed to mature and dry, they can be a severe fire hazard; however, a controlled (mowed) mat of weeds or cover crop allows equipment to move on to wet soil with less compaction than on cultivated soil.

Weeds are beneficial in some operations where they reduce ero-

1. Monsanto Agriculture Products Company, Lodi, CA. 2. University of California Cooperative Extension, Davis, CA. 3. University of California Cooperative Extension, Parlier, CA.

Figure 1. Strip weed control is practiced in many tree (left) *and vine* (right) *crops. Photos courtesy C.L. Elmore.*

sion during periods of heavy rain or wind. They also help keep the soil open for good water penetration in soils likely to form impervious layers. For these and other reasons, vegetation can be managed in horticultural crops where their presence for all or part of the year is desirable, particularly if a clean strip down the tree or vine row is maintained (fig. 1).

The grower/manager must consider several key points in planning an individual vegetation management system. They are:

- Crop (variety/rootstock, age, stage of growth, date of harvest)
- Weeds (species, life habit, population(s))
- Cultural practices (irrigation cover crop, nontillage) (fig. 2)
- Environmental conditions (soil type, weather, rainfall, residual leaves or other organic matter) (fig. 3)
- Method of vegetation management (mechanical, cultural or physical, chemical)
- Desired results (maintain low vegetation growth, strip systems, nontillage)

WEEDS IN HORTICULTURAL CROPS

A thorough survey of winter and summer annuals and perennials in individual crops should be made in order to identify species. Examples of survey forms may be found in Chapter 10. The species present will determine the choice of the vegetation management program.

Both annuals (winter and summer) and perennials can present problems in horticultural crops. In orchards, it was estimated a few years ago that approximately 75% of the major weeds were annuals and 25% perennials. Today, due primarily to mowing (which reduces or eliminates most annuals) or the use of preemergence herbicides (which control

Figure 2. Three methods of orchard irrigation are: furrow (left), flood (center), and sprinkler (right). Photos courtesy J.K. Clark and C.L. Elmore.

most annuals but not all perennials), a higher percentage of weeds in orchards are perennials.

Winter annual weeds germinate in the late fall and winter and, due to weather conditions, are generally slow in growing. Common winter annual species include redstem and whitestem filaree, London rocket, sowthistle, common groundsel, wild oat, annual bluegrass, chickweed, and ripgut brome. Control of the winter weeds is important since they compete with crops for moisture and nutrients at the onset of spring (fig. 4). Large weeds are difficult to control and if left unchecked will produce many seeds.

Summer annual weeds germinating in the spring grow much faster than winter annuals. These weeds should be controlled with the residual winter-applied soil herbicides or as young plants in the spring. If they are controlled early in mature trees or vines, the shading effect of the crop foliage will suppress later growth of the weeds. Some of the particularly troublesome summer annual weeds include barnyardgrass, horseweed, purslane, cupgrass, annual morningglory, lambsquarters, knotweed, black nightshade, pigweed species, and puncturevine. Some plants becoming more common include sprangletop, the panicums, and prostrate pigweed. If not controlled, many summer annuals can severely hamper harvest operations.

Biennial plants are sometimes a problem in horticultural crops. They are somewhat difficult to control because there is a mixed population of seedlings and second-year plants. Two species include little mallow and bristly oxtongue. Little mallow is common in most growing areas, but bristly oxtongue is generally a coastal weed.

Perennial weeds are the most troublesome. They are more difficult to control than annuals and thus require extensive programs of selec-

Figure 3. Using an air blower to remove leaves from the soil surface before application of preemergence herbicides. Photo courtesy E.E. Sieckert.

tive treatment plus cultivation. They are especially competitive to trees and vines during the first five years. Perennial weeds are best controlled prior to planting crops. Established stands can be controlled with postemergence herbicides and cultivation before orchard or vineyard establishment. If a preemergence herbicide or mechanical mowing program is started and perennial weeds such as bermudagrass, dallisgrass, johnsongrass, field bindweed, or nutsedge are present, these weeds will eventually dominate. After a period of years, bermudagrass develops a dense sod if left unchecked, and a disc may just roll over the top without reaching the soil. Heavy shade from mature trees reduces its vigor.

Dallisgrass is frequently found on fine soils. It is found in low areas at the ends of checks where water stands.

Johnsongrass can be as tall or taller than young trees, reducing photosynthesis and therefore decreasing vigor. If weeds are left unchecked, a young tree will not survive. It is costly to remove aboveground portions and rhizomes from around a tree, and there is no guarantee that all portions of the extensive rhizome system, which may number 1000 segments, will be removed.

When an orchard is crossdisked, an island of johnsongrass may be found around the tree trunk. This trashy area makes harvest difficult in tree fruit or nut crops. Johnsongrass also hosts insects that easily transfer to trees and feed in maturing fruit.

Field bindweed is particularly prevalent on fine soils. Trees planted into an infested area will result in total envelopment if left unchecked. Mites are often found on field bindweed. They tend to increase on bindweed and can form bridges to the trees and move into tree foliage.

Nutsedge has become an increasing problem primarily for two reasons in orchard culture: (1) drip irrigation provides constant moisture around the plant which favors the growth and development of nut-

Figure 4. An orchard heavily infested with winter weeds. Photo courtesy C.L. Elmore.

sedge; (2) residual herbicides have reduced the competition from annuals, allowing nutsedge populations to increase.

METHODS OF VEGETATION MANAGEMENT

The three basic methods of managing vegetation in trees and vines are mechanical, cultural and physical, and chemical. Brief reviews of each method follow.

Mechanical

Mechanical methods of weed control have been used for many years in both tree and vine crops. These methods include hand hoeing as well as the use of such implements as disc harrows, power rototillers, French plows, spring-hoe weeders, mowers, and others (figs. 5 and 6). Detailed information on the use of these implements for weed control may be found in Chapter 4.

Cultivation in the spring is used to reduce weed growth and to prepare a firm surface wherever frost may present problems. This should be done several weeks prior to bloom in most deciduous trees and prior to leafing out in grapes. If cultivation is used, it should be done when soil moisture content is dry enough to avoid compaction. During wet years, mowing is often used to reduce soil compaction. A too-early cultivation in rolling hills, bench lands, or at higher elevations may cause severe erosion problems.

Figure 5. Weeds removed around vines with a 'French'-type hoe-plow (left) *and in between tree rows with a disc* (right). *Photos courtesy J.K. Clark.*

Cultural and Physical

Burning, using propane gas jets mounted on booms—either short booms for strip treatments or long booms for complete coverage—is expensive. It leaves no soil residues but requires retreatement as new weeds germinate or regrowth occurs. Tree injury can occur if enough dry weed residue is around the tree base to sustain a fire.

Chemical

Chemical weed control in horticultural crops has reduced tillage operations, improved time management, and provided a higher return on investment. Three primary methods of chemical weed control in use today are:

Herbicide Strips Under Crop Rows and Disc Centers
Disking the center and reestablishing irrigation basins is labor-intensive and costly. Weeds generally grow quickly in the summer and compete for water and nutrients. During the winter, moving equipment on medium to fine soils is difficult and may increase soil compaction in the disc area.

Herbicide Strip and Mow-Sod Centers
The strip, generally 2–8 feet, is established during the winter with a post-emergence plus a residual herbicide. The sod center is mowed every three to four weeks during the period of active growth. This method

Figure 6. Vegetation managed in-between tree rows with rotary or flail-type mower. Photo courtesy J.K. Clark.

allows equipment entry after rainfall in the winter months, reduces dust during the year, and provides a clean surface under the tree to facilitate mechanical or hand harvesting. Perennial weeds are controlled with applications of a herbicide either as a broadcast or spot treatment. Disadvantages of this method are competition of the sod with the tree for nutrients and water, mowing costs, and the possibility of allowing perennial weeds to spread (fig. 7).

Complete Herbicide Nontillage

The addition of new, safe herbicides for stone fruits has brought about more interest in this method, which is currently being used in citrus. The herbicides are applied from tree row to tree row during the winter months to provide a weed-free soil surface. The advantages of this method are maximum frost protection, labor and equipment savings, improved water and nutrient utilization, and earlier orchard maturity. The cost at the outset of this program is slightly higher than that of other methods, but the benefits outweigh the disadvantages.

The key disadvantages occur with problem soils, high in silt, that may form a crust (surface seal), thus reducing water infiltration. Periodic or light cultivation may be required to reduce this problem. Prunings should be chopped (shredded) or disked in periodically to reduce problems associated with cultural practices and the application of herbicides. This method has significant potential for improved orchard management practices.

All references to acreage and value included herein were obtained from the California Agricultural Statistics Service for 1986–87.

Figure 7. Repeated applications of herbicides for annual weed control can result in release of perennial weeds such as field bindweed (left) *and johnsongrass* (right). *Photos courtesy J.K. Clark.*

FIGS

by Ron Vargas[1]

Figs are a perennial member of the deciduous, subtropical plant group which has been an important fruit throughout the world dating back to 1600 B.C. In Greek mythology the fig tree was sacred to the god of fruitfulness and vegetation, and at one time figs were man's principal sustenance in the Greek peninsula.

In California, the fig, like many other fruits, dates from the establishment of the mission at San Diego in 1769. Commercial culture started in 1885 with Adriatic figs. Smyrna figs were introduced into California in 1880, but it was not until about 1900 that the fig *(Blastophaga psenes)* was established and used successfully to transfer caprifig pollen to Smyrna-type figs to obtain fruit set. This success stimulated interest in commercial production of Calimyrna figs in California, and acreage expanded in the early 1900s.

California produces more than 99% of the U.S. fig crop. About 90% is used as dried figs, while the rest is sold fresh or canned. California dried fig production is located primarily in the San Joaquin Valley, with more than 98% of the acreage in Fresno, Madera, Kern, and Merced counties. Kadota figs for canning are concentrated in Merced County, while fresh figs are shipped from Riverside County in the south, from

1. University of California Cooperative Extension, Madera County, CA.

the San Joaquin Valley in central California, and from Coastal Valley counties.

Acreage in 1987 of all fig varieties totaled 18,184, of which 18,065 were bearing acres. The value of the crop in 1986 was estimated at $12,288,000.

Site Preparation

Once a suitable site has been selected, site preparation can have a decided effect on subsequent weed problems.

If the orchard is going to be located on flat land where irrigation is to be practiced, proper land-leveling is essential in eliminating high and low spots on the orchard floor, which can create environments conducive to weed growth.

If the orchard is to be located in the rolling, hard-pan soils of the eastern portion of the San Joaquin Valley, deep ripping, especially down the tree row (up to 60 inches in depth), is essential to allow uniform water penetration and infiltration. Weeds can become a problem in saturated soils with little aeration as herbicides biodegrade much faster under anaerobic conditions.

Control of persistent perennial weeds such as johnsongrass and bermudagrass should be considered the summer before planting. The use of a nonselective, translocated herbicide such as glyphosate in late summer has proven to be very effective in controlling persistent perennial weeds.

Varieties

Few varieties are available for commercial fig production in California. Dried figs are produced from the Calimyrna and Mission cultivars while fig paste is produced from Adriatic, Kadota, Calimyrna, Mission, Conadria, and Di Redo. Kadota is also the principal fig used in canning.

Varietal selection plays an important role in the development of the weed-management program. Dried figs and paste figs are allowed to mature on the tree and drop to the ground, where they are picked up either by hand or mechanically; therefore, the orchard floor must be free of weeds and trash. Fresh-market or canning figs need not have an orchard floor completely bare of vegetation because the fruit is hand-picked from the tree. In this system a strip-nontillage program is adequate. Kadota, Mission, and Conadria varieties bear two crops per year; the first crop ripens in June and July, and the second or main crop ripens August through October, depending upon the variety. Weed-free conditions must prevail during each harvest season. This may require additional attention to controlling weeds either mechanically or chemically, or by a combination of the two.

Soil Type

A large portion of the fig orchards in the San Joaquin Valley are grown on the San Joaquin soil series. This series consists of shallow, iron-silica-cemented, hardpan soils normally associated with a rolling or undulating topography.

These soils are not suited to a weed-management system requiring repeated mechanical tillage to prepare for harvest. Such a system would lead to soil compaction and reduced water infiltration, causing weed problems and adverse tree growth. Therefore, a chemical strip nontillage program is best suited to the hardpan soils of the San Joaquin soil series. Many of the older fig orchards produced under these conditions, however, are kept weed free and readied for harvest solely by mechanical means. Only the newer orchards, established from 1970 on, normally use a chemical strip with mowing or disking of centers as a weed-management system.

Associated with this soil series, along with common winter and summer annual weeds, are inherent weed problems such as mulleins, vinegar weed, and Fitch's spikeweed, which require different approaches for effective control. These summer annuals are not effectively controlled with present preemergence herbicides, so additional postemergence herbicidal use or hand weeding is necessary.

Some figs are grown on soil that will allow a weed-free environment with mechanical tillage and with little impact on soil and tree growth. In such cases, a mechanical weed-free system may be preferred.

Cultivation

The main purposes of cultivation are to facilitate the distribution of irrigation water, to incorporate organic matter with the soil, and to eliminate the competition of weeds for the available soil moisture.

The common method of controlling unwanted vegetation and preparing the orchard floor for harvest has been repeated disking, harrowing, land-leveling, cultipacking, and rolling.

This is accomplished by two-way disking to destroy weeds between and within the tree rows. Often hand shoveling is required to destroy the vegetation adjacent to the tree trunk. Normally, irrigation methods, including furrow, basin, and contour flood, are associated with this system of cultivation.

In the undulating orchards of the San Joaquin soil series, control of unwanted vegetation is best accomplished with a chemically treated strip, 6–10 feet wide down the tree row, and repeated diskings or mowing of vegetation between rows which account for the system name—'strip-nontillage.' Drip-irrigation systems are always associated with this type of cultivation regime.

Irrigation

The type of irrigation method employed in a particular orchard also has a decided influence on the weed-management program. Methods of applying irrigation water to fig orchard soils are not essentially different from those used in other deciduous orchards. Furrow, flood, border check, or contour flood are all methods of irrigation found in fig orchards grown on relatively flat lands. Irrigation is normally coupled with mechanical tillage to control unwanted vegetation.

Drip irrigation via low-volume emitters or sprinkler drag lines is practiced in fig orchards which are grown on hilly or rolling topography where leveling is neither practiced nor economically feasible. A chemical strip-nontillage system of weed management is best adapted to this type of irrigation regime. Continuous monitoring of the performance of the drip line and emitters is required for maximum water-application efficiency, so it is imperative to have a weed-free strip down the tree row. Also, soils of these orchards are usually of hardpan origin which do not lend themselves to the repeated tillage operations necessary to mechanically control unwanted vegetation.

Besides the influence irrigation methods or systems have on the weed management program, the water requirements of the fig tree also have a direct effect on weed management. Fig orchards require 2½ acre-feet of water per year from rainfall and irrigation, with the first application normally occurring during the winter. Another irrigation is applied during the spring months. Because only moderate vegetative growth and maximum fruiting is desired, irrigation is minimal, dependent on soil type, during the hot, dry summer months.

Summer irrigation can also cause splitting of the fruit. Due to this practice, summer weed populations are not normally as great or severe as early-spring or winter weed problems. Only minimal tillage or contact herbicide use is necessary to control weeds during this time period because of the lack of soil moisture.

Fertilization

Fertilization has little effect on the weed-management program. Sometimes soil fertility is improved with the use of a cover crop to be turned under the orchard floor as green manure. Therefore, it may be desirable to allow vegetation to grow during the winter months and then mechanically disk it under early in the spring before the frost season.

Chemical Control

The following herbicides are registered for use in nonbearing and bearing California fig orchards:

- Preemergence: napropamide, oryzalin, and oxyfluorfen
- Postemergence: paraquat and weed oil

Harvest

Figs grown for dried use, which are allowed to fall to the ground, require an orchard floor completely free of weeds and trash.

Fresh-market and canning figs are picked from the trees as they mature. Harvest is by hand, and figs are placed in buckets or boxes. This harvest system does not require a weed- and trash-free orchard floor. A weed-free strip down the tree row accomplished with a preemergent herbicide is all that is required.

Rotation to Other Crops

The major concern regarding weed management, when planning the removal of the orchard, is the effect herbicides applied to the figs may have on the subsequent crop. The herbicides used to control unwanted vegetation in fig orchards do not normally have a long persistent carryover in the soil. But preemergence herbicide use should be reduced if not eliminated at least one to two years before removal of the orchard. This may require supplementing mechanical tillage in place of herbicides during these last two years.

Summary

In order to produce high yields of good quality figs that are an economically feasible crop for the grower, close attention must be given to weed management programs.

In California two systems of weed management are practiced—mechanical tillage and strip-nontillage—depending upon variety, soil type, topography, and irrigation methods.

Where land is level and furrow or flood irrigation is practiced for dried figs, the best weed-management system may be complete mechanical tillage. But when figs are grown on an undulating topography where repeated tillage is not desirable and drip irrigation is practiced, the best weed program is a strip-nontillage system.

REFERENCES

Condit, Ira J. *Fig culture in California,* Calif. Ag. Ext. Ser., Cir. 77, October 1983.
Dried Fig Advisory Board, California Fig Institute. *Statistical review of the California dried fig industry. 1982.*
Fischer, Bill B., G.L. Obenauf, M.H. Gerdts, A.H. Lange. Runcina Vol. 17, *Evaluation of herbicides for vegetation management in fig orchards,* A progress rpt., Univ. of Calif. Coop. Ext., Fresno County.
Obenauf, G.L. M.H. Gerdts, G. Leavitt, J. Crane. Leaflet 21051, *Commercial dried fig production in California.* Div. of Agric. Sci., Univ. of Calif.
United States Dept. of Ag. Soil Conservation Ser., *Soil Survey, Madera Area, Calif.*

NUT CROPS

by Arthur H. Lange[1]

The three primary nut crops chosen for discussion—almonds, pistachios, and walnuts—are almost exclusively grown in California. Production and value (almonds based on shelled commodity, others on in-shell) for these crops in 1987 was as follows: Almonds—423,375 acres and $649,635,000; pistachios—54,120 acres and $44,317,000; and walnuts (English and black)—199,098 acres and $194,400,000 (value for 1986). About 85% of the almonds, 80% of the pistachios, and 60% of the walnuts are treated for weed control.

Weed control costs figure relatively little in the overall financial burden imposed on orchardists bringing their trees into production. Nevertheless, weeds represent an annual cost that may total a substantial outlay over the first several years, i.e., by the time the average crop is commercially productive.

Weeds compete with newly planted deciduous trees until they are about four years old, depending on the growth of the trees and the intensity of weed growth. Perennial weeds such as field bindweed and johnsongrass may compete longer. Bermudagrass, the nutsedges, and, to a lesser extent, annual grasses tend to be shaded out as trees get larger.

Another major reason for controlling weeds is to help in the control of field mice and gophers to reduce the incidence of losses due to bark girdling. Poisonous snakes sometimes hide in tall grasses near the base of trees in some of California's northern counties.

Orchard Weed Problems

Important annual or biennial weeds in California nut orchards include: barnyardgrass, black nightshade, large crabgrass, lovegrass, pigweeds, lambsquarters, common purslane, puncturevine, mustards, flaxleaved fleabane, horseweed, and little mallow.

Important perennial weeds include: bermudagrass, johnsongrass, nutsedges, field bindweed, and silverleaf nightshade.

Weed Control in Nut Orchards

Weeds in nut tree orchards are controlled today in California principally by a combination of tillage, mowing, and chemicals. Burning is used occasionally in some areas, particularly for cleanup just before harvest.

Principal tillage tools include the hoe, disc harrows, and power rototillers. Tillage has the disadvantage of sometimes increasing disease

---

1. *University of California Cooperative Extension, Parlier, CA.*

and insect problems and, in some soils, developing impervious layers, often called plow or tillage pans.

Mowing is inexpensive and rapid but does not control weeds directly adjacent to the trees. As many as eight to 10 mowings per year are often required.

Burning, using propane gas jets, is expensive, but leaves no soil residues. It may require as many as 20 treatments for perennial weed control, which is becoming uneconomical.

Chemicals are used generally in 4–6-foot strips down the tree row, which results in inexpensive weed control. The centers are either tilled or mowed, but the total distance is cut in half because travel is in only one direction, i.e., parallel with the tree row. In order for strip chemical treatment to be successful, the eradication of perennial weeds by the use of repeated postemergence-herbicide applications and tillage is essential.

The ideal combination of preemergence weed control down the tree or vine row with mowing or tilling the centers is a growing practice throughout California's nut orchards. Mowing is practiced on contour plantings especially where sprinklers are used or where rainfall is the major source of moisture, such as in some coastal walnut orchards.

Strip treatment using a number of herbicides with tilled centers is being used in furrow- and flood-irrigated nut orchards throughout California. Weed control in the strip is accomplished with preemergence herbicides or in some orchards with repeated summer postemergence herbicides, usually glyphosate or combinations with paraquat or other postemergence herbicides. Weed control in the centers and/or in the strip down the tree row with a burn-down herbicide has proven to be cost-effective and is being used extensively. In some orchards because of the low rates of postemergence herbicides, tolerant species, especially nutsedge and bermudagrass, have increased. This ultimately requires that higher rates be used at least part of the time.

During the summer harvest period weeds often tend to get ahead of the grower. Also props, ladders, surface irrigation pipe, etc., can make frequent spray jobs more difficult during summer. The tendency is to delay spraying and allow the weeds to prosper. However, overall summer weed control is another workable tool for the orchardist.

Complete coverage with herbicides is being practiced in many almond orchards but less in walnuts and pistachio. However, some walnut and pistachio orchards are also treated with complete-coverage herbicides.

Chemical Weed Control

There are important reasons for using chemicals to control weeds in orchards. The practice of mechanical tillage, mowing, or burning wastes energy, considering the number of times each season it is necessary to traverse the orchard. Hand hoeing around the tree is expensive, and labor is not always available. Furthermore, nut crops are machine harvested. Mechanical harvesting equipment requires weed-free conditions for successful operation.

The ultra-low-volume sprayers with flotation tires have been used effectively for both preemergence and postemergence herbicides. In some soils, nontillage has increased water penetration. Less frost injury during bloom has been reported in weed-free, nontilled orchards.

The following herbicides are registered for use on the indicated nut crops in California:

Herbicide	Almond	Pistachio	Walnut
Preemergence			
dichlobenil	B	—	B
diuron	B	—	B
EPTC	B	—	B
metolachlor	B	—	B
napropamide	B	B	B
norflurazon	B	—	B
oryzalin	B	B	B
oxyfluorfen	B	B	B
pendimethalin	B	N	B
simazine	B	—	B
trifluralin	B	B	B
Postemergence			
2,4-D	B	B	B
glyphosate	B	B	B
MSMA	N	N	N
paraquat	B	B	B
sethoxydim	N	N	N
fluazifop-P	N	N	N
weed oil	B	B	B

B = Bearing
N = Nonbearing
— = Not registered

Individual Crops

Walnuts, grown largely in California, are deep-rooted, widely spaced trees, usually furrow or broad-basin irrigated. Simazine and diuron are registered and recommended for use in walnuts in California. Annual applications are made on coarse soils. With fine soils and heavy weed populations, walnut orchards may receive split applications; half in the late fall or winter and half in the spring. Sometimes simazine is applied in the fall for broadleaf winter annual control and diuron or oryzalin is applied in the spring for the summer grasses. Overall treatments are being used, but most are single-tree treatments or strips down the tree rows.

Almonds, like peaches, are usually grafted on peach rootstock. Rootstocks and scions vary in their susceptibilities to some herbicides. For example, Mission almond scion is more sensitive to simazine than Nonpareil stock. The cultural requirements of almonds are similar to those of peaches except that they are usually grown on coarse soil, partially to facilitate soil preparation for harvest. Because of the sweeping procedure used in harvest, almond farmers must have a weed-free orchard. At the same time, noncultivation is desirable to reduce dust which favors mite infestation. Mowing weeds also produces some dust, but less than cultivation. Oryzalin and simazine have been satisfactory, the latter at low rates in the finer soils. In the coarser, sandy soils, simazine has been applied to raised beds with furrow or flood irrigation with success, but care must be exercised.

Pistachios are usually grafted on to one of three *Pistachia* species, *terebinthus, atlantica,* and, more recently, *integerrima.* Most of the herbicide testing has been done on the two earlier rootstocks which in general seems to be somewhat susceptible to simazine and norflurazon. Less has been done with the more vigorous *integerrima.* The 1983 University of California screening trials included *integerrima,* and it appeared to be quite resistant to most herbicides. Most of the pistachios are grown in loams and clay loam soils. Nonetheless, pistachio appears to be sufficiently tolerant of most herbicides to allow their judicial use. Weeds appear to present a great deal more hazard in being carriers of Verticillium wilt and competing for expensive water than even the marginally safe herbicides. A wide, weed-free strip with one or two drip lines is common in California pistachio orchards. For the most part there are adequate chemicals available for satisfactory weed control, but more are needed, especially for control in the wet zone of the drip emitter. There are no preemergence herbicides currently available to effectively control weeds through emitters. Weeds are controlled with timely post-emergence applications of glyphosate and other foliar-applied herbicides.

Pecans are of limited importance in California, but the interest in growing them is on the increase. In 1987 there were 2,708 acres in the state. The weed problems in California are similar to those in other crops. The lack of herbicides available in California for pecans is probably the biggest weed control problem since there are very few registered.

Annual Weed Problems

The principal annual weed problems in almonds and walnuts and where pistachios are knocked to the orchard floor are those that occur at harvest time. Such weeds as purslane, barnyardgrass, and other annual grasses must be controlled in order to harvest nuts off the orchard floor. Cultivation at this time often produces clods that are swept up with the nuts. EPTC surface applied and sprinkled in or applied in the irrigation water has been very successful at preventing annual weed growth after floating and before harvest.

Perhaps an even more important problem is the early-germinating Compositae family of weeds which are resistant to almost all the currently registered herbicides used in nut orchards. The most troublesome species are flaxleaved fleabane, horseweed, groundsel, and cudweed. This complex is resistant to all but simazine. Postemergence applications of either glyphosate, 2,4-D, or paraquat applied when the weeds are small are effective.

Perennial Weed Problems

Deep-rooted perennials grow well after simazine or diuron is applied for preemergence annual weed control. Bermudagrass, johnsongrass, and field bindweed have increased rapidly in preemergence weed-control trials where mixtures of these weeds and annual weeds were present. It is of paramount importance that perennial weeds be controlled—most cheaply with a combination of frequent tillage and postemergence herbicides—before a program of annual weed control with preemergence herbicides is initiated. Norflurazon will give control of bermudagrass, silverleaf nightshade, and nutsedge with continued use. It also has considerable effect on johnsongrass but little or no effect on field bindweed. Trifluralin alone or in combination has been effective on the perennial grasses and field bindweed.

Herbicide Residues in Soils

Herbicides are as organic as any of nature's products in the soil. Being man-made, they are usually simpler and relatively unstable. It is true that some herbicides are more persistent than others. These longer-lasting herbicides are the ones that have been selected for weed control in perennial crops such as the nut orchards. However, even the longest-lasting break down. They disappear from the soil at unpredictably variable rates. Therefore, the use of preemergence herbicides should be discontinued about one or two years before pulling an orchard so as to prevent effects on subsequent crops.

REFERENCES

Bryant, L.R. and L.W. Rasmussen. 1951. The use of 2,4-D in orchard bindweed control. Proc. Soc. Hort. Sci. 58:131–135.

Burnside, O.C., E.L. Schmidt and R. Behrens. 1961. Dissipation of simazine from the soil. Weeds 9:477–484.

Chaney, D., L. Buschman, A. Lange, V. Carlson, L. Hendricks, J. Smith and C. Elmore. 1966. Weed control in deciduous fruit nurseries. Proc. Calif. Weed Conf. 18:56–57.

Curtis, O.F. 1965. Weeding apple orchards. FM. Res. 30:12. Weed Abst. 14:201.

Elmore, C.L., D.E. Bayer, A.H. Lange, L.L. Buschman, and R.B. Jeter. 1966. Perennial weed control in orchards. Proc. Calif. Weed Conf. 18:61–62.

Holly, K. and H.A. Roberts. 1963. *Persistence of phytotoxicity residues and triazine herbicides in soil.* Weed Res. 3:1–10.

Jaynes, R.A. 1969. *Handbook of North American Nut Trees. The Northern Nutgrowers Assoc.* W.F. Humphrey Press, Inc., Geneva, N.Y. pp 51–59.

Kearney, P.C., T.J. Sheets and J.W. Smith. 1964. *Volatilization of seven s-triazines.* Weeds 12:83–87.

Kortleve, C. and H.J. Slotboom. 1967. *Weed control in the autumn and night frosts.* Fruitteelt 57:1132–1133. Weed Absttr. 17(6):437.

Lange, A.H. and J.C. Crane. 1967. *The phytotoxicity of several herbicides to deciduous fruit tree seedlings.* J. Amer. Soc. Hort. Sci. 90:47–55.

Lange, A.H., B.E. Day, L.S. Jordan, R.C. Russell. 1967. *Preemergence herbicides for weed control in walnuts.* Calif. Agr. 21:2–4.

Lange, A.H., and C.L. Elmore. 1967. *Rootstock-scion-herbicide interrelationships in almond.* J. Amer. Soc. Hort. Sci. 90:56–60.

Lange, A.H. 1968. *Postemergence weed control studies in young deciduous fruit trees.* Univ. of Calif. Agr. Ext. Serv. AXT281. 12 pp.

Lange, A.H. and C.L. Elmore. 1969. *Moisture and the use of simazine on* Prunus. Hort. Sc. 4(1):30–32.

Lange, A.H., C. Elmore, B. Fischer, L. Buschman and N. Ross. 1969. *Combination for preemergence weed control in California orchards.* Univ. of Calif. Agr. Ext. Serv. AXT312. 54 pp.

Lange, A.H. and B.B. Fischer. *Phytotoxicity and irrigation effects in orchard weed control with herbicides.* Calif. Agr. 23:6–8.

Lange, A.H. 1970. *Weed control methods, losses and costs due to weeds, and benefits of weed control in deciduous fruit and nut crops.* Weed Science Society of America F.A.O. International Conference on Weed Control, pp. 143–162.

Lange, A.H. and B.B. Fischer. 1970. *Herbicide screening trials in* Prunus. West. Soc. Weed Sci., Res. Rept. pp. 29–34.

Lange, A.H. and J. Schlesselman. 1976. *Weed control in trees and vines.* Weed Control Notes Prog. Rept., Series 76:1.

Lange, A.H., H.M. Kempen, B.B. Fischer, J. Schlesselman, L. Nygren, and E.E. Stevenson. 1977. *Weed control in almonds.* Weed Control Notes Prog. Rept. Series 77:1.

Lange, A.H., J.T. Schlesselman, Harold Kempen, Ron Vargas, and Lonnie Hendricks. 1978. *Weed control in almonds 1978.* Weed Control Notes Prog. Rept. Series 78:5.

Lange, A.H., B.B. Fischer, R. Vargas, and Harold Kempen. 1980. *Weed control in pistachios for 1980.* Weed Control Notes Prog. Rept. Series 80:1.

Lange, A.H., H.M. Kempen, Clyde L. Elmore, B.B. Fischer and R.N. Vargas. *Weed Control Notes Prog. Rept. Series 80:3.*

Lange, A.H. and R.N. Vargas. 1981. *Weed control in pistachio 1981.* Weed Control Notes Prog. Rept. Series 81:5.

Lange, A., R. Vargas and H. Kempen. 1982. *Weed control studies for 1982 in almonds.* Weed Control Notes Prog. Rept. Series 82:4.

Lange, A.H., R. Vargas and W.D. Edson. 1983. *Weed control studies for 1983 in almonds.* Weed Control Notes Prog. Rept. Series 82:3.

Lange, A.H., R.N. Vargas and W.D. Edson. 1983. *Weed control in pistachio.* Weed Control Notes Prog. Rept. Series 83:4.

Lord, W.H., D.A. Marini, and E.R. Ladd. 1967. *The effectiveness of fall application of granular simazine and granular dichlobenil for weed control in orchards and the influence of weed control on mouse activity.* Proc. No. East Weed Contr. Conf. 21:213–217. Weed Abst. 16:364.

Meith, C.L. and A.D. Rizzi. 1964. *Nontillage and strip weed control in almond orchards.* Univ. of Calif. Agr. Ext. Serv. AXT164 Rev. 19 pp.

Mellenthin, W.M., G. Crabtree, and F.D. Raugh. 1966. *Effects of herbicides and weed competition on growth of orchard trees.* Proc. Amer. Soc. Hort. Sci. 88:121–126.

Yarwood, J.D. 1969. *Tillage increases plant diseases.* Calif. Agr. 23(3):4–6.

SOFT FRUITS

by Arthur H. Lange[1]

Strawberries and cane-bushberries are the primary soft fruits discussed in this section. Strawberries were produced on 16,800 acres in 1987 with a value of $407,657,000. In terms of value, approximately 85% of the crop

1. *University of California Cooperative Extension, Parlier, CA.*

is produced for the fresh market, while 15% is processed. Caneberries (boysenberries, olallieberries, and raspberries) were produced on a total of 1,020 acres in 1987 with a value of $8,963,000.

Strawberries and caneberries are extremely susceptible to competition from weeds. Annual weeds reduce their growth and yield. Perennial weeds left uncontrolled eliminate such crops by shading strawberries and by competing with caneberries for water. Pigweed and lambsquarters are continuous broadleaf-annual problems in soft fruits. Annual grasses include barnyardgrass, lovegrass, crabgrass, and others. Bluegrass and volunteer grains are problems along the coast. Puncturevine is also a problem in the coarse soils of the San Joaquin Valley. Along the coast, the weeds include mostly common broadleaf species such as sweet clover, pigweeds, nettleleaf goosefoot, annual sowthistle, common groundsel, chickweeds, nightshade, little mallow, burning nettle, shepherdspurse, purslane, pineappleweed, lambsquarters, burclover, filarees, and three difficult-to-control perennial weeds—nutsedge, bermudagrass, and field bindweed. Perennial-weed-infested soils must be avoided when planting soft fruit crops.

Strawberries

Strawberries are grown primarily as an annual crop in California, with some plantings carried over for production in the second year. Weeds not only compete with newly planted and established crops but also interfere with harvesting operations. Although costly (approximately $1200 per acre) the application of methyl bromide and chloropicrin, as soil fumigants, prior to planting will provide excellent weed control and also control other pests and diseases. Weed control can be particularly expensive in strawberries if the fields are not fumigated prior to planting. Annual weeds are the main problem in strawberries. These develop during the rainy season or appear in new plantings when the beds must be kept comparatively wet so the plants can become established. Under wet soil conditions, cultivation is not possible, and the weeds often take over.

Cultural and Physical Methods
A good approach to weed control in strawberries is to prevent weeds from developing. Wherever possible, fields selected for strawberry culture should be relatively free from weeds. When weeds do emerge, they should not be allowed to go to seed. Weeds that can reproduce vegetatively, such as purslane and the perennial weed species, should be hand cut, carried out of the field, and destroyed.

When weather or soil conditions permit, various types of cultivation tools (shovels, duckfoot, or blades) should be used to remove annual weeds from the furrows and shoulders of the beds. Most annual weeds on the top of the bed can be controlled by using a black polyethylene-plastic film as a mulch. Usually, however, this does not increase the soil temperature and can delay fruit maturation. Clear plastic film usually increases the soil temperature and hastens fruit maturation, but will increase the weed problems unless weeds are eliminated by other means. Cultivation of furrows is difficult when plastic film is used.

Chemical Control

Herbicides should be used in combination with good crop management and tillage to control weeds in strawberries. Several herbicides are approved for use in strawberries but differ in weeds controlled and in soil persistence.

Preplant Fumigation

In California, fields for strawberries are usually fumigated before planting with a mixture of methyl bromide and chloropicrin. Methyl bromide is the most important ingredient in this mixture. This treatment kills many weed seeds and the reproductive organs of some perennial weeds as well as soilborne disease organisms, such as Verticillium and nematodes. Weeds that are not adequately controlled by this treatment include burclover, filaree, and little mallow.

Methyl bromide and chloropicrin are gases under pressure sold as liquids in pressurized containers. The materials are applied simultaneously by shank injection to depths in the range of 6–10 inches. The treated area is sealed immediately with a gas-tight plastic cover (polyethylene) for at least 48 hours. Fumigant injection and covering are completed in one operation with all equipment mounted on a single tractor (see photo in the Fumigation section of Chapter 7). Strawberries may be planted 14 days after removing the plastic cover.

Metham, long considered a fumigant, is more correctly a water-transported biocide. It appears to kill germinating weed seeds by contact. Like methyl bromide, it kills weeds, disease organisms, and insects in the soil. Unlike methyl bromide, metham does not move well in the gas phase. Furthermore there is a longer waiting period between treatment and planting young strawberry plants. Metham applied through sprinklers, drip systems, or in a water drench gives excellent weed control which will last from one month to several depending on the method of application, the rate, and the soil type.

New Plantings

If weeds emerge prior to planting, then paraquat or weed oil will provide acceptable control. DCPA should be applied immediately after transplanting before weeds germinate. Sprinkler irrigation should be used to ensure adequate incorporation.

Napropamide is labeled for use on newly planted strawberries and is sprinkler incorporated. Napropamide provides only partial control of little mallow but is effective on the clovers and filarees.

Sethoxydim is also available as a postemergence treatment for the control of grasses.

Established Plantings

DCPA and napropamide may be applied to the soil to control annual weeds as they germinate and will not control weeds that have already emerged. Therefore, a hand weeding and/or cultivation may be required in conjunction with application for effective use in established plantings. Sprinkler irrigation should be used to ensure adequate incorporation.

Sethoxydim is also available as a postemergence treatment for the control of grasses.

Chemical Considerations

Soil differences have been observed in the response of strawberries to several preemergence herbicides. The coarse soils, low in organic matter, can be a problem with some herbicides.

Because of the standard practice of using plastic mulch, mechanical cultivation is used very little. Some hand weeding is used where resistant or perennial weeds are present.

Drip irrigation within the emitter area causes more rapid breakdown of herbicides than other irrigation methods. Sprinkler irrigation is often used to set new plantings and for activating preemergence herbicides. Strawberries are then primarily drip-irrigated.

Caneberries

The most frequently planted caneberries in California are boysenberries, raspberries, and olallieberries. Minor acreages of blackberries are grown in the coastal counties of California.

All caneberries suffer competition from annuals (e.g., pigweeds and lambsquarters) and perennials (e.g., bermudagrass and nutsedge) in the Central Valley and from field bindweed in the coastal areas.

Cultural Methods

One method of controlling weeds in caneberries is to prevent weeds from developing by field selection and by sanitation. With the rising cost of field labor and the difficulty of hand weeding with hoes, traditional physical methods can be prohibitively expensive. The use of preemergence weed control in the vine row is considerably cheaper. The centers are usually disked or power tilled and the vine row treated with preemergence herbicides such as oryzalin. Many surface roots are damaged during disking of the centers. Power tilling is somewhat less damaging to shallow boysenberry roots.

Perennials such as bermudagrass are essentially impossible to control once established in the vine row. The berry plants can become so intermingled with the stolon of bermudagrass that they cannot be controlled without injury to the plant.

Chemical Weed Control

In the coastal strawberry production areas, some growers fumigate with methyl bromide and chloropicrin prior to planting, while others follow fields that were planted the previous year to strawberries, which provides some weed control from the fumigation treatment.

Boysenberries and olallieberries are quite resistant to several of the more active preemergence herbicides. They are particularly herbicide tolerant in the finer soils of the Watsonville area where much of California's caneberries grow. In the coarser soils of the central San Joaquin Valley (i.e., Modesto and Fresno), some of the more active herbicides must be either used judiciously or avoided. In these soils, it is more efficient to use herbicides like napropamide or oryzalin. Combinations of these herbicides with low rates of herbicides such as simazine will give season-long weed control with adequate safety. Sethoxydim can be used on raspberries to control grasses.

REFERENCES

Ashton, F.M., H.S. Agamalian and A.H. Lange. 1980. *Weed control in strawberries. Leaflet 2926, rev. August 1980.*

Humphrey, W., A.H. Lange, H.S. Agamalian, V. Voth, P. LaVine, and E. Koch. 1966. *Weed control in strawberries and brambles. Proc. 18th Annual Calif. Weed Conf., January 1966, pp. 54–55.*

Lange, A.H., H.S. Agamalian, V. Voth, and W.A. Humphrey. 1967. *Weed control in strawberries. Calif. Agric. 21(12):8.*

Lange, A.H. 1972. *Postemergence weed control in strawberries. Western Soc. of Weed Sci. 1972 Res. Prog. Rpt.*

Lange, A.H., W.A. Humphrey, and V. Voth. 1973. *Relative phytotoxicity of 16 herbicides to strawberries. A progress report.*

Lange, A.H., V. Voth, R.S. Bringhurst, H.S. Agamalian and L.H. Francis. 1973. *Annual weed control in strawberries. A progress report. #MA-67. November 1973.*

Lange, A.H. 1977. *The control of annual weeds in strawberries. Western Soc. of Weed Sci. Res. Prog. Rpt. March 1977, p. 60.*

Lange, A.H. 1978. *The effect of postemergence sprays on newly planted Tioga strawberry plants. Western Soc. of Weed Sci. Res. Prog. Rpt. Sparks, Nev. March 14–16, 1978.*

GRAPES

by Robert J. Meyer[1]

Acres: Value and Importance

In California in 1987, there were 692,940 total acres of grapes. The greater portion of this acreage was devoted to the production of wine grapes

1. *Weed Control Management, Inc., Bakersfield, CA.*

(323,533), followed by raisin grapes (276,998) and table grapes (92,409). The total value of all grapes produced in California in 1987 was $1,135,950,000. In 1986, grapes ranked third in leading farm products, exceeded only by milk and cream and cattle and calves.

Grape production in California is generally divided into four major growing areas: northern coast, central and southern coast, northern and southern San Joaquin Valley, and Coachella Valley. The type of grapes grown in each of these areas varies with the temperature and climate. The warmer dry areas grow raisins, table, and wine varieties.

Weed Problems

Weed control is an important part of the overall operation in the production of grapes. Weeds are always controlled in the vine row. Weeds compete with the grapevine for nutrients, water, and sunlight. In newly planted vineyards weeds will easily outgrow young vines. As the vineyard comes into production, weeds will interfere with mechanical or hand harvest. This will increase harvest costs and reduce the quality of the grapes.

The presence of weeds in the vineyard may increase insect problems, especially as the weeds dry and the insects move into the green grapevines. Drying weeds will also produce seed that attracts birds which can also cause damage to the grapes. Rodents are attracted to the cover the weeds provide. They multiply and cause damage to the vine trunk, roots, and crop.

Weeds may be used as a cover crop to control soil erosion and dust and to improve water penetration. This vegetation cover should be kept under control by mowing and not allowed to grow in the vine row.

Cultural Control

Varieties

Grapes are produced mainly for three types of markets: fresh, raisins, and wine. Fresh, or table grapes, are grown with much more care in order to produce a grape with appeal to the buyer. Careful production includes grape shoot thinning during the early stage, reducing the number of berries on the bunch by brushing or flower cluster thinning, and later berry and cluster thinning. Next, vine girdling and spraying with gibberellin are done to increase the berry size. The canes are rearranged, and some leaves may be removed to expose the grapes to more indirect light during maturing. Harvesting is selective to obtain good quality, and the grapes are cooled soon after harvesting to extend the market life of the table grapes. As a result of these processes, the cost of producing table grapes is considerably higher than that of raisins or wine grapes.

Most fresh and raisin grapes are grown in the warmer areas because heat is needed to produce sugar in the grapes and for drying the raisins. The majority of the raisins are grown in the San Joaquin Valley. Although the cooler areas are generally thought of as producing most of the wine grapes, about half of them are produced in warmer areas.

All varieties of grapes are started from cuttings, rootings, or hothouse plants. Cuttings are usually started in a healing bed to start the roots, and are then planted directly into the field the same year. Rootings are planted and grown in closely planted rows called a nursery. The following spring, they are dug and planted in the field. Hothouse plants are grown from short cuttings planted in a small container of potting soil. They are grown in the hothouse for several months and are then planted in the field.

Once the young plant has been placed in the field, every effort is made to get the plant growing quickly. Weed competition at this time should be avoided. Staking the vine is delayed until the second year to allow for cross cultivation until the vine grows large enough to tie to the stake. Grapes usually start production in three to four years; however, some growers are pushing for production in the second year. This may weaken the young vine and may even cause the vine to collapse if it is forced to produce when too young. In the past, vineyards produced grapes for more than 80 years. Today, growers produce them for about 25 years, depending on the variety and its production.

Vineyards are usually set out with 12-foot rows to accommodate equipment; however, some are set at 11- or 10-foot rows. The narrower the row, the more equipment damage will occur to the vines. The spacings of vines in the row has been 8 feet, but growers are now planting as close as 5 feet. Closely planted vines will produce a canopy of growth sooner and shade out weeds, but the vines may compete with each other for production space if not properly managed.

Soil Types

Grapes grow better in deep soils that are porous for good drainage. Hardpan and other layered soils can be improved by deep ripping to a depth of 3–4 feet, or slip plowing 5–7 feet deep. Best results are achieved by slip plowing where the vine row will then be at a cross angle. The slip plow not only penetrates layers but also mixes the layers of soil. Soils high in boron or alkali are not good for vineyards, although these elements may be leached out after ripping.

Many grapes are grown in coarse soils, but they may require additional fertilizer and water. Root-knot nematode is generally found in coarse-textured, sandy soils and is controlled prior to planting. Weed control on these coarse soils is done with caution because the lack of clay and organic material may allow some herbicides to be moved deep into the soil by water and may injure the vine.

Wine grape areas have been developed on hillsides. This causes problems from water runoff, erosion, and shallow soils. Ripping hillside soils before planting will improve water penetration and reduce runoff and erosion. Terracing is another method used to prevent runoff and to allow equipment to operate without turning over.

Cultivation

The plow was the first tool used to cultivate vineyards, but this created a plow pan and poor water penetration. Next, the disc was popular, and it still is, although in many soils the disc develops a shallow, impervious layer. Many growers are presently using spring-tooth cultivators, or they are alternately using the spring-tooth cultivator and the disc. In drip-irrigated vineyards the weed knife is being used to undercut weeds in the dry middle. It is a blade that runs in the row center and is operated 2–4 inches under the surface. The spring-hoe weeder is run several inches deep next to the vine. It will destroy small weeds and work around the vine. The soil surface in the vine row is either flat or has been built into a raised berm. This berm is where the weeder works best. The weeder will not control well-established annual or perennial weeds. This is an important tool but must be used properly to avoid injuring the vine.

The French plow, or row plow, will plow the soil out of the vine row. It has a trip arm that hydraulically moves the plow around the vine. After the French plow has been used to plow the vine row, the soil directly around the vine is removed and usually replaced by hand or by running a spring-hoe weeder in the French plow furrow next to the vine. The French plow is an excellent tool to remove bermudagrass clumps out of the vine row. Once the vine row has been plowed, a disc may be used to throw back the soil. A preemergent herbicide, which must be mechanically incorporated, may be included at this time. This is accomplished by directing the spray of several nozzles into the tumbling soil. This produces good mixing of the herbicide in the top 2 inches of soil surface. Several companies are now making a mulcher that works the vine row and hydraulically moves around the vine. These tools do an excellent job of eliminating weeds, tilling the soil, and incorporating herbicides, but are slow in operation.

Once a surface has been treated with a soil herbicide, any cultivation of that area may move the herbicide and reduce its activity. During cultivation of middles, any untreated soil that is thrown onto a treated area may grow weeds. If weed growth does develop, the growth may be sprayed, hand weeded, or cultivated with a spring-hoe weeder.

Irrigation Methods

Basically, there are three types of irrigation: furrow, sprinkler, and drip. Furrow, or flood irrigation is the oldest and least expensive to install. It wets most of the ground, and furrows can be blocked if more water is needed in some areas. The berm area tends to stay drier and, because of shading from the vine, weed growth in the vine row is less than in vineyards under sprinkler or drip irrigation. Incorporation of residual herbicides must depend on rain or mechanical incorporation when using furrow irrigation.

Sprinkler irrigation wets the entire surface, and the amount of water to be applied can be controlled accurately. Sprinkler irrigation is an excellent means of incorporating most surface-applied, residual herbicides. In coarse soils or low-organic soils, simazine or diuron may cause toxicity symptoms on some vines when sprinklers are used. Usually herbicides become adsorbed by clay particles or by organic matter. If these are lacking, the herbicide may move deeper and is picked up by the feeder roots. In areas with these coarse soils, simazine or diuron are avoided or rates are reduced when using sprinkler irrigation.

Drip irrigation is a fine way to conserve water and yet irrigate to a greater depth close to the vine. The row middles are usually kept dry so that little weed growth develops. The row has drip areas on each side of the vine that are kept saturated for a period of time. In this saturated area, herbicides tend to leach and may cause toxicity symptoms on the vines. Many herbicides tend to break down prematurely due to bacterial action and leaching. One of the worst weeds to develop in this area is nutsedge. It becomes very aggressive under this condition and is extremely difficult to control. The addition of a registered herbicide into the drip-irrigation water may help to control weeds in the wet area of the drip system, but will not usually control weeds beyond this area.

Fertilization

Fertilization is accomplished by placing the fertilizer in the soil near the vine's feeder roots. This prevents loss of nitrogen into the air and reduces the loss to weeds. Many growers inject their fertilizer just prior to bud break in the early spring. Others believe that fertilizer applied during the growing season and in the fall influences the features of the next year's buds. Normally, the level of nitrogen available to table grapes should be high until the grapes are well developed, but reduced during July so that quality and color will improve during the final stage. Legume cover crops, planted between grape rows, will not only add nitrogen to the soil from the nitrogen-producing nodules on the roots but also will add organic material to the soil and can improve water penetration. Legumes are planted in every other middle row so that equipment can get into the vineyard for weed control and other cultural practices during wet periods. Broadcast plantings of crops into the vine row is undesirable because the cover crop may become a weed problem.

Chemical Weed Control

The following herbicides are registered for use in California:

- Preemergence—nonbearing: metolachlor, pendimethalin.
  bearing: dichlobenil, diuron, napropamide, norflurazon, oryzalin, oxyfluorfen, pronamide, simazine, trifluralin.
- Postemergence—nonbearing: fluazifop-P, MSMA, sethoxydim.
  bearing: 2,4,-D, glyphosate, paraquat, weed oil.

Frost damage in grapes can be a serious problem. The practice of controlling green growth in the vineyard middles has proven to be beneficial during frost periods. Treating the middles at least 30 days prior to frost with glyphosate, paraquat, or combinations with oxyfluorfen will provide a smooth, firm soil surface with no vegetation, which usually raises the temperature by one or two degrees.

Harvesting Techniques

The quality of handpicked wine grapes is generally better than machine-harvested. Weeds that have grown up into the vine row greatly reduce the efficiency and quality of harvest. Certain poisonous weeds such as American black nightshade could cause problems if quantities of their berries were mechanically harvested with the wine grapes.

Raisin grapes are usually picked by hand and placed on paper to dry. Recent developments show that grapes may be mechanically harvested and laid on a strip of paper to dry. They are then sun dried for raisins. Weeds left in the vine row interfere with this harvest, and the raisins' quality is reduced when weedy trash is present.

Table grapes are handpicked only. Weeds such as horseweed or nettle will greatly interfere with harvest and may reduce the quality.

Rotation to Other Crops

Many vineyards have been treated with residual herbicides for many years. As a result, these herbicides may have a toxic effect on the next planted crop. Simazine and diuron are known to cause injury to many rotational crops. There are two methods which help prevent injury.

- Incorporate 2.3 to 3.5 pounds of activated charcoal for each pound of active chemical ingredient calculated as remaining in the soil. Spread it evenly over the area and incorporate it with a rototiller to a depth of 4–6 inches. Water thoroughly every day for three to four days. Then wait several days before seeding or planting.
- If there is time after the grapes have been pulled out, plow the soil and plant to irrigated grain. The next year, plant another annual crop that contains a heavy amount of organic matter. After two years it may be possible to plant a crop with little or no herbicide injury.

Pruning and Thinning

Grapevines are pruned each year to maintain their vigor and to control their shape. Each spur is pruned leaving two to five buds. This will produce a compact growing area that will protect and shade the crop and also shade out weeds that grow under this canopy. Suckers are always removed because they take strength from the vine. A sucker that is accidentally sprayed with a systemic herbicide may injure the vine.

Summary

Planning is essential for effective weed-control in grapes. First, all weeds in each field are identified and the information catalogued for reference. This will help to develop the weed-control program for the following year. Each field is evaluated separately because different weed problems may require different herbicide programs in each field.

Timing of mechanical cultivation is important. Cultivation is done to eliminate existing weeds, to shape the surface of the vineyard, to incorporate soil herbicides, and to break up soil so that water penetrates. Avoid cultivation of wet soil to prevent clod formation and compaction. However, when the soil is too dry it is too difficult to cultivate.

Timing is also important in applying different herbicides. Annual weeds are sprayed when they are small. If glyphosate is used, perennial grass weeds should be sprayed when they are in the boot to heading stage. Soil-residual herbicides are usually applied during the winter because they need rain for soil incorporation. Mature weeds and trash are removed before residual herbicides are applied. Herbicide tank mixes are used because no single herbicide controls all weeds. When a herbicide is applied, some resistant weeds may continue to grow. To help avoid this, a herbicide with a different weed-control spectrum may be mixed with it.

Current weed-control information may be obtained from product manuals, university bulletins, and periodicals. Professional advisers are also a source of information. Time spent in keeping informed of new methods of cultivation, irrigation, fertilization, and new herbicides will result in a better product for the consumer and more profit for the grower.

KIWIFRUIT

by Clyde L. Elmore[1]

Kiwifruit is a large, deciduous vine that is native to China. Male and female plants are interplanted in the vineyard. Kiwifruit was first planted commercially in New Zealand about 1950 and in California in 1967. It is now grown principally throughout the Sacramento and San Joaquin valleys.

The acreage of kiwifruit in 1987 was estimated at 7,137 acres with a

1. University of California Cooperative Extension, Davis, CA.

value of $20,482,000. The principal production areas are in Butte, Sutter, Glenn, and Yuba counties in the north, and Fresno, Tulare, and Kern counties in the south. Parcels of kiwifruit are generally from 2 to 10 acres, though there are larger plantings.

Establishment costs are high, ranging from $20,000 to $25,000 per acre for the four years to get them into production. Plants are transplanted bareroot or from containers. The T-bar trellis system is extensive and limits access except down the rows. Rows are usually 15 feet wide, and the vines are planted 17 to 20 feet apart down the row.

Nonchemical Weed Control

Weed control is critical around the base of the plant in young plantings because of the early weed competition. However, because the plants are transplanted, complete control is not required. Several methods of weed control are used. The most common one has been mowing the vineyard floor. Usually it is necessary to mow 10 times per year for the first four years to keep weeds under control. By the fourth year there is usually some shade available which will reduce weed growth. The weeds around the base of the vine are usually hand-hoed or, after the vines are three or four years old, a swing mower (a mower that moves in and out of the vine row) is used. In some young plantings, synthetic mulches (polyethylene or polypropylene) have been spread around the base of young plants to suppress weeds and conserve moisture.

Chemical Weed Control

A preferred method of weed control is to use selective herbicides in a strip down the vine row. This keeps the hoe or equipment away from the trunk yet removes most of the weeds. Postemergence and/or preemergence herbicides are available for this method. The area between the rows may be planted to cover crops, or resident plant populations are used and mowed.

Complete chemical control of weeds is used in some vineyards. Preemergence herbicides are applied for annual weeds then followed with postemergence materials for perennial weeds and tolerant annuals as needed to keep the vineyard weed-free. The following herbicides are registered for use in California:

Preemergence	Postemergence
napropamide, N, B	fluazifop-P, N
oryzalin, N, B	glyphosate, B
oxyfluorfen, N,B	paraquat, N, B

N = registered on non-bearing crops in California
B = registered on bearing crops in California

Annual weeds are a common problem in kiwifruit. However, they are usually relatively easily controlled with any of the methods described. In mowed vineyards, annual weeds such as crabgrass, purslane, knotweed, puncturevine, and prostrate spurge may become problems. More commonly the perennial weeds, particularly bermudagrass, field bindweed, dandelion, clover, and yellow nutsedge become problems. Once there is heavy shade from the vines, bermudagrass and field bindweed are not as severe.

In vineyards that are strip treated or completely treated with chemicals, the annual weeds are controlled with preemergence herbicides plus a postemergence material or with repeat applications of contact materials. If there is a low level of management, prostrate spurge, crabgrass, and nutsedge can still become major weed species. Unless additional herbicides are registered for their control, perennial weeds will continue to pose a major problem. Currently, the registered preemergence materials will only control seedlings of some perennial weeds. Repeat postemergence treatments are required to control perennials. With these treatments there is always some concern of injury to vines from careless applications.

REFERENCES

Beutel, J. 1981. Kiwifruit propagation. Mimeo. Univ. of Calif. Coop. Ext.
Beutel, J. 1982. World kiwifruit production. Mimeo. Univ. of Calif. Coop. Ext.
Hasey, J., B. Olson, J. Beutel, and K. Klonsky. 1987. Costs of establishing and producing kiwifruit—Sacramento Valley. Univ. of Calif. Coop. Ext.

OLIVES

by Bill B. Fischer[1]

Olives are one of the world's oldest cultivated crops. They were grown on the island of Crete as early as 3500 B.C. In Greece at the time of Homer, 900 B.C., olive oil was a highly prized luxury for anointing the body. In California, olives were first planted in 1800 from seeds and cuttings brought to the missions from Mexico by the Franciscan padres. Today, California produces 99% of the olives grown in the United States and about 1% of the total world production. Arizona is the only other state where olives are grown commercially. In California, olives are grown in 20 counties, on 33,175 acres of land with a value of $20,482,000. Tulare County has the most acreage (14,299), followed by Tehama (5,194), Kings (3,153), Butte (2,641), and Glenn (2,035). The industry is based on the production of canned ripe olives (black ripe and green ripe). California

1. University of California Cooperative Extension, Fresno County, CA.

supplies only 2% of the olive oil used in the United States; the remainder is imported from Spain and Italy.

The five major varieties of olives produced in California are: Sevillano, Ascolano, Barouni, Manzanillo, and Mission. Orchard-floor management and other cultural practices followed in producing these varieties do not differ significantly, but the methods of harvesting them do.

Soil Types

Olives are grown in California on a wide range of soil types. The trees grow well and produce on rather shallow, moderately acid, or alkaline soils. They will tolerate soils where many other crops will fail; however, prolonged wet, alkaline soils with pH of 8.5 or higher will cause poor growth. Olive trees will grow well in soils relatively high in calcium and boron.

Irrigation

In California, unlike other major olive-producing areas of the world, all commercial olive orchards are irrigated. Olives tolerate prolonged periods of drought and high temperatures. However, for the production of profitable crops of acceptable canning-size olives, irrigation comparable to that required by other tree crops is essential.

In olive orchards in California, irrigation water is applied by furrow, basin flood, contour flood, sprinklers, and by low volume emitters (drip or microsprinklers). Any one of these methods that provides ample, though not excessive, water is acceptable.

Pruning

Moderate annual pruning is commonly practiced by most growers. Harvesting costs are high; therefore trees are kept relatively low to facilitate the use of ladders. Pruning has moderate influence on the management of unwanted, competing vegetation in the orchards. In orchards where branches on the trees are allowed to grow close to the ground (where low skirts are maintained), shading will minimize weed growth under the trees.

Harvesting

At the present time a major portion of the crop is hand harvested. Rough handling of the fruit causes bruises and reduction in grade. Since harvesting represents a major production labor cost, there is increased interest in mechanical harvesting.

Training of the trees for mechanical harvest must begin while young. Generally, the low fruiting branches must be sacrificed (pruned) to accommodate the catching frame.

Orchard Management

Effective weed control is an indispensable component of proper orchard management for the economical and efficient production of olives. In recent years, a limited amount of applied research has been conducted on weed-control practices in olive orchards; therefore, there is a scarcity of information on the performance of newly introduced herbicides in olive orchards. The lack of interest in generating research results may be due to the effectiveness of diuron and simazine, which have long been registered for use.

Weed Problems

Olives are grown in California from Shasta County, in the northern part of the Sacramento Valley, to San Diego County in Southern California. Weeds that infest olive orchards vary greatly from one area of production to another. Summer annual as well as winter annual grasses and broadleaf weeds can be serious problems. Perennial weeds, such as johnsongrass, bermudagrass, field bindweed, and yellow and purple nutsedge, also infest many orchards.

Uncontrolled weeds will interfere with the performance of all necessary cultural operations required for the efficient management of the orchard. In newly planted orchards, weeds can significantly reduce the growth and vigor of young trees. In established orchards, they can increase the frequency of irrigation and the amount of water needed for tree maintenance and optimum production. They can serve as hosts to insects and diseases that attack the tree and fruit. Weeds can interfere with the efficiency of harvest.

Vegetation Management

There are several management systems used to control unwanted vegetation in olive orchards. The more common ones are:

Tillage
Conventional tillage practice is to disk the orchard floor to destroy unwanted vegetation before they use much moisture and nutrients. This usually involves disking and furrowing after every second or third irrigation during the summer. Weeds are allowed to grow during the winter months. Most of the roots of olive trees are in the top 2 or 3 feet of soil. Repeated cultivations or subsoiling destroy much of the root sys-

tem in the top 6–8 inches of soil. Frequent cultivation compacts the soil and reduces movement of water and air into it. Where olive trees grow on shallow or rocky soil, eliminating tillage allows tree roots to completely penetrate the available soil profile.

Sod Culture

Many olive growers, especially in the Sacramento Valley, utilize permanent sod culture. Well-constructed, permanent furrows or border checks are established. If a sprinkler irrigation system is used, the orchard is graded sufficiently to eliminate pockets where water might collect. Vegetation is allowed to grow and its growth is kept under control by repeated mowing.

Properly handled, sod culture permits the root system to be undisturbed; erosion is controlled, and orchard operations may be carried on soon after irrigation or rain. However, sod culture requires both fertilizing and irrigation to satisfy the needs of trees and sod. Perennial grasses and clovers can be planted; however, the resident vegetation makes satisfactory sod. Sod culture is inadvisable if quantities of water or nitrogen are limited.

Strip-nontillage

In many orchards, repeated cultivation can cause soil compaction. Working close to the tree with heavy tillage and mowing equipment can injure the trunks of trees. Treating a narrow band of soil, 2–3 feet wide on each side of the tree rows, with a soil-persistent herbicide can eliminate the need for the use of heavy equipment close to the trees. The area between the rows can be cultivated, or the vegetation can be allowed to grow and repeatedly mowed, as in sod culture, or they can be treated with foliar-applied herbicides to control their growth. Under strip-nontillage management, the orchard is managed similarly to a row crop. Cultivation is performed only in one direction. The need for cross tillage is eliminated, and travel through the orchard with tillage equipment is reduced by 45–50%.

Complete Nontillage

Complete nontillage management, whereby all vegetation is controlled with pre-and postemergence herbicides, is very popular in many olive producing areas of the state. With increasing costs of fuel, equipment, and labor, olive growers find that complete nontillage management is one of the more economical ways to control unwanted vegetation in their orchards. It can be used under all methods of irrigation and on many soils, except those on rolling terrain, where soil erosion is a potential problem.

The soil-persistent and foliar-applied herbicides labeled for use in olive orchards are listed in the following table:

HERBICIDES LABELED FOR USE IN OLIVE ORCHARDS

Preemergence	Postemergence
diuron	glyphosate
napropamide	paraquat
oryzalin	fluazifop-P, N
oxyfluorfen	sethoxydim, N
simazine	

N = non-bearing only

There is limited interest in the registration of new herbicides for use in olive orchards. This may be attributed to the fact that in the United States the total acreage of olives is only 35,000–40,000. However, presently registered herbicides can provide effective control at a relatively low cost.

Planning the Weed-control Program

Prevention is a good beginning in planning a weed-control program. It should start prior to planting the orchard. This is especially important if the area to be planted is infested with perennial weeds.

Established grasses such as bermudagrass and johnsongrass can be eradicated by dehydrating the roots and rhizomes by repeated plowing and disking of the infested area during the summer months, prior to planting the orchard. Systemic herbicides coupled with timely tillage can also be used to control perennial grass as well as perennial broadleaf weeds.

Proper Land Preparation

Proper land preparation is an essential part of a good weed-control program, regardless of the method of irrigation used. In furrow-, contour-, or basin-flood-irrigated orchards, proper leveling and/or grading is essential to ensure uniform water distribution and to avoid excessive ponding. In sprinkler-irrigated orchards, the system should be designed to ensure that the rate of water application does not exceed the infiltration rate of the soil. In areas where water ponds, the herbicides can leach and degrade more rapidly; therefore, their residual activities will be shortened. In areas where the soil remains saturated for prolonged periods, annual and perennial grasses establish and become especially troublesome. Sprangletop and dallisgrass commonly infest poorly drained areas and those where water ponds.

Weed control is more difficult to maintain in drip-irrigated orchards. The continued saturation of the soil adjacent to the emitters favors the rapid breakdown of herbicides through hydrolysis and microbiological degradation. In drip-irrigated orchards, repeated application of foliar-applied herbicides is required for weed control around the emitters.

REFERENCES

Fridley, R.B. et al. Olive harvest mechanization in California. Calif. Exp. Sta., Bull. 855, November 1971.

Hartman, H.T., K.W. Opitz, and J.A. Beutel. Olive production in California, Div. of Agric. Sci., Univ. of Calif., leaflet 2474, October 1980.

Hartman, H.T. and K.W. Opitz. Pruning olive trees in California. Calif. Agric. Exp. Sta., Ext. Ser., Circular 537, January 1966.

Summary of county agricultural commissioner's reports. California 1981 & 1982. Calif. Crop and Livestock Rep. Ser., July 1983.

POME FRUITS (Pears and Apples)

by Dick Bethell[1] and Clyde L. Elmore[2]

In 1987 there were 24,837 acres of pears in California with a value of $64,241,000, and 29,396 acres of apples with a value of $69,550,000.

Approximately 60% of the pear crop is processed into fruit cocktail, fruit mixes, and canned pears. The fresh market absorbs around 20%, and 15–25% is fermented into wine.

Pears are grown primarily in the cooler, deciduous fruit districts of Northern California. The major pear producing counties and their associated acres in 1987 were: Sacramento, 6,465; Lake, 5,451; Mendocino, 3,086; Solano, 2,333; Yuba, 1,479; and El Dorado, 1,120.

The California apple crop is sold 20–30% as fresh fruit, 20–25% canned, 30–50% juiced, and less than 10% dried.

The California apple industry is characterized by diversity in growing areas, varieties, utilization, marketing outlets, and weed problems. Various attempts to organize and promote the industry statewide have been short-lived.

Traditionally, apples have been grown in the coolest of the state's deciduous fruit districts. The major apple producing counties and their associated acres in 1987 were: Sonoma, 5,813; Santa Cruz, 5,237; Kern, 4,230; and Merced, 2,495. Apples are also grown in other coast counties, the Sierra Nevada foothills, and several mountain communities in Southern California. Recent plantings suggest that the San Joaquin and Sacramento valleys are going to become important in apple production, where the Granny Smith variety has been heavily planted.

Annual and perennial weeds can create major problems in the production of both apples and pears. Buckhorn plantain, a common weed

1. University of California Cooperative Extension, El Dorado County, CA. 2. University of California Cooperative Extension, Davis, CA.

in many apple growing areas, acts as the principal host for the rosy apple aphid, the most damaging apple aphid in California. Swamp smartweed has become a very common and competitive perennial in individual apple and pear orchards, while whitetop (hoary cress) is also a problem in certain apple areas.

Cultural Practices

Varieties

One variety, Bartlett, has dominated the California pear industry for many years and currently accounts for 95% of the acreage.

Bartlett pears without a pollenizer require 60°F temperatures to set parthenocarpically. Other pome fruit varieties requiring cross pollination must have bees working in the trees rather than in the weeds.

The questionable economic future for processed Bartletts is causing growers to look for other varieties. The Bosc variety is proving its adaptability and profitability in the late-harvested California pear districts. It is doubtful that the fresh market could accommodate a substantial conversion to this variety. Most other pear varieties are more successfully grown in Oregon and Washington. The high-quality but hard-to-handle Comice variety has potential for growers using direct-to-consumer marketing methods.

The major apple varieties being produced in California and their associated acres in 1987 were: Granny Smith, 9,855; Red Delicious, 3,961; Newton Pippin, 2,904; Golden Delicious, 2,528; Gravenstein, 1,746; and Rome Beauty, 1,074.

Seedlings of Winter Nelis pears, *Pyrus communis,* are usually used for rootstock for new pear orchards. Seedlings often suffer from inadequate weed control and shading when interplanted in mature orchards.

MM 106, MM 111, M7-A, and M 26 are dwarf-type apple stocks in current use. Seedling stock is still used with some spur-type varieties and for replants.

Older pear and apple orchards are widely spaced with pear trees 18–24 feet apart and apples 24 to over 30 feet apart. Square and triangular planting systems are best suited for widely spaced plantings. They are well adapted for mechanical weed-control methods.

New pome fruit orchards are generally more closely planted with 170 to 400 trees per acre. Rectangular plantings are common, with trees spaced 7–14 feet apart within the row and rows 15–20 feet apart. They make earlier production possible but tend to form hedgerows that restrict movement around trees. This limits weed-control options and may restrict other practices such as the use of portable sprinkler systems for irrigation.

Pears require seven or more years to reach profitable production and 10 to 15 years to reach full production. Orchards are long-lived, often producing well for over 75 years.

Apple varieties start to bear economic crops in six to nine years on seedling rootstock. Spur-type strains are available for many of the important varieties, and these start producing at three to four years of age. Clonal rootstocks also encourage earlier production. Profitable production can be achieved several years sooner in orchards using spur types and/or clonal rootstocks.

Most apple varieties are long-lived like pears. A reduction in quality of fruit and wood decay may hasten removal of some apple orchards after 40 years on seedling rootstocks and probably sooner on dwarfing rootstocks.

Soil Types

Pears and, to a lesser extent, apples, can tolerate moderate soil problems. In older fruit districts such as Placer County, stone fruits were located on the higher frost-free and better-drained soil sites. Pears inherited what was left. Pears survive on marginal sites because few trees die of crown rot. But low vigor and poor yields are often associated with high water tables, shallow soils, and poorly drained soils. Weeds are a constant problem in such orchards because they receive ample sunlight there for growth.

Pears and apples are best located on loam soils 4 or 5 feet deep for good performance. While there are some examples of excellent performance on 2-foot soils, they are always accompanied by outstanding water and weed management.

Though there are procedures to reduce the risks of layered and compacted soils, high water tables, and alkali, the already high investment costs and the long wait for profitable production make the selection of marginal sites for pears nowadays very risky and questionable.

The same holds true for apples where clonal, size-controlling rootstocks are employed. These stocks may not have adequate vigor for marginal sites. Apples are quicker than pears in expressing distress to soil-related problems. Trial plantings should be made before stocks are selected or orchards planted on questionable sites. New pome fruit orchards should be "forced" to promote rapid establishment. Once tree growth slows and fruiting commences, it can be difficult to obtain the necessary vigor to bring trees to full size. Thorough weed control and restriction of early cropping are important in maintaining tree vigor on most orchard sites.

Most of the good loam-soil sites in better deciduous fruit districts are already planted. Growers may find it necessary to develop land with steeper slopes. There are about a half-million acres of good loam soils in the 1500–3500-foot elevation zone of the Sierra Nevada foothills. Coastal foothills also contain some excellent loam soils. Slopes of up to 20% can be farmed effectively using good site-management practices.

Tree rows are laid out on cross-slopes to reduce equipment drift downhill without giving up any appreciable degree of erosion control. Slopes of over 20% may be terraced. However, they should be reserved for wine grapes or dwarf apple trees that don't require tall ladders.

Cultivation

Cultivation is a common practice in California pome fruit orchards. It is carried out in dry-farmed Sonoma County apple orchards to prevent weeds from using up soil-stored winter rainfall. Though conserving stored water is important in irrigated orchards, cultivation is practiced for many other reasons as previously discussed. Possibly the most important reason is that well-cultivated orchards perform better than weedy orchards, as was especially noticeable during the time of pear-decline disease where trees declined more rapidly under a sod or weedy regime.

Vigorous orchards tend to shade out weeds, and such orchards are less likely to be affected by weeds. Strip spraying of tree rows and mowing of row centers is a common practice in vigorous orchards.

Sod cover crops have been planted in many orchards at one time or another over the years. Few of these have been maintained as originally planted, either because the sod chosen was accompanied by problems or because it did not establish well over the long term. The search for the ideal, low-growing, low-water-using, problem-free sod is being intensified to provide better erosion control and water management.

Apples can perform well under a sod culture and, where fruit color is a concern, grass sods may enhance color development by lowering the soil nitrogen prior to harvest. Apples with high nitrogen retain their greenish skin color instead of developing a normal yellow or red color on maturing.

Where "grounders" are picked up for juice or fermentation, low-growing sod covers reduce cuts and subsequent rot of fruit that falls on the ground.

Newly planted orchards on square and triangular spacing are usually cultivated in all directions to obtain maximum weed control. Orchards on rectangular spacings or that have drip or permanent-set sprinklers are strip treated with chemicals in the row and mowed or disked in between rows.

Pear and apple growers often have a tracklayer tractor to pull cultivation equipment and spray rigs. Four-wheel drive and high-horsepower wheel tractors are becoming popular for these tasks. Tracklayers are safer on slopes and less apt to get stuck. Discs are more common than the more expensive rototillers. Most growers have equipment for mowing or shredding brush, which is usually drawn by wheel tractors.

Irrigation Methods

Most pome fruit growers prefer sprinklers over surface flooding and drip irrigation, even though many orchards are still flood irrigated. Growers view sprinkler irrigation as providing better irrigation results and tree performance. Permanent under-tree systems provide important flexibility in carrying out many practices.

Sprinklers are usually placed on 12–18-inch risers in between every other tree in every other row. It affords precision in timing and in amounts of water applied during irrigations. It also facilitates spray operations, irrigations between picks during harvest, incorporation of herbicides and fertilizers, and results in some frost protection and uniform soil moisture for cultivation and efficiency in irrigation labor requirements. Because these benefits eventually offset the high costs of system installation, growers are converting to such under-tree systems as they are financially able. Permanent under-tree systems are not well adapted for hedgerow and closely spaced plantings. The new micro- or mini-sprinkler systems appear suitable and economical for such plantings, however. Some over-tree sprinkling systems are used in apples for frost protection and climate modification.

Many portable sprinkler systems are still in use, especially on hillsides. Sprinkler irrigation is recommended for use on slopes to minimize erosion. Sprinklers can also be used to stabilize freshly cultivated soil and to irrigate up a winter cover crop.

In surface flooding, berms and levees can become sites of weed problems. Because it is difficult to incorporate herbicides on berms, perennials such as field bindweed or bermudagrass may become established on them. Cultivation and mowing are more difficult, and sometimes dust is a problem.

Dust can be a very severe problem when drip irrigation is used in pome fruit orchards. Heavy traffic for spraying and other cultural practices creates a dusty soil surface. This can result in dirty fruit, especially around apple stems where, with rainfall, a mudcake can form. Dusty slopes are very erodible, and with drip systems there is no way of irrigating up a cover crop to protect the slopes.

Pome fruits have high water requirements. They are usually harvested late in the growing season and must be irrigated to obtain good fruit size and yields. Deep loams and clay soils with high water-holding capacities may need only a few irrigations a season. In contrast, a foothill orchard with 3 feet of coarse-textured soil may require as many as 12 sprinkler applications a season, which is enough to make almost any weed grow vigorously.

Fertilization

Most pome fruit orchards require one or more applications of nitrogen annually to maintain adequate tree vigor and good fruit set and growth. The best time to apply nitrogen to enhance fruit set and growth is in the late summer or early fall. This is because the tree stores the nitrogen which makes it available the following spring when the demand for nitrogen is high.

A fall application well before leaf drop is very efficient and usually provides an apple tree with its total nitrogen requirements for a year. Applications may be applied to the ground and irrigated in, or fertilizer-grade urea may be sprayed on the foliage immediately after the harvest.

A urea spray gives a combination of benefits. Because nitrogen moves directly through the foliage into the tree, rapid nutrient uptake is ensured. When the old leaves drop, rot organisms can decompose the leaves more rapidly with ample nitrogen for their nutrition. Decomposed leaves produce fewer spores for apple scab infections the following spring. The urea sprays cause trees to defoliate earlier, which may disrupt rosy apple aphids from laying overwintering eggs. The sprays also reduce the amount of nitrogen on the ground surface and the amount available for weed growth. Thirty to 40 pounds of urea are used per 100 gallons of water, and 300–400 gallons are sprayed per acre to achieve these effects.

Spring soil applications may also be used on pears to improve vigor in old trees, trees suffering from pear decline, or orchards on sandy or shallow soils. Fertilizer applications should be made when the trees' shoots are about 4–6 inches long.

Nonbearing pear and apple orchards benefit from several nitrogen applications a season. The first is applied at the 4–6-inch-shoot stage and later applications about a month to a month and a half apart. These applications must be accompanied by good weed control to avoid nitrogen-stimulated weed competition.

Potassium deficiency occurs in most of the major pear districts. Some weeds are heavy potassium users and compete for available soil potassium. They should be controlled on heavy crop years when pear trees have difficulty obtaining their potassium requirements.

Phosphorus deficiency occurs with high iron content in some foothill areas. Pears, apples, and weeds all respond to phosphorus applications under these conditions. Sometimes weeds will even fail to establish on phosphorus-deficient sites. Although phosphorus stimulates weed growth, application may be desirable to promote weed or cover crop establishment for erosion control and organic-matter production.

Chemical Weed Control
The following herbicides are registered for use in California:
- Preemergence—bearing: dichlobenil, diuron, napropamide, norflurazon, oryzalin, oxyfluorfen, pronamide, and simazine.
- Postemergence—nonbearing: MSMA.
      bearing: 2,4-D, glyphosate, paraquat, weed oil.

Harvest Techniques
Nearly all pears are hand harvested to avoid bruise damage, except some

that are fermented. Many apple crops are hand harvested to obtain fresh-market-grade fruit with processing grades sorted out at the packing plant. Pear crops going directly to processors for juice may be mechanically harvested.

Apples and pears are harvested from midsummer until November. Pears are picked when hard and green in color, and they ripen best at comfortable room temperature. Some varieties ripen better after a period of cold storage. Asian varieties are exceptions, achieving optimum eating quality on the tree.

Apples can be picked ahead of optimum eating maturity for storage and later ripening, or they can be harvested tree ripe.

Tall weeds interfere generally with the harvest operation and are mowed or disked prior to harvest. Apple and pear limbs in older orchards are often propped, making vehicular travel difficult. Travel through newer dense plantings is also difficult because fruit-laden branches bend downward into the drive rows.

Rotation to Other Crops

When pome fruit orchards are removed for replanting or planting to other crops, soil-applied, residual applications of herbicides should be stopped two years before removal and replanting. Perennial weeds should also be controlled before planting because they will be harder to cope with and more damaging after planting.

Pruning/Thinning

Pears and apples should be pruned annually to maintain regular bearing, good fruit size, and adequate light throughout the tree. When weed growth is severely depressed from shading, it is evident that tree tops have not been adequately pruned to permit light entry for the health and fruiting of lower tree limbs. These lower limbs produce fruit that is less expensive to grow, and their health should be carefully watched and maintained.

French pear varieties are usually not thinned in California unless a very heavy crop load persists after the June drop. Asian pears are thinned to obtain the large size that brings the best market prices. Many apple varieties require thinning. This is usually done with chemical sprays from during bloom to a month after bloom. Some touch-up thinning is practiced where crops are largely marketed fresh.

Summary

Close attention needs to be given to weed control to obtain the best cropping performance in pears and apples. These fruits have a long growing season and require ample soil moisture to obtain optimum fruit size for the fresh market and high per-acre yields.

Because of the long time required to establish pome fruit orchards, good weed control is especially important in hastening nonbearing trees into production. Better weed management may also be required where size-controlling stocks are used for apples.

REFERENCES

Calif. Tree Fruit Agreement. 1981. California tree fruit agreement, p. 17.

AVOCADOS

by L.S. Jordan[1] and J.L. Jordan[2]

Production

In 1987 California had 75,300 acres of avocados, mostly grown in the south coastal counties of San Diego, Ventura, and Santa Barbara, for a total value of $91,356,000. The two principal varieties are Hass and Fuerte. San Diego County has the largest avocado acreage.

Production problems associated with avocados include erratic fruit yield and diseases; mainly root rot (fungus), sunblotch (virus), and black streak (cause unknown). Irrigation water is expensive and often contains a high chloride content which causes leaf damage. Insects are not generally a problem, but rodents must be controlled.

Weed Control

Weeds are controlled in avocado orchards by mowing, tillage, and herbicides. Mowing is used extensively in San Diego County to establish permanent cover crops. Mowing quickly eliminates broadleaved weeds with an upright growth habit. Regular mowing, plus adequate irrigation, creates an ideal environment for bermudagrass or other sod-forming grass, which becomes well established and crowds out many other low-growing weed species which survive mowing. Even frequent mowing does not adequately lessen water consumption by bermudagrass, and indications are that up to one-half of the irrigation water applied to an orchard covered with a solid stand of bermudagrass is used by the grass. Bermudagrass competes heavily with the trees for plant nutrients. Competition is especially severe in young orchards. Dense shade under older trees inhibits bermudagrass growth. Gophers and field mice are protected by the grass cover. Snails may become a serious problem in mowed orchards. Mowing, especially in strips, may be justified as a

1, 2. University of California, Riverside, CA.

weed-control method on steep hillsides where vegetation is necessary to prevent soil erosion and where tillage is impossible.

Tillage, however, is undesirable in most orchards. Frequent tillage may be used to discourage growth of some perennials. Bermudagrass and dallisgrass remain present but do not form solid sods in frequently tilled soil. However, perennial weeds are spread with tillage. Furthermore, continuous tillage deteriorates soil structure and results in a plow sole which retards water penetration. Most avocado roots are located in the top 2 feet of the soil. The cutting off of roots near the soil surface and plow sole formation severely restricts the soil area in which avocado roots can grow. Erosion is frequently a problem in tilled avocado orchards.

Proper use of herbicides will eliminate many of the problems associated with mowing and tillage. Removal of the weeds eliminates competition for water and nutrients. Bare soil is warmer, and danger from frost injury is reduced. Harvesting, pest control, irrigation, and other orchard practices are more easily accomplished in a weed-free orchard with a firm soil surface.

The following herbicides are registered for use in California:
- Preemergence—bearing: napropamide, oryzalin, and simazine.
- Postemergence—nonbearing: fluazifop-P and sethoxydim.
  bearing: glyphosate, paraquat, weed oil.

Three types of herbicides are used in avocado orchards for weed control; they are contact, soil active, and systemic. Weed oil and paraquat are contact herbicides used to control annual weeds. They are both most effective when weeds are small; the roots die because they are deprived of necessary foliage. Perennial weeds, such as bermudagrass, johnsongrass, and dallisgrass, are very difficult to control with contact herbicides because they can regrow from untreated underground stems called 'rhizomes.' Effective bermudagrass control is obtained when it is sprayed for two years or longer each time the grass reaches about 20% regrowth. Care must be taken to prevent contact sprays getting on the trees because injury may occur.

Soil-active herbicides are used to prevent growth of weeds from seedlings in avocado orchards. Simazine is the most widely used soil-active herbicide in avocado orchards. It is effective only against germinating weed seedlings and has little postemergence activity to foliage. Tolerant weeds in a simazine-treated orchard must be controlled either by mechanical methods or with contact or systemic herbicides.

Glyphosate is the only systemic foliar-applied herbicide used in avocado orchards. It is effective for controlling growing annual and perennial weeds. Since glyphosate is not soil active, it does not injure avocado trees unless it is sprayed directly on green tissue. Many growers use ultra-low-volume application sprayers to apply glyphosate to weeds in avocado orchards.

The combination of herbicides with mowing in strip culture is used on slopes. The strip system leaves mowed vegetation in the row middles, while weeds are controlled in the tree rows with herbicides. A combination of simazine and glyphosate is often used in the nontilled tree row. Simazine controls many weeds arising from seedlings, while glyphosate controls emerged weeds that escape the soil-active herbicide treatment. Thus, strip culture takes advantage of the merits of both mowing and herbicides for weed control in avocado orchards.

REFERENCES

Div. of Agric. Sci., Univ. of Calif., Weed control for orchards, Coop. Ext. Flyer CP-117-1000, March 1976.
Div. of Agric. Sci., Univ. of Calif., Weed management guide for citrus, Leaflet 2979, 1980.
Div. of Agric. Sci., Univ. of Calif., The citrus industry. 1967, 1973.
Div. of Agric. Sci., Univ. of Calif., Economic trends in the California avocado industry, Leaflet 2356, 1980.
International Society of Citriculture. Proc., Benefits and problems of herbicide use in citrus. 1978.

STONE FRUITS (Apricot, Cherry, Nectarine, Peach, Plum, and Prune)

by Edwin E. Sieckert[1]

The stone fruit crops discussed in this section were grown on 248,266 acres in California in 1987. The 1987 acres and their associated values for each individual crop were: apricots, 23,100 acres, $33,451,000; cherries, 11,512 acres, $28,445,000; nectarines, 25,586 acres, $65,545,000; peaches—clingstone, 35,781 acres, $95,612,000; peaches—freestone, 27,503 acres, $68,212,000; plums, 42,752 acres, $75,361,000; and prunes, 82,032 acres, $81,081,000 (for 1986). The major counties, in terms of acreage, involved in stone-fruit production are listed in table 1.

TABLE 1. PRIMARY STONE FRUIT PRODUCTION AREAS IN CALIFORNIA IN 1987

Crop	Major counties
Apricot	Stanislaus, San Joaquin, San Benito
Cherries	San Joaquin
Nectarine	Fresno, Tulare
Peaches	
Freestone	Fresno, Tulare
Clingstone	Sutter, Stanislaus, Yuba, Merced, Butte, San Joaquin
Plums	Fresno, Tulare, Kern
Prunes	Sutter, Yuba, Butte, Tehama, Tulare, Colusa

Weeds are a severe threat to developing stone fruit, and if left unchecked, can reduce the vigor by 50%, which will extend the time re-

1. Monsanto Agriculture Company, Lodi, CA.

quired to reach the first harvest year. Weeds compete for light, nutrients, and water, especially in the first five years. As a tree matures, many weeds are shaded and competition is reduced, but perennial weeds remain a problem. Weeds will interfere with harvest and also cause workers or pickers to select orchards with fewer weeds when choosing work. Cultural practices affect weed control and must be considered prior to planning any programs. This section will discuss varieties, soil types, cultivation, irrigation, fertilization, herbicides, harvesting techniques, crop rotation, and pruning-thinning practices in relation to weed control.

Varieties

Most rootstocks of stone fruits are planted from seed in late winter-early spring, and the varieties are generally grafted in June or T-budded onto the rootstocks. Varieties are grown in special nurseries for about one year and removed as bare-root plantings in November or December. They are sold in bare-root form and planted by the grower in early spring in the orchard. There are too many varieties in just fresh-market peaches or nectarines to allow discussion of the importance of each variety in the stone fruit group. The length of time each is grown in the field varies from 15 to 40 years. Some fresh-market peach varieties may become obsolete eight to 15 years after planting and are then removed. Some orchardists will interplant young trees in an established orchard and will remove the older trees in one to two years. This practice is not ideal as it reduces the amount of light available to the young trees, and secondly, if certain residual herbicides are used and the tree is planted into treated soil, reduced vigor can occur.

Stone fruits, especially fresh-market peaches and nectarines, may be spaced at 7-by-12-foot intervals for hedgerow type of planting. This will bring them into production earlier than normally spaced planting; however, crossdisking will be eliminated as a choice for weed control, and a good program for strip treatment must be established instead. Most stone fruits are planted on square, diamond, or hexagonal spacings of from 16 to 24 feet.

Consideration of spacing is important for effective weed control. Narrow rows or improperly pruned scaffold limbs can cause disc injury or decrease driver safety. Crossdisking is effective, although it leaves vegetation around the tree trunks which injures and destroys young, developing roots close to the soil surface.

Soil Types

Stone fruits require a deep, porous soil with a minimum of restricted layers. Clay pans or alluvial hardpans create poor drainage and require deep ripping prior to tree establishment in both the Sacramento and San

Joaquin valleys. Well-drained, porous, aerated soil is ideal for fast development and continued growth of the stone fruit tree.

Utilization of a sod center composed of natural vegetation or clover provides a minimum of soil erosion from heavy precipitation and provides access during the wet winter months for applications of dormant sprays, fungicides, and herbicides. Weeds grow quickly in the fall, and if wet soil inhibits equipment movement, additional herbicides may be required to control tall weeds. Placement of the herbicides may not be adequate to reach the ground, and poor preemergence control will be evident. Careful planning can prevent low spots that occur due to high water tables. Adequate slope is also important to minimize flooding and standing water which reduces the available amount of oxygen to the roots and may leach some herbicides into the root zone, possibly injuring the tree. Many orchards are planted on raised areas (berms) down the row. These berms keep the tree base out of standing water and reduce the chance of injury from soil-applied herbicides.

Cultivation

Cultivation is practiced in stone fruits to incorporate fertilizer and to reduce weed populations. The disc is the main implement used prior to planting and for crossdisking the orchard for weed control. A newly planted orchard may be crossdisked or disked down the center with a herbicide strip under the row or with a sod center which is mowed. The continual disking of the centers is not cost effective; it reduces the root system and nutrient availability and promotes a disc pan. The remedy for disc pan is to rip alternate rows in the fall to improve water penetration. A selection of sod centers with a herbicide strip or a complete herbicide program will increase root development in the upper soil strata and improve nutrient uptake and tree vigor. A nontillage program reduces dust on fruit and mite buildup on foliage. Dust particles on a fresh-market peach lessen both color and taste quality for the consumer. Continuous cultivation produces a loose, aerated soil which interferes with dormant and foliar spray applications, especially with heavy equipment.

Irrigation

Since there is little rainfall from April to November in California, stone fruit orchards are irrigated to provide water for developing the proper size fruit, flower bud formation, and overall vigor. Local temperatures play a key role in irrigation, as they are 50% higher in the Central Valley than in the coastal areas. Several types of irrigation systems are utilized: contour-flood, border-check, drip, furrow, and sprinkler. Contour-flooding and border-check methods are used where water is inexpensive and on land that has not been graded. Weed-control strip cannot be used, and crossdisking is the only practical tool. Crossdisking increases the annual and perennial weed growth at the tree base. A residual herbicide around the tree base applied in the winter months will reduce annual weeds and the habitat for insects and rodents. A follow-up spray for perennials then can be applied in the early summer months.

Furrow or border-check irrigation requires a special implement, and the border must be removed monthly to maintain a weed-free environment resulting in improved water movement. This method allows weeds to increase significantly around young trees as there is no shade to reduce weed growth. A raised berm may be placed in the tree row to manage water flow and reduce herbicide movement downward.

Sprinkler irrigation is an effective practice for trees because a precise amount can be applied uniformly to supply moisture for developing roots. Proper timing to maintain the tree can be selected by the use of moisture-determining devices such as the neutron probe, gypsum block, or tensiometer. Sprinkler irrigation can provide the exact amount of moisture necessary to activate a soil-residual herbicide and reduce the dependence on rainfall. A disadvantage of sprinklers is that, on coarse-textured soils, they move some residual herbicides downward into the soil profile, resulting in later damage to the crop.

Drip irrigation conserves water and can be used on sloping land. A ⅜- or ½-inch-diameter black polypropylene line is laid down the tree row with one or more emitters placed at each tree base. The advantage of an emitter is that it allows slow and deep watering around the tree. Certain herbicides, however, will degrade faster due to high microbial activity and leaching, leaving weeds to develop around the moist surface areas. Additional spot treatments of postemergence herbicides are required to maintain a weed-free area.

Fertilization

Fertilizers play an important role in the early development of the tree, continued growth, and fruit production as the tree matures. Applications of ammonium nitrate or urea can be made on the orchard floor in the fall after harvest for maximum uptake to increase blossom and fruit set in the spring. Spring applications are made to increase fruit sizing. A sod center with native vegetation requires additional nitrogen input during the growing season as it competes with the tree for nutrient uptake. The clover sod is used on a small number of acres. However, one reason for orchardists' increasing interest in growing clover sod is that it provides a portion of the needed nitrogen. Clover sod is dense when well established and will compete with weeds. But if clover grows into the tree row it may become a severe weed problem in itself. The clover will also withstand mowing. At this time, little is known of the effects of various sod-plant mixes or about how clovers affect growth of other plants.

Herbicides

The following table is provided to indicate those herbicides registered for use in California.

Herbicide	Apricot	Cherry	Nectarine	Peach	Plum	Prune
Preemergence						
dichlobenil	—	B	B	B	B	B
diuron	—	—	—	B	—	B
metolachlor	—	—	B	B	B	B
napropamide	B	B	B	B	B	B
norflurazon	—	B	B	B	B	B
oryzalin	B	B	B	B	B	B
oxyfluorfen	B	B	B	B	B	B
pendimethalin	N	N	N	N	N	N
pronamide	—	B	B	B	B	B
simazine	—	B	B	B	—	—
trifluralin	—	—	B	B	B	B
Postemergence						
2,4-D	B	—	B	B	B	B
fluazifop-P	—	N	N	N	N	N
glyphosate	B	B	B	B	B	B
MSMA	N	—	—	N	N	N
paraquat	B	B	B	B	B	B
sethoxydim	N	N	N	N	N	N
weed oil	B	—	B	B	B	B

B = Bearing
N = Nonbearing
— = Not registered

Harvesting Techniques

Stone fruits are hand or machine harvested, depending on whether they are destined for the fresh or the processing market. Handpicked crops are plums, peaches, nectarines, cherries, and apricots. Machine-picked crops, in order of greatest use, are: prunes, peaches, and apricots. Several pickings of fresh-market fruits into bins for further cooling, washing, sizing, and packaging constitute a major energy output.

Machine-picked prunes or cling peaches require large, canvas, expandable, covered catching frames, plus pneumatic shaker units attached under them. Three types of units are currently in use: (1) roll-out sheets, (2) two-unit catching frame (Kilby-type), and (3) wraparound frame. The shaker unit vibrates the tree quickly, causing the fruit to drop to the canvas from where it is then moved into a field box which is transported to the cannery or dryer.

A weed-free area around the tree trunk is necessary for mechanical and fresh harvest alike. Weeds promote rodent populations which cause unsafe footing for pickers on ladders. Weeds also increase the relative humidity in some orchards with a greater chance of fruit loss due to rot.

Crop Rotation

As an orchard becomes mature or there is a demand for change in a fresh-market variety, an orchardist must consider planning for a new orchard or alternate crop. The use of some residual herbicides should be discontinued during the last one to two years as they may severely reduce vigor on the newly planted tree. Two options are available: (1) in the last one to two years, apply a postemergence herbicide such as glyphosate or paraquat in crops for which they are registered; or (2) use 2.5–3 lb of activated charcoal for each pound of active ingredient calculated to be left in the soil; spread evenly over the soil surface and incorporate to a depth of 4–6 inches; irrigate for three days, and wait several days before planting. The period prior to planting new trees affords an excellent opportunity to control perennial weeds that compete strongly in the first five years of development. Rotation and considerations for planting the new crop may mean success or failure in orchard development.

Pruning

Pruning can affect the incorporation and placement of pre- and post-emergence herbicides on the orchard floor. Pruning is conducted during the dormant period (December to February), and the brush is either shredded or disked into the soil or removed and burned. Pruning operations should be done as early as possible to coordinate with the herbicide application because wet soil and prunings may cause weeds to grow larger and require higher rates of herbicides for control. Brush removal may displace the herbicides as the brush is removed from the orchard or interferes with placement on the soil surface.

In summary, varieties, tillage, irrigation, fertilizers, herbicides, crop rotation, pruning, and harvest must be considered when planning an orchard weed management program. Such planning is one of the prime factors in early development and increased yields in stone fruit.

REFERENCES

Aldrich, Tom, et al. 1978. *Irrigation, fertilization and soil management of prune orchards. Univ. of Calif. Leaflet 21026, pp. 1–20.*
Davis, A.R., S. Severson. 1981. *California fruit and nut acreage, Calif. Crop and Livestock Rep. Ser.*
Lange, A.H., C.L. Elmore, et al. 1981. *Weed control in peach and nectarine orchards, Univ. of Calif. Leaflet, pp. 1–19.*
LaRue, J.H., M.H. Gerdts. 1976. *Commercial plum growing in California, Univ. of Calif. Leaflet 2458, pp. 1–22.*

Meith, C., T. Browne. 1975. *Nontillage and strip weed control in almond orchards,* Univ. of Calif. Leaflet 2770, pp. 1–9.

Ramos, D.E. et al. 1981. *Prune orchard management.* Univ. of Calif. SP 3269, pp. 1–156.

Reed, A.D., A.H. Horel. 1977. *Orchard development costs,* Univ. of Calif. Leaflet 2717, pp. 1–55.

Reuther, W., J.A. Beutel, et al. 1981. *Irrigating deciduous orchards,* Univ. of Calif. Leaflet 2455, pp. 1–7.

Ross, N., A.D. Rizzi. 1976. *Cling peach production,* Univ. of Calif. Leaflet 2455, pp. 1–7.

Security Pacific Bank, 1981, *Calif. Agric.* pp. 1–41.

Stevenson, E.A., A.H. Lange, C.L. Elmore, N.W. Ross. 1974. *Weed control in deciduous trees,* Univ. of Calif. pp. 1–31.

Westwood, M.N. 1978. *Temperate Zone Pomology,* W.H. Freeman Co., pp. 1–427.

CITRUS

by L.S. Jordan[1] and J.L. Jordan[2]

In 1987 there were approximately 265,500 acres of citrus being produced in California. The 1987 acres and values for the three primary citrus types produced in California were: oranges, 185,528 acres, $427,520,000; lemons, 49,365 acres, $152,890,000; and grapefruit, 21,481 acres, $59,127,000.

Commercial citrus production areas of California are located in southern coastal, interior valley, and southern desert regions, each with different climatic and soil conditions. Citrus is planted at elevations ranging from 175 feet below sea level in the southern desert to over 2500 feet above sea level in the Central Valley. Soil texture ranges from coarse to fine. Alluvial valley soils may be deep, while hillside soils may be shallow and fine.

California citrus-growing areas have a wide range of climates. Rainfall occurs mostly from November to April. The southern coastal area has a mild climate with relatively high humidity, mean temperature of 61°F and 10–20 inches of rainfall. Interior valley districts have medium humidity, medium-hot summers, comparatively colder winters, and 10–30 inches of rainfall. The southern desert area has low humidity, low rainfall, and a mean yearly temperature of about 72°F, with a minimum of 13°F and a high of 128°F. Freezing may occur occasionally in California citrus-producing areas.

Cultural Practices

Most California citrus is irrigated six to 10 times a year. Irrigation water is applied by furrows, sprinklers, and low-volume drip systems. Routine care of trees includes minor element sprays, chemical fertilization, chemical and biological pest control, and pruning. Leaf and soil analyses are widely used for fertilization and irrigation guides. Pest control is often accomplished by trained, licensed pest control advisers.

1, 2. *University of California, Riverside, CA.*

Cultural problems include small fruit, irrigation, soil salinity, hardpans in cultivated soil, diseases, rodents, insects, mites, and weeds.

Weed Control

The wide range of soil and environmental conditions under which California citrus is grown provides favorable conditions for diverse weed populations. Weed growth is undesirable because it competes with trees for water and nutrients, provides cover for rodents and insect pests, and interferes with orchard heating, harvesting, and other cultural practices.

Cultural, Physical, and Mechanical Methods
Several methods of cultural weed control are practiced in citrus orchards, depending upon soil, topography, and weed species present. The two practices most widely used are mowing and disking.

Mowing is used in orchards where low-growing ground cover is desired to prevent soil erosion on sloping land. For a few soil types, water penetration is increased by maintenance of controlled plant growth. Continuous mowing encourages establishment and spread of perennial grass sod, which competes with trees for nutrients and water.

Tillage by disking is practiced in citrus orchards to control annual weeds, to bury vegetation, and to suppress perennial weed growth. For annual weed control, tillage is most effective when timed to eliminate each new crop of weeds while the weeds are small and before seeds are produced. Perennial weed control with tillage is more difficult, and eradication is rarely, if ever, obtained. Tillage for perennial weed control is effective for some species provided that it is properly timed to exhaust underground stored food supplies. Infrequent or poorly timed tillage provides short-term weed control and may increase weed populations by bringing buried weed seeds near the soil surface where they can germinate, and by spreading vegetative portions of perennial weeds.

Chemical Control
Herbicides are the most widely accepted, efficient, and economical means of controlling weeds in California citrus orchards. Most chemical weed-control programs are based on the use of preemergent, soil-acting herbicides to control most annual species. Supplemental spraying of perennial weeds and resistant annuals with weed oil or a contact herbicide may be required in summer.

The following herbicides are registered for use on one or more types of citrus crops in California (please refer to individual label directions for specific crop registrations and directions for use):
- Preemergence—bearing: bromacil, diuron, EPTC, napropamide, norflurazon, oryzalin, oxyfluorfen, simazine, and trifluralin.

- Postemergence—nonbearing: cacodylic acid, fluazifop-P, pendimethalin, sethoxydim.

bearing—glyphosate, MSMA, paraquat, weed oil.

Soil-active Herbicides. Soil-active herbicides are applied directly to the soil surface and, to be active, must be carried into the soil either by rainfall or irrigation. In practice, these herbicides are generally applied to most citrus orchards in fall or early winter at the start of the rainy season. In sprinkler-irrigated orchards, they may be applied at any time of the year.

Some herbicides used in citrus orchards are both foliar- and soil-active and can be used to control growing plants as well as germinating seedlings. A surfactant can be added to increase foliar activity, e.g., diuron and bromacil.

Several factors determine the selection of the proper soil-acting herbicide for a particular citrus orchard: the age of the trees, the type of soil, and the variety of weed growth. Either simazine or diuron may be used in plantings one year old or older. On coarse soils or soils of low organic content, simazine affords a greater margin of safety to young citrus than does diuron. At rates used in citrus orchards, both herbicides control *only* seedling weeds of most species. Diuron will control some annual grasses and sensitive broadleaved weeds, such as chickweeds, at more advanced stages of growth. Both herbicides are ineffective against perennial weeds such as bermudagrass, johnsongrass, field bindweed, and nutsedge. Separate spray programs using other herbicides are required in orchards where perennials are established.

In addition to perennials, a number of annual weeds are resistant to either simazine or diuron. Barnyardgrass and many other summer grasses are resistant to simazine. Groundsel and turkey mullein are resistant to diuron. Spurge and puncturevine are poorly controlled by either herbicide. In orchards three years old or older, a commercial mixture of diuron and bromacil is generally more effective than are diuron and simazine in controlling these more resistant species, and provides more effective control in summer. The mixture also provides better control of germinating weeds in furrow bottoms under conditions of heavy leaching during summer irrigation than do other specific herbicides used alone. This combination tends to reduce scattered infestations of bermudagrass and johnsongrass over several years of usage.

Heavy infestations of puncturevine can be controlled by spot or broadcast applications of bromacil applied in late winter or early spring. Treatment over one or two growing seasons may eliminate or greatly reduce puncturevine infestations.

Trifluralin may aid weed control in some situations where simazine, diuron, or bromacil are used.

Contact Herbicides. Contact herbicides are applied as direct sprays to the plant foliage and kill only the aboveground parts of the plant contacted. Weed oil and paraquat can be used to control both the annual and perennial weed growth in the citrus orchard at any time. They are nonselective herbicides and must be kept off the green bark or young trees, the foliage of young trees, and the foliage of all citrus. One or two treatments will generally control all winter annual weed growth. Summer annuals and perennial weeds may require several treatments during the growing season. The effectiveness of both weed oil and paraquat depends upon wetting all plant parts. Because higher volumes are required to control older, mature weeds, it is more economical to spray weeds when they are 1–6 inches tall. Annual weeds should be treated before they produce seed.

When applied to weeds in the seedling stage, weed oil can be used as an oil-water emulsion in mixtures containing from 40 to 60 gallons of oil per 100 gallons of spray mix.

Paraquat affects most, but not all, of the same weeds controlled by weed oil but is usually ineffective against little mallow and common lambsquarters. It has some advantages in storage and handling, but it is a Category I poison and requires special protective equipment. A nonionic surfactant should be used with paraquat spray mixtures. Drift to the tree foliage or adjacent plants should be avoided.

Systemic Herbicides. Systemic herbicides are translocated in either the xylem or phloem of plants and are often more effective for control of perennial weeds. Glyphosate has been most effective when applied to perennial weeds in the fall when weeds are still growing somewhat slowly and are in flower. Late-fall applications, a few days before frost, have also provided good control. Even with optimum conditions, however, it is often necessary to use follow-up applications of this herbicide or a contact application in spring. Spring applications of glyphosate, although sometimes less effective than those in fall, give a margin of control especially on johnsongrass and bermudagrass. Even field bindweed and nutsedge show some control from spring applications.

Care should always be taken to keep herbicide spray off citrus foliage, although citrus has shown more resistance to drift amounts of spray than have some stone fruits and grapes. Spray shields should be used, and low-hanging tree skirts should be pruned up off the ground to prevent injury to citrus foliage.

Perennial Weed Control. Perennial weed control requires a preventive program. Perennial grasses, nutsedges, and field bindweed may thrive during the warm season in some orchards where annuals are controlled with residual herbicides.

In orchards four years old or older, bermudagrass and nutsedges can be controlled by one or two applications of bromacil. Treatments should be made during the late rainy season in furrow-irrigated orchards, but they can be made in summer under sprinkler irrigation. Bermudagrass and nutsedges require treatment rates higher than those used for control of annual weeds. Bromacil should not be used on coarse soils or on soils low in organic matter. Spot treatments require the same degree of precision as do broadcast treatments. Bromacil will control young johnsongrass plants germinating from seed, but it will not control plants established from rhizomes.

Field bindweed, johnsongrass, and dallisgrass require repeated applications of weed oil or paraquat; plants should be sprayed during early stages of growth to reduce the amount of spray material required.

MSMA will effectively control johnsongrass and yellow nutsedge in nonbearing citrus. Three or more repeated sprays are needed for adequate control. For yellow and purple nutsedge, more may be required to control delayed emerging shoots. MSMA will not control bermudagrass but has sometimes given some control of field bindweed.

14

ORNAMENTALS AND TURF

by Clyde L. Elmore[1]

The production of ornamental plants in California for local use and for shipment elsewhere in the United States is a large industry. Plants produced and their 1986 values in California include: deciduous and evergreen trees, shrubs, and vines ($424 million); cut flowers and cultivated greens ($316 million); potted plants for both flowers and foliage ($273 million); bedding plants ($98 million); rose plants ($55 million); and other ornamental propagative material, including bulbs, corms, and flower seeds ($40 million). It is estimated that this production occurs on less than 20,000 acres.

Weed control is a costly, labor-intensive expense in ornamental plant production. It is also an expensive item in the establishment of landscape plant material that gives no return to the producer, user, or home owner. Costs of weeding range from $150 to $250 per acre on some of the cleaner ground for field-grown flowers to $2000–3000 per acre for establishing ground covers along freeways. In a study at one of the container-grown ornamental nurseries (in juniper plantings), the weeding cost for six months without herbicides was $2,418 per acre. When two applications of oxadiazon were used in addition to hand weeding, the cost was reduced to $468 per acre.

Deciduous and Evergreen Trees, Shrubs, and Vines

The majority of ornamental shrubs and trees is grown in containers in California. Many of them are grown in lightweight, artificial or modified soil mixes containing bark, chips, or sawdust. The organic-matter con-

1. *University of California Cooperative Extension, Davis, CA.*

Figure 1. Container-grown ornamentals treated with boom-type spray equipment. Photo courtesy C.L. Elmore.

tent of the soils may range from 3.5% to 30%. The percentage depends upon the amount of sand or soil in the mix compared to organic material. Since the organic material added to the mix varies in particle size, the adsorptive characteristics of the mixes for various herbicides are not constant. It is not known how to match the herbicide rate to the organic content of the mix. Although many shrubs and trees are used in California, many of these lighter-weight containers are shipped out-of-state to eastern markets. Because of the long and favorable growing conditions, some plants are marketed within six months to one year, whereas the slower-growing plants (junipers, etc.) or those that can be moved to larger containers are held into the second season.

Irrigation of the containers may be either by hand watering with hoses or more commonly with overhead sprinklers. Large containers (5 gal to tubs) are often irrigated with a drip system or by hand with hoses. Fertilizer is often injected into the irrigation system to automatically fertilize the plants at the same time that they are being irrigated. Frequent irrigations are required to keep mature plants from becoming water-stressed in the light soil mixes. Accumulated amounts of water used may equal as much as 7 acre-feet per year. When this much water is applied, previously applied herbicides must have the characteristics of being insoluble in water and adsorbing tightly to organic matter to maintain residual control. Herbicides must be used that will control weeds but not get into the water supply and later injure other plants. Registered herbicides that currently meet these criteria include napropamide, oryzalin, oxadiazon, oxyfluorfen, and pendimethalin. Alachlor, metolachlor, and isoxaben are also registered for use in some container-grown plants. When herbicides are applied broadcast over ornamentals, some of the herbicides fall to the soil and control weeds between and under the container areas (fig. 1).

The weed spectrum found in a nursery is usually narrow, and the species tend to be those that propagate within the nursery or arrive as wind-blown seed from peripheral areas. The dominant ones include common groundsel, creeping woodsorrel, prostrate spurge, and lesser-seeded bittercress. Weeds sometimes found but not dominant include sowthistle, horseweed, sprangletop, annual bluegrass, cudweed, fireweed (*Epilobium* spp.), and the lower plant liverwort. One species, pearlwort, has become more common because of its tolerance to oxadiazon. Other preemergence herbicides, such as oryzalin and pendimethalin, will control pearlwort as well as the combination products (pendimethalin plus oxyfluorfen, and oryzalin plus oxyfluorfen). Because of the weed spectrum found, herbicides are frequently used in sequence or they are alternated to control different species.

Many species of annual and some perennial weeds can be found growing under or between containers if the soil or rock base for the containers is not treated with a soil-residual herbicide. Simazine is frequently used on the soil if rock or gravel is used as a base for the containers. If the containers are placed onto compacted soil, dichlobenil, oxadiazon, or oryzalin have been used. These herbicides afford greater safety to broadleaf ornamentals than simazine if roots of rapidly growing plants grow out of the container and into the soil. These same herbicides, with the addition of a contact or translocated material, are used around the periphery of the nursery to reduce weeds and prevent weed seeds from reinfesting the area. Some nurseries use ultraviolet-light-inhibited polypropylene plastic mulches under containers instead of gravel or rock and don't use herbicides. Weeds do not root through these tightly woven materials. However, if soil is spilled, weeds will grow.

Field- and Greenhouse-grown Cut Flowers

Cut flowers are produced both in greenhouses (principally roses, carnations, and chrysanthemums) and outdoors. Common field-grown flowers include marguerite and Shasta-type daisy, Dutch iris, daffodils, heather, gladiolus, baby's breath, statice (perennial and annual), strawflower, bachelor's button, column stock, and many others. Crop culture varies considerably for each crop and by locality. Daisy, heather, baby's breath, statice, strawflower, and bachelor's button are planted as transplants, whereas daffodils, Dutch iris, and gladiolus are started from bulbs or corms. Column stock can be transplanted, or, as with many flowers, may be direct-seeded. Annual flowers used in seed production are also direct-seeded.

Because most flower crops are often grown in small blocks and are from various families and genera, it is difficult to use selective herbicides on them. Annual flower crops are short term and are rotated frequently. Hand labor is used with most flower crops in conjunction with

Figure 2. Weeds are common in field-grown flower crops (left), *and can be controlled with pre- or postemergence herbicides* (right). *Photos courtesy C.L. Elmore.*

mechanical cultivation for weed control. By planting on beds in rows, close mechanical cultivation will control most weeds with a minimum of handwork.

Selective preemergence herbicides are used in some field-grown crops (fig. 2). Several herbicides have been tested on individual crops. These materials must be fitted to each crop and frequently to soil type. The manufacturer's label should be consulted for the latest registration.

Weed control in greenhouses depends greatly on crop and crop culture. Chrysanthemums and carnations are planted as transplants generally in raised beds either on the floor or sometimes on elevated benches. Fumigation of the soil with steam or methyl bromide is frequently practiced before planting, thus controlling diseases, insects, nematodes, and weeds. Methyl bromide–fumigated soil is leached with water before planting carnations so that injury will not occur. Unfumigated beds may be treated with preemergence herbicides (trifluralin for chrysanthemums, and oxadiazon for carnations). Many plantings are hand-weeded until the crop shades the soil.

Greenhouse roses are planted as bareroot plants into artificial soil mixes high in organic matter that provide excellent drainage. There are currently no registered preemergence herbicides for use in greenhouse crops. Hand weeding may be needed to keep the beds weed-free. Glyphosate or diquat have been used as translocated or contact materials for established weeds on the floor or between beds. Simazine and diuron have been used on the dirt floors or between beds. Care must be taken that the herbicides cannot get into the beds or wherever roots of ornamentals can pick them up. There is always a concern when using herbicides in greenhouses. They should be used with care or not at all.

Around greenhouses, weeds are controlled with soil-residual herbicides such as simazine or diuron. If weeds are present, glyphosate is applied to the existing weeds alone or in combination with simazine, diuron, or similar herbicides.

Roses sold as bareroot stock are grown in fields. They are planted as cuttings into paper-covered beds or beds that are treated with pre-plant herbicides in late fall and early winter. The preplant treatment (primarily trifluralin) or a preemergence treatment of oryzalin usually controls annual weeds into the second season of a two-year crop. Oxadi-azon applications are sometimes used in fields where populations of weeds tolerant to trifluralin occur. A minimum of mechanical tillage is used so that the propagation materials are not disturbed. Any disturbance from cultivation reduces the rooting of the cuttings. After the cuttings are es-tablished and grafting has occurred, mechanical cultivation is used be-tween irrigations to control annual weeds and open up the soil for in-creased water penetration. Where weeds or diseases have been severe, fumigation has been used to clean up a field before planting.

Oryzalin and oxadiazon have been used preemergence on estab-lished field grown roses. Metolachlor has been partially effective for nutsedge control in field-grown roses.

Bulb crops grown principally for flowers are Dutch iris, daffodils, and gladiolus. The bulbs are planted in raised beds (30–36 inch spac-ings) and treated with preemergence herbicides. Short-to-medium length (two-to-four-month) residual herbicides are needed for season-long control but should not remain active long enough to affect following crops.

Other flowers such as begonias and calla and Easter lilies are grown for bulbs and not principally as cut flowers.

Field-Grown Nursery Planting

Fruit tree nurseries grow a variety of trees using seed or rootstock cut-tings. These may be two-year crops from planting to lifting. Plantings are usually established in coarse-to-medium-textured soil free of peren-nial weeds. Most growers fumigate prior to planting for disease and nematode control and consequently control many weeds. But if little mallow, field bindweed, California burclover, or sweet clover are pres-ent, they will remain after fumigation and must be cultivated or hand weeded. Preemergence herbicides are usually not used in the first year but have been used in the second year of culture. Weed control in the first season is accomplished with mechanical cultivation.

The same preemergence herbicides are used for ornamental field plantings as for container-grown plants. Oxadiazon, oryzalin, and na-propamide are the principal ones among them. Postemergence herbi-cides are used around the nursery periphery for control of perennial and invasive annual weeds. Selective postemergence materials have been used for grass control in ornamental plantings. Great care is used to keep weeds from seeding and thereby establishing new populations.

Ornamental Landscape Plantings

A large quantity and a broad spectrum of ornamental materials are used for commercial and residential ornamental plantings.

Bedding plants are usually annual, though some perennials are also used. Bedding plants are placed in soil free of weeds at the time of planting, but there may be many seeds or plant propagules remaining in the soil. Because bedding plants are treated as annuals, they may be removed from a site and a second planting of a different species may be planted for growth during the alternate season. A preplant herbicide is sometimes used with little use of preemergence materials.

Ground covers are normally perennial and are planted as rooted transplants from cuttings or sometimes from seed. There is a broad range of prostrate perennial plant material used as ground covers, including Algerian or English ivy, large-leaf ice plant and other ice plants, stonecrop, capeweed, African trailing daisy, junipers, strawberry, spring cinquefoil, and many more. These ornamentals are planted to completely cover the soil.

Weeds must be controlled during the establishment period. This period varies by plant spacing, vigor, and care of the plants. Rapidly closing plants include ice plant, capeweed, and African trailing daisy. Plants that are slow covering include ivy (Algerian and English) and *Hypericum*. Annual weeds are often controlled by the competition from the ground cover once the ornamental is established.

Woody shrubs or trees are perennials frequently planted from 1-gallon containers. Some trees and specimen shrubs are planted from 5-gallon containers or boxes. These plants have large, established root systems within the container. When soil-applied herbicides that inhibit rooting, e.g., trifluralin, oryzalin, or napropamide, are used, plants from containers are less likely to be suppressed than unrooted cuttings, shallow planted cuttings, or rooted liners.

Weeds are major problems in many new plantings and in some mature plantings. In ornamental ground covers, annual weeds usually do not develop in mature plantings unless part of the stand is lost and the cover is opened to weed invasion. Perennial weeds are a common problem in most mature plantings. In commercial plantings there is often no effort made to eliminate perennial weeds before planting. Preemergence herbicides are used shortly after planting rooted ornamental materials (bedding plants and shrubs). A second application following a weeding is usually made two to four months later. Hand weeding is almost always necessary one or more times during establishment.

Perennial weeds pose a major problem in ornamentals. By planning ahead, weeds such as bermudagrass, kikuyugrass, johnsongrass, and, to some extent, field bindweed and yellow nutsedge, can be controlled before planting. Perennial grasses can be controlled in established plantings with selective postemergence materials. There is no selective control measure for broadleaf weeds and nutsedge, thus glyphosate is used as a nonselective herbicide postemergence. With the introduction of diluted forms of glyphosate in retail nurseries, there is widespread dependence on this material for weed control in the home landscape. Home owners look upon it as a panacea. They are sometimes dissatisfied with the degree of control achieved, or discouraged because of damage to ornamentals. Such mishaps are generally caused by misuse of the material, or by lack of understanding about the timing of application.

Annual and perennial weeds are frequently found in woody shrub beds. Annual weeds in many shrub plantings are controlled with mulches, which can include almost all organic materials, e.g., sawdust, rice hulls, cottonseed hulls, barks, composted plant litter, etc. Mulches must be 4–6 inches thick to completely shade out weed seedlings. In some permanent plantings, black plastic mulch is placed on the soil, and bark, wood chips, or rock is placed over the plastic. As dust accumulates or the bark degrades, weeds grow in the surface areas above the plastic. These weeds usually are those species whose seed are easily disseminated by wind.

Newer woven or nonwoven synthetic mulches of polypropylene or polyesters are also being used in the landscape for weed control. Bark or mulches are used over the top of these materials. They allow air and moisture exchange with the soil, which is an advantage over the polyethylene plastic. Some are light or open enough that grass will grow through the mulch.

One of the greatest problems of weed control in the landscape is to get the landscape contractor or home owner to use preventive practices rather than depend on curative measures. Frequently, weeds cannot be controlled selectively with chemicals once the planting has been made because of lack of herbicide selectivity, and hand weeding them must be the primary means of control. The selective, preemergence herbicides DCPA, trifluralin, EPTC, oryzalin, and dichlobenil are available for the control of many weeds in ornamental plantings, but in mixed plantings great care must be exercised in their use.

Another frequently encountered problem is the lack of identification of common weeds in the landscape. Many consumers refer to 'weeds' or 'weeds and grasses' without identifying the particular plants. Control measures with herbicides must be precise, and identification is essential for complete control.

Turfgrass Weed Control

Turfgrass has a direct effect on the lives of many people living in California. Many residential areas and recreational facilities have areas of turf which are viewed or used frequently. In a 1977 survey, residential

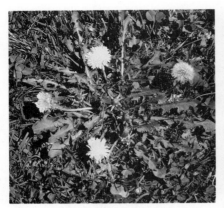 

Figure 3. Dandelion (left) *and dallisgrass* (right), *common perennial weeds found in turfgrass. Photos courtesy C.L. Elmore.*

turfgrass in California was estimated to cover 860,000 acres. An additional 75,000 acres was in golf courses, 42,000 acres in parks, 68,000 acres on school grounds, and 34,000 acres in cemeteries. Roughly 2500 acres of turfgrass were grown for sod. Another 297,000 acres were found around airports, highways, industrial lawns, and motels. All together, turfgrass was grown on 1.38 million acres in California. And since 1977, recreational, sod-growing, and golf-course turfgrass acreages have increased.

Turfgrass adds to the beautification of residential property and institutional buildings. Uniform dense swards also add greatly to the monetary values of these sites. Turfgrass adds to the beauty of sporting events and has been known to reduce the extent of injuries to players.

Turfgrass varies greatly throughout California. In the northern half of the state, the principal turfgrass species are blends of Kentucky bluegrass or perennial ryegrass varieties, or a mixture of the two. Many recreational fields, parks, and home lawns are planted to the newer, finer-leaved, tall fescues. Golf-course greens are predominantly creeping bentgrass. In the Central Valley, common bermudagrass is sometimes found as a turf but more often as a weed.

The central and southern areas are transitional zones where any turf species can be grown. The cool-season grass species (Kentucky bluegrass, perennial ryegrass, and tall fescue) are dominant, but warm-season grasses such as bermudagrass (hybrids and common) also are grown. Lawns of St. Augustine, Zoysia and dichondra can likewise be found. A new species from Australia, *Paspalum vaginatum,* is planted in some southern California lawns.

Interior southern California turfgrasses are predominantly bermudagrass. Hybrid bermudagrasses (Tifgreen, Santa Ana, and Tifway) as well as common bermudagrass are well adapted. More cool-season species are being planted in this zone, particularly turf-type tall fescues, but they require more careful irrigation and more sophisticated maintenance to maintain good swards. Zoysia, St. Augustine, and dichondra, and, more recently, *P. vaginatum,* are also found.

Irregular areas or patches of weeds in turf reduce its beauty and usefulness. Turf weeds recover from mowing more rapidly than most turfgrasses, causing a rough texture in a few days. Annual bluegrass or ryegrass in the winter and tall fescue (in Kentucky bluegrass) or buckhorn plantain in the summer are examples of weeds that must be mowed frequently to maintain a uniform turf species. Weed problems can be reduced or, in certain cases, eliminated with treatments of herbicides prior to turf establishment. Preplant fumigation of a turf site can kill bermudagrass, nutsedge, and other perennials as well as all existing annual plants and many seeds. Postemergence herbicides can be used for turfgrass or weed renovation to establish new lawns. The choice of nonselective treatments must be evaluated carefully. Some have longer soil-residual properties than others and may injure subsequent seedlings of plantings of turfgrasses.

Management Practices

Weedy turf often results from a breakdown somewhere in the management program (fig. 3). Overwatering of turf encourages the establishment of seedlings of crabgrass, annual bluegrass, and other winter annual grasses. Underwatering of cool-season grasses (perennial ryegrass and Kentucky bluegrasses) stresses turf to the point that drought-tolerant broadleaf weeds (narrow-leaf plantains, clover, or knotweed) and bermudagrass become dominant. Soil that is wet for long periods of time, often due to poor drainage, favors red sorrel, curly dock, and annual bluegrass.

Summer weeds tend to establish in cool-season turfgrasses when they are mowed below 1½–2 inches in height. There are instances of prostrate spurge being larger and more frequent in ryegrass mowed at ¾ inch instead of at 1½–2 inches. Weeds will invade bermudagrass when mowed too high (above 1 inch). Mowing height for cool-season grasses (bluegrass, ryegrass, and fescue) is 2 inches, and for bermudagrass below 1 inch, to maximize competitiveness for weed control.

Fertilization requirements (primarily nitrogen) vary by turfgrass species being grown, species adaptation to a particular site, and season. Fertilizing at times or rates not conducive to turfgrass growth encourages weed growth. By maintaining a vigorous, dense turf, weeds such as crabgrass, dandelion, and clovers can be excluded.

Other factors contributing to the decline of turfgrasses, such as excessive wear, diseases, insect damage, soil compaction, and excessive shade, all allow weeds to invade turf. Any condition that exposes the soil surface to additional sunlight tips the competitive balance in favor of invading weed species.

Herbicides are used as tools in turf management where high-quality turf is desired. Selective, preemergence materials are routinely used for control of crabgrass (large and smooth) and annual bluegrass (table 1). Fall applications of these materials control winter annual grasses. When applied in the late winter, some summer annual broadleaf weeds are also controlled.

TABLE 1. HERBICIDES FOR PREEMERGENCE CONTROL IN VARIOUS TURFGRASSES

Herbicide	Bentgrass	Bermudagrass	Kentucky bluegrass	Perennial ryegrass	Tall fescue	Zoysia
benefin	−	+	+	+	+	+
bensulide	+	+	+	+	+	+
DCPA	−	+	+	+	+	+
oxadiazon	−	+	+	−	+	−
pronamide	−	+	−	−	−	−

+ = *tolerant (Note: certain hybrid or fine-leaved varieties are more sensitive to herbicides)*
− = *not tolerant to the herbicides in most areas*

Golf Courses

Many golf-course greens are planted to creeping bentgrasses. The newer greens are usually planted on sand as a base. Older greens are on native soils or are modified with topdressings of sand and peat moss plus turf thatch. When preemergence herbicides are used on sand greens, leaching may occur. This gives reduced control of the principal weed, annual bluegrass. In the central coast area particularly, perennial biotypes of annual bluegrass are found, further reducing control. Annual bluegrass is used sometimes in this area as the principal turf on greens.

Fairways and tees receive less maintenance than greens. Crabgrass is controlled with preemergence materials. Against broadleaf weeds, mixtures of broadleaf herbicides are applied in the spring or fall. In worn or heavy-traffic areas, goosegrass or knotweed may become a problem, as well as any other common annual grasses (annual bluegrass, large or smooth crabgrass, or wild barley). Kikuyugrass has become a common invasive plant along central and southern coastal regions, and some of it has been found in the Central Valley. It is becoming more common in inland southern California. Dallisgrass and tall fescue are the most common clumpgrass weeds in turfgrass. Velvetgrass is also becoming more common in various turf areas, particularly in the coastal regions. Velvetgrass is found in cool-season turfgrass in the northern half of the state when the turf is watered frequently.

Parks, Landscapes, Public Buildings, and School Facilities

Turf areas in parks are frequently on medium-to-low maintenance schedules because of budget restraints. Broadleaf weeds are commonly found in these turfgrass areas. Public concern has been expressed about the use of phenoxy-type herbicides in public access turf areas because of the possible inadvertent contact by children with these herbicides. The superintendents of some parks and school grounds and city officials have responded by restricting the use of these herbicides for the control of broadleaf weeds, though research has shown a good safety record. There are no equally effective materials currently available as substitutes. Broadleaf weeds in the turf at some public buildings and school facilities remain uncontrolled because of the proposed restrictions on the uses of 2,4-D and other phenoxy herbicides.

Since overall levels of fertilizing, watering, mowing, and other practices may be lower on these turf areas, weeds are more likely to invade and become established. However, in most instances, there is less need or demand for a monoculture turf.

Crabgrass is frequently controlled with preemergence herbicides. If application of preemergence crabgrass herbicides is too late, postemergence applications of DSMA or other forms of the organic arsenicals can be used. These same materials effectively control dallisgrass and johnsongrass and suppress nutsedge. Repeated applications are necessary, and frequently some temporary turf injury can be observed. Preemergence herbicides are also used for control of dallisgrass seedlings. Other materials available for suppression and reduction of nutsedge include 2,4-D and bentazon.

Homeowners who demand weed- and pest-free landscapes must provide frequent, diligent maintenance and, where needed, apply pesticides themselves or have them applied by the landscape-gardening and turf-maintenance industry.

Sod Culture and Production

The production of sod in California is a relatively small but rapidly growing industry. Many types are grown, including tall fescues, bermudagrass (hybrids), Kentucky bluegrass, perennial ryegrass, plus blends of Kentucky bluegrass and perennial ryegrass, St. Augustine, Zoysia, Adalaydgrass, bentgrasses, and the broadleaf dichondra.

New turf areas to be planted to sod are usually fumigated before planting. This reduces or eliminates the need of a preemergence herbicide which can suppress growth and slow establishment of the new sod. Kentucky bluegrass, perennial ryegrasses, bentgrasses, tall fescue, and dichondra are established from seed. The warm-season stoloniferous or rhizomatous grasses are vegetatively propagated. Common bermudagrass can be either seeded or stolonized. Second crops of the stoloniferous grasses are grown from strips of sod or from shallow rhizomes.

If the site has not been fumigated prior to planting, all types of weeds may be present. Common problem weeds include little mallow, field bindweed, and clovers. Seeds of these species survive fumigation. Field bindweed also regrows from its deep rootstock. Annual bluegrass and sowthistle are also frequently observed weeds in sod. Sometimes grass sod is grown on ground where cereal grains have grown a year earlier. Cereals then are frequent weeds.

Such postemergence herbicides as 2,4-D, mecoprop, bentazon, or mixtures of 2,4-D, mecoprop, and dicamba have been used for broadleaf weeds. Mowing and some hand weeding are usually adequate to clean up sod fields.

Summary

Weed control in ornamental plant production and management is complex partly because of the many species grown. The same principles that apply in other plant systems apply in these and must be followed. All methods of weed control are usable; but as always when using herbicides, labels must be followed and related to information on existing local conditions.

REFERENCES

Elmore, C.L., V.A. Gibeault, D.L. Hanson, Et. al. 1979. *Turfgrass renovation. Leaflet 21132, Univ. of Calif., Div. of Agri. Sci. Publ.*

Elmore, C.L., and K.A. Hesketh. 1980. *Weed control in the home landscape. Leaflet 21152, Univ. of Calif., Div. of Agri. Sci. Publ.*

Elmore, C.L., W.A. Humphrey, and K.A. Hesketh. 1979. *Container nursery weed control. Leaflet 21059, Univ. of Calif. Div. of Ag. Sci. Publ.*

Gibeault, V. 1979. *Importance of turfgrass in California. Calif. Turfgrass Culture 29(4):25–26.*

SUGGESTED READING

California turfgrass culture. Univ. of Calif. Coop. Ext., Div. of Agri. Sci. Publ.

Elmore, Clyde L., W.A. Humphrey, W.D. Hamilton, and D.L. Hanson. 1985. *Weed control in ground covers. Leaflet 2782, Univ. of Calif., Div. of Agric. Sci. Publ.*

Flower and nursery reports. Univ. of Calif., Coop. Ext. Div. of Agric. Sci. Publ.

Madison, J.H. 1971. *Practical Turfgrass Management. Van Nostrand Reinhold Co., New York. 466 pp.*

Madison, J.H. 1971. *Principles of Turfgrass Culture. Van Nostrand Reinhold Co., New York. 420 pp.*

Schery, R.W. 1961. *The Lawn Book. The MacMillan Co., New York. 207 pp.*

Turfgrass pests. 1980. *Leaflet 4053, Univ. of Calif., Div. of Agri. Sci. Publ.*

Turgeon, A.J. 1980. *Turfgrass Management. Reston Publishing Co., Inc. Reston, VA. 391 pp.*

Weed control in the home garden. 1975. *Brooklyn Botanic Garden, Record Plants and Gardens. 31(2):64.*

15

FOREST, RANGELAND, AND CHRISTMAS TREES

INTRODUCTION

by W.B. McHenry[1]

The land area of California is 100.2 million acres, of which approximately 85% is occupied by forests, grassland, brush, and other wildlands. Nearly 40% of the state is in forests and 43% in rangeland. Some 85% of the water used in California originates in the forests and grasslands. Christmas trees are harvested in timber-thinning operations as well as from single-purpose tree plantations. There is no figure for the total Christmas-tree acreage in California.

In terms of economic value, retail Christmas-tree sales amount to an estimated $80–100 million annually. In 1975, forest and forest-product industries provided 70% of the manufacturing employment in 13 counties (90% in Humboldt County alone), and over 20% of the total employment in 20 counties. The forage produced on the California rangelands has an estimated annual value of $300 million for the production and keep of cattle and some horses, goats, and dairy stock. This feed supplies approximately 60% of the total need for meat animals raised on California farms and ranches.

Common forage and weed species, chiefly winter annual types, possess well-developed survival characteristics for the long summer drought that characterizes the Mediterranean-type climate of California. The vegetative-growth stages culminate in seed production by late March in the south to June in the north. Seeds, dormant in the summer, perpetuate the species when they germinate in the fall following the first soil-moistening rains. Thus the life cycle of principal rangeland forages and numerous weeds of Christmas tree plantations and forests is repeated. The highly developed survival adaptation of naturalized

---

1. University of California Cooperative Extension, Davis, CA.

annuals and of native shrubs and hardwood trees creates significant obstacles to the successful establishment and growth of improved rangeland forages and of conifers grown for Christmas trees or for timber. Where survival of the planted species is achieved, forage yields and tree growth can be severely impeded by weeds, principally from competition for soil moisture. Moisture-stressed plants experience shorter daily and seasonal growing periods because of extended periods of stomate closure, a survival adaptation to reduce moisture loss. Stomate closure in turn reduces carbon-dioxide utilization and carbohydrate production.

Application of practical management practices that reduce competition can result in dramatic increases in survival and growth. In a timber crop requiring 60–125 years to attain harvest, competition from greenleaf manzanita or bearmat (mountain misery), for instance, can reduce boardfoot yields by 20% to 60% or more (Fiske, 1983). Weed-control studies with Monterey pine Christmas trees demonstrated growth increases of 67–78% when herbaceous weeds were controlled compared to unweeded trees. Weedy direct-seeded Monterey pine in a nursery yielded 209 marketable trees per 100 square feet. With weed control, the quality increased to 401 saleable trees per 100 square feet.

On rangeland, few practices are employed for selectively controlling herbaceous competitors in herbaceous forage seedlings, although technology exists to do so. For instance, on a northeastern California range site, applying atrazine to reduce competition from medusahead increased wheatgrass (*Agropyron intermedium* var. 'Amur') from 36 pounds per acre with no weed control to 571 pounds per acre, a 95% increase (Christensen, Young, and Evans 1974).

The categories of vegetation-management methods used in the text— e.g., cultural and physical, mechanical, biological, and chemical—apply equally to irrigated farm commodities and the three commodity or crop categories included in this chapter. Also, as prescribed (controlled) fire is an integral part of weed control in both forest and rangeland, a separate section dealing with the details of this method is included. Prescribed (or controlled) fire has had a long history of use as a management tool for brush control on rangeland.

FOREST VEGETATION MANAGEMENT

By W.B. McHenry[1] and Steven R. Radosevich[2]

Natural seeding and, more commonly, artificial planting have generally kept pace with forest removal by wildfire and logging in recent

1. *University of California Cooperative Extension, Davis, CA. 2. Oregon State University, Corvallis, OR.*

times. There remain, however, extensive areas of approximately 5 million acres that have been burned or were logged in the past. Previously timbered sites now are occupied by brush or hardwood trees and are inadequately stocked with conifers. The conifers that do occur on these brush or hardwood sites—in the Cascades, Sierra, and Coast Range— live under conditions of intense competition and thus accumulate little annual volume growth and are often severely stunted in height. Application of improved management methods to provide release from severe competition through brush removal and replanting on 2.9 million of these previously forested acres alone could increase softwood production in California 10% over a single year.

Conifer regeneration by natural seed fall has often proved inadequate to reestablish forests lost to fire and early-day logging. Natural regeneration, left to its own resources, requires a sequence of biological events that span 60 to 100 years or longer before conifers begin to attain dominance. This lengthy time for conversion back to timber in most of California is largely influenced by the Mediterranean climate characterized by two seasons, a cold precipitation period in the winter, and dry, warm weather during the summer. It is the dry period that imposes difficult environmental constraints on conifer survival and growth. Competition reduction can shorten the rotation at times by decades.

Following forest canopy removal, the initial pioneer plants are typically herbaceous grass and broadleaved species and brush. The appearance of conifers is usually delayed for decades. The abilities of herb, shrub, hardwood tree, or conifer species to prevail on a site with its specific resources (principally adequate soil depth, nutrients, moisture, and light) depend on how quickly they establish and on their innate ability to sur-

TABLE 1. EXAMPLES OF COMMON WEEDY GRASSES, BROADLEAVED PLANTS, AND FERNS BY PLANT FAMILY FOUND ON FOREST SITES

Fern family (Polypodiaceae)
    western bracken
    western swordfern
Figwort family (Scrophulariaceae)
    common mullein
Grass family (Gramineae)

blue wildrye	medusahead
California stipa	orchardgrass
downy brome	perennial ryegrass
Elmer stipa	squirreltail
Italian ryegrass	western stipa

Sunflower family (Compositae)
    Australian burnweed
    bull thistle
    American burnweed
    mulesears

vive, grow, and reproduce. In time, the herbs are forced to yield in the competition for site resources to increased stands of brush and surviving conifers. Common competitors of forest land are listed in tables 1 and 3. Shrub and sprouting hardwood tree cover is tenacious and yields slowly to conifers as they gradually grow above the competing cover and join their canopies to eventually dominate. The relative ability of each successional plant community to dominate has been described as *species-dominance potential*. If two species with different dominance potentials germinate and establish, the one with the highest potential will ultimately replace the other. It should be noted that if a specie with a *relatively* short-term dominance potential (e.g., herbs or shrubs) becomes established first following disturbance it will prevail for many years. Although conifers have a long-term dominance potential, they nevertheless must become established the first year following wildfire or logging if they are to prevail. Post-fire salvage logging, logging debris disposal, and limited seedling-tree availability are often logistic barriers to timely seedling planting.

Weedy species are classified as either herbaceous (grasses or broad-leaved types) or woody (shrubs or hardwood trees). Herbaceous species are annual, biennial, or perennial in longevity.

Herbaceous Competitors

Grass and broadleaved communities (table 1) are among the first successional plants to appear. Although their dominance potential is relatively short-lived, they can exploit site resources for many years if they establish ahead of shrubs, hardwood trees, or conifers. The more limited the moisture during the typical California summer, the more intense the competition between species and individual plants.

Herbaceous cover often encourages high gopher populations that can result in unacceptable conifer mortality in addition to weeds competing with conifers for soil moisture. In a Northwest study, control of western needlegrass, a perennial, with atrazine resulted in survival of

TABLE 2. AVERAGE SURVIVAL OF SEEDLING PONDEROSA PINE PLANTED (1) WITH NEWLY SEEDED FORAGE GRASSES, (2) ONE YEAR, AND (3) TWO YEARS FOLLOWING GRASS SEEDING

| | Survival of transplanted pines by tree planting year | | | Survival of direct-seeded pines by year of seeding | | |
	First year	Second year	Third year	First year	Second year	Third year
Grasses seeded	55%	21%	6%	45%	1%	1%
No grasses seeded	57%	68%	26%	49%	14%	8%

Figure 1. A forest site that has reverted to an earlier successional (shrub) stage as the result of wildfire. Some sites remain dominated by brush for 70 years or longer if left to the time scale of natural succession. Photo courtesy W.B. McHenry.

1,375 ponderosa pine (*Pinus ponderosa* Dougl. ex P. & C. Lawson)/A, as compared to 120 pines/A with no grass control. Losses were attributed to a combination of gopher activity and moisture stress.

Delayed planting following timber fires enables early site occupancy by herbaceous plants. This typically results in heavy conifer mortality if control measures are not practiced. Results given in table 2 illustrate the adverse results of delayed planting of pines on an experimental site that had been seeded in separate sites with three to eight forage grasses. Seedling pines were planted on grass-seeded sites over consecutive years. Deer, rabbit, and mice populations increased with time and added stress to the trees by feeding on them. Presumably, tree predation by animals affected pines in the unseeded controls, though to a lesser extent.

Some grasses can initiate active root growth in the winter or early spring when soil temperatures are still relatively cold. Root growth of downy brome and medusahead is active at 36°F, while ponderosa pine roots grow little at 50°F. Young conifers can therefore be placed at a distinct disadvantage as transpiration rates climb and soil moisture declines during the late spring and into summer.

Woody Competitors

Site domination by shrub and hardwood tree species represents the second successional stage following removal of a closed forest canopy by logging or wildfire (fig. 1). If the forest canopy prior to its removal is sufficiently open to support a lower story of partial brush cover, shrubs will rapidly occupy the site following conifer removal. In this event, grasses may establish minimally, if at all. Successional events of forest lands do not always include three distinct sequential plant communities. There is often an intermixing of communities in varying proportions. As each new community appears, it initially adds to the species diversity.

Shrub occupancy represents the longest lived subclimax stage due to the ability of shrub species to survive and reproduce under exceedingly harsh environmental constraints. Shrub communities are particularly adapted to repeated wildfires. Common shrubs and sprouting hardwood tree species that occupy forest acreage are listed in table 3.

TABLE 3. EXAMPLES OF COMMON SHRUB AND SPROUTING HARDWOOD TREE SPECIES BY PLANT FAMILY GROWING ON PRODUCTIVE FOREST SITES

Birch family (Betulaceae)
    red alder
Heather family (Ericaceae)
    Pacific madrone   pinemat manzanita
    greenleaf manzanita   whiteleaf manzanita
    pine manzanita   salal
Buckthorn family (Rhamnaceae)
    deerbrush ceanothus   snowbrush ceanothus
    mountain whitethorn   varnishleaf ceanothus
Sunflower family (Compositae)
    big sagebrush
Legume family (Leguminosae)
    Scotch broom
Oak or beech family (Fagaceae)
    bush chinquapin   tanoak
    golden chinquapin   California black oak
    shrub tanoak
Rose family (Rosaceae)
    bearmat (mountain misery)
    bitter cherry
    salmonberry

For decades, regeneration foresters have viewed shrub communities as the most difficult to manipulate in reforestation programs. The impact of brush competition on conifer seedlings has been measured in several studies (fig. 2). Douglas fir (*Pseudotsuga menziesii* Mirb.) and white fir (*Abies concolor* Gord. & Glend. Lindl.) seedling survival was observed under conditions of full and partial shade (partial over-canopy of conifers or oaks), and full sun with either bearmat or ceanothus. First-year seedling survival ranged from 80% to 94% in full sun with squawcarpet ceanothus to 1% to 6% in the presence of bearmat. Relatively pure stands of varnishleaf ceanothus often dominate burns and logged sites. In one study this shrub was seen to serve as a protective 'nurse crop' for Douglas fir seedlings for the first year or two. After the fir was established, the shrub species then competed with the forest crop. Height

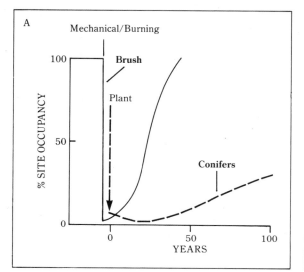

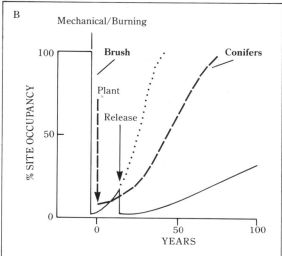

Figure 2. A diagramatic illustration of (A) natural succession, and (B) accelerated succession through the use of a conifer-release method. Management option A allows established root crowns of brush (solid line) to sprout and recapture the site. Option B introduces a control method that interrupts the successional brush stage, allowing the conifer population to dominate many years sooner.

growth of Douglas fir was observed to have increased from 130% to 255% after five years, depending on height class and the ceanothus control measure. On the north coast, Douglas fir basal growth was observed to increase 260% to 451% 10 years following application of control measures to a tanoak overstory as compared to 79% to 94% increase where tanoak was not disturbed.

The competition effect of brush and/or hardwood trees on seedling conifer survival and growth rates is further complicated by competition between the crop trees themselves. More widely spaced trees develop wood volume more rapidly than closely spaced conifers if there is an insignificant shrub population. At one locale, severely retarded 70-year-old ponderosa pine (averaging 1-inch diameter and 8.2 feet in height) were thinned to five different spacings ranging from 6.6 (1000 trees/A) to 26.4 feet (62 trees/A). Understory brush at the widest spacing was still substantially reducing growth 12 years following thinning. Diameter growth continued to be superior where understory shrubs were removed in all but the closest spacing at 12 years following thinning.

In another tree-spacing study, predawn plant-moisture stress was significantly higher in 12-year-old ponderosa pine at a 6-foot spacing than in trees at wider spacing. Needle retention was shorter-lived on the closest spaced trees. Carbohydrate utilization in needle replacement is thus not available for root and top growth.

The influence of older seed trees on the survival of young conifers has been investigated. Naturally regenerated ponderosa pine of three age classes, five, nine, and 13 years, located at four distances from seed trees were monitored. Reduced growth for up to 14 years was observed to the maximum distance from associated seed trees, i.e. 40 feet. Growth loss is reflected in delayed attainment of harvestable wood volumes.

Differences in drought tolerance between conifer species are illustrated in a study where soil moisture was allowed to be depleted to the permanent wilting point. White fir seedlings died first in an average of 35 days, then incense cedar (*Libocedrus decurrens* Torr.) in 44 days, ponderosa pine survived for 65 days, and Jeffrey pine (*Pinus jeffreyi* Grev. & Balf. in A. Murr.) for 95 days. Moisture stress, aggravated by water use by herbs, shrubs, and unwanted trees, can have a dramatic impact on conifer survival and growth. Conifers that are subject to extended periods of moisture stress just above or occasionally to the permanent wilting point will receive less atmospheric carbon dioxide and thus experience lower growth rates restrictions in photosynthesis.

Weed Control Methods

There are several general methods of weed control applicable to forest vegetation management. Often two or more techniques are employed in sequence depending on the type or complex of weeds and the peculiarities of the site.

These methods are cultural, hand, mechanical, biological, prescribed burning, and chemical.

Cultural Methods

Cultural methods include selection of genetically site-adapted conifers seeded or transplanted in a manner that will maximize survival and growth. To realize potential survival and growth usually requires competition control measures. Tree planting density will in time impose distinct influences on the potential development of herbs and shrubs. Closer spacing will ultimately limit understory competition but increase competition among conifers. Wider spacing may require one or more additional competition control measures early in the rotation. Alternatively, wide spacing can reduce cost of later pre-commercial thinning (destruction of small, unmarketable conifers to reduce crowding).

Hand Methods

Control of competition by cultural, physical, or mechanical methods includes the use of hand tools for herbaceous growth or chain saws and portable brush saws to remove woody growth near young conifers. An efficiency study in Oregon of chainsaw brush cutting at three seasons indicated a brush height reduction of 44–56% and 0–16% less canopy ground cover compared to uncut brush one year later. At a more drought-prone Sierra Nevada site, snowbrush ceanothus and greenleaf manzanita regrowth following hand removal had from 37% to 76% less shrub ground cover two years later as compared to uncut brush. Because of relatively high costs of hand brush control, its use has been limited to specialized conditions such as steep slopes or buffer zones near streams. Hand brush and hardwood-tree or sprout cutting becomes the most cost-effective if combined with precommercial conifer thinning or in the preparation of sites for prescribed burning. Hand cutting, like mechanical brush mowing/shredding or fire, offers short-term relief from competition because of the strong sprouting characteristics of nearly all forestland shrub and hardwood-tree species in California.

Mechanical Methods

The most commonly employed method of mechanical control is the use of crawler tractors fitted with brush blades or rakes for preplant weed control. Early-day methods in the 1930s involved removal of alternate strips of brush, approximately 6 feet wide and 20 feet apart, with a bulldozer. Conifers were planted in the brush-free strips. The undisturbed brush, however, continued to provide cover for mice and rabbits who found tree seeds and seedlings attractive food sources. A survey of reforestation programs conducted over 18 years on 27,700 acres beginning in 1930 revealed a survival rate of 40%. Only 3% of the transplanted acreage was adequately stocked at harvest time.

Since 1956, emphasis has shifted to complete brush and debris removal as a standard practice to prepare sites for reseeding or planting. Although significant advances have been made in increasing tree survival and growth, losses remain relatively high. The U.S. Forest Service, for example, has been experiencing about a 39% plantation failure with plantings over the last decade.

Generally, the use of a tractor-mounted brush rake is preferred over that of a conventional blade for brush removal. Less soil is displaced, and more brush roots can be worked out of the ground, allowing them to desiccate. Dry as opposed to wet soil conditions favor removal of underground plant parts and reduce the opportunity for equipment to compact the soil. Initial survival of seedling conifers depends heavily on the efficiency of root and rhizome removal prior to planting. Live underground plant parts commence vigorous sprouting almost immediately and can quickly dominate a plantation. In ease of mechanical uprooting, deerbrush ceanothus and mountain whitethorn are more readily killed than are manzanita species. Chinquapin and bearmat require tedious soil displacement for complete removal and therefore sprout readily.

A number of tractor-mounted brush cutter/shredders have been developed in recent years and have been employed on a limited scale. An advantage of powered brush cutters over brush raking or blading is that little, if any, soil disturbance occurs to aggravate soil erosion. However, since underground parts of shrubs are undisturbed, sprouting quickly restores the canopy density to unacceptable levels if not repeated or supplemented by alternative control methods such as grazing or herbicide application. All wheeled and tracklayer equipment is limited to more gentle terrain for operator and equipment safety.

Mechanical removal of dead brush, often used in combination with prescribed burning, is far more effective than the use of herbicides alone for preparing reforestation sites. Nearly all brush species, with the possible exception of deerbrush or ceanothus, become increasingly tolerant to currently available foliar-active herbicides after they mature.

Neither bulldozing nor hand-scraping of grass-dominated sites in preplant preparation has proved successful beyond the first year.

Biological Methods

Biological control of herbs and shrubs has been accomplished with cattle or sheep grazing. Cattle are far less susceptible than sheep to predation by coyotes and marauding domestic dogs near mountain communities. Livestock prefer the more palatable species of herbs and shrubs. Deerbrush ceanothus and bitterbrush rank among the shrub species most acceptable to livestock. Unfortunately, manzanita, one of the most common successional shrubs, is low in acceptance by livestock and deer. If grazing is employed early in a plantation when manzanita is young, cattle can keep manzanita under control. According to one report, continuous cattle and deer use for four years held brush cover at near 25% that of ungrazed areas. There was little loss in crown diameter and height growth of ponderosa pine, sugar pine (*Pinus lambertiana* Dougl.), Douglas fir, and white fir. To minimize cattle concentrations and conifer injury, it is important to provide readily accessible, diverse forage areas. Additional grazing experiments are needed in order to better understand livestock utilization in forest management. Use and recycling of plant nutrients by livestock may provide a financial return for the forest owner as opposed to the high expenditures involved in other weed-control strategies. Practical problems standing in the way of wider adoption of livestock grazing are unknowns in predicting conifer damage and widely varying palatabilities between shrubs' species and age.

The development of conifer-safe pathogens or insect modes of biological weed control for forest sites may not be environmentally sound for native plant species. Population epidemics extending beyond the targeted zones could have devastating impacts on living systems. There is a need for host-specific biological agents, however, for introduced species such as Scotch broom and common mullein.

Prescribed Burning

In prescribed burning, the threat of fire escape beyond the burn zone is moderated by manipulating fuel moisture on the burn site. Prescriptions include planning establishment of adequate fuel breaks at high-risk points around the perimeter, selection of meteorological conditions to help retain the fire, and the availability of fire-fighting crews and equipment prior to ignition. Crushing brush with a tractor or controlling it with a herbicide application a year ahead of a fire to ensure a dry biomass will result in a more complete burn. Prescribed burning is often the least costly method of disposing of brush biomass. But additional control methods are required in preparing reforestation sites for planting because of the need to control brush seedlings and crown sprouts. Burning is the only practical means of slash disposal on steep terrain.

Fire is used to dispose of logging and naturally occurring wood debris prior to planting; fuel reduction also reduces future wildfire hazard. A counter point in the use of fire is that seeds of fire-adapted shrub and herb species lie dormant for decades until fire alters the seed coat, allowing water uptake and germination. A forested site with low shrub densities may experience population explosions of shrub species following preplant use of fire.

Prescribed burning for control of understory shrubs and hazardous fuel accumulations in established timber prior to logging can reduce competition and thus complement dominance by conifers. However, preharvest burning of forest floor fuels may stimulate germination of brush and herb seeds.

Additional information on this important technique is found later in this chapter.

Chemical Methods

The employment of chemical energy to selectively reduce competition in the production of food, fuel, fiber, and timber crops has been adopted worldwide. The introduction of the phenoxy herbicides in the late 1940s ultimately became of considerable interest to forest managers. The compound 2,4,5-T was found to be particularly useful because it is more effective than 2,4-D on many common shrub species, notably the ceanothus group, tanoak, and the true oaks. Of equal importance was the fact that conifers exhibit appreciably more tolerance to 2,4,5-T than to 2,4-D. At this writing, 2,4,5-T is no longer registered in California.

Forest herbicides can be classified as foliar-active or soil-active. All herbicides currently registered for silviculture uses in California are translocatable, that is, they possess varying degrees of mobility in the plant vascular system. Some are effective at use rates only on dicotyledenous species, i.e., broadleaved (herbaceous or woody); others are effective in controlling both herbaceous narrowleaved and broadleaved species. Application rates and timings are important in maximizing weed control and degree of conifer tolerance. The most common application method is by helicopter, using an application water volume generally of

10 gallons per acre. Directed ground applications with backpack sprayers, however, are coming into increasing use.

Foliage-Active Herbicides

The most effective timing for shrub control with this category of herbicides is during the first or second growing season following development from seed or sprout establishment from root crown or rhizomes. Sensitivity decreases markedly with increased maturity due to either more restricted transport of photosynthates in older tissues or increased cuticular waxes on the leaf surfaces, or both. Attempts to control more mature brush when it is under severe moisture stress during the summer or fall results in poor root-crown kill.

At this writing, 2,4-D in low volatile (heavy) ester forms is the most widely used herbicide principally directed at the suppression of sprouting shrubs. The maximum application rate for competition release is limited to 3 lb ai/A to minimize conifer injury. Pines are the least tolerant, and incense cedar is the most tolerant to 2,4-D. For conifer release, applications are delayed until late summer or fall to help assure conifer dormancy and thus reduced tree susceptibility. This necessary delay is accompanied by reduced shrub sensitivity as well.

If conifer planting is delayed a year or two, more efficacious spring applications and higher use rates can be employed on brush. Also, enhanced foliage and stem penetration can be achieved through the addition of oils such as diesel fuel. These options of higher herbicide rates and addition of oil must not be used over conifers. The same use of higher rates and addition of oil should be followed to desiccate brush a year in advance of prescribed burning. Use of glyphosate, low-volatile esters of 2,4-D, hexazinone, or triclopyr are alternatives in forest brush control.

Asulam is notably effective in controlling western bracken (fern) and can be employed either as a site preparation or conifer-release treatment in the spring or early summer.

Glyphosate offers considerable utility for the control of herbaceous competitors including western bracken and a number of shrub and broadleaved tree species. Deerbrush ceanothus, bearmat, bittercherry, and Scotch broom appear to be among the most sensitive, followed by greenleaf manzanita (very juvenile resprout stage) and snowbrush ceanothus. California chinquapin and mature greenleaf manzanita are least sensitive. To minimize conifer injury under aerial application, the rate must not exceed 2 lb ai/A, and applications should be delayed until conifers have completed their annual growth. Directed ground application with backpack equipment offers more effective timing and flexibility, as direct tree exposure can be reduced.

Triclopyr appears promising for the control of a number of woody competitors. It is very phytotoxic to pines and true firs when they are exposed to topical applications during their growth period. Douglas fir and redwood (*Sequoia sempervirens* (D. Don) Endl.) appear to be more tolerant than other conifers.

Translocatable, foliage-active herbicides have found acceptance for the control of unwanted hardwood trees by application directly into the vascular system. This is accomplished by applying undiluted or partially diluted herbicide into basal stem (trunk) cuts or frills or to the freshly cut surface of stumps. Water-soluble derivatives of 2,4-D, triclopyr, etc., are commonly selected.

Solutions of ester formulations of herbicides applied in oil to the basal portions of shrub and small hardwood tree stems typically are effective alternatives to cut-surface applications. Effectiveness is usually limited to stems with 4-inch diameters or smaller because of penetration problems encountered with thicker bark.

Soil-active Herbicides

The term soil-active implies movement into soil and uptake by roots of species. Rainfall or melting snow is effective in leaching soil-active herbicides into the rooting zone. The period of effective weed control for a given application rate is shortened by environmental conditions that favor leaching to depths below the roots of target species and that hasten microbial degradation in soils. Thus, weed control with this herbicide group is extended under the harsh conditions of frozen soils during the winter season, low precipitation (under 20 inches per year) and relatively short-lived soil moisture in the spring—in effect, a short growing season. The ultraviolet spectrum from sunlight can photodegrade appreciable amounts of many herbicides that remain exposed at the soil surface. This is more likely to occur when precipitation is inadequate and at higher altitudes where solar radiation is strong. See Chapter 7 for a discussion of the influence of soil texture (sand, silt, clay) and organic matter on the movement and fate of herbicides in soil.

Atrazine is applied either preplant or postplant over seedling conifers to control many annuals and some herbaceous perennials. It is effective on weeds either preemergence or postemergence. In contrast, simazine must be applied and leached into the soil before target species germinate, as it has little postemergence activity. Conifers growing on forest soils are quite tolerant of atrazine and simazine.

Hexazinone is another soil-active compound possessing pre-and postemergence activity for control of annual or perennial herbaceous species and several shrubs. Data on conifer tolerance is limited.

Summary

There is abundant evidence from both historical records and research that competition imposes enormous losses in initial conifer seedling survival and subsequent growth. Competition studies on older conifers are few in number, but results to date suggest that growth increments continue to be reduced well beyond the first decade of a tree's life. Planning is essential to circumvent successional events that yield only reluctantly to reforestation efforts. Consideration should be given to tactics that could have long-term benefits if imposed even before the timber is harvested.

Advances have been made in better understanding threshold densities of shrubs that can be tolerated before serious tree growth reduction and high mortality levels occur. However, current guidelines offer only relatively crude insights on which to base forest-management decisions because of the great diversity of site characteristics and the related growth impacts on shrubs and conifers. Forest managers should recognize that there are positive and negative attributes of shrub-conifer associations to be considered in developing their forest-management strategies. New methods of employing and integrating cultural, biological, mechanical, and chemical vegetation-management strategies will further improve conifer seedling survival and growth, as indeed it must to meet future needs. The incentive for increased forest productivity relates in part to the fact that the amount of California forest land is declining as land is diverted to other uses.

REFERENCES

Baron, Frank J. 1962. *Effects of different grasses on ponderosa pine seedling establishment. USDA For. Ser., Res. Note PSW 199.*

Barrett, James W. 1973. *Latest results from the Pringle Falls ponderosa pine spacing study. USDA Forest Service, Pac. N.W. For. & Range Exp. Sta., PNW-209.*

Bartolome, James W. 1981. *Livestock grazing for vegetation management. Proceedings 3rd An. For. Veg. Mgt. Conf.*

Beaufait, William R. 1982. *National forest vegetation treatment. Trends Proc. 4th An. Veg. Mgt. Conf.*

Bolsinger, Charles L. Aug., 1980. *California forests: trends, problems, and opportunities. Pac. N.W. For. & Range Exp. Sta. Res. Bul. PNW-89.*

Calif. Dept. of Forestry. 1979. *California Forest Resources Preliminary Assessment.*

Conrad, S.G. and S.R. Radosevich. 1982. *Growth responses of white fir to decreased shading and root competition by montane chaparral shrubs. For. Sci., Vol. 28, no. 2.*

Crouch, Glenn L. and Erwin Hafenstein. 1977. *Atrazine promotes ponderosa pine regeneration. USDA For. Ser. Res. Note PNW-309.*

Fowells, H.A. and Duncan Dunning. 1948. *A survey of national forest planting in Calif. since 1930. Calif. For. & Ran. Exp. Sta. (20 pp mimeo).*

Gratkowski, H. and P. Lauterbach. 1974. *Releasing Douglas fir from varnishleaf ceanothus. Jour. of For., March, Vol. 72, no. 3.*

Harris, Grant A. and A.M. Wilson. 1970. *Competition for moisture among seedlings of annual and perennial grasses as influenced by root elongation at low temperature. Ecol. Vol. 51, no. 3.*

Heidmann, L.J. 1969. *Use of herbicides for planting site preparations in the Southwest. Jour. of For., July, Vol. 69, no. 7.*

Jarvis, P.G. and Margaret S. Jarvis. 1963. *The water relations of tree seedlings. IV. Some aspects of the tissue water relations and drought resistance. Physiologia Plantarum, Vol. 16.*

Jenkinson, James L. 1980. *Improving plantation establishment by optimizing growth capacity and planting time of western yellow pines. USDA For. Ser. Res. Paper PSW-154.*

McDonald, Philip M. 1976. *Inhibiting effect of ponderosa pine seed trees on seedling growth. Jour. of For., Vol. 74, no. 4.*

Newton, Michael. 1973. *Forest rehabilitation in North America: Some simplifications. Journ. of For., Vol. 71, no. 3.*

Oliver, William W. 1979. *Early response of ponderosa pine to spacing and brush: Observations on a 12-year-old plantation. USDA, For. Ser. Res. Note PSW-344.*

Radosevich, S.R., P.C. Passof, and O.A. Leonard. 1976. *Douglas fir release from tanoak and Pacific madrone competition.* Weed Sci., Vol. 24, no. 1.

Rice, Elroy L. 1979. *Allelopathy—An update.* The Bot. Rev., Vol. 45, no. 1.

Rietveld, W.J. 1975. *Phytotoxic grass residues reduce germination and initial root growth of ponderosa pine.* USDA For. Ser. Res. pap. RM-153.

Roberts, Catherine. 1980. *Second year report—Cooperative brush control study.* Corvallis, OR.

Schubert, Gilbert H. and Ronald S. Adams. 3rd print. 1975. *Reforestation Practices for Conifers in California.* Calif. State Board for For., Div. of For.

Stewart, R.E. and T. Beebe. 1974. *Survival of ponderosa pine seedlings following control of competing grasses.* Proc. West. Soc. of Weed Sci., Vol. 27.

Stone, Edward C. 1957. *Dew as an ecological factor. II. The effects of artificial dew on the survival of Pinus Ponderosa & Associated Species.* Ecol., Vol. 38, no. 3.

Tappenier, J.C, II, and J.A. Helms. 1971. *Natural regeneration of Douglas fir and white fir on exposed sites in the Sierra Nevada of Calif.* Amer. Mid. Nat., Vol. 86, no. 2.

WEED MANAGEMENT OF CALIFORNIA RANGELAND

by W.B. McHenry[1] and A.H. Murphy[2]

California rangeland is a discontinuous and exceedingly diverse agricultural sector of the state occupying approximately 36–46 million acres (36%–46% of the total surface area). Within the boundaries of the rangeland province can be found nearly every combination of topography, climate, soils influence, precipitation, and plant types existing elsewhere in the United States. Although soil resources have a large influence on forage productivity and nutritive value, California climate and weather have an overriding impact. The principal grassland provinces lie between sea level and about 4000 feet elevation.

The widely varying amounts of precipitation from one rangeland sector to another and the high variation from year to year create immense management challenges. Precipitation variables coupled with the annual summer drought exert a significant influence on species and carrying capacity. Only the outer north coast ranges escape the severe desiccation of the summer heat.

The immense diversity of California rangelands can be visualized by considering the piñon-pine-juniper-grass associations ranging eastward from the southern Sierra, thence northward to the Great Basin sagebrush-grass complex, and then on from the oak-grassland communities of the western slopes of the Sierra and Cascade mountains and interior coast range to the north and south coastal uplands. Average annual precipitation ranges from a few inches in the southeast to 80 inches and more on the north coast. Any more general perception of California rangeland as a single entity would be misleading.

The principal type of livestock using rangelands are cattle and sheep. In certain localities, such as the high desert area in Modoc and Lassen

---

1. *University of California Cooperative Extension, Davis, CA.* 2. *University of California, Hopland, CA.*

counties, some bands of wild horses are of importance, and in the central foothills of the Sierra Nevada Mountains brush area, goats use grazing land. Most rangeland is used by livestock as well as by deer with an estimated population of over one million animals.

Historical Changes

The early Spanish travelers, commencing about 1770, and later the European settlers, found a vastly different forage composition than exists today. The herbaceous plant communities of the Central Valley and inter-mountain valleys of the coast ranges were dominated by perennial grasses, principally needlegrasses of the genus *Stipa*. Associated with the needlegrasses were wildrye, junegrass, pine bluegrass, melicgrasses, and deergrass, all perennials. On the north coast ranges, California oatgrass, fescues, and tufted hairgrass largely outnumbered the needlegrasses. A number of annual grasses and broadleaved species added to the floral spectrum and forage diversity.

What has followed since the appearance of early settlers and missions, and more particularly following the discovery of gold, has been a wholesale replacement of the plant species of California rangeland. Importations of crop seed and livestock feed containing weed seed, overgrazing, and the annual summer drought, appear to have combined to replace the original perennials with annuals. To a very large extent the events leading to the replacement of the native flora west of the Cascade-Sierra crest occurred within 20 years, between 1845 and 1865.

A similar major plant community alteration occurred on the rangeland of northeastern California and elsewhere in the Great Basin. The original community was comprised of an overstory of sagebrush species with an understory of perennial grasses such as bluebunch wheatgrass and Idaho fescue in the northern reaches. Thurber needlegrass was prevalent in the more arid sector to the south. By 1890, overuse by livestock had severely depleted the perennial grass community, and adapted annuals again became dominant. Downy brome was the first highly successful alien species. Though utilized to a degree, it provides 10% of the productivity of the species it replaced. Downy brome was followed in the 1930s and 1940s by halogeton, which was in turn followed by medusahead in the 1950s and Russian thistle in the 1960s.

The principal market demand of the growing populations of settlers was for hides and tallow, and stock were bought and sold by the head rather than by weight. As a result, cattlemen managed their herds to maximize numbers of livestock rather than striving for weight gains. In a relatively few years this early-day range utilization took its toll on the native plants. Today, the "new natives" west of the Cascade-Sierra crest include yellow starthistle, redstem and whitestem filarees, mustards, wild radish, wild oat, soft chess, perennial and Italian ryegrass, medusahead, burclover, milkthistle, and a host of other species. However, many of the imported and now dominant annuals proved to be valuable forages, e.g., burclover, the filarees, soft chess, wild oat, ripgut brome, and the ryegrasses. The reader will immediately realize that a good many of the annual "new natives" comprising valued rangeland forage are elsewhere considered weeds.

From a crop perspective, the forage production from the new natives has an estimated value of $300 million for the production or keep of cattle, sheep, and some horses, goats, and dairy stock. This feed supplies approximately 60% of the total requirement for meat animals produced on California farms and ranches. The annual production is about 480 million pounds of meat.

Herbaceous Competition

Seedling survival of improved and resident species is a complex struggle. Some 200 to 300 resident species per square mile have been identified at the San Joaquin Experimental Range in Madera County. Because of the intense competition, an immense proportion of the resident germinating annual plants die prior to reaching maturity. Soft chess population densities averaged 17,433 plants per square foot, foxtail fescue 20,875, and broadleaf filaree 1,048; and additional species averaged 1600 at one study site. Seedling population densities at other locations have been determined to range from 3000 to nearly 14,400 plants per square foot early in the season. Resident competitors have been measured to produce up to 400 pounds of seed per acre.

A number of improved forage grasses and legumes have been introduced to lengthen the productive grazing season and to increase the nutritional quality of forages. Seeded perennial grass species such as hardinggrass possess low seedling vigor, and first-year survival is poor under conditions of severe competition. Perlagrass possesses greater seedling vigor and is more inclined to establish. It is little wonder that the microenvironment must be compatible for a range seeding of 10 pounds or less of seed per acre (0.1 gram per square foot).

The perception of what constitutes a forage species or a weed in the rangeland setting can be quite fickle. Soft chess, wild oat, and filaree if grazed are clearly forage species, but may quickly become weeds if they cause a seedling failure from competition with perlagrass, rose clover, and subterranean clover. In a new seeding the critical stage of clover and grass development is the first growing season. If seeded plants have to compete with an abundance of weeds they will be stunted and seed-set decreased. Competition reduction from simultaneous seed drilling and band-applied paraquat can be seen in table 4. A limitation of delay in seeding to gain postemergence competition control is that the seeding operation must be compressed into a short period of time before declining fall temperatures inhibit plant growth. Once established, hardinggrass or perlagrass provide a good companion forage species for winter annual legumes. Introduction of adapted perennial grasses and annual legumes have nearly doubled forage yields on Sierra foothill ranges. Relatively small reductions in competition can have marked influence on clover and hardinggrass establishment.

Similar problems of successfully establishing perennial wheatgrasses occur following sagebrush removal on the Great Basin rangelands. Downy brome and medusahead grasses exert intense competition for soil moisture on seedlings of improved forage species. A strategy that depletes medusahead seed reserves with atrazine applied a year in advance of seeding has been particularly fruitful. In one study, the use of atrazine at 1 lb ai/A resulted in an herbage yield of 500 lb/A three years after seeding; intermediate wheatgrass comprised 93% of the herbage. With no competition control, wheatgrass made up 9% of the forage.

TABLE 4. ENHANCEMENT OF HARDINGGRASS AND SUBTERRANEAN CLOVER ESTABLISHMENT ON RANGELAND WITH AND WITHOUT COMPETITION CONTROL WITH SIMULTANEOUS DRILLING AND PARAQUAT APPLICATION

Paraquat application method	Number of seeded plants per foot of row	
	hardinggrass	subterranean clover
5.5-inch band	58	148
11-inch band	60	160
100% coverage	75	162
no control	0	96

Woody Competition

Chamise constitutes the most prevalent shrub species in California and infests over 7 million acres. Population densities have been reported from 2,075 to 5100 shrubs per acre. The average per-acre chamise density was 3750. The principal hardwood tree species of consequence are blue, black, interior, live, and scrub oaks. Oak densities may be 100–200 per acre. Blue oak is most common at 300–2500-foot elevation, and black oak at above 2000 feet. Interior liveoak occurs throughout the foothills; scrub oak is a problem species chiefly in Southern California.

On deeper soils where grasses are adapted, well-planned and executed brush management can lead to very significant increases in livestock carrying capacities. The initial phase in brushland management typically focuses on the planning for and use of prescribed burning to dispose of the accumulated above ground biomass. But for a type-conversion from brush to grass to endure, follow-up measures such as a grazing management, additional use of fire, and use of herbicides are necessary. Proper grazing pressure on resprouting shrubs, particularly by sheep, after the herbaceous forage dries will greatly reduce shrub reinvasion. In one study, useable forage on a recently burned chamise range was reduced from 640 lb/A the first year following a burn to 201 lb/A the fourth year as the result of shrub encroachment.

Competition between shrubs and grasses for resources has been demonstrated in the Great Basin as well. The release of Idaho fescue, squirreltail, and western stipa, all native grasses, by killing big sagebrush resulted in a 115% increase in fescue, 379% more stipa, and 748% increase in squirreltail. The composite average forage increase (dry weight) for all three species was 125%. If perennial forage species are not present in sufficient density—no greater than 30 inches apart on the average— best management practices indicate that a seeding operation be combined with big sagebrush or rabbitbrush removal.

Where oak tree populations approach or exceed 100 trees per acre, considerable reduction in herbaceous forage production can occur. Forage yields have been measured from samples taken under oak trees and away from trees. In the first year following application of 2,4-D into blue oak trunks, forage yields increased from 960 lb/A to 2170 lb/A under the tree canopy and 1580 lb/A away from the trees. Yield increases were significant in 11 of the 13 years of study with most of the increase as soft chess.

In addition to increased contributions to forage production for livestock, there are three additional major benefits of significance to California residents:

- Brush modification by prescribed burning greatly reduces the risk of extensive losses from uncontrolled wildfire and the cost of extinguishing them.
- Conversion of brushlands to grass or use of scheduled reburning to retard brush regrowth can provide significant increases in available groundwater.
- Brush thinning often provides improved habitat and feed resources for deer and other wildlife.

An over-zealous program in the past of limiting the extent of brushlands fire has resulted in enormous accumulations of dry brush. Woody fuel accumulations of up to 45 tons per acre have been measured. Grass fuel accumulations, by comparison, are in the range of $1/3$–1 ton per acre. The reintroduction of prescribed burning has only begun to bring back effective brushland management in California.

Over 30 million of the nearly 65 million acres of principal watershed land could be managed to increase water yields. Where dense brush has been replaced with grass, water flow has shown consistent increases of 50% or more. About one-half the increase occurs during the summer-fall seasons when water need is greatest. Greatest increases in flow occur on sites where annual precipitation exceeds 15–20 inches.

Weed control measures play a role in the overall management of rangeland to suppress unwanted woody or herbaceous competition or

TABLE 5. COMMON HERBACEOUS WEEDS OF RANGELAND

Borgae family (Boraginaceae)
    coast fiddleneck
    Douglas fiddleneck
Fern family (Polypodiaceae)
    western bracken
St. Johnswort family (Hypericaceae)
    Common St. Johnswort (Klamathweed)
Goosefoot family (Chenopodiaceae)
    halogeton
    Russian thistle
Grass family (Gramineae)
    downy brome
    medusahead
    nitgrass
Legume family (Leguminosae)
    locoweed
    Scotch broom
Sunflower family (Compositae)

artichoke thistle	milk thistle
Italian thistle	virgate tarweed
Malta starthistle	yellow starthistle

to reduce numbers of poisonous plants. Principal herbaceous and woody species are listed in tables 5 and 6. Weed control methods used in rangeland management are cultural, biological, mechanical, and chemical.

Cultural Methods

Prescribed (controlled) burning is often used as a management "tool" to maintain brush in a younger, more palatable condition and to reduce competition for soil moisture. The California Department of Forestry and Fire Protection is the lead agency in assisting landowners with brush-burning plans and permits. Fire is a natural environmental component of California brushlands and should be viewed as an appropriate method of vegetation management.

Frequent burn cycles of two- to five-years' duration will eventually deplete the landscape of nonsprouting shrub species. However, short-frequency burn strategies have been observed to increase species with horizontal rhizome or rootstocks such as Pacific poison oak, yerba-santa, and globemallow.

When in the planning stage of reseeding for forage improvement, rangeland operators should carefully choose the best adapted selection of grasses and legumes for their site. Use of legume seed innoculum and recommended fertilizers will improve success in establishing new forage seedlings. Successful introduction of perennial grasses has gradually reduced several annual residents such as yellow starthistle.

TABLE 6. COMMON WOODY WEEDS OF RANGELANDS

Beech family (Fagaceae)

blue oak	interior live oak
California scrub oak	scrub oak

Buckwheat family (Polygonaceae)

California buckwheat

Heather family (Ericaceae)

big manzanita	mariposa manzanita
bigberry manzanita	whiteleaf manzanita

Mint family (Labiatae)

black sage
whiteleaf sage
purple sage

Phacelia family (Hydrophyllaceae)

California yerba-santa
wooly yerba-santa

Pine family (Pinaceae)

digger pine
western juniper

Potato family (Solanaceae)

tree tobacco

Rose family (Roseaceae)

chamise
redshank chamise
salmonberry

Sumac family (Anacardiaceae)

poison oak

Sunflower family (Compositae)

big sagebrush	Douglas rabbitbrush
California sagebrush	rubber rabbitbrush
coyotebrush	

Biological Methods

Livestock browsing of young shrub resprouts is a very effective management method to slow brush growth and to utilize additional carbohydrates. Sheep utilize browse much more than do cattle. Browsing typically increases during the summer when the herbaceous forage has dried. Therefore, prescribed burning every two to five years retains the brush growth in a more palatable and nutritious stage for both livestock and deer, as young sprouts have greater acceptance by deer as well.

Mohair and Spanish goats are used very successfully in a few counties to control and kill resprouting brush and oak stumps without depleting herbaceous forage plants. Goats prefer sprouts of scrub oak, chamise, and manzanita, in that order. Grazing may change the chemical composition of these shrub species, which could influence the degree of utilization as grazing time proceeds.

In the past, a number of insects and disease organisms have been carefully researched and released for several weedy pests that include

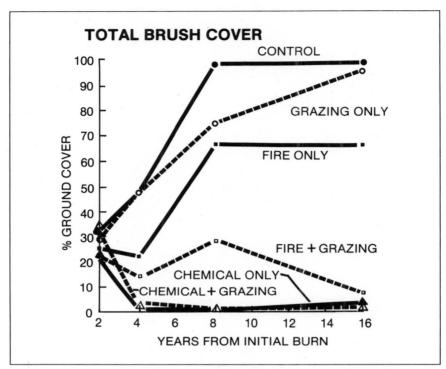

Figure 3. Results of six alternative methods of brush management on rangeland following prescribed (controlled) burning.

rangeland in their distribution. None have had more dramatic effect than the Klamathweed beetle. Common St. Johnswort (Klamathweed) infested over 2 million acres in California, primarily on north-coast rangelands. The release of beetles in 1945 proved to be highly successful. At one initial release site, Klamathweed populations declined from 70% to 15% of the vegetation one year after the beetles had been established.

Another example of biological control was the introduction of insects to control the prickly pear cactus on Catalina Island. Several other insect release programs have been less than successful—for instance, those for the control of Scotch broom and yellow starthistle.

Biological control measures offer the potential for reducing infestations of such widespread introduced rangeland weeds as Scotch broom, medusahead, and Italian thistle.

Mechanical Methods

Relatively little direct weed control with bulldozers or discs is practiced on California rangeland. In northeastern California, heavy discs are employed to remove big sagebrush and to prepare a seedbed for the drilling of wheatgrasses and other improved forages. Occasionally, bulldozers are used to push out oak stumps to prevent resprouting, but expense restricts the use of equipment in this manner. More typically, tracklayer tractors are used to pull heavy anchor chains or ball and chain to break down brush and trees in preparation for controlled burning. Bulldozers are commonly used to prepare fire breaks in preparation for burning.

Limited manual effort is employed to supplement bulldozers in fuel-break construction and maintenance and in ignition of controlled fires. The greatest utility of manual operations is in hand-applied herbicides for tree control wherein a herbicide is applied to a freshly cut stump or into hand-chopped cuts or frills near the tree base.

Chemical Methods

Herbicides offer utility in rangeland management principally to retard or kill brush and resprouting oak stumps. At one time, this could be accomplished with 2,4-D and/or 2,4,5-T or silvex. At this writing, neither 2,4,5-T nor silvex is now registered in California. Therefore, if a type conversion from brush to grass is the management goal, herbicides such as ester derivatives of 2,4-D and/or triclopyr are selected. Shrubs and tree species vary widely in susceptibility to herbicides. Among the most easily controlled are purple and white sage of the south coast and southern Sierra, and sagebrush in northeastern and southeastern California. The most difficult shrubs and trees to control with foliar applications are the oaks, notably interior live oak, scrub oak, and blue oak. Best response to foliage applications in oaks and most resprouting brush is achieved when ground or aerial applications are made to resprouts that are one year old or no older than two. Poison oak and sages are exceptions, as these groups can be controlled when mature. Poison oak requires several annual or biennial applications to be controlled.

Optimum herbicide translocation occurs in woody and herbaceous plants when soil moisture is sufficiently high to avoid plant moisture stress. This applies to cut surface, basal, and foliar applications. The optimum period of translocation is from late April to mid-June but will vary with the presence of spring rainfall, with latitude, and with aspect (south- and west-facing slopes will reach stress conditions earlier).

Summary

In summary, rangeland weed problems are often best managed by integrating grazing flexibility, use of prescribed burning with reseeding, and herbicides when needed (fig. 3). It is hoped that biological strategies with insects and pathogens will play a larger role in the future.

If all these techniques were judiciously applied in accordance with local needs, the management of range vegetation could result in at least a three- to four-fold increase in value. For example, optimized vegetation management on grasslands has a potential improvement value of $50 million, woodland-grass $24 million, and chaparral range $9 million for California's grazing land.

REFERENCES

Adams, Theodore E. 1976. Brush management—Modified & smooth chains. Leaflet 2922, Div. Agr. Sci., Univ. of Calif.

Adams, Theodore E. 1976. Brush management—Straight dozer blade & brush rake clearing. Leaflet 2923, Div. Agr. Sci., Univ. of Calif.

Adams, Theodore E. 1976. Brush management—The ball & chain. Leaflet 2920, Div. Agr. Sci., Univ. of Calif.

Adams, Theodore E. 1976. Brush management—The brushland disk. Leaflet 2921, Div. Agr. Sci., Univ. of Calif.

Biswell, H.H. & C.A. Graham, 1956. Plant counts & seed production on Calif. annual-type ranges. Jour. Range Mgt., vol. 9, no. 3, pp. 116–118.

Burcham, L.T. 1957. California Range Land. Div. of Forestry, Dept. Nat'l. Resources. Grasslands of the Central Valley & Inter-mountains of the Coast Range.

Burcham, L.T. 1973. Fire & chaparral before European settlement. Proceedings of symposium on living with the chaparral. pp. 101–120.

Burcham, L.T. 1975. Climate, structure, and history of California's annual grassland ecosystem. In Love, R. Merton, (ed). The Calif. annual grassland ecosystem, Inst. of Ecol. Publ. No. 7, Univ. of Calif., Davis.

Burgy, Robert H. and Theodore E. Adams, Jr. 1977. Wildlands and watershed management. In Calif. Agr., vol. 31, no. 5, pp. 9–10.

Buttary, R.F., J.R. Bentley, and T.R. Plumb, Jr. 1959. Season of burning affects follow-up chemical control of sprouting chamise. P.S.W.F. & R.S., Res. Note no. 154.

Christensen, M. Dale, James A. Young, and Raymond A. Evans. 1974. Control of annual grasses and revegetation in ponderosa pine woodlands. Jour. Range Mgt., vol. 27, no. 2, pp. 143–145.

Cornelius, Donald R. & Charles A. Graham. 1951. Selective herbicides for improving Calif. forest ranges. Jour. Range Mgt., vol. 4, no. 2.

George, Melvin R., Theodore E. Adams, Jr., and W. James Clawson. 1983. Seeded range plants for Calif. Leaflet 21344. Coop. Ext. Div. Agr. Sci., Univ. of Calif.

Green, Lisle R. 1981. Prescribed burning in the Calif. Mediterranean ecosystem. Proc. of the symposium on dynamics & management of Mediterranean-type ecosystems. Pac. SW For. & Range Exp. Sta., Gen. Tech. reports PSW-58, pp. 464–471.

Heady, Harold F. 1956. Evaluation & measurement of the annual type. Jour. Range Mgt., vol. 9.

Kay, Burgess L. 1966. Paraquat for range seeding without cultivation. Calif. Agr., vol. 20, no. 10, pp. 2–4.

Kay, B.L. 1969. Hardinggrass & annual legume production in the Sierra foothills. Jour. Range Mgt., vol. 22, pp. 174–177.

Kay, Burgess L. and O.A. Leonard. 1979. Effect of blue oak removal on herbaceous forage production in the north Sierra foothills. Symp. on the ecology, mgt., & utilization of Calif. oaks, Claremont, CA.

Kay, Burgess L. and Cyrus M. McKeil. 1963. Preemergence herbicides as an aid in seeding annual rangelands. Weeds, vol. 11, no. 4, 260–264.

Kay, B.L. and R.E. Owen. 1970. Paraquat for range seeding in cismontane. Weed Sci., vol. 18, no. 2, pp. 238–243.

Leonard, O.A. 1956. Studies of factors affecting the control of chamise (Adenostoma fasiculatum) with herbicides.

Leonard, O.A. and C.E. Carlson. 1957. Control of chamise & brush seedling by aircraft spraying. Calif. Div. For., Range Impr. Studies No. 2.

Leonard, O.A., and W.A. Harvey. 1965. Chemical control of woody plants. Univ. of California Agric. Exper. Sta. Bull. 812.

Longhurst, W.M., A.S. Leopold, and R.F. Dasmann, 1952. A Survey of California deer herds their ranges and management problems. Department of Fish and Game, Game Bull. #6.

McKell, C.M. & B.L. Kay. 1964. Chemical fallow aids perennial grass establishment. Calif. Agr., vol. 18, no. 2, pp. 14–15.

Murphy, Alfred H. 1955. Range cover after noxious Klamathweed. Calif. Agr., vol. 9, no. 5.

Murphy, A.H., M.B. Jones, J.W. Clawson and J.E. Street. 1973. *Management of clovers on California annual grasslands. Univ. of Calif. Agric. Exper. Sta. Cir. 564.*

Murphy, Alfred H. and Oliver A. Leonard. 1974. *Chaparral shrub control as influenced by grazing, herbicides, & fire. Calif. Agr., vol. 28, no. 1.*

Reed, A.D. June 1974. *The contribution of range land to the economy of Calif. MA-82.*

Sampson, A.W. and L.T. Burcham. 1954. *Costs & returns of controlled brush burning for range improvement in Northern California. Calif. Div. of For. Range Improvement Studies #1.*

Sampson, Arthur W., Agnes Chase, and Donald W. Hedrick. 1951. *Calif. grasslands and range forage grasses. Bul. 724, Agr. Exp. Sta., Col. of Agr., Univ. of Calif.*

Sidamed, S.R. Radosevich, J.G. Morris, L.J. Koong. 1982. *Nutritive value of chaparral for goats grazing in fuelbreaks. California Agric. vol. 36, no. 5 & 6.*

Sumner, D.C. and R.M. Love. 1961. *Seedling competition from resident range cover often cause of seeding failures. Calif. Agr., vol. 15 no. 2.*

Wright, H.A. 1951. *Why squirreltail is more tolerant to burning than needle-and-thread. Jour. Range Mgt., vol. 24, pp. 277–284.*

Young, J.A., R.A. Evans, & R.E. Eckert, Jr. 1981. *Environmental quality and the use of herbicides on Artemisia grassland of the U.S. Intermountain area. Agr. & Environment, vol. 5, pp. 53–61.*

PRESCRIBED BURNING IN CALIFORNIA

by Richard Winterrowd[1] and Richard Clanton[2]

History

Historically, fire has played an important role in the development of California's wildland ecosystems. Since the early 1900s, prevention and suppression of wildland fires has become routine practice. As fire-suppression practices became more effective, undesirable changes in age and composition of wildland vegetation occurred. In attempting to exclude fire from the wildlands, modern man has been altering a succession that once was established and maintained by periodic occurrences of fire either from natural causes or introduced by primitive man. In so doing, modern man has allowed vast amounts of decaying, overage vegetation in the wildlands.

Of the many adverse effects of this situation, the most spectacular is the extreme fire hazard contributing to large, high-intensity wildland fires during periods of hot, windy weather. Other adverse effects of the exclusion of fire are reduction in available browse and forage for wildlife and livestock, reduced water yield, reduction in quality of wildlife habitat, increase in less desirable forest species, and decreased access to forest and wildland areas.

Today's forest and wildland managers are reintroducing fire as a cost-effective method of maintaining vegetation in conditions that are more ecologically diverse, and of meeting land management goals. By combining fire with other methods of vegetation manipulation, land managers can more effectively duplicate the historically natural occurrences, and shift the ecosystem back toward its natural condition.

1, 2. California Department of Forestry, Sacramento, CA.

Controversy

Controversy still exists on the "to-burn-or-not-to-burn" issue. Both fire exclusionists and pro-burners present strong arguments for their sides. Only by understanding and evaluating both sides of the issue can one draw rational conclusions upon which sound decisions can be made. In brief, the major points presented by each side are as follows:

Arguments Against Burning

- Escape fires are costly and possibly disastrous.
- Deterioration of air quality will occur.
- Fire kills and displaces wildlife.
- Burning may cause an unwanted vegetation-species change.
- Burning will increase soil erosion and stream sedimentation.
- Burning may damage undiscovered archaeological sites.

Arguments For Burning

- Fire reduces volume, continuity, and dead-fuel accumulation of vegetation, which materially increase wildfire threat and intensity.
- Burning will increase water yields.
- Burning will decrease soil erosion and downstream sedimentation by reducing number of large-scale wildfires, replacing them with planned, small fires.
- Fire will improve wildlife habitat.
- Burning increases forage and browse for wildlife and livestock.
- Fire improves long-term air quality due to reduction of wildfires.
- Burning opens access for recreational purposes.

Taken together, the points presented by each side are useful as a guide for evaluating where, when, and under what conditions fire is a viable land-management tool. In cases where the negatives can be mitigated and the benefits achieved in a cost-effective manner, fire becomes a desirable method of attaining management goals.

Definitions

The two types of fire intentionally set for land-management purposes are known as *controlled burning* and *prescribed burning*. Although to many the two terms are synonymous, there are real differences between them primarily in the comparative sophistication of the processes of planning and conducting the operations they describe.

The term *controlled burn* serves to define any vegetation fire set for a beneficial purpose, with the intent of keeping the fire confined to a

Figure 4. Prescribed (controlled) burning (note firebreak) is one common method of reducing undesirable brush biomass and fire hazard in forests and rangelands. Photo courtesy U.C. Hopland Field Station.

specific area by use of control lines or other measures of containment (fig. 4). The process of planning and conducting the burn is usually limited to only those measures necessary to prevent the fire from escaping and to achieve the desired results. This type of burning has been conducted for years in California, primarily by ranchers for the elimination of brush encroaching on rangelands. Timber interests also use fire to eliminate logging-slash residues, and farmers burn crop residues in preparation for subsequent planting.

Prescribed burning, on the other hand, is a relatively new method of conducting burns. Years of research on the effects of fire on the various elements of forest, range, and watershed ecosystems have provided land managers with a sounder information base from which fire-use decisions can be made. When goals have been identified and the total effect on the area of the burn evaluated, the land manager can, by use of modern fire-predictive technology, write a prescription for conditions of weather and fuel that will produce fire behavior necessary to achieve the desired results. Thus, the term *prescribed burning*.

Benefits

Prescribed burning is conducted for a variety of purposes. It must be remembered that even though each burning operation has a primary purpose, many other benefits may be achieved at the same time. Some of the more common land-management purposes for burning are:

Fire Hazard Reduction

One of the most beneficial uses of prescribed burning is to reduce volume and composition of vegetative material in forest, brush, and rangelands. Fire intensity increases in direct proportion to the increase in volume of fuel available. Prescribed burning not only reduces the volume of fuel, but materially reduces the dead-to-live ratio which contributes to flammability.

Silviculture

Prescribed burning can be used to accomplish many silvicultural objectives. Site preparation for natural regeneration seeding or planting may be achieved by removing slash accumulations, shrubs, or grass from the site by use of fire. Various frequencies, intensities, and seasons of fires favor different plant communities. Species management may be implemented through correct timing and intensity of prescribed burns. Excessive or unwanted understory vegetation may also be removed by prescribed burning.

Disease and Insect Control

Prescribed burning has been used to some extent for controlling disease or pest infestation in forest stands. Although high-intensity wildfires damage trees and make them susceptible to insect attack, judicious use of prescribed fire will often effectively rid sites of infected slash or trees. Spores of the deadly *Fomes annosus* fungus, which infects pine root systems, are killed by exposure to wood smoke.

Wildlife-Habitat Management

Prescribed burning, particularly in heavy chaparral-type fuels, is an effective method of opening up areas for access by several species of wildlife such as deer, quail, and raptors. Certain species of brush or vegetation can be regenerated or caused to resprout, thus providing increased browse. If this is done in small patches (2–10 acres), the adjacent unburned areas provide escape cover and more diverse habitat accommodating many species.

Range Management

Due to overgrazing and fire exclusion, much usable rangeland has become overgrown with brush species. Proper use of prescribed burning, combined with follow-up practices such as seeding and erosion control, can reverse this situation and return many of these areas to satisfactory grazing conditions.

Recreation and Access

Prescribed burning is a method of maintaining forests in an open, park-like condition. Thick undergrowth of vegetation can be reduced to provide access and more open vistas, pleasing to the eye, as well as offering greater safety from destructive wildfires.

Safety
As we become more knowledgeable about the factors (weather, fuel, topography) affecting fire behavior, the likelihood of fire-related death and property and/or resource damage will be diminished as a result of better planning in both fire suppression and prescribed burning.

From an analysis of 40 tragic or near-tragic fires, researchers identified six common denominators that significantly affected fire behavior in each incident. These common denominators are:
- Fatal incidents occurred in relatively small fires or isolated sectors of large fires.
- "Unexpected" winds were often recorded as the major cause of "erratic fire behavior."
- Most fires appeared relatively harmless prior to blow-ups.
- Blow-ups generally occurred in deceptively light fuels.
- Fires ran uphill in "chimneys, gullies, or steep slopes."
- Aircraft adversely modified fire behavior by causing localized wind disturbances (vortices).

These common denominators can be a real asset to fire managers for planning and developing operational procedures in combating wildland fires and conducting prescribed-burn projects. From a consensus of several experienced wildland fire fighters, in addition to the information provided by the above tragedy-fire analysis, the following situations were identified that clearly signal "Watch out":
- You are building a line downhill toward a fire.
- You are fighting a fire on a hillside where rolling material can ignite a fire below you.
- The wind begins to blow, increase, or change direction.
- The weather turns hotter or drier.
- You are on a fireline located within heavy fuel, with unburned fuel between the fire fighter and the fire.
- You are in an area where the topography and/or cover makes travel difficult and slow.
- You are in unfamiliar country.
- You are in an area where the fire fighters are not familiar with local factors influencing fire behavior.
- You are attempting a frontal assault on a fire with "pumpers."
- Frequent spot fires are crossing the line.
- You cannot see the main fire, and you are out of communication with anyone who can see it.
- You do not clearly understand your assignment or instructions.
- You are drowsy and feel like taking a nap near the fire line.
  Awareness of the above, potentially dangerous situations helps

protection agencies to develop safer methods for dealing with fire. The two major wildland fire fighting organizations in California are currently operating under the guidance of *10 standard fire fighting orders:*

1. Keep informed of fire-weather conditions and forecasts.
2. Know what your fire is doing at all times—observe personally, use scouts.
3. Base all action on current and expected behavior of fire.
4. Provide escape routes for everyone and make them known.
5. Post a lookout when there is possible danger.
6. Be alert, keep calm, think clearly, act decisively.
7. Maintain prompt communication with your crew, your boss, and adjoining forces.
8. Give clear instructions and be sure they are understood.
9. Maintain control of your crew members at all times.
10. Fight fire aggressively but provide for safety first.

Prescribed burning, using fire in a controlled set of environmental conditions for designated purposes, is providing new and veteran fire fighters with the best training possible. This experience teaches safe, thorough control of fire and a better understanding of fire behavior.

With minor variations among regulatory agencies, prescribed burns conducted in California must include an approved safety plan completed by the fire boss or prescribed fire manager. An additional plan is required if firing is to be done by an aerial source (e.g., helitorch). Included in these safety plans is a list of nearest burn-treatment facilities and contingency plan: a statement of who does what if the fire escapes.

The following outline enumerates the responsibilities of the prescribed-fire boss on all burn projects:

Prescribed-fire boss will:

Be responsible for performance, safety, and welfare of all employees participating in the project.

I. Preburn (Tailgate Session):
    A. Prepare plan of action.
    B. Organize forces according to plan.
        1. Assign personnel equipment.
        2. Organize forces into needed units.
    C. Define techniques of ignition to assure good fire behavior.

II. Operation Duties
    A. Check welfare and safety of all personnel.
        1. Personal protective gear required.
        2. Radio communications.
    B. Maintain high level of performance.
    C. Take required action on all cases of personnel deficiency.

III. Postburn (Tailgate Session):
    Debrief all personnel after each burn, placing emphasis on burn technique, fire behavior, and safety.

WEED CONTROL IN PLANTATION-GROWN CHRISTMAS TREES

by Clyde L. Elmore[1]

Christmas trees are conifers, usually pines or firs, grown in plantations or as managed natural stands that are cut in the late fall or early winter for the Christmas season. Some trees are grown for "living" trees and are planted in portable containers so the tree may be planted into the landscape after indoor use. In choose-and-cut operations, 68% of the trees are Monterey pine and 17% Douglas fir, with small percentages of other species aking up the balance. In 1987 a conservative estimate of farm-gate value for Christmas trees was $30.1 million. Counties of principal production were San Mateo, Humboldt, Shasta, Orange, San Diego, Los Angeles, and Siskiyou.

Weed species found in Christmas tree plantations vary by location within the state and from site to site within a locale. Although any weed species can be found somewhere in the state, a list of common weeds within separate regions follows.

North State, Coastal
Annual and perennial ryegrass, wild mustard, red sorrel, bristly oxtongue, catsear, broadleaf plantain, buckthorn plantain, hardinggrass, dandelion, poison oak.

North State, Foothill Region
Wild blackberry, bracken fern, johnsongrass, tall fescue, filaree and clover species, poison oak, and other brush species.

South State
Prostrate spurge, large crabgrass, sprangletop, wild mustard, lovegrass, London rocket, annual sowthistle, pigweed, bristly oxtongue.

Central Valley
Crabgrass, pigweeds, lambsquarters, wild radish, annual bluegrass, annual ryegrass, purslane, knotweed, ryegrass, dallisgrass.

Plantation trees planted near high-population areas consist principally of Monterey pine (*Pinus radiata* D. Don), Scotch pine (*Pinus sylvestris* L.), and Douglas fir (*Pseudotsuga menziesii* (Mirb. Franco)). In growing areas further from populations, Douglas fir and true firs are the principal species. A lesser number of California incense cedar (*Libocedrus decurrens* Torr.), giant sequoia (*Sequoia sempervirens* (D. Don) Endl.), Bishop pine (*Pinus muricata* D. Don), white fir (*Abies concolor* (Gord.)),

1. *University of California Cooperative Extension, Davis, CA.*

and California red fir (*Abies magnifica* A. Murr.) are used for Christmas trees. Monterey pine matures most rapidly, producing some saleable trees in three years with most of the trees being marketed by the fifth year. In plantations, Monterey pine tree growth is so rapid that shearing is used to form a more compact pyramidal shape.

Weed growth in new plantings severely suppresses tree growth and reduces tree survival. This problem is especially prevalent in natural rainfall areas but even occurs in sprinkler-irrigated sites. In a study on the impact of weeds in a Mendocino County Bishop pine plantation, a 128% increase in growth occurred when weeds were controlled with atrazine at 2 lb ai/A compared to trees growing in a weedy area. With weed control, there is an increased amount of water available for trees. Soil moisture increased from 11% and 6.8% at the 0–6-inch and 6–12-inch depths, respectively, in the untreated weedy blocks to 16.0% and 13.2% in the area where weeds were controlled. A similar response could be expected from thorough but careful hand weeding. Where supplemental irrigation water can be supplied there may be less growth reduction from competition, but production costs would be higher. There have been instances where there has been excessive tree growth between whorls where weeds have been controlled with herbicides. This has increased the pruning required to retain market quality.

When preemergence, selective herbicides are used, often there is excellent control of annual weeds. If perennial weeds are present in the same plantation, this control of annual plants often leads to the release of perennial weeds just as the conifer is released, a characteristic commonly observed by orchardists and vineyardists. The escape of perennial weeds requires followup postemergence control, or the plantation will be overrun by perennials. Frequently, when a single chemical or family of chemicals (triazine, for example) is used without alternating to other chemical groups of soil-applied herbicides, a shift to tolerant annual weed species occurs. These tolerant annual or biennial species usually are controlled by changing chemicals or cultural practices. Postemergence treatments may also be required for control of these weeds.

Weeds growing around the bases of trees also form an ideal habitat for various species of rodents. Young trees can be severely injured by these rodents. By removing weeds, the rodent activity close to the tree trunks is significantly reduced.

Site Preparation

How a site is prepared for planting depends on its present and potential composition of vegetation. If the site has been cultivated or has remained fallow with a vegetative cover of mostly annual grasses, it may be most easily prepared either by spraying with an appropriate chemical or by cultivation. When proposed planting sites support hard-to-control per-

Figure 5. Competition from weeds in young Christmas trees can be reduced by preemergence herbicides (left) *or mowing* (right). *Mowing, however, does not eliminate weeds in the tree rows which compete for light, water, and nutrients. (Note difference in tree growth between the two techniques.) Photos courtesy C.L. Elmore.*

ennial herbaceous or brush species, such as johnsongrass or other perennial grasses, field bindweed, poison oak, or blackberries, they are best controlled before planting. Tough perennial plants require repeated cultivation or one or more treatments with translocated herbicides to bring them under control. Mechanical and chemical methods are frequently combined for effective preparation of a site. Use of herbicides prior to planting should be carefully considered in order to avoid soil-persistent chemicals that could jeopardize young trees.

New Plantings

On fine soils (containing over 4% organic matter) preemergence herbicides are often used prior to tree planting. They should be uniformly mixed into the top 2–2½ inches of soil. When planting, tree roots should be carefully placed at the bottom of the planting hole to minimize contact of chemically treated soil with the roots. A mechanical planter will open a planting furrow and cover the bare roots without herbicide contact occurring. Most trees are planted as bare root 1-0, 2-0, or 2-1 stock before the site is treated. Hand hoeing around young trees will effectively control weeds; however, tree roots and often trees are inadvertently destroyed. Most preemergent herbicides are applied after planting and before weed emergence. The soil-active herbicides atrazine, simazine, and hexazinone control a very broad spectrum of annual weeds and are safe for most trees. Atrazine and hexazinone have postemergence activity especially when application is followed by a rain or irrigation. In coarse, sandy soils atrazine and hexazinone should not be used because tree injury can result. Simazine is safer to use on these soils.

Tree species such as coast redwood or, more commonly, giant sequoia will be injured by atrazine or simazine in coarse, sandy soil. In these soils, simazine frequently does not control weeds like crabgrass and sprangletop. To control these weeds a material such as napropamide, oryzalin, oxyfluorfen, or pronamide can be combined with atrazine or simazine. Hexazinone is also an effective treatment and is much safer to use on Scotch or ponderosa pine than on Douglas fir or the true firs. Hexazinone should not be used on Monterey pine.

Isolated perennial plants that survive from the site preparation or that establish in new plantings should be spot treated when they are small and few in number to keep them from taking over a plantation. The postemergence herbicides glyphosate, amitrole, and, in the case of bracken fern, asulam, will control perennial grasses and many broad-leaf and woody species. Grasses can also be selectively controlled with postemergent applications of fluazifop-P or sethoxydim.

Established Tree Plantings

Weeds in established plantings are controlled by combining mechanical and chemical control methods. Frequently herbicides are used preemergence around the tree in a strip centered on the tree row, and the areas between the trees are mowed or in some plantations mulched with chips. Mowing resident vegetation provides a mulch between the tree rows which aids during pruning and harvesting operations. It must be done frequently so that weeds do not become large. Mowing promotes a shift of species to low-growing plants such as common knotweed, bermudagrass, or toadflax.

Fall or winter treatments of preemergent, soil-active herbicides should give a clean plantation, free of annual weeds (fig. 5).

It should be remembered that some annual, biennial, or perennial weeds will tolerate certain herbicides. This should be anticipated by identifying the weed species and matching the species to the control program.

When conifers are grown on upland areas without irrigation, there is often a greater need for brush and stump control to reduce competition. This growth is best controlled before trees are planted and then with postplant followup spot spraying as new growth appears. Stumps of sprouting species are removed, while nonsprouting species are left in the soil to decompose. Brush control is discussed in greater detail in this chapter under "Forest Vegetation Management."

REFERENCES

Elmore, C.L., D. Donaldson, and G.E. Veerkamp. 1988. Christmas Tree Weed Control, Univ. of Cal. Coop. Ext., Div. of Ag. and Nat. Res., Pub. 21445.

16

NONCROPLAND AND AQUATICS

NONCROP VEGETATION MANAGEMENT

by Paulo Moraes[1], Thomas Heffernan[2], Howard Rhoads[3], and Dennis Stroud[4]

Although many of the same tools and products are common to both, there are vast differences in the parameters involved with crop and noncrop vegetation management. The former remains necessary and much more important to the consumer largely because of the pressures for increased crop production through elimination of weed competition. Other factors, including numbers of field personnel and demands for additional control measures (with agricultural chemicals related to these same crop patterns), team up to make crop vegetation management paramount in the eyes of those who manufacture or supply vegetation-management products and those who are advisers in the field.

Noncrop vegetation management, as practiced by people who specialize in this field, requires a more individualistic approach. For the most part, noncrop consumers must be educated individually to the needs and expected results of such management techniques. The suppression or removal of vegetation does not usually provide these consumers with increased yields of oil, plant production, electricity, or faster trains. However, many noncrop areas require, through either state or local regulations or ordinances (e.g., fire protection, impaired visibility, noxious weed control programs, weed abatement ordinances, etc.) that vegetation either be removed or reduced to the extent that it will meet such regulatory requirements. In many noncrop areas that require minimum weed populations, the most predominant and effective long-term controls are accomplished through the use of preemergent herbi-

1. Monsanto Agricultural Company, Mission Viejo, CA. 2. Custom Weed Control, Fresno, CA. 3. California Polytechnic State University, San Luis Obispo, CA. 4. Barber Rowland Inc., Geyserville, CA.

cides in combination with, or applied sequentially after, postemergent herbicides. Mowing, burning, soil tillage (disking), scraping, or the physical removal of undesirable vegetation are the usual alternatives. However, this latter form of management yields very short-term results, primarily because weed seeds and viable plant parts are spread thereby from one area to another.

There are several factors that are common to most types of noncrop weed control. The following factors should be considered prior to initiating the management of weeds in noncrop areas:

Reasons for Weed Management

The reasons for weed control or suppression (e.g., fire hazard, visibility, abandoned or neglected property or crops, public nuisance, noxious weed control, reduction or elimination of insect or disease hosts, personnel safety, aesthetic value, etc.) play important roles in the method of noncrop weed control selected or required for a specific site. Some examples are as follows:

- If the site is relatively small and may be used in the future for any landscaping or agricultural activities, then soil-active residual herbicides should not be used. Instead, use alternate methods of control, which include mowing, disking, scraping, burning, or the use of contact or foliar translocated herbicides that do not have soil persistence.
- If bare ground is required, then soil-residual herbicides, either applied alone or in combination with a complementary residual material, offer the most efficient and economical means of providing the desired results. If there are weeds present at the time of application, then the addition of an appropriate postemergent herbicide may be desirable.
- If encroachment (e.g., iceplant or ivy on road shoulders or around signs) is the primary consideration, then repeated treatments of foliar-applied herbicides (contact or translocated) or growth regulators applied to the desired area, or trimming, mowing, scraping, or disking can provide the desired result.
- If a ditchbank or similar area (e.g., edge of pond) requires weed control, then consideration should be given to both the length of desired control and the maximum expected water level.

Weed Spectrum

If the weed spectrum is known, then the choice of control method is greatly simplified. Maintaining weed population records (see examples in Chapter 10) for individual sites will ensure that the control method selected will provide the optimum results.

Annual vs. Perennial

Most winter annual weeds are more easily controlled than summer annuals. Additionally, there is always the potential to eliminate one or more weed species and release other annual or perennial species that may not be controlled by the treatment. Consideration should always be given to combining or using herbicides with different spectrums of weed activity in alternate years to reduce the potential to create new or unanticipated problems.

Length of Desired Control

Most noncrop areas lend themselves to seasonal (approximately one year) weed-control programs. However, many sites do not require this length of control, and therefore any planned program should consider the short- or long-term needs of the individual site.

Time of Application

Applications of many soil-applied residual herbicides require rainfall either prior to or shortly after application to ensure maximum effectiveness and minimum off-site movement. Most herbicide applications to noncrop areas are made in either the fall/winter or spring/summer periods. Reduction of vegetation by scraping, disking, mowing, or burning (where permissible) requires properly timed treatments to ensure minimum regrowth. Applications of plant growth regulators also require properly timed treatments to ensure the desired result.

Application-Related Issues

Individual noncrop herbicides and other methods of vegetation management require specific methods of application, and in many cases applications must comply with state or local regulations or ordinances. Additionally, Toxicity Category 1 herbicides (see Chapter 9) present potential hazards to operators during application and require special handling. Knowledge of all regulations and adherence to label instructions are necessary requirements prior to the use of any method of weed control.

Potential Off-target Problems

Noncrop herbicides are, for the most part, nonselective and either control or suppress a wide range of weed species. Extreme care should be taken when selecting an individual herbicide or herbicide combination treatment to reduce the following potential application-related problems:

Figure 1. Most soil-applied noncrop herbicides are nonselective and persistent in the soil. Extreme care should be taken during application to avoid off-site movement and the potential for associated crop loss, in this case cauliflower. Photo courtesy H.S. Agamalian.

drift during application; movement of the herbicide off the target site (fig. 1) following the application (e.g., in dust, or from excessive rainfall or flooding); slope of application site; encroachment of roots of desirable species into treatment zone; allowance for fluctuation in water levels on ditchbanks and other water-related applications; movement of herbicide into groundwater; and any other potential short- or long-term effects of the treatment.

Regulatory Issues

A review of many individual issues is presented in Chapter 9. Two areas of concern to noncrop weed control are:

- At the federal level, the Endangered Species Act requires that every effort be made to protect endangered species, including weed species. The impact of this act has yet to be determined, but it will require careful consideration when choosing a weed control program in areas in which endangered species are present.
- At the state level, the Pesticide Contamination Act of 1985 has resulted in the establishment of Pest Management Zones (PMZs) and new restrictions associated with the applications of individual herbicides in California. It is expected that the use of noncrop herbicides (e.g., atrazine) may be affected by this legislation.

Aesthetic Value

Many noncrop areas are highly visible to the public and require aesthetic value to aid in public acceptance. Some areas are landscaped to help beautify the site. The influence of the public on the use of herbicides or other methods of vegetation management, near residential areas, or in environmentally sensitive areas, has been and will continue to be an area of concern that must be addressed with any method of weed control or suppression. Extreme care must be taken to ensure that the weed-control method, whether it is disking, scraping, mowing, burning, the application of growth regulators, or the use of herbicides, will consider the potential impact on the public and the environment.

The following weeds, along with many others, depending upon locale, present specific problems in many noncrop areas:

- Broadleaves: alkali mallow, annual burweed, buckhorn plantain, chicory, common fennel, common mullein, field bindweed, puncturevine, Russian thistle, and yellow star thistle.
- Grasses: bermudagrass, dallisgrass, Hillman's panicum, Italian ryegrass, johnsongrass, Jubatagrass, quackgrass, saltgrass, wild oat, and witchgrass.
- Brush: coyotebrush, Himalaya blackberry and other *Rubus* spp., poison oak, wedgeleaf ceanothus, and whiteleaf manzanita.

Most weed management decisions for noncrop areas are designed to provide seasonal weed control. This can usually be accomplished through the use of a single preemergent, or a combination treatment of two unrelated preemergent herbicides applied as a tank mix. The advantage of using two or more soil-active herbicides, if required, is to broaden the spectrum of weed control and/or to reduce the rate of application to provide acceptable weed management objectives. If weeds have already emerged, then a postemergent material should be added to the selected treatment.

Timing of applications for weed management is essential to obtain the desired results. When preemergence herbicides are used, they must be applied in a manner that will ensure maximum weed control or suppression with a minimum possibility for off-target related problems. When postemergence herbicides are applied, especially when they are combined with preemergent materials, they should be used when annual weeds are small to provide optimum control with the postemergent herbicide and ensure that the preemergent material will reach the soil surface. This does not necessarily hold true for all perennial species.

The following postemergence herbicides are available for use in most noncrop sites: amitrole, bromoxynil, diquat, 2,4-D, glyphosate, oxyfluorfen, paraquat, and weed oil. These materials should be applied under nonwindy conditions or with application techniques that reduce the potential for drift to adjacent off-target sites.

A complete list of herbicides in relation to persistence is provided in Chapter 7. A partial list of herbicides that are soil applied and provide control or suppression of various noncrop weed species is included in table 1.

TABLE 1. PARTIAL LIST OF SOIL-APPLIED NONCROP HERBICIDES INCLUDING THEIR RELATIVE SOIL PERSISTENCE

Relative persistence	Herbicides
1–3 months	linuron, metribuzin, oxyfluorfen
3–12 months	atrazine, diuron, hexazinone, oryzalin, simazine, sulfometuron, trifluralin
More than 12 months	bromacil, chlorsulfuron, prometon, tebuthiuron

TYPES OF NONCROP VEGETATION MANAGEMENT

Roadsides

Most of the vegetation management on these sites is conducted by the State of California (Department of Transportation or Caltrans), counties, city public works departments, and departments of parks and recreation. To a lesser degree, private contractors and private subdivision districts also practice vegetation management on these sites.

Weed management programs under the direction of Caltrans or individual counties comprise the primary activities in this area. Individual county programs vary from county to county and within counties. Some counties maintain weed control programs on 50–75% of the roadside miles and other areas of their counties, while some have no programs at all.

Caltrans maintains an active vegetation management program throughout the state, with annual expenditures in excess of $17 million. Many methods of vegetation management are practiced by Caltrans; however, reports indicate that the use of pesticides (herbicides) is 40% more efficient and cost effective than mowing or any other alternative practice (fig. 2). Examples of areas maintained by Caltrans on an annual basis are as follows:

- 15,109 center lane miles of highway
- 20,085 acres of landscape plantings
- 225,000 acres of roadsides
- 90 safety roadside rest areas
- 100 vista points
- 200 park-and-ride lots

The primary benefits derived from roadside and structural weed control include:

Figure 2. The primary method of weed control in such noncrop areas as roadsides and railroads is spray applications. Photo left shows herbicide application along a freeway using low-drift nozzles, while photo right shows "hi-rail" truck application which allows on- or off-track treatments to railroads. Photos courtesy Caltrans and B. Washburn.

Visibility
For safe vehicle operation, it is necessary to maintain weed control on road shoulders, and around signs, intersections, guard rails, and parking areas. Visibility also aids in the ability of road maintenance crews to locate and repair problem areas.

Fire Prevention
Prevention of fire damage to areas adjacent to roads can be reduced by vegetation-free road shoulders, particularly in high-risk areas.

Longevity of Road Surfaces
Effective control measures reduce the weed-encroachment problems that can prematurely destroy road surfaces.

Railroads

There are four major railroads that currently maintain facilities in California as well as some 30 short line, or municipal railroads. It is estimated that there are over 7000 miles of railroad track in California and that approximately 95% of these miles are treated on an annual basis. Track mileage is treated by either the individual railroad companies or by independent contractors.

The railroads also maintain portions of their other properties (i.e., yards, spurs, and buildings) for weed-control purposes.

Railroad application equipment is unique and specialized. Equipment commonly used includes "spray trains" or "hi-rail" trucks (fig. 2) meant for on- or off-track travel.

The primary objectives in railroad weed control include:

Fire Prevention

Rail wheels under heavy loads traveling on steel rails often produce sparks and embers that can contact and ignite adjacent vegetation.

Personnel Safety

Railroad worker unions require weed control in all areas where train crews and/or repair and maintenance workers may be walking. The goal in this instance is safe, visible footage that is also free of snakes, rodents, and other nuisances.

Visibility

To aid in safe and efficient operations, railroads maintain maximum weed-free areas around signs, road crossings, buildings, and other areas where vegetation can encroach. In addition, weeds are controlled on the track itself to facilitate visual inspection of the railroad components.

Water-handling Facilities

These facilities include irrigation districts, reclamation districts, flood-control districts, water districts, etc. It is estimated that there are some 25,000 miles of agency-operated lined and/or unlined canals in California. Most of the larger districts have their own personnel and equipment for chemical and mechanical control. Smaller ones do their own work or in many instances contract the work out to a professional contractor.

Weed-control practices for water-handling facilities do not stop at the waterline. Districts are also concerned about and involved in the control of true aquatic vegetation (see "Aquatic Weed Control" portion of this chapter).

The primary objectives of water-handling weed management include:

Erosion

Some soil types (i.e., coarse soils) in conjunction with steep slopes create situations that are conducive to erosion. High-velocity water flows also tend to aggravate bank erosion under certain conditions.

Weed Seed Source Reduction

Water is a primary source of weed seed introduction. Removing unwanted vegetation eliminates the potential for weed seed development and subsequent movement in irrigation water to agricultural areas and other sites.

Rodent Control

Vegetation control eliminates the habitat of rodents and allows burrowing or tunneling along canals to be detected, which results in the reduction of leaks or wash-outs.

Figure 3. Examples of two types of vegetation management under utility lines are: complete elimination of all vegetation under power poles on which are mounted a potential fire source (left) *and selective suppression of vegetation under utility lines in forest areas* (right) *which allows easier access for maintenance, creates a fire break, does not promote erosion problems, and aids in wildlife management. Photos courtesy PG&E.*

Reduction in Mosquito Breeding Areas

Vegetation can restrict water flows; slow moving or quiescent water provides an ideal habitat for mosquito breeding.

Utilities

The bulk of the acreage programmed for vegetation control in this group is managed by Pacific Gas and Electric (PG&E), Southern California Edison, and Pacific Bell. The remainder is operated by private or municipally owned companies. In most cases, vegetation control, both mechanical and chemical, is done by professional contract applicators. Their services vary from herbicide application at substantial rates to the selective removal or retardation of growth, through the application of growth regulators, of tall-growing species from under transmission lines. Many utility rights-of-way are valuable areas for wildlife habitation. In planning a vegetation-management program for a right-of-way, the wildlife and its needs should be considered and planned around. In addition to wildlife, erosion is a constant consideration, and erosion-control measures through vegetative manipulation are of the utmost importance (fig. 3).

Examples of facilities that require maintenance by PG&E in California are:

- 90,000 miles of distribution
- 18,000 miles of transmission
- 2,250,000 poles
- 187,000 towers

The primary objectives for utility company weed control are:

Fire Prevention

Certain pieces of equipment used by utility companies have capacities to emit sparks or to act as lightning rods. Both can be the source of a fire if the immediate area is not kept free of problem vegetation. In areas of extreme fire risk, total vegetation control and bare ground is required (fig. 3).

Preserving and Maintaining Equipment

Good vegetation management around utility sites helps prevent premature corrosion of expensive equipment including fences, pipelines, transmission lines, and other structures. Vegetation control also increases the ease and effectiveness of visual inspection of the various sites and equipment.

Maintenance and Operations

This need is secondary to fire prevention but is of great importance. Regular inspection of equipment at these sites is critical in maintenance and performance of many mechanisms. A weed-free work area greatly facilitates the accomplishment of this task.

Miscellaneous Noncrop Sites

This category includes all sites for noncrop weed control that have not previously been discussed. Examples of such sites include new construction sites, parking lots, airports, military facilities, athletic facilities, schools, and agricultural facilities (e.g., on-farm related buildings and storage areas, roads and roadsides, power sources, pumps, etc.). These sites vary in both need for weed control and the weed-control practices used. However, they share with the major sites the basic reasons and objectives for effective weed-management programs.

Summary

Noncrop vegetation management is an area where multiple vegetation-control practices are used. In most cases, noncrop sites lend themselves to chemical, mechanical, and physical means of control. The successful vegetation manager dealing with these sites is the one who can design a program that maximizes the objectives and minimizes the overall environmental impact.

AQUATIC WEED CONTROL

by Terry McNabb[1] and Lars W.J. Anderson[2]

Plant life is an essential component of almost all ecosystems, and aquatic environments are no exception. An amazing variety of plants have become adapted structurally and biologically for life on, in, and near lakes, ponds, reservoirs, streams, canals, and drainage ditches. Whether naturally occurring or man-made, these aquatic sites are occupied by many different species of algae, true mosses, ferns, and flowering plants. Aquatic plants in general play an important role by providing oxygen, habitats, shelter, and food, and by recycling nutrients in the aquatic ecosystem. Taken together, aquatic plants form the basis of nearly all aquatic food chains, many of which culminate in production of fish, waterfowl, and many other commercial and game species.

Why then is there a need for aquatic-plant control? When do some aquatic plants become aquatic weeds? To answer this, we must view aquatic sites as dynamic and responsive ecosystems in which many different species of plants and animals compete for resources such as space, light, and nutrients. Each type of plant (including algae) has its own particular set of these requirements, as well as certain inherent limitations or tolerances for other physical surroundings as temperature, water movement (wave action, for example), pH (acidity of the water), light levels, and salinity.

It follows then that changes in the availability and nature of resources can lead to changes in species diversity and amounts of aquatic vegetation. Changes in environmental conditions, whether seasonal or man-induced, can lead to rapid increases or decreases in certain species and affect the use of aquatic sites. In some cases, an exotic species, new to a geographical area, is introduced (most often by human activity) and simply out-competes the native plants. The success of these exotic weeds is typically due to a lack of limiting conditions such as other competitive plants, pathogens, foraging or grazing fish, or insects.

The Physical Aquatic Environment

Light

The availability of adequate *quality* (wave length) and *amount* (radiant energy) of light is the most important physical requirement for all aquatic plants. Though there is generally no problem for plants living on the shorelines of ponds, ditches, and canal banks, species that grow under water are often light-limited. This is because water attenuates the total amount of light which passes through it, and because certain parts of

1. Aquatics Unlimited, Concord, CA. 2. United States Department of Agriculture, Davis, CA.

the photosynthetically active radiation (PAR) are reduced very readily (e.g., the red and red-orange region). This decrease in available light is especially rapid in turbid water. Above-water light intensity can be reduced by more than 95% in just 1–2 feet in some cases. The general reduction in light normally restricts the occurrence of aquatic plants to the upper 10–20 feet. It should be noted that water clarity is also affected by microscopic algae (phytoplankton) which can become so numerous that they block out light even at shallow depths. Other types of algae, which form floating mats, can also produce shade and reduce penetration of light.

Nutrients

Aquatic plants require nutrients similar to those of land plants, i.e., nitrogen (usually as nitrate or ammonia), phosphorus (as inorganic phosphate), potassium, calcium, magnesium, and many so-called micronutrients. However, aquatic plants have one very important advantage over land plants: many species can obtain essential resources either from the hydrosoil or directly from the water. The ability to acquire nutrients dissolved in the water is due in part to the relatively large surface area of aquatic plant stems and leaves and to the fewer waxy cuticle layers on leaves. This interesting feature of aquatic plants also leads to weed-control strategies involving herbicides that can be applied into the water. Finally, it should be recognized that seasonal hydrologic cycles in ponds and flowing waters can lead to regular, somewhat predictable maximums and minimums in dissolved nutrients.

Gases

Both oxygen and carbon dioxide (CO_2) are as vital to aquatic plants as they are to land plants. Oxygen, dissolved in water, is available continuously to aquatic plants for respiration. However, since aquatic plants also produce considerable amounts of oxygen during photosynthesis, this often results in daily fluctuations in quantities of dissolved oxygen. Normally, high levels occur from midday to early afternoon; lowest levels occur just before sunrise. The dissolved oxygen levels at night can be low enough to cause fish kills. Extremely low oxygen levels usually occur if the aquatic vegetation is extraordinarily dense. They may also occur during the day if a large plant biomass has been treated with a herbicide. There can be two possible causes of oxygen depletion: (1) blockage of photosynthesis and (2) decomposition of dead plants by bacteria and fungi, which take up oxygen. Therefore, whenever large areas of an aquatic site are infested with undesirable plants, herbicide treatments should be staggered in time or space to prevent precipitous reduction in dissolved oxygen.

Carbon-dioxide levels can also fluctuate due to absorption by plants during the day and production by both plants and animals during the night. (It should be noted that water temperature can affect how much CO_2 and oxygen are dissolved; these gases are more soluble in colder water.)

Another important distinction between land plants and aquatic plants with regard to CO_2 is that in the water carbon may exist as (1) dissolved CO_2, (2) bicarbonate (HCO_3^-), and (3) carbonate (CO_3^-). The relative amounts of these forms of inorganic carbon are very dependent upon the pH of the water. At high pH—e.g., 8–9—bicarbonate predominates, while at pH below 7, carbon dioxide predominates. At extremely high pH—e.g., 9.5–10.5—carbonates predominate. This can be important for two reasons: (1) most aquatic plants utilize CO_2 readily, but only some are able to use bicarbonate, and (2) some aquatic herbicides (e.g., copper sulfate) are rendered inactive when carbonates are abundant.

Temperature

Water serves as an excellent buffer against rapid changes in temperatures. Plants growing under water therefore are somewhat insulated from the shocks of extreme temperature changes. Long-term seasonal changes are just as significant for aquatic plants as land plants. Also, water temperatures usually decline with depth, particularly in deep lakes in summer. This, coupled with progressive loss of light, often restricts the depth at which aquatic plants can grow rapidly. Low growth rate often limits herbicide effectiveness, so seasonal temperature patterns must be considered when chemical control is planned.

Types of Aquatic Weeds

With this background on the physical environment of aquatic plants, let's look at the major types of aquatic plants. The most commonly used classification relies on the general structures and growth habits of the plants. It is not a classification based upon evolutionary or phylogenetic relationships. However, it can be very useful in understanding where a particular plant can grow, how it can reproduce, how it can become a weed, and what control methods may be effective.

The general classifications of aquatic plants are summarized in table 1, which lists examples of aquatic plants in each category. (Sometimes a more simplified classification scheme is used, which includes: (1) emersed weeds, (2) floating weeds, (3) submersed weeds, and (4) algae. But this scheme often does not provide sufficient information about growth habit or type of plant.) A careful study of the summary table shows that successful control or management of aquatic weeds requires reliable information, including:

Weed Species

The importance of proper identification cannot be overemphasized. Just as with terrestrial weeds, aquatic weeds vary in their response to herbicides and in their reproductive capacities. A list of useful guides for identification is given at the end of this chapter.

Relative Abundance
Relative abundance of weed species and approximate extent of infestation: e.g., is 30% of surface covered or 90–100%?

Location of Weeds
Are they only in near-shore areas? Are they only along sides (not bottom) of a canal? The location is extremely important since it usually relates to the ecological or growth-form category of the weed (e.g., attached-submersed, attached-emergent, free-floating, etc.). (See table 2.) The growth habit in turn will often dictate the alternative control methods available.

Age of Infestation
This is important because new ones (less than one or two seasons) may not have produced sufficient seed/vegetative reproductive and overwintering capacity.

Use of the Aquatic Site and Fate of Water
Beyond knowing what weed is present, this is the next most important fact. It determines the limitations on mechanical and herbicidal approaches to control. Potential uses and fates include:
- Industrial (e.g., cooling systems).
- Irrigation or frost control (sensitivity of crops to herbicides or temporary restriction of water must be considered).
- Domestic (potable).
- Livestock watering.
- Swimming, boating, fishing (frequency of use of aquatic site and what types of fish are important).
- Waterfowl habitat.
- Downstream flows (e.g., to natural waterways or to other use sites).

Any need for temporary cessation or modification of these uses can be determined. The ability to curtail downstream flows can be particularly useful when herbicidal methods are planned. Temporary, alternate sources of water should be explored also. In many cases, no change can be tolerated.

Time of Year
Unfortunately, most problems with aquatic weeds are recognized only after dense populations of them have become established. The most effective time for control is usually spring. As indicated earlier, water temperature is a major determinant of growth and should be measured

where the weeds occur. Generally, when water temperature begins to exceed 60–65°F, growth begins to increase sharply.

Strategies for Aquatic Weed Control

General Methods
Once sufficient information is obtained about a weed infestation, many control methods (unfortunately, often the simplest) can be ruled out. For example, most aquatic herbicides require a specified posttreatment waiting interval before water can be used for fishing, drinking, or irrigating crops. In other cases, use in irrigation water is completely prohibited. Awareness of such limitations is a must, and information regarding them can be obtained directly from the herbicide label. Often herbicide use is simply not permissible.

Mechanical control can provide relief but may also encourage the spread of weeds if it results in fragmentation of vegetative parts that sprout new plants. Such a situation usually results from cutting hydrilla, eurasian watermilfoil, or elodea.

Natural growth cycles in aquatic sites must be considered. In this regard, two concepts are important:

- Even without human intervention, plant populations rise and fall seasonally, and there is often a succession of plant species as the seasonal conditions change, and as conditions change over several years.
- Nature abhors a vacuum—which means that even if a weed is removed, chances are good that another plant will occupy the new opening or niche. The new species may or may not be weedy. Removal of a weed species may sometimes allow introduction of more desirable species.

Types of Aquatic Weed Control
Prevention. Obviously most existing aquatic weed problems have moved beyond the option of an initial prevention strategy. However, when construction of new water-holding or conveyance systems is planned, or if significant refurbishing of old systems is needed, then the following should be considered:

- Can light be eliminated or greatly reduced (e.g., by deepening the body of water)? Can storage systems be covered? Can highly turbid water be tolerated?
- Can nutrient inputs be reduced? Since most aquatic weeds grow well at low nutrient levels, this may be an impractical approach, but reducing runoff from adjacent fertilized areas (e.g., cropland, landscaped sites) into holding ponds or small reservoirs can help slow aquatic weed growth. Placement of berms or gutters can keep out runoff waters.

TABLE 2. GENERAL CLASSIFICATION OF AQUATIC WEEDS

Type of aquatic plant and growth habit	Mode of reproduction and associated structures	Potential weed impacts	Control methods
I. Algae			
A. Unicellular or microscopic colonies			
1. Free-floating and suspended in water, e.g., phytoplankton	• Mostly cell division (asexual)	• Reduced aesthetic value of ponds, lakes	• Reduced nutrient availability
2. Some attached to substrate, e.g., diatoms	• Some resistant or "resting" stages	• Toxic secretions can kill fish, livestock	• Encourage aeration, mixing of water
		• Can reduce nighttime oxygen and kill fish	• Herbivorous fish
		• Fouling of irrigation system, e.g., of drip emitters	• Algicides applied on a concentration basis, e.g., to water column
			• Filtration to remove as above, and mechanical removal (screens, rakes)
			• Use of fish to increase turbidity
			• Use dye to block light e.g., Aquashade
B. Filamentous or colonial (visible to naked eye)			
1. Attached and/or floating on surface, e.g., *Cladophora, Spirogyra, Nostoc*	• Cell division with or without branching	• Blockage of waterways from commercial, recreational use	
	• Some sexual stages and "resting" stages	• Blockage of water delivery for irrigation, domestic use	
		• Destruction of fisheries habitats	

II. Vascular plants (mosses, ferns, flowering plants)

A. Attached by roots and rhizomes

Type	Reproduction	Problems	Control

1. Completely submerged with no obvious "floating leaves," e.g., sago pondweed, hydrilla, eurasian watermilfoil, some true mosses and ferns
 	
2. Submersed but with obvious "floating"-type leaves, e.g., many "waterlillies," American pondweed, arrowhead
	• Primarily by asexual vegetative structures:
	  a) fragmentation
	  b) rhizomes and runners
	  c) specialized buds
	    (1) subterranean "turions," "winterbuds," "tubers"
	    (2) stem-produced turions, buds
	• Some sexual reproduction by seed
	• Spores (mosses, ferns)
		• Reduced volume and flow of canals
		• Reduced recreation (fishing, swimming, boating)
		• Damage to canals
		• Blockage of hydroelectric production
		• Increased mosquito habitat
		• Interference with crop production, e.g., rice
			• Cutting and removal
			• Dredging, excavation (removal of roots/rhizomes)
			• Herbicides (water- or soil-applied after drawdown) or foliar-applied at drawdown or when "floating leaves" occur
			• Herbivorous fish
			• Seasonal drawdown
			• Cement lining of canals

3. Emergent: large portion of plant above water, e.g., cattails, bulrushes, grasses	• Both asexual and sexual • Rhizomes, stolons • Seeds • Overwintering vegetative structure, e.g., tubers, rhizomes	• Blockage of recreational uses • Interference with crop production, e.g., rice • Blockage of irrigation and drainage canals • Increased siltation	• Cutting, burning • Excavation (removal of roots/rhizomes) • Foliar-applied herbicides
B. Free-floating (roots not attached to substrate)—e.g., waterhyacinth, duckweed, Azolloa and Salvinia (ferns)	• Asexual is primary mode with production of "daughter" plants which are sometimes interconnected by stolons • Fragmentation of whole plants • Sexual by seeds and spores	• Blockage and cover of water surface • Restriction of light for desirable aquatic plants • Increased mosquito habitat and increased habitat for other disease vectors, e.g., snails • Decrease in dissolved oxygen below dense populations	• Mechanical removal • Mechanical restrictions of movement (via booms, floating fences) • Biological control, e.g., of waterhyacinth and Salvinia • Foliar-applied herbicides

- Other design and construction considerations: Deep, straight-walled ponds/reservoirs offer the poorest conditions for aquatic weed growth. Alternatively, designs which allow for partial separation (compartmentalization) of storage systems can allow use of aquatic herbicides that require posttreatment waiting periods without interrupting water uses. These compartments (or dual ponds) may even be drained individually (at least partially) to permit mechanical removal of weeds or use of less herbicide or algicide.

Mechanical Control. Several approaches can be used in canals and ponds. Before adopting these methods you must decide if further spread of the weeds is likely to result. Also, large masses of vegetation can be uprooted or freed, and this may require screening or removal to prevent downstream problems with clogging or fouling of canals and pipelines.

Typical practices include:

- Harvesting and removal: This can be effective in relieving small areas of ponds or sections of channels for access, water delivery, boat traffic, etc. Since most aquatic plants contain 90–95% water, the removal/transport steps often require large equipment (e.g., barges, trucks). This general method has the advantage of removing any plant biomass that contains nutrients, thus reducing recycling of them into the water.
- Cutting: Aquatic weeds can be removed by various cutting devices which are usually barge- or boat-mounted. The cutting mechanism can usually be adjusted vertically. These systems can be quite effective in providing limited open areas, and as with several aquatic herbicides, they usually require repeated maintenance cutting as regrowth occurs. Cutting also releases parts of plants that can resprout and reroot. Therefore, unless substantial infestation is already present, there is a high risk of spreading the problem.
- Chaining/disking: The physical disruption and tearing off of root plants can provide immediate (but usually temporary) relief in canals. This may be especially feasible when canals have access roads on both banks from which trucks or tractors can operate. Large-link chains or discs can be towed by pairs of vehicles moving along the canal. As with cutting methods, large masses of plants are freed and must be removed at a downstream point.
- Drag-lining, backhoeing, telescooping: Drag-lining consists of repeated scraping and removal of plants and substrate with a crane-operated bucket. Similarly, small canals can be cleared with a backhoe. Both approaches are slow and expensive. However, when done as part of maintenance of a canal's shape, they can be economically feasible. Likewise, large, hydraulically operated scooping buckets (telescoops) can remove plants and substrate fairly well. The advantage of substrate removal is that it can also eliminate or reduce

the number of subterranean reproductive structures, e.g., winter-buds, turions, tubers, root crowns, and rhizomes.

- Burning: Though mainly used to remove bank or shoreline weeds, some rooted-submersed plants can be burned if they are allowed to dry sufficiently. This requires well-planned drawdown at times when the plants are exposed to bright sunlight. Since damp soil is a good thermal insulator, burning will not usually kill roots, rhizomes, or subterranean propagules.

- Physical suppression or restraints: Some types of physical, screen-type materials are available for placement directly on top of sub-mersed plants. These "screens" reduce light but also physically restrain the upward growth of some plants. They are usually held in place with weights or rods driven into the substrate. For very localized areas, such as small swimming beaches, this can be a practical approach. For floating weeds, skirted floating booms may be useful in restricting the spread of plants.

Water Management. This method includes a variety of possibilities, such as a seasonal drawdown, intermittent (within-season) drawdown, partial drawdowns, ponding of flowing water, deferring of water use or release, wasting of herbicide-exposed water, and alternation of sources. Unfortunately, most aquatic storage-and-delivery systems are designed with a complete disregard for the benefits of water management for aquatic weed control. Therefore, water management may have limited application, although all possibilities should be explored because the ability to even moderately alter water management can greatly increase the range and types of methods applicable.

Drawdown alone, even for days or weeks, can often reduce production of large biomass. Timing drawdowns to block production of reproductive structures can also be useful. Finally, the ability to hold, pond, or partially drain a system can allow use of some aquatic herbicides which might otherwise be ineffective.

Chemical Control. A variety of aquatic herbicides and algicides are available. However, various characteristics of these herbicides and algicides often limit their use to specialized aquatic sites or even to certain geographic areas. In addition, aquatic plants vary in their susceptibility to these chemicals. Likewise, effects on nontarget species (other plants, animals, man) must be considered. Most of the limitations on chemical control are associated with the use or potential use of herbicide-exposed water.

Herbicides can be broadly grouped as either contact, meaning they only affect that part of the plant directly exposed, or systemic, meaning the herbicide can *move* within the plant away from the site of uptake. Recalling the types or classifications of aquatic plants, you will see that the growth habit of a plant often determines the most efficient method for exposing the plant to herbicides. Thus, floating plants can be exposed by foliar-applied sprays (contact or systemic) without large amounts of herbicide being put directly into the water. Attached-submersed plants can be controlled by herbicides applied in the water, or those that can be placed around or near the roots and rhizomes. In such cases, drawdown can be used, followed by soil application of herbicides (with or without soil-incorporation). Thus, we can group aquatic herbicides and algicides by the location or mode of exposure:

- Direct foliage applications above water: Floating plants, emersed plants, or submersed plants after drawdown. Note that application rates are usually on an area basis.
- Water applications: Submersed weeds, algae. Applications can be subgrouped under: (1) whole water columns, (2) bottom acre-foot, and (3) bottom layered. The application rates may be based on total amount needed to produce a required concentration (e.g., 1 part per million = 1 mg per liter = 2.71 lb per acre-foot). They may also be based on area coverage.
- Direct soil applications at drawdown.

Adjuvant or formulation selection is important since herbicides must contact plants in order to get into them, and the contact must be long enough to allow a sufficient amount of the compound to enter the plant. Therefore, some water-applied herbicides that may be very effective in ponded or standing water may be less effective in flowing water due to shorter contact time. Likewise, effectiveness can be diminished in water that is diluted by untreated water. In fact, very few herbicides are registered for flowing water applications.

Because of specialized techniques often used for aquatic herbicide applications, the sensitivity of nontarget plants (e.g., crops) and animals and the potential for exposure of water used for irrigation and domestic purposes, thorough knowledge of the aquatic site, water uses, herbicide labeling, and federal/state regulations is essential.

Biological Control. This may be subdivided into methods of direct and indirect impact on weeds. Biocontrol agents that directly attack or infest aquatic plants include herbivorous fish, insects, fungi, bacteria, and waterfowl. Beneficial organisms that indirectly affect aquatic plant growth include the mirror carp *(Cyrpinus carpoi),* an active fish that increases turbidity through its bottom-feeding, which in turn decreases the light available to rooted aquatic weeds. Beneficial competitive plants are also among these indirect biocontrol agents. These are species that do not in themselves become weeds and that tend to exclude the weedy plants. The small sedge called dwarf spikerush *(Eleocharis coloradoensis)* and the related slender spikerush *(E. acicularis)* have received most attention as potential competitive and beneficial plants. Establishment of these species is difficult in canals but can be done in some ponds, lakes, or reservoirs. Again, it is not a quick-cure option, but it is an approach that is suitable in some circumstances.

Of those organisms that directly attack or infest plants, two types have shown promise: various weevils and moths for control of water-hyacinth and alligatorweed, and the white amur ("grass carp"), a herbivorous fish. The white amur can consume large quantities of various submersed aquatic weeds, and there is considerable interest in developing a non-reproducing fish for general use. Since this fish is not native to the United States, and since it is such an efficient forager, fish and game managers are concerned that uncontrolled populations could adversely impact native fisheries habitats.

The most promising development in this area to date is the production of a "triploid" grass carp. This abnormal chromosome number (3N vs. normal diploid, or 2N) results from a brief exposure of normal, newly fertilized eggs to hydrostatic pressure or heat treatments. When these fish mature, they are generally unable to form normal sperm and ova, thus dramatically decreasing the chances of successful spawning and reproduction. Attempts by researchers will also be made soon to produce a "monosex" triploid, which would further reduce the possibility of reproduction.

At present, the grass carp, whether diploid or triploid, is not permitted for release or use in California, though about 14 other states do allow its use. There are two research programs operating under special permits from the Department of Fish and Game: in the Imperial Irrigation District as part of the Hydrilla Eradication Project; and at the USDA Aquatic Weed Control Research Laboratory at UC Davis. Research on the reproductive capacity of the triploids is also being conducted by scientists at UC Davis.

An important feature of biological control is the need for a long-term management program. Biocontrol agents are simply not off-the-shelf items to be applied like herbicides.

Integrated Control of Aquatic Weeds. The previous descriptions of aquatic plants, their requirements for growth, modes of reproduction, and responses to the environment suggest that there are optimal times and conditions for use of various control methods. The complexity of each aquatic site requires that the best timing, water-management, and control(s) must be determined quite specifically.

The economic threshold is a very important component of integrated weed control, but it is often difficult to define. Simply stated, this threshold is the level or extent of weed infestation above which economic losses occur. If this level is known, then the relative merits of the available control methods can be judged. Unlike crops, which have very well-defined monetary value, the worth of infested aquatic sites (and water) is usually difficult to determine. (Studies are under way to determine economic thresholds in several California irrigation districts.) Lack of this "threshold" value means that the integrated approaches used now are simply a best estimate of potential economic losses.

TABLE 3. GENERALIZED DECISION SCHEME TO DETERMINE POTENTIAL AQUATIC WEED CONTROL METHODS IN LAKES, PONDS, AND OTHER IMPOUNDMENTS

I. ALGAE

What Is Use of Water?

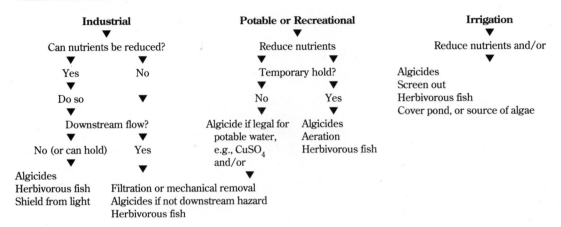

II. ATTACHED-SUBMERSED WEEDS

What Is Use of Water?

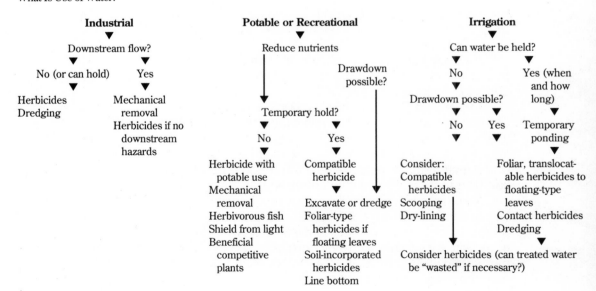

III. ATTACHED—EMERGENT

What Is Use of Water?

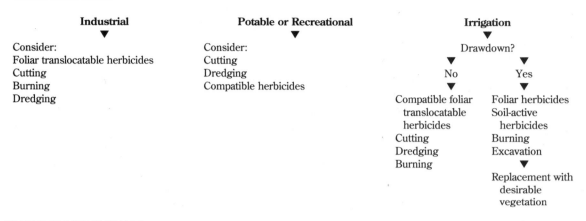

Industrial
▼
Consider:
Foliar translocatable herbicides
Cutting
Burning
Dredging

Potable or Recreational
▼
Consider:
Cutting
Dredging
Compatible herbicides

Irrigation
▼
Drawdown?
▼   ▼
No   Yes
▼   ▼

No:
Compatible foliar translocatable herbicides
Cutting
Dredging
Burning

Yes:
Foliar herbicides
Soil-active herbicides
Burning
Excavation
▼
Replacement with desirable vegetation

IV. FREE-FLOATING PLANTS

What Is Use of Water?

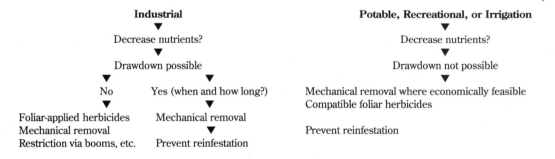

Industrial
▼
Decrease nutrients?
▼
Drawdown possible
▼   ▼
No   Yes (when and how long?)
▼   ▼

No:
Foliar-applied herbicides
Mechanical removal
Restriction via booms, etc.

Yes:
Mechanical removal
▼
Prevent reinfestation

Potable, Recreational, or Irrigation
▼
Decrease nutrients?
▼
Drawdown not possible
▼
Mechanical removal where economically feasible
Compatible foliar herbicides

Prevent reinfestation

It is clear, however, that by using water management and seasonal variations, the effectiveness of both chemical and biological methods can be enhanced. For example, one can use such mechanical methods as cutting or chaining, or contact herbicides, to produce springlike "new growth" in established, submersed plants. This approach may be useful in combinations with herbicides that are most effective at the preemergent or early-postemergent growth stages. Likewise, removal of established growth may allow biocontrol agents, such as herbivorous fish, to keep subsequent regrowth in check. This strategy may also be effectively used in some floating species (e.g., waterhyacinth) except that a growth retardant could be used rather than a herbicide. The growth retardant could slow the production of new plants, thus allowing intro-

TABLE 4. GENERALIZED DECISION SCHEME TO DETERMINE POTENTIAL AQUATIC WEED CONTROL METHODS IN IRRIGATION AND DRAINAGE

Special remarks: Many irrigation canals carry water that is used for other purposes, e.g., livestock watering, domestic (potable), and recreational (boating, fishing, swimming). Drainage canals may also return water to natural aquatic sites, e.g., rivers, lakes, streams, estuaries. Therefore, the fate of the irrigation water should be carefully determined.

Also, controlling weeds on the "crown," "berms," or "inside ditchbank" is not the same as controlling weeds within the wetted perimeter. Herbicides that can be used outside the wetted area often cannot be used on weeds in the water or emerging from it.

I. ALGAE

(NOTE: This assumes water is normally flowing)

No drawdown possible and ponding not possible ▼	**Drawdown possible** ▼	**Ponding possible** ▼
Algicide compatible with water use, e.g., $CuSO_4$ with potable use as acrolein is not ▼	Determine if timing will allow use of contact algicides or desiccation of algae ▼	Determine if timing and duration will permit use of algicides ▼
Mechanical removal, e.g., "traveling screens"	Mechanical removal	Pond sections of canal and treat with algicide(s)
Another option: Bypass irrigation during chemical treatment		

II. ATTACHED—SUBMERSED

No drawdown possible and ponding not possible ▼	**Drawdown possible** ▼	**Ponding possible** ▼
Herbicide compatible with fate of water Mechanical: Draglining Chaining Cutting Scooping Dredging Biological: Herbivorous fish	Determine if timing and duration will permit use of contact or translocatable or soil-applied herbicides Can water be managed to induce terrestrial-type leaves? If yes, use foliar herbicides Mechanical: Excavation Disking Scooping Draglining Drawdown alone Biological: Establish beneficial plants Line canal with concrete	Determine if timing and duration will permit use of contact, water-applied herbicides Mechanical: Cutting and removal

III. ATTACHED—EMERGENT (see LAKES, PONDS, etc.)

IV. FREE-FLOATING (see LAKES, PONDS, etc.)

duced insects to increase their numbers to a level that can keep the waterhyacinth population at a low density.

The use of beneficial, competitive plants generally requires well-coordinated water management and perhaps mechanical or chemical control. For example, dwarf and slender spikerushes are able to grow (albeit slowly) during the winter drawdown in northern California when noxious aquatic weeds such as sago pondweed and curlyleaf pondweed do not grow. But canals that are poorly drained (i.e., have standing water) do not provide the best conditions for encouraging spikerush since they may also allow weed populations to persist.

Other Considerations

The decision schemes in tables 3 and 4 can be used to determine possible control methods. They should be considered *starting points*. Once the options are clear, further considerations must include:

- Existence of state/federal-approved label if herbicides are to be used.
- County or other local permit requirements for either herbicide applications or mechanical work (e.g., dredging).
- State/local permits for introduction of biological control agents (e.g., fish or insects).
- Requirement for applicator's license (certification).
- The advisability of contacting your local Cooperative Extension Service weed representative for information about new approaches available or particular circumstances that limit your planned weed-control strategy.

This has been a brief introduction to a rather complex area of weed control. Since aquatic weeds don't grow in prepared fields (except in rice), even gaining access to them can present problems. It is best to seek practical, field-oriented experience with a knowledgeable person. General information on aquatic-herbicide application techniques is presented in another section. It is important to remember that water doesn't stay in one place forever, it eventually gets cycled and recycled. It is advisable always to consider the best, environmentally compatible alternatives when attempting to control aquatic weeds.

SUGGESTED READING

General Monographs
Hutchinson, G.E. 1975. *A Treatise on Limnology, Vol. 3, Limnological Botany.* John Wiley & Sons, Inc., New York. 660 pp.
Sculthorpe, C.D. 1965. *The Biology of Aquatic Vascular Plants.* Edward Arnold Ltd., London. 610 pp.
Periodicals Containing Research and General Interest Articles
Journal of Aquatic Plant Management Society
Aquatic Botany
Aquatics (publication of the Florida Chapter of Aquatic Plant Management Society).
Aquatic Plant Identification Guides
Fasset, N.C. 1957. *A Manual of Aquatic Plants.* Univ. of Wisconsin Press, Madison. 405 pp.

Hotchkiss, N. 1967. Underwater and Floating-Leaved Plants of the United States and Canada. U.S. Dept. of Interior, Fish, and Wildlife Ser., Bur. of Sport Fisheries and Wildlife. No. 44. 124 pp.

Mason, Herbert W. A Flora of the Marshes of California. Univ. of Calif. Press.

Muenscher, W.C. 1944. Handbook of American Natural History, Vol. IV. Aquatic Plants of the United States. Comstock Co., Cornell Univ., NY. 374 pp.

Otto, N.E., Bartley, T.R., Thullen, J.S. 1980. Aquatic Pests on Irrigation Systems—Identification Guide, 2nd ed. U.S. Bur. of Reclamation. 90 pp.

Tarver, David P., John A. Rodgers, Michael J. Mahler, Robert L. Lazor. 1978. Aquatic and Wetland Plants of Florida. Bur. of Aquatic Plant Research and Control. Florida Dept. of Natural Resources. 127 pp.

Aquatic Plant Control Recommendations

Ag Consultant and Fieldman. 1985 Weed Control Manual. Meister Publishing Co. (Write to: Ag Consultant and Fieldman, Willoughby, OH 44094.)

USDA-ARS. Suggested Guidelines for Weed Control. pp. 310–330. USDA Agriculture Handbook No. 565. 330 pp.

GLOSSARY

Many of the terms and definitions in this glossary were compiled by the Herbicide Handbook Committee of the Weed Science Society of America. They are recommended by the society for use in all weed science publications. Some terms not included in the WSSA glossary but used in the present text have been added.

The glossary is published in the *Herbicide Handbook* of the Weed Science Society of America, Fifth Edition, 1983, and is used here with permission of the society.

Absorption The process by which a chemical passes from one system into another; e.g., a herbicide that passes from the soil solution into a plant root cell or from the leaf surface into the leaf cells.

Acid equivalent (AE) The theoretical yield of parent acid from the active ingredient content of a formulation.

Activate The process by which a surface-applied herbicide becomes phytotoxic after rainfall or irrigation. Activation results from movement of the herbicide into the soil where it can be absorbed by roots of weed seedlings, and usually not from any chemical change in the active ingredient.

Active ingredient (AI) The chemical in a herbicide formulation primarily responsible for its phytotoxicity and which is identified as the active ingredient on the product label.

Acute toxicity The quality or potential of a substance to cause injury or illness shortly after exposure to a relatively large dose.

(See *chronic toxicity.*)

Adjuvant Any substance in a herbicide formulation or added to the spray tank to improve herbicidal activity or application characteristics.

Adsorption The process by which a herbicide associates with a surface (e.g., a soil-colloidal surface).

Agitation The process of keeping a herbicide mixed, or preventing it from separating or settling in a spray tank.

Allelopathic substances Chemical compounds produced by plants which affect the interactions between different plants, including microorganisms.

Allelopathy Any direct or indirect effect of one plant on another through the production of chemical compounds that escape into the environment.

Annual A plant that completes its life cycle in one growing season.

Antidote 1) A chemical applied to prevent the phytotoxic effect of a specific pesticide on desirable plants. (Synonymous with *protectant.*) 2) A substance used as a medical treatment to counteract pesticide poisoning.

Apoplast The total, nonliving continuum in a plant, including cell walls, intercellular spaces, and the xylem vessels, that forms a continuous permeable system through which water and solutes may move.

Aqueous suspension (AS) A finely divided dry formulation (similar to a wettable powder) that is suspended in a viscous liquid.

Band treatment Application of herbicide to a restricted linear strip

on or along a crop row rather than continuous (broadcast) application over the field area.

Basal treatment An application that encircles the stem of a plant essentially at ground level so that foliage contact is minimal. The term is used mostly to describe treatment of woody plants.

Bed 1) A relatively level piece of soil raised above the furrows for planting crops in rows. 2) An area in which seedlings or transplants are grown for transplanting later in the field.

Biennial A plant that grows vegetatively during the first year and fruits and dies during the second year.

Bioassay Determination of the biological activity or potency of a substance, such as a pesticide, by testing its effect on the growth or survival of a living organism.

Biological control (biocontrol) The use of natural enemies to reduce a plant's pest population to the level at which it is no longer an economic problem.

Bioherbicide A living organism which is effective in weed control that can be applied in a similar fashion to chemical herbicides.

Biotechnology Techniques that use living organisms or parts of organisms to produce a variety of products (from medicines to industrial enzymes) to improve plants or animals or to develop microorganisms for specific uses such as removing toxics from bodies of water, or as pesticides.

Biotype A population within a species that has distinct genetic variation.

Blind cultivation Cultivation

before seeded crops emerge.

Broadcast rate equivalent For band treatments, the rate for a broadcast treatment which would be equivalent to the rate applied to the band area, or the rate of herbicide applied per unit area when only the band area is considered. All rates for band treatment should be expressed as the broadcast rate equivalent.

Broadcast treatment Uniform application of a herbicide to an entire area.

Brush control Control of woody plants such as brambles, sprout clumps, shrubs, trees, and vines.

Carbohydrate A chemical compound that is composed of carbon, hydrogen, and oxygen and that is produced by plants in photosynthesis.

Carcinogenic Capable of causing cancer in animals.

Carrier A gas, liquid, or solid substance used to dilute or suspend a pesticide during its application.

Chemical name The name applied to the active ingredient of a herbicide which describes its chemical structure according to rules prescribed by the American Chemical Society and published in the *Chemical Abstracts Indexes.*

Chlorosis Loss of green color (chlorophyll) from foliage without desiccation.

Chronic toxicity The ability of a substance to cause injury or illness after repeated exposure to small doses over an extended period of time. (See *acute toxicity.*)

Common name An abbreviated name applied to the active ingredient of a herbicide usually agreed upon by the American National Standards Institute and the International Organization for Standardization.

Compatibility The ability of an agent to mix in a formulation or in a spray tank for application in the same carrier without undesirably altering the characteristics or effects of the individual components.

Competition A tendency of neighboring plants to make simultaneous demands for the same resources (light, water, nutrients) such that the immediate supply of the resources is below their combined demand.

Concentration The amount of active ingredient or herbicide equivalent in a quantity of diluent expressed as percent, pounds per gallon, kilograms per liter, etc.

Contact herbicide A herbicide that causes localized injury to plant tissue where contact occurs.

Controlled burn Any vegetation fire set for a beneficial purpose which is contained by control lines.

Cool-season crop A crop that is normally grown under cool temperature regimes—e.g., artichokes, broccoli, cauliflower, Brussels sprouts, celery, lettuce— as opposed to one that is grown under warm temperatures *(warm-season crop).*

Cotyledons Seed leaves; the first leaves or the first pair or whorl of leaves on plants.

Crop oil A nonphytotoxic petroleum oil used as a diluent and adjuvant with pesticides.

Crop rotation The sequence of crops grown in succession in a given field.

Cultivation Mechanical soil disturbance during and after crop emergence to uproot weeds, aerate the soil, and facilitate irrigation.

Cuticle The waxy layer on the outer wall of epidermal cells of the plant shoot.

Cytoplasm The protoplast of a cell outside of the cell nucleus.

Defoliant A chemical that causes leaves to drop from a plant.

Desiccant Any substance or mixture of substances used to accelerate the drying of plant tissue.

Dicotyledon A plant whose embryo has two cotyledons.

Diluent Any gas, liquid, or solid material used to reduce the concentration of an active ingredient in a formulation.

Direct seeding Planting seed in the field where the crop is grown to harvest as opposed to planting seed in a greenhouse or other location for later transplanting to the field.

Directed application Precise application to a specific area or plant organ such as to a row or bed or to the leaves or stems of the plants.

Dispersible granule A dry granular formulation that will separate or disperse to form a suspension when added to water.

DNA (deoxyribonucleic acid) The primary genetic material of all cells or organisms.

Dormancy The state of inhibited germination or plant-organ growth in the presence of the required conditions for initiating growth.

Drift See *spray drift* and *vapor drift.*

Dry flowable (DF) A dry granular formulation that is relatively dust-free and can be readily suspended in water.

Ecotype A population within a species which has developed a distinct morphological or physiological characteristic (e.g., herbicide resistance) as an adaptation to a specific environment. When individuals of an ecotype are moved to a different environment, the characteristic persists.

Emergence The event when shoots of seedling or perennial growth become visible by pushing through the soil surface.

Emersed plant A rooted or anchored aquatic plant adapted to grow with most of its leaf and stem tissue above the water surface.

Emulsifiable concentrate (EC) A single-phase liquid formulation that forms an emulsion when added to water.

Emulsifier A substance that promotes the suspension of one liquid in another.

Emulsion One liquid suspended as minute globules in another liquid; e.g., oil suspended in water.

Encapsulated formulation Pesticide enclosed in capsules (or beads) of thin polyvinyl or other material that controls the rate of chemical release and thereby extends the period of activity.

Endangered species Animals, birds, fish, plants, or other living organisms threatened by extinction by man-made or natural changes in their environment, as defined by requirements for declaring a species endangered in the Endangered Species Act.

Epidermis The surface layer of cells occurring on all parts of the primary plant body, both above and below ground.

Epinasty That state in which more rapid growth occurs on one side of a plant organ or part (especially a leaf), which causes the organ or part to bend or curl downward.

Extender A chemical that increases the longevity of a herbicide.

Fallow Crop land left idle, for any period of time, during one or more seasons.

Floating plant A free-floating aquatic plant adapted to grow with most of its vegetative tissue at or above the water surface.

Flowable (F) A two-phase formulation that contains a solid herbicide suspended in liquid and that forms a suspension when added to water.

Formulation 1) A pesticidal preparation supplied by a manufacturer for practical use. 2) The process, carried out by manufacturers, of preparing pesticides for practical use.

Fumigation Subsurface application of liquid pesticides that vaporize and spread through the soil in a gaseous state.

Genetic engineering Genetic manipulations that use recombinant DNA methods (gene splicing) to change the genetic make-up of an organism.

Germination The process of growth initiation in seeds.

Granular (G) A dry formulation consisting of discrete particles of generally less than 10 cubic millimeters (0.006 cubic inch) that is designed to be applied without a liquid carrier.

Groundwater The supply of fresh water found beneath the earth's surface, usually in aquifers, which often supplies wells and springs. Groundwater is a major source of drinking and irrigation water.

Growth stages, cereal crops
  1) **Tillering** Development of shoots from the crown.
  2) **Jointing** When stem internodes begin elongating.
  3) **Booting** When the upper leaf sheath swells due to the growth of developing head.
  4) **Heading** When the seed head is emerging or has emerged from the sheath.

Herbaceous plant A vascular plant that does not develop persistent woody tissue and dies down to the ground each year.

Herbicide A chemical used to control weed populations by suppressing (severely interrupting their normal growth processes), or killing plants.

Herbicide resistance The trait or quality of a population of plants within a species (or plant cells in tissue culture) of tolerating a particular herbicide, which is substantially greater than the average for the species. Such tolerance is created through enhancement of naturally occurring tolerances by exposure to the herbicide during several reproductive cycles.

Indigenous Native, not exotic.

Irrigate up Application of water to bring the moisture in a field up to the level required for germination and emergence.

Incorporate To mix or blend a pesticide into the soil.

Invert emulsion The suspension of minute water droplets in a continuous oil phase.

Label The directions and precautions for using a pesticide which are approved through the registration process.

Lateral movement Movement of a pesticide through soil, generally in a horizontal plane, from the original site of application.

Lay-by application Applied and incorporated with or applied after the last cultivation of a crop.

LC_{50} The concentration of a chemical in air (inhalation toxicity) or water (aquatic toxicity) that will kill 50 percent of the organisms in a specific test situation.

LD_{50} The dose (quantity) of a chemical calculated to be lethal to 50 percent of the organisms in a specific test situation. It is expressed in weight of the chemical (mg) per unit of body weight (kg). The toxicant may be fed (oral LD_{50}), applied to the skin (dermal LD_{50}), or administered in the form of vapors (inhalation LD_{50}).

Leachate Liquid obtained by a mild form of leaching such as would occur under natural conditions of plant growth.

Meristem A tissue type composed of cells that are not differentiated and that are capable of active cell division and differentiation into specialized tissues.

Metabolite A compound derived from metabolic transformation of a pesticide by plants or other agents.

Molecular biology A branch of biology which deals with the study of biology using the established principles of chemistry and physics. In many modern uses, this term has been more specifically related to the study of genetics using established principles of chemistry and physics. This branch of biology gave rise to genetic engineering.

Monocotyledon A plant whose embryo has one cotyledon.

Mutagenic Capable of causing genetic changes.

Mutation breeding The use of detectable and inheritable changes in the genetic material not caused by genetic segregation or genetic recombination as a means of selecting unique individuals for variety development.

Mycoherbicide A fungus applied for weed control, using chemical application techniques and equipment.

Necrosis Localized death of tissue, usually characterized by browning and desiccation.

Nonselective herbicide A herbicide that is generally toxic to all plants. Some selective herbicides may become nonselective if used at very high rates.

Nontarget species Species that may be unintentionally affected by a pesticide.

No-till Planting crop seed directly into stubble or sod with no more soil disturbance than is necessary to place the seed into the soil.

Noxious weed A weed specified by law as being especially undesirable, troublesome, and difficult to control. Precise definition varies according to legal interpretations.

Oncogenic Capable of producing or inducing tumors, either benign (noncancerous) or malignant (cancerous), in animals.

Overtop application A broadcast or banded application above the plant canopy.

Pelleted formulation A dry formulation consisting of discrete particles, usually larger than 10 cubic millimeters (0.006 cubic inch), and designed to be applied

without a liquid carrier.

Perennial A plant that continues to live from year to year, usually with new growth each year.

Persistent herbicide A herbicide that, when applied at the recommended rate, will harm susceptible crops planted in normal rotation after harvesting the treated crop, or that interferes with regrowth of native vegetation in noncrop sites for an extended period of time. (See *residual herbicides.*)

Pest An insect, mite, rodent, nematode, fungus, weed, or other form of terrestrial or aquatic plant or animal life or virus, bacterium, or microorganism that is injurious to plant health or the environment (except viruses, bacteria, or other microorganisms on or in man or other animals).

Pesticide Substance or mixture of substances intended for preventing, destroying, repelling, or mitigating any pest. Also, any substance or mixture of substances intended for use as a plant regulator, defoliant, or desiccant.

Pesticide interaction The action or influence of one pesticide upon another and the combined effect of the pesticide on the pest(s) or crop system.

Pesticide tolerance The amount of pesticide residue allowed by law to remain in or on a harvested crop. By using various safety factors, EPA sets these levels well below the point where the chemicals might be harmful to consumers.

Photosynthesis A process carried out by green plants in which the radiant energy of the sun is used to chemically join carbon dioxide and water to form a carbohydrate.

Phytotoxic Injurious or lethal to plants.

Phloem The living tissue in plants that functions primarily to transport metabolic compounds from the site of synthesis or

storage to the site of utilization.

Plant-growth regulator A substance used for controlling or modifying plant-growth processes without appreciable phytotoxic effect.

Plasmodesma (plural, plasmodesmata) Threadlike streams of protoplast that pass through the cell wall and serve as connections between the protoplasts of two cells.

Postemergence (POE) 1) Applied after emergence of the specified weed or crop. **2)** Ability to control established weeds.

Preemergence (PE or PRE) 1) Applied before emergence of the specified weed either before or after the emergence of the crop. **2)** Ability to control weeds before or soon after they emerge.

Preirrigation Application of water to improve soil tilth and to bring the moisture in a field up to the level required to germinate weed seeds before planting.

Preplant Applied before planting or transplanting a crop, either as a foliar application to control existing vegetation, or as a soil application to control weed seedlings as they emerge.

Preplant incorporated (PPI) Applied and tilled into the soil before seeding or transplanting.

Prescribed burn A controlled burn that is prescribed by a land manager on the basis of fire-predictive technology.

Propagules Plant parts used in asexual reproduction.

Protoplast The organized living unit of a single cell.

Rate The amount of active ingredient, acid equivalent, or formulated product applied per unit area or other treatment unit.

Recirculating sprayer A herbicide sprayer system with the nozzle aimed at a catchment device to recover and recirculate herbicide that does not hit plants or weeds passing between nozzles and catchment device.

Registration Approval for use of a product as required by the Federal Insecticide, Fungicide, and Rodenticide Act (FIFRA), which is administered by the Environmental Protection Agency (EPA) and enforced by state departments of agriculture.

Release treatment A forest-vegetation-management term equivalent to postemergence weed control in agronomic crops. Herbicide is applied selectively after tree seeding or transplanting, and after weed emergence.

Residue That quantity of a pesticide remaining in or on the soil, plant parts, animal tissues, whole organisms, and other areas.

Residual herbicide A herbicide that persists in the soil and injures or kills germinating weed seedlings over a period of time. (See *persistent herbicide.*)

Rhizome A below-ground stem that is capable of starting new plants by growing roots below and shoots above ground level.

Shielded application A postemergence application of a nonselective herbicide directed toward weeds growing at the base of plants. A hood or shield is attached to the spray apparatus to prevent herbicide from contacting the crop.

Silviculture A branch of forestry dealing with the development and care of forests.

Soil injection Placement of pesticide beneath the soil surface with a minimum of mixing or stirring of the soil as with an injection blade, knife, or tine.

Soluble concentrate (S) A liquid formulation that forms a solution when added to water.

Soluble powder (SP) A dry formulation that forms a solution when added to water.

Solution A homogenous or single-phase mixture of two or more substances.

Spot treatment A pesticide applied to restricted area(s) of a whole unit, e.g., treatment of spots or patches of weeds within a larger field.

Spray drift Movement of airborne spray away from the intended area of application.

Stolon A rootlike branch that grows horizontally on the ground from the base of a plant and starts new plants by sending down roots and growing shoots from buds.

Stoma (plural, stomata) A tiny opening in the epidermis of leaves and stems, bordered by guard cells, through which gases pass.

Submersed plant An aquatic plant that grows with all or most of its vegetative tissue below the water surface.

Surfactant A material that improves the emulsifying, dispersing, spreading, wetting, or other surface-modifying properties of liquids.

Susceptibility The sensitivity to, or degree to which a plant is injured by, a herbicide treatment. (See *tolerance.*)

Suspension A mixture containing finely divided particles evenly dispersed in a solid, liquid, or gas.

Sward A European term equivalent to turf.

Symplast The total mass of continuous living cells in a plant connected by plasmodesmata and including the phloem.

Synergism An interaction of two or more chemicals such that their combined effect is greater than the predicted effect on the basis of the activity of each chemical applied separately.

Systemic herbicide Synonymous with *translocated herbicide,* but *systemic* is more often used to describe the action of insecticides or fungicides.

Tank-mix combination Mixing of two or more pesticides or agricultural chemicals in the spray tank at the time of application.

Teratogenic Capable of producing birth defects.

Thinning The removal of surplus crop plants in order to obtain the most desirable population density for production.

Tillage Mechanical soil disturbance or displacement for the purpose of improving soil tilth, uprooting and/or burying weeds and crop residues.

Tissue culture The growth and maintenance of cells from a higher organism outside of the tissue of which they are normally a part. The growth of cells *in vitro.*

Tolerance 1) Ability to withstand herbicide treatment without marked deviation from normal growth or function. (See *susceptibility.*) 2) The concentration of pesticide residue allowable in or on agricultural products. (See *pesticide tolerance.*)

Toxicity The quality or degree of being toxic.

Toxicology The study of the principles or mechanisms of toxicity.

Trade name A trademark applied to a herbicide formulation by its manufacturer.

Translocated herbicide A herbicide that is moved within the plant. Translocated herbicides may be either phloem-mobile or xylem-mobile, but the term is frequently used in a more restrictive sense to refer to herbicides that are applied to the foliage and move downward through the phloem to underground parts.

Translocation The transport of food materials or products of metabolism through the plant.

Transpiration The evaporation of water vapor from the surface of leaves and stems.

Tuber An enlarged, short, fleshy underground stem that functions in food storage.

Turgid Swollen, distended, as a cell that is firm due to water uptake.

Undercut The process of pulling a blade under the crop bed to kill undesirable vegetation and dry the tops of crops (e.g., onions and garlic), or to aid harvesting (e.g., green bunching onions and carrots).

Vapor drift The movement of chemical vapors from the area of application. Some herbicides, when applied at normal rates and normal temperatures, have sufficiently high vapor pressure to change them into vapor form, which may cause injury to susceptible plants distant from the site of application. Note that vapor injury and injury from spray drift are often difficult to distinguish.

Vascular tissue A group of specialized cells in the plant, including the xylem and the phloem, that serve as the conducting tissue of the plant.

Vegetative growth Growth of nonreproductive plant parts, e.g., leaves and stems.

Volatility Capability of a solid or liquid substance to change to a gaseous state.

Volunteer crop Crop plants that are considered weeds and have grown from seed or vegetative material remaining in the field from the previous season.

Warm-season crop A crop that is normally grown under warm-temperature regimes; e.g., cotton, melons, tomatoes, as opposed to one that is grown under cool temperatures. (See *cool-season crop*.)

Water dispersible granules (WDG) A pelletized dry formulation that can be readily suspended in water.

Weed Any herbaceous or woody plant that is objectionable or interferes with the activities or welfare of man.

Weed control The process of reducing weed growth and/or infestations to acceptable levels or levels at which economic loss does not occur.

Weed eradication The total elimination of all live plant parts and viable seeds of a weed from a site.

Wettable powder (W or WP) A finely divided dry formulation that can be readily suspended in water.

Wetting agent **1)** A substance that serves to reduce the interfacial tensions and causes spray solutions or suspensions to make better contact with treated surfaces. (See *surfactant*.) **2)** A substance in a wettable-powder formulation that causes it to wet readily when added to water.

Wick/wiper A postemergence herbicide applicator that selectively applies contact-translocated herbicides to weeds growing several inches taller than the crop. The applicator consists of a rope or pad of absorbent material mounted on a raised boom in front of a vehicle; the absorbent material is soaked with herbicide which is wiped onto tall-growing weeds. Also called a *ropewick applicator*.

Woody plants Vascular plants that develop persistent woody tissue above ground.

Xylem The nonliving tissue in plants that functions primarily to conduct water and mineral nutrients from roots to the shoot.

CONVERSION FACTORS

Area equivalents
One acre = 43,560 square feet
= 160 square rods (rd)
= 0.405 hectares (ha)
= 4,840 square yards
One are = 100 square meters
One hectare = 100 are = 2.471 acres

Liquid equivalents
One U.S. gallon = 4 qt = 8 pt = 16 cups
= 3.785 liters = 3785 ml = 128 fluid ounces
= 231 cu inch
= 8.3370 pounds of water
= 3785.4 cu cm
One quart = 0.9463 liters = 946.3 ml = 2 pt = 32 fl oz = 4 cups = 64 tbs
One tablespoon (tbs) = 14.8 ml = 3 teaspoons = 0.5 fl oz
Ounce (U.S. fluid) = 29.57 ml = 2 tbs = 6 tsp
Ounce (British fluid) = 28.41 ml

Weight equivalents
One pound = 453.6 grams = 16 oz
One ounce = 28.35 grams
One kilogram = 1000 grams = 2.2 lbs
One gram = 1000 milligrams = 0.35 oz.

Temperature equivalents
(°F − 32) × 5/9 = degrees Centigrade
(°C × 9/5) ÷ 32 = degrees Fahrenheit

Length equivalents
centimeter = 0.394 inch
meter = 3.28 feet = 39.4 inches
kilometer = 0.621 statute mile
inch = 2.54 centimeters
foot = 30.48 centimeters
yard = 0.914 meters
rod (16.5 feet) = 5.029 meters
statute mile (1,760 yards) = 1.61 kilometers

Parts per million equivalents
1 part per million (ppm) = 1 milligram/liter
= 1 milligram/kilogram
= 0.0001 percent
= 0.013 ounces by weight in 100 gallons of water
1 percent = 10,000 ppm
= 10 grams per liter
= 10 grams per kilogram
= 1.33 ounces by weight per gallon of water
= 8.34 pounds/100 gallons of water
0.1 percent = 1000 ppm = 1000 milligrams/liter
0.01 percent = 100 ppm = 100 milligrams/liter
0.001 percent = 10 ppm = 10 milligrams/liter
0.0001 percent = 1 ppm = 1 milligram/liter

INDEX